MW00813859

The fourth volume in John Frame's Theology of Lordship series, *The Doctrine of the Word of God*, is the best of them—and that is high praise. In a 700-page "draft" of what he hopes will be a longer and more definitive work, Frame thinks through what Scripture is, what authority means, how to understand inspiration, canon, and a host of other categories intrinsic to any responsible treatment of revelation, especially the revelation provided by Holy Scripture. Frame's style is highly personal, occasionally sliding all the way to an almost stream-of-consciousness set of associations, but his reflections are invariably so fresh (even when he is articulating old truths) and so thought-provoking (not least where one wants to demur or introduce a caveat) that this reader, at least, overlooks the style he would otherwise have found a bit cloying. More so than the other volumes in the series, this book works hard at developing its theology, the theology of the word of God, out of Scripture itself—and without descending to vicious circularity. This is an important book, and those who write on this subject in the near future without wrestling with Frame will merely testify to their own narrowness.

> —**D. A. Carson**, Research Professor of New Testament,
> Trinity Evangelical Divinity School, Deerfield, IL

I thank God for raising up John Frame in our day. We are the wiser, the more biblical, and the healthier because of it. And because he has written so deeply and so well about such great truths about a great God, this will, I believe, be the testimony of generations to come.

> —**John Piper**, Pastor for Preaching and Vision,
> Bethlehem Baptist Church, Minneapolis

Too often, the Bible is considered an academic text to be evaluated, rather than a Scripture to guide our piety. This book goes a long way toward correcting that mistake. And what a feast it is! To be sure, it leaves no stone unturned. Just about every significant issue connected with God's Word is tackled with clarity and with faithfulness to the highest view of biblical authority. Still, this is far more than a solid apologetic for inspiration and inerrancy. John Frame pleads for the "personal-word model" of the sacred text. With enormous wisdom and cogency, he leads the reader to discover the wonder of the Scripture, and thus to discover the wondrous love of its magnificent author, the Lord God himself.

> —**William Edgar**, Professor of Apologetics, Westminster
> Theological Seminary, Philadelphia

John Frame's course on the doctrine of the Word of God had a profound influence on me as a student at Westminster Seminary in 1971, and it has significantly affected my understanding of theology for my entire life. I am thrilled to see that Frame's excellent material is finally being published for a wider audience.

> —**Wayne Grudem**, Research Professor of Theology and
> Biblical Studies, Phoenix Seminary

Frame's work offers rich, vigorous, deep, biblically sound exposition of the Bible's own teaching about the word of God and about the Bible's character as the written Word of God. We have needed this vigorous defense of orthodoxy, which answers modernist deviations and now deviations cropping up even within evangelicalism. I highly commend it as a fitting capstone to Frame's Theology of Lordship series.

—**Vern S. Poythress**, Professor of New Testament Interpretation, Westminster Theological Seminary, Philadelphia

John Frame's fourth (possibly final) contribution to his Theology of Lordship series evidences this septuagenarian theologian's lifetime study of God's word. While writing in the spirit of Warfield, Young, Murray, and Van Til, the author freely merges his own (sometimes provocative or contemporary) thinking into the foundational works from previous generations. Commendably, he aspires to be presuppositional, exegetical, expositional, and Reformed in his conclusions and applications. This monumental volume certainly qualifies as a "must-read" for advanced students of theology.

—**Richard Mayhue**, Senior Vice President and Dean, The Master's Seminary, Sun Valley, CA

John Frame's *Doctrine of the Word of God* is, by his own reckoning, his magnum opus, and I wholeheartedly agree. It is a rare event when evangelical theologians publish primary rather than secondary texts, but Frame has done it with this work—a constructive proposal that is as creative as it is conservative, "something close to biblicism" concerning the Bible itself. He has kept references to other theologians to a minimum (mainly confined to the several appendices) in order to focus on the biblical text itself, the personal Word of God. This book is a fitting capstone not only to Frame's Theology of Lordship series but also to his whole career. It demands not only our admiration but, more importantly, our attention. Those who do take up and read will come away with an expanded and enhanced vision of biblical authority and a renewed confidence in Scripture as the compelling personal communication of the triune Lord.

—**Kevin J. Vanhoozer**, Blanchard Professor of Theology, Wheaton College Graduate School, Wheaton, IL

In my estimation, there has never been a book that deals with the word of God so carefully, thoroughly, and practically. I cannot imagine a follower of Christ who will not be transformed into a more humble and loyal disciple by pondering its wisdom. The content is up to date, exegetical, and systematic. The style is crystal clear. You will never forget this book.

—**Richard L. Pratt Jr.**, Third Millennium Ministries, Fern Park, FL

I trust John Frame! I am a cynical old preacher and trust comes hard; but when John Frame speaks or writes, I trust him—his mind, his heart, and his faithfulness. But mostly I trust the God whom John Frame worships with such passion. A case in point is *The Doctrine of the Word of God*. This (along with the three other volumes in this series) will be one of the most valuable books in your library, and you'll rise up and call me blessed for recommending it to you.

—**Steve W. Brown**, Professor of Preaching Emeritus, Reformed Theological Seminary, Orlando

A distinguished teacher and author for over four decades, John gives us a wonderful fourth volume in his Theology of Lordship series. The book is accessible, concise, and saturated with Scripture. I heartily recommend his description of how God's word, in all its aspects, is his personal communication with us, with echoes of John's own lifelong faithfulness to the Lord.

—**J. Lanier Burns**, Research Professor of Theological Studies, Senior Professor of Systematic Theology, Dallas Theological Seminary

I am delighted to recommend John Frame's *Doctrine of the Word of God*. It is a fitting finale to the Theology of Lordship series. Frame has profited much from the biblical theology of Vos, Murray, Kline, and Clowney; the result here is, as it is in his other books, a deeply biblical account of his subject. God's covenants are never far from the discussion. John is equally at home in biblical exegesis and in resolving the questions of our uncertain times regarding Scripture. Easy to read, yet penetrating, the argument carries us along. I especially admire John's "personal-word model" of Scripture. After reading *DWG*, students will be convinced of the sovereign power, truthfulness, and authority of the Bible. Even in areas where I question some of John's views, such as the usefulness of confessions of faith, I was encouraged and challenged to follow Holy Scripture more faithfully. Thank you, John, for this book!

—**Howard Griffith**, Associate Professor of Systematic Theology and Academic Dean, Reformed Theological Seminary, Washington DC

We all need to read John Frame. At different times, he provokes, informs, irritates, illuminates, and excites. He is—thankfully!—not easily categorized, and therefore he must be wrestled with and not simply embraced or dismissed. This is the case in his most recent offering in his massive Theology of Lordship series. In some ways, Frame is at his best when exploring questions of methodology and the dynamics of revelation. In *The Doctrine of the Word of God*, Frame approaches issues in a fresh and stimulating way, anchored in classic Reformed orthodoxy, but often asking unexpected questions or giving surprising analysis and reaction. Yes, supporters and opponents should read this volume by John Frame because it proves to be a truly significant addition to literature on the Word of God.

—**Kelly M. Kapic**, Professor of Theological Studies, Covenant College. Lookout Mountain, GA

When I first began teaching systematic theology nearly thirty years ago, one of the first things I did was to contact the bookstore of Westminster Seminary California to order several of the syllabi of John Frame on the various heads of theology. I considered him a leader in theological thinking then, and all these years later, I still do. I have often thought of him as something like a combination of a meticulous brain-surgeon and a keen-nosed bloodhound. With deep biblical faith and massive erudition in the entire Christian theological tradition, he painstakingly reads all the relevant material and clearly isolates the matters at hand. He does not then "cut or bite," but rather fairly and charitably reveals each problem or issue in light of the ever-new, ever-ancient biblical faith. He never jumps to conclusions, and always seeks to believe the best about those who may be opponents, without relinquishing honesty and realism in the process.

I will be using this book in my own classes and teaching, and I am delighted to have such a rich resource to hand.

> —**Douglas F. Kelly**, Professor of Systematic Theology,
> Reformed Theological Seminary, Charlotte

In many ways, Frame's *Doctrine of the Word of God* is the crowning achievement of his career. If Barth was designated the theologian of revelation, Moltmann the theologian of eschatology, and Cullmann the theologian of salvation history, Frame could rightly be labeled the theologian of the Bible. No theologian in recent memory has more frequently and doggedly held up the Bible as the divine norm for all human thought and action; and no English bibliology in the last century matches the present work in scope, fervor, logic, and fidelity to the Bible's view of itself. This work is an evangelical landmark, likely to be unsurpassed for generations.

> —**P. Andrew Sandlin**, Center for Cultural Leadership,
> Church of the King, Santa Cruz

The Doctrine of the Word of God strengthened my faith in the authority, the sufficiency, and the thorough jurisdiction of God's Word in my daily life. I cannot ask for more from any human book.

> —**Andrée Seu**, Senior Writer, *WORLD* Magazine

THE DOCTRINE
OF THE
WORD OF GOD

A THEOLOGY OF LORDSHIP

A SERIES BY JOHN M. FRAME

Also available in the series:

The Doctrine of the Knowledge of God
The Doctrine of God
The Doctrine of the Christian Life

THE DOCTRINE
OF THE
WORD OF GOD

JOHN M. FRAME

P&R

P U B L I S H I N G

P.O. BOX 817 • PHILLIPSBURG • NEW JERSEY 08865-0817

Library of Congress Cataloging-in-Publication Data

Frame, John M., 1939-
  The doctrine of the Word of God / John M. Frame.
     p. cm. -- (A theology of Lordship)
  Includes bibliographical references (p.   ) and indexes.
  ISBN 978-0-87552-264-7 (cloth)
  1. Word of God (Christian theology) 2. Reformed Church--Doctrines. I. Title.
  BT180.W67F73 2010
  220.1'30882842--dc22
                              2010030270

In Memory of
Edmund P. Clowney
(1917–2005)

And he gave to Moses, when he had finished speaking with him on Mount Sinai, the two tablets of the testimony, tablets of stone, written with the finger of God. (Ex. 31:18)

Now this is the commandment, the statutes and the rules that the LORD your God commanded me to teach you, that you may do them in the land to which you are going over, to possess it, that you may fear the LORD your God, you and your son and your son's son, by keeping all his statutes and his commandments, which I command you, all the days of your life, and that your days may be long. Hear therefore, O Israel, and be careful to do them, that it may go well with you, and that you may multiply greatly, as the LORD, the God of your fathers, has promised you, in a land flowing with milk and honey.

Hear, O Israel: The LORD our God, the LORD is one. You shall love the LORD your God with all your heart and with all your soul and with all your might. And these words that I command you today shall be on your heart. You shall teach them diligently to your children, and shall talk of them when you sit in your house, and when you walk by the way, and when you lie down, and when you rise. You shall bind them as a sign on your hand, and they shall be as frontlets between your eyes. You shall write them on the doorposts of your house and on your gates. (Deut. 6:1–9)

This Book of the Law shall not depart from your mouth, but you shall meditate on it day and night, so that you may be careful to do according to all that is written in it. For then you will make your way prosperous, and then you will have good success. (Josh. 1:8)

The law of the LORD is perfect, reviving the soul; the testimony of the LORD is sure, making wise the simple; the precepts of the LORD are right, rejoicing the heart; the commandment of the LORD is pure, enlightening the eyes; the fear of the LORD is clean, enduring forever; the rules of the LORD are true, and righteous altogether. More to be desired are they than gold, even much fine gold; sweeter also than honey and drippings of the honeycomb. Moreover, by them is your servant warned; in keeping them there is great reward. (Ps. 19:7–11)

In God, whose word I praise, in the Lord, whose word I praise, in God I trust; I shall not be afraid. What can man do to me? (Ps. 56:10–11)

Do not think that I have come to abolish the Law or the Prophets; I have not come to abolish them but to fulfill them. For truly, I say to you, until heaven and earth pass away, not an iota, not a dot, will pass from the Law until all is accomplished. Therefore whoever relaxes one of the least of these commandments and teaches others to do the same will be called least in the kingdom of heaven, but whoever does them and teaches them will be called great in the kingdom of heaven. (Matt. 5:17–19)

In the beginning was the Word, and the Word was with God, and the Word was God. He was in the beginning with God. All things were made through him, and without him was not any thing made that was made. (John 1:1–3)

Lord, to whom shall we go? You have the words of eternal life. (John 6:68)

Scripture cannot be broken. (John 10:35)

If anyone thinks that he is a prophet, or spiritual, he should acknowledge that the things I am writing to you are a command of the Lord. (1 Cor. 14:37)

From childhood you have been acquainted with the sacred writings, which are able to make you wise for salvation through faith in Christ Jesus. All Scripture is breathed out by God and profitable for teaching, for reproof, for correction, and for training in righteousness, that the man of God may be competent, equipped for every good work. (2 Tim. 3:15–17)

And we have something more sure, the prophetic word, to which you will do well to pay attention as to a lamp shining in a dark place, until the day dawns and the morning star rises in your hearts, knowing this first of all, that no prophecy of Scripture comes from someone's own interpretation. For no prophecy was ever produced by the will of man, but men spoke from God as they were carried along by the Holy Spirit. (2 Peter 1:19–21)

Jesus loves me, this I know,
For the Bible tells me so;
Little ones to him belong,
They are weak, but he is strong.

Yes, Jesus loves me! *[3×]*
The Bible tells me so. *[repeat after each verse]*

Jesus loves me, he who died,
Heaven's gates to open wide;
He will wash away my sin,
Let his little child come in.

Jesus loves me, loves me still,
Though I'm very weak and ill;
From his shining throne on high
Comes to watch me where I lie.

Jesus loves me, he will stay
Close beside me all the way:
If I love him, when I die
He will take me home on high.[1]

1. "Jesus Loves Me, This I Know," by Anna B. Warner, 1859.

Contents

Analytical Outline

4. Revelation and Reason
   A. Reason Itself a Good Gift of God
   B. Reason Affected by Sin
   C. Logical Reasoning Presupposes God
   D. Reason Is a Test of Divine Truth, if Done Right
   E. Reason Goes Astray When It Assumes Autonomy
   F. Circularity of True Reasoning
   G. Limitation of Our Creatureliness

5. Revelation and History
   A. History Is a Rational Study
   B. Centrality of History a Unique Feature of Biblical Revelation
   C. Divine Words Necessary to the Interpretation of Events
   D. Modern Theologians Try to Interpret History Autonomously
   E. Barth on *Historie* and *Geschichte*
   F. Lessing's Big Ditch
   G. Solution to These Problems: Renounce Autonomy

6. Revelation and Human Subjectivity
   A. Schleiermacher: Autonomous Reasoning *about* the Inner Life
   B. Kierkegaard, Barth, and Others
   C. Reformed Theology: Both Objective and Subjective Revelation
   D. Objective and Subjective Senses of "Revelation"

7. Revelation and God Himself
   A. "God Doesn't Reveal Information; He Reveals Himself"
   B. Barth's View
   C. The Identity of Revelation with Christ Doesn't Exclude the Authority of Personal Words

PART THREE: THE NATURE OF GOD'S WORD

8. What Is the Word of God?
   A. The Word Is All of God's Communications
   B. It Is Also God Himself

9. God's Word as His Controlling Power
   A. Creation and Providence
   B. His Words to People

Foreword

Recently a former student wrote to me as follows:

> Dr. Packer, is there a reasonably recent work on the nature of Scripture that you would consider "magisterial" or close to indispensable, other than the Bible?

At that time, I could not name a book that met these specifications. But now I can, and this is it.

It concludes a heavyweight group of four, together titled A Theology of Lordship. The earlier items were *The Doctrine of the Knowledge of God*, *The Doctrine of God*, and *The Doctrine of the Christian Life*. *The Doctrine of the Word of God* crowns the design it completes. The author ventures the opinion, "I think this book is my best work ever," and I agree. Clinically and climactically, it rounds off the series, which in broad terms has focused on the word of God from the start. Pulling together threads from the previous volumes into a single systematic survey, it now stands on its own, as something of a landmark in its own right. I count it a huge privilege to introduce so good a book.

It must be all of sixty years since I picked up, from James Denney as I recall, the thought that in teaching systematic theology, the doctrine of Holy Scripture will ideally be handled twice—once at the start, to establish epistemology and method; and once at the end, to integrate the full wisdom about Scripture as a product, instrument, and conveyor of God that the process of gathering and synthesizing its overall, multiform doctrinal content has brought to light. Denney never attempted this himself, and indeed the Ritschlian streak in his thought would have made it impossible for him to do it coherently. I have never tried it, nor has any instructor I know. But although this was not John Frame's conscious agenda, it is pretty much what he has actually achieved. Epistemology and methodology begin the series, and Denney's proposed return to full-scale bibliology completes it. And the job, first to last, has been done thoroughly and well.

Frame has taught in conservative Reformed seminaries for over forty years, among his other labors going over the doctrine of the word of God in some form annually. He has won himself many admirers in his own circle, but in the wider evangelical and Christian world his influence has not been great. The Lordship series, and this book in particular, will, I hope, change that. For here we find breadth and precision, lucid accessibility, disciplined theocentricity, alertness to real questions, analytical depth, consistent commonsensical Christian wisdom, and wholehearted faithfulness to the written Word, all coalescing into a convincing and heartening worldview before the argument is done. Two of the book's special excellences call for separate mention here.

First, the "big idea" that holds everything in this big book together is *pastoral*, and that to my mind is as it should be. As I was writing this foreword, I learned of a Chinese lady, a seventy-year-old watermelon grower named Jin, who said, "Reading the Bible is like having God talk to you." This is precisely the truth that Frame follows through, start to finish, angling it, as one would expect, in his own ministerial-formational way. In his opening paragraph he writes:

> The main contention of this volume is that God's speech to man . . . is very much like one person speaking to another. . . . My thesis is that God's word, in all its qualities and aspects, is a personal communication from him to us.

Elsewhere he states that *person-revelation* is his theme, and he maintains this theme as the necessary framework within which all sound theologizing does and must take place. The profound rightness of this approach is surely obvious.

Second, the complex specifics of God and godliness as the Bible presents them are here set forth in terms of the triadic *perspectivalism* that has become John Frame's trademark. In this conceptuality, each item in each triad is distinct yet inseparable from the other two, and must always be linked with them. For Frame holds that we have here an analogical shadow of what Scripture tells us about our triune Creator, the so-called economic Trinity, within whose unity the Father initiates, the Son mediates, and the Holy Spirit effectuates, all three acting together at all times. So the sovereignty—that is, the lordship—of God entails control, authority, and presence. God's revelation to us involves event, word, and person, and thus is in itself circumstantial, verbal, and relational, while from our standpoint as recipients it is normative, situational, and existential. And response to revelation embraces belief, obedience, and participation, all together. Biblically grounded and theologically focused, these thought-diagrams that Frame gives us will stretch minds and clarify vision, very much to Christians' advantage. The same must be said of Frame's mapping of theology as application of God's Word to our lives. The perspectives that perspectivalism highlights are in truth integral to the God-man relationship, and should be prized as such.

So where are we? "Magisterial"? Yes. "Close to indispensable"? Yes again. Would John Calvin, Jonathan Edwards, Abraham Kuyper, and B. B. Warfield, Reformed theology's Fabulous Four (in my book, anyway), enthuse about this volume as I have done? Pretty much, I think.

There, I have had my say. Now read on, and taste the good food for yourself.

J. I. Packer

Preface

I turned seventy in April 2009. My father died at age seventy-one, in 1980. They discovered that he had acute leukemia, and he was gone in six months. So I find myself more and more often calculating the implications of mortality. I am not morose, and for now I am in good health. I believe in Jesus Christ and anticipate a glorious reunion with him before too long. But while I am here, I need to put a fresh emphasis on redeeming the time. There are a lot of affairs I would like to put in order, if God wills. This book is one of them.

I have published three big fat books in the series A Theology of Lordship. These are *Doctrine of the Knowledge of God* (DKG), *Doctrine of God* (DG), and *Doctrine of the Christian Life* (DCL). The present volume, *DWG*, is the final planned volume of the series. In a way, I have been planning this book longer than the others. I worked on the doctrine of revelation and Scripture during my doctoral program at Yale (alas, leaving the dissertation unfinished). Through forty-one years as a seminary teacher, I have taught Doctrine of the Word of God as a locus of systematic theology every year, and I have written a great many articles and book reviews on this subject. I have accumulated about six hundred pages of reading notes on the literature of the field, typed, single-spaced, and concise. I have long hoped to finish *DWG* before God takes me home.

But there are many other things to do, and writing such a big book is a large job. About fifteen years elapsed between *DKG* and *DG*. That happened because my Lordship books require a lot of research, and because my other work required me to do a lot of other things, labeled *Urgent*. Those other urgent things continue to beckon me, and I think it humanly impossible that I could finish *DWG*, as originally planned, in two or three years.

So I decided, just in case God doesn't allow me to finish *DWG* according to my original plan, to leave behind the present draft, a more concise version of what I had originally hoped to write. I have in my mind a pretty clear idea of the basic case I'd like to set forth. So I think I can summarize the book now, and add to it later, if God permits. This summary will contain very little documentation: relatively few citations of historical and current writers. I will be more careful than I usually am to avoid rabbit trails. Here I will simply outline my basic contentions and their basic arguments, so that these will be on the table for discussion, even if all my research is not.

I'm not worthy of being compared to John Calvin, but perhaps this book will grow over the years like the successive editions of Calvin's *Institutes*. Or perhaps I will write an additional book or two, dealing with the history and contemporary discussion of the word of God and Scripture.

On the other hand, maybe I will not expand this project at all. To tell the truth, I rather like this concise version, and I have some worry that it might even be harmed if I add to it a great deal of interaction with historical and contemporary literature. Regular readers of my work know that I am critical of the typical method of modern theologians (including evangelical theologians), who include in their writing a great deal of interaction with other theologians and very little interaction with Scripture itself. This is an inheritance from the academic model of theology, which I have criticized elsewhere.[1] Interaction with the theological literature is useful in a number of ways. But most important by far is what Scripture itself tells us. It has always been my purpose to emphasize the latter, even though more of the former might have gained for my work a greater level of acceptance. Focus on Scripture without the theological environs gives my argument a kind of starkness, a kind of sharpness, that I want it to have. So this concise version of *DWG* may turn out to be the final version, regardless of how many more years God gives me.

And the more I think about it, the more I think this book is my best work ever.

Thanks to many who have shared kind words and constructive criticisms of the other books in this series. To those who have noted that these books are too "self-referential," that I refer too often to other writings of mine, I reply that that is the nature of the Theology of Lordship series. In my view, this series is a single project, setting forth a unified vision of the theology of Scripture. I believe most of my readers understand this, and that I am doing them a service by referring to parallel discussions of issues from volume to volume. This is simply a supplement to the indices, analytical outlines, and tables of contents—a reference tool. I hope this practice doesn't draw too much attention to myself; I don't believe that it does, and I don't intend it to. But in any case, I think these references perform a service to those who are interested in the Lordship project as a whole.

1. See my "Proposal for a New Seminary," available at http://www.frame-poythress.org/frame_articles/1978Proposal.htm.

If the "self-referential" comment has to do with my use of the first-person pronoun and my occasional stream-of-consciousness mode, again I will not apologize or change. I have often said that theology is not primarily an academic discipline, observing the impersonal academic conventions. It is rather (as in the NT) a highly personal communication, a testimony of faith. Our God is personal, and the Christian *didache* is also personal. I will never change in that respect. If the theological community has adopted rules that conflict with this vision, then it ought to change them.

Does this personalist approach detract from the God-centeredness of my theology? Readers are invited to make their own judgment about that. But if this approach to theology is scriptural, it can never detract from the God-centeredness of the theology. And Psalm 18 (among many other Scripture passages) shows concretely that a large number of personal references are compatible with God-centeredness and can actually enhance it: "The LORD is *my* rock and *my* fortress and *my* deliverer" (v. 2). The psalmist here shows explicitly God's centrality to his whole life.

A few words about the dedication of this book. Edmund P. Clowney was the first president of Westminster Seminary in Philadelphia. He was a teacher, friend, and mentor to me during my student years at Westminster (1961–64) and until his death in 2005. From 1968 to 1980 we were colleagues at Westminster in Philadelphia, and through most of 1980–2000 at Westminster in California. Westminster in Philadelphia during my student days was a wonderful place in which to study the doctrine of Scripture. Practically every professor made some major contribution to the defense of biblical authority. But Ed Clowney seemed to me to be the best at setting forth the big picture, that Scripture asserts the authority of God's word on nearly every page, in one way or another, and that the Christian life in its essence is a faithful response to the Word of God. Ed never wrote a major work on this subject, but the present volume seeks to set forth his vision.

Ed and I disagreed on a number of things that were important to both of us: the regulative principle of worship, the appropriateness of contemporary songs and instrumentation in worship, the preeminence of biblical theology in sermon preparation, the "two kingdoms" view of Christ and culture, and the value of Norman Shepherd's theology. These issues have produced factions in Reformed circles, with one party trying to exclude another from the Reformed community. But the friendship between Ed and me was never disrupted by this kind of division. He respected my Reformed commitment, even when others questioned it, and I treasured his faithfulness, wisdom, and kindness to the end of his life. I seek to honor him here, as well as to emulate his theology of the word of God.

The analytical outline is not a mirror image of the internal structure of *DWG*'s chapters because, generally speaking, those chapters are not divided into precise sections. It is, however, a fair outline. I think it actually adds something to the book, unlike the outlines of the earlier books in the Lordship series, because readers will be able to see developments in the arguments that they might not have thought of simply by reading the chapters. Therefore, although it is not terribly different from previous analytical outlines in the Lordship series, in my judgment it is actually an improvement.

DWG uses *word of God* and *word* (as shorthand for *word of God*) in a variety of ways. When *word of God* or *word* refers to the written, inscripturated Word of God, *word* is capitalized in this book. *Word* is also capitalized when it refers to Christ as the Word incarnate. Otherwise, *word of God* and *word* are lowercased.

I wish to express thanks to the board, administration, and faculty of Reformed Theological Seminary for granting me a study leave for the spring term of 2007, which helped with my preparation to write this book. Thanks again also to P&R Publishing for supporting my work over many years, and especially to John J. Hughes and Karen Magnuson, who edited this volume.

Abbreviations

AGG	*Apologetics to the Glory of God*
ASV	American Standard Version
CalCon	*Calvinist Contact*
CRC	Christian Reformed Church
CVT	*Cornelius Van Til: An Analysis of His Thought*
CWM	*Contemporary Worship Music*
DCL	*The Doctrine of the Christian Life*
DG	*The Doctrine of God*
DKG	*The Doctrine of the Knowledge of God*
DWG	*The Doctrine of the Word of God*
ER	*Evangelical Reunion*
ESV	English Standard Version
GKN	Gereformeerde Kerken in Nederland
Guardian	*The Presbyterian Guardian*
IRB	*International Reformed Bulletin*
JETS	*Journal of the Evangelical Theological Society*
JPP	*Journal of Pastoral Practice*
KJV	King James Version
LXX	Septuagint, the Greek translation of the Hebrew Bible widely used in the time of Jesus and the apostles
NASB	New American Standard Bible
NEBA	*The Nature and Extent of Biblical Authority*
NIV	New International Version
NKJV	New King James Version
NLT	New Living Translation
NOG	*No Other God*
NT	New Testament

OT	Old Testament
RES	Reformed Ecumenical Synod
RESTB	*RES Theological Bulletin*
SBL	*Salvation Belongs to the Lord*
WCF	Westminster Confession of Faith
WLC	Westminster Larger Catechism
WSC	Westminster Shorter Catechism
WTJ	*Westminster Theological Journal*

PART ONE

ORIENTATION

CHAPTER 1

The Personal-Word Model

The main contention of this volume is that God's speech to man is real speech. It is very much like one person speaking to another. God speaks so that we can understand him and respond appropriately. Appropriate responses are of many kinds: belief, obedience, affection, repentance, laughter, pain, sadness, and so on. God's speech is often propositional: God's conveying information to us. But it is far more than that. It includes all the features, functions, beauty, and richness of language that we see in human communication, and more. So the concept I wish to defend is broader than the "propositional revelation" that we argued so ardently forty years ago, though propositional revelation is part of it. My thesis is that God's word, in all its qualities and aspects, is a personal communication from him to us.

Imagine God speaking to you right now, as realistically as you can imagine, perhaps standing at the foot of your bed at night. He speaks to you like your best friend, your parents, or your spouse. There is no question in your mind as to who he is: he is God. In the Bible, God often spoke to people in this way: to Adam and Eve in the garden; to Noah; to Abraham; to Moses. For some reason, these were all fully persuaded that the speaker was God, even when the speaker told them to do things they didn't understand. Had God asked me to take my son up a mountain to burn him as a sacrifice, as he asked of Abraham in Genesis 22, I would have decided that it wasn't God and could not be God, because God could never command such a thing. But somehow Abraham didn't raise that question. He knew, somehow, that God had spoken to him, and he knew what God expected him to do.

We question Abraham at this point, as did Søren Kierkegaard in *Fear and Trembling*.[1] But if God is God, if God is who he claims to be, isn't it likely that he is able to persuade Abraham that the speaker is really he? Isn't he able to unambiguously identify himself to Abraham's mind?

Now imagine that when God speaks to you personally, he gives you some information, or commands you to do something. Will you then be inclined to argue with him? Will you criticize what he says? Will you find something inadequate in his knowledge or in the rightness of his commands? I hope not. For that is the path to disaster. When God speaks, our role is to believe, obey, delight, repent, mourn—whatever he wants us to do. Our response should be without reservation, from the heart. Once we understand (and of course we often misunderstand), we must not hesitate. We may at times find occasion to criticize one another's words, but God's words are not the subject of criticism.

Sometimes in the Bible we do hear of "arguments" between God and his conversation partners. Abraham pleaded for the life of his nephew Lot in Sodom (Gen. 18:22–33), and Moses pleaded that God would not destroy Israel (Ex. 33:12–23). But no human being, in such a conversation, ought to question the truth of what God says, God's right to do as he pleases, or the rightness of God's decisions. The very presupposition of Abraham's argument, indeed, is "Shall not the Judge of all the earth do what is just?" (Gen. 18:25), a rhetorical question that must be answered yes. Abraham's argument with God is a prayer, asking God to make exceptions to the coming judgment he has announced. Abraham persists in that prayer, as all believers should do. But he does not question the truth of God's words to him (Rom. 4:20–21) or the rightness of God's plans.[2] Sometimes, to be sure, believers in Scripture do find fault with God, as did Job (Job 40:2), but that is sin, and such people need to repent (40:3–5; 42:1–6).

God's personal speech is not an unusual occurrence in Scripture. In fact, it is the main engine propelling the biblical narrative forward. The thing at issue in the biblical story is always the word of God. God speaks to Adam and Eve in the garden to define their fundamental task (Gen. 1:28). All of human history is our response to that word of God. God speaks to Adam again, forbidding him to eat the forbidden fruit (2:17). That word is the issue before the first couple. If they obey, God will continue to bless. If they don't, he will curse. The narrative permits no question whether the

---

1. Søren Kierkegaard, *Fear and Trembling: The Sickness unto Death* (1941; repr., Garden City, NY: Doubleday, 1954).

2. On the question whether God can change his mind, see *DG*, 559–72. And see ibid., 150, which is also relevant to the question whether God's decrees are in any sense dependent on events in history, that is, how God's foreordination is related to his foreknowledge.

couple knew that it was God who spoke. Nor does it allow the possibility that they did not understand what he was saying. God had given them a personal word, pure and simple. Their responsibility was clear.

This is what we mean when we say that God's word is *authoritative*. The *authority* of God's word varies broadly according to the many functions I have listed. When God communicates information, we are obligated to believe it. When he tells us to do something, we are obligated to obey. When he tells us a parable, we are obligated to place ourselves in the narrative and meditate on the implications of that. When he expresses affection, we are obligated to appreciate and reciprocate. When he gives us a promise, we are obligated to trust. Let's define the *authority* of language as its capacity to create an obligation in the hearer. So the speech of an absolute authority creates absolute obligation. Obligation is not the only content of language, as we have seen. But it is the result of the *authority* of language.

As we know, Adam and Eve disobeyed. Many questions arise here. How did people whom God had declared "very good," along with the rest of creation (Gen. 1:31), disobey his word? The narrative doesn't tell us. Another question is why they would have wanted to disobey God. They knew who God was. They understood the authority of his word and his power to curse or bless. Why would they make a decision that they knew would bring a curse on themselves? The question is complicated a bit by the presence of Satan in the form of a serpent. Satan presumed to interpose a word rivaling God's, a word contradicting God's. But why would Adam and Eve have given Satan any credence at all? The most profound answer, I think, is that Adam and Eve wanted to be their own gods. Impulsively, arrogantly, and certainly irrationally, they exchanged God's truth for a lie (cf. Rom. 1:25). So they brought God's curse upon themselves (Gen. 3:16–19). Clearly, they should have known better. The word of God was clear and true. They should have obeyed it.

Noah, too, heard God's personal speech, telling him to build an ark. Unlike Adam, he obeyed God. He might have thought, like his neighbors, and like Adam, that God couldn't have been right about this. Why build a gigantic boat in a desert? But Noah obeyed God, and God vindicated his faith. Similarly with Abraham, Isaac, Jacob, Moses, Joshua, Gideon, David. All these narratives and others begin with God's personal speech, often saying something hard to believe or commanding something hard to do. The course of the narrative depends on the character's response, in faith or unbelief. Hebrews 11 summarizes the faithful ones. Faith, in both Testaments, is hearing the word of God and doing it.

That's the biblical story: a story of God speaking to people personally, and people responding appropriately or inappropriately.

Scripture is plain that this is the very nature of the Christian life: having God's word and doing it. Jesus said, "Whoever has my commandments and keeps them, he it is who loves me" (John 14:21). Everything we know about God we know because he has told us, through his personal speech. All our duties to God are from his commands. All the promises of salvation through the grace of Christ are God's promises, from his own mouth. What other source could there possibly be, for a salvation message that so contradicts our own feelings of self-worth, our own ideas of how to earn God's favor?

Now, to be sure, there are questions about where we can find God's personal words today, for he does not normally speak to us now as he did to Abraham. (These are questions of *canon*.) And there are questions about how we can come to understand God's words, given our distance from the culture in which they were given. (These are questions of *hermeneutics*.) I will address these questions in due course. But the answer *cannot* be that God's personal words are unavailable to us, or unintelligible to us. If we say either of those things, then we lose all touch with the biblical gospel. The idea that God communicates with human beings in personal words pervades all of Scripture, and it is central to every doctrine of Scripture. If God has, in fact, not spoken to us personally, then we lose any basis for believing in salvation by grace, in judgment, in Christ's atonement—indeed, for believing in the biblical God at all. Indeed, if God has not spoken to us personally, then everything important in Christianity is human speculation and fantasy.

Yet it should be evident to anyone who has studied the recent history of theology that the mainstream liberal and neoorthodox traditions have in fact denied that such personal words have occurred, even that they can occur. Others have said that although God's personal words may have occurred in the past, they are no longer available to us as personal words because of the problems of hermeneutics and canon. If those theologies are true, all is lost.

The present book is simply an exposition and defense of the biblical personal-word model of divine communication. As such, it will be different from many books on the theology of revelation and Scripture. Of course, this book will differ from the liberal and neoorthodox positions, but it will not spend a great deal of time analyzing those. Nor will it resemble the many recent books from more conservative authors that have the purpose of showing how much we can learn from Bible critics and how the concept of inerrancy needs to be redefined, circumscribed, or eliminated.[3] I don't

---

3. For examples of how I respond to such arguments, see my reviews of recent books by Peter Enns, N. T. Wright, and Andrew McGowan, Appendices J, K, and L in this volume.

doubt that we can learn some things from Bible critics, but that is not my burden here. As for inerrancy, I think it is a perfectly good idea when understood in its dictionary definition and according to the intentions of its original users. But it is only an element of a larger picture. The term *inerrancy* actually says much *less* than we need to say in commending the authority of Scripture. I will argue that Scripture, together with all of God's other communications to us, should be treated as nothing less than God's personal word.

To make that case, I don't think it's necessary to follow the usual theological practice today, setting forth the history of doctrine and the contemporary alternatives and then, in the small amount of space that remains, choosing among the viable options. I have summarized my view of the liberal tradition here in chapters 3–7, and I do hope that in later editions of this book and in other writings I will find time to interact more fully with those writings.[4] But although we can learn from the history of doctrine and from contemporary theologians, the final answers to our questions must come from the Word of God itself. And I don't think you need to look hard to find those answers. You don't need to engage in abstruse, complicated exegesis. You need only to look at the obvious things and be guided by them, rather than by Enlightenment skepticism. This book will attempt to set forth those obvious teachings and explore some of their implications.

The main difference between this book and other books on the doctrines of revelation and Scripture is that I am trying here, above all else, to be ruthlessly consistent with Scripture's own view of itself. In that regard, I'm interested in not only defending what Scripture says about Scripture, but defending it by means of the Bible's own worldview, its own epistemology,[5] and its own values.[6] That there is a circularity here I do not doubt. I am defending the Bible by the Bible. Circularity of a kind is unavoidable when one seeks to defend an ultimate standard of truth, for one's defense must itself be accountable to that standard.[7] Of course, I will not hesitate to bring extrabiblical considerations to bear on the argument when such considerations are acceptable within a biblical epistemology. But ultimately I trust the Holy Spirit to bring persuasion to the readers of this book. God's communication with human beings, we will see, is supernatural all the way through.

4. For examples of such interaction, see Appendices A, E, F, H, M, and Q in this volume.
5. I have formulated what I think a biblical epistemology looks like in *DKG*.
6. *DCL* focuses on biblical values. *DKG* makes the case that biblical epistemology can be understood as a subdivision of biblical ethics.
7. See *DKG*, 130–33.

CHAPTER 2

Lordship and the Word

If we are to understand the nature of the word of God, we must certainly understand something about the God who speaks. In my other writings (see especially the first seven chapters of *DG*), I have listed some important ways in which the God of Scripture differs from all the gods of other religions and the principles of philosophers. I will summarize these here.

GOD IS AN ABSOLUTE PERSONALITY

The biblical God is the supreme being of the universe—eternal, unchangeable, infinite. He is self-existent, self-authenticating, and self-justifying. He depends on no other reality for his existence, or to meet his needs. In these senses he is absolute. But he is not only absolute. He is also personal, an *absolute personality*.

Further, the biblical God is not only personal, but tripersonal. His self-love, for example, in Scripture is not based on the model of a narcissist, an individual admiring himself (though God would not be wrong to love himself in that way). Rather, his self-love is fully interpersonal: the Father loving the Son, the Son loving the Father, and the love of both embracing the Holy Spirit and his own love for them. God is for us the supreme model not only of personal virtues, but of interpersonal ones as well.

Other religions and philosophies honor absolute beings, such as the Hindu Brahman, the Greek Fate, Aristotle's Prime Mover, Hegel's Absolute. But none of these beings are personal. They do not know or love us, make decisions, make plans for history. Significantly in our present context, they do not *speak* to us.

Other religions and philosophies do honor personal gods, as with the polytheisms of Canaan, Greece, Egypt, Babylon, India, and modern paganism. Yet none of these personal gods are absolute. Only in biblical religion is the supreme being an absolute personality. Only in biblical religion does the supreme being *speak*. And only in biblical religion is the speaking God absolute, a being who, significantly, needs nobody or nothing outside himself to validate his speech.

Consider the immense significance of the fact that the Creator of heaven and earth, who sovereignly governs all the affairs of the universe, actually knows, befriends, even loves human beings—and that he *speaks* to us.

There are, of course, other religions that approach the biblical idea of an absolute personal God. These include Islam, Judaism, the Jehovah's Witnesses, and Mormonism. These present themselves as believing that the supreme being is an absolute person. I believe this claim is inconsistent with other things in these religions. Certainly, none of these religions embraces the absolute tripersonality of biblical theism. But my present point is that even in these religions the claim to believe in an absolute personal God arises from the Bible. For all these religions are deeply influenced by the Bible, though they have departed from it in many ways.

GOD IS THE CREATOR

God, the absolute tripersonality, is related to the world in terms of the *Creator-creature distinction*. He is absolute, and we are not. Cornelius Van Til expressed this distinction in a diagram with a large circle (God) and a small one under it (the creation). God and the world are distinct from each other.

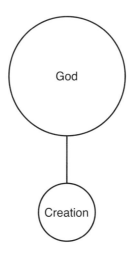

Fig. 2.1. Two circles

The world may never become God, nor can God become a creature. Even in the person of Christ, in which there is the most intimate possible union between God and human nature, there is (according to the formulation of the Council of Chalcedon, A.D. 451) no mixing or confusion of the two natures. In the incarnation, God does not abandon or compromise his deity, but takes on humanity. In salvation, we do not become God; rather, we learn to serve him as faithful creatures.

At the same time, the Creator and creature are not distant from each other. This, too, is evident from the person of Christ, in which deity and humanity are inseparable, though distinct. Indeed, the Creator is always present to his creatures. The most important thing about any creature is its relation to the Creator. The creature's life, in every respect, at every moment, is possible and meaningful only because of that relationship. In him we live and move and have our being (Acts 17:28).

GOD IS THE COVENANT LORD

The Creator is related to the creature as its *covenant Lord*. *Lord* represents the Hebrew *Yahweh* (Ex. 3:15), the name by which he wants his people forever to remember him. So the chief confessions of faith in the Bible are confessions of God's lordship (Deut. 6:4–5; Rom. 10:9; 1 Cor. 12:3; Phil. 2:11). God performs all his mighty works so that people will "know that I am the LORD" (Ex. 6:7; 7:5, 17; 8:22; 10:2; 14:4; etc.). The chief message of the OT is "God is the Lord." The chief message of the NT is "Jesus Christ is Lord."

To say that God is Lord is to say that everything else is his servant. The relationship between Lord and servant is called *covenant*. As in the section on God as Creator above, there is to be no confusion between Lord and servant.

In Scripture, God's covenant lordship has three major connotations: (1) God, by his almighty power, is fully in *control* of the creation. (2) What God says is ultimately *authoritative*, in the sense we have discussed previously. (3) As covenant Lord, he takes the creation (and parts of the creation, such as Israel, or the church) into special relationships with him, relationships that lead to blessing or cursing. So he is always *present with* them. He was literally present with Israel in the tabernacle and the temple. He became definitively present to us in the incarnation of Jesus Christ. And his Spirit indwells NT believers, making them his temple. Truly God is "God with us," Immanuel.

I describe God's control, authority, and presence as the three *lordship attributes*. I think there is some relationship between these and the three persons of the Trinity: in general, the Father formulates the eternal divine plan of nature and history (authority), the Son carries out that plan (control), and the Spirit applies it to every person and thing (presence). This triad is echoed in many areas of the teaching of Scripture, and as we will see, it is reflected throughout the biblical doctrine of the word of God.

As in previous Lordship books, I will also distinguish three *perspectives* by which we can look at all of reality, corresponding to the three lordship attributes: in the *situational* perspective, we will examine nature and history as they take place under the controlling power of God. In the *normative* perspective, we will look at the world as God's authoritative revelation to us. And in the *existential* perspective, we will focus on our own inwardness, our personal experience, in which God has chosen to be near to us. These are perspectives, for we cannot fully understand reality under one perspective without considering the other two.

If God is to communicate with his creatures, clearly he must communicate as the Lord, for that is what he is. He cannot abandon his lordship while speaking to us. So his word must come to us with absolute power (able to accomplish its purposes, Isa. 55:11), authority (beyond criticism, Rom. 4:20, as we earlier described the authority of language to create obligation), and presence (the Word as God's personal dwelling place, John 1:1; Heb. 4:12–13). The word of God is the word of the Lord. So it can be nothing other than the personal word we discussed earlier.

PART TWO

GOD'S WORD IN
MODERN THEOLOGY

The rest of this book will follow the pattern of my three perspectives. In Part 2, I will discuss the views of revelation and Scripture held by mainstream liberal theologians. That is our situational perspective, the theological situation into which we teach and preach the authority of God's Word. Part 3 will expound how Scripture itself defines the word, the normative perspective. Part 4 will discuss the means by which God's word comes from God's lips to our hearts, the existential perspective.

CHAPTER 3

Modern Views of Revelation

Following the example of Scripture, I prefer the term *word of God* to *revelation* when considering God's communication with his creatures. Scripture uses both terms, but *word* far more often. *Word* is God's communication. *Revelation* is the content disclosed by the word. The two terms can be used interchangeably, but I prefer to use the more common biblical terminology. Yet the mainstream modern theology of around 1650 to the present has chosen to speak most often of *revelation*, and perhaps it is best to present those modern concepts in terminology different from that emphasized in Scripture.

I will speak of *modern* and *liberal* theology somewhat synonymously: as those types of theology that do not accept the absolute authority of the Bible. There are, of course, nuances in these terms that I cannot discuss in this summary; so I will be describing as liberal some who, like Karl Barth, prefer not to be described that way. It is usually best to describe people in the terms they have chosen to describe themselves, but that cannot be an absolute rule.

What distinguishes modern views of revelation from orthodox (to my mind biblical) views is their affirmation of human *autonomy* in the realm of knowledge.[1] Intellectual autonomy is the view that human beings have the right to seek knowledge of God's world without being subject to God's

---

1. My emphasis on autonomy is very much influenced by the work of Cornelius Van Til. Herman Dooyeweerd also protested, at great length and in great depth, the "pretended autonomy of theoretical thought." See Dooyeweerd's *A New Critique of Theoretical Thought* (Lewiston, NY: Edward Mellen Press, 1997). I have some disagreements with Van Til, and

15

revelation. It first appears in the history of thought in Genesis 3's narrative of the fall, in which Adam and Eve make their decision to disobey God's personal word to them. In their decision, they affirm their right to think autonomously, even to the point of contradicting God himself.

The spirit of autonomy underlies every sinful decision of every human being. As I noted earlier, it is irrational in an important sense. Paul tells us in Romans 1:18–32 that human beings know God clearly from his revelation to them in creation, but that nevertheless they choose to repress this knowledge and exchange it for a lie. How could anyone imagine that contradicting the Master of the universe could be a wise decision? This foolishness mirrors the biblical paradigm of irrationality, the foolishness of Satan himself, who (again in the face of clear knowledge) tries to replace God on the throne of the universe.

In this satanic project, man seeks to become his own lord. He denies God's ultimate control, authority, and presence. Either he denies that there is such a Lord or he ascribes lordship to something in creation. If he denies that there is a Lord, he embraces *irrationalism*, the view that there is no ultimate meaning in the universe. If he ascribes lordship to something finite (i.e., idolatry), he embraces *rationalism*, the view that a godlike knowledge can be obtained from the creation alone.

Of course, Satan and his followers embrace rationalism irrationally, for they have no right to insist that their minds are the ultimate criterion of truth. Similarly, they embrace irrationalism rationalistically, assuming the ultimate authority of their own minds. So in unbelieving thought, rationalism and irrationalism are two sides of a single coin, though they actually contradict each other. That contradiction is part of the irrationality of it all. That irrationality permeates the whole fabric of human knowledge. So we can understand how the assumption of intellectual autonomy destroys knowledge.

Of course, as Romans 1 shows, Satan and his disciples do have a clear knowledge of God, which they repress. But they have that clear knowledge of God in spite of, not because of, their commitment to autonomy. If they were consistent with their commitment to autonomy, they could not know anything at all.

We can see this spirit of autonomy in all sin. As in Genesis 3, sin assumes autonomy. It assumes that God does not exist, or that he has not given us a personal word. That is true of the sins of individuals, families, and nations. It is true of all types of sin: stealing, adultery, murder, deceit. It is also true

more with Dooyeweerd. But I believe these two thinkers deserve far more attention than they have received by the philosophical and theological communities.

of intellectual sin: denying the truth in the face of clear knowledge. Why should anyone imagine that the intellect could be left out of our account of sin? The mind is part of our being. It contributes to sin as much as our wills and feelings, as much as our arms and legs. So the spirit of autonomy appears in the history of human thought.

In the history of religion, human beings devise idols (false gods) and ascribe to them some kind of ultimacy, though pagans at their best have understood that their false gods had no ultimate control, authority, or presence. But around 600 B.C. something new appears in Western thought, beginning among Greek thinkers in Asia Minor. These thinkers, such as Thales, Anaximenes, and Anaximander, were given a unique name, because their thought was significantly different from that of the previous religious teachers and writers. The name was *philosopher*. In itself, the term is a good one, designating love of wisdom. Christians, too, should engage in philosophy in this sense. But the Greek philosophers received that name not because of their general love of wisdom, but because of a unique feature of their thought. The feature was a commitment to intellectual autonomy. The philosophers rejected the authority of religion and tradition and insisted on the sole ultimate authority of human reason.[2]

Greek philosophy fell into the paradox I have ascribed to all would-be autonomous thought, that of rationalism and irrationalism. Greek philosophers were rationalists, in that they embraced the ultimate authority of human reason, and irrationalists in that they denied the existence of any adequate source of order in the world. Their project, sophisticated as it became in such later thinkers as Plato and Aristotle, was the impossible task of imposing a rational order on an essentially irrational world—or, as they put it, categorizing matter by form.

In the early centuries after Jesus' resurrection, biblical thought came to influence the philosophical discussion. The Christian thinkers made use of Greek philosophy, but they modified it considerably by their allegiance to the biblical worldview. They did not, however, break away entirely from the Greek conception. The *Summa Theologiae* of Thomas Aquinas (1225–74) begins with a distinction between two disciplines: philosophy, which operates by "natural reason" alone, and theology, which appeals to divine revelation. In Thomas's thought, these two spheres overlapped in certain ways. But in his work there was always some confusion as to the role of revelation in the sphere assigned to natural reason. He at least suggests

2. For more reflection on philosophical ideas that influence the theological understanding of revelation, see my review of Norman L. Geisler, ed., *Biblical Errancy*, Appendix M in this volume.

that intellectual autonomy is possible and legitimate in some degree and at some areas of thought.

The seventeenth century A.D. brought a change analogous to the birth of philosophy around 600 B.C. The medieval "scholastics" such as Aquinas had tried to combine biblical thought with Greek philosophy, and they had created their own Christian philosophical traditions to which all later philosophers were expected to subscribe. But as Thales rejected the traditions of the Greek priests and poets, René Descartes (1596–1650) and others rejected the traditions of scholasticism.

Wanting to achieve absolute certainty, Descartes resolved to doubt anything that he did not "clearly and distinctly perceive to be true." For him, all the teachings of the church, as well as the philosophical traditions, were in this sense subject to doubt. The only idea that he clearly and distinctly perceived to be true was the fact that he himself was thinking. So the famous *cogito, ergo sum*, "I think, therefore I am." From this foundational truth, Descartes proposed to erect, by logical deduction, the whole fabric of human knowledge. Among the truths in that fabric was the existence of God. Descartes did profess to be a Christian. But his philosophy and theology were built on a foundation of human autonomy, which, as we have seen, is radically unbiblical.

Intellectual autonomy has been the rule in philosophy down to the present, with a few exceptions. Indeed, this principle has deeply infected theology as well.

A younger contemporary of Descartes, Baruch (or Benedict) Spinoza (1634–77), attempted to carry on Descartes' program more consistently, by developing his philosophy in the form of a geometric system in his *Ethics* (1674). But Spinoza also applied the principle of intellectual autonomy to more explicitly theological subjects. In 1670, he published his *Tractatus Theologico-Politicus*, in which he dealt with the nature and interpretation of Scripture and its implications for politics. In this volume, he defends freedom of thought in society by attacking superstition. He contends that the Bible, rightly interpreted, leaves reason absolutely free. Rational knowledge is just as much revelation as anything in Scripture. Prophecy cannot give knowledge of phenomena beyond that available to reason alone. Miraculous events, which contravene the laws apprehended by reason, can never take place. Spinoza denies the Mosaic authorship of the Pentateuch and many other traditional ideas about the origin of Scripture. Essentially, he proposes that we read the Bible as any other ancient text, subjecting it to the criteria of human reason. It is God's Word only in the sense that God endorses all the conclusions of reason. And of course, Spinoza understands reason to be autonomous.

Spinoza's approach to Scripture (similar to that of others in the seventeenth century, such as Thomas Hobbes and Richard Simon) rather quickly became the dominant view of mainstream academic theology. The Cambridge Platonists in seventeenth-century England, such as Ralph Cudworth and Benjamin Whichcote, affirmed the primacy of reason, as did the Deists, such as Lord Herbert of Cherbury and Matthew Tindal. These were the harbingers of the so-called Enlightenment of the eighteenth century, of which Voltaire, Denis Diderot, and Gotthold Ephraim Lessing are well-known representatives. In the eighteenth through the twentieth centuries, the Germans led in the field of biblical criticism, with names such as H. S. Reimarus, D. F. Strauss, F. C. Baur, Julius Wellhausen, Johannes Weiss, Albert Schweitzer, and Rudolf Bultmann contributing to the liberal tradition. Today the "Jesus Seminar" in the United States (John Dominic Crossan, Robert Funk, Marcus Borg, and others) makes regular headlines for its pronouncements on what can and cannot be believed in the NT.

Some of these are more positive, some more negative as to the historical and doctrinal value of Scripture. But I can safely say that nobody in this succession ever took seriously the central issue: the acceptability of autonomous reasoning. Conservative scholars and churchmen did take issue with this principle, or at least they refused to accept it. But within the liberal movement itself, there was no consideration of the alternative. Intellectual autonomy was accepted as a presupposition, as something fundamental, not to be argued about. It was thought that anyone who disagreed was simply not a scholar, not qualified to do serious research.

Many did disagree and therefore maintained the authority of Scripture as the church had always done before Spinoza. We recall in this connection the names of biblical scholars E. W. Hengstenberg, J. F. K. Keil, Franz Delitzsch, Theodor Zahn, B. B. Warfield, Robert D. Wilson, Geerhardus Vos, J. Gresham Machen, George E. Ladd, F. F. Bruce, Edward J. Young, Meredith G. Kline, Ned Stonehouse, Donald Carson, Richard Bauckham, and Craig Blomberg. Certainly, these men qualify as scholars, if we are permitted to employ a less tendentious definition of scholarship than that common in the liberal community.

But the major university faculties were nonetheless dominated by those who embraced the principle of intellectual autonomy. It all happened very quickly. There was no academic debate on whether it is right for human beings to exercise reason without the authority of God's revelation. There was not much argument about whether the universities should change their time-honored commitments to divine revelation. Rather, major figures simply began teaching from the new point of view, and there was no significant resistance. They accepted the assumption of autonomy and saw to it that their successors accepted it, too. Campus politics certainly played a major role in this development. The conservatives did not know what hit them.

Soon, because pastors were trained in universities, the liberal view spread to the churches, so that by the late nineteenth century most mainstream denominations in America were tolerating that approach. In 1924, 1,274 ministers of the Presbyterian Church USA signed a document called the *Auburn Affirmation*, which denied that the inerrancy of Scripture, the virgin birth of Christ, the substitutionary atonement, the resurrection of Christ, and his miracles should be tests of orthodoxy in the denomination. In the 1930s, ministers in the denomination were disciplined for insisting that the church's missionaries believe in the above-listed doctrines. The liberal commitment to intellectual autonomy had made these doctrines optional, and many church leaders regarded them as literally untrue. Those who objected to these developments (contrary to liberal claims of "tolerance") were given no respect or power in the councils of the church.

This change was astonishing. The adoption of intellectual autonomy as a theological principle was certainly at least as important as the church's adoption of the Nicene doctrine of the Trinity in 381, or the doctrine of the two natures of Christ in 451. Yet without any council, without any significant debate, much of the church during the period 1650 to the present came to adopt the principle of intellectual autonomy in place of the authority of God's personal words. But this new doctrine changed everything. Given intellectual autonomy, there is no reason to accept supernatural biblical teachings such as the doctrine of the Trinity and the two natures of Christ. The virgin birth, miracles, atonement, resurrection, and glorious return of Jesus are on this basis no longer defensible. J. Gresham Machen showed, in *Christianity and Liberalism*, that liberalism rejected the historic Christian teachings about the Bible, God, Christ, the atonement, salvation, and the church.[3] Some thinkers rejected these traditional doctrines outright. Others reinterpreted them in some symbolic fashion. In both cases, these doctrines had to meet the criteria of autonomous human reason.

If these doctrines are true, they must be true because of God's personal testimony. There is no way that they can be validated on the authority of autonomous reason. Indeed, if human reason is autonomous, the God of the Bible does not exist, for his very nature as the Creator excludes the autonomy of his creatures. And in fact nothing at all can be validated by autonomous reason, for as we have seen, such reasoning leads to a rationalist-irrationalist dialectic, which destroys all knowledge. For that pottage, much of the church has forsaken its birthright, God's personal word.[4]

---

3. J. Gresham Machen, *Christianity and Liberalism* (Grand Rapids: Eerdmans, 1923).
4. For more discussion on the antithesis between biblical and unbiblical thought on the subject of the Word of God, see "Antithesis and the Doctrine of Scripture," Appendix A in this volume.

CHAPTER 4

Revelation and Reason

For the next several chapters, I will describe and evaluate in more detail the liberal theologies of revelation. I will organize this discussion under my three perspectives, normative, situational, and existential. Under the normative perspective, I will consider the relation of revelation to reason. Under the situational, I will discuss revelation and history. And under the existential, revelation and human subjectivity. Then there will be a chapter on the important relationship between revelation and God in these views.

I have said a great deal already about the relation of revelation and reason, and the liberal view of it. But there is more to be said.

I hope it is understood that my complaint against liberalism is not a complaint against reason itself, but against the propositions (1) that human reason operates autonomously, and (2) that autonomous reason provides the ultimate criteria of truth and falsity, right and wrong, by which everything (including Scripture) is to be judged.

Reason itself is a good gift of God. English translations of Scripture do not use the term *reason* in anything like a philosophical sense. But the Bible is full of what we call reasoning. For example, God often gives us reasons for his commands. In Exodus 20:11, God commands Israel to keep the Sabbath day, "for in six days the LORD made heaven and earth." Israel is not only to rest one day a week, but to rest for that reason. Deuteronomy 5:15 adds another reason: God rescued Israel from bondage in Egypt and gave them rest, so they should give rest to their households. In Isaiah 1:18,

God calls Israel, "Come now, let us reason!" Paul's letters often contain the term *therefore*, as in Romans 8:1 and 12:1. Paul uses it to indicate the reasons why God's people should hope in God and obey him.

Even when God's commands appear arbitrary, as in his command to Adam to abstain from the forbidden fruit, there is a reason: "for in the day that you eat of it you shall surely die" (Gen. 2:17). Even if there is no obvious connection between eating the fruit and bearing God's judgment, a rational person will not make a choice that opposes God's desires, that brings estrangement from God and death.

Service to God, then, is rational service. Service of the head as well as the heart. Those who disbelieve and disobey are not reasonable people; they are "fools" (Ps. 14:1; Prov. 1:32; 1 Cor. 1:20).

But Scripture does distinguish between right and wrong reasoning. In the parable of the talents (Matt. 25:14–30), the fellow who chose not to invest his talent but to hide it in the ground thought he had good reasons for doing so: "Master, I knew you to be a hard man, reaping where you did not sow, and gathering where you scattered no seed, so I was afraid, and I went and hid your talent in the ground. Here you have what is yours" (vv. 24–25). This is actually fairly plausible reasoning—reasoning that I might well have used myself in the same situation. But Jesus condemns it as not only fallacious, but "wicked" (v. 26). Reason is a good gift of God, but it is fallible, and it is affected by sin.

It is best, I think, to define reason as a human faculty, like our ability to see, hear, or touch. Reason is our ability to judge consistency and logical validity. It enables us to see whether two statements are logically consistent or inconsistent and when an argument is valid or invalid. Like our sight and hearing, it is not always accurate, and it can be distorted by sin. Sin gives us a bias against God's authoritative reasoning. And it commits us to intellectual autonomy, which, as we've seen, destroys knowledge the more consistently it is carried out.

The term *reason* can be used either descriptively (referring to the faculty just described) or normatively (referring to the right use of this faculty). In the first usage, even bad reasoning is reasoning. In the second usage, bad reasoning is not really reasoning at all; it is unreason.

It is then important to ask what constitutes good reasoning. There is, of course, a close relation between reason and logic, so that we regard violations of the laws of logic to be violations of reason as well. But an argument can lead to a false conclusion even when it is a logically valid syllogism. For example, consider: "All professors of theology eat rats. Dr. Clark is a professor of theology. Therefore Dr. Clark eats rats." This is a valid argument. But because the first premise is false, the conclusion may be false as well. That is to say, sound syllogisms require not only logical validity, but also true premises. Logic alone does not tell us whether our premises are false or true. That knowledge must come from elsewhere. One cannot, therefore, judge the rational strength of arguments by logic alone. Logical reasoning presupposes knowledge of reality beyond knowledge of logic.

In the context of a biblical worldview, logical reasoning presupposes God, the author and ultimate standard of logical truth and all human rationality. Denying God, as we have seen, leads necessarily to irrationality (and to rationalism as well!).

Now, as we have seen, the liberal theologies of revelation began among philosophers such as Baruch Spinoza of the rationalist tradition.[1] It seemed obvious to them that reason should have the final word in evaluating claims to revelation. Indeed, the only alternative appeared to be that we should make those evaluations *unreasonably*. I will surprise readers by saying that Christians, too, ought to believe in the ultimate authority of reason. But in saying this, I take *reason* in the normative sense, reason functioning at its best. Reason has the last word because it presupposes the reality of God and subjects itself to the "premises" of God's revelation to us.

The point was often made (as in Immanuel Kant's *Religion within the Limits of Reason Alone*[2]) that even if an angel speaks to us, our reason must determine whether it really is an angel, and whether the angel's words deserve to be followed. This point is just as cogent (if a bit more startling) applied to the personal words of God himself. Even if God himself were to speak to you, as to Abraham (Kant would say), your reason must determine whether it is really God speaking, and whether God deserves to be obeyed.

In my surprising mode again, I agree with this argument. Yes, indeed, our reason should evaluate every claim to revelation, including the claims of the biblical God. But what constitutes a sound rational analysis of these claims? The problem with the argument as presented by Spinoza and Kant is its assumption about how reason should function. It simply assumes, without raising the issue, that reason should function autonomously. As we have seen, this assumption must be challenged. It leads to rational unintelligibility as well as to spiritual disaster.

1. I am here using the term *rationalist* in a narrower sense than before. In the wider sense, as I discussed it in chapter 3, all would-be autonomous thought is rationalist (and of course irrationalist as well). In the narrower sense, *rationalist* refers to a distinct school of philosophy: philosophers who give more authority to reason than to sense experience. In this sense, the rationalist school is opposed to the *empiricist* school (e.g., John Locke, George Berkeley, and David Hume), which favored the primacy of sense experience. René Descartes and Spinoza were rationalists in both broader and narrower senses.

2. Many editions, such as 1934; repr., NY: Harper and Bros., 1960.

A legitimate rational evaluation of God's personal words will consider the authority of God and conclude that the hearer should certainly believe these words, without objection. In making this evaluation, reason is doing its proper work in the proper way, and it is completely trustworthy.

Later liberal thinkers, as we will see, didn't like the idea of subjecting God to human reason, but they still conceived of reason as functioning autonomously. Indeed, it was the autonomous character of reason that led them to be suspicious of reason. So they subordinated reason to history (Albrecht Ritschl, Oscar Cullmann), feeling (Friedrich Schleiermacher), Jesus Christ (Karl Barth), personal encounter (Martin Buber, Emil Brunner), self-understanding (Rudolf Bultmann), community (Roman Catholic thinkers and some Protestants), the experience of an oppressed community (Gustavo Gutiérrez, James Cone, Elizabeth Johnson), hope in an open future (Jürgen Moltmann), and others.

But these alternatives offer no remedy to the problem. If "history" means anything, it is a rational account of events, to be analyzed by rational people. It is not an alternative to reason, but a rational inquiry. Schleiermacher's "feeling" generated a great deal of rational reflection on Schleiermacher's part. Certainly, he intended his account of feeling, and his assertion of the primacy of feeling, to be a rational account. The same is true of the others, including Barth's "Jesus Christ." For Barth himself emphasized that in our understanding of Christ, there must be no *sacrificium intellectus*, no sacrifice of the intellect.

Evangelical Christians, too, should not claim that there is anything wrong with reason as such, or that it is unfit to identify and evaluate God's revelation. Scripture never suggests that there is any defect in human reason as such. The problem with reason is not that it is naturally unfit to examine revelation, but that it is fallen. The problem is that fallen man tries to use his reason autonomously. All his arguments are founded on the false premise that God is not the author and final standard of truth. We should not seek to be less rational, or to substitute something else for reason. Rather, our reason, with all the rest of us, should be regenerated by God's grace. Then we should learn to use reason in a new way, suited to regeneration, under the authority of our covenant Lord.

There is a certain circularity in saying that we should base our reasoning on God's Word, while evaluating God's Word. I have discussed this circularity in *DKG* and in chapter 1 of this book, and I will discuss it in later chapters as well,[3] because it is important for many issues that arise on these topics. Arguments are always circular when they seek to validate an

---

3. I have developed the topic especially in Appendix E.

ultimate principle of thought. To show that reason is ultimate, one must appeal to reason. To show that sense experience is ultimate, one must show that this view is warranted by sense experience itself. Similarly with history, feeling, experience, and so on. Christians should not fear charges of circularity when they are proving God's Word by God's own principles of rationality. All alternative systems of thought are in the same boat. And as we have seen, reasoning in accord with God's Word is the only kind of reasoning that doesn't dissolve into meaninglessness.

There is one limitation of reason that I have not so far referred to in this section. That is that reason, like all other human faculties, is incapable of knowing God exhaustively, knowing God as he knows himself. This fact implies that there may be arguments that seem sound to us that God himself (because of his superior understanding of logic and because he has a better knowledge of the truth of the premises) disallows. And there may be, for the same reason, arguments that seem invalid to us, but not to God, or conjunctions of sentences that seem inconsistent to us (such as "God is good, but he foreordains evil") but not to God.[4]

Reason, however, ought to acknowledge the limitation of being less than divine, of being creaturely. That is, paradoxically, the rational thing for reason to do. The Creator-creature distinction applies to reasoning as well as everything else. So God's higher knowledge is a limitation of human logic, but it is also a presupposition of it and a condition of its validity. To deny this limitation is to deny the ultimacy of God's thought and to assert human autonomy in its place. And autonomy leads to incoherence.[5]

4. I have discussed the problem of evil and the paradox of divine sovereignty and human responsibility in *DG*, chapters 8–9.
5. For more discussion of the relation between revelation and reason, see *DKG*, 242–301, 329–31, and my article "Rationality and Scripture," Appendix B in this volume.

CHAPTER 5

Revelation and History

As we have seen, theologians debating revelation have often discussed reason as a norm for evaluating revelation. So I have presented reason as the normative perspective of the debates.

We have also seen, however, that some theologians have wanted to deny or limit the authority of reason in the interest of some other category. The most common of these is history. I argued in the last section against the notion that history could somehow be a substitute for reason in Christian theology. Rather, the discussion of history requires reason. To discuss history is to engage in rational analysis.

Sometimes, however, we think of reason as a faculty for constructing abstract systems of thought, like Euclid's geometry, in which every idea is linked to every other by a tight chain of logical deductions, based on self-evident axioms. Certainly, it is often observed, Christian theology cannot be such a system. For it does not deal primarily with abstract or general truths, as does Euclid's system. Nor does it, like geometry, deal primarily with truths that are timeless, that are always true. Rather, Christian theology is about a *gospel*, good news: news about events in history. In that sense it is true that revelation is historical. So if we identify reason with axiomatic systems and timeless truths, then revelation is historical rather than rational.

Of course, it should be evident that I think it wrong to identify reason with axiomatic systems and timeless truths. These are some forms of rational thought. But rationality is not limited to them. Reason is also important in examining history, in understanding things that happen in time. So as we begin to discuss history, I don't intend to leave rationality behind. Reason is crucial in the examination of history. But it must be a reason that is subject to God's Word, not conceived as autonomous.

Or look at it this way: in the previous section, we looked at reason as a norm, as a tool of analysis. In this section we look at the data that theological reason seeks to analyze. As a norm, reason seeks to understand a situation. History is that situation, conceived in broadest terms. So reason is the normative perspective, history the situational.

The term *history* can refer either to a series of significant events or to a (rational!) account of such events. In both senses, therefore, history is crucial to Christian theology, even though the term is not often found in English translations of Scripture. As events, history provides the content of Christian faith. Revelation (well, "special" revelation) is an account of those events. So revelation is history and history is revelation.

The content of Scripture has often been summarized by three events: creation, fall, redemption. These can be further subdivided into many other events: God's creative acts over six days, Satan's temptation, the sin of our first parents, God's curses on and promises to them, the flood, God's covenant with Abraham, and so on. This series of events leads to the coming of Christ, his perfect life and teachings, and his atoning death, resurrection, and ascension. Events following the work of Christ on earth are the outpouring of the Spirit on Pentecost and the spread of the gospel through the earth. Revelation also holds out the promise of future events: Jesus' return, the final judgment, and the eternal destinies of the saved and the lost.

In chapter 2, I discussed three ways in which the biblical God is different from all other beings that have been called *god*. The biblical God is an absolute tripersonality, he relates to the world as Creator to creature, and he holds the office of covenant Lord over all things. The centrality of history is also a unique feature of biblical religion. For biblical faith, everything turns on the historical events of creation, fall, and redemption.

In Buddhism, there are, to be sure, stories of the Buddha's life, focusing on his enlightenment under the bodhi tree. But what the Buddha learns under the bodhi tree is not about specific historical events. Rather, he learns general truths, such as that life is suffering. On the Buddhist view, these are true at all times. They are true whether or not Gautama Buddha discovered them, and they would be true even if Buddha had never lived. Some forms of Buddhism, to be sure, honor stories about miracles performed by the Buddha. But to most sophisticated Buddhists, these miracle tales are an embarrassment. They detract from the main thrust of Buddhist theology, in which the path to enlightenment is not through miracle, but through a life based on the four noble truths and the noble eightfold path.

The same is true of Hinduism, Taoism, and other religions. Judaism and Islam seem to be exceptions. But neither of these admits to any historical basis for human salvation. As with Buddhism, they refer to history only to cite teachers such as Moses and Muhammad, who tell us how to live. If indeed these two religions are exceptional to some extent, however, it is because they are both strongly influenced by the Bible. This is the same point I made about their views of God in chapter 2.

So the centrality of historical events is foundational to biblical faith, and unique to it. It is therefore not surprising that many theologians in the liberal tradition came to assert that revelation is historical events, not spoken or written words. The Bible itself points to the mighty acts of God (Pss. 106:2; 145:4, 12; 150:2) as the subject matter of our praise. Obviously, God's acts in the context of creation, fall, and redemption do reveal him. They show us what kind of God he is. For example, the NT often singles out the atonement as the chief revelation of, indeed the definition of, God's love (John 3:16; Rom. 5:8; Eph. 2:4–5; 1 John 3:16; 4:8–11; Rev. 1:5).

It is tempting to say, therefore, as some theologians have, that these events are a more fundamental revelation of God than the words about those events. On the other hand, it is the words that make the events accessible to us. A frequent pattern in Scripture is that a prophet will predict an event, then a passage narrates the event, and then further commentary interprets the event. Word, event, word. But even the narrative of the event is by word. The nature of an event is that it occurs at a specific time and place. Words are the *news* of the event, the necessary media to report that event to people who weren't there, and to interpret its significance. If the event, say, of Jesus' atonement had taken place without witnesses to spread the news in words, we would not benefit from it today.

So James Barr, in *Old and New in Interpretation*, says:

> The progression of the story is given not only by what God does but also by what he says. Indeed, yet more, there is no progression given by God's deeds and sayings alone, but only one when both of these are combined with the deeds and sayings of men. It is possible to make a chain of things done by God, and regard the sayings attributed to him as human meditation upon the things done. If we do this, we should be frank that it is also a modern

rationalizing device, which departs from the form, and therefore from the spirit, of the literature itself.[1]

Barr was no fundamentalist; indeed, he was a very sharp critic of conservative Christianity. Yet he was also a sharp critic of the theologians who tried to limit revelation to the actions of God narrated in Scripture and to disparage the authority of his words reported there. It's fairly obvious when you think about it. Scripture represents God both as acting and as speaking, and it doesn't prefer the one to the other.

Those who prefer God's acts to his words do so not because of anything in Scripture, but because they demand the right to consider biblical history autonomously. Divine words get in the way when human beings try to place their own interpretations on God's actions.

Hence, through the history of liberal theology, a number of theologians have sought to place emphasis on history, the acts of God, as opposed to revealed words. Among these are Albrecht Ritschl (1822–99), "acts of God" theologians of the mid-twentieth century such as Oscar Cullmann (1902–99) and G. Ernest Wright (1909–74), and the later school of Wolfhart Pannenberg (1928–). In Ritschl's understanding, theology should be based on the attempt of historians to find and understand the "historical Jesus." For Cullmann, revelation consists of historical events interpreted by faith. For Pannenberg, revelation is general history, understood by reason to validate the Christian faith. Others such as Karl Barth (1886–1968) also had much to say on the role of history in revelation, as part of his larger theology of revelation.[2]

For Ritschl, history is history interpreted by autonomous reason. What is authoritative in the historical events is not the events themselves, or truths derived from those events, but "value judgments" that arise from the work of the historian. Pannenberg's thought is similar, except that Pannenberg is more interested in Jesus' resurrection as a reference point for understanding the Bible's interpretations of its history. For Cullmann, the events in question may be perfectly natural in themselves, perhaps unremarkable; but

1. James Barr, *Old and New in Interpretation* (London: SCM Press, 1966), 21. He adds, "Such a device has more serious consequences than at first appears, for it damages the picture of the personal God of the Bible."

2. Readers may also be interested in my paper "Muller on Theology," *WTJ* 56 (Spring 1994): 133–51, also available at http://www.frame-poythress.org/frame_articles/1994Muller.htm and as Appendix C in this volume. In this review article I take issue with Richard Muller's book *The Study of Theology: From Biblical Interpretation to Contemporary Formulation*, Foundations of Contemporary Interpretation 7 (Grand Rapids: Zondervan, 1991). Muller presents an evangelical version of the thesis that theology is a form of history. I complain that he does not give Scripture an adequate role in his understanding of theological method.

when one looks at them in faith, they become significant. In a way, what is important for Cullmann is not the event itself, but faith's interpretation of the event. So although he speaks much of the primacy of the acts of God, he actually ascribes more authority to interpretation than to fact.

None of these repudiates the principle of human intellectual autonomy. Indeed, all presuppose it. For all of them, history is events interpreted by autonomous human thought. This is why, I think, in the end Cullmann should be seen as backing away from history, embracing faith instead. But the relation between faith and event in his thought is obscure.

Barth distinguished between two concepts of history, expressed by two German words, *Geschichte* and *Historie*. *Historie* consists of events available for the inspection of secular historians, who use the standard techniques of autonomous historiography. Barth, like Cullmann (but not like Ritschl or Pannenberg), hesitates to base the Christian faith on *Historie*, so defined. But he recognizes in Scripture the centrality of such events as Christ's incarnation, atonement, and resurrection.[3] So he explains these events as history, taken in a different sense: *Geschichte*. It is very difficult from Barth's writings to get a clear idea of what *Geschichte* is. Barth's main concern, I think, is to insulate it from the methods of autonomous, "objective" historians. *Historie* is indeed accessible to them. In it, they are free to believe or disbelieve, to determine for themselves its significance. But Barth does not want to give them such freedom with the great events of redemption.

Nevertheless, if *Geschichte* is to be truly independent of autonomous historical science, Barth thinks that it must be of a very different character from *Historie*. Events of *Historie* take place at particular times and places. Those times and places can be investigated, so that the historian can make an authoritative judgment whether they happened or not. *Geschichte* must, however, be immune to such profane analysis. So the events of *Geschichte* must be removed from calendar time and space.

Another distinction: events of *Historie* can affect only those who directly experience them when and where they can occur, or those who hear authoritative reports from scientific historians. But events in *Geschichte* can affect all people equally.

3. Many in the church have attempted to make major distinctions between events such as the atonement and resurrection, and "secular" events such as the Battle of Waterloo. Compare (1) the medieval distinction between nature and grace, (2) Martin Luther's distinction between the "two kingdoms," (3) attempts among liberal theologians and some evangelicals to distinguish between Scripture's authority for "faith and practice" and for supposedly secular areas of life, and (4) Meredith G. Kline's attempt to distinguish between the "realm of the holy" and the "realm of the common." I reject all of these as lacking biblical support. (For argumentation, see *DCL*.) God's lordship, and therefore the scope and authority of his Word, extends to all of life.

The idea of *Geschichte* as a series of events without specific time and place, that affect all people, and that can be known apart from the mediation of historical scholarship is an odd notion. It seems even odder for Barth to place the incarnation, atonement, and resurrection into that realm. So all sorts of questions have arisen as to whether Barth believes these events "really happened" in the time-and-space world. To say the least, Barth's answer to this question is unclear. He does believe that the resurrection, for example, took place in literal history; but he represents this event as a pointer to a higher reality that can only be described as *geschichtlich*.

Clarification of this issue will have to be left to Barth scholars more expert than I. I should say, however, that this unclarity arises because Barth accepts the notion of intellectual autonomy. *Historie* is precisely the sphere in which such autonomy holds sway. So Barth believes that secular scholars should be perfectly free to criticize the historical assertions of the Bible. But as a Christian, Barth senses the danger of exposing the central truths of redemption to such negative criticism. *Geschichte*, whatever other purposes it may serve, supports that concern, but it introduces much confusion.

It would be better simply to repudiate the legitimacy of autonomous historical scholarship. Then there is no need for two histories. There is only one, which occurs in time and space, and which is accessible to historians who regard God's Word as their ultimate standard of truth. Nothing in the Bible suggests the kind of distinction that Barth sets forth, and Barth's formulation brings nothing but confusion to discussions of biblical epistemology. In Scripture, it is simple: we believe in the incarnation, the cross, and the resurrection because of the apostolic testimony (as 1 Cor. 15:1–2, 11), which amounts to God's personal words.

The whole discussion began with Gotthold Ephraim Lessing (1729–81), who said in his "On the Proof of the Spirit and of Power"[4] that there was a "big, ugly ditch" between "accidental truths of history" and "necessary truths of reason." Now, it is right to say that necessary truths of reason, like $2 + 2 = 4$, are not derived from an examination of historical events. And it is true that most historical inquiries do not yield the kind of certainty that we associate with mathematical and logical truths. But Lessing intended to draw a theological implication from this observation. As an Enlightenment rationalist, he believed, like Baruch Spinoza, that autonomous reason is the ultimate criterion of faith. So his "ditch" was a ditch not only between history and the necessary truths of reason, but also between history and faith.

---

4. In H. B. Nisbet, ed. and trans., *Lessing: Philosophical and Theological Writings* (Cambridge: Cambridge University Press, 2005).

Many have been troubled by Lessing's ditch. How can we believe in Christ on the basis of historical events, when those events are so uncertain? No historical event is absolutely certain, it seems, let alone events that took place in a vastly different time and culture. The theologians of history that we have considered in this chapter were all somewhat intimidated by this chasm. Ritschl and Pannenberg thought they could cross the chasm by autonomous historical scholarship. Cullmann felt the need of something else to bridge the gap, which he called faith. Barth thought that he had to distinguish a new kind of history, in which there was no gap, but in which historical scholarship played no role.

In this respect, Barth follows Immanuel Kant. For Kant, the world of ordinary experience in time and space, the world of "phenomena," is knowable by autonomous human reason; indeed, its fundamental structure is created by reason. Even "religion within the limits of reason" is subject to the criteria of autonomous rationality, as I indicated in the previous chapter. That would include knowledge of the historical events recorded in the Bible. But Kant also speaks of the "noumenal" realm, the realm of things as they are in themselves, in which reason is incompetent. We can, nevertheless, imagine what the noumenal world is like and develop beliefs about it by a kind of "faith." Although the existence of God, for example, cannot be demonstrated by reason, we should believe that God exists for the scientific and moral advantages that belief gives us. Barth's *Historie* is much like Kant's phenomenal realm; Barth's *Geschichte* is much like Kant's noumenal. Barth leaps Lessing's ditch by placing faith in *Geschichte*, much as Kant placed it in a posited noumenal. Both Barth and Kant do this because they agree with Lessing as to the autonomy of reason in historical scholarship. They concede ordinary history in time and space to secularists, in order to be able to make theological statements concerning a different realm, unfettered by historical scholarship.

But if we renounce the autonomy of historical scholarship, then the gap disappears. If God's own testimony resolves all controversy, then the truths of redemptive history are not dubious or merely probable. They are certain, because God's Word is our ultimate criterion of certainty.[5] Histori-

---

5. I will indicate later that even with a soundly biblical epistemology, a believer may not become certain about everything in Scripture. There are questions of interpretation, and of course our level of understanding is subject to the sovereign decision of the Holy Spirit. But the uncertainties in our faith do not spring from the fact that history is essentially unknowable or uncertain. Nor should we imagine that there are no certainties in our faith. It is hard to conceive of any disciple of Christ who is uncertain, for example, that Jesus lived, or that he rose from the dead. For such a disciple, these events become the *criterion* of certainty, the certainty by which all other certainties are tested. See chap. 41.

cal scholarship that proceeds with this presupposition will attain certainty about the main redemptive events of Scripture.

Then we are free to regard God's revelation as it is in the Bible: both divine acts and divine words, the words interpreting the acts and the acts as the subject matter of the words. We study the events in the authoritative light of God's words, and we study the content of the words, which tell us of God's acts.[6]

6. For more discussion of the relation between revelation and history in modern theology, see "Antithesis and the Doctrine of Scripture," Appendix A in this volume.

CHAPTER 6

Revelation and Human Subjectivity

We have seen that modern theologians have developed ideas of revelation drastically different from the traditional views of the church. They have substituted human reason for the personal words of God, as the ultimate test of truth. Some have also tried to locate revelation in history rather than in divine words, not only because of the actual prominence of history in Scripture, but because history seems more amenable to autonomous rational thought than divine words. I have tried to show that it is biblically wrong to substitute either history or human rationality for the ultimate authority of God's personal words.

Another approach to revelation in liberal theology has been to identify it with a subjective event, something that takes place within the human heart. This view is most often associated with Friedrich E. D. Schleiermacher (1768–1834), often called the "father of modern theology." Schleiermacher was not pleased with the rationalism of earlier modern thinkers such as Baruch Spinoza and Immanuel Kant. He thought the focus on reason was unsuitable to the distinctive nature of religion. To him, religion was based not on reason, but on *Gefühl*, a German term that can be translated "feeling" or "intuition." Religion begins, he thought, with a "feeling of absolute dependence," and *God* is, in the first instance, a name for that reality we feel dependent on. The Christian faith interprets that reality in terms of Jesus Christ. So Christian theology expresses the Christian religious affections in the form of speech. The feeling is first, the words (of Scripture and theology) a secondary expression of and reflection on the feeling.

So for Schleiermacher, revelation is not the deliverances of reason as such, or the history presented in Scripture, but the feeling of God, the religious consciousness, that interprets the biblical history. Revelation is primarily subjective, not objective. It is not objective truths, but our subjective responses to objective truths.

Although Schleiermacher tries to lessen the emphasis on reason that was so strong in the work of his predecessors, we should note that Schleiermacher's voluminous writings are not just expressions of feeling. They are rational *analyses* of religious feeling. And as with others we have discussed, Schleiermacher gives no indication of bringing reason under the authority of divine words. His reasoning seeks to be *autonomous*. Autonomous feelings interpreted by autonomous reasoning. In fact, one suspects that Schleiermacher has limited revelation to feeling in part to avoid making religious feeling subordinate to divine words. So Schleiermacher's differences from the rationalists are not as great as he would have us believe.

Emotion and reason, I believe, are not sharply separate aspects of the mind.[1] Each affects the other, of course. Moreover, each defines the other in an important sense. Emotion can be understood as a kind of reasoning, in the sense that it is an appropriate or inappropriate response to data given to the person.[2] And reason is a kind of emotion: for when we arrive at conviction following a process of rational analysis, that conviction is very much a feeling, what I have elsewhere called "cognitive rest."[3]

So when we pass from Spinoza to Schleiermacher, from reason to feeling as a judge of truth, we have not passed very far. The real issue is between those who accept and reject autonomy, not between autonomous reason and autonomous feeling. Similarly, there is not a great difference between Schleiermacher and those liberal theologians who have identified revelation with history. For what they consider history is either an achievement of autonomous reason (Albrecht Ritschl, Wolfhart Pannenberg) or a datum malleable to subjective faith (Oscar Cullmann). Rationalism, historicism, and subjectivism are three perspectives on autonomous human thought. None are capable of dealing properly with God's personal words.

Nevertheless, we should look at some more recent representatives of theological subjectivism, for many have followed Schleiermacher's emphasis. Although Søren Kierkegaard (1813–55) recognized an objective revelation in Scripture, he considered the objective truth of Scripture to be far less important than our subjective response to God. Emil Brunner (1889–1966)

---

1. For more discussion of this relationship, see *DKG*, 337–39; *DG*, 608–11; *DCL*, 370–82.
2. Emotional responses tend to be more spontaneous, rational responses more labored; but there is a continuum between these, not a sharp division.
3. *DKG*, 152–62.

was deeply critical of Schleiermacher. Yet, following suggestions of Martin Buber (1878–1965) and Ferdinand Ebner (1882–1931), Brunner came to think that revelation in its highest sense was a personal encounter between God and the individual. The divine-human encounter cannot be described objectively. Indeed, the use of words depersonalizes it. Factual knowledge "about" God compromises the integrity of our knowledge of God himself. So revelation can never be identified with a spoken discourse or a written document. In this sense, it is subjective rather than objective.

Karl Barth, though his emphasis is elsewhere as we will see, also identifies revelation with human subjectivity at a certain level. For him, Scripture is the word of God only as it "becomes" the word of God to an individual by a present event.[4] Its being, as the word of God, is entirely in its becoming the word. We never "have" God's word, but only the recollection of its being given in the past and the expectation or hope that we will hear it again in the future. Otherwise, Barth thinks, God's words become objects, to be "possessed," "manipulated," or "preserved" by human beings. Thus, he believes, God loses control over his own words. So the biblical text should never be simply equated with God's word. It is a human document, prone to error, even in its theological assertions. But that is of no concern to faith, in Barth's view. Whether there are errors in the biblical text is of no consequence: errors do not prevent God from speaking his instantaneous, unpreservable words. The erroneous text may "become" the word of God anytime God wants it to.

I have some sympathy with Kierkegaard, who was wrestling with dead orthodoxy in the Danish Lutheran state church. He recognized the biblical importance of a living experience with God, in which God actually enters time and enters the experience of the individual. But his contrasts between objective and subjective tend to set asunder what Scripture brings together. In Scripture, subjective revelation is the Spirit's illumination of objective revelation. It brings the objective truth of Scripture into our hearts, communicating to us a vital personal relationship with Christ.

I have less sympathy for Brunner. His insistence that objective words and facts compromise the personal character of relationships is nonsense. It is not true on the human level. A friendship may sometimes be compro-

---

4. More recent Barth scholars emphasize that for Barth, the Bible "is" the word of God; it does not only "become" the word. Indeed, it "becomes" because it "is." But its "being is in becoming," so its "being" the word of God is simply its capacity to become the word of God. In my judgment, the consequences are the same, whether the Bible "is" the word in its becoming, or whether the Bible merely becomes the word without being it. In neither case are we authorized to receive the words of Scripture as God's personal words, except on those special occasions when he chooses to speak through the Bible.

mised when facts come to light, but more often factual knowledge enriches such relationships. And Scripture never suggests that a factual knowledge of God's character, his words, and his deeds diminishes the quality of our friendship with him—quite the contrary.

As for Barth, his conception is also unbiblical. Scripture never says that "the being of God's word is in its becoming." Rather, in Scripture God simply speaks his personal words, and people are expected to believe, obey, rejoice, mourn, give thanks, and so forth. Revelation in Scripture is not something instantaneous, appearing for a moment and then disappearing, leaving only its "recollection and expectation," as Barth says. Rather, revelation is to be preserved from one generation to the next (as Ps. 78:1–8). The Ten Commandments, written by the finger of God, were to be kept by the ark of the covenant, the holiest place in Israel (Deut. 10:5). That document is to be read over and over again, in every sabbatical year (Deut. 31:10–13). The apostolic tradition of the gospel of Christ is also something given once for all that is to be preserved and guarded (Jude 3).[5]

Does the objective preservation of the text compromise God's sovereignty over his Word? Certainly not. The document is the constitution of God's covenant people. It is the very expression of his sovereign authority. It validates God's sovereign right to impose on his people everlasting ordinances. The objectivity of revelation is precisely what protects it from human manipulation.

Orthodox Reformed theology does not reject a subjective element in revelation, but it formulates it rather differently. In a Reformed understanding, there is both objective and subjective revelation. God reveals himself in creation and in Scripture, objectively. But that objective revelation is of no use to us unless the Holy Spirit illumines our hearts and minds. As sinners, we suppress God's revelation (Romans 1 again). It is the gracious, regenerating work of the Spirit that enables us to understand, believe, and obey. So on the Reformed view, there is a sense in which revelation is not completed until it becomes subjective by the Spirit's work.[6]

The term *revelation* has various uses, some objective, some subjective. When a government official announces the year's budget in a document, we say that the budget has been "revealed," even though nobody may have actually read the document. Einstein revealed his general theory of relativity to all, publicly, in 1915, even though few people on the earth could actually understand it. That is objective revelation, like the natural

---

5. On this point, see chapter 16.
6. On this point, see chapters 41–44.

revelation in Romans 1, which reveals God clearly no matter how man chooses to respond.

But there are other cases in which something does not become revelation until someone actually knows it. The price of grain in China is public knowledge, but I don't know it. It has been objectively revealed, but it has not been revealed *to me*. Now, in Romans 1, the revelation is both objective and subjective. The passage does not contemplate anyone who is ignorant of this revelation or who has not responded to it. Rather, everybody knows it, and knows God (v. 21) through it.

A further distinction is also important if we are to understand the debate over revelation. There are different human responses to revelation: responses in unbelief and in faith. In Romans 1, the response of the pagans is to repress the truth, exchange it for a lie, and so on. But in Matthew 11:27, Jesus says that "no one knows the Father except the Son and anyone to whom the Son chooses to reveal him." Now, Jesus here refers to a subjective revelation, a revelation that brings knowledge to the hearer, and indeed knowledge as part of a close saving relationship with the Father and the Son, a knowledge in faith. This meaning of *revelation* can also be found in Ephesians 1:17, where Paul prays that God will give to the Ephesians "a spirit of wisdom and of revelation in the knowledge of [Christ]."

So we may distinguish three kinds of revelation: (1) objective revelation, (2) subjective revelation received in unbelief, and (3) subjective revelation received in faith.

Now, since Schleiermacher, liberal theologians have tended to say that revelation doesn't exist unless it is subjective, until someone knows it. I have sometimes described this tendency as the "subjective turn" in the history of the doctrine of revelation. Liberals have tended to disparage the idea of objective revelation, the revelation that is "just there" in nature and Scripture regardless of what anybody thinks. Further, they have tended to believe that revelation is not revelation unless it is received *in faith*. So if someone has not come to believe, then he has not actually received revelation. This idea contributes to the universalistic tendencies in liberalism, for it regards those who reject God as those who have not received revelation, rather than (as in Romans 1) those who have received it and have rejected it.

Scripture, however, as we have seen, speaks of both objective and subjective revelation, and of revelation received both in unbelief and in faith. All these kinds of revelation are important. Objective revelation is important, both because it actually exists and because it creates an obligation to believe. (Romans 1:20 puts the point negatively: it takes away our excuses.) Subjective revelation received in unbelief is important as an illustration of human depravity: man represses the truth, even when it is presented clearly to him. And subjective revelation received in faith, by the grace of God and the power of the Spirit, shows that God drives his Word home to the hearts and minds of those he intends to communicate with as a Father and friend.

So for orthodox Reformed theology, there are both subjective and objective forms of revelation. For Schleiermacher and the subjectivist tradition, there is only subjective.[7] And thereby Schleiermacher loses the element of *obligation*, which we earlier associated with the concept of *authority*. Revelation is not just what we feel, or even what we believe on the basis of feelings. It is what we *ought* to believe, what we are *obligated* to confess.

The present event, in which the Spirit draws our hearts into God's embrace, is an illumination of the Word of God, the gospel of Christ, already and permanently revealed (1 Thess. 1:5; 2:13).

There really is a subjective element in God's revelation, for God intends his words to be apprehended and understood. All true communication is objective (the content and the transmission) and subjective (the hearing and the response). But the subjective element is a human response to God's objective personal words to us. Liberal theology has often sought to avoid the authority of God's personal words by eliminating the objective side of the communication. This enables man to judge God's Word with his autonomous reason. That concept is unacceptable to Christian believers.

7. As we will see in the next chapter, Barth regards revelation in Christ as objective in a certain sense. But our knowledge of him is a subjective occurrence that cannot be expressed in objective truths.

CHAPTER 7

Revelation and God Himself

I have considered modern liberal views of revelation in terms of three themes representing our normative (reason), situational (history), and existential (feeling) perspectives. The word *perspective* indicates my judgment that these three approaches are not very different from one another. Rather, they represent three aspects of a single approach, one that subordinates God's personal words to human autonomous thought.

In my judgment, these views are more right in what they affirm than in what they deny. It is not wrong to say that reason should judge matters of religion. It is wrong to say that such judgments should be made autonomously. It is not wrong to say that revelation centers on historical events. But it is wrong to insist on interpreting and evaluating these by autonomous historiography. Further, it is not wrong to say that revelation consists of feelings; that, too, is a legitimate perspective! But it is wrong to insist that those feelings be understood, interpreted, and evaluated by autonomous thought.

There are other features of liberal thought about revelation that we will consider later in this text, on subjects such as hermeneutics, canon, and the accuracy and purpose of Scripture. I postpone them because these matters concern written revelation specifically rather than revelation in general, and because they have attracted more or less equal interest both in liberal and in orthodox theological traditions.

But something should be said here about one more theme that has often appeared in liberal theology, especially in the neoorthodox writers of the mid-twentieth century. That is the theme that revelation is essentially identical with God himself. This broad statement puts talk of reason, history, and subjectivity into a larger context. Whatever we say about reason, history, and subjectivity, some theologians say, they are nothing more than means of putting us in touch with God himself.

We may recall the slogan common during that period: "God doesn't reveal information; he reveals himself." The purpose of this slogan was to demean the idea that God speaks to us in personal words, particularly words that state propositions. As a general refutation of the personal-word model of revelation, this slogan is not very impressive. On the human level, there is no reason why someone cannot reveal himself through revealing information about himself. In fact, we regularly do that. It's almost impossible to imagine revealing yourself to someone without at the same time revealing information about yourself. And whenever we reveal information about ourselves, we are to some extent (not exhaustively, to be sure) revealing ourselves.

On the divine level, there is certainly no scriptural support for the notion that God never reveals information about himself, that such information tells us nothing about God himself, or that God's giving of information is not revelation. Consider the uses of "reveal" in Daniel 2:47; Matthew 11:27; and Philippians 3:15 and of "revelation" in Romans 16:25; 1 Corinthians 14:6, 26; Galatians 1:12; 2:2; Ephesians 1:17; 3:3; and Revelation 1:1. These constitute most of the NT occurrences of this word group. All of these passages present revelation as God's communicating information. First Peter 1:13 uses "revelation" to refer to Jesus' return, probably in view of the fact that it is informative. The return of Jesus is glorious, a public display of his lordship that reveals Christ himself, and also many things about him.

Nevertheless, the equation of revelation with God himself can be understood in ways that merit serious theological discussion. Karl Barth's view is a case in point. We have seen that Barth engages the continuing discussions about the relation of revelation to reason, history, and subjectivity. But the heart of his view is that revelation is nothing less than Jesus Christ himself. Barth develops this position by showing that revelation has a Trinitarian structure: the Father is the Revealer, the Son the Revelation, and the Spirit the Revealedness. So when Barth defines revelation, he focuses on the Son. He distinguishes three forms of revelation: Christ, Scripture, and Preaching. These are hierarchically structured. Christ alone is revelation in the fullest sense. Scripture may be called revelation insofar as it witnesses to Christ and insofar as the Spirit uses it as an instrument to bring God's Word (Christ) to its recipient. Preaching is revelation insofar as it witnesses to Scripture and thereby puts us in touch with Christ and the Spirit. Scripture and Preaching are not in themselves the word of God, but they can "become the word," and they "are" the word "in becoming."

It is theologically right to say that in a sense God is revelation. God is a being who in his very nature is communicative. He speaks not only to creatures, but within his Trinitarian existence, Father to Son, Son to Father, both to the Spirit, and the Spirit to both of them.[1] And we should note the specific biblical references to Christ as the Word of God, which we will examine more directly in chapter 11. This attribution is most explicit in John 1:1, but is also evident in Hebrews 1:1–3 and 1 John 1:1–3. Note also Paul's use of Deuteronomy 30:11–14, which speaks of the nearness of God's word to Israel, to refer to the nearness of Christ in Romans 10:6–8. Note also the related ideas that Christ is God's wisdom (1 Cor. 1:30) and that he is God's name (Phil. 2:10–11; cf. Isa. 45:23). When the Word becomes flesh, he speaks with authority greater than any scribe (Matt. 7:29).

But it is also evident in Scripture that the triune God reveals himself through personal words, received through such means as reason, history, and human subjectivity. Should we say with Barth that Christ is the true revelation and that the personal words are revelation in a lesser sense, as witnesses to Christ? Or would it be better to say that in those personal words Christ himself comes to us and speaks? I will argue the second possibility later on.

What is clear from Scripture, however, is that the identity of revelation with Christ does not compromise the authority of God's personal words. If anything, it underscores that authority. For to dishonor God's personal word is to dishonor Christ. To disobey the personal word is to disobey Christ. To disbelieve the personal word is to disbelieve Christ.

Even if God's personal words, from an ontological point of view, are something "less" than Christ himself, they are not less authoritative, less reliable, or less powerful.

When the Word became flesh and dwelt among us, he did not merely stand somewhere so that people could look at him and absorb some silent influence from him. Rather, he *taught*. That is what we would expect from an absolute *person*. He said to Pilate, "For this purpose I was born and for this purpose I have come into the world—to bear witness to the truth. Everyone who is of the truth listens to my voice" (John 18:37). His word was uniquely authoritative (Matt. 7:29) because *he* was uniquely authoritative. The fact that he was the Word meant that his words were of ultimate authority.

1. See *DG*, 470–75, and my further discussion in chapters 8, 11, and 42 of this book.

So the Christological nature of revelation does not permit us to disparage God's personal words in any way. Rather, it enhances their authority and power. Peter says, "Lord, to whom shall we go? You have the words of eternal life" (John 6:68).

It is best to see Christ not as a "form" of revelation superior to other forms, but as the *speaker* of God's personal words.[2] So our response to God's personal words is nothing less than our response to Christ himself. In God's personal words, Christ himself comes to engage our belief and obedience.

Barth does make the value judgment that Christ himself is somehow more authoritative than the words given in Scripture, or any words or sentences given to human beings. We ought to reject that judgment. Christ as Lord is our supreme authority. But to say that he is more authoritative than his own words (i.e., more authoritative than himself) is nonsense. And Scripture itself never makes any such value judgment. Rather, it calls us to give to Jesus' words the same reverence, obedience, and belief that we give to Jesus himself.

Nevertheless, we should thank Barth for drawing our attention to the identity between the Word and Christ. As with the other themes in modern theology that we have considered, we should agree with what Barth affirms, but not with what he denies. He affirms rightly that Christ is God's Word; but he is wrong to deny that God's personal words, the very words of Christ, are ultimately authoritative.[3]

2. Christ is, of course, also central to forms of revelation other than word-revelation. He is the one who performs the mighty acts of God, what I will call *event-revelation* in chapter 13. And he is the person who most reveals the Father, as I will indicate in chapter 42.

3. For more discussion of liberal theologies of revelation, see Appendices A, F, H, and Q in this volume.

PART THREE

THE NATURE OF
GOD'S WORD

In Part 2, I summarized and evaluated approaches of representative modern theologians in dealing with revelation and the Word of God. That is the theological situation in which we live, and in which we are called to rethink these doctrines. But the determining voice in our deliberations must be that of God himself.[1] His voice in Scripture must be our norm, our rule for determining what we should say today. So I describe the modern theological discussion as our *situational perspective*, Scripture's self-witness as the *normative perspective*. The Bible itself will show us how to apply its teaching to the situation we are in.

Some may think this approach is circular, for in determining the Bible's own view of revelation I will be assuming at the outset some of my conclusions. For example, since I maintain that God is the author of Scripture, I will assume that Scripture is consistent with itself, that it presents (across its sixty-six books) a single view of its own authority.

I defended this circularity in chapters 1 and 4, above, and elsewhere.[2] Circularity is necessary when any system of thought seeks to defend its first

---

1. So I reject the common pattern of theology today in which a writer cites all the contemporary literature on his subject and then tries to come to a conclusion by triangulating among the different views with little reference to Scripture. To determine the truth of any theological proposal, we must look at Scripture itself in depth, even at the expense of neglecting some historical and current thought.

2. *DKG*, 130–33; *AGG*, 9–14; Appendix E in this volume.

principle, its supreme authority. A rationalist must defend his rationalism by appealing to reason. A Muslim must ultimately defend his religion by appealing to the Qur'an. And one who believes in the supreme authority of Scripture must appeal to Scripture.

Nevertheless, those who are not committed in advance to the authority of Scripture should at least take an interest in what it says. Certainly, if Scripture were to deny its own authority, Christians (and everybody else) should deny it, too. But if it affirms its own authority, and gives sufficient reasons for believing in that authority, then Christians (and everybody else) should accept its claim.

CHAPTER 8

What Is the Word of God?

The WLC asks in Question 3, "What is the Word of God?" And it answers, "The holy Scriptures of the Old and New Testaments are the Word of God, the only rule of faith and obedience."

Many Christians would give this answer almost instinctively: the word of God is the Bible. It is true, as I will argue, that the Bible is God's Word, supremely authoritative. And certainly (and I think this is the main point that the catechism wishes to make) Scripture is God's sufficient revelation to us today, for all of life. But it would not be right to say that the Bible is the *only* word of God that has ever been spoken. The Bible itself tells us that Paul, as an inspired apostle, wrote two letters to the Corinthians that never became part of the Bible (1 Cor. 5:9; 2 Cor. 2:4). Further, it is evident that the prophets, apostles, and Jesus all uttered inspired spoken words that did not end up as part of the canon of Scripture. And God speaks also to angels (Ps. 103:20) and to the natural world (Pss. 147:15–18; 148:8), words that we do not have in written form. Such words are the means by which God created all things (Gen. 1:3, 6, 9, etc.; Ps. 33:6, 9). And as we have seen, Christ himself is the divine Word (John 1:1, 14).

So the word of God is more than just the Bible, although the Bible is the Word of God. The Bible is one utterance, or a series of utterances, of God's word. But it does not exhaust the word of God. We should not be embarrassed about this fact. To acknowledge the broader dimensions of the word of God is not to disparage the written Word in any way. Indeed, we can get a clearer and stronger view of the importance of Scripture when we understand its relationship to the other utterances of God. Psalm 19 shows us that God's written Word ("the law of the LORD," v. 7) is as powerful and reliable as the words of God that govern the natural world (vv. 1–6). A similar argument is implicit in Psalm 147:15–20.

How, then, should we define *word of God?* God's word is, certainly, the sum total of his communications, everything that he has said, is saying, and will say. But it is even more than that, for as we saw in chapter 7, there is a sense in which God's word is God himself. God eternally communicates his love and purposes within the Trinity: Father to Son, Son to Father, both to the Spirit, and the Spirit to both. This communication is essential to God's nature. He is, among all his other attributes, a *speaking* God.[1] This is part of what I meant in chapter 2 by saying that God is absolute personality. For speaking is a quality unique to personal beings. As with the broader concept of absolute personality, the concept of a speaking God is unique to biblical religion.

We can say, then, that God's eternal inter-Trinitarian speech is a necessary divine attribute, an attribute without which God would not be God. As such, speech, like all other necessary attributes, designates the essence of God, what God really and truly is.[2] Ultimately, God's word is God, and God is his word.

And given the teaching of John 1:1–14 (see again chapter 7), the term *Word* also designates specifically the second person of the Trinity. There is no contradiction between thinking of the word as a divine attribute and thinking of *Word* as the name of the eternal Son of God. Fatherhood is a divine attribute, but *Father* is also the name of the first person of the Trinity. Similarly *Spirit:* a divine attribute, and the name of the third person of the Trinity.

So God's word is God himself, understood as a speaking God, one who eternally communicates. His inter-Trinitarian communications are essential and necessary to who he is. But by his grace and free decision[3] he also speaks to his creatures. These communications do not exhaust his word, but they are truly his utterances, his expressions.

It is important, therefore, to distinguish the word of God itself, which is purely divine, from the created media through which the word comes to us (which I discuss in chapter 12 and thereafter). The Creator-creature distinction in Scripture is fundamental and nonnegotiable.

1. See *DG*, 470–75.
2. Ibid., 225–37, 387–94.
3. Ibid., 230–36.

So nature, for example, is not the word of God; it is a created medium by which the word of God comes to us.[4]

I therefore define the word of God as (1) God himself, understood as communicator, and (2) the sum total of his free communications with his creatures. Usually in this book I will be using definition (2), but of course we will need to explore (1) as well and understand the relation between the two.[5]

4. This was one of the major issues in my controversy with the followers of Herman Dooyeweerd. See Appendix D in this volume.

5. The Greek word *logos*, which is usually translated "word" in the English Bible, has various meanings, such as "thought," "reason," "account," "discourse," "teaching," "intellectual content." In Heraclitus, Philo, and other ancient writers, the term refers, even more broadly, to some kind of cosmic principle of rationality. I see this as a dim memory of the truth that the supreme reality is an absolute personal communicator.

CHAPTER 9

God's Word as His Controlling Power

When God speaks to us, he speaks as Lord, for that is his relation to us. We should therefore expect that his speech, like all his actions, will express his lordship attributes: his control, authority, and presence. Indeed it does.

We look first at the controlling power of his word. It is important that we understand God's word not only as a communication of linguistic content to our minds, though it is that, but as a great power that makes things happen.

When God first utters his word in the first chapter of Genesis, he speaks not to rational beings, but to inanimate objects. And in the first instance, he addresses that object before it exists. He says, "Let there be light" (Gen. 1:3), and light comes into existence. Such is the power of his word that he is able to "call [*kalountos*] into existence the things that do not exist" (Rom. 4:17).

So Scripture often extols the power of God's word. Summarizing Genesis 1, Psalm 33:6 and 9 say, "By the word of the LORD the heavens were made, and by the breath of his mouth all their host. . . . For he spoke, and it came to be; he commanded, and it stood firm." Cf. Ps. 148:5; John 1:3, 10; Heb. 1:2; 11:3; 2 Peter 3:5–7.

After God makes the world, he continues to govern it by the word of his power. Note what is ascribed to the "voice of the LORD" in Psalm 29 and to the words and commands of God in Psalms 147:15–18 and 148:7–8. God's word governs providence as well as creation. Cf. Gen.

1:9, 11, 22; 8:21–22; Job 37:12; Pss. 18:15; 33:11; 119:89–91; Matt. 8:27; Heb. 1:3; 2 Peter 3.

When God speaks to rational creatures, the word continues to be powerful. God's word brings judgment on sinful people, and often the power of that judgment-word is palpable (Ps. 46:6; Isa. 30:30–31; 66:6; Hos. 6:5; Joel 2:11; Amos 1:2). In 2 Peter 3:5–7, the apostle compares the judgment of Noah's flood with the original creation by the word of God. Just as God's word was powerful enough to bring the world into being, so it will destroy all the works of wickedness. The fire of judgment is one that comes out of God's mouth (Job 41:19–21; Ps. 18:7–8, 13–14; Jer. 5:14; 20:9; 23:29). Fire is God's "answer" to unbelief (1 Kings 18:24). He answers with fire upon the sacrifice that stands in place of the sinner (1 Chron. 21:26). To change the metaphor, God's word is the mighty sword (Isa. 49:2) or hammer (Jer. 23:29) that brings defeat to his enemies (Hos. 6:5). Compare Paul's reference to the word of God as the "sword of the Spirit" in Ephesians 6:17.

But God's word is also powerful to save, powerful in grace. In Genesis 18:14, after God has promised a miraculous child to Abraham and Sarah in their old age, he ascribes the miraculous power to his word. He asks, "Is anything too hard for the LORD?"—literally, "Is any word too wonderful for the LORD?" In Luke 1:37, the angel Gabriel, having announced to the virgin Mary that she would bear the Messiah, echoes Genesis 18:14: "nothing will be impossible with God"—literally, "no word [*rhema*][1] will be impossible for God."[2]

When a centurion asks Jesus to heal his servant, he tells Jesus not to come personally to his home, but only to "say the word" (Luke 7:7). He adds:

> For I too am a man set under authority, with soldiers under me: and I say to one, "Go," and he goes; and to another, "Come," and he comes; and to my servant, "Do this," and he does it. (v. 8)

Indeed, Jesus does heal the servant from afar. And he comments, "I tell you, not even in Israel have I found such faith" (v. 9). What is remarkable about the centurion's faith? Perhaps his request to "say the word" gives the answer. In Greek, this phrase is redundant, "speak with a word" (*eipe logo*). The unusual emphasis on the *verbal* nature of this healing indicates the centurion's belief in the power of Jesus' *word* to heal the servant.

---

1. In Greek, *logos* is a broader term than *rhema*, though both can be translated "word." *Logos* can refer to an individual saying, as does *rhema*, but *logos* can also refer to a discourse, rationale, rational account, principle of rationality, and so forth.

2. Cf. also Jer. 32:17, 27.

And when the apostles bring the gospel of Christ to the world, they rejoice that it is not only a content, but also a power (Rom. 1:16; 1 Thess. 1:5; 2:13). Not only is it accompanied by signs of God's power (Rom. 15:19), but the word itself changes hearts and strengthens believers (Rom. 16:25). It is the "word of life" (Phil. 2:16; see John 1:1), the gospel that brings life and immortality to light (2 Tim. 1:10).

So the word of God is powerful both in judgment and in blessing. These are the twin covenant sanctions. In the covenant, the Lord promises blessing to the obedient, judgment to the disobedient (Deut. 27–28). So the commandments of God have a double edge; they can be blessing (Ex. 20:12) or curse (v. 7). Obedience to God's commands is the path of life (Lev. 18:5; Deut. 8:3; Pss. 19; 119:25, 50), but the commandments themselves can give opportunity for sin (Rom. 7:7–25). God tells Isaiah that his message will be mostly one of hardening and curse: "Make the heart of this people dull, and their ears heavy, and blind their eyes; lest they see with their eyes, and hear with their ears, and understand with their hearts, and turn and be healed" (Isa. 6:10). God sends Isaiah to people who doubtless have already hardened their hearts against the Lord. But in this context it is Isaiah's words, the words of God, that bring the hardening. Jesus and the apostles invoke the words of Isaiah 6 to characterize their own preaching (Matt. 13:14–15; Mark 4:11–12; Luke 8:10; John 12:37–40; Acts 28:26–28; Rom. 11:8; cf. John 15:22).

The power of the word brings wonderful blessings to those who hear in faith, with a disposition to obey. But it hardens those who hear it with indifference, resistance, rebellion. In considering this biblical teaching, I often warn my seminary students to pay heed to what God is telling us here. For seminarians typically spend two or more years intensively studying Scripture. It is so important that they hear in faith, lest the Word actually harden their hearts and become a fire of judgment to them. God's Word never leaves us the same. We hear it for better or worse. So we should never hear or read God's Word merely as an academic exercise. We must ask God to open our hearts, that the Word may be written on them as well as in our heads.

So God accomplishes all his works by his powerful word: creation, providence, judgment, grace.[3]

The power of the word is the power of God's Spirit (1 Thess. 1:5), though the Spirit is not always mentioned in contexts that speak of the word's

---

3. If we add God's eternal plan to this list, we have a good summary of all the works of God reported in Scripture. God's eternal plan is also an exercise of his word. It is the agreement between Father, Son, and Spirit to carry out their program for creation, fall, and redemption. See Pss. 2:7–9; 110; Matt. 11:25–27; John 4:34; 5:19–30; 6:38; 17:1–26.

power (as 1 Thess. 2:13). That is to say that the power of the word is personal, not impersonal. So when the word of the gospel leads one hearer to faith and hardens another, that is God's sovereign decision. The difference is not that some hearers are better able to resist God's word than others, as some Lutherans have claimed. That would mean that the word, like an impersonal force of electricity or gravity, works uniformly on everyone, and that the only differences in response come from those who hear. Scripture, however, teaches that God himself determines who will respond favorably to his word. That is Paul's argument in Romans 9:1–28.

To say this is not to say that the word is powerful only when the Spirit accompanies it and is powerless otherwise. The word is never powerless, as we have seen from Genesis 18:14 and Isaiah 55:11. That implies that the word is never without the power of the Spirit. But sometimes that power effects a blessing, sometimes a curse, depending on God's sovereign intent.

How powerful is the power of the word? The power of God's word is nothing less than his own omnipotence. As we saw earlier, *no* word of God is too hard for him to accomplish. In Isaiah 55:11, we read, "So shall my word be that goes out from my mouth; it shall not return to me empty, but it shall accomplish that which I purpose, and shall succeed in the thing for which I sent it." What God says with his mouth he fulfills with his hand (2 Chron. 6:15; cf. Ezek. 1:3; 3:22).

CHAPTER 10

God's Word as His Meaningful Authority

The second of the lordship attributes is divine authority. As I indicated in chapters 1 and 2, God's word expresses that authority that is unique to God, his *ultimate* authority. As we saw in chapter 1, the authority of language is its capacity to create obligations in the hearer. God's language is authoritative not only in telling us what to believe and do, but in directing our emotions, our preoccupations, our priorities, our joys and sorrows. That is to say, God's words are authoritative in all the ways that language can be authoritative, and their authority is ultimate.

Authority is a function of the *meaning* of language. Here it is important to observe that God's word is not only powerful, but also meaningful. The power of language is what it does; meaning is what it says. Of course, saying is one kind of doing, so meaning is one of the powers of language.[1] But it plays such an important role among the powers of language that it deserves special attention.

In the history of liberal theology, we may observe that the "older liberalism" (Albrecht Ritschl, Adolf von Harnack, Wilhelm Herrmann) saw the words of Scripture as meaningful, but without divine power. They were merely words of men, to be examined and evaluated like any other

---

1. And in the case of God, the power of his language is an aspect of its meaning. For the power of God's word comes from his authority to command things to happen. Thus, in God's word, power and meaning are perspectives on each other.

words of men. In neoorthodoxy (Karl Barth, Emil Brunner—even Rudolf Bultmann) there was a greater understanding of the Word as a divine power, but a denial that the Word was meaningful language. The same power-centered view of God's Word can be found among some disciples of the Dutch philosopher Herman Dooyeweerd.[2]

In traditional theology, and in Scripture itself, God's word is both powerful and meaningful. We have seen Bible references to its power. But Scripture also regards God's word as having meaningful content. The word is never a blind force.[3] When God creates the world by the word of his power, he not only makes things happen. He commands them to happen by intelligible speech, giving names to things that interpret their function. In Genesis 1:5, 8, and 10, God "calls" (*qara'*) things by names: Day, Night, Heaven, Earth, Seas. (Cf. Ps. 147:4; Isa. 40:26.) In the remaining verses of Genesis 1, he determines, in other language, the nature and function of each created thing, and by the word *good* he evaluates the work of his hands. In verses 27–28 he defines by his word the nature and task of mankind.[4]

Note also that in 2:19 God gives an analogous task to Adam, to give names to the animals, as God has already given names to the things in creation. In the ancient world, a name was not merely an arbitrary label. God asked Adam to create a system of meaningful words that would indicate the nature and characteristics of the animals.

In chapter 9, we saw how the powerful word of God accomplishes all of God's actions. Not only do his words accompany what he does; they empower everything he does. Whatever God does, he does by his word; whatever God does, the word does. Now, we should note that all these

2. See my *The Amsterdam Philosophy*, available at http://www.frame-poythress.org /frame_books/1972Amsterdam.htm and in *The Collected Works of John M. Frame*, CD and DVD collection, vol. 1 (Phillipsburg, NJ: P&R Publishing; Whitefish, MT: Bits & Bytes, Inc., 2008). See also the essays in Appendix D in this volume.

3. Preachers and others sometimes point out the relationship between the Greek word for *power*, *dynamis*, and the English word *dynamite*. In some contexts, the power of God's word can profitably be compared to that of dynamite, but there is a major difference. Dynamite only destroys, sending debris every which way. But the power of God's word builds up God's kingdom, rather than merely tearing things down. It creates an order, not a chaos: a rational structure. So does the power of God's word create the universe, turning what is "without form and void" (Gen. 1:2) into a beautiful, orderly universe. In the first three days of creation, God produces locations (heaven and earth, seas and land, growing fields). In the next three, he produces beings to dwell in those locations (heavenly bodies, sea creatures and birds, animals and men). In God's creative work we find the very definition of order: a place for everything and everything in its place.

4. Note the analogue in the realm of redemption. As God gave names to all the creation in Genesis 1, so in redemption he calls us by name (Isa. 43:1) and gives us a new name (Isa. 62:2; 65:15), God's name (Isa. 43:7; Jer. 7:10; Amos 9:12).

words constitute meaningful communication. Everything God does is informed by his wisdom (Ps. 104:24). So the world as a whole is meaningful, its meaning determined by God's plan.

Similarly, when God speaks to rational beings (himself, angels, humans), his word conveys meaning. In his word, he expresses his wisdom, knowledge, desires, intentions, love, grace. That meaning is authoritative. When God shares his love with us, we have the obligation to treasure it. When he questions us, we should answer. When he expresses his grace, we are obligated to trust it. When he tells us his desires, we should conform our lives to them. When he shares with us his knowledge and intentions, we ought to believe that they are true.

In chapter 1, I showed how the whole course of the biblical narrative is structured as a dialogue: God speaks, man responds. The course of subsequent history is the result of man's response to God's word. When man disobeys, there is curse. When he obeys, there is blessing. So biblical history is covenantal. The covenant Lord sets forth his will, and history describes the covenantal sanctions.

So every page of the Bible teaches or illustrates the authority of God's word. Everything that human beings do or say is a response to God's word or a consequence of their response. Let us look at some examples in a brief survey of redemptive history.

ADAM AND EVE

In Genesis 1:28, the first recorded experience of the first human beings was that of listening to God's word. In that experience, they learned their fundamental task as human beings, the task of filling and subduing the whole earth. In Genesis 2:16–17, God supplies food for Adam, authorizing him to eat of every tree in the garden. But he adds a negative command, that Adam is not to eat of the tree of the knowledge of good and evil.

The narrative in chapter 3 of Genesis underscores the centrality of the word of God. A talking serpent enters a dialogue with the woman. Aesop's fables, of course, are full of talking animals, but these are rare in Scripture.[5] God had told Eve, along with Adam, to have dominion over the lower creation (1:28), not to listen to the word of an animal as if it were God's. Satan, speaking through the serpent[6] (Rev. 12:9), here sought

---

5. I think Balaam's ass in Numbers 22:27–30 is the only other instance.
6. Scripture often identifies Satan in verbal terms. He is a liar, a deceiver, an accuser. The serpent figure well illustrates the negative power of Satan's tongue, for a poisonous serpent attracts by his fluttering tongue and kills through the bite of his mouth.

precisely to overturn the system of authority that God had instituted. Instead of God's having the supreme authority, then man, then wife, then the animal creation,[7] Satan the talking animal wanted to rule over the wife, who would rule her husband, who would seek to overturn the authority of God. We see this in the aftermath (Gen. 3:8–13) in which Eve blames the serpent, Adam blames the woman, and both implicitly blame the providence of God.

The contest is precisely between two words claiming supreme authority: God's and Satan's. Satan's attack is precisely on the word that God had spoken. He questions whether God had uttered such a word (3:1), and then, assuming that God had spoken it, Satan contradicts it (3:4–5).

Adam and Eve had no third authority to arbitrate the dispute. They had no means, scientific, philosophical, or religious, to test whether God or Satan was telling the truth. In effect, what happened was that they trusted their own word, their own judgment, as if it were divine. This is the origin of the autonomous rationality that we discussed in chapters 3–7. But clearly the text condemns such autonomy. What Adam and Eve should have done was to accept the naked word of God—without verification from any other source—even though it was contradicted by another source claiming expertise.

In the narrative, God's word prevails, for human disobedience brings death on the first couple and on the whole creation (vv. 14–19). God imposes the wages of sin. But amazingly, he also proclaims his grace, for he says that a descendant of Eve will one day crush the head of the serpent (v. 15). This is the first intimation in Scripture of Messiah's coming, and it also implies that the physical death that the first couple deserves will not be immediate. They will live to reproduce and enjoy the fruits of their labors, albeit with pain and suffering.

Adam and Eve have no reason to expect such grace, except by the word of God. As with the original prohibition, there was no verification. In their own wisdom, Adam and Eve could not possibly have determined that God would show grace to them; in fact, they had every reason to doubt that. Nor could they possibly have guessed that the Messiah would come many centuries later to redeem them.

But this time, they believed—without verifying, without testing, without trying to evaluate God's word by their autonomous judgment. Adam named his wife Eve, "life" (v. 20). He might have named her Death, given her role in the narrative to this point. But he believed God, whose word said

---

7. I realize that this notion of authority is not politically correct these days. For my general view of the relations between the sexes, see *DCL*, 622–47.

that she would bring forth life, children to till the earth and to bring forth the messianic line. When Eve bore the first child, she named him Cain, saying: "I have gotten a man with the help of the LORD" (4:1). In the birth of Cain, she believed, according to God's word of promise, that God was fulfilling his plan to redeem the earth through a seed of the woman.

NOAH

The story of Noah, too, begins with God's favor (6:8) and with God's word (6:13–22). The science of meteorology being what it was at the time, Noah had no way of confirming the unlikely possibility that God would send a flood to destroy humanity. Nor would his human wisdom alone have motivated him to construct a large boat in the desert. Still, against the objections of unbelief, "Noah did this; he did all that God commanded him" (v. 22; cf. 7:5, 9). The word of God was enough.

The NT teaches that the last days of our present age will be like the days of Noah. People will be carrying on their daily work and recreations without any attention to God's warnings (Matt. 24:37–39). These will be "swept away." But those who hear and obey Jesus' warnings will be ready for the new deluge (vv. 43–44).[8]

Hebrews 11:7 commends Noah's faith as a model of Christian faith: he was "warned by God concerning events as yet unseen" and responded to God's word "in reverent fear." Indeed, he not only obeyed God's word, but also proclaimed it to others (2 Peter 2:5).

ABRAHAM

Of all characters in the OT, Abraham is the chief NT model of saving faith (Rom. 4:1–25; Gal. 3:6–9; Heb. 11:8–19; James 2:21–24). What was the object of his faith? The word of God. The narrative begins with God's telling him to leave Ur, his home city, and go to another land (Gen. 12:1). God promises blessing to him (vv. 2–3), but as with Adam and Noah,

---

8. Second Peter 3:5–7 finds the word of God in still another dimension of the flood story: "The heavens existed long ago, and the earth was formed out of water and through water by the word of God." It was nothing else than God's word that held the water up in the sky. And the word not only warned Noah that the water was to fall, but *caused* the water to fall. (Recall the discussion of the last chapter: the word governs all the events of nature.) Similarly, says verse 7, "by the same word the heavens and earth that now exist are stored up for fire." Surely, then, the word gives the best testimony concerning its own actions.

Abraham has no independent means to test whether God is telling the truth. He must simply accept God's word for God's word's sake.

Later, God tells him that he and his wife Sarah will have a son (Gen. 17:15–21), but that promise is unfulfilled until Abraham is over a hundred years old and his wife is well past the age of childbearing. In this case, not only is there no independent means of verification, but all the evidence points in the opposite direction. Everybody knows that old men and women don't have babies. Sarah laughed at the very thought (18:12–15).[9]

Abraham's record of trusting God was not spotless; note the episodes in 12:10–20 and 16:1–16. But Paul presents the broader picture in Romans 4:16–25:

> That is why it depends on faith, in order that the promise may rest on grace and be guaranteed to all his offspring—not only to the adherent of the law but also to the one who shares the faith of Abraham, who is the father of us all, as it is written, "I have made you the father of many nations"—in the presence of the God in whom he believed, who gives life to the dead and calls into existence the things that do not exist. In hope he believed against hope, that he should become the father of many nations, as he had been told, "So shall your offspring be." He did not weaken in faith when he considered his own body, which was as good as dead (since he was about a hundred years old), or when he considered the barrenness of Sarah's womb. No distrust made him waver concerning the promise of God, but he grew strong in his faith as he gave glory to God, fully convinced that God was able to do what he had promised. That is why his faith was "counted to him as righteousness." But the words "it was counted to him" were not written for his sake alone, but for ours also. It will be counted to us who believe in him who raised from the dead Jesus our Lord, who was delivered up for our trespasses and raised for our justification.

Abraham believed the word of God, even though in doing so he had to believe that God could raise the dead. So should our faith be, says Paul, a faith in God's promise, regardless of those who say that Jesus' resurrection is impossible.

In fact, God did give a son to Abraham and Sarah, and his name, Isaac ("laughter"), mocked Sarah's mockery. But later, God again spoke to

---

9. Recall my discussion in chapter 9 of Genesis 18:14: "Is anything too hard for the LORD?"—which can be translated: "Is any word too wonderful for the LORD?"

Abraham, telling him to take this very son, the son of the promise, to a mountain in the land of Moriah to offer him as a sacrifice (Gen. 22). In this case, too, Abraham had no independent way of verifying whether he should do this, and indeed he may well have seen it as violating God's own moral law.[10] Even more seriously, if Isaac were to die, it would seem, God could not fulfill his promise of blessing the world through Isaac's descendants. So Abraham might have seen this commandment as contradicting God's own previous words.

Yet somehow God identified himself to Abraham as the one who was speaking (cf. my discussion in chapter 1), and so Abraham had no choice but to do what God told him, whatever might be the result. As we know, it was a test, and Isaac did not die. God provided a substitute, foreshadowing the work of Christ (Gen. 22:11–14). James says that Abraham's obedience in this test completed his faith (James 2:22). The letter to the Hebrews says, "He considered that God was able even to raise him from the dead, from which, figuratively speaking, he did receive him back" (Heb. 11:19)—another example of Abraham's resurrection faith.

So God tested Abraham's faith in regard to both the promises of the covenant: land and seed. He trusted God's promise of land, even though he owned no part of the land of promise. He trusted God's promise of seed, even though God himself appeared to threaten that promise.

JESUS

I will discuss Moses with the prophets and apostles at a later point. Of course, they, too, received a word from God that required absolute obedience. But we need to look at Jesus here and now, for he is not only a recipient of the word, but the Lord who speaks.

Since Jesus is both perfect God and perfect man, he is both the most authoritative speaker and the most faithful hearer of the word of God. As a human hearer, he speaks just what his Father teaches him (John 8:28; 10:18; 12:49–50; 14:10; 15:15). He does not question, contradict, or hesitate.

But he is also the Word of God incarnate (John 1:1, 14). As I argued in chapter 7, the fact that Jesus is the Word does not detract at all from the authority of God's personal words to human beings. In fact, Jesus himself, as the Word of God, brings verbal testimony to the truth (John 18:37).

---

10. God later prohibited human sacrifice explicitly in Deuteronomy 18:10, but one would think that even people living long before would have seen this practice as wickedness.

He presents this testimony as the reason why he came into the world. His mission was revelatory: to follow Moses' revelation of the law with a revelation of grace and truth (John 1:17). He has made the Father known to us (v. 18; cf. Matt. 11:27). His mission is not *merely* revelatory. He came to accomplish redemption, not just to tell us about it. But his redemptive act reveals his grace, and the revelation of his grace interprets the redemptive act. Revelation and redemption are two aspects of—two perspectives on—his ministry to us.

Jesus' personal words are of utmost importance to the message of the NT. There is no trace of any development from a word-centered revelation in the OT to a nonverbal revelation in the NT. Quite to the contrary. Jesus' personal words are crucial to his ministry. In the community of his disciples, his word is the supreme criterion of discipleship. Jesus teaches that calling him Lord is meaningless unless we do the will of his Father (Matt. 7:21–23). The will of his Father is to be found in the law of Moses (Matt. 5:17–20), and also in Jesus' own words (7:24–29). Those who hear Jesus' words and do them will be like the wise man who built his house on the rock. Those who do not hear and obey will be like the fool who built his house on sand.

When he returns in glory, Jesus will be ashamed of those who have been ashamed of him—notably those who have been ashamed of his words (Mark 8:38; Luke 9:26). His mother and brothers are those who "hear the word of God and do it" (Luke 8:21).

The Gospel of John, which begins by identifying Jesus with the Word of God, is, of the four, the most preoccupied with the importance of the words of Jesus. In John 6:63, Jesus says, "The words that I have spoken to you are spirit and life." Five verses later, Peter asks, "Lord, to whom shall we go? You have the words of eternal life."

In John 8:47, Jesus identifies his own teaching with the "words of God" and insists that anyone who is "of God" will hear and obey them.

John 12:47–50 is remarkable:

> If anyone hears my words and does not keep them, I do not judge him; for I did not come to judge the world but to save the world. The one who rejects me and does not receive my words has a judge; the word that I have spoken will judge him on the last day. For I have not spoken on my own authority, but the Father who sent me has himself given me a commandment—what to say and what to speak. And I know that his commandment is eternal life. What I say, therefore, I say as the Father has told me.

Note here (1) the equation between rejecting Jesus and rejecting his words (v. 48), (2) the word of Jesus (particularly in contrast with his personal presence during his earthly ministry) as the judge of men (v. 48), (3) the determination of Jesus' words by the Father, both in content ("what to say") and in form ("what to speak") (v. 49),[11] and (4) the commandment of the Father (both his commands in general and his commands given to Jesus specifically) as the means and substance of eternal life (v. 50).

Some lessons from John 12: (1) If we are critical of Jesus' words, we may not appeal beyond them (neoorthodox fashion!) to Jesus himself (vv. 48–49). (2) We may not appeal to the substance or content of Jesus' words, beyond the forms in which they are presented (v. 49). (3) We may not claim eternal life while rejecting the demand of Jesus' words upon us (v. 50).

It is also the Johannine literature that identifies most clearly our love for Christ as his disciples with our obedience to his commands. See John 14:15, 21, 23; 15:7, 10, 14; 17:6, 17; 1 John 2:3–5; 3:22; 5:2–3; 2 John 6. John's visions of Revelation identify God's people as those who "keep the commandments of God and hold to the testimony of Jesus" (Rev. 12:17; see 14:12).

Paul refers less often to the words Jesus spoke in his earthly ministry, more often, understandably, to his own apostolic revelation. But note Luke's account of his message to the Ephesian elders at Acts 20:35. And in 1 Timothy 6:3–4, Paul follows Jesus himself in making agreement with Jesus' words a test of fellowship: "If anyone teaches a different doctrine and does not agree with the sound words of our Lord Jesus Christ and the teaching that accords with godliness, he is puffed up with conceit and understands nothing."

To hear the words of Jesus, then, is the same as hearing the words of the Father. We are to hear the words of Jesus as Abraham heard the words of Yahweh, as words of supreme authority. We are not in any position to find fault with the words of Jesus. They rather create obligations on our part: to hear, believe, obey, meditate, rejoice, mourn—whatever the words may demand of us.

---

11. This seems to be the best way to render in English the Greek distinction between *ti eipo* and *ti laleso*. The first is from the verb *lego*, the second from *laleo*. These are often interchangeable and translated "to speak." But the former tends to emphasize content, the second manner—the sounds that come out of the mouth.

CHAPTER 11

God's Word as His Personal Presence

The third of the lordship attributes is the divine presence. Because God is Lord, he lives in and with his creation. Indeed, he chooses people to encounter his presence in a special measure. So Israel is his special people, and he is their God. In the tabernacle and temple, he is literally "God with them." His Son is named Immanuel, "God with us" as he takes on human form and takes the place of sinners before God's judgment. And his Spirit dwells with us and in us as his temple.

We have seen that in his word, God speaks as Lord. His word is his controlling power and his meaningful authority. Should we see the word also as God's personal presence? I believe so.

From a general theological perspective, this conclusion is unavoidable. God's speech is, as we have seen, a necessary divine attribute, so that wherever God is, his word is. We have also seen that *Word* is a title of the second person of the Trinity, and whenever one divine person acts in the world, the other two persons act together with him. God *is* the word, and the word is God. So we conclude that wherever God is, the word is, and wherever the word is, God is. Whenever God speaks, he himself is there with us.

The same conclusion follows from God's attribute of omnipresence. Since God is everywhere, God and his word are always near to us.

But the presence of God in the word is not only a deduction from broader theological principles. Scripture is often very specific about it.

GOD'S NEARNESS TO HIS PEOPLE
IS THE NEARNESS OF HIS WORDS

In Deuteronomy 4:7–8, God says that he is especially near to Israel and connects that nearness with the rightness of his statutes:

> For what great nation is there that has a god so near to it as the LORD our God is to us, whenever we call upon him? And what great nation is there, that has statutes and rules so righteous as all this law that I set before you today?

Deuteronomy 30:11–14, then, speaks of the nearness of the word to Israel in the same terms as God's own nearness:

> For this commandment that I command you today is not too hard for you, neither is it far off. It is not in heaven, that you should say, "Who will ascend to heaven for us and bring it to us, that we may hear it and do it?" Neither is it beyond the sea, that you should say, "Who will go over the sea for us and bring it to us, that we may hear it and do it?" But the word is very near you. It is in your mouth and in your heart, so that you can do it.

In Romans, Paul quotes this Deuteronomy passage, with some adjustments. Here, the nearness of the commandments in Deuteronomy becomes the nearness of Christ, particularly in the gospel message:

> But the righteousness based on faith says, "Do not say in your heart, 'Who will ascend into heaven?'" (that is, to bring Christ down) or "'Who will descend into the abyss?'" (that is, to bring Christ up from the dead). But what does it say? "The word is near you, in your mouth and in your heart" (that is, the word of faith that we proclaim). (Rom. 10:6–8)

WHERE THE WORD IS, THERE
IS GOD'S SPIRIT

In many biblical texts we see the word accompanied by the Spirit, and vice versa. In Genesis 1:2, God's Spirit hovers over the waters as God prepares to create all things by his word. Psalm 33:6 couples God's "word" and "breath" as the sources of creation. God's breath is his Spirit.[1] Cf. Isa. 34:16; 59:21. Jesus says his words are both Spirit and life (John 6:63).

In John 16:13, Jesus says that the Spirit will "speak" to bring the disciples into all the truth. Throughout the book of Acts (note, e.g., 2:1–4), when the Spirit falls upon people, they often begin to speak of Jesus. In 1 Thessalonians 1:5, Paul couples word and Spirit as factors that are always equally present when people receive the gospel in faith. Negatively: in 2 Thessalonians 2:2, Paul tells people to ignore either a false word or a false spirit, suggesting that Satan's counterfeit words also come with a counterfeit spirit.

Scripture also connects the written Word of God to the Spirit. Second Timothy 3:16 tells us that Scripture is *theopneustos*, "God-breathed," again invoking God's Spirit-breath as the source of the Word. Similarly, 2 Peter 1:21 indicates that the written Word has come about by the Spirit's direction of the human writers.

GOD PERFORMS ALL HIS ACTIONS THROUGH SPEECH

In chapter 9, I noted that all of God's works could be summarized thus: his eternal plan, creation, providence, judgment, grace. In that context I indicated how all these actions reveal his controlling power. But of course, where God's power is, his authority and presence are there, too. We considered in chapter 10 the inseparability of his power and authority. Now we should note the inseparability of both of these from his personal presence.

Since God is not a physical being, his presence with us is different from the presence of a physical object or person. With a physical being it is possible to measure its distance from us, but that is not possible with God. How, then, could we judge when a nonphysical person is present with us? Such a person, evidently, is present wherever he can exercise his controlling power, and wherever he can enforce his authoritative commands. But God, of course, exercises his power and authority throughout the universe; so he is present everywhere.[2]

---

1. The biblical words for *Spirit*, the Hebrew *ruach* and the Greek *pneuma*, are both often translated "wind" or "breath."

2. By *presence* in this context, of course, I refer to God's general omnipresence. Scripture also refers to other kinds of presence, in which God reveals himself to us more intensely: the burning bush, Mount Sinai, the Holiest Place in the tabernacle and the temple. In these forms, too, his presence is not separated from his speech. My larger

So if God performs all his actions by powerful and authoritative speech, then his speech is never separated from his personal presence.

GOD IS DISTINGUISHED FROM ALL OTHER GODS BECAUSE HE IS THE GOD WHO SPEAKS

Idols are "dumb" or "mute" (1 Cor. 12:2). Cf. Pss. 115:5–7; 135:16; Hab. 2:18–20. In 1 Kings 18:24–35, the contest between Elijah and the priests of Baal concerns which deity will "answer." God's answer, of course, is by fire. Speaking is unique to God, an attribute that distinguishes what he is from all other supposed gods.

THE PERSONS OF THE TRINITY ARE DISTINGUISHED FROM ONE ANOTHER IN SCRIPTURE ACCORDING TO THEIR ROLE IN THE DIVINE SPEECH

This is not the only scriptural way of representing the Trinitarian distinctions, but it is one significant way: The Father exerts his lordship through speech (Pss. 29; 147:4; Isa. 40:26; 43:1; 62:2; 65:15; Eph. 3:14–15). The Son is the Word spoken (John 1:1; Rom. 10:6–8 [cf. Deut. 30:11–14]; Heb. 1:1–3; 1 John 1:1–3; Rev. 3:14; 19:13). The Spirit is the powerful breath that drives the word along to accomplish its purpose (Gen. 1:2; Ps. 33:6; 1 Thess. 1:5; 2 Tim. 3:16; 2 Peter 1:21). I will later refer to this pattern as the *linguistic model of the Trinity*. So in still another way we see that God's speech is inseparable from his Trinitarian being.

THE SPEECH OF GOD HAS DIVINE ATTRIBUTES

These include righteousness (Ps. 119:7), faithfulness (119:86), wonderfulness (119:129), uprightness (119:137), purity (119:40), truth (119:142; John 17:17), eternality (Ps. 119:89, 160), omnipotence (Gen. 18:14; Isa. 55:11; Luke 1:37), perfection (Ps. 19:7ff.). These attributes are not merely the attributes of something in creation, such as human faithfulness, righteousness, or truth. Clearly, in context these passages are saying that the

---

point is that in even the broadest kind of divine presence, general omnipresence, his word is there, too.

words of God are different from merely human words because they embody the unique qualities of God's own nature.

THE WORD DOES THINGS THAT ONLY GOD CAN DO

In Hebrews 4:12–13, the author says:

> For the word of God is living and active, sharper than any two-edged sword, piercing to the division of soul and of spirit, of joints and of marrow, and discerning the thoughts and intentions of the heart. And no creature is hidden from his sight, but all are naked and exposed to the eyes of him to whom we must give account.

Verse 12 speaks of the word of God discerning the most hidden aspects of our being. That clearly is something that only God can do. Verse 13 seems to mark a transition from talking about the word to talking about God. But there is no grammatical indication of a change to a new subject. In both verses the author speaks of the powers of the word, and in both the powers of God. There is no distinction between one and the other. What the word does, God does, and vice versa. So the word not only has distinctively divine attributes, but also performs distinctively divine acts.

THE WORD OF GOD IS AN OBJECT OF WORSHIP

The psalmists view the words of God with religious reverence and awe, attitudes appropriate only to an encounter with God himself. The psalmist trembles with godly fear (Ps. 119:120; cf. Isa. 66:5), stands in awe of God's words (Ps. 119:161), and rejoices in them (v. 162). He lifts his hands to God's commandments (v. 48). He exalts and praises not only God himself, but also his "name" (Pss. 9:2; 34:3; 68:4). He gives thanks to God's name (Ps. 138:2). He praises God's word in Psalm 56:4, 10. This is extraordinary, since Scripture uniformly considers it idolatrous to worship anything other than God. But to praise or fear God's word is not idolatrous. To praise God's word is to praise God himself.

Does this worship justify "bibliolatry"? The Bible, as we will see later, is God's word in a finite medium. It may be paper and ink, or parchment, or audiotape or a CD-ROM. The medium is not divine, but creaturely. We should not worship the created medium; that would be idolatry. But through the created medium, we receive the authentic word of God, and that word of God should be treasured as if God were speaking it with his own lips. It should be received with absolute trust, obedience, and, yes, worship.

Opponents of evangelicalism commonly say that it is idolatrous to accept any human word as having divine authority. Scripture, however, teaches that we should accept the divine-human words on its pages precisely as God's own. Evangelicals are often too sensitive to the charge of bibliolatry. That charge is illegitimate, and it should not motivate evangelicals to water down their view of Scripture.

FINALLY, THE WORD IS GOD

John 1:1 comes right out and says this, together with other passages we have mentioned that correlate God's word with Jesus Christ (Heb. 1:1–3; 1 John 1:1–3; Rev. 3:14; 19:13). We are inclined to focus on the Christology of John 1:1–14 and thus to take it as identifying Jesus Christ with the word of God and therefore with God. But we should also note the fact that this verse identifies God with the creative word of Genesis 1. We have seen that in Genesis 1, God creates all things by his word. When John's Gospel starts "In the beginning," any Jewish reader would have caught the allusion back to Genesis 1:1. John 1:1–14 is about *that* word, the word that created all things. The allusion becomes more obvious in verse 3: "All things were made through him [i.e., through the word], and without him was not any thing made that was made." So when verse 1 says that "the Word was God," it indicates not only the deity of Christ, but also the deity of the creative word. So the passage teaches not only an identity between God and Christ, but a threefold identity, between God, Christ, and the creative word.

So the word is God. When we encounter the word of God, we encounter God. When we encounter God, we encounter his word. We cannot encounter God without the word, or the word without God. God's word and his personal presence are inseparable. His word, indeed, is his personal presence. Whenever God's Word is spoken, read, or heard, God himself is there.

PART FOUR

HOW THE WORD
COMES TO US

Part 1 of this book was orientation. Part 2 (representing my situational perspective) dealt with the theological environment in which we investigate the word of God. Part 3 (representing my normative perspective) attempted to define the word of God, based on Scripture. Now Part 4 will attempt to show how the word gets from God's mind to our hearts, the existential perspective. Of course, Part 4 will be highly normative as well, since I will be mainly concerned to set forth what Scripture says about how God's word reaches our inner being.

CHAPTER 12

The Media of God's Word

In chapters 8–11, we have been thinking about the fundamental nature of God's word. It is an eternal, necessary, defining attribute of God, his capacity for communication, together with the sum total of God's actual communications, within the Trinity and with creatures. God's communication with creatures expresses his lordship, controlling power, meaningful authority, and personal presence. Now we must look at the media God employs to bring his word to creatures.

Media refers to the means by which a speaker's words are connected with the hearer's mind and heart. We are familiar today with the term as it is used for radio, television, films, newspapers, magazines, and we often express some trepidation about the effects of the media on our culture. The problem, of course, is not with the media themselves, but with fallen man's use of them. That there are pure and righteous ways to employ media becomes evident when we consider that God himself makes use of media to communicate his word.

We are concerned here with *created* media. Certainly, God's inter-Trinitarian communication does not require created media, so in terms of the present discussion, we should refer to the inter-Trinitarian communication as *unmediated*. But I'm inclined to think that when God speaks with human beings, he almost always uses one medium or other. We sometimes speak of God's revealing himself "directly," as when he speaks on Mount Sinai to all Israel, or when he speaks to a prophet like Moses "mouth to mouth" (Num. 12:8). But even in those situations, God evidently uses created media. God's voice on these occasions uses the atmosphere to carry sound waves to the ears of his audience and thence to their brains. He uses the Hebrew language, or some ancestor of it: a language of creatures, certainly not the divine language by which the persons of the Trinity communicate with each other. So even when God's revelation is "direct," it employs created media.

An exception might exist when and if God determines to place a message immediately into a person's mind, without any seeing, hearing, or reasoning. God certainly has the power to do this. Perhaps the Holy Spirit acts in such an immediate way to persuade us that some revelation of God is true. But if unmediated revelation occurs in this world, that would be hard to prove from Scripture. The forms of revelation that theology describes must be limited to those described in Scripture. So we must confine ourselves to considering mediated revelation. And therefore it is necessary to make some effort to understand the media.

I distinguish three categories of revelation media: events, words, and persons. These categories correspond roughly to the lordship attributes: events are brought about by God's controlling power; words bear God's meaningful authority; and persons embody the personal presence of the Lord. But we should not press the parallel too far. It would be wrong, for example, to say that event-revelation embodies God's control, but not his authority or presence. Rather, through all the media of revelation, God expresses all the aspects of his lordship. In event-revelation, God reveals himself not only as the supremely powerful controller, but also as the supremely meaningful authority and the supremely personal presence. Similarly for word-revelation and person-revelation. Scripture treats all revelation as mediated, and it treats all of God's revelation, as we've seen, as supremely powerful, authoritative, and personal.

Indeed, the three kinds of media are inseparable from one another and perspectivally related. We gain our knowledge of event-revelation by means of word-revelation, words narrating and explaining the events. But God's giving of words is also an event. And the words have no value to us except as they convey to us the events of creation, fall, and redemption. Further, the narrative of events expressed in words is a narrative about persons, divine, angelic, and human. And the narrative is also addressed to persons, including ourselves. So the events, words, and persons are all necessary to one another; indeed, they constitute one another.

These three forms of revelation also explain and interpret one another. One cannot fully understand revelation in events without the commentary of God's verbal revelation. On the other hand, one cannot fully understand the verbal revelation of the Bible without understanding something of biblical languages, ancient history, and ancient culture, which requires a study of extrabiblical event-revelation. Similarly, event- and word-revelation cannot be understood without an understanding of revelatory persons, and vice versa.

So all these media are essential to the revelation that God has chosen to give us. It is not our place to pick and choose among them what we would prefer to hear, to believe, or to obey. To question the words is to question the events described in the words and the persons who participated in those events. Similarly for the other media.

So it would be wrong to say that the media of revelation somehow detract from the power, authority, and divine presence of the revelation. The media are inseparable from the revelation. If they are defective, there is no way for us to reclaim an uncorrupted version of God's truth. If we are to accept God's revelation, we must accept what we hear and see through his media.

So we must never regard the media as barriers to God's communication. God is never prevented by the limitations of creation, or the finitude of people, from saying what he wants to say to them. Rather, the media are God's chosen instruments for bringing his absolute power, authority, and presence to the attention of finite hearers.

This is the fundamental answer to the question whether the "humanity" of revelation detracts from its divine character. It is often pointed out that God's revelation through prophets, apostles, and biblical writers is human as well as divine.[1] But human beings do make mistakes. So, the argument goes, we should expect mistakes in the revelation, not because of God, but because of the human instruments. But note:

1. Human beings do not *necessarily* err. Even unregenerate people sometimes speak the truth. So we should not think it impossible that God could reveal himself through human agents, keeping them from error, without violating their humanity.
2. If humanity necessarily entails error, then *all* of God's revelation in Scripture, every sentence, is erroneous, for all of it comes through human mediation. Nobody has ever argued such an extreme position.
3. Christ was fully human, but he did not speak error.
4. Most of the biblical statements we noted in chapters 8–11 about the power, authority, and presence of God in revelation pertain

---

1. Indeed, even the most direct revelation of God, such as his speaking from Mount Sinai in the presence of Israel, has a human element; for on such occasions he speaks a human language.

to revelation through the mediation of human beings. There is no suggestion in any of these passages that human media somehow detract from or compromise the divine quality of the message; indeed, these passages exclude that possibility.

5. On the argument that human *language* is somehow incapable of truly referring to God, see my article "God and Biblical Language."[2]

6. In general, the humanity of God's word is not a liability, but a perfection. God's intent in revelation is to communicate with people. To do that, he must speak their language so that they may understand it. This language, therefore, must be a fully human language. Scripture shows that God has indeed succeeded in putting his word into human words, words that human prophets, apostles, and biblical writers utter as their own. For that, he deserves praise, not suspicion.

2. In John W. Montgomery, ed., *God's Inerrant Word* (Minneapolis: Bethany Fellowship, 1974), 159–77. See Appendix E in this volume and http://www.frame-poythress.org/frame_articles/1974BiblicalLanguage.html.

CHAPTER 13

God's Revelation through Events

First, we consider *event-media*, the revelation of God through the mediation of events. We may further distinguish events of nature and events of history. Nature is everything that takes place in God's creation. History is a set of events significant to human beings. We also use the term *history* to refer to spoken or written accounts of those events. We will look at history in that sense under the second class of media, *word-media*.[1]

History in the first sense, the set of events significant to human beings, may be divided into general history and redemptive history. General history is the usual content of secular history books: the records of the earliest humans, the rise of civilization in China, Egypt, and Babylon, and the course of civilization since. Redemptive history comprises those events by which God redeems his people from sin. Redemptive history is preeminently the work of Christ in his incarnation, atonement, resurrection, and ascension. But redemptive history also includes those events that prepared for Christ, such as God's covenants with Abraham, Israel, and David, the application of Jesus' redemption in the church's mission, the return of Christ, and the final judgment.

In one sense, redemptive history is a portion of general history, but I will speak of general history in a narrower sense: namely, the nonredemptive portion of human history. This is not to deny that redemptive and nonre-

1. This discussion should be compared with the discussion of history in modern theology, chapter 5, above.

demptive history influence each other, each forming a context in which the other should be understood.

NATURE AND GENERAL HISTORY

Let me consider first nature and general history as media of revelation. Clearly, everything that God has made, and every event that takes place, reveals God in some way. For everything in the world is God's creation, and everything that happens is God's providence.[2] Indeed, no fact can be rightly understood apart from God.

So Scripture recognizes the natural world as a revelation of God. As Psalm 19 says, "The heavens declare the glory of God, and the sky above proclaims his handiwork." God's awesome deeds in the natural world bring the psalmists to express awe, wonder, and praise, as in Psalms 46:8–10; 65; 104. In chapter 9, I listed many Scripture passages in which the power of God displayed in nature is the power of his *word*; nature is God's self-expression. Nature behaves as it does because God's word tells it what to do.

It is important to remember that nature is not the word of God, but only a medium of the word. The word, as we saw in chapter 11 and elsewhere, is God. It is divine, not something created. Theologians have sometimes written loosely about the "creation word" or the "word in creation." But to be precise, the word is something *above* creation that speaks *through* creation.[3]

Natural revelation shows us the kindness of God. Paul tells the pagans at Lystra that God "did not leave himself without witness, for he did good by giving you rains from heaven and fruitful seasons, satisfying your hearts with food and gladness" (Acts 14:17; cf. Matt. 5:45).

But natural revelation can also have a negative meaning. It has a particularly important role in convicting human beings of sin. In Romans 1:18–21, Paul says:

> For the wrath of God is revealed from heaven against all ungodliness and unrighteousness of men, who by their unrighteousness suppress the truth. For what can be known about God is plain to them, because God has shown it to them. For his invisible attri-

2. Note the discussion of God's providence in chapter 14 of *DG*, and also chapter 4 of *DG*, which argues that all things are under God's sovereign control.

3. I discuss in more detail the relation between the divine word of God and the created media in Appendix D in this volume. This was a major issue in my debates with the followers of Herman Dooyeweerd in the 1970s.

butes, namely, his eternal power and divine nature, have been clearly perceived, ever since the creation of the world, in the things that have been made. So they are without excuse. For although they knew God, they did not honor him as God or give thanks to him, but they became futile in their thinking, and their foolish hearts were darkened.

God has given human beings a clear revelation of himself (v. 19), including a revelation of his "invisible attributes" (v. 20), from the natural world ("in the things that have been made," v. 20). The knowledge we gain from this is not only a knowledge of information about God, but a knowledge of God himself, a personal knowledge (v. 21). That revelation has a moral content (v. 32) that requires human beings to honor God and give thanks to him (v. 21). But, Paul says, human beings fail to honor him as they should. Rather, they "suppress" the truth (v. 18), they "exchanged the truth about God for a lie" (v. 25), and they "did not see fit to acknowledge God" (v. 28). Though they fail to worship God, they do not abandon religion altogether. Rather, they worship idols (v. 23), and that idolatry leads them into Paul's full catalogue of sins. He mentions first sexual sins (vv. 24–27), then "all manner of unrighteousness" (vv. 28–31). So the revelation is a revelation of the "wrath of God" (v. 18).

Natural revelation, therefore, is a clear and personal revelation of the true God, which makes authoritative demands on human beings. As in Acts 14, it displays God's kindness, his "common grace."[4] But when people betray that kindness, as they always do apart from faith in Christ, it serves as a basis for judgment, to leave them "without excuse" (Rom. 1:20). Romans 1 does not indicate that anybody can find a means of forgiveness of sins through natural revelation. Later on, Paul indicates that salvation comes through a different form of revelation: the preaching of Christ (Rom. 10:14–17).

But for those who have received God's saving grace, natural revelation has a more positive meaning. Like the psalmist, we come to praise God for the revelation of him in the heavens and the earth. Nature also provides signs for redemptive covenants: the regularity of the seasons (Gen. 8:22), the rainbow (Gen. 9:16), and "heaven and earth" (Deut. 4:26; 30:19; 31:28; 32:1) serve to witness the promises and threats of God's covenants.

Nature is fallen because God placed a curse on man's labor after Adam's fall (Gen. 3:17–19). Yet it "waits with eager longing for the revealing of the sons of God" (Rom. 8:19; cf. vv. 20–23). So nature is not entirely separate from redemption, as one might suspect from Romans 1 alone. Indeed,

4. See *DG*, 429–37.

nature is preoccupied with the hope of redemption, and it cannot rightly be understood apart from that hope.

Another blessing of natural revelation to Christian believers is this: nature is a means of applying redemptive revelation, Scripture, to our daily lives. To apply Scripture to the world, we must know some things about the world, not only about Scripture. For example, the eighth commandment tells us not to steal. But to apply that commandment to the question of cheating on taxes, we must know something about taxes (natural revelation) as well as about Scripture. So to obey God, we need to know nature as well as Scripture.

One might ask how natural revelation fits the personal-word model of revelation that I have recommended in this book. There is some awkwardness here, because events aren't words, at least in and of themselves. As I pointed out, natural events are not the word of God, but media of the word. In natural revelation, we do not hear a literal voice (Ps. 19:3). So some might ask whether natural revelation conveys the same power, authority, and divine presence as God's personal words.

But natural revelation does have some important characteristics of personal-word revelation. It is clear (Rom. 1:19–20) and makes clear demands of us, so that when we disobey we have no excuse (v. 20; cf. v. 32). As in our personal-word thought-experiment, we have no right to talk back to God. His authority comes through as absolute and unconditional.

Similarly with his other lordship attributes. Many biblical texts on natural revelation stress the controlling power of God revealed therein (as Ps. 29:3–11). That power fills the believer with awe and wonder, and he ascribes glory to God. The heavens and earth become a temple for God's worship, a temple of his personal presence (Ps. 29:1–2, 10–11; cf. Isa. 66:1; Matt. 5:34–35).

So although natural revelation does not consist of literal divine words, it is an infallible *medium* of such divine words. As such, natural revelation conveys to us God's power, authority, and presence.

There is therefore no room for human autonomy in dealing with God's natural revelation. We may interpret the creation only by thinking God's thoughts after him. And this means that when we analyze the creation, we must listen to God's words in other media, such as the written Word, if we are to understand nature as he made it to be. As John Calvin said, we are to understand the natural world through the "spectacles" of Scripture.[5] For it is the gospel message of Scripture that takes away our unrighteous desire to suppress God's truth.

5. *Institutes*, 1.6.1.

REDEMPTIVE HISTORY

Redemptive history, as I defined it earlier, is that series of events by which God redeems his people from sin, a narrative fulfilled in Christ. It is the principal subject matter of Scripture. Redemptive history constitutes the mighty acts of God that he performs for the sake of his people, those acts by which people come to know that he is the Lord (Ex. 7:5; 14:18). When God brings Israel over the Red Sea on dry land, both Israel and the Egyptians come to know his lordship. In Deuteronomy 8:11–18, God tells Israel that when they are prosperous in the land of promise, they should not forget the acts of the Lord. Their wealth comes from God alone, and he can take it away if they are not faithful. God's great deeds should be warnings to the nations outside Israel (Ps. 66:5–7). God's mighty acts are a theme that resounds through the OT. For a sense of its importance to God's people, see Psalms 135; 136; 145:4, 12.

Similarly, the Gospels are preoccupied with the mighty deeds of Jesus. The Gospel of John is structured according to the "signs" Jesus wrought in his earthly ministry (John 2:11; cf. Acts 2:22). Of course, the greatest of Jesus' mighty acts are his sacrificial death on the cross, his resurrection, and his ascension to God's right hand.

Jesus also performs mighty acts in the history of the early church.[6] In Acts 15:12, Barnabas and Paul relate the "signs and wonders God had done through them among the Gentiles."[7] Cf. Heb. 2:4; Rev. 15:3–4.

Redemptive history supplies what is lacking in natural revelation, the means by which God forgives sin. So it is tempting to say that natural revelation is "law," while redemptive history is "gospel." But the matter is more complicated than that, as we have seen. In the conventional distinction, law is unmitigated "bad news," gospel unmitigated "good news." But as we have also seen, nature reveals God's kindness as well as his severity. And when believers look at natural revelation from a perspective of grace, it reinforces the gospel in many ways, in covenant signs, in its eager longing for the consummation of redemption, and in its help to believers in living the Christian life.[8]

Similarly, redemptive history contains negative as well as positive elements. It shows us the glory of Christ in his redemptive work. But it also

6. Acts 1:1 says that the Gospel of Luke concerns what Jesus *began* to do and teach, suggesting that the book of Acts presents what Jesus *continued* to do and teach.

7. "Signs and wonders" is a name for what English speakers often call "miracles." For a somewhat nontraditional account of miracle, see *DG*, chapter 13. Miracle is a form of revelation, which I define as "an extraordinary demonstration of God's lordship."

8. See my discussion of law and gospel in *DCL*, 182–92.

displays the judgments of God on those who reject Christ and who will not bow before his lordship. The blessings and the judgments are inseparable: God blesses Abraham, but he curses Sodom and Gomorrah. He redeems Israel, but in the same act curses Egypt (and later Canaan). When Jesus returns, his people will rejoice, but the wicked will weep and wail.[9]

Redemptive history, like natural revelation, is a medium of God's word, rather than the word itself. But it conveys all the power, authority, and divine presence of God himself. The mighty redemptive acts of God are a biblical paradigm of his controlling power, especially the miraculous birth of Isaac (Gen. 18:14), God's deliverance of Israel from Egypt (Ex. 15:4–12), the cross of Christ (1 Cor. 1:18), and Jesus' resurrection from the dead (Rom. 1:4; 2 Cor. 13:4; Eph. 1:19–21; Phil. 3:10).

The mighty acts of God also bear God's lordship authority, in the sense that they demand a favorable human response. God's deliverance of Israel from Egypt ought to motivate Israel's obedience. The preface to the Decalogue is "I am the LORD your God, who brought you out of the land of Egypt, out of the house of slavery" (Ex. 20:2). Then come God's commands, "You shall have no other gods before me" (v. 3), and so on. Israel in its disobedience is all the more culpable because of the powerful and clear revelation it has received (Deut. 29, among many other passages). God gave Israel much more revelation of himself than he gave to the other nations, and "to whom much was given, of him much will be required" (Luke 12:48).

God's redemptive deeds are also a revelation of his personal presence. God does, of course, bring all events to pass (Eph. 1:11). But God's presence is all the more intense when he is acting to carry out redemption and judgment. These are "acts of God" par excellence. God's wonderful works typically elicit religious awe (as Ex. 15; many psalms). In Luke 5:1–10, Jesus grants to the disciples a miraculous catch of fish. Peter's response is surprising: "Go away from me, Lord; I am a sinful man!" (v. 8 NIV). Peter's eyes are not on the fish, or on the event as such, but on the presence of God in Jesus. In the miracle, God himself is present.[10]

So, as with natural revelation, redemptive history is an unambiguous, clear revelation of God. This fact is contrary to the liberal views of redemptive history noted in chapter 5. Human beings have no freedom to interpret the event as they wish. There is no role here for human autonomy. It is not

9. There is a theory that Christian preaching should focus exclusively on redemptive history. I would agree, if *redemptive history* is taken broadly enough to include the whole content of Scripture. But if (as I sometimes suspect) *redemptive history* is defined as an exclusive focus on narrative, excluding the moral, wisdom, and literary content of Scripture, then I take issue. See *DCL*, chap. 16, and this volume, chap. 35.

10. See the discussion of miracle in chapter 13 of *DG*.

as if the event were somehow "neutral," accessible indifferently to unbelief or faith. Nor is it the case that the unbelieving, secular interpretation is somehow normative. Faith is essential, of course; but faith is obligatory. Faithful interpretation of these events is the only legitimate interpretation, not one of many.

And we cannot say with the neoorthodox tradition that the historical event is only a "pointer" to a higher (*geschichtlich*) event that is the true revelation. God reveals himself precisely in the events of calendar time and space, where we live. This fact does not imply that secular historians may dictate the meaning of the event, as if calendar time and space were a realm where such historians could function autonomously. "Secular history" is illegitimate in any sphere of inquiry. Events of time and space can be fully understood only by those who, as with Scripture, view them through the spectacles of God's revelation.

So Gotthold Ephraim Lessing was wrong. There is no "big, ugly ditch" between history and faith. Rather, history necessitates faith, and history cannot be rightly understood apart from faith. There is no need for faith to retreat to some mysterious events occurring above and beyond time and space. God has acted in literal history to redeem his people, and through that history he calls us to trust him.

CHAPTER 14

God's Revelation through Words:
The Divine Voice

The second type of medium is revelation through human words. Because of Scripture's emphasis on this kind of revelation, and because of the many theological controversies over this concept, this particular medium will occupy our attention from chapters 14 to 41. Then we will turn to the third type of medium, person-revelation, in chapters 42–44.

This revelation is "verbal" in two senses: it is a revelation of the word of God, and it is a revelation using human words as a medium. We will see, however, that in such revelations the word of God and the human words are not actually distinct from one another. In the verbal medium, God creates an *identity* between his own words and some human words, so that what the human words say, God says. This identity between God's words and human words is, I think, the best definition of *inspiration*.[1]

I mentioned earlier that in an obvious sense event-revelation is not verbal: events are not words. But word-revelation is precisely verbal. So there is a difference between event-revelation and word-revelation. But the difference is not great. As I indicated in the previous chapter, revelatory events bring to us clear revelation, embodying God's own lordship:

---

1. See chapter 23 for more discussion of inspiration. Some have questioned whether it is possible for a human word to be identical to a divine word: is it possible for God to speak in human language? Or is it even possible to speak truly *about* God in human language? The transcendence of God seems in some minds to be an insuperable barrier to verbal revelation. I discuss these issues in some detail in "God and Biblical Language," Appendix E in this volume.

his controlling power, meaningful authority, and personal presence. Revelatory events, therefore, bring to us the same kind of content that verbal revelation brings.

Why, then, does God give us both? Because of the differing potentials of the two media. We say that a picture is worth a thousand words. We could substitute *event* for *picture* in this saying. Someone who saw Jesus resurrected from the dead received revelation beyond what words could say. But there are also senses in which a group of words is worth a thousand events. For words can interpret events in ways that events themselves cannot do. A witness to Jesus' resurrection saw something wonderful, overwhelming. But a verbal description and interpretation of that event could add much to the witness's understanding of what happened.

And words can be preserved. Memories of events tend to fade over time. But words can be written down, even passed from generation to generation. We will see in chapter 16 the importance of *permanent* verbal revelation.

In the present and following chapters, we will consider several kinds of divine revelation through verbal media: the divine voice, the word through prophets and apostles, and the written Word.

I will use the phrase *divine voice* to refer to the most direct kind of verbal revelation, in which God speaks to human beings without any human mediator. The paradigm of the divine voice can be found in Exodus 20, the only occasion on which all Israel is gathered in one place (camped around Mount Sinai) to hear words from God's own lips. God here declares the covenant (Deut. 4:13) establishing Israel as his people and himself as their God. He identifies himself as the one who delivered them from Egypt (Ex. 20:2), and he declares how they should serve him (vv. 3–17). The people are afraid and stand far off (v. 18), and they say to Moses, "You speak to us, and we will listen; but do not let God speak to us, lest we die" (v. 19). God accepts this arrangement (Deut. 5:28–31), and from then on God's revelation to Israel is largely indirect, rather than direct.

People often say that if God spoke to them directly, they would believe. And Christians sometimes imagine that hearing God directly would be the height of spiritual joy. They do not know what they are asking. For Israel, the experience was terrible, frightening. They wanted nothing more than for it to end.

Nevertheless, many other people have heard the divine voice, unmediated. Moses himself is the chief example of this. Note the description of the intimacy between God and Moses in Numbers 12:8:

> With him I speak mouth to mouth, clearly, and not in riddles, and he beholds the form of the LORD.

Unlike Moses, Israel did not "behold the form of the LORD" at Mount Sinai (Deut. 4:12),[2] but like Israel, Moses heard the word of God directly. The same, of course, was true of Adam, Cain, Noah, Abraham, and many others. The prophets regularly heard the divine voice. That indeed is part of the definition of a prophet. Like Moses, a prophet hears the word of God directly and passes it on to the people (Deut. 18:18).

When Jesus came into the world, the divine voice was heard once more in the public arena. At his baptism, the Father said, "This is my beloved Son, with whom I am well pleased" (Matt. 3:17). More privately, the Father spoke from heaven to three disciples at Jesus' transfiguration, using the same words, adding "listen to him" (Matt. 17:5). But we should also not forget that throughout his earthly ministry Jesus himself was the divine voice. He himself was the Word. And though he had the right to speak on his own authority, he spoke only what the Father required him to say (both content and manner, John 12:49). And on the last day his word will judge those who reject him (v. 48).

Now, the divine voice is a medium for conveying God's mind to man. And there is a human-creaturely element even in the divine voice, though we have been calling it a "direct" form of revelation. For the divine voice evidently uses a human language and created elements (atmosphere, sound waves, human hearing mechanisms and brains). These created elements distinguish the divine voice from the eternal language spoken between the persons of the Trinity. The divine voice speaks in the created world, in time and space, to creatures, employing parts of the creation.

But it is not *merely* a medium. The divine voice is the word of God. It brings God before people in all his lordship attributes. The power of this voice terrified the Israelites at Sinai. Its authority was absolute. And clearly, when the divine voice speaks, God himself is personally present.

Place yourself as an Israelite hearer of the divine voice in Exodus 20. Can you imagine that you would ever find fault with what God said then? Comedians may joke about how people today translate the Ten Commandments into "ten suggestions." But of course, no Israelite would have understood them that way. When the divine voice speaks, you obey, and that is all there is to it. No authority is higher. If you disobey, you incur God's curse. If you obey, blessings abound.

The only problem here is the identification of God's voice. How do I know that it is really God speaking to me, especially if, as with Abraham, the voice tells me to do something really outrageous? The problem is exac-

---

2. When God reveals himself under a visible form, the revelation is called *theophany*, "divine appearance." See further *DG*, 585–87, and this volume, chap. 42.

erbated when we consider that there are counterfeits. Lying spirits have sometimes claimed to be the voice of God (1 Kings 22:20–23; cf. Matt. 24:24; 2 Thess. 2:2; Rev. 13:5–6; 16:13; 19:20; 20:10), and God sometimes permits people to be deceived by the counterfeits.[3] Everyone who hears the authentic word of God knows that God has spoken to him. But not everyone who claims that God has spoken to him has heard the authentic word of God.

Scripture doesn't tell us directly or systematically how the divine voice identifies itself. Exodus 19 tells us that God's voice at Mount Sinai followed frightening phenomena: thunders, lightnings, a thick cloud, a "very loud trumpet blast" (v. 16), and "the whole mountain trembl[ing] greatly" (v. 18). The people were cautioned "lest the LORD break out against them" (vv. 22, 24). These phenomena contributed to Israel's frightened reaction in 20:18–21. But this display of phenomena occurred only on this occasion. On other occasions there were signs: the burning bush in Exodus 3, the angelic display in Isaiah 6. Sometimes Jesus worked miracles to underscore his words.

Nevertheless, it does not seem that such displays regularly accompanied the divine voice. No such thing is recorded in God's visits to Abraham, except for God's fire passing through the animal pieces in Genesis 15:17. God's speech to the prophets was often quiet. God seems to make a point of that with Elijah in 1 Kings 19:12: his presence is not in the wind, earthquake, or fire, but in a "low whisper." And although Jesus performed wonders that validated his claims, not every word of his was accompanied by miracles.

The conclusion seems to be that ultimately God himself identifies himself to his hearers. That is part of the revelation.[4] Natural phenomena and miracles do impress, but Satan, too, can produce spectacle (2 Thess. 2:9). The phenomena are not our fundamental source of assurance; their main function is to underscore the nature and the seriousness of the encounter. Abraham *just knew* that God wanted him to leave Ur, that he would grant a son, that he wanted him to take his son to the mount of sacrifice.

As for the counterfeits of the divine voice, Jesus' words in Matthew 24:24 are reassuring: "For false christs and false prophets will arise and perform great signs and wonders, so as to lead astray, if possible, even the elect." He implies that the false christs and prophets will in fact deceive many, and that they will try to lead astray "if possible" even the elect. But

---

3. For a discussion of God's permission of evil, see chapter 9 of *DG*.

4. Recall our earlier argument (chap. 4; Introduction to Part 3) that in the end revelation must authenticate itself. Similar circularity always occurs in any argument purporting to validate the ultimate standard of truth in any system of thought.

the *if*-clause is contrary to fact. The elect will not ultimately be deceived. How can that be? Evidently because assurance is supernatural. We know that the false revelation is false, just as we know that the true revelation is true—by God's sovereign self-testimony.

The importance of God's sovereignty in identifying his own word cannot be overestimated. If that is the case in regard to the divine voice, it certainly is the case for other kinds of word-media. When we discuss those, we will discuss the self-identification of the word in terms of the testimony of the Holy Spirit. And in chapter 42 we will discuss the witness of the Spirit more systematically.

CHAPTER 15

God's Revelation through Words: Prophets and Apostles

In the theological literature, writers often admit that God's divine voice is infallible, perfect, but they claim that imperfection necessarily enters the picture when God's word comes through human lips. In chapter 12, however, I argued that in general the humanity of revelation never detracts from its divine character, for God is sovereign over all things human. There is humanity even in the language of the divine voice, but nobody would dream of saying that on that account the divine voice is imperfect or fallible. The same must be said for those cases in which the word of God comes through human lips rather than God's own, through prophets and apostles.

When Israel no longer wished to hear the word of God directly from God's lips, they turned to Moses: "You speak to us, and we will listen; but do not let God speak to us, lest we die" (Ex. 20:19). So they called on Moses to speak as a prophet. A prophet is someone who has God's words on his lips, as we see from the virtual definition of *prophet* in Deuteronomy 18. In that chapter, God forbids Israel from seeking revelation from pagan fortune-tellers, wizards, necromancers, diviners (vv. 9–14). But how are they to learn God's will? Here, God approves Israel's desire to hear his word indirectly rather than directly, and he promises this to Moses:

> I will raise up for them a prophet like you from among their broth-
> ers. And I will put my words in his mouth, and he shall speak to

them all that I command him. And whoever will not listen to my words that he shall speak in my name, I myself will require it of him. (vv. 18–19)

Note that (1) the prophet's words are God's words (v. 18); and (2) God's words in the mouth of the prophet are fully authoritative, so that God will discipline anyone who refuses to "listen" (v. 19).[1]

Evidently Moses himself is something of a model for the whole series of prophets that appear through Israel's history. Let us look further at his prophetic office.

When Moses first meets God at the burning bush, God commissions him to bring a message to Israel and to Egypt (Ex. 3:7–22). Moses complains to God, however, that he is not an eloquent speaker (4:10). God replies:

Who has made man's mouth? Who makes him mute, or deaf, or seeing, or blind? Is it not I, the LORD? Now therefore go, and I will be with your mouth and teach you what you shall speak. (Ex. 4:11–12)

God is sovereign over Moses' speech. God will supply the words. But Moses still is not satisfied: "Oh, my Lord, please send someone else" (v. 13).

Then the anger of the LORD was kindled against Moses and he said, "Is there not Aaron, your brother, the Levite? I know that he can speak well. Behold, he is coming out to meet you, and when he sees you, he will be glad in his heart. You shall speak to him and put the words in his mouth, and I will be with your mouth and with his mouth and will teach you both what to do. He shall speak for you to the people, and he shall be your mouth, and you shall be as God to him." (vv. 14–16)

In this extraordinary exchange, God establishes a hierarchy: God, Moses, Aaron, Israel. God gives his words to Moses. Moses gives these divine words to Aaron. Aaron gives them to the people. Throughout the hierarchy the words are God's. Indeed, in verse 16, Moses is called "God."[2] He functions as God because he gives God's words to Aaron, his prophet. There is no decrease in authority among God himself, Moses (Aaron's

---

1. Here, "listening" is not just physical hearing, but obedient hearing. In verse 14, by contrast, God says that they may not "listen" to the wizards and diviners. The older English term *hearken* better conveys the idea of hearing with an obedient disposition.

2. Compare Psalm 82:6 in the light of John 10:35: even wicked rulers can be called "gods" because the word of God comes to them.

God), and Aaron.[3] Moses and Aaron have the authority of God because they speak God's words. And not only do Moses and Aaron have God's words, they have his presence as well, for God says that he will be "with" their mouths.

Here, as in Deuteronomy 18, the prophet is one who has God's words in his mouth. Note similar language in the call of Jeremiah:

> Now the word of the LORD came to me, saying, "Before I formed you in the womb I knew you, and before you were born I consecrated you; I appointed you a prophet to the nations." Then I said, "Ah, Lord GOD! Behold, I do not know how to speak, for I am only a youth." But the LORD said to me, "Do not say, 'I am only a youth'; for to all to whom I send you, you shall go, and whatever I command you, you shall speak. Do not be afraid of them, for I am with you to deliver you, declares the LORD." Then the LORD put out his hand and touched my mouth. And the LORD said to me, "Behold, I have put my words in your mouth. See, I have set you this day over nations and over kingdoms, to pluck up and to break down, to destroy and to overthrow, to build and to plant."
>
> And the word of the LORD came to me, saying, "Jeremiah, what do you see?" And I said, "I see an almond branch." Then the LORD said to me, "You have seen well, for I am watching over my word to perform it." (Jer. 1:4–12)

Like Moses, Jeremiah pleads his own inadequacy. God remedies that inadequacy with his own adequacy: the words are to be God's own, in Jeremiah's mouth. Here the emphasis is on the power of the word, rather than its authority as in Deuteronomy 18, though of course the two are inseparable. Because Jeremiah has God's words in his mouth, he has powers that belong only to God, to build up or destroy nations. Jeremiah sees a vision of an almond branch. God interprets this vision: "I am watching over my word to perform it."[4] The word in Jeremiah's mouth is God's, and so God will see that whatever the word declares will be done. The word has the same power in the prophet's mouth as in God's own.

So the prophet is a divinely approved substitute for the divine voice itself. When Moses spoke to Israel in the name of God, his speech was less frightening than God's own, but no less authoritative or powerful. Earlier, in Exodus 19:9, God told Moses, "Behold, I am coming to you in a thick

---

3. Cf. Ex. 7:1–2. This is the background of the idea that people "to whom the word of God came" may be called "gods" (Ps. 82:6; John 10:34–35).

4. The interpretation of the vision is based on a pun in the Hebrew language. Both "almond tree" and "watch" are from the root *shaqad*.

cloud, that the people may hear when I speak with you, and may also believe you forever." To hear Moses is to hear God. When Moses speaks to Israel, he speaks "according to all that the LORD had given him in commandment to them" (Deut. 1:3). Moses teaches Israel the statutes of God that bear the covenant sanctions: those who obey are blessed; those who disobey are cursed (Deut. 4:1–8). Moses' statutes are God's. Cf. 5:1, 22–33; 6:1–9. Israel promises to obey all of God's words; but most of those are words they hear from Moses' lips, not directly from the divine voice.

Jesus himself acknowledges the authority of Moses' words. He tells the Jews:

> Do not think that I will accuse you to the Father. There is one who accuses you: Moses, on whom you have set your hope. If you believed Moses, you would believe me; for he wrote of me. But if you do not believe his writings, how will you believe my words? (John 5:45–47)

Jesus' main point here, of course, is to testify to his own authority. But he does that by invoking and supporting the Jews' reverence for the words of Moses. Indeed, in verse 47 believing the words of Moses is a kind of prerequisite for believing the words of Jesus. Compare also Luke 16:29–31, when in Jesus' parable "father Abraham" tells the rich man that if people will not hear Moses and the Prophets, they will not be convinced even if someone rises from the dead.

So it is clearly wrong to think there is a decrease in power, authority, or divine presence between the divine voice and the word of God in the mouth of the prophet. If we may not criticize the divine voice, no more may we criticize the prophetic word. The prophetic word is human in ways that the divine voice is not, but the additional humanity of the prophetic word does not inject any fallibility or weakness into the message. Nor does the speaker's sin impart error to the divine words. By whatever means (and such passages as Exodus 4; Deuteronomy 18; and Jeremiah 1 leave no question that it is miraculous), the prophet speaks God's word perfectly well, and we must not find fault with it.

Though Moses is the biblical paradigm for the office of prophet, he is neither the first nor the last to have the prophetic gift. Certainly, Noah spoke prophetically when he declared many centuries in advance how God would deal with the descendants of his sons Shem and Japheth and his grandson Canaan (Gen. 9:24–27). Isaac's blessings on Jacob (Gen. 27:27–29) and Esau (vv. 39–40) were prophetic, as were Jacob's final blessings on his large family (Gen. 49:1–27). Whether we construe these utterances as foretelling the future (divine knowledge) or as bringing about future states of affairs (divine power), they are clearly divine words.

Elijah begins his prophetic ministry by announcing that there would be no rain "except by my word" (1 Kings 17:1). As with Jeremiah, the prophet's word has the power that only God's word has. Then "the word of the LORD came to him" (v. 2), as it would throughout his career. God cleanses Isaiah's lips (Isa. 6:5–7) and gives to his words the power to harden the hearts of the people (vv. 9–10; cf. Matt. 13:14–15; Mark 4:12; Luke 8:10; Acts 28:26–27).

There are also prophets in the NT church. These are numerous, and of both sexes, fulfilling the prophecy of Joel 2:28–32, which Peter quotes in his Pentecost sermon (Acts 2:17–18). These prophets predicted the future (Acts 11:27–28; 21:9–14), received orders from the Holy Spirit (13:1–3), encouraged and strengthened fellow believers (15:32), identified spiritual gifts in people (1 Tim. 1:18; 4:14),[5] witnessed for Christ amid persecution (Rev. 11:3–13). Paul urges the church at Corinth to give more emphasis in worship to the gift of prophecy, less to uninterpreted tongues, because prophecy brings edification to the congregation (1 Cor. 14:1–40). The book of Revelation is a specifically prophetic writing (Rev. 1:3; 22:7). Other texts simply mention prophets, or the prophetic gift, without mentioning a specific function (Acts 19:6; Rom. 12:6; 1 Cor. 11:4–5; 12:10; 1 Thess. 5:20).

I see no reason to understand these prophets any differently from the prophets of the OT. The concept of a prophet, one who has God's word in his mouth, was familiar to Jews and Christians of the NT period. There is no explicit indication in the NT that the office of prophet had changed in any way. Certainly, the presence of the word of God in their mouths adequately accounts for the functions of the NT prophets in the texts cited above,[6] and it would be difficult to account for those functions otherwise than by their unique access to God's word. But the NT does not contain a passage, like Deuteronomy 18, specifically setting forth the meaning and power of the prophetic gift.

The NT, however, is more explicit about the apostles, who are certainly true successors of the OT prophets, and more.[7] Jesus at the beginning of

---

5. Or did the prophets rather predict the course of Timothy's ministry? In either case, they displayed supernatural knowledge.

6. To the contrary, see Wayne Grudem, *Systematic Theology* (Grand Rapids: Zondervan, 1994), 1049–61, who believes that prophecy in the NT had less authority than prophecy in the OT. He says that the NT apostles, however, were the true successors of the OT prophets, in that their word was supremely authoritative.

7. The apostles rank higher than the prophets, according to 1 Corinthians 12:28.

his ministry chooses twelve who are to have a special relationship to him, during his earthly ministry and beyond.[8] Anticipating their later persecution, Jesus assures them:

> When they deliver you over, do not be anxious how you are to speak or what you are to say, for what you are to say will be given to you in that hour. For it is not you who speak, but the Spirit of your Father speaking through you. (Matt. 10:19–20)

They are to have divine assistance when they are called to witness for Jesus. That assistance comes specifically in a divine gift of extraordinary speech. They are to be supported by God's people both as prophets and as righteous men (Matt. 10:40–41).

In the Johannine passion discourses, Jesus is more explicit about the apostles' role in revelation:

> But the Helper, the Holy Spirit, whom the Father will send in my name, he will teach you all things and bring to your remembrance all that I have said to you. (John 14:26)

> But when the Helper comes, whom I will send to you from the Father, the Spirit of truth, who proceeds from the Father, he will bear witness about me. And you also will bear witness, because you have been with me from the beginning. (15:26–27)

> When the Spirit of truth comes, he will guide you into all the truth, for he will not speak on his own authority, but whatever he hears he will speak, and he will declare to you the things that are to come. (16:13)

From the first two passages, we learn that the Spirit will empower the memories of the apostles, so that they will remember Jesus' words. Recall from chapter 10 of this book the great importance of Jesus' words for the salvation of his people. Jesus, as the divine voice, has given to his disciples teaching that is an absolutely necessary foundation for their life and ministry. Remember Peter's "Lord, to whom shall we go? You have the words of eternal life" (John 6:68). But Jesus wrote no books. So the question is urgent as to where the words of Jesus can be found since his ascension to heaven. If we cannot identify them, we have no hope. John 14:26 and 15:26–27 answer that urgent question. The words of the apostles preserve the words of Jesus. When we seek the precious words of Jesus, it is to the apostles that we must go.

---

8. The "beyond," of course, does not include Judas, the betrayer.

John 16:13 enlarges this view of the scope of apostolic revelation. Here the Spirit not only reminds the apostles of what Jesus said. More than that, he will guide them into all truth. And he will show to the apostles things that are to come in the future. As the prophets were both forthtellers and foretellers, so the Spirit empowers the apostles to proclaim the truth and to foretell events to come in the future. So the Spirit gives them revelation about the past (the words of Jesus), the present ("all the truth"), and the future ("things that are to come").

When God pours out the Spirit on the day of Pentecost, the apostles begin to preach Christ.[9] The coming of the Spirit empowers the church for its worldwide witness (Acts 1:8). When the Spirit comes down in wind and fire, "they were all filled with the Holy Spirit and began to speak in other tongues as the Spirit gave them utterance" (2:4). I cannot here discuss the meaning of the gift of tongues, except to say that it enables the disciples to preach the gospel to Jews of many cultures who are gathered in Jerusalem for the feast.[10] The tongues partially reverse the curse of Babel (Gen. 11:1–9), bringing people together under the word of God. When the Spirit comes on the Christians, they speak of Jesus. Spirit and word come together. The book of Acts often presents that correlation (4:8, 31; 6:3–5, 10; 7:55–56; 9:17–20; 13:9–10).

After his miraculous conversion in Acts 9, Paul joins the group of apostles. He is, by his own admission, "untimely born" (1 Cor. 15:8), "the least of the apostles" and "unworthy to be called an apostle" (15:9) because he once persecuted the church. Some in the church questioned his apostolic authority, perhaps on those grounds, perhaps out of their opposition to his doctrine, an issue to which he responds in Galatians and elsewhere. But Paul has seen the resurrected Lord and is therefore a witness to the resurrection, even though he has not been with the disciples from the beginning (Acts 1:22). More significantly, he claims to be an apostle by special appointment of God himself and by the Lord Jesus Christ (Rom. 1:1; Gal. 1:1, 12). Sixteen times in his writings, he applies the title *apostle* to himself. In time, even his opponents accepted that title, so that he was able to ask them as a rhetorical question, "Am I not an apostle?" (1 Cor. 9:1). In the postapostolic age, Paul's status as an apostle was unquestioned, and it has been recognized by the church through all ages, together with his writings that constitute most of the NT.

9. Recall in chapter 9 my discussion of the regular biblical correlation between word and Spirit.

10. In chapter 32 I make some comments about the relation of charismatic theology to the sufficiency of Scripture.

The apostles themselves teach that their message comes from God and therefore has divine authority. In 2 Corinthians 4:1–6, Paul claims that the apostles never tamper with God's word, but rather state it openly and honestly. God who brought light out of darkness has, Paul says, "shone in our hearts to give the light of the knowledge of the glory of God in the face of Jesus Christ" (v. 6).

In Galatians 1:11–12, Paul insists against his opponents:

> For I would have you know, brothers, that the gospel that was preached by me is not man's gospel. For I did not receive it from any man, nor was I taught it, but I received it through a revelation of Jesus Christ.

Since God has appointed him an apostle, his message also comes from God by revelation. (Compare also the reference to revelation in 2:2.)

Speaking for all the apostles, Paul in 1 Corinthians 2:10–13 says of the wisdom of his gospel:

> These things God has revealed to us through the Spirit. For the Spirit searches everything, even the depths of God. For who knows a person's thoughts except the spirit of that person, which is in him? So also no one comprehends the thoughts of God except the Spirit of God. Now we have received not the spirit of the world, but the Spirit who is from God, that we might understand the things freely given us by God. And we impart this in words not taught by human wisdom but taught by the Spirit, interpreting spiritual truths to those who are spiritual.

Note that for Paul the Spirit's revelation gives not only understanding of divine mysteries, but also the words in which the apostles teach these mysteries. Paul also appeals to the Spirit as the source of his counsel in 1 Corinthians 7:40, to revelation as the source of his knowledge of God's mystery in Ephesians 3:3.

The apostles are "stewards of the mysteries of God" (1 Cor. 4:1). "Mystery" in the NT does have some of the connotations of our modern English word—something hard to grasp, beyond our usual understanding. But it also designates more precisely those elements of God's revelation that have been hidden for centuries, now made known through the apostolic preaching and writing. See Rom. 16:25–26.

So God gives to the apostles, like the prophets of the OT, revelation in words, which they communicate in their proclamation. In this revelation, their words are words of God (1 Thess. 2:13). So they display the qualities of the divine voice itself: power (Rom. 1:16–17), authority (Gal. 1:9), and divine presence (1 Thess. 1:5). There is no decrease in any of these qualities when the word of God moves from the lips of God to the lips of the prophets and apostles.

Now, one problem arises at this point that we also discussed in connection with the divine voice in chapter 14. That problem is that of identifying the true revelation. We asked how Abraham knew that the one who spoke to him was the true God. And how we can identify the true voice of God among the counterfeits. In chapter 14, my response to that problem was to emphasize God's sovereignty in revelation. God is sovereign, not only to speak as Lord, but also to assure his hearers that they are hearing the Lord.

When we pass from the divine voice to the words of prophets and apostles, a similar problem emerges. Just as there are lying spirits who counterfeit the divine voice, so there are false prophets (Jer. 14:14; Lam. 2:14; Matt. 7:15; etc.) and apostles (2 Cor. 11:13; Rev. 2:2). As with the divine voice, our ultimate assurance of who speaks truth is supernatural. So Paul attributes the persuasiveness of his gospel to the Holy Spirit's testimony (1 Thess. 1:5). But Scripture also provides tests of prophetic claims that help the people of God to discern which are authentic. Recall that Deuteronomy 18 established the basic definition of a prophet, a person with the words of God in his mouth. The passage also says this:

> "But the prophet who presumes to speak a word in my name that I have not commanded him to speak, or who speaks in the name of other gods, that same prophet shall die." And if you say in your heart, "How may we know the word that the LORD has not spoken?"—when a prophet speaks in the name of the LORD, if the word does not come to pass or come true, that is a word that the LORD has not spoken; the prophet has spoken it presumptuously. You need not be afraid of him. (vv. 20–22)

Here there are two sure marks of false prophets: (1) speaking in the name of a false god,[11] and (2) making predictions that don't come true.

These are marks of false prophets, however, not tests of true prophets. If someone speaks in the name of the true God, and he makes a prediction that comes true, does that mark him as a true prophet? Or what if he makes no predictions at all? Deuteronomy 18 does not anticipate all possible

---

11. Notice how 1 John 4:2–3 brings this principle into the new covenant: "every spirit that confesses that Jesus Christ has come in the flesh is from God, and every spirit that does not confess Jesus is not from God." And believing that Christ has come in the flesh includes believing in the whole apostolic witness (v. 6).

situations. It does not give us infallible marks of all true prophets of God, though it excludes some prophetic claims as false.

Beyond Deuteronomy 18, signs and wonders attested to the prophetic ministry of Moses, and later of Elijah and Elisha. Certainly, the same was true of Jesus' prophetic ministry. Paul speaks, too, of the "signs of a true apostle" that God performed for him (2 Cor. 12:12). But no miracles are mentioned in the ministries of many of the OT prophets or NT apostles. And as we mentioned in chapter 14, Satan counterfeits God's signs and wonders so that some (not the elect) will be deceived (Matt. 24:24). And Jesus rebukes people who *demand* a sign (Matt. 12:38–39; 16:1–4). If people will not hear Moses and the Prophets, he says, they will not believe the word of a resurrected saint (Luke 16:31).[12]

So evidently the attestation of the prophets and apostles, like the attestation of the divine voice, is fundamentally supernatural. God comes with the prophetic and apostolic word and convinces hearers that that word is his own. Miracles and predictions give the hearers a nudge, alert them that something remarkable is happening. But these wonders are not the ultimate argument that identifies a true prophet. God's Spirit is the one who persuades.

This is all the more evident when we consider that true prophecies often seem to break the rule of Deuteronomy 18:22. They make apparent predictions that do not literally come to pass; yet the prophets are accepted, by God and by God's people, as true prophets. The most obvious example is the book of Jonah, where the prophet proclaims, "Yet forty days, and Nineveh shall be overthrown!" (3:4). But Nineveh is not overthrown, at least at that time. Rather, the king and the city repent (3:6–9), and "God relented of the disaster that he had said he would do to them, and he did not do it" (v. 10).

The apparent failure of this prophecy does not arise from the humanity of Jonah as God's messenger. The passage identifies Jonah's words in verse 4 with God's in verse 10. As is the normal pattern in Scripture, the words of the prophet are the words of God, even when that relationship is problematic. If Jonah is a false prophet, then the divine voice is also false.

But the passage offers no solution to that problem. It does, however, see this pattern as rather typical of God and his prophets. The king of Nineveh urges repentance, based on the possibility that "God may turn and relent and turn from his fierce anger, so that we may not perish" (v. 9). God's

12. The relation between signs and faith is complex. See my discussion of miracles, chapter 13 of *DG*.

response showed that the king had supposed rightly (v. 10). Jonah himself is displeased, probably because Nineveh was a great enemy of Israel. But he himself had suspected that this might happen:

> But it displeased Jonah exceedingly, and he was angry. And he prayed to the LORD and said, "O LORD, is not this what I said when I was yet in my country? That is why I made haste to flee to Tarshish; for I knew that you are a gracious God and merciful, slow to anger and abounding in steadfast love, and relenting from disaster." (Jonah 4:1–2)

Jonah here is quoting Yahweh's description of his covenant lordship in Exodus 34:6–7, adding the reference to God's "relenting." He sees God's action as typical of God, not some odd exception to God's general behavior.

Jeremiah 18:5–10 formulates this "relenting" as a general principle of God's action and of his announcements through prophets of covenant blessing and curse:

> Then the word of the LORD came to me: "O house of Israel, can I not do with you as this potter has done? declares the LORD. Behold, like the clay in the potter's hand, so are you in my hand, O house of Israel. If at any time I declare concerning a nation or a kingdom, that I will pluck up and break down and destroy it, and if that nation, concerning which I have spoken, turns from its evil, I will relent of the disaster that I intended to do to it. And if at any time I declare concerning a nation or a kingdom that I will build and plant it, and if it does evil in my sight, not listening to my voice, then I will relent of the good that I had intended to do to it."

The reversal of God's intent for Nineveh is an instance of this principle, as are similar instances in Exodus 32:9–14; Joel 2:13–14; and Amos 7:1–6. Cf. Isa. 38:1–5; Jer. 26:3, 13, 19; 42:10.

In this discussion, I am relying on Richard Pratt's important article, "Historical Contingencies and Biblical Predictions."[13] In that article, Pratt discusses a wide range of biblical data that display the above principle. He argues that Israelites and NT believers regularly took account of the possibility that historical circumstances might prevent the literal fulfillment of prophetic prediction. He believes this principle provides a possible understanding of the NT passages that appear to predict a very soon return of Jesus Christ.

13. Available at http://reformedperspectives.org/newfiles/ric_pratt/TH.Pratt.Historical_Contingencies.html.

But does this principle, then, make prophecy a dead letter? If prophecy does not necessarily find literal fulfillment, is it then the case that anything can happen, following a prophecy? Does this mean that prophecies can safely be ignored? Pratt argues that the prophets' messages must be understood in covenantal terms. The covenant is conditional: it promises blessings for obedience, threatens curses for disobedience. The prophets are God's prosecuting attorneys, bringing the "covenant lawsuit." The people must listen, because God himself, through the prophets, is calling them to repent of their disobedience. They know that the predictions of blessing and judgment are subject to historical contingency, as in Jeremiah 18. But they *must* obey the prophet's words. They must repent, or they can be sure that the worst will happen. And if they do repent, they can expect the best. Sometimes, to be sure, prophecies are qualified by divine oaths or assurances that limit the possible variations in the results of the prophecy (Amos 4:2; 6:8; 8:7). In Jeremiah 11:11, 14, God excludes even the possibility that people can save themselves by repentance. But even in these cases, the details of the fulfillment may be subject to historical contingency.

Pratt points out that the content of the prophecy limits what can happen even when historical contingencies are relevant. Jonah's prophecy indicated that *destruction*, not mere famine or defeat, would result if Nineveh did not repent. The prophecy does not specify *how* Nineveh would be destroyed, or how long it would take, or by what means. Nor does it indicate specifics about Nineveh's future if Nineveh does repent. But it does limit expectations on either alternative. It is therefore a meaningful word from God. So if a prophet predicts a range of results, blessings and cursings contingent on the behavior of his hearers, and if after the people's response God's actions do not fall within that range, the prophet is a false prophet.

But of course, it is not always easy to determine when God's actions do and do not fall within such a range. On a literal reading of Deuteronomy 18:22, it seems fairly simple: if the prophet predicts something, and it doesn't happen, he is a false prophet. But on Pratt's view, a true prophet may predict something that doesn't happen, or a fairly vague range of events, because of a historical contingency. That certainly makes it harder than Deuteronomy 18:22 suggests to determine which prophets are true and which false.

We should remember here, however, that prophets are primarily forthtellers, only secondarily foretellers. Only a very small amount of biblical prophecy contains specific prediction of the future, and most of that is clearly subject to the principle of historical contingency. But at times there are specific predictions. First Samuel 10:1–7, which describes the anointing of King Saul by the prophet Samuel, is an example:

Then Samuel took a flask of oil and poured it on his head and kissed him and said, "Has not the LORD anointed you to be prince over his people Israel? And you shall reign over the people of the LORD and you will save them from the hand of their surrounding enemies. And this shall be the sign to you that the LORD has anointed you to be prince over his heritage. When you depart from me today, you will meet two men by Rachel's tomb in the territory of Benjamin at Zelzah, and they will say to you, 'The donkeys that you went to seek are found, and now your father has ceased to care about the donkeys and is anxious about you, saying, "What shall I do about my son?"' Then you shall go on from there further and come to the oak of Tabor. Three men going up to God at Bethel will meet you there, one carrying three young goats, another carrying three loaves of bread, and another carrying a skin of wine. And they will greet you and give you two loaves of bread, which you shall accept from their hand. After that you shall come to Gibeath-elohim, where there is a garrison of the Philistines. And there, as soon as you come to the city, you will meet a group of prophets coming down from the high place with harp, tambourine, flute, and lyre before them, prophesying. Then the Spirit of the LORD will rush upon you, and you will prophesy with them and be turned into another man. Now when these signs meet you, do what your hand finds to do, for God is with you."

Samuel tells Saul that when he leaves he will encounter precisely three men, bearing precisely three goats and one skin of wine. He mentions other precise details. Verse 9 tells us that "all these signs came to pass that day." Clearly, Samuel is giving to Saul a group of signs to validate the anointing of verse 1. These signs verify to Saul that Samuel is a true prophet of the Lord and that the Lord has truly anointed him to be king. Samuel's ability to describe precisely such future events vindicates his prophetic office, as Deuteronomy 18:22 indicates. The kinds of historical contingencies that we have mentioned are unlikely to affect the outcome of this particular set of predictions, so they serve as an unambiguous example of the prophet's ability to predict the future. Another example is the first recorded statement of Elijah, "As the LORD the God of Israel lives, before whom I stand, there shall be neither dew nor rain these years, except by my word" (1 Kings 17:1). This prediction is literally fulfilled. Prophets may have often employed literal predictions of the future in order to establish their divine credentials.

But the usual work of the prophet is different. At times it may be appropriate for him to display his power of detailed, unconditional prediction; but generally it is not. As forthtellers, prophets are covenant attorneys. The historical contingencies are understood to be part of the prophecy. So when a prophet says, "God will judge you," the audience understands the implicit "unless you repent." Interpreting the prophecy must take this conditionality into account. So that if a prediction made by a prophet does not literally take place because of a historical contingency, believing hearers may legitimately judge that the prophecy has nevertheless "come to pass or come true" (in terms of Deuteronomy 18:22), and that this result confirms the authenticity of the prophet.

So identifying true prophets is more difficult than Deuteronomy 18:22 might appear to suggest. But the ultimate test is whether the prophet truly represents God's covenant sanctions. Only then does he speak in the name of the true God (the first test of Deuteronomy 18:20), and only then do his words, understood in the covenant context, "come to pass or come true" (v. 22).

But someone who wishes to test a prophet by this means must bring to his evaluation a subtle understanding of God's covenant and the condition of the prophet's audience. Therefore, a certain level of spiritual maturity and discernment is needed here, as Paul suggests in 1 Corinthians 14:29, "Let two or three prophets speak, and let the others weigh what is said." The weighing or authenticating of prophecy is not a simple task.

But that difficulty underscores the importance here of God's own witness to himself. We saw in chapter 14 that in his divine voice God not only speaks, but also identifies himself as the speaker. In prophecy, too, it is God's Spirit who identifies the true prophets and distinguishes them from the false. There are marks of true prophecy (Deut. 18; 1 John 4:1–6), but those are not always easy to apply. But as with the divine voice, so also with the prophets and apostles: somehow God drives his message home to the hearts of God's people. Would any Christian believer today seriously doubt that Isaiah was a true prophet, that Paul was a real apostle?

By his Spirit God sovereignly opens the eyes of his people to the signs of true prophecy, such as true prediction, miracles, and orthodox content (1 John 4:2–3), pressing our minds to see in these an authenticity that goes beyond mere probability, an authenticity that can only be the self-authenticating voice of God. When we receive that supernatural verification by God's grace, we confess that the words of the prophets and apostles are nothing less than the word of God, bearing supreme power, authority, and divine presence. In these lordship attributes there is no difference between the words of prophets and apostles and the voice of God himself. These words are therefore God's personal words to us.

CHAPTER 16

The Permanence of God's Written Word

Now, would these words be any less personal if they were to be written down? Emil Brunner and others have argued to this effect. There is some truth in this view. John, for example, tells his "elect lady" that he would rather not use paper and ink to communicate certain things, but rather hopes "to come to you and talk face to face, so that our joy may be complete" (2 John 12). As we will see later in our discussion of person-media,[1] there are some ways in which person-to-person meetings communicate beyond the capacity of written words. But there are also some ways in which written words are better than personal visits. For one thing, written words are more permanent and therefore more suitable for official and public functions.

And we will also see that according to Scripture, God himself has appointed written revelation to play a central role in his communication with human beings. In fact, that revelation (illumined by the Spirit and ministered through the teaching of the church) is our main access to God's personal words in the present age. So written revelation will be the main focus of the rest of this book, with some digressions.[2]

1. See the discussion of the *apostolic parousia* in chapter 43.
2. For a briefer summary of what Scripture says about itself, see "Scripture Speaks for Itself," Appendix F in this volume. Note also my review of John Wenham, *Christ and the Bible*, in Appendix G.

To begin, therefore, we should set aside the prejudice of the contemporary theological community against the idea of written revelation from God. The literature often seems to suggest that divine revelation comes from the divine voice and the prophets/apostles, but that written Scripture is a merely human record of revelation. But in fact, Scripture contains a doctrine of Scripture. It teaches us that God's personal words often come to us through written words—indeed, that written words are of major importance.[3] They have the same authority as the divine voice itself. And God himself has ordained that these written words serve as the constitution of his church.

Before we look directly at this teaching, we should consider an important assumption that underlies the Bible's doctrine of written revelation. That is that divine revelation is not just a momentary experience given to an individual. It is rather to be preserved and passed on to others and to subsequent generations. Even before the beginning of the written canon, we see this emphasis on permanence, for example in the covenant memorials of the patriarchs. In Genesis 8:20, we read that Noah builds an altar in response to God's delivering him through the flood. God responds by reestablishing his covenant. The rainbow (9:12–17) is the sign of the covenant, a permanent witness to God's promise.[4] Abram later builds an altar in Shechem (12:7) to memorialize God's promise that his descendants would possess the land. Cf. also 13:18. After Jacob experienced his revelatory vision of God, he erected a pillar and poured oil on it (28:18), in remembrance of the divine speech to him (35:14). These stone pillars are less than written revelation, of course. But they indicate the patriarchs' desire, and God's, to leave permanent witness to God's covenantal words.

God's covenants are with families, not only with individuals. He does not renew the covenant, by divine voice, individually to each member of the covenant community. Rather, he appoints the recipients of the covenant words to preserve those words and to pass them on to later generations. Although oral tradition plays a role, the normal way of preserving words is through writing.

The same is true in the NT. As we saw in chapter 15, Jesus empowered his disciples to remember all the words he spoke to them (John 14:26). He

3. On the circularity of appealing to Scripture for a doctrine of Scripture, see my brief remarks and references in chapters 1, 4, 8, 14, and Appendices C and E. Briefly, (1) any argument in favor of a supreme authority must appeal to that authority and therefore be circular; and (2) in this case, we are merely using the same procedure by which the church establishes all its doctrines. Scripture is our chief authority for the doctrine of God, of sin, of Christ, of salvation; it must also be our chief authority for the doctrine of Scripture.

4. Rainbows individually disappear, of course; but the *institution* of the rainbow is permanent.

was concerned not only for his disciples, but for those who come to believe through the disciples' word (17:20). The revelation is to be "passed down" as a *tradition*, first "handed over" (*paradidomi*) from the Father to the Son (Matt. 11:27) and then "revealed" to those whom the Son chooses. The revelation of Jesus' resurrection is one that Paul "received" (1 Cor. 15:3) and then "delivered" (*paradidomi*) to the churches. So Paul exhorts the Thessalonian church, "So then, brothers, stand firm and hold to the traditions [*paradosis*] that you were taught by us, either by our spoken word or by our letter" (2 Thess. 2:15). And:

> Now we command you, brethren, in the name of our Lord Jesus Christ, that you keep away from every brother who leads an unruly life and not according to the tradition [*paradosis*] which you received from us. (2 Thess. 3:6 NASB)

Later, Paul exhorts Timothy to "guard the deposit [*paratheke*] entrusted to you" (1 Tim. 6:20). Cf. 2 Tim. 1:12–14; 2:2; 2 Peter 2:21. These passages indicate that the gospel of Christ is a specific content, a tradition (indicated by the *paradidomi* and *paratheke* terminology), passed from the Father, to the Son, to the apostles, to the churches. That tradition[5] serves as the criterion of discipleship, of doctrine and behavior. It is to be defended and preserved, passed from one generation to the next. As Jude says:

> Beloved, although I was very eager to write to you about our common salvation, I found it necessary to write appealing to you to contend for the faith that was once for all delivered [*paradidomi*] to the saints. (Jude 3)

The prominent twentieth-century theologian Karl Barth is well known for the view that revelation cannot be preserved, but exists only in a crisis moment, leaving us only with "recollection and expectation." He believes that if revelation becomes permanent, it then becomes something that we can possess, master, manipulate, and so forth. Intuitively, we will probably agree that Christians, not least theologians, have fallen into the trap of treating God's word as a commodity of which they are masters, though it is difficult to identify when this happens and to prove guilt. The only certain way to prove someone guilty of such an attitude is to read his heart. Certainly, nobody ever admits guilt in this respect. In any case, Barth is right to insist that God's word must be sovereign over us, not the other

---

5. Of course, in the NT there are bad traditions as well as good. The bad traditions are the merely human traditions of the Pharisees that make "void the word of God" (Matt. 15:6). These traditions add to and supplant the true word of God, and so we should reject them. Cf. Col. 2:8. See chap. 38.

way around. But to deny the permanence of God's revelation is no help. Such a denial is unscriptural, as we have seen. And my impression is that Barthian theologians are no more or less prone than anyone else to use revelation as a tool to magnify themselves and to disrespect others, as if they were masters of the word.

In Scripture itself, God ensures the sovereignty of his revelation not by making it momentary and evanescent,[6] but by establishing it as a permanent part of the human landscape, like the pillars and altars of the patriarchs. God commissioned Israel to put the Book of the Law in the holiest part of the tabernacle (Deut. 31:26) and to have the commandments read publicly to the nation as God's witness against their sins (vv. 10–11). The permanent law of God maintained God's sovereignty over his people. And later, during a time of national apostasy, Hilkiah the high priest discovered a copy of the law of God in the temple and brought it to King Josiah, leading to national repentance (2 Kings 22:8–20). Humans may try to add to the word, subtract from it, ignore it, misuse it, or hide it, but they can never be sovereign over it. It will always be God's word, and its very permanence is a sign of that: "The grass withers, the flower fades, but the word of our God will stand forever" (Isa. 40:8).

6. Barth's approach amounts to sovereignty by retreat. In his view, for God's word to be sovereign, it must escape the scrutiny of human beings. But such sovereignty is to no purpose. It cannot command, promise, or guide, as it must if it is to be God's covenant word.

CHAPTER 17

God's Written Words in
the Old Testament

As I indicated in the last chapter, God's revelation even in the earliest books of Scripture is permanent, a content to be preserved and communicated to other people and to later generations. We saw this emphasis in the covenant memorials: pillars and altars erected in memory of God's revelation to the patriarchs.

THE GENERATIONS

The book of Genesis also contains indications of revelation from that time that is specifically verbal. Genesis is divided into a number of sections, each beginning "These are the generations." This and similar phrases occur at 2:4; 5:1; 6:9; 10:1; 11:10; 11:27; 25:12, 19; 36:1, 9; 37:2 (cf. Matt. 1:1). Each introduces the content of the material that follows it. Evidently, these are a literary device governing the structure of Genesis. This pattern does not continue into Exodus or the other books of the Pentateuch. That it is a literary pattern is suggested by the distinctive language of Genesis 5:1, which speaks of a "*book* of the generations of Adam." P. J. Wiseman argued that all these references to generations were in fact titles of books, sources later used by Moses.[1] If this view of the generations is true, it doesn't prove

1. P. J. Wiseman, *Ancient Records and the Structure of Genesis* (Nashville: Thomas Nelson, 1985).

105

that these sources were divinely inspired. If Moses used them in his writing of the Pentateuch, however, then we may conclude that even at the times of Noah, Abraham, Isaac, and so on, God was preparing literary materials for inclusion in the eventual canon.

If the "generations" are not book titles, Moses nevertheless must have gotten the material for the book of Genesis from somewhere other than his own experience. That might have been direct divine revelation, oral tradition, or written sources other than those supposed by Wiseman. On any of these alternatives, plainly God intended the stories of Noah, Abraham, and others to be permanently available to his people, eventually in written form.

THE COVENANT DOCUMENT

What I have said about the generations is somewhat speculative. But there is no question that written revelation is a central part of God's covenant with Israel in the time of Moses. As we saw in chapter 14, God met with Israel at Mount Sinai, where the whole nation heard the divine voice. This was the great "day of the assembly" (Deut. 9:10; 10:4; 18:16) on which God appointed Israel to be his people. After God spoke to them, they told Moses that they did not want to hear the voice of God himself. They asked Moses to hear God's direct voice in their place and to communicate that word in turn to them. Both God and Moses approved that request. So Moses was prophet and mediator of the covenant.

But God's communication with Israel was not only through Moses' prophetic words. In Exodus 24:12:

> The LORD said to Moses, "Come up to me on the mountain and wait there, that I may give you the tablets of stone, with the law and the commandment, which I have written for their instruction."

Note that these tablets have been written by God before Moses even ascends the mountain. The words on the tablets are not only God's words, for he is the speaker throughout the document, but also God's actual writing. God here is not only the author, but the publisher. In 31:18, there is an even more vivid picture of the divine authorship:

> And he gave to Moses, when he had finished speaking with him on Mount Sinai, the two tablets of the testimony, tablets of stone, written with the finger of God.

The very finger of God! The work is not only God's words, but God's penmanship!

When Moses comes down the mountain to rejoin the people (and to grieve over their idolatry), he brings the tablets with him, and again there is an emphatic expression of divine authorship: "The tablets were the work of God, and the writing was the writing of God, engraved on the tablets" (Ex. 32:16). Moses breaks the tablets out of anger for their sin, or perhaps as a symbolic gesture. But then Moses intercedes with God, and God announces reconciliation. He invites Moses to come up the mountain again. This time, Moses is to bring tablets with him:

> The LORD said to Moses, "Cut for yourself two tablets of stone like the first, and I will write on the tablets the words that were on the first tablets, which you broke." (Ex. 34:1)

Since Moses broke the first tablets, he must replace them. But again, God is the one who does the writing. Nevertheless, at one point the narrative also gives Moses a role in the writing:

> And the LORD said to Moses, "Write these words, for in accordance with these words I have made a covenant with you and with Israel." So he was there with the LORD forty days and forty nights. He neither ate bread nor drank water. And he wrote on the tablets the words of the covenant, the Ten Commandments. (34:27–28)[2]

It is not quite clear what role Moses played as distinguished from the writing of God's own finger. But that doesn't matter much in this context. If Moses was God's agent, if indeed Moses was himself God's "finger," his humanity does not detract one bit from God's personal authorship of the document.[3] The words of the document are God's own personal words to Israel.

The document should be seen in the context of the suzerainty treaties of the ancient Near East. Meredith G. Kline, in *The Structure of Biblical Authority*,[4] points out that in Hittite and other ancient cultures, a great king would sometimes make a treaty with a lesser king and inscribe the terms of that treaty in a written document. Kline believes that the Decalogue, the document written by God's finger on tablets of stone, shares a literary form with the Hittite suzerainty treaties. He also finds the treaty-form in the book of Deuteronomy.

2. Deuteronomy repeats much of this same language (4:13; 5:22; 9:10–11; 10:2–4).
3. On the relationship between the human element in revelation and its divine authority, see chapter 12.
4. Grand Rapids: Eerdmans, 1972.

Later in this book (especially chapter 24), I will note many parallels between Moses' tablets and the Hittite suzerainty treaties. For now, the important thing to remember is that as with those treaties, God's relation to Israel is structured by a written text.

1. As the great king in the Hittite treaties began by identifying himself as the author of the document, so Yahweh identifies himself as the author, "I am the LORD your God," and he speaks throughout the document in the first person.
2. As with the suzerainty treaties, God unilaterally lays down the terms of his covenant. There is no negotiation.
3. As with the suzerainty treaties, the words of the document are the "words of the covenant" (Ex. 34:28). Indeed, they are identified with the covenant. Deuteronomy 4:13 says:

> And he declared to you his covenant, which he commanded you to perform, that is, the Ten Commandments, and he wrote them on two tablets of stone.

The tablets are "the tablets of the covenant" (Deut. 9:9, 11, 15). These and subsequently revealed laws are words of the covenant (Deut. 29:9, 21; 33:9).

4. The covenant words are a *holy* text. As the Hittite suzerainty treaties were placed in the sanctuaries of the great king and the lesser king, so God's covenant words were put by the ark of the covenant, the holiest place in Israel (Deut. 31:26), the most intense manifestation of God's presence. Compare Paul's description of the OT as the *holy* Scriptures in 2 Timothy 3:15. Holiness indicates a special relationship to God, and a locus of the divine presence.
5. The placing of the covenant document in the sanctuary also guards its permanence. The holy books were placed in the tabernacle, and later in the temple in Jerusalem, until the Romans destroyed the temple in A.D. 70.
6. The divine text is God's witness against Israel. In modern theology it has been common to refer to Scripture as man's witness to God. The account of God's written words in Exodus and Deuteronomy turns this upside down. God says:

> Take this Book of the Law and put it by the side of the ark of the covenant of the LORD your God, that it may be there for a witness against you. For I know how rebellious and stubborn you are. Behold, even today while I am yet alive with you, you have been rebellious against the LORD. How much more after

my death! Assemble to me all the elders of your tribes and your officers, that I may speak these words in their ears and call heaven and earth to witness against them. (Deut. 31:26–28)

Far from being an account of man's opinions about God, the covenant document is God's witness against all of man's false notions and disobedience.

7. By implication, the covenant document is the highest law in Israel. It is, we may say, Israel's *constitution*. As with the United States of America, Israel's highest authority is a written document.

8. As with the suzerainty treaties, God orders that the law be publicly read to all Israel. In this case, it must be officially read every seven years (Deut. 31:9–13).

9. God's word is Israel's very life:

He said to them, "Take to heart all the words by which I am warning you today, that you may command them to your children, that they may be careful to do all the words of this law. For it is no empty word for you, but your very life, and by this word you shall live long in the land that you are going over the Jordan to possess." (Deut. 32:46–47)

The Decalogue document is not the last of God's written words to Israel. Toward the end of his life, Moses writes "this law," probably including much of Deuteronomy. He gives it to the priests who carry the ark of the covenant (Deut. 31:9), and mandates that it be publicly read (vv. 11–13). Cf. 31:24–29. The "Song of Moses," chapter 32, is especially to be preserved, taught, and heeded (31:19–22) as God's "witness."

After Moses dies and Joshua replaces him as Israel's leader, God exhorts him to follow the written law:

Only be strong and very courageous, being careful to do according to all the law that Moses my servant commanded you. Do not turn from it to the right hand or to the left, that you may have good success wherever you go. This Book of the Law shall not depart from your mouth, but you shall meditate on it day and night, so that you may be careful to do according to all that is written in it. For then you will make your way prosperous, and then you will have good success. (Josh. 1:7–8)

At the end of his life, when Israel had conquered much of the Promised Land, Joshua made a covenant with the people that day, and put in place statutes and rules for them at Shechem. And Joshua wrote these words in the Book of the Law of God. And he took a large stone and set it up there under the terebinth that was by the sanctuary of the LORD. And Joshua said to all the people, "Behold, this stone shall be a witness against us, for it has heard all the words of the LORD that he spoke to us. Therefore it shall be a witness against you, lest you deal falsely with your God." So Joshua sent the people away, every man to his inheritance. (Josh. 24:25–28)

That Joshua would add words to the sacred covenant words of God, indeed "in the Book of the Law of God," would at first glance seem arrogant, especially in light of the prohibition in Deuteronomy 4:2 and 12:32 against adding to or subtracting from the word of God. But in Joshua 24 we see that his writing was in the context of a covenant with God. Certainly, this covenant was a covenant between God and Israel, with Joshua serving only as mediator. As with the words of Moses, the words of Joshua are God's words, put with the other words of God with the ark, in God's sanctuary, with a stone as God's witness against Israel. Thus a pattern is established for additions to the canon.

WRITTEN PROPHECY

Prophets after the time of Moses and Joshua also produced written documents setting forth the words that God gave to them. In Isaiah 8:1–2, we read:

Then the LORD said to me, "Take a large tablet and write on it in common characters, 'Belonging to Maher-shalal-hashbaz.' And I will get reliable witnesses, Uriah the priest and Zechariah the son of Jeberechiah, to attest for me."

Maher-shalal-hashbaz ("haste to the spoil") is the name of the son whose birth will signal the coming defeat of Damascus and Samaria by the king of Assyria. The written tablet containing the prophecy is authorized by God and witnessed (as the earlier covenant document) for authenticity. The document preserves the prophecy, so that when the event takes place it will identify Isaiah as a true prophet.

In 30:8–11, God again authorizes written prophecy, again as a witness against Israel's unbelief. Israel will not heed the prophecy, so it takes written form "that it may be for the time to come as a witness forever." A later generation may be more attentive and will take Israel's past disobedience as cautionary.

For other references to written prophecy, see Isaiah 34:16–17; Jeremiah 25:13; 30:2; 51:60–61; and Daniel 9:1–2. David is called a prophet in Acts 2:30, on the basis of his written text, Psalm 16. Jesus and the apostles also quote David's psalms as anticipating Jesus' work as Messiah (as Matt. 22:42–45).

In Jeremiah 36, a scroll of written prophecy plays an important role in the narrative. At God's behest, Jeremiah dictates God's words to Baruch, his scribe. Baruch reads the scroll publicly and to the Israelite officials. The unbelieving king Jehoiakim burns the scroll, but God calls on Jeremiah to write the same words on another scroll, plus divine condemnation on Jehoiakim, "and many similar words were added to them" (v. 32).

In some OT passages, one writer quotes another from what is evidently a written source. Cf. Jer. 26:17–18 with Mic. 3:12–13; Isa. 2:2–4 with Mic. 4:1–5; Isa. 11:9 with Hab. 2:14. A number of OT writers show familiarity with the written law of Moses (Dan. 9:9–15; Pss. 19:7; 94:12; 119:1 and throughout Ps. 119). So it is evident that during the OT period itself, a body of writings developed that could be quoted as divinely authoritative.

WISDOM

The wisdom literature (Job, Proverbs, Ecclesiastes, Song) stands somewhat separate from the laws of Moses and the prophets. But it, too, presupposes written revelation from God. The first four chapters of the book of Proverbs urge readers (especially young ones) to attend to wisdom as a guide to their lives. That wisdom comes from God (Prov. 2:6–8), and the fear of the Lord is the beginning of wisdom and knowledge (1:7; 9:10; 15:33; cf. Ps. 111:10). The benefits of wisdom in Proverbs, chapters 1–4 and 8–9, are essentially the same as those of God's words, statutes, and testimonies in Psalm 119. Proverbs 30:5–6 also relates God's word to wisdom:

> Every word of God proves true; he is a shield to those who take refuge in him. Do not add to his words, lest he rebuke you and you be found a liar. (Prov. 30:5–6)

The wisdom itself began in oral teaching, but was eventually, like the law, put into writing. Israel came to recognize it as written words from God and therefore of permanent importance:

> The words of the wise are like goads, and like nails firmly fixed are the collected sayings; they are given by one Shepherd. (Eccl. 12:11)

CHAPTER 18

Respect for God's Written Words in the Old Testament

In none of the passages we have considered is there any suggestion that the written form of the word is less authoritative than the oral, or, for that matter, than the divine voice. In the narrative of Jeremiah 36, Jehoiakim should have taken heed to Baruch's scroll. When he burned it, he added to his condemnation. The scroll was God's personal word to him, and he despised it. When one prophet quotes the written word of another, or when Psalm 119 refers to the written law, the written words are referred to with utmost reverence, as the supreme authority for all of life.

N.B.: Contrary to many liberal writers, the concept of a written word of God does not begin with twentieth-century fundamentalism, or seventeenth-century orthodoxy, or medieval scholasticism, or postapostolic defensiveness, or late Jewish legalism.[1] It is not even the product of late

---

1. To disparage an idea, or praise it, because it comes from a particular time or place is to commit the genetic fallacy. It's like Nathanael's early disparagement of Jesus, "Can anything good come out of Nazareth?" (John 1:46). Yet this sort of thing happens all the time in theology. Some eras, such as the time of Paul, the Trinitarian fathers, Augustine, and the Protestant Reformation, are supposed to be fonts of wisdom, and others (those listed above) are considered dark days for the church. If you want to defend a theological idea, you would be wise to trace its historical pedigree to one of the favored eras. Certainly you should never claim (or admit) to have gotten an idea from twentieth-century American fundamentalists! I have often heard the idea of biblical inerrancy disparaged by European theologians on the ground that it is an "American" idea. (I believe myself that it is rather, by other names, the view of the whole church before 1650.) But even if we grant the legitimacy

NT documents like 2 Timothy 3:15–17 and 2 Peter 1:19–21, which some critics dismiss as postapostolic or legalistic. It is embedded in the original constitution of the people of God and is assumed throughout Scripture.

In one sense, the written document is actually weightier than the oral messages of the prophets. For it is the written document that, as only a written document can, serves as the formal constitution of the people of God. It governs Israel long after the prophets have gone. The covenant document is the fundamental law of Israel, as the written Constitution is the fundamental law of the United States of America. N. T. Wright is critical of the tendency in the postapostolic church to regard Scripture

> as a "court of appeal," the source-book or rule-book from which doctrine and ethics might be deduced and against which innovations were to be judged.[2]

But there is no doubt that the covenant document, and the whole Torah that developed from it, served (among other functions) as a rulebook, as law, as a court of appeal, in ancient Israel.

Open randomly to almost any page of Deuteronomy 4–11, and you will find admonitions like these:

> And now, O Israel, listen to the statutes and the rules that I am teaching you, and do them, that you may live, and go in and take possession of the land that the LORD, the God of your fathers, is giving you. You shall not add to the word that I command you, nor take from it, that you may keep the commandments of the LORD your God that I command you. Your eyes have seen what the LORD did at Baal-peor, for the LORD your God destroyed from among you all the men who followed the Baal of Peor. But you who held fast to the LORD your God are all alive today. See, I have taught you statutes and rules, as the LORD my God commanded me, that you should do them in the land that you are entering to take possession of it. Keep them and do them, for that will be your wisdom and your understanding in the sight of the peoples, who, when they hear all these statutes, will say, "Surely this great nation is a wise and understanding people." For what great nation is there that has a god so near to it as the LORD our God is to us, whenever we call upon him? And what great nation is there, that

---

of such genetic reasoning, it cannot be brought against the idea of a divinely authoritative written Word; for that idea goes back to Israel's beginnings as a nation.

2. N. T. Wright, *The Last Word: Beyond the Bible Wars to a New Understanding of the Authority of Scripture* (San Francisco: HarperCollins, 2005), 65.

has statutes and rules so righteous as all this law that I set before you today? (Deut. 4:1–8)

Now this is the commandment, the statutes and the rules that the LORD your God commanded me to teach you, that you may do them in the land to which you are going over, to possess it, that you may fear the LORD your God, you and your son and your son's son, by keeping all his statutes and his commandments, which I command you, all the days of your life, and that your days may be long. Hear therefore, O Israel, and be careful to do them, that it may go well with you, and that you may multiply greatly, as the LORD, the God of your fathers, has promised you, in a land flowing with milk and honey.

Hear, O Israel: The LORD our God, the LORD is one. You shall love the LORD your God with all your heart and with all your soul and with all your might. And these words that I command you today shall be on your heart. You shall teach them diligently to your children, and shall talk of them when you sit in your house, and when you walk by the way, and when you lie down, and when you rise. You shall bind them as a sign on your hand, and they shall be as frontlets between your eyes. You shall write them on the doorposts of your house and on your gates. (Deut. 6:1–9)

And the LORD commanded us to do all these statutes, to fear the LORD our God, for our good always, that he might preserve us alive, as we are this day. And it will be righteousness for us, if we are careful to do all this commandment before the LORD our God, as he has commanded us. (Deut. 6:24–25)

You shall therefore be careful to do the commandment and the statutes and the rules that I command you today. (Deut. 7:11)

Take care lest you forget the LORD your God by not keeping his commandments and his rules and his statutes, which I command you today. (Deut. 8:11)

In Deuteronomy, the statutes, laws, commandments, ordinances, rules, words, and so on (note the eloquent redundancy) are spoken by Moses in his final addresses to the nation of Israel. They are prophetic words. But they are also permanent requirements imposed on Israel, to be remembered and observed beyond the lifetime of Moses. And so Moses writes down the Deuteronomic law, places it with the sacred stone tablets, and arranges for its regular public reading (Deut. 31:9–13). Once that is done, the statutes are a *written* revelation, a book. So God tells Joshua to do according to the law that Moses placed in a book:

> Only be strong and very courageous, being careful to do according to all the law that Moses my servant commanded you. Do not turn from it to the right hand or to the left, that you may have good success wherever you go. This Book of the Law shall not depart from your mouth, but you shall meditate on it day and night, so that you may be careful to do according to all that is written in it. For then you will make your way prosperous, and then you will have good success. (Josh. 1:7–8)

At the end of Joshua's life, he urges Israel to do the same:

> Therefore, be very strong to keep and to do all that is written in the Book of the Law of Moses, turning aside from it neither to the right hand nor to the left. (Josh. 23:6)

Compare Deuteronomy 5:32; 28:14; and Joshua 11:15 on the language of "neither to the right hand nor to the left."

The theme of praise for God's written words is frequent in the psalms. In Psalm 12, when David bemoans a world of lies, flattery, and oppression, corrupted by evil speech, he reflects on the one form of language that is pure:

> The words of the LORD are pure words, like silver refined in a furnace on the ground, purified seven times. (Ps. 12:6)

In Psalm 19, after a section on praise for God's revelation of himself in the creation, David continues:

> The law of the LORD is perfect, reviving the soul; the testimony of the LORD is sure, making wise the simple; the precepts of the LORD are right, rejoicing the heart; the commandment of the LORD is pure, enlightening the eyes; the fear of the LORD is clean, enduring forever; the rules of the LORD are true, and righteous altogether. More to be desired are they than gold, even much fine gold; sweeter also than honey and drippings of the honeycomb. Moreover, by them is your servant warned; in keeping them there is great reward. (Ps. 19:7–11)

In Psalm 78, Asaph reflects on the requirement of Deuteronomy 6:6–9 that parents should saturate the minds of their children with the words of God:

> He established a testimony in Jacob and appointed a law in Israel, which he commanded our fathers to teach to their children, that

> the next generation might know them, the children yet unborn, and arise and tell them to their children, so that they should set their hope in God and not forget the works of God, but keep his commandments; and that they should not be like their fathers, a stubborn and rebellious generation, a generation whose heart was not steadfast, whose spirit was not faithful to God. (Ps. 78:5–8)

With these compare Psalms 18:30; 111:7; and the many other references in the psalms to God's laws, commandments, and so on.

Psalm 119 is, of course, the most extensive source of these references. It is the longest psalm, the largest chapter in the Bible, and its chief theme is the word of God. Nearly every verse uses one of the synonyms of our "eloquent redundancy": God's law, testimonies, ways, precepts, statutes, commandments, word, rules, promise. Each of these verses brings out the perfection of God's law and the importance of not straying from it.

The psalm is not merely about obeying commands, however. It displays a highly personal relationship between the psalmist and his Lord through the word: God's testimonies are his greatest delight (vv. 15–16, 24, 47), his source of wonder (v. 18), his consuming object of longing (vv. 20, 40), the means of giving him life in a desperate situation (vv. 25, 50), his strength in sorrow (v. 28), his object of worship (v. 48), hope (v. 49), and comfort (vv. 50, 52). He sings them (v. 54). God's law is better to him "than thousands of gold and silver pieces" (v. 72). We can continue with this type of exposition all the way to verse 176.

Recall that in chapter 11, I referred to a number of biblical passages and principles to defend the conclusion that God's word is God himself, his own personal presence. One of the arguments was that believers regard God's word as a proper object of religious worship. In that connection, I mentioned such passages as Psalms 56:4, 10; 119:48, 120, 161–62, and the worship offered to God's name in Psalms 9:2; 34:3; 68:4; 138:2.

Now, we should remind ourselves that the chief object of this religious praise, and the chief object of all the other acclaim for God's laws, statutes, commandments, and so on, is specifically the *written* Word of God. The psalmists' primary focus here is not on the divine voice heard directly, nor on the oral words of prophets, but on the written documents constituting God's law, statutes, commandments, ways, precepts, and so forth.

It should be clear from this discussion that OT religion is focused on divinely authored written words. Those written words govern all aspects of an Israelite's life, and they function in many ways: for example, as indicatives, imperatives, sources of delight, and objects of worship. No passage suggests that these written words are of less authority than the oral prophetic word or the divine voice itself. There is no suggestion that the influence of the human writer injects any falsehood or inadequacy into the sacred texts.

Israel's awareness of being subject to God's words begins in Genesis and continues throughout the OT, indeed on nearly every page, for as I said in chapter 1, the entire biblical narrative is governed by the pattern of God's speech followed by man's response.

It could not have been otherwise, for OT revelation is covenantal. It is an aspect of Israel's relationship to her Lord. The Lord-servant relationship is a relationship in which language is essential. The Lord sets forth the terms of the covenant in words; the servant accepts these and seeks to abide by them. Without words, there can be no covenant, no Lord. Further, in a covenant, the words take on permanent form, in writing, and they are preserved from one generation to another. So the very nature of covenant implies that there will be written revelation, and that that revelation will have the same power, authority, and divine presence as direct, personal revelation from the covenant Lord. So the written words of the OT are the personal words of God to his people.

CHAPTER 19

Jesus' View of the Old Testament

In chapters 7–8, I expounded the teaching of John 1 and other passages that Jesus Christ is himself the Word of God. But in God's plan of salvation, he became a man in total subjection to the Father's will, obeying the Father's word (John 5:36; 8:42). In his earthly ministry, he did nothing merely on his own authority, but on that of his Father (10:18). He spoke only as the Father taught him to speak (8:28; 12:49), and he spoke all that the Father gave him to speak (15:15).

So in chapter 10 I emphasized not only that Jesus *is* the Word of God, but that he is the chief *speaker* of that word. Therefore, his words are supremely important as the criterion for Christian discipleship. Here I will argue that Jesus, the supreme speaker of God's word, validates through his word the authority of God's written Word.

The Gospels emphasize that Jesus was subject not only to the Father's direct communication to him, but also to the written words of God in the OT. He regularly and intentionally acts and speaks in such a way as to fulfill Scripture (Matt. 4:14; 5:17; 8:17; 12:17; 13:35; 26:54), and he says that the great events of his own life have taken place to fulfill Scripture (Matt. 13:14; 26:56; Luke 24:44–47). Further, he says that the OT Scriptures as a whole "bear witness about me" (John 5:39; cf. Luke 24:25–27; John 5:45–47).

Further, Jesus cites OT passages as authoritative words of God. The authority of what we call the OT was commonly accepted among the Jews of Jesus' day. It represents common ground between Jesus and his Jewish

118

opponents. In this regard, he did not merely accommodate his views to theirs. He did not hesitate to disagree with Jewish traditions when he thought it necessary. But he never questioned the Jews' understanding of scriptural authority. There is not a shred of evidence that he personally held a view of Scripture different from theirs.

Jesus refers to the OT, describing it as "Law" and "Prophets" (Matt. 5:17–18; 7:12; 11:13; 12:5; 22:40; 23:23), which, as we have seen, reflect on the authority of the text as God's Word. The term *Scripture* (*graphe, grammata*) in citations carries the same connotation (Mark 12:10; Luke 4:21; John 7:38).[1] So the formula "It is written" (*gegraptai*) should be taken the same way (Matt. 4:4, 7, 10; 11:10; 21:13; 26:24, 31).

This understanding is consistent with Jesus' explicit reflections on the nature of the OT, the chief of which is this:

> Do not think that I have come to abolish the Law or the Prophets; I have not come to abolish them but to fulfill them. For truly, I say to you, until heaven and earth pass away, not an iota, not a dot, will pass from the Law until all is accomplished. Therefore whoever relaxes one of the least of these commandments and teaches others to do the same will be called least in the kingdom of heaven, but whoever does them and teaches them will be called great in the kingdom of heaven. (Matt. 5:17–19)

This passage serves as an introduction to Jesus' treatment of the Ten Commandments in the Sermon on the Mount. In that sermon, Jesus often differs from traditional Jewish interpretations of the commandments, indicating his disagreement by the phrase "You have heard that it was said" (vv. 21, 31, etc.), but he does not criticize the commandments themselves. In verse 27, he does quote the actual words of the seventh commandment "You shall not commit adultery" with the phrase "You have heard that it was said," but here he uses that phrase not to diminish the authority of the commandment, but rather to criticize those Jewish teachers who merely refer to the commandment, without acknowledging the depth of its requirement. In fact, verses 27–30 contain a strong affirmation of the authority of the seventh commandment. The seventh commandment, to Jesus, governs not only our outward behavior, but also the desires of our hearts.

In John 5:45–47, Jesus addresses the Jews as follows:

1. See Benjamin Breckinridge Warfield, "The Terms 'Scripture' and 'Scriptures' as Employed in the New Testament," in Warfield, *The Inspiration and Authority of the Bible* (Grand Rapids: Baker, 1970), 229–41.

> Do not think that I will accuse you to the Father. There is one who accuses you: Moses, on whom you have set your hope. If you believed Moses, you would believe me; for he wrote of me. But if you do not believe his writings, how will you believe my words?

Here Jesus agrees with his opponents on the authority of Moses, who as we saw in chapters 14 and 15 is the very paradigm of the OT prophets. By this time, of course, Moses himself has been dead for centuries; so to "believe Moses" is to believe his written words. Yet Moses himself lives with God and accuses the Jews of unbelief because, according to Jesus, they do not believe Moses' writings as they claim to. Those writings, Jesus says, are about him, about Jesus. In verse 47, Jesus in effect makes believing Moses' writings a prerequisite for believing Jesus himself. The Jews do not *truly* believe Moses, but they must do that if they are ever to trust in Jesus. So the words of Moses have a high importance over a thousand years after they were written.

We should also note John 10:34–36:

> Jesus answered them, "Is it not written in your Law, 'I said, you are gods'? If he called them gods to whom the word of God came—and Scripture cannot be broken—do you say of him whom the Father consecrated and sent into the world, 'You are blaspheming,' because I said, 'I am the Son of God'?"

Jesus here responds to the charge of blasphemy with a formal rather than substantive argument. Rather than entering into Trinitarian nuances, which his opponents could never have understood, he appeals to the broad meaning of the term "god" in the Scriptures, which his opponents would have acknowledged. His example is Psalm 82:6, which refers to the (wicked!) rulers of Israel as "gods." Jesus argues that he has far more reason than those rulers to apply the term to himself, because the Father consecrated him and sent him into the world.

In the course of his argument, Jesus calls Psalm 82:6 "your Law," even though in the Jewish categories of Law, Prophets, and Writings, the psalms were among the Writings, not the Law. This usage ascribes legal authority to this text, simply because it is part of the Scriptures (John 10:35). Jesus certainly regarded it this way, and most likely the Jews did also.

In verse 35, Jesus says that "Scripture cannot be broken." Here again, Jesus is on common ground with the Jews. Because Psalm 82:6 is Scripture, it is God's personal word, which can never become anything less. It cannot fail or lose its authority.

CHAPTER 20

The Apostles' View of
the Old Testament

The apostles' view of the OT does not differ from that of Jesus himself. The apostles use the same titles Jesus used to denote Scripture, such as "Law," "Prophets," and "Scripture." They sometimes modify these titles, as with Paul's "*holy* Scriptures" (2 Tim. 3:15 NIV), which recalls the placing of the tablets of the covenant into the Holiest Place in the tabernacle.[1] James speaks of the "perfect law" (James 1:25), the "law of liberty" (1:25; 2:12), and the "royal law" (2:8). Paul refers to Scripture by the title "oracles of God" (Rom. 3:2; cf. Acts 7:38; Heb. 5:12; 1 Peter 4:11).[2] The oracles, he says, give the Jews an advantage over the Gentiles.

All these references underscore the authority of the OT written Word. Often, to be sure, Paul uses "law" with a negative connotation, when he is

1. See chapter 17 on the placing of the law into the Holiest Place in the tabernacle and later the temple. We should not pass quickly over the use of "holy" in Romans 7:12 and 2 Timothy 3:15, as we often do. It is no accident that most Bibles today bear the title *Holy Bible*. The book is holy not because it engenders religious feelings, but because it stands in the closest proximity to God himself, as it did in the tabernacle and temple. It is "holy ground," like the burning bush Moses approached on Mount Sinai, the place of God's presence (Ex. 3:5).

2. Benjamin Breckinridge Warfield explores the meaning of this phrase in "The Oracles of God," in Warfield, *The Inspiration and Authority of the Bible* (Grand Rapids: Baker, 1970), 351–407. He concludes on page 406, "We have unobtrusive and convincing evidence here that the Old Testament Scriptures, as such, were esteemed by the writers of the New Testament as an oracular book, which in itself not merely contains, but is the 'utterance,' the very Word of God; and is to be appealed to as such and as such deferred to, because nothing other than the crystallized speech of God."

121

arguing that nobody can become right with God through obedience to the law. But Paul does not doubt for a minute that the written law is God's holy Word and represents God's standard of judgment. For him, "the law is holy, and the commandment is holy and righteous and good" (Rom. 7:12).

The apostles, like Jesus, quote the OT with phrases connoting authority, such as "it is written" (Rom. 1:17; 3:4; many others). B. B. Warfield observes a remarkable pattern in these quotations, particularly "Scripture says" and "It says." He notes two classes of passages:

> In one of these classes of passages the Scriptures are spoken of as if they were God; in the other, God is spoken of as if He were the Scriptures: in the two together, God and the Scriptures are brought into such conjunction as to show that in point of directness of authority no distinction was made between them.[3]

In Galatians 3:8, God is spoken of as if he were the Scriptures: "And the Scripture, foreseeing that God would justify the Gentiles by faith, preached the gospel beforehand to Abraham, saying, 'In you shall all the nations be blessed.'" Romans 9:17 is similar. The other class of passages includes Matthew 19:4–5; Acts 4:24–25; 13:34–35; and Hebrews 1:6; 3:7, where the NT writer cites sayings from the OT as coming from God, which in the OT context are not directly spoken by God, but by the human writer. The subjectless verbs *legei* and *phesi*, both translated "it says" or "he says," cite Scripture and God interchangeably in Romans 9:15; 15:10; 1 Corinthians 6:16; 15:27; 2 Corinthians 6:2; Galatians 3:16; Ephesians 4:8; 5:14; Hebrews 8:5; and James 4:6. Warfield discusses opposing interpretations of these texts, but concludes that for the NT writers, God and Scripture were interchangeable in such contexts because the Scriptures were nothing less than the Word of God. Acts 4:25 is representative: God "through the mouth of our father David, your servant, said by the Holy Spirit, 'Why did the Gentiles rage, and the peoples plot in vain?'" God is the speaker, giving his utterance through the human writer (David), inspiring him to speak by the Holy Spirit. So even though David is the speaker, we may take his utterance as God's personal word to us.

This is the view of Scripture that the apostles teach when they are reflecting on the subject. For James, following his brother Jesus (Matt. 7:21, 24–27), the written Word is something we should do, not merely hear (James 1:22). Scripture never speaks "to no purpose" (4:5). James sees

---

3. Benjamin Breckinridge Warfield, "'It Says:' 'Scripture Says:' 'God Says,'" in *The Inspiration and Authority of the Bible*, 299.

great blessing in the doing of it (1:25), great dangers in neglecting any part of it. He says, "For whoever keeps the whole law but fails in one point has become accountable for all of it" (2:10). And note the following:

> Do not speak evil against one another, brothers. The one who speaks against a brother or judges his brother, speaks evil against the law and judges the law. But if you judge the law, you are not a doer of the law but a judge. There is only one lawgiver and judge, he who is able to save and to destroy. But who are you to judge your neighbor? (4:11–12)

There are many good reasons to avoid judging one another. But James mentions a reason we normally don't think of: such behavior amounts to speaking evil of the law. And in James's mind, slandering the law is one of the worst things you can do. If you speak evil of the law, you are judging the law, making yourself the supreme lawgiver (i.e., claiming autonomy). You are claiming a prerogative that belongs only to God. You are seeking to replace him on the throne of the universe.

Paul agrees with James. According to Acts 24:14, he announces to the Roman governor Felix:

> But this I confess to you, that according to the Way, which they call a sect, I worship the God of our fathers, believing everything laid down by the Law and written in the Prophets.

In his letter to the Romans, after quoting Psalm 69:9, Paul explains his reason for appealing to the OT:

> For whatever was written in former days was written for our instruction, that through endurance and through the encouragement of the Scriptures we might have hope. (Rom. 15:4)

Here, Paul says that the Scriptures, though written centuries before his time, were written for the specific purpose of instructing and encouraging believers of the first century A.D. There are, of course, many ancient books that have the ability to instruct people centuries later. We think of the works of Aeschylus, Plato, and many others. But none of these ancient writings were composed *for the purpose of* instructing people of later ages. Paul says that the Scriptures were written intentionally for the benefit of people living centuries later. If this is true, then there must have been a divine intention underlying the intentions of the human writers of the OT. Cf. 1 Cor. 10:6, 11.

Thus we come to the most famous passage in the NT dealing with Scripture, 2 Timothy 3:15–17:

> From childhood you have been acquainted with the sacred writings, which are able to make you wise for salvation through faith in Christ Jesus. All Scripture is breathed out by God and profitable for teaching, for reproof, for correction, and for training in righteousness, that the man of God may be competent, equipped for every good work.

We should remember that Paul writes this letter late in his life, with a clear awareness that his own ministry is drawing to its end (4:6–8). In the Pastoral Epistles, Paul is passing the torch to younger men. His concluding admonitions are important, not only because he will soon be gone, but also because the coming times will be especially difficult (3:1–9). The church will be invaded by people "having the appearance of godliness, but denying its power" (v. 5). These are false teachers, who practice all kinds of immorality.

In this coming darkness, where does a young pastor like Timothy turn for light? How can he determine what is true and what is false, and how can he deal with what is false? Paul gives two answers to these questions. The first: "remember me" (vv. 10–14). Paul's successors should remember Paul's life and doctrine and be imitators of him.

Yes, but memories fade over time, and generations will arise who do not have personal memories of Paul. How do they discern between true teachers and "impostors"? Here Paul's second answer becomes especially important: turn to Scripture. From childhood, raised by a Jewish mother and grandmother (1:5), Timothy has known the Scriptures of the OT. These Scriptures convey wisdom (3:15) that brings salvation through faith in Christ. Paul continues, "All Scripture is breathed out by God" (v. 16). "Breathed out by God" is the ESV's literal translation of the Greek *theopneustos*, which is found only here in the Bible. Warfield defended this translation against various alternatives,[4] and I believe his argument is cogent. I take issue with Warfield on only one point. He summarizes his findings as follows:

> The Scriptures owe their origin to an activity of God the Holy Ghost and are in the highest and truest sense His creation. It is on this foundation of Divine origin that all the high attributes of Scripture are built.[5]

It seems to me, rather, that to say Scripture is "breathed out by God" is to say more than that Scripture has a divine origin and is God's creation.

---

4. Benjamin Breckinridge Warfield, "God-Inspired Scripture," in *The Inspiration and Authority of the Bible*, 245–96.

5. Ibid., 296.

Everything, after all, has a divine origin and is in some sense God's creation. What Paul says here is that the Scripture is breathed out, not created. What can that mean? Well, to breathe out words is simply to *speak* them. Paul is saying that the OT words are the *speech* of God, his personal utterances. Speech is not the same thing as creation. In chapters 7, 8, and 11, I argued that the word is God, that it is divine, and that it is therefore precisely *not* a created thing. That is true of the living Word, Jesus Christ, and it is true of all divine utterances. The written Word is, of course, expressed on a created medium, whether stone tablets, papyrus, paper, or digital media. But the Word that is written on these media is divine. It is the personal word of God himself. So "breathed out by God" means "spoken by God."

That is a fairly common biblical way of describing the inspiration of the OT. The *pneu* syllable of *theopneustos* connotes both God's breath and God's Spirit. We saw already in chapter 11 that God's word is always found with his Spirit. In chapter 11, I noted the linguistic model of the Trinity, that the Father is the speaker, the Son the Word, and the Spirit the breath that conveys the word to its hearers. Matthew 22:43; Acts 1:16; 4:25; 28:25; Hebrews 3:7; 9:8; and other passages ascribe specific texts of the OT to the Spirit. These passages are the Spirit's words, addressed to us today.

It is important to note that *theopneustos*, often translated "inspired by God," in the one place where it occurs in Scripture, is a quality of the *written* Word. Indeed, the same is true of the list of passages above, beginning with Matthew 22:43. Theologians have often developed theories in which inspiration is a quality of human prophets, even biblical writers, but not a quality of the written text itself. Such theories are plainly inadequate as accounts of the *theopneustos* of 2 Timothy 3:16. Even more bizarre is Karl Barth's contention that the work of the Spirit in this verse does not produce a permanent written word of God. In Barth's view, revelation can never be made permanent, preserved, identified with a finite object. So the "inspiration" of 2 Timothy 3:16 yields not a written word of God, but only "recollection" of past revelation and "expectation" of revelation in the future. But this idea goes directly against Paul's purpose in this verse, to give to Timothy a permanent source of divine revelation that will enable the church at any time to discern the truth and identify error.

In verse 17 of the passage, Paul adds that the words of the OT are not only authoritative but *sufficient*: "that the man of God may be competent, equipped for every good work." We will discuss the sufficiency of Scripture in chapter 32. But while we are looking at 2 Timothy 3:17, it is interesting to note that Paul here is still talking about the OT. For him, evidently, the OT, even apart from the NT, is sufficient to identify false teaching and to equip the young pastor to do the work of God.

We come next to another famous NT passage dealing with the nature of OT Scripture, 2 Peter 1:19–21. The context of this passage is very similar to that of 2 Timothy 3:15–17. Like Paul in the latter passage, Peter in context anticipates his soon death (2 Peter 1:13–15) and seeks to prepare his successors to lead the church without him. And as with Paul, Peter anticipates hard times ahead for the church. The second chapter of the letter is very much like 2 Timothy 3:1–9, anticipating the coming of false prophets and teachers into the church who "secretly bring in destructive heresies" (2 Peter 2:1) and many forms of immorality (v. 14). So in effect Peter poses to his younger colleagues the same question that Paul raised to his: how will you deal with this situation after I am gone? How will you distinguish true and false, right and wrong?

Interestingly, Peter gives two answers, the same as Paul's. The first is "remember me":

> For we did not follow cleverly devised myths when we made known to you the power and coming of our Lord Jesus Christ, but we were eyewitnesses of his majesty. For when he received honor and glory from God the Father, and the voice was borne to him by the Majestic Glory, "This is my beloved Son, with whom I am well pleased," we ourselves heard this very voice borne from heaven, for we were with him on the holy mountain. (1:16–18)

Peter's preaching of the gospel was not based on myths,[6] but on his own eyewitness experience. He refers in verses 17–18 to the transfiguration of Jesus, recorded in Matthew 17:1–8; Mark 9:2–9; and Luke 9:28–36.

But there will come generations of believers who do not remember Peter directly. For them, as well as for his contemporaries, Peter's second answer (again the same as Paul's) is important:

> And we have something more sure, the prophetic word, to which you will do well to pay attention as to a lamp shining in a dark place, until the day dawns and the morning star rises in your hearts, knowing this first of all, that no prophecy of Scripture comes from someone's own interpretation. For no prophecy was ever produced by the will of man, but men spoke from God as they were carried along by the Holy Spirit. (2 Peter 1:19–21)

"More sure" here is the Greek *bebaioteron*. The ESV takes the phrase "more sure, the prophetic word" to mean that the written prophetic words are more

---

6. One wishes that Peter's disavowal of "myth" here (Greek *mythos*) would make modern theologians more cautious about applying this term to the content of Scripture.

certain even than Peter's eyewitness experience. Others have taken it to mean that because of Peter's experience, the prophetic word is "*made* more sure." I prefer the first interpretation, but both interpretations commend the certainty of the written Word. The "dark place" is the culture of false prophets and destructive heretics that he refers to later in chapter 2.

Verse 20 denies that these written words come from a merely human source. The rendering "interpretation" here is misleading, though it is a permissible translation of the Greek *epiluseos*. "Interpretation" suggests that Peter's concern is about hermeneutics, about finding the meanings of difficult passages. The older translation "of private interpretation" stimulated the Roman Catholic/Protestant debate as to whether individuals could understand the Bible without submitting themselves to the church's teaching authority. But in fact the passage is not about interpretation; it is about origin—more precisely, about the basis of Scripture's authority. The passage actually tells us that the Scriptures do not originate from men who interpret reality out of their own experience, like modern-day pundits.

That is plain from verse 21, which denies that Scripture is produced by the will of a human being. This is not to deny that human writers were involved, but only to say that those writers were not the source of biblical authority. The human writers, rather, spoke from God, being carried along by the Holy Spirit. That is to say, they wrote what the Spirit directed them to write, not what they autonomously chose to write. The authority of their words, therefore, is the authority of the Spirit, not the authority of a mere human writer.

Second Timothy 3:15–17 and 2 Peter 1:19–21 are powerful testimonies to the authority of the OT as a written revelation of God. It is possible, however, to put too much emphasis on them in our general argument for biblical authority. Liberal writers often argue that these two passages do not actually come from Paul and Peter, and that they come from a period when the church was losing its spontaneous vitality, a time when it had a more static[7] focus, on church government and written standards. Thus, the argument goes, what they say is not very important for our lives today.

Of course, I disagree with this view. But it is important to emphasize that these two passages don't stand alone. Indeed, they are the capstone of a theme that pervades the entire Scripture, that God rules his people by a written document. That theme begins with the stone tablets written by the

---

7. *Static* is a theological buzzword that comes up in many contexts, contrasted with *dynamic*. Everybody tends to honor the dynamic, to disparage the static. But this is foolish. In some situations it is good to be static, in others dynamic. For example, when undergoing surgery, it is usually best for the patient to remain static. He could cause all sorts of problems for his surgeons if he got up and started to dance.

finger of Yahweh on Mount Sinai in Exodus (note again Ex. 24:12; 31:18). As we have seen, in all periods of redemptive history God urges obedience to his written Word, and psalmists extol its wisdom. Jesus concurs, as we have seen. So it should not be surprising that Paul and Peter, toward the end of their lives, call the churches back to the standard that has always ruled the people of God. The teaching of these two passages is clear and specific, but it is hardly novel.

What these two passages tell us is that there will come a time in which no one can personally recall the living voice of a prophet or apostle, and that in that time especially we should turn to the written Word. We are now living in that time. It is not a time to turn back to autonomous thinking. It is a time to read in Scripture God's personal words to us.

CHAPTER 21

The New Testament as God's Written Words

No single NT text teaches the authority of the NT as one complete document. That is, no text speaks of the NT the way 2 Timothy 3:15–17 and 2 Peter 1:19–21 speak of the OT. That should not surprise us. In the nature of the case, the NT could not speak of itself as a completed collection because when the NT writers wrote, the collection was still incomplete.

Nevertheless, there is plenty of biblical evidence that God intends our NT to function as his written personal word to us.

The NT cannot be considered apart from its OT context, for it claims to continue, indeed to complete, the story of Yahweh's redemption begun in the former volume. As we have seen, that former volume calls attention to itself as a written Word of God. Jesus and the apostles recognize the OT as such, as God's own written account of his covenants with Adam, Noah, Abraham, Moses, and David. Is it likely that the greatest covenant of all, the new covenant that God made with his people in Jesus, would have no written attestation?

As I said in chapter 10, there is no reason for thinking that the new covenant is any less verbal than was the old. Covenants by their very nature are verbal transactions, in which the covenant Lord identifies himself in word to the covenant servant, gives his name, cites their historical relations, sets forth his law, and so on. Jesus and the apostles revered the OT as God's Word (chaps. 19–20), and they also identified themselves as God's prophets, bringing God's words to the world (chap. 15). The only

129

remaining question for us to consider is whether they recorded that prophetic message in writing.

Remember that covenants are lasting arrangements (chap. 16), and therefore the covenants between God and man have always been recorded in writing. God's covenant with Moses, inscribed with his own finger, was kept in the Holiest Place, to be regularly read to the people. The words of Jesus and the apostles were also intended to be preserved for later generations. They are the "tradition" (see chap. 16) passed from the Father, to the Son, to the apostles. It would have been anomalous in the extreme if this decisive, final revelation of God (Heb. 1:1–3) were not written down. In 2 Thessalonians 2:15, Paul identifies the traditions that he and other apostles passed on to the church, "either by our spoken word or by our letter."

Or look at it this way: The words of Jesus as the divine voice and as the prophet par excellence are absolutely crucial to the believer's life (John 6:68). As we saw, Jesus appoints the apostles to remember these words (John 14:26) as well as to receive additional revelation. By their own oral teaching, the apostles could preserve the memory of Jesus' words for only one or two more generations. A written record would seem to be the only way in which generations of believers after the apostolic period would have access to Jesus' words. Without a written record of them, and of the apostles' testimony to them, those words would be lost to us forever. And without those words, we do not have Jesus as our covenant Lord or as our Savior. Without these words, there can be no Christianity, no Christian church. Only a written document can preserve these words as God's personal words to us.

As we saw in chapter 15, Jesus appointed his apostles to be his spokesmen. After Jesus' ascension, they presented their preaching and teaching as the word of God, given by Christ through the Spirit, not by any human source. A number of the apostles, at least, put their teaching into writing. Is it likely that this teaching is less authoritative than their oral witness? I think not. As we saw in chapter 17, the writings of the prophets were as authoritative as their speaking. The apostles' writings could have no less authority.

The documents themselves claim that they have full authority over their recipients. For one thing, they are not optional reading, but mandatory. Paul says to the Colossians:

> And when this letter has been read among you, have it also read in the church of the Laodiceans; and see that you also read the letter from Laodicea.[1] (Col. 4:16)

1. The "letter from Laodicea" may be a letter from Paul now lost, or it may be one of the canonical Epistles under another name. This letter and Colossians were evidently

This reading took place during the worship service, as is implied by the language of this passage ("in the church") and stated later by the church fathers. To receive a letter from an apostle was a momentous event, and it was important that everyone had a chance to hear the actual letter, not just to hear the truths of the letter taught secondhand. But more than that, the reading of the letter was a *solemn* event, one to be done in worship, in the presence of the Lord himself. In 1 Thessalonians 5:27, this reading is again a solemn responsibility: Paul says, "I put you under oath before the Lord to have this letter read to all the brothers."

We are reminded here of the OT pattern, in which the leaders of Israel read the law publicly to the people (2 Kings 23:2; Neh. 8:1–8), as God's own witness against them (Deut. 31:19–22, 26).

In 2 Thessalonians 3:14–15, obedience to Paul's letter is a matter of discipline:

> If anyone does not obey what we say in this letter, take note of that person, and have nothing to do with him, that he may be ashamed. Do not regard him as an enemy, but warn him as a brother.

Similarly, in 1 Corinthians 14:37–38:

> If anyone thinks that he is a prophet, or spiritual, he should acknowledge that the things I am writing to you are a command of the Lord. If anyone does not recognize this, he is not recognized.

The Corinthians had in their church a number of prophets and others who had, or who claimed, spiritual gifts (1:7). Those who had "greater gifts" were sometimes proud and lorded it over those whose gifts were "lesser" (chaps. 12, 13). In 14:37–38, Paul says that the contents of his letter, his written word, take precedence over the authority of anyone else in the church. Indeed, Paul says, no one should be recognized as a prophet or as having a spiritual gift unless that person recognizes Paul's written word as a command of the Lord. Clearly, Paul here identifies his *written* word as the word of God.

Indeed, even while the NT was still being written, there are indications that parts of it are regarded as *Scripture*. In 1 Timothy 5:17–18, Paul says:

> Let the elders who rule well be considered worthy of double honor, especially those who labor in preaching and teaching. For the

---

intended as "round robin" letters, to be passed from church to church, as Paul indicates here. In that case, "Laodiceans" could be the letter we know as Ephesians, a letter written about the same time as Colossians and with much parallel content. The church in Ephesus was a center for the churches in Asia Minor and may have been a clearinghouse for Paul's letters. But that is only one suggestion.

Scripture says, "You shall not muzzle an ox when it treads out the grain," and, "The laborer deserves his wages."

The "honor" here is a payment for service, what we today call "honorarium." In support of this exhortation, Paul quotes Deuteronomy 25:4, indicating that even oxen should receive remuneration for their work. The other passage he quotes, "The laborer deserves his wages," is not found in the OT. The source is most likely Luke 10:7. So Paul quotes the Gospel of Luke alongside the OT, implying that the two have the same authority.

Peter says the same about Paul's letters. In 2 Peter 3:15–16, he exhorts the people:

> And count the patience of our Lord as salvation, just as our beloved brother Paul also wrote to you according to the wisdom given him, as he does in all his letters when he speaks in them of these matters. There are some things in them that are hard to understand, which the ignorant and unstable twist to their own destruction, as they do the other Scriptures.

Peter commends Paul's writings to the church, but he admits that they can be misused. Of course, the "ignorant and unstable" misuse all the *other* Scriptures as well. By this language, Peter places Paul's writings into the category of Scripture. There are the Pauline Scriptures, and then there are also the other Scriptures.

There can be no doubt, then, that the apostles functioned as prophets, not only in their oral preaching and teaching, but in their written ministry as well. As there is an authoritative written account of the old covenant, there is also an authoritative written account of the new. These are both God's personal words to us.

CHAPTER 22

The Canon of Scripture

The next logical question is this: where may we find these written words of God? In what written texts? This is the question of *canon*. *Canon* refers to the body of writing that God has given to rule the church.

Identifying the books of the canon can be made to seem like a terribly difficult task. Roman Catholics and Protestants have disputed the list of OT books since the time of the Reformation. And the list of NT books accepted by the churches as canon varied (from church to church and from time to time) in the first four centuries A.D.

Irenaeus, however, who died around A.D. 202, clearly cites in his *Against Heresies* almost all the books of our present NT canon as authoritative texts. The only books he does not quote are Philemon, 2 Peter, 3 John, and Jude. He does also mention 1 Clement and Shepherd of Hermas (which the church did not finally recognize as canonical) as worth reading. He dismissed the Gnostic Gospel of Truth as heretical. So the NT canon of Irenaeus (and he was very concerned about questions of canon in his opposition to the heretic Marcion) is very close to ours.

Recently there has been much publicity about early documents concerning Jesus that were eventually excluded from the NT canon, such as the Gospel of Thomas and the Gospel of Judas. Some scholars have suggested that these represent a legitimate party in the early church that was disenfranchised by ecclesiastical politics, so that the process of canonization was essentially a matter of one faction's trying to exclude another. Others argue that Thomas and Judas represent forms of Gnosticism rightly condemned by the church as heretical. I agree with the latter position.[1] But even books that are now well accepted in all parts of the church, such as 2 Peter, 2–3 John, and Revelation, are not found on some of the early canon lists. So some have thought that ascertaining the books that God inspired to rule the church, even given that there are such books, is a formidably difficult task. Those who accept this difficulty and seek nevertheless to undertake the task, and those who try to show that it is impossible, have produced a large amount of literature.

The present volume cannot enter into the details of this debate. My book is a systematic theological treatment, not a historical study. My purpose is not to enter into this complicated history and to determine inductively whether a canon somehow emerges from it and what books constitute that canon. Indeed, I'm inclined to think that that kind of study is unfruitful. Studies of the historical process by which the church came to identify the canon certainly do reveal interesting facts, and believers can see the hand of God throughout this process. But inductive study alone is unlikely to show us with certainty which books God has given to rule the church. My purpose here, rather, is to present the teachings of Scripture itself relevant to the doctrine of the word of God, and now relevant to the specific question of canonicity.

No biblical text sets forth a definitive list of books to be included in the Bible. We should not expect to find one, since while the biblical texts were being written the canon was not yet complete. But there are some biblical principles that direct us on a sure path.

As we have seen, it is God's intention to speak personal words to us, words that have more authority than any other. These words govern our use of all other words, of all other sources of knowledge. For God's words to have this kind of authority, they must be distinguishable from all other words, from words that are merely human. So there must be a canon, a body of divine words that God's people can identify as his.

We have also seen (chap. 16) that these words are not to be received as momentary experiences by individuals and then allowed to disappear into past history. Rather, they are to be kept permanently so that God can continually witness against the sins of his people (Deut. 31:24–29), both present and future generations. So God places the Ten Commandments by the holy ark of the covenant and places other words beside them. Doubtless other copies were made as well, which circulated among the people of Israel. The people knew that these were

---

1. See, e.g., Peter R. Jones, *Spirit Wars: Pagan Revival in Christian America* (Escondido, CA: Main Entry Editions, 1997). For my evaluation of Gnosticism and similar worldviews, see *DG*, 216–20.

God's words, the words of supreme authority, clearly distinct from all merely human words.

So at every stage of Israel's history, there was a canon, a definite body of divine writings, that spoke to the nation and its individuals with supreme authority. The first canon was the two tablets of the covenant. A later canon added to these the Deuteronomic law of Moses (Deut. 31:24). Still a third added words of Joshua (Josh. 24:25–28).

Scripture does not continue an explicit narration of each stage in the growth of the canon. But as we have seen, it describes occasions in which prophecy was written down for future generations. There are also many places in the OT where one writer indicates a knowledge of the work of another, either through quotation (as Jeremiah 26:18, which quotes Micah 3:12) or through awareness of symbols, historical narrative, and themes found in previous books.[2] The NT indicates, as we noted, that during Jesus' earthly ministry he was able to appeal to the Law, Prophets, and Writings of the Hebrew Bible, which we call the *Old Testament*, as common ground with his Jewish opponents. We note that although Jesus and his opponents disagreed about a great many things, they never disagreed about what texts could be authoritatively cited.

Evidently, then, we should identify the OT canon as consisting of those books acknowledged by the Jews, in the time and place of Jesus' earthly ministry. We can determine that list of books by investigating the history of the time, verifying our conclusions by looking at what texts Jesus cites and doesn't cite. In my judgment, the data indicate clearly that this canon is identical with the canon endorsed by Protestants since the Reformation.

Given God's intention to rule the church by a written document consisting of his personal words, it would be anomalous in the extreme if he put them in a place where we couldn't find them. Through OT history, God has taken pains to put these words in an *obvious* place, the tabernacle, and later the temple. Josephus says that the books kept in the temple, before its destruction in A.D. 70, were the books recognized as canonical by the Jews. Although the Jews read other books for edification, the temple books were those with fully divine authority. So there is no mystery about the extent of the OT canon. God put the books in a place where they could function as he intended, where they would be recognized as his.

The extent of the NT canon is on the surface a more difficult problem, because in the nature of the case no inspired writer could refer to the NT writings as a completed collection. But we have seen that the NT writers

---

2. See John Sailhamer, *Introduction to Old Testament Theology: A Canonical Approach* (Grand Rapids: Zondervan, 1995), 212–13. This phenomenon is known as *intertextuality*.

speak of a "tradition" that was to be passed down from generation to generation and guarded against distortion. And we have seen that there is written revelation attesting the new covenant as there was attesting the old (chap. 21). As with the OT, we should note how anomalous it would be if this revelation were hard to find. Our salvation depends on our access to the words of Jesus (John 6:68) and to the gospel preached by the apostles (Rom. 1:16; Gal. 1:6–9; Eph. 1:13).

The problem with much current literature on the canon is that it does not take account of God's expressed intentions. It seeks, rather, through autonomous reasoning (see chap. 3), to determine whether any first-century books deserve canonical status, and using that method it arrives at conclusions that are uncertain at best. But once we understand God's use of a canon from the time of Moses, we must approach our present problem with a presupposition: that God will not let his people walk in darkness, that he will provide for us the words we need to have, within our reach.

So we reach out, and we find before us twenty-seven books—from Matthew to Revelation. God did not put them in the Jerusalem temple, for that temple is gone. He placed them in his temple the church (1 Cor. 3:16–17; Eph. 2:21; Rev. 3:12), that is, among the people of God, where, as in Deuteronomy 30:11–14, the word is very near us.

The early church was divided by many controversies concerning basic doctrines, including the Trinity and the person of Christ. There were differences among the churches, too, as to what books were canonical. But it is remarkable how little they fought about this. Some of the differences had to do with geography: some books reached parts of the church before other parts. Some of the differences had to do with views of content and authorship. But remarkably, when in A.D. 367 Bishop Athanasius of Alexandria published a list of books accepted in his church, there was no clamor. From that time on, Christians of all traditions—Eastern Orthodox, Roman Catholic, and Protestant—agreed on the NT canon. Indeed, through the centuries since, agreement on the NT canon has been more unanimous than on the OT canon, though on the surface it might seem that ascertaining the former would have been more difficult.

What happened? Jesus' sheep heard his voice (John 10:27). Or, to put it differently, the Holy Spirit illumined the texts so that God's people perceived their divine quality. Recall that in chapter 14 I discussed a similar problem in connection with the divine voice: how can we be sure that the voice is God? The answer I proposed was that our assurance is supernatural. When God speaks, he at the same time assures us that he is speaking.[3] In

---

3. Compare also my discussion of Abraham's revelatory experience in chapter 1.

chapter 15, I proposed the same answer to the problem of identifying true prophets and apostles. In this case Scripture does give objective criteria (Deut. 18), but those criteria are difficult to apply in view of the relation between prophecy and historical contingency. In this case, too, our ultimate assurance is supernatural. So it is, I believe, with the question of identifying canonical books.

In this case, as with the identification of prophets, the Christians used some objective criteria. Apostolic authorship was an obvious criterion. Jesus had appointed the apostles to remember his words and to lead the church into all truth. So if the Christians believed that a book was written by an apostle, they received it, without further argument, as canon.

But of course, they also received books that were not written by apostles, such as Mark, Luke-Acts, Hebrews, James, and Jude. The criterion of apostolicity was relevant to these as well, of course. These books were thought to have come from the apostolic circle, to have somehow been certified by the apostles. Mark was thought to have been a close associate of Peter, and Paul himself testifies in his writings that Luke was his associate (Col. 4:14; 2 Tim. 4:11; Philem. 24). See also the "we" sections of Acts, which indicate that Luke traveled with Paul on his missionary journeys (Acts 16:10–24; 20:5–21:18; 27:1–28:16). Hebrews was sometimes thought to be the work of Paul, though most scholars deny that today. James and Jude were most likely blood brothers of Jesus and part of the apostolic church leadership, though not technically apostles.

The connection of these books with the apostles, even when indirect, is certainly in their favor. Since the apostles are the main recipients of NT revelation, we naturally look favorably on any text that they may have approved in some way. And we should grant that the first- and second-century Christians were closer to the writing of these books than we are, and that they probably had more knowledge than we of who wrote the books and the grounds on which the church accepted them. But this is only a probable argument, if we look at the historical evidence alone. We cannot prove decisively that the apostles officially warranted all the books of the NT and withheld their certification from books that were excluded.

Other criteria used by early Christians were antiquity, public lection (those read in worship), and orthodoxy of content.[4] But these criteria are

---

4. Martin Luther questioned the canonicity of James because he thought it did not set forth a clear doctrine of justification by faith alone. In this judgment, he was using a doctrinal standard to determine which books belonged in the canon. He actually held a very high view of Scripture. He questioned James precisely because he didn't think James met the very high standards he assigned to the Word of God. But the church as a whole, in all branches, has disagreed with Luther on this matter: James's teaching is indeed consistent

also insufficient to *prove* that any book belongs in the canon, or to disprove claims to canonicity on behalf of other books.

Nor should we rest our conclusion on the testimony of the church alone, and certainly not on the testimony of a particular denomination, as in the Roman Catholic view of the matter. The Roman church has claimed that the authority of the canon rests on that church's pronouncement. But (1) the church's conviction on this matter, unanimous since A.D. 367, precedes any statement by a Roman Catholic pope or council; and (2) as we have seen, God intends to rule his church by a book, not a church authority. So the authority of the church rests on the authority of the canon, not the other way around.

We should, however, join with the church of all ages (the early church and all Christian denominations since then) in the presupposition that God intended the new covenant in Christ to be attested in writing, and that the apostles were charged with bringing the written Word, as well as the oral word, before the world. Nor can we doubt that God's intention to provide such written revelation was successful. Thus does Scripture attest itself, together with the witness of the Holy Spirit. Our assurance that these books are canon, like our assurance of the divine voice and of prophecy, is supernatural. So we can be sure that the canon of twenty-seven NT books, now universally accepted in the church, is God's personal word to us today.

Is the canon "closed," or should we expect God to add more books to the canon in our time and in the future? In one sense, the canon is always closed. God forbids people to add to or subtract from it (Deut. 4:2; 12:32; cf. Prov. 30:6; Rev. 22:18–19). Jesus upbraided the Pharisees for putting their traditions on a par with Scripture and therefore making "void the word of God" (Matt. 15:6). We are to be satisfied with what God has given us, and not long for more. In every age, God has given his people all the written words we need to live faithfully before him.

Nevertheless, God himself has added to the canon, as we have seen. Moses added the Deuteronomic revelation to the original Decalogue. God

---

with Paul's doctrine of justification. Like Paul, James teaches that we are saved only by a faith that is living and active (cf. Paul in Gal. 5:6). The church has agreed that the books of the canon agree with one another in doctrine. Luther's example illustrates the danger of trying to determine the canonicity of a book by applying doctrinal tests alone, and apply-ing them in an individualistic way, without corroboration from the community. The case of James requires some hard exegetical thinking on which faithful scholars can disagree. Consistency of doctrine with other canonical books is a legitimate criterion, however, when it is used as one among others. God's written words must be in agreement with one another. But discerning agreement and disagreement for this purpose requires discernment and corporate consensus, given by the Spirit of God.

accepted that revelation as worthy to be placed alongside the Decalogue in the Holiest Place. Joshua added his words to those of Moses. God added the Prophets and Writings to the Law, and the NT to the OT. Of course, God has the freedom to do this, though he forbids any mere man to do so.

God adds revelation as needs for it arise in history. The revelation made to Adam would not have been sufficient for Noah, because he had to prepare for the flood. The revelation made to Noah would not have been sufficient for Abraham, to define God's covenant with him. And the OT, though sufficient to meet the challenges of the NT church after Paul's demise (2 Tim. 3:17), was not sufficient to tell the whole story of Jesus.

The NT teaches, however, that with the coming of Christ, with his atonement, resurrection, and ascension, and the coming of the Spirit at Pentecost, redemptive history has reached a watershed. The work of Christ is final, in a way that the work of Abraham and Moses is not. In Christ, God has spoken (past tense, Heb. 1:2) a final word to us, attested (also past tense, Heb. 2:2) by Jesus' original hearers. As the redemptive work of Christ is once for all, so the word of Christ and the apostles is once for all. For God to add more books to the canon would be like his adding something to the work of Christ, something that Scripture teaches cannot be done.

So the canon is closed today, not only in the sense that human beings dare not add to it, but also in the sense that God himself will not add to it. The closing of the canon does not, however, put an end to revelation in general. God still communicates with us in general revelation, in the Spirit's work of writing the word on our heart, and of course in Scripture itself. The writing of Scripture is once for all, but God continues to speak to us *through* Scripture day by day.[5]

---

5. Compare on these matters my discussion of the sufficiency of Scripture in chapter 32. There I discuss the distinction made here at greater length.

CHAPTER 23

The Inspiration of Scripture

I believe I have established that there is among us a collection of God's written words, which we may call *canon*. These are God's personal words to us. Now we must look at some questions that pertain to the entire canon. In this chapter, I will consider the relationship between God's personal words and the human writers of Scripture. Scripture is both a divine book and a human book. God is the author, and there are also human authors.

The relation between God and the human writers is often called *inspiration*. The term is not found in Scripture itself, except in 2 Timothy 3:16, where older translations render the Greek *theopneustos* "inspired of God." The ESV prefers a more literal translation, "breathed out by God," as I indicated in chapter 20. The term may be extended to oral revelation by prophets and apostles, and to the human writers of Scripture, because certainly there is an act of God by which God's words are identical with their own.

So I define *inspiration* as a divine act that creates an identity between a divine word and a human word. Such inspiration takes place in all verbal revelation. In this chapter, we will look more closely at the event of inspiration and focus on the relation between the divine and human authors of Scripture.

Many recent books on the doctrine of Scripture begin with human authorship, assuming that the human writers of Scripture made mistakes and at times misrepresented the divine word.[1] Such books, then, have

1. This is the error common to the books of Peter Enns, N. T. Wright, and Andrew McGowan, which I discuss in the reviews found in Appendices J, K, and L in this volume.

to deal with the problem of how God can reveal himself authoritatively in such writings. In this book, I have chosen, rather, at the risk of being criticized as old-fashioned, to begin with God's intention to speak personal words to his people. I assume here that God is able, one way or another, to get his words to us. This method avoids the problem of the other books, but it does render somewhat problematic the very presence of human writers on the scene. Are these writers mere secretaries, mere recipients of "dictation"? Does God operate upon them in a "mechanical" fashion?

Among writers who hold the traditional view of Scripture, almost all have answered no. Some older writers, including John Calvin,[2] have spoken favorably of divine dictation, and others have used mechanistic analogies, such as Athenagoras's illustration: God is like the flute-player, and the prophets were like flutes.[3] But neither of these writers was dealing with the precise question before us. One can agree that dictation and flute-playing are meaningful *analogies* of the relation between God and the human authors of Scripture, without accepting these as literal *analyses* of inspiration.

Most advocates of the traditional view reject the idea that God literally dictated to the human writers the contents of the Scriptures, and most deny that the relationship is well described as "mechanical." Some theologians, I think, have been *too* eager to avoid suspicion of a dictation theory. Certainly, there are places in Scripture where God literally dictates words for human beings to write down. God dictated to Moses the words of the law, according to Ex. 34:27. Note also Jeremiah 36:4: "Then Jeremiah called Baruch the son of Neriah, and Baruch wrote on a scroll at the dictation of Jeremiah all the words of the LORD that he had spoken to him." And Revelation 2–3, where the risen Jesus tells John to write as he dictates letters to the seven churches of Asia.

Does divine dictation degrade the humanity of those who receive it? Theologians sometimes say that it does, but I do not find this representation persuasive. The work of a secretary, amanuensis, or (as we now say) administrative assistant is a noble calling. The apostle Paul made use of such amanuenses, such as Tertius in Romans 16:22. To be God's secretary must be a wonderful thing indeed. Speaking for myself, I would consider it a transcendent privilege to receive dictation from God. What a wonderful experience it must have been, for Moses, Baruch, and John.

---

2. *Calvin's Commentaries*, at 2 Tim. 3:16, available at http://www.ccel.org/ccel/calvin/commentaries.i.html.

3. In Athenagoras, *Plea for the Christians*, available at http://www.monachos.net/content/patristics/patristictexts/313-athenagoras-plea-link.

But of course, this sort of dictation is rare in Scripture. There is no record of Joshua, or Samuel, or David, or Luke, or even Paul, receiving literal dictation from the Lord. The regular pattern, rather, is that God appointed the biblical writers to be prophets, apostles, or associates of the apostles, and those writers wrote what they chose to write. In their writing, their individual human qualities appear vividly. David writes in a very different way from Moses. Luke's writing is very different in style from that of John, or of Paul. But as we have seen, all of these very different writers were chosen by God to convey his personal word to the world.

The result of their writing is nothing less than the Word of God, the personal word of God to us. It is *like* dictation, because what Luke writes is exactly what God wants us to hear. It is *like* mechanical inspiration, because God is in full control of the process. But how *unlike* mechanical dictation it is! God's dealings with Luke, for example, are person to person, as are all of God's dealings with human beings. God uses Luke's gifts as a historian and as a physician, his careful accuracy, and his association with Paul to add distinctive elements to Luke's Gospel and the book of Acts. He uses Luke's intellect and style to convey the truth with the nuance that he desires. God also uses the very different endowments of John and of Paul to present other perspectives on the gospel of Christ.

Abraham Kuyper and Herman Bavinck called this process "organic" inspiration, to distinguish it from dictation or mechanical inspiration. Organic inspiration means that God used all the distinct personal qualities of each writer. God used the differences of heredity, environment, upbringing, education, gifts, talents, styles, interests, and idiosyncrasies to reveal his word. These differences were not a barrier that God had to overcome. Rather, they were God's chosen means of communicating with us. God's Word is complex and nuanced, multiperspectival. God used the organic complexity of human persons and the diversities among persons to communicate the complexity of his own personal word. He used human persons to communicate with us in a fully personal way.

Remember that God's Word is not *merely* propositional. God's purpose is not merely to convey information to us, though he certainly does that. His purpose is to do for us all that can be done by language. He means to convey not only information, but tone, emotion, perspective. He means to convey his love to us, along with the sternness of his justice. Human language is rich in this way, conveying a wide variety of content. God's language is all the richer. And to communicate it, he employs a wide variety of writers with a rich diversity of experience.

And the final result is exactly what he wanted to say to us. Just *like* dictation or mechanical inspiration, but with vast riches of meaning. What an amazing treasure is the written Word of God.

I have defined *inspiration* as a divine act creating an identity between a divine word and a human word. To describe the conformity of the text to God's intention, theologians have also used other technical terms. *Plenary* inspiration simply means that *everything* in Scripture is God's Word. To say this is merely to say that the entire canon is God's Word, as we have already seen. If the Bible is plenarily inspired, we may not pick and choose within the Scriptures, regarding one part as God's Word and another part as merely human.

Verbal inspiration means that the *words* of Scripture, not only the ideas of the biblical writers, are God's Word. In the light of our discussion in this book, that should be obvious. God's intention is to speak personal *words* to human beings. He has identified those words with the canonical text. We recall Peter's question, "Lord, to whom shall we go? You have the words of eternal life" (John 6:68). The emphasis on the *words* of God, Christ, and the apostles is pervasive in the NT. See Matt. 7:24–28; 24:35; Mark 8:38; 13:31; John 3:34; 5:47; 6:63; 8:47; 14:10, 24; 17:8; Acts 15:15; 1 Cor. 2:13; 1 Tim. 4:6; 6:3; 2 Tim. 1:13; 2 Peter 3:2; Jude 17; Rev. 1:3; 19:9; 21:5; 22:6–10, 18–19. In the singular, *word* can sometimes be read as designating thoughts or ideas apart from their formulation in words and sentences; but the plural, *words*, cannot be.

Our whole discussion since chapter 14 has underscored the point that God's intention is to give us *words*, personal words, not just thoughts or ideas. The divine voice, as on Mount Sinai, spoke words in the hearing of Israel. So did the voice of Jesus in his earthly ministry. So did the prophets and apostles. And so did the text of God's written Word, from covenant document to complete canon. At no point in this redemptive history is God content to give thoughts or ideas to his spokesmen, without giving them words in which to express those thoughts.[4] Rather, he assigns them the role of speaking and writing his words.

Therefore, it should not be surprising that the only time we find the word *inspiration* in the English Bible (2 Tim. 3:16), it refers to the written Word—

---

4. To say that inspiration is restricted to *thoughts* or *ideas* is to give the doctrine of inspiration a very intellectualist cast. (Normally, liberals charge conservatives with intellectualist views of inspiration, but the shoe is on the other foot.) *Thought*-inspiration suggests the notion that God reveals to the writers a set of *concepts*. But as we have seen, God wants to reveal to us a wide variety of things: not only propositions or concepts, but events, promises, feelings, tone, and so on. These don't fit very well into the notion of God's revealing *ideas*, but they fit very well into the revelation of *words*, for words (not ideas) are capable of communicating in all these ways.

not to the ideas of prophets and apostles, not even to their oral speech, and not to the biblical writers as such, but to the very *text* of Scripture. Now, it is not wrong to ascribe inspiration to the prophets and to the writers of Scripture. The NT frequently refers to the Holy Spirit as governing the words of prophets and apostles: Matt. 10:20; 22:43; Acts 1:16; many other texts (see chaps. 15 and 20). There is no reason why we should not describe this influence of the Spirit as *inspiration*, using the same definition as above. But we should never say, as some have, that inspiration properly pertains to persons rather than to written texts. In Scripture, the Spirit inspires not only prophets, apostles, and biblical writers, but also *texts*. As we have seen, Jesus and the apostles regard the texts of the OT as fully authoritative, just as authoritative as God's direct voice. The text has no less authority than the divine voice itself, or than the prophets and apostles.

Because inspiration is verbal, it is also, often, textual. You can't put an idea or a thought exhaustively on paper; but you can put a *word* on paper. Inspiration is of words, whether spoken orally or put on a material medium (stone tablets, parchment, paper, digital media, etc.). So there is no reason to deny that God's personal words take written form in the canonical books he has given to us.

CHAPTER 24

The Content of Scripture

I have argued that God has spoken to us. But certainly it is not enough to know the bare fact that God has spoken. The life-and-death question is: what has he said to us?[1]

In chapter 13, I discussed what God says to us through the events of nature and history, what theologians often call *general revelation*. God tells us there who he is and what he requires of us, and he reveals his wrath against us for disobeying him (Rom. 1). Apart from grace, our response is to "suppress the truth" (Rom. 1:18), to exchange the truth for a lie (v. 25). I also pointed out, however, that natural revelation is a great blessing to those who have been saved from sin by God's grace, as a testimony to God's glory and as a means of showing us how to apply God's commands. From God's creation we learn all sorts of things of relevance to the sciences and humanities and to our practical life, everything we need to take dominion of the earth (Gen. 1:28). Natural revelation, then, proclaims our estrangement from God, but it also provides us with broad knowledge about his world and his providential supervision of his world.

Scripture tells us how to escape the wrath of God revealed from heaven against us. It brings to us the good news of Jesus Christ, the gospel (Luke 24:27; John 5:39; 20:31). But it presents Christ in a broad historical context,

---

1. David H. Kelsey argues that theologians differ greatly on the nature of Scripture's content and therefore on the uses we should make of it. He thinks these issues, rather than our view of inspiration or inerrancy, govern what we mean when we talk about doing theology "according to Scripture." See my review of his book *The Uses of Scripture in Recent Theology*, Appendix H in this volume.

showing how God prepared the world for him, by entering relationships called *covenants* with Adam, Noah, Abraham, Moses, and David, and with many others through these. Scripture presents this covenant history in a wide variety of ways, through many different kinds of literature, many styles, many different perspectives.

This diversity has given some readers another occasion (in addition to arguments that we have already considered) to find disunity in Scripture—contradictions, factual disagreement, and so on. In my view, however, the covenantal content of Scripture enables us to see a fundamental unity among these sixty-six books. These books didn't just happen to come together. As we have seen, God intentionally provided them for his people. Through all the diversities, they are his speech to us. The covenant structure enables us to see God's reasons for structuring Scripture as he has. This structure does not by itself answer every problem raised by Bible critics. But it does help us to look at the Bible in a way different from them, in a way that suggests design rather than accident, harmony rather than discord.

Reformed theologians have commonly found in the covenant motif a helpful way to show forth the unity of the Bible.[2] Traditionally, these writers have found in Scripture two major covenants, sometimes called the covenant of works and the covenant of grace. The former embraces the pre-fall period. In it God offers an eternal life of blessedness (symbolized by the tree of life) to Adam and Eve on the condition that they abstain from the fruit of the tree of the knowledge of good and evil. After the fall into sin, God sets forth the covenant of grace: a promise of redemption through the divine Messiah received through faith alone.

The covenant of grace, in turn, encompasses, on the traditional view, all the post-fall historical covenants, including those with Adam, Noah, Abraham, Moses, and David, and the "new covenant" effected by the blood of Jesus himself, of which the earlier covenants are but anticipations.

On this understanding, the whole Bible, diverse in content as it may appear at first sight, can be seen as a story of God making covenants and man responding to them. The books of law show what God expects of his covenant people. The books of history indicate man's actual response. The psalms contain the praise, the laments, the questionings, the blessings and

---

2. What follows is, with minor changes, a paper that I wrote some years ago called "Covenant and the Unity of Scripture." The book for which I wrote the article was never published, but it is now available at http://www.frame-poythress.org/frame_articles/1999Covenant.htm under the title "Covenant and the Unity of Scripture." Readers will note that the style and approach of this section differs from the rest of the present volume in various ways, such as in its interaction with some modern theologians. I have not taken pains to eliminate every redundancy between this section and the rest of this book.

cursings that should be on the lips of a covenant people. The wisdom books contain applications of the covenant law to human problems. The Prophets bring God's covenant lawsuit against the covenant-breakers while at the same time promising covenant renewal. The Gospels and Acts present the history of the new covenant, which is applied to believers and to world history in the Epistles and Revelation.

In chapter 17, I referred to Meredith G. Kline's analyses of biblical covenants in terms of the ancient Near Eastern suzerainty treaties. In the earlier chapter, I focused on the treaty as an analogy of the written revelation that God gave to Israel. As the treaty is written by the great king, so God is the author of the Decalogue. In this chapter, we will consider the content of the treaties, as a parallel to the content of Scripture.

The Hittite suzerainty treaties have a fairly standard form consisting of the following elements:

A. Name of the great king
B. Historical prologue
C. Stipulations (laws)
   1. Exclusive loyalty (= love)
   2. Specific requirements
D. Sanctions (blessings and curses)
E. Administration

Kline finds this literary form in the Decalogue (Ex. 20:1–17), and he identifies the book of Deuteronomy as a whole as a suzerainty treaty between Yahweh and Israel.

Section A makes it clear, as we saw in chapter 17, that the great king, not the vassal, is the author of the document, and that its provisions are his own will. So Yahweh in Exodus 20:2 announces, "I am Yahweh your God." So other passages of Scripture also emphasize the divine authorship (even divine publication!) of the document (Ex. 24:12; 31:18; 32:15f.; 34:1, 27f., 32; Deut. 4:13; 9:10f.; 10:2–4).

Section B indicates the previous benefits conferred upon the vassal by the suzerain: "who brought you out of the land of Egypt, out of the house of slavery." Here Yahweh indicates that the deliverance of Israel from Egypt was by his sovereign grace.

Section C shows how the suzerain expects the vassal to respond to these benefits: "You shall have no other gods before me," and so on. The first of the Ten Commandments is a love commandment, for *love* was the term used for the kind of exclusive covenant loyalty required in the covenant law. This is followed by various specific commandments spelling out how one should behave if he is exclusively loyal to Yahweh.

Section D indicates the consequences of obedience (blessing) or disobedience (curse). In the Decalogue, these are not put into a separate section (although they are in Deuteronomy: see chaps. 27 and 28), but are found in and with other commandments—curses in the second and third, blessings in the fifth. Note that one's good standing in the covenant relation depends on his obedience or disobedience to the written covenant document.

Section E indicates how the covenant is to be administered. Copies of the covenant document are to be placed in the religious sanctuaries of suzerain and vassal (cf. Deut. 31:26), there is provision for periodic public reading (vv. 9–13), and there are rules of dynastic succession (vv. 1–8). The covenant document stands as a witness: not man's fallible witness concerning God, but God's infallible witness *against* his disobedient people (v. 26). Again, the emphasis is on the divine authority of the document.

Kline holds that the original covenant document, the Ten Commandments, written by the finger of God (Ex. 31:18; 32:16) on two tables of stone, is the seed of the biblical canon. Additional writings were added to the covenant document as history progressed (see Josh. 24:25f.). These described the history of Israel's response to the covenant (Genesis–Esther), the covenant servant's praises, laments, questions (Psalms), and covenantal wisdom (Job, Proverbs, Ecclesiastes, Song). The prophetic books describe, as we saw earlier, God's covenant lawsuit and promises of covenant renewal. Kline offers a similar analysis of the NT—which, nevertheless, he regards as a new and separate canon setting forth a "new" covenant.

This covenantal model of canonicity is enormously helpful in dealing with questions concerning biblical authority, infallibility, and inerrancy. On this model, God is the ultimate author of Scripture,[3] and we vassals have no right to find fault with that document; rather, we are to be subject to it in all our thought and life.

What I would like to do now is to show that Kline's thesis is also helpful to our understanding of the *unity* of Scripture. Let us assume for now that Kline's model is correct; those who have doubts may pursue his arguments for themselves. And then let us ask what that model implies with regard to the unity of the biblical text.

The treaty form, as described above, is certainly a diversity-in-unity. It is a single document, with a single purpose: to govern a vassal people in the name of a great king. Yet to accomplish this single purpose, five different sections are necessary, as we have seen. These five sections define five types of revelation found within Scripture:

---

3. But meaningful human participation in the production of Scripture is by no means excluded; see Exodus 34:27–28 in comparison with verse 1.

A. Revelation of the name of God
B. Revelation of God's mighty acts in history
C. Revelation of God's law
   1. Love
   2. Specific requirements
D. Revelation of God's continuing presence to bless and curse
E. Revelation of God's institutional provisions: Scripture, church, sacraments, discipline, etc.

Name-revelation (A) is an important form of revelation in Scripture. In a narrow sense, we may think of God's names as the various words used to designate him: *Yahweh, Elohim, Adon, Theos,* and so on. Those names are an important aspect of scriptural revelation. Dramatically, God appears to Abram and says, "I am God Almighty [*El Shaddai*]; walk before me, and be blameless" (Gen. 17:1). Inaugurating another era of revelation, God comes to Moses in the burning bush and declares his name to be "I AM WHO I AM" (Ex. 3:14) and *Yahweh* (v. 15, evidently related in some fashion to the verb *to be*; cf. 6:1–3). God performs his mighty acts "that they may know that I am Yahweh" (see Ex. 14:18; 1 Kings 8:43; Pss. 9:10; 83:18; 91:14; Isa. 43:3; 52:6; Jer. 16:21; 33:2; Amos 5:8). As *El Shaddai* marked God's covenant relation with Abraham, so *Yahweh* marks the covenant relation between God and the nation Israel. All of God's mighty acts he performs in order to proclaim, display, and advance that covenant relation. In the new covenant, it is the name of Jesus into which people are to be baptized (Acts 2:38), in which we trust (1 John 3:23), through which we are to pray to God (John 16:23f.), and in which we perform all our labors (Col. 3:17).

God's names also have meaning. *Yahweh,* for instance, connotes God's sovereign control over the world, his ultimate authority to determine standards for intelligent beings, and his covenant solidarity and presence with his people.[4] When God reveals himself as *Yahweh,* he stresses those elements of his character.

In a still broader sense, God's "name" (*shem* or *onoma,* without a proper name) is a way of referring to God himself in all his self-revelation; cf. Josh. 7:9; Ezek. 20:9. In this respect it is a near-synonym of "word of God." To praise the name of God is to praise him; to dishonor the name is to dishonor him. Note the unity between the name of God and God himself (e.g., Ex. 33:19; 34:5f.; Pss. 7:17; 9:10; 18:49; 68:4; 74:18; 86:12; 92:1; Isa. 25:1; 26:8; 56:6; Zech. 14:9; Mal. 3:16).

The second form of revelation (B) is also prominent in Scripture. Scripture may be called the story of God's mighty deeds performed

---

4. See my *DG,* 1–102.

for the salvation of his people. Whether called "signs," "wonders," or "mighty acts," God's amazing works accomplish the redemption of his people and the judgment of the wicked, from the flood of Genesis 6–9 to the final judgment. In the biblical history, especially important roles are given to the deliverance of Israel from Egypt and to the greatest miracle, the resurrection of Jesus Christ from the dead. This is, essentially, the message of God's grace. It tells us what God has done for his people; it enumerates his free gifts. It includes all of what is called redemptive history, but also creation and providence: Pss. 104; 136:4, 25; 145:4–6, 12.

Law-revelation (C) is also important within Scripture. The *torah* is the heart of the old covenant, giving instruction in God's standards, which are invoked throughout the OT. Throughout the historical, poetic, wisdom, and prophetic books, God calls his people back to obey his commandments. The written *torah* is that law in which the righteous man meditates day and night (Ps. 1:2); it is the law that is "perfect, reviving the soul" (Ps. 19:7). It is the Word of God to which praises are sung in Psalms 56:4, 10; 119:161–62; etc.

Jesus also comes bringing commandments that his disciples are to obey. Though rejecting the attempt to save oneself by keeping the law, the NT nevertheless stresses our obligation to keep the commandments of Jesus: Matt. 7:21ff., 24f.; Mark 8:38; Luke 8:21; 9:26ff.; John 8:47; 12:47ff.; 14:15, 21, 23f.; 15:7, 10, 14; 17:6, 17; 1 Tim. 6:3; 1 John 2:3–5; 3:22; 5:2f.; 2 John 6; Rev. 12:17; 14:12.

Sanction-revelation (D) can also be found throughout Scripture. God's covenants are two-edged. Those who are faithful to the covenant receive blessing; those who are not faithful receive curse. Many in Israel falsely trusted in their covenant membership, as if being children of Yahweh allowed them to sin with impunity. But God responded to them with devastation and exile, preserving the faithful remnant. In time it becomes evident that only Jesus is the perfectly faithful remnant. He bears the curse for his people—for all who are joined to him by God's election (Gal. 3:13; Eph. 1:4). Yet even under the new covenant, there are those who attach themselves to God's church who later prove to be devoid of true faith and outside of God's electing love. Those receive exceptionally severe curses as those who rebelled against Christ in the face of intimate knowledge (Heb. 6:4–6; 10:26–31). Biblical writers never tire of presenting the enormous consequences of faith or unbelief: the rewards coming to God's people, the dreadful judgments upon the wicked.

Finally, Scripture is also concerned with the continuing life of God's people, with those arrangements (E) by which the Word of God is preserved and applied to each generation. The original covenant document was placed by the ark of the covenant, the holiest place among the people of God. It was, as we have seen, to be read publicly from time to time. God established prophet, priest, and king to rule his people according to his word. In the new covenant, Jesus fulfills these offices; but he, too, is concerned that his church be built on a firm foundation (Matt. 16:18ff.). He appoints the apostles to remember his words (John 14:26) and to convey new truth from the Spirit (John 15:26; 16:13). The apostles, in turn, establish the offices of elder and deacon (Acts 6:1–6; 1 Tim. 3:1–7; etc.).

Therefore, even if we have reservations about Kline's thesis that the Scripture historically developed from the original covenant document, we must admit that the five major elements of the covenant form each represent an important aspect of biblical revelation.

Now we ask our main question: How do these covenant elements testify to the unity of Scripture? My threefold answer: by their pervasiveness, their mutual complementarity, and their perspectival relationship. Let me expound each of these in turn.

PERVASIVENESS

First, each of these covenantal themes is fundamental to all parts of Scripture, as should be evident from the survey above. The five forms of covenantal revelation are equally at home in Old and New Testaments, in books of history and books of prophecy, in Gospels and Epistles, in apocalyptic.

The one area in which a question might arise is the wisdom literature. Certainly, the "name" (A) and the "mighty acts" (B) of God are not common themes of these books, at least in so many words. But the fundamental premise of the book of Proverbs is that "the fear of the LORD is the beginning of knowledge" (Prov. 1:7; cf. Pss. 111:10; 112:1; Prov. 9:10). The wisdom to be gained in Proverbs begins with covenant faithfulness to the Lord. Thus, this literature presupposes, though it does not verbally emphasize, the covenant relationship. Certainly, its teaching can be seen to spring from the covenant law (C). Ecclesiastes concludes that to fear God and keep his commandments is the whole duty of man (Eccl. 12:13–14), thus echoing the connection between keeping the law and wisdom found in Deut. 4:6. The consequences of obedience and disobedience (D) are well illustrated in the wisdom books, and these books are themselves part of the structure (E) by which the covenant law is passed down and applied from generation to generation (cf. Prov. 1:8).[5]

Thus, the covenant consciousness pervades the Scriptures. Each of the five themes ties Scripture together, as each part of the Bible seeks to advance that theme. Despite Scripture's diversity of authorship, style, and specific interest, all parts of it are united by its strong covenant interest.

COMPLEMENTARITY

The pervasiveness of these covenant themes, however, would not be conducive to the unity of Scripture if the themes themselves were inconsistent with one another. Are the five elements of the covenant complementary, or do they present to us different concepts of God, of his works, of salvation, of the believer's life?

Within the covenant model, there is no evident tension. The name of the Lord (A) is the name of the one who performs the mighty works (B), lays down the law (C), executes the sanctions (D), establishes the institutions (E). The mighty works of the historical prologue present a strong motivation for the loyalty demanded in the law and a reason for the severity of the sanctions. The law itself must have teeth; thus it requires sanctions. And a people cannot truly be "under" law unless there are institutional ways in which the law can be preserved, taught, enforced. Thus, the different parts of the covenant reinforce one another.

The consistency of these covenant elements is sharply at odds with the picture of Scripture found in many forms of modern theology. Typically, the various schools of liberal theology find in the Bible many discordant elements, which cannot be reconciled or fit together in a single theological system. Thus, the theologian thinks he is forced to choose some of those motifs to use in his own theology and to discard (or de-emphasize) others. There is necessarily a certain arbitrariness in this procedure, though of course these theologians typically claim that they have chosen those motifs most fundamental to Scripture itself. Yet among these theologians there is wide disparity over which themes are affirmed and which ones discarded, which ones are considered central and which ones are relegated to the periphery. Thus, we have had in our time a great number of "theologies of" this or that: the word of God, crisis, personal encounter, history, love, hope, being, process—and the list goes on. Each of these appeals to some

---

5. Compare Kline's larger discussion of the wisdom literature in *The Structure of Biblical Authority* (Grand Rapids: Eerdmans, 1972), 64–67.

aspect of Scripture, maintaining that other aspects may be denied, ignored, or minimized. Consider some examples:

Person and Proposition (A)

In modern theology, especially the personalism of Martin Buber[6] and Emil Brunner,[7] there is often a sharp opposition between the revelation of a person and the revelation of propositions or information. As John Baillie puts it, in the NT, "the content of revelation is not a body of information or of doctrine. [Rather,] what is revealed is God himself."[8] We certainly cannot doubt that God through Scripture reveals himself as a person.[9] But must we choose between person-revelation and propositional revelation? Granting the first, must we deny the second? Baillie assumes that we do.[10]

The covenant form, however, presents us with a model of revelation that is both highly personal and highly propositional. God reveals his name, which is virtually equivalent to himself. He authors the entire treaty, revealing himself throughout its pages. He communicates love, by revealing his past blessings and by promising future ones to those who are faithful. He speaks intimately to his people.[11] He promises that he will be personally involved with his people to bless, to punish, and to chastise.

At the same time, the covenant is propositional. It is a document containing words and sentences. It functions as a legal constitution for God's people. It is to be kept, passed on, from generation to generation (Deut. 6:4ff.; Jude 3). It contains information about God's name, his mighty deeds, his will for our lives, his sanctions, and his established institutions.

In the light of the covenant model, surely the burden of proof is on modern theologians to tell us why we must place personal and propositional

---

6. Martin Buber, *I and Thou* (New York: Scribner, 1958).

7. Especially in Emil Brunner, *Truth as Encounter* (Philadelphia: Westminster Press, 1964).

8. John Baillie, *The Idea of Revelation in Recent Thought* (New York: Columbia University Press, 1956), 60.

9. F. Gerald Downing, however, argues in *Has Christianity a Revelation?* (London: SCM Press, 1964) that this is not the case, that we cannot say that God in Scripture reveals "himself." Downing's argument is not cogent, in my opinion, but it is interesting in that it shows how one can, with some plausibility, argue for theological choices quite different from those of Buber, Brunner, and Baillie.

10. So far as I can tell, Baillie offers no argument to prove that the person/proposition distinction is an exclusive disjunction. Brunner does, saying that information about one of the parties detracts from the personal character of a relationship. But I find that idea utterly implausible.

11. In the Decalogue, God addresses Israel as if the nation were one person: *thou!*

revelation in sharp opposition to each other. Or perhaps they should admit that their theological construction is simply a capitulation to the demands of "historical-critical" scholarship, setting the scholar free to find fault with biblical propositions as long as some vague "person-revelation" still shines through. But to do that is to rebel against God's requirements for human thinking (2 Cor. 10:5).[12]

ACT AND WORD (B)

It was once fashionable among modern theologians to emphasize very strongly that God reveals himself in *events* (acts, deeds, etc.) rather than in words (propositions!) about those events. That sort of contrast can be found in Karl Barth[13] and Emil Brunner, as was the last. Baillie[14] also assumes this dichotomy, as he did the last. But one wonders, then, how revelation can be both *person* and *event*, and why we don't have to choose between them. Baillie gives very little indication of how *person* and *event* are related in the evidently complex reality called revelation.[15]

Somewhat more consistent was the proposal of George Ernest Wright[16] that God reveals himself only in events interpreted through the eyes of faith. Events, not propositions—again, that was the contrast. James Barr, however, certainly a man with no sympathies for fundamentalism, refuted Wright's thesis with the obvious point that in the scriptural narrative God reveals himself not only by doing things but also by speaking directly to man.[17] Barr added that we may wish, as modern people, to reject the idea of direct speech from God to man; but in all honesty we should not pretend that that idea is absent from the Bible itself.

On the covenantal model, there is no opposition between God's acts and God's words. Both exist harmoniously in the treaty form. The whole document consists of God's words. But among those words are words that tell of God's mighty acts. These accounts of God's acts are not, as on Wright's view, the stumbling attempts of human beings to interpret their

12. See my *DKG*.

13. Barth's concept of *event* is, however, quite idiosyncratic.

14. Baillie, *The Idea of Revelation*, 62–82.

15. Gordon D. Kaufman, in his *Systematic Theology: A Historicist Perspective* (New York: Scribner, 1968), actually describes Christ as a "person-event," but that idea remains as obscure in his thought as in Baillie's. See my review of Kaufman's book in *WTJ* 32, 1 (November 1969): 119–24.

16. George Ernest Wright, *God Who Acts* (London: SCM Press, 1952); George Ernest Wright and Reginald Horace Fuller, *The Book of the Acts of God* (Garden City, NY: Doubleday, 1957).

17. James Barr, *Old and New in Interpretation* (London: SCM Press, 1966).

experiences (cf. 2 Peter 1:20); they are rather God's own descriptions and interpretations of what he has done. Modern man may, like Barr, resist the possibility of such divinely formulated interpretation; but in doing so he resists the very notion of a sovereign God who can do what he wishes in and with his creation.

GRACE AND LAW (C)

Not only among modern liberal theologians, but also throughout the history of Christianity there has been disagreement over the precise relation between grace and law. Because of certain expressions in the NT referring negatively to law, there has been a tendency in theology to radically oppose grace and law—even to remove law from any positive function in the Christian life.[18] This tendency has in my view been reinforced in the modern period by the craving for absolute autonomy expressed by modern philosophers and literary writers. Even among evangelicals there has been a substantial controversy as to whether salvation involves a commitment to obey Jesus as Lord, or whether such a commitment takes place sometime after salvation, at the point when one becomes a "disciple."

Orthodox Reformed theology has traditionally avoided the sharp opposition between grace and law found in other traditions (e.g., Lutheran, dispensationalist). While acknowledging that salvation is by the grace of God and not by any good works of man, Reformed theology has had no trouble saying that from the beginning of the Christian life we are obligated (indeed, privileged) to live according to God's law. It is grace alone that saves, but the grace that saves is never alone (cf. James 2:14–26).

The covenant model vindicates this Reformed understanding of the relation between grace and law. God proclaims his grace in section B. This is unmerited favor. He did not choose the people of Israel because they were more numerous than other peoples, but simply because he loved them (Deut. 7:7; cf. 4:37; 9:4–6; 10:15). But at the same time, Israel from the very beginning of its existence is to obey God's law (C). Similarly, Jesus makes it clear that although salvation is by the free gift of the Father (John 6:65), believers are expected from the very beginning to obey him (14:21–24), so that keeping his words is the test of covenant faithfulness. And indeed, obeying Jesus brings more grace, more blessing (D). Grace and law are harmonious. They become antagonistic only when someone tries to save himself by his own works.

---

18. This sort of controversy may have existed during the NT period itself; certainly it was a major element in the second-century controversy over the views of Marcion.

Indeed, the covenant message of grace (B) is already understood to be the word of the Lord (A). There is no separation here between lordship and salvation. It is the Lord who accomplishes salvation (cf. Jonah 2:9). Only the Lord has the requisite authority and power to save his people. To confess trust in God's salvation is at the same time to acknowledge him as Yahweh, the Lord. Similarly in Romans 10:9–10, confession of Jesus' resurrection is inseparable from the heart belief that "Jesus is Lord."

Love and Law (D)

The antagonism in modern theology between love and law goes back at least to Friedrich Schleiermacher.[19] Emil Brunner[20] and Joseph Fletcher[21] are among many well-known theological ethicists of the last century who have urged an ethic of love without any absolute divine legal standards. Surely Scripture puts love in first place as the distinguishing mark of the Christian (John 13:35). But (modern theologians to the contrary) in Scripture, the love mandate is part of the law.[22] And Jesus says over and over that if we love him, we will keep his commandments (John 14:15, 21, 23f.; 15:7, 10, 14; cf. 1 John 2:3–6; 5:2f.; 2 John 6).

Modern theologians assume too readily that since love and law are not perfectly synonymous, one must take precedence over the other in the Christian life. They assume that the two must conflict with each other at some point. But why should we make that assumption? Is it not a fundamentally atheistic assumption? For if God exists, he is certainly able to create a world in which love and law both dictate precisely the same ethic.

Such assumptions are radically negated by the covenant model. The love command is the first stipulation (C, 1), while what we normally think of as "law" (C, 2) follows that first stipulation. They are together in the body of stipulations, indicating that they are not to be considered antagonistic toward each other. Indeed, in the suzerainty treaties and in God's covenant with Israel, "love" means "exclusive covenant loyalty." Law is the outworking of love, the particular applications of it. Love is that whole-souled, exclusive loyalty we owe to our Great King, while the detailed stipulations show us the practical, detailed outworkings of that covenant loyalty. If we love God exclusively, then we will not worship idols, take his name in vain,

---

19. Friedrich Schleiermacher, *The Christian Faith* (Edinburgh: T&T Clark, 1928).

20. Emil Brunner, *The Divine Imperative*, trans. Olive Wyon (Philadelphia: Westminster Press, 1947).

21. Joseph Fletcher, *Situation Ethics* (Philadelphia: Westminster Press, 1966).

22. When Jesus cites the two great commandments of loving God and neighbor, he quotes Deuteronomy 6:5 and Leviticus 19:18 from the Mosaic law (Matt. 22:37–40).

and so on. The details spell out the meaning of love, rather than presenting an alternative ethic that we may or may not wish to choose.

Redemptive Focus and Comprehensive Application (E)

Much has been written in recent years about the "purpose" of Scripture and how that purpose affects its reliability, inerrancy, and sufficiency.[23] Many have argued that the purpose of Scripture is to present a message of redemption and therefore not to teach us anything of interest to (e.g.) science, history, or philosophy as such. Therefore, if there are errors in the details of biblical history, for example, those do not affect the reliability of Scripture, which is only to give us a redemptive message.

This issue is also relevant to those who maintain that "redemptive history" should be the chief or only subject matter of biblical preaching, as opposed to ethical principles, apologetic defenses of biblical reliability, and the like.

There is no doubt that the covenant is redemptive in its thrust. The historical prologue (B) is a message of redemption. It tells of God's grace in redeeming his people from the realm of sin and death. But to proclaim the covenant is not merely to inform people of those redemptive facts. Rather, to proclaim the covenant is to proclaim it in toto: the message of grace together with the obligations that constitute our thanksgiving for grace (C), the consequences of obedience and disobedience (D), and the institutional, social structure that God has planted on earth (E). Further, those obligations are comprehensive: the love commandment requires a radical reorientation of life so that all things are done to God's glory (Deut. 6:4f.; cf. Rom. 14:23; 1 Cor. 10:31; Col. 3:17, 24). That includes all aspects of life, such as our intellectual work, our studies in history, science, and philosophy. All human work must be done out of faith, presupposing and embracing all that God has told us in his Word.

So the covenant is redemptive, but not in any narrow sense—not in any sense that forbids God to speak to us on certain subjects. Even more fundamental to the covenant than the emphasis on redemption is the declaration of God's lordship (A). And that lordship is absolutely comprehensive.

Scripture does not teach any general distinction between the sacred and the secular. There are degrees of holiness: the Holiest Place of the tabernacle/temple, with the ark of the covenant, is the maximum place of

23. Some examples: G. C. Berkouwer, *Holy Scripture* (Grand Rapids: Eerdmans, 1975); Dewey M. Beegle, *The Inspiration of Scripture* (Philadelphia: Westminster Press, 1963); Jack B. Rogers and Donald K. McKim, *The Authority and Interpretation of the Bible: An Historical Approach* (San Francisco: Harper and Row, 1979).

holiness, in comparison with which all else is common. The Holy Place is less holy than the Holiest, but more holy than anything else. And so, in descending levels of holiness, we may distinguish the tabernacle as a whole, the holy city (Jerusalem), the Holy Land (the land of promise), and the heavens and earth as God's throne and footstool.[24] But nothing is "secular" in the sense of being outside the scope of God's lordship and lacking responsibility to all of God's words.

I would offer a similar response to the related question whether revelation consists of "events" or of "timeless truths" (see also section B above). God's lordship itself is certainly eternal; but the application of that lordship to our situation is, of course, conditioned on our history. Our relation to God depends on how in history we have responded to him, and further revelation always presupposes these events. His covenant law is a reflection of his eternal character, but it also relates that eternal character to the concrete situation of God's people. And although God is changeless, the specific applications of his law do change from one situation to another.

Judgment and Blessing (F)

Nineteenth-century liberalism uniformly disparaged the idea of divine judgment. Barth and Brunner restored the discussion of judgment to centrality (as did, in a different way, the consistent eschatological school of Johannes Weiss and Albert Schweitzer and the recent theologians of hope and liberation). But even this more recent theology regards judgment either as a mere symbol or as an event fully or largely overcome by grace.

We all wonder, of course, how a God of love can send people to hell. It is not wrong to rethink this matter from time to time. What the covenant structure reminds us is that God is a God of both justice and blessing and that neither of these is to be compromised. If we do not completely understand how grace and retribution can coexist, we must accept both on faith, trusting that God knows better than we what is truly just and what constitutes mercy.

God's Word and Man's Response (G)

Much has been written about the relation between revelation and the human response to revelation. Most theologians since Schleiermacher have said that revelation does not exist without human response, for only when man responds is there true communication. Indeed, that response must be

---

24. See the diagram in *DCL*, 417, with the accompanying discussion.

one of faith, or else the communication has not been *properly* received. Since revelation (according to these theologians) is nonpropositional, it is virtually defined by them as that event in which faith is aroused.

Conservatives have objected that in Scripture itself, "revelation" is used in various senses. Certainly, there is one sense in which revelation is inseparable from response; that is the sense in which revelation is defined as individual illumination (e.g., Matt. 11:27; Gal. 1:16; Eph. 1:17; Phil. 3:15). But this is not the same sense in which the idea of revelation appears, for example, in Romans 1:18; for there revelation is given precisely to those *without* faith so as to leave them without excuse. Further, *revelation*, with its apocalyptic connotations, is not the only, or even the standard, term used for divine-human communication in Scripture. Much more common is the phrase *word of God*, which, of course, applies to publicly written documents, as well as to divine communication with prophets, and which never (so far as I can see) refers to inward illumination. Even more obviously does this argument apply to such terms as *law*, *statutes*, and *testimonies*.

The confusions over this point are linked to the widespread ignorance and neglect of the covenantal model. For within the covenant there is a clear relation between divine revelation and human response. God is the author of the covenant document and identifies himself as such (A). The history, laws, sanctions, and administrative ordinances are by his authorship. But the covenant *requires* a response by the vassals (D), and the nature of that response will lead to curse or blessing. Further, in the ratification of the covenant, the vassal takes an oath, agreeing to the treaty conditions (cf. Deut. 27:12–28:68). And future covenants will record the enacting of blessing and curse sanctions as prologue to the new covenant.

Such is the fundamental relation, in Scripture, between divine revelation and human response. Of course, just as the curse sanctions of the covenant are borne by Jesus on behalf of God's elect, so the elect also receive a special kind of revelation: a communication of the Spirit eliciting faith. All of this happens by God's grace. Thus, there is more than one kind of revelation within the covenant. The actual publication of the covenant document is available to all who can read or hear. But inward illumination is only for those whom God has united to Christ by grace.

History and Eschatology (H)

Since the time of Schweitzer and Weiss, who argued that Jesus' message was wholly eschatological, many have sought to understand the relation of history to eschatology in Scripture. To what extent is Christian faith oriented toward once-for-all past events, and to what extent is it oriented toward the future? "Future-oriented" theology has been highly popular recently, under the names *theology of hope*[25] and *liberation theology*,[26] and in the neo-Hegelian theology of Wolfhart Pannenberg.[27] The earlier existential theologians, such as Rudolf Bultmann, presented the gospel as a kind of "openness to the future," somewhat anticipating the more recent developments.

In the covenant structure, however, there is no hint of any tension between concerns with past and future. Past events are the necessary conditions for bringing the covenant into being (B). Indeed, the covenant servant of Yahweh always looks back with thankfulness on the grace given in past history. Yet there are also in the covenant present (C) and future (D, E) foci. In the present, we look to God's law to know how he wants us to live. We look forward to the outworking of God's covenant sanctions, and we expect in the future to have continued access to the covenant by God's own administrative arrangements. The future focus within the covenant does not conflict with the focus on the past. On the contrary, the past events are the foundation for God's future working.

And the future orientation of the covenant is not vague in the way that Bultmann's "open future" is, or as are the unspecified futures of Moltmann and Pannenberg. God tells us, making some allowances for mystery, what is going to happen. We can confidently look forward to God's future in a way in which we certainly cannot look forward to the future that Bultmann speaks of.

Divine Sovereignty and Human Responsibility (I)

The covenant model cannot do everything, and I don't think it leads to any radically new insights into the sovereignty/responsibility question.[28] Yet it does speak to those theologians (especially of the "process" tradition) who would insist that God's plans are changeable and dependent on man's decisions. The covenant model does, as we've seen (especially section G above), put a great emphasis on man's responsibility, but also on the sovereignty of God, who identifies himself as Lord, who unilaterally establishes the covenant morality, who declares what will happen in the future. To be sure, the covenant sanctions (D) are dependent on whether man responds in obedience or disobedience. But the divine plan is fully set

25. Jürgen Moltmann, *Theology of Hope* (New York: Harper and Row, 1967).
26. As in Gustavo Gutiérrez, *A Theology of Liberation: History, Politics, and Salvation* (Maryknoll, NY: Orbis Books, 1973).
27. E.g., Wolfhart Pannenberg, *Jesus, God and Man* (Philadelphia: Westminster Press, 1968).
28. The main treatment of this question in the Lordship series is in *DG*, chapters 4 and 8.

in either case. God will not have to make new plans in order to deal with some unforeseen possibility.

Nature and Scripture (J)

Far from nature and Scripture's being two competing sources of revelation as in much theology, God appears in the covenant as the controller of nature, the one who establishes its course. Nature therefore behaves as the covenant document says it will. It confirms, but never contradicts, the written covenant. And only those who see nature through the "spectacles" (John Calvin) of the covenant document see nature aright. Thus, the covenant calls the created world ("heaven and earth") as witnesses (Deut. 4:26; 30:19; 31:28; 32:1) together with the chief witness, which is the covenant document itself (Deut. 31:14–29). Cf. Rom. 8:19–22.

We have seen, then, many ways in which the covenant model displays the unity in diversity of various aspects of scriptural revelation. It is not necessary for theology to posit disunity and then to pick and choose what elements it prefers. Rather, to do so is to ignore or violate the basic structural principle of the biblical genre.

PERSPECTIVAL RELATION

A third way in which the covenant structure shows the unity of Scripture is by the *perspectival relation* of its elements to one another.

It is possible to divide Scripture into various parts, each reflecting a particular element of the covenant structure. The revelation of the name (A) would include such passages as Exodus 3:14; 6:1ff.; 33:19ff.; 34:6f.; Isaiah 40:25ff.; 41:1–4; Malachi 3:6; John 8:58; and so on. The historical prologue (B) would consist of the historical books of the OT and the Gospels of the NT. (But notice that categories (A) and (B) already overlap.) The law (C) would include the OT *torah*, the Sermon on the Mount (Matt. 5–7), and other ethical portions of Scripture. The sanctions (D) would include some passages in Psalms and Proverbs and other books, particularly prophecy and apocalyptic. Administration (E) would also be found in the Pentateuch, and in such passages as Matthew 18 and the Pastoral Epistles.

But when you think more deeply about it, the following thought occurs: One cannot really get a full understanding of the name of God (A) except by understanding the totality of Scripture. The whole Bible, then, is the revelation of the divine name. Same for history. The full history of God's people includes the laws God gave them, and the poetic, wisdom, prophetic, and apocalyptic literature that molded their thinking. Similarly for law, for the application of God's laws requires an understanding of our historical circumstances. To know what God requires of us, we must know where we are in the history of redemption. Same for sanctions and administration.

So the whole Bible is a revelation of God's name; it is all history; it is all law; it is all sanctions; it is all administration. Each element of the covenant is a way of looking at the whole Bible. Each element includes all the others.

The point is not that the various elements of the covenant are synonymous. History is not synonymous with law, for instance. But for us, *understanding* history is the same as *understanding* law. We cannot understand and use one part of God's revelation adequately if we neglect others. Of course, we do learn by bits and pieces, and the most fragmentary knowledge of God's book is better than nothing, if it is part of a process of continuing study under the guidance of the Holy Spirit. But theologians often make serious blunders by arbitrarily chopping the Scriptures into segments and reporting on those segments in isolation.

I think this perspectival relation of the various covenant elements is a further testimony to the unity in diversity of Scripture. To pit these elements against one another as modern theologians like to do is to miss something very important.

This covenantal model may suggest other perspectival ways of looking at the text. For instance, consider the discussion over whether God's revelation is *propositional truth*. I would say that propositional truth is one perspective on Scripture; but Scripture also contains questions, imperatives, and poetry. Yet to understand the propositional message that God gives to us, we must study the whole Bible—commands, questions, and poetry as well. So in a sense the whole Bible is propositional. But the whole Bible is also command (it demands something of us), question (it solicits an answer), poetry (it engages our deepest selves).

CONCLUSION

In all these sorts of ways, the covenant model helps us to view Scripture as a unity, amid the undoubted differences among its authors and books. God the Three-in-One has given his revelation to us as a unity in diversity. Thus, he manifests the unity of his speech to us ("I am the Lord") in all its manifold applications. Truly the Word of God is *rich*. If it is simple enough for little children, it also contains depths challenging to the brightest scholars. And for all believers it sets forth a reliable, clear, unified expression of our sovereign God.

CHAPTER 25

Scripture's Authority, Its Content, and Its Purpose

The question of Scripture's content, which I discussed in the preceding chapter, has been thought to have implications for the nature of its authority. As I indicated in the previous chapter, some have supposed that Scripture has a narrowly redemptive content and purpose, and therefore that it should not be expected to give us revelation from God in matters of interest to science, history, psychology, philosophy, and so on. I replied that the purpose of Scripture is redemptive, but not narrowly redemptive in this sense. Redemption itself is very broad, renewing every area of human life. And since Scripture is God's personal word to us, we dare not limit its scope, telling him, in effect, that we will listen to him only on certain subjects. Would we ever lay down such an ultimatum if he addressed us personally and directly? Rather, we should listen at his feet, ready to accept whatever he should choose to say to us.

In this chapter, I would like to present some more analysis of the relations between Scripture's authority, content, and purpose, by way of responding to some influential (but to my mind inadequate) views of the subject.

In the 1970s there was some controversy among the Reformed churches, particularly those of Dutch background, over the "relationship between the authority of Scripture to its content." In Reformed circles, we continue to hear of this debate from time to time.

In 1972, a study committee presented its report, *The Nature and Extent of Biblical Authority*,[1] to the Synod of the Christian Reformed Church (CRC), an American denomination of Dutch background. Today, this document is commonly referred to as *Report 44*. It was in response to a request from the Reformed Ecumenical Synod (RES), which, in turn, was prompted by a request for joint discussion by the Gereformeerde Kerken in Nederland (GKN). The discussion led to the GKN study *God with Us*, which was presented to the Synod of Delft in 1980. The RES (and the CRC also) had made earlier declarations about the authority of Scripture, but the GKN questioned whether these documents were adequate to deal with the contemporary issues. In particular, these documents failed to discuss the "connection between the content and purpose of Scripture as the saving revelation of God in Jesus Christ *and* the consequent and deducible authority of Scripture."[2]

To accept the GKN's formulation of the problem at this point, of course, is to prejudice significantly the sort of answer that one will arrive at. The GKN lays it down as an assumption of the discussion that the authority of Scripture is somehow "consequent to" and "deducible from" its content. Then it asks us to discuss the connections between these. But its assumption already asserts certain connections.

We need to discuss, not assume, the proposition that the authority of Scripture is consequent to and deducible from its content. What does this proposition mean, and is it true?

I think it is true in several ways: (1) Most of us come to know Jesus first, the authority of Scripture second. We are attracted to Scripture because it tells us of Christ. Nobody, to my knowledge, first determines that the Bible is God's Word and then later inquires to discover what it has to say. (2) As we have seen, if we are to trust Scripture as God's Word, we must do so on the basis of its own teachings about itself—part of its content. (3) In the final analysis, it is the content of Scripture that is authoritative. The content of Scripture tells us what God wants us to believe, do, and feel, what his promises are, and so on. The doctrine of Scripture, including the concept of biblical authority, is part of that content and arises out of that content.

But there are some dangers in making the content of Scripture the source of Scripture's authority. Some have drawn false conclusions from this assumption, such as (1) that our belief in Scripture is not based on

1. Committee on Biblical Authority of the Christian Reformed Church, *The Nature and Extent of Biblical Authority* (Grand Rapids: Board of Publications of the Christian Reformed Church, 1972). See my review of the document itself in Appendix I in this volume.

2. Ibid., 16 (emphasis theirs).

Scripture's self-attestation, but on our autonomous value judgment concerning the significance of Scripture's message, and (2) that some parts of Scripture are somewhat irrelevant to the central message and can therefore be treated as merely human words.

The relationship between the content and authority of Scripture is more complex than the GKN assumed in its call for discussion. It is true that human beings cannot confess the authority of Scripture if they have no idea of its content. But the content of Scripture is not the ultimate source of its authority. That content does not give it the unique authority that pertains to Scripture alone. Many other books present the biblical gospel, but they do not on that account deserve a place in the canon. What gives Scripture an authority above that of any human being is that it is God's Word. WCF 1.4 puts it this way:

> The authority of the Holy Scripture, for which it ought to be believed, and obeyed, depends not upon the testimony of any man, or Church; but wholly upon God (who is truth itself) the author thereof: and therefore it is to be received, because it is the Word of God.

Divine authorship is the ultimate reason why Scripture is authoritative. Its authority is absolute because God's authority is absolute, and Scripture is his personal word to us.

Since Scripture is God's personal word, *all* of it is authoritative, for as Paul says, "*All* Scripture is breathed out by God" (2 Tim. 3:16), not just those parts that we find attractive, cogent, relevant, or culturally respectable.

There are nevertheless many writers who believe that the purpose of Scripture is redemptive in a narrow sense, rather than in the comprehensive sense I argued earlier (chap. 24). On their view, the purpose of Scripture is to get us right with God through Christ, but not to tell us what to believe in areas of history, science, and so on. Jack Rogers and Donald McKim, for example, say:

> Calvin, in common with the early church fathers, held that the authority of Scripture resided in its function of bringing people into a saving relationship with God through Jesus Christ.
>
> Turretin, on the other hand, held that the authority of Scripture was based on its form of inerrant words. The Bible was a repository of information about all manner of things, including science and history, which had to be proven accurate by then-current standards.[3]

3. Jack B. Rogers and Donald K. McKim, *The Authority and Interpretation of the Bible: An Historical Approach* (San Francisco: Harper and Row, 1979), xvii.

Rogers and McKim follow John Calvin as they understand him and reject Francis Turretin's approach. The authority of Scripture, they say, resides in its evangelistic function. But then how does its authority differ, say, from the authority of Billy Graham? I don't think this quote adequately describes Calvin's view of the matter—nor, more importantly, does it describe Scripture's own account of its authority.

And did Turretin actually believe that "the authority of Scripture was based on its form of inerrant words"? If the authority of Scripture had this kind of basis, then its authority would not differ from the authority of an accurate mathematics text. Rather, both Calvin and Turretin held that the authority of Scripture resides in the fact that God is its author.

My purpose here is not, however, to evaluate Rogers and McKim's view of Calvin or Turretin, or of the many other historical figures they discuss in their book. In my own view, the critique of this book by John Woodbridge is definitive.[4] Woodbridge argues and documents extensively the view that neither Calvin nor the earlier church fathers observed any sharp distinction between the saving truth of Scripture and matters of science and history.

But our own view of the matter cannot be ultimately based on church history, however much such a study may help us. Our view of Scripture must, in the end, be warranted by Scripture itself. And as I have argued, Scripture itself does not limit its authority the way Rogers and McKim seek to limit it. It claims, rather, (1) that God is the author of the whole biblical canon, (2) that we live by all of it (Matt. 4:4), (3) that God has the right to speak to us about anything at all, (4) that the purpose of Scripture is redemptive in a broad sense, not a narrow sense, and (5) that the redemptive purpose of Scripture is so broad that no area of human life is excluded from its concern.

4. John D. Woodbridge, *Biblical Authority: A Critique of the Rogers-McKim Proposal* (Grand Rapids: Zondervan, 1982).

CHAPTER 26

The Inerrancy of Scripture

One of the most fiercely debated subjects in the doctrine of the word of God is that of biblical inerrancy, and we must now enter that debate.

It is important, first of all, to understand what we are talking about. The term *inerrancy*, not found in English translations of the Bible, has been given a number of different definitions. James Orr says that the term refers to "hard and fast literality in minute matters of historical, geographical, and scientific detail."[1]

There is also a position called *limited inerrancy*,[2] which claims that Scripture is inerrant only in matters of salvation.[3] On Orr's definition, this position is not inerrancy at all. For to him, the only purpose of the term *inerrancy* is to assert the accuracy of Scripture in matters *not* related to salvation.[4]

1. James Orr, *Revelation and Inspiration* (New York: Scribner's, 1910; repr., Grand Rapids: Baker, 1969), 199.
2. See, e.g., Richard Coleman, "Reconsidering 'Limited Inerrancy,'" *JETS* 17 (1974): 207–14. Note also Vern Poythress's response, "Problems for Limited Inerrancy," *JETS* 18, 2 (Spring 1975): 93–102, also available at http://www.frame-poythress.org/poythress _articles/1975Problems.htm#_ftn2.
3. The definition contains ambiguities, as Poythress brings out in his response to Coleman (previous footnote).
4. Jack Rogers and Donald McKim, whom we mentioned in the previous chapter, agree with Orr in his general position and in his distaste for the term *inerrancy*. They prefer to describe their own position, and the one they attribute to John Calvin and the church fathers, as *infallibility*. But as we will see, there are problems with that usage.

A third approach to defining the term might be to look at the dictionary. It is not common for theologians to rely on dictionary definitions, since theological terms often have a history ignored by secular dictionaries, and since theologians have assumed a remarkable freedom to come up with their own terms and their own definitions of existing terms. Yet dictionaries have a far more intuitive and logical understanding of the term *inerrancy* than is implied in either definition mentioned above. The *American Heritage College Dictionary* defines *inerrancy* simply as "freedom from error or untruths."[5] *Inerrant* means:

1. Incapable of erring; infallible.
2. Containing no errors.[6]

This dictionary also cites a meaning for *inerrantism*, namely, "Belief in the inerrancy or literal truth of a particular writing or document."[7] On the basis of my own reading in the literature, I don't think that *inerrantism* is widely used, or that it is uniformly used with this precise definition.[8] But generally I think the dictionary is our best guide here.

While we are looking at the dictionary, we should also take note of the term *infallible*, often found in the literature either as a near-synonym of *inerrant* or as an alternative to it. Note that the first definition of *inerrant* above cites *infallible* as a synonym. The same dictionary lists the following definitions of *infallible*:

1. Incapable of erring.
2. Incapable of failing; certain.
3. *Rom. Cath. Ch.* Incapable of error in expounding doctrine on faith or morals.[9]

The third definition is similar to what we earlier called *limited inerrancy*, and of course in the Roman Catholic context it applies both to Scripture and to the *ex cathedra* deliverances of the pope. But what is interesting here for our purposes is the word *incapable* in all three definitions. *Infallible* is what philosophers call a modal term, as indicated by its *-ible* ending. It deals not merely with the presence of error, but with the *capability*, the *possibility* of error.

5. 3rd ed. (Boston and New York: Houghton Mifflin Co., 2000), 695.
6. Ibid.
7. Ibid.
8. I think, too, that it is a misunderstanding to bring the word *literal* into the sphere of inerrancy. Inerrancy is a belief about the truth of a document, not about the interpretation of it. I think Orr's definition makes the same mistake.
9. *American Heritage College Dictionary*, 695.

Since *inerrant* is not a modal term in the same way, it is most natural to say that *infallible* is a *stronger* term than *inerrant*. To say that a text is inerrant is to say that there are no errors in it. To say that a text is infallible is to say that there *can be* no errors in it, that it is *impossible* for that text to contain errors. So it is rather perplexing, I would say, and lexically irresponsible, for theologians such as Rogers and McKim to urge the use of *infallible* as a *weaker* term than *inerrant*, or to say that an infallible text (as opposed to an inerrant text) may have errors in it.[10]

The dictionary suggests that distinction by the difference between the second definition of *inerrant* and the first two definitions of *infallible*. It somewhat compromises the distinction, however, when in the first definition of *inerrant* it makes it a synonym of *infallible*. That shows us, of course, that language is not a precise instrument, that words and concepts shade off into each other. *Inerrant* does not have to have a modal ending to serve as a modal term and therefore as a synonym for *infallible* in some contexts.

I do think, however, that our brief lexical study justifies the following usage: *inerrant* means, simply, "without error." *Infallible* denies the *possibility* of error. In those senses (though certainly not in Orr's), I would say that Scripture is both inerrant and infallible. It is inerrant because it is infallible. There are no errors because there *can be* no errors in the divine speech.

This conclusion follows from our previous discussions of God's personal words, particularly his words to us in human words. In chapter 1, I proposed a thought-experiment in which we imagined God speaking to us face-to-face. In that direct encounter, it would have been unthinkable for any of us to accuse God of error or wrongdoing. We would recognize that God spoke with absolute authority (the right to impose obligation on his hearers).

Error arises from two sources: deceit and ignorance. Deceit is intentional error, lying. Ignorance may lead to unintentional error. But God does not lie (Num. 23:19; 2 Tim. 2:13; Titus 1:2; Heb. 6:18), and he is ignorant of nothing (Ps. 33:13–15; Heb. 4:12–13). If Scripture is his Word, therefore, it contains no errors. It is inerrant.

Some have objected that this is a conclusion from a deductive argument, rather than an explicit statement of Scripture. True. But (1) the term *inerrant* is not found in the English Bible itself, so any conclusion about it, affirmative or negative, must of necessity be determined by implication from the actual language of Scripture. (2) Theology inevitably engages in logical deduction because its mandate is not just to repeat the biblical language, but to apply that language to questions and situations not

---

10. Rogers and McKim's concept of infallibility does correspond somewhat with the third dictionary definition of *infallible*, which it identifies as specific to the Roman Catholic Church.

explicitly mentioned in Scripture.[11] All use of Scripture to define doctrine engages in logical deduction. (3) There are also many explicit statements of Scripture that are relevant to the question before us.

To elaborate on (3): Scripture says in a number of places that God's word is true, or truth. He is a God of truth. He desires truth in the inward being (Ps. 51:6). His word is the word of truth (119:43, 160). His law is true (119:142, 151). Jesus prays for his disciples, "Sanctify them in the truth; your word is truth" (John 17:17). Paul says:

> Let God be true though every one were a liar, as it is written, "That you may be justified in your words, and prevail when you are judged." (Rom. 3:4, quoting Ps. 51:4)

Paul's statement brings us back to our thought-experiment. If there is any disagreement between God's words and our own ideas, his must prevail. And if we should be so arrogant as to judge what he says, he must prevail in that judgment.

True and *truth* have several meanings in Scripture: (1) metaphysical truth, what is complete and ultimate (as John 17:3); (2) propositional truth, language that correctly states what is the case (e.g., Deut. 17:4; 1 Kings 10:6; Eph. 4:24); (3) ethical truth, the light by which we walk (1 John 1:6; 2:4; 2 John 4).[12] God is truth in all these senses. Our present concern is mainly with (2). What God says is reliable, correct, and accurate, so that we can always trust what he says to us.

In my definitions presented earlier, *inerrancy* simply means "truth," in the propositional sense.[13] I could wish that we could be done with all the

---

11. For a defense of the concept of theology as the application of Scripture to all areas of human life, see *DKG*, 76–85, 93–98. Cf. also chap. 37 of this volume. I have also defended the use of logical deduction in theology in *DKG*, 242–60, taking account of the limitations of logic when practiced by human beings. The WCF says that logical deductions from Scripture are part of the authoritative teaching of Scripture: "The whole counsel of God concerning all things necessary for His own glory, man's salvation, faith and life, is either expressly set down in Scripture, or by good and necessary consequence may be deduced from Scripture" (1.6).

12. For a longer discussion of truth as it applies to God, see *DG*, 475–79.

13. In chapter 24, toward the end, I indicated that Scripture employs many types of speech: questions, imperatives, promises, propositions, and others. Propositions are assertions of fact. In one sense, then, Scripture incorporates many kinds of language other than propositions. Propositional language is only one of many aspects of biblical revelation. But remember that to know what propositional information God is revealing to us, we must consult the whole Bible. In that sense, the whole Bible is propositional. That is to say, in terms of chapter 24, propositional truth is both a single aspect of Scripture and a perspective on the whole Bible. Now, inerrancy is a quality of propositions. So in one sense it pertains to only one aspect of Scripture; in another sense it pertains to the whole. It is possible to put too great a stress on inerrancy, neglecting the authority of the Bible's nonpropositional

extrabiblical technical terms such as *infallible* and *inerrant* and simply say that the Bible is true. But in the contexts of historical and contemporary theological discussion, that alternative is not open to us. Theologians are too inclined to distort the word *truth* into some big theological construc‐ tion that has nothing to do with simple propositional correctness. As we have seen, there are several ways in which *truth* is used in Scripture, and in John 14:6 it is a title of Christ himself. Theologians have taken license from these facts to ignore or deny the more common propositional use of the term, or its relevance to the doctrine of the word of God.

So it seems that to express what we want to say, we must choose another term instead of (or as a supplement to) *truth*. *Infallibility* is a good term, as we have seen, arguably stronger than mere *truth*, for it denies the very possibility of untruth. It also has the advantage of a historical usage going back to the Protestant Reformation. But as we have seen, such writers as Rogers and McKim have hijacked *infallibility* also, going against responsible lexical usage to turn it into a *weaker* term than either *truth* or *inerrancy*.

So although I still prefer the word *truth*, I will hold on to *inerrancy* as an alternative, along with the adjective *infallible*, not to mention *reliable*, *accurate*, *correct*, and others, so there can be no doubt as to the view I am defending, the view that Scripture teaches and the church has affirmed until the advent of seventeenth‐century rationalistic theology.

The word *inerrancy* does have a certain disadvantage, however, suggested by Orr's rather extreme distortion of its lexical meaning. The word has come to suggest to many the idea of precision, rather than its lexical mean‐ ing of mere truth. Now, *precision* and *truth* are not synonyms, though they do overlap in meaning. A certain amount of precision is often required for truth, but that amount varies from one context to another. In mathematics and science, truth often requires considerable precision. If a student says that 6 + 5 = 10, he has not told the truth. He has committed an error. If a scientist makes a measurement varying by .0004 cm of an actual length, he may describe that as an *error*, as in the phrase *margin of error*.

But outside of science and mathematics, *truth* and *precision* are often much more distinct. If you ask someone's age, the person's conventional response (at least if the questioner is entitled to such information!) is to tell how old he was on his most recent birthday. But this is, of course, imprecise. It would be precise to tell one's age down to the day, hour, min‐ ute, and second.[14] But would that convey more *truth*? And if one fails to

---

language. But of course, in our time, the danger is largely on the other side: of denying or neglecting inerrancy.

14. Even that would be somewhat imprecise. What of milliseconds and nanoseconds? Of course, when one tries to give his age that precisely, he finds that his age has changed

give that much precision, has he made an error? I think not, as we use the terms *truth* and *error* in ordinary language. If someone seeks to tell his age down to the second, we usually say that he has told us more than we want to know. The question "What is your age?" does not demand that level of precision. Indeed, when someone gives excess information in an attempt to be more precise, he actually frustrates the process of communication, hindering rather than communicating truth. He buries his real age under a torrent of irrelevant words.

Similarly, when I stand before a class and a student asks me how large a textbook is, say that I reply, "400 pages," but the actual length is 398. Have I committed an error, or told the truth? I think the latter, for the following reasons: (1) In context, nobody expects more precision than I have given in my answer. I have met all the legitimate demands of the questioner. (2) 400, in this example, actually conveys more truth than 398 would have. Most likely, 398 would leave the student with the impression of some number around 300, but 400 presents the size of the book more accurately.[15]

So the relation between precision and error is more complicated than many writers suggest. "What is an error?" seems like a very straightforward question, as if errors were always perfectly easy to identify once we know the facts. But actually, identifying an error requires some understanding of the linguistic context, and that in turn requires an understanding of the cultural context.[16] A child who says in his math class that $6 + 5 = 10$ may not expect the same tolerance as a person who gives a rough estimate of his age or a professor who exaggerates the size of a book by two pages.

We should always remember that Scripture is, for the most part,[17] ordinary language rather than technical language.[18] Certainly, it is not of the

---

before he gets the words out of his mouth! So in this case, absolute precision is impossible *in principle.*

15. Grocery and department stores often take advantage of this psychological quirk in their shoppers, by pricing goods at $3.98, for example, rather than $4.00. The first digit of the number makes a far greater impression than the others. To encourage shoppers to buy, the stores keep that digit as low as possible. It may be too much to call this practice deception, but the plausibility of that charge indicates the extent to which precision can actually detract from truth.

16. In debates about Scripture, those who oppose inerrancy often charge those who defend it with ignorance of culture and the dynamics of language. In this case, however, the shoe is clearly on the other foot.

17. I qualify this statement merely out of abstract scholarly caution, not because I have any actual exceptions in mind.

18. It is interesting that liberals often complain that conservatives read the Bible as a "textbook of science," imagining it to address the technical issues of modern life. Sometimes that sort of criticism is fair. But both parties should recognize that it is the genius of the inerrantist position to see the Bible as *ordinary* language, subject to *ordinary,* not technical,

modern scientific genre. In Scripture, God intends to speak to everybody. To do that most efficiently, he (through the human writers) engages in all the shortcuts that we commonly use among ourselves to facilitate conversation: imprecisions, metaphors, hyperbole, parables, and so forth. Not all of these convey *literal* truth, or truth with a precision expected in specialized contexts; but they all convey truth, and in the Bible there is no reason to charge them with error.

Inerrancy, therefore, means that the Bible is true, not that it is maximally precise. To the extent that precision is necessary for truth, the Bible is sufficiently precise. But it does not always have the amount of precision that some readers demand of it. It has a level of precision sufficient for its own purposes, not for the purposes for which some readers might employ it.

It is helpful to consider that propositional language makes *claims* on its hearers. When I say that the book is on the table, I am claiming that in fact the book is there. If you look, you will find it, precisely there. But if I say that I am age twenty-four (do I wish!), I am not claiming that I am precisely twenty-four. I am claiming, rather, that I became twenty-four on my last birthday. And if I say, as in the previous example, that there are 400 pages in a textbook, I am not claiming that the book contains precisely that number of pages, only that the number 400 gives a pretty reliable estimate of the size of the book. Of course, if I worked for a publisher, and gave him an estimate of the size of the book that was two pages off, I could cost him a lot of money and myself a job. In that context, my imprecision would certainly be called an error. But in the illustration of the professor's making an estimate before his class, it would have been inappropriate to say that he was in error. Even though I use the same language in the two situations, I am making a different claim in the first situation from the claim I make in the second. And so the amount of precision demanded and expected in one case is different from what is demanded and expected in the other. In the one case I have made an error, in the other case not.

A claim in this sense can be explicit or implicit. If someone asks me to quote a Bible passage, and I say, "This is inexact," I am making an *explicit* claim, namely, "I will give you the gist of it, but not the exact words." But of course, it is rare in language for someone to make his claims explicit in that way. When a person gives his age, he rarely says, "I am giving you an approximate figure." Rather, he simply accepts the custom of approximating one's age by the last birthday, assuming that people will understand that custom and will not be misled into thinking that his answer is absolutely

---

standards of truth. So here, as in the "ignorance of culture" charge mentioned in a previous note, the shoe is on the other foot. For another example of anti-inerrantists' using the Bible as a "textbook of science," see chapter 28, "Bible Problems."

precise. In following this custom, people understand that he is making an *implicit* claim.

So in reading the Bible, it is important to know enough about the language and culture of the people to know what claims the original characters and writers were likely making. When Jesus tells parables, he does not always say explicitly that his words are parabolic. But his audience understood what he was doing, and we should as well. A parable does not claim historical accuracy, but it claims to set forth a significant truth by means of a likely nonhistorical narrative.

So I think it is helpful to define *inerrancy* more precisely [!] by saying that *inerrant language makes good on its claims*. When we say that the Bible is inerrant, we mean that the Bible makes good on its claims.

Now, many writers have enumerated what are sometimes called qualifications to inerrancy: inerrancy is compatible with unrefined grammar, nonchronological narrative, round numbers, imprecise quotations, prescientific phenomenalistic description (e.g., "the sun rose"), use of figures and symbols, and imprecise descriptions (as Mark 1:5, which says that everyone from Judea and Jerusalem went to hear John the Baptist). I agree with these points, but I do not describe them as "qualifications" of inerrancy. These are merely applications of the basic meaning of inerrancy: that it asserts truth, not precision. Inerrant language is language that makes good on its own claims, not on claims that are made for it by thoughtless readers.

Take "unrefined grammar" as an example. In natural languages, there are many variations in grammar, style, and accent. Grammarians tend to elevate one group of variations as a standard. So the predominant speech in Berlin is considered to be "good German." The predominant speech of Amsterdam is "good Dutch," and so on.[19] There may be some value in this as a means of encouraging uniformity of language in public writing and speech. But it is somewhat arbitrary. We need to remember that it comes from human grammarians, not from divine revelation. No divine norm requires us to speak in what grammarians may describe as "good" language. God never tells us to speak the language of the academic elite, or to disparage variations from that language as "errors."

The NT itself is written not in the literary Greek of Thucydides and Plato, but in Koine Greek, the language of the people. Within the NT, some writers, such as Luke and the writer to the Hebrews, excel others in the impressiveness of their literary style. But Scripture never claims to be written in the most impressive language, or even in perfect grammar. What

19. One suspects, however, that such "good speech" is often determined by the speech on university campuses, where the grammarians themselves feel most at home.

it claims is *truth.* And truth can be expressed in any dialect. In English, "I ain't goin'" is considered less proper than "I am not going." But the meaning of both phrases is clear. They say the same thing, and they can both express truth.

People sometimes think that if Scripture is the Word of God, it must be written in the most elevated language, language worthy of God. Can we imagine God speaking anything less than the King's English? But that is a misunderstanding. God's intent is to speak to ordinary people. He "accommodates," as John Calvin put it; he "lisps" to us.[20] So he speaks both in the elevated language of Luke the physician and in the simpler language of the fisherman Peter. If they or anyone else uses poor grammar in the judgment of modern linguists, that fact has no bearing on the Bible's inerrancy.

Consider nonchronological narrative. In modern historical writing, we assume that the author is portraying events in chronological order, unless he says otherwise, or unless there is some kind of novelistic intent. But (1) the historical portions of Scripture (chiefly Genesis–Esther and the four Gospels) are not academic histories in the modern sense. Their purpose is to narrate the acts of God to redeem his people. (2) The Bible makes no *claim* to tell all these events in a precise chronological order. Sometimes there is such a claim for a specific group of events: for example, in Matthew 8:1, we read, "When [Jesus] came down from the mountain, great crowds followed him." This passage does make the claim that Jesus taught on the mountain, and that the crowds followed him afterward. But more often there is no such claim.

Nor does Scripture usually claim that its accounts of people's words are verbatim.[21] In ordinary language we often paraphrase the words of a speaker. Usually people understand that we are doing this so that we don't need to claim explicitly that our citation is imprecise. Of course, in scholarly articles, quotations of the words of others require quotation marks or indentation, footnoting, and/or bibliographical documentation. These indications constitute, among other things, an affirmation that our quotations are precise. But these conventions did not exist in the biblical period. In the original manuscripts of Scripture, there are no quotation marks; there is no apparatus for formal documentation. When Jesus

---

20. Accommodation does not mean, as some have claimed, that God speaks error to us. Rather, it means that he speaks truth in such a way that we can understand it, insofar as it can be understood by human beings. Theologians often compare divine accommodation to a parent's accommodation to his young children. But a wise parent, while choosing simple language to use with his children, does not lie to them.

21. One exception is Galatians 3:16, in which Paul makes an interpretative point depending on the singular form of "seed" (ESV "offspring") in Genesis 22:18.

quotes Moses, there is usually no reason to expect that his quotation will be precise. In ordinary language it is perfectly proper to give the gist of someone's words without precision, or even to alter the quotation to bring out something that might otherwise be ignored. And Scripture, again, is ordinary language.

I conclude that Scripture is inerrant because the personal word of God cannot be anything other than true. When he gives us propositional information—and he certainly does—that information is reliable, though expressed in ordinary, not technical, language. The written Word, further, is just as inerrant as the oral message of the prophets and apostles. And their word is just as inerrant as the divine voice itself.[22]

22. For critical interaction with other views of biblical inerrancy within evangelicalism, see my reviews of books by Peter Enns, N. T. Wright, and Andrew McGowan, Appendices J, K, and L in this volume.

CHAPTER 27

The Phenomena of Scripture

The view that Scripture is inerrant has two major objections. The first is that this view misunderstands the *purpose* of Scripture. The second is that it is inconsistent with the *phenomena* of Scripture.

Concerning Scripture's purpose, many have argued that Scripture is written to tell us of salvation, not about matters of history, geography, science, and so on. I addressed that objection somewhat in chapters 24 and 25 when we discussed the content of Scripture, and I will discuss it further in chapter 31.

To review and amplify:

1. Scripture does not distinguish in any general way between the sacred and the secular, between matters of salvation and mere worldly matters.
2. Scripture speaks not only of salvation, but also of the nature of God, creation, and providence as the presuppositions of salvation. But these deal with everything in the world and with all areas of human life. So Scripture makes assertions not only about salvation narrowly considered, but about the nature of the universe.
3. The salvation that Scripture talks about is a comprehensive renewal of human life, extending to every aspect of human life and thought. So no area of human life is beyond the concern of Scripture.
4. The salvation that Scripture speaks of took place in the space-time world. The atonement and resurrection of Jesus are events of real history, which occurred in a real time and place. Our

understanding of history, geography, and science must be consistent with this narrative, and with its OT prehistory.

5. Scripture is God's personal word to us. As we are confronted by that personal word, it is not our place to pick and choose the areas concerning which God may address us authoritatively. After he speaks to us, we may discern, in a general way, the subject matter that he has chosen to address. But that understanding does not give us the right to limit his speech to that subject matter or to assume that every other word of God must deal with the same subject.

For these reasons, it is not possible to draw a sharp line between one area (matters of salvation) about which Scripture speaks inerrantly and another area (the secular world) in regard to which it may err.

The other objection concerns the *phenomena* of Scripture. Phenomena are appearances, the way things look to us. Immanuel Kant distinguished between the phenomena, appearances, and the *noumena*, the world as it really is, apart from our experience. Now, when many readers look at Scripture, it *appears* to them to contain errors. So many writers have urged that we should not derive our doctrine of Scripture merely from its teachings about itself, but that we should take into account the phenomena. And if we take the phenomena seriously, they tell us, we will not be able to conclude that Scripture is inerrant. This approach is sometimes called an *inductive* approach, as opposed to the *deductive* approach presented in chapter 26, which derives inerrancy as a conclusion from Scripture's teaching about itself.

I believe the inductive method, so described, is a faulty method for determining the character of Scripture. Of course, Scripture contains "difficulties," problems, apparent errors. But what role should these play in our formulation of the doctrine of Scripture? It is important to remember that *all* doctrines of the Christian faith are beset by problems. The doctrine of God's sovereignty seems in the view of many readers to conflict with the responsibility of human beings, and that apparent contradiction has led to many theological battles. The doctrine of the Trinity says that God is both three and one, and the relation between his threeness and his oneness is not easy to put into words. When speaking of Christ, we face the paradox that he is both God and man, both eternal and temporal, both omniscient and limited in his knowledge. Would anyone argue that because of these problems we should not confess that God is sovereign, that man is responsible, that God is three and one, that Jesus is divine and human?

The very nature of Christian faith is to believe God's Word *despite* the existence of unresolved difficulties. When God told Abraham that he and his wife Sarah would have a child, that promise was beset by difficulty. How could a man father a child when he was over a hundred? How could a woman bear a child when she was far past the age of childbearing? From a human point of view (even in the time of Abraham), the fulfillment of such a promise seemed highly improbable. But Romans 4:19–21 says this:

> He did not weaken in faith when he considered his own body, which was as good as dead (since he was about a hundred years old), or when he considered the barrenness of Sarah's womb. No distrust made him waver concerning the promise of God, but he grew strong in his faith as he gave glory to God, fully convinced that God was able to do what he had promised.

Abraham did not weigh God's word over against the problems and conclude that God's promise could not be fulfilled. Nor did he withhold judgment, waiting for the problems to be solved before he would make a commitment. Nor did he even think that the problems decreased the *probability* of God's word being fulfilled. He did not distrust at all, despite the difficulties. He grew strong in faith and gave glory to God. He was "fully convinced." And verse 22 continues, "That is why his faith was 'counted to him as righteousness.'" Paul tells us about Abraham's faith as a model for our own.[1] We, too, ought to trust God's promise, despite the difficulties.

So the proper method in theology is not to withhold judgment until the problems are solved. It is rather to believe God's personal word, despite the problems. We will never solve all the problems in this life. So we live by faith, not by sight. That must also be our attitude when we seek to formulate the doctrine of Scripture. When we say that Scripture is inerrant, we encounter many problems. But Scripture's claim to inerrancy is entirely clear; it is not in doubt. It is God's personal word to us. We must believe it, despite what we may be tempted to believe through an inductive examination of the phenomena.

The situation would be different if Scripture's claim were itself uncertain. If Scripture's claim to be the Word of God were itself problematic, and then we discovered from the phenomena that the biblical text is full of unsolved problems, we might well reconsider our initial assumption. But as we have seen, no one can fairly doubt that Scripture *claims* to be God's written Word. On nearly every page of Scripture, we learn that God speaks personal words to his people, words of highest authority, words that we need for our eternal salvation and our life here on earth. And we learn that

---

1. Abraham's faith was not perfect, as is evident in Genesis 12:10–20; 16:1–4; and 20:1–18. But he did not doubt God's promise that he and Sarah would have a son, or that God would preserve the son's life (Gen. 22:1–19).

that Word takes written form, for it is God's intention to rule his church by means of a book. Given the pervasiveness of this biblical teaching, we cannot question it on the basis of problems found in the phenomena.

This is not to say at all that we should ignore the phenomena, or even that we may do so. To ignore the phenomena would be to ignore the Word itself. God calls us to meditate on his Word (Ps. 1:2) and to live by every word of it (Deut. 8:3; Matt. 4:4). As we enter into a deep study of God's Word, we must investigate the problems. For when we have a problem, it means that our understanding is incomplete. We must think about the problems and solve them, if possible, for our own edification and that of those we teach.

In dealing with problems, however, we must not revert to intellectual autonomy (recall chaps. 3–7), assuming that human reason serves as the final criterion of truth. Rather, we should study the problems in faith, presupposing that God is real and that he has given us his personal words in Scripture. His Word, not our own wisdom, is to be our ultimate standard. That is true of all our activities, so it is certainly true of the study of Scripture itself.

And we must not demand that all problems be solved before we receive Scripture in faith. As we have seen in the case of Abraham, that is not how Christian faith works. In Christian faith, the Word of God determines how we should look at problems.

Once we come to faith, problems look different. Problems test our faith, but they do not carry anywhere near the weight of God's self-witness. That was true for Abraham, even though he had only a few individual encounters with God. We have had far more than that: three thousand years of history in which God has spoken to his people and attested his word (by divine voice, prophetic-apostolic proclamation, and written Word, and of course through his Son Jesus Christ) as true. Those revelations have led to the formation of a Christian way of thinking, a Christian mind. To that mind, attacks on Scripture are never credible because they must overcome a vast weight of God's own testimony.

We have problems with Scripture for two reasons: finitude and sin. Because of our finitude, we have problems understanding the vast depths of God's nature and actions: how he can be both one and three, how he can be eternal and yet enter history, how he can be good and yet permit evil, how he can be sovereign and yet hold us responsible for what we do.

Our finitude also bars us from an exhaustive knowledge of God's world, of the course of nature and history. It is difficult for us to understand cultures such as those described in the Bible, far removed from ours in space and time. It is not easy for us to understand the social working of tribal and monarchical cultures, the customs underlying biblical stories, the nature of biblical poetry, the ways in which the meaning of texts is affected by literary practices.

When we deal with Bible problems, then, it is important for us to be aware of these limitations, that is, to read humbly. When we are faced with a problem, it is no dishonor to say, "I don't know how this can be resolved." Scientists do that all the time, when they encounter a phenomenon that seems to run contrary to a theory they believe. When the evidence for the theory is otherwise substantial, the scientist rightly assumes that the phenomenon can *somehow* be reconciled to the theory, even if he doesn't know how that will happen.

The other reason why we have problems with Scripture is sin. Romans 1, as we have seen, tells us that sinners "repress" the truth of God's clear natural revelation, exchanging it for a lie. They do the same with Scripture, until or unless the Spirit causes a radical change in their outlook (Luke 24:25; John 5:37–40; 2 Cor. 3:14). Because of the Spirit, believers have the means to overcome the sinful distortion of Scripture. But we are not sinlessly perfect in this life, and we are subject every day to Satan's temptation. Satan tempts us to unbelief as well as wrong behavior. Indeed, unbelief *is* wrong behavior.

So sometimes believers think like unbelievers. Often believers will ascribe authority to liberal scholarship—scholarship committed, as we have seen, to read the Bible like any human book. Such scholarship regularly assumes that the biblical worldview *cannot* be true: that miracles cannot occur, that predictive prophecy is impossible, that God cannot speak words and sentences to human beings.

The would-be autonomous kind of scholarship is often arrogant in its claims. In the past, such scholars have often spoken of the "assured results of modern scholarship." One does not hear that phrase so much these days; most all these "assured results" have been questioned. But one stands amazed at how easily modern scholars can claim that this portion of a verse in Genesis must have been written by a different author from that one, or that this sentence ascribed to Jesus in one of the Gospels must have originated in a setting different from that set forth in the Gospel itself. In reply to Rudolf Bultmann's claim that the personality of Jesus was unimportant to Paul and John, C. S. Lewis, himself a scholar of ancient literature, replies:

> Through what strange process has this learned German gone in order to make himself blind to what all men except him see?[2]

2. C. S. Lewis, "Modern Theology and Biblical Criticism," in *Christian Reflections*, ed. Walter Hooper (Grand Rapids: Eerdmans, 1967), 156.

And then:

> These men ask me to believe that they can read between the lines of the old texts; the evidence is their obvious inability to read (in any sense worth discussing) the lines themselves. They claim to see fern-seed and can't see an elephant ten yards away in broad daylight.[3]

The difference between liberal Bible critics and believing Christians is not merely academic, a difference in point of view; nor is it merely a difference in presupposition (though it is certainly that). It is a moral difference. The liberal reads the text with an incredibly exalted view of his own competence to understand ancient cultures and writers in finest detail. Christians should remember that our faith divides us from the liberal tradition in the most profound way. We are often tempted to reply to their arrogance with more arrogance. We should avoid that temptation, by God's grace. Often, as we will see, this means that we respond to Bible problems with an honest "I don't know."

3. Ibid., 157.

CHAPTER 28

Bible Problems

A great many writers have dealt with specific difficulties in the Bible, difficulties that some have claimed imply the existence of errors in Scripture. There are many such difficulties. Norman L. Geisler and Thomas A. Howe believe that their book *When Critics Ask*[1] gives "answers to all the major questions ever raised about the Bible—over 800 in all."[2] Whether or not that number is entirely accurate, clearly there are too many of these questions to be discussed in the present volume. My book is primarily a *doctrine* of the word of God and Scripture, a systematic theological treatment of the subject. My interest is in what Scripture teaches about itself. Typically in books such as this one, there is not much discussion of specific Bible difficulties, if any. Still, readers ought to receive some guidance in how to deal with such problems. I will try to provide that here—based, of course, on the doctrinal and epistemological foundation I have laid in earlier chapters.[3]

First, however, we should be aware that Bible difficulties are not a recent discovery. Many of these were known to the early church fathers. In approximately A.D. 178, the Platonist philosopher Celsus wrote *True Discourse*, a critique of Christianity. The Christian writer Origen (185–254) replied at length in *Against Celsus*. He deals there with many of the same

1. Wheaton, IL: Victor Books, 1992.
2. Ibid., 10. On page 605, the authors include a bibliography of fourteen other books devoted to the discussion of specific Bible difficulties.
3. See also my reviews of books by Peter Enns, N. T. Wright, and Andrew McGowan, Appendices J, K, and L in this volume.

Bible difficulties that are with us today. Today, the body of literature on Bible difficulties is huge. My impression is that for every problem raised by critics of the Bible, at least three solutions have been proposed by Christian theologians, Bible scholars, and apologists. So no one should assume that Christian thinkers have been stymied by any of these questions. Not all of their solutions have been plausible, but many are, in my judgment.

Our faith does not depend on our ability to solve any of these problems. As I indicated in the last chapter, it is perfectly legitimate to set unsolved problems aside, given that the positive evidence for the truth of Scripture is enormous. But it is reassuring to know that there are *possible* solutions, at least, for most every Bible problem.

Evangelical writers have often said that although there are many Bible difficulties, nobody has ever *proved* the existence of a single error. This is true. It takes only a *possible* solution to a problem to refute the dogmatic assertion that there is *no* solution, that is, that the problem amounts to an error. But more profoundly: no problem has such weight as to overturn the fundamental premise of Christian epistemology: that the Bible is God's permanent personal word, given to us to be believed and obeyed.

In the rest of this chapter, I will list the general types of Bible problems and some resources for dealing with them.

THEOLOGICAL PROBLEMS

These include such problems as reconciling God's oneness with his tripersonality, God's sovereignty with human responsibility, God's goodness and omnipotence with the existence of evil, God's eternity with his revelation in time, Adam's original goodness and his fall into sin, Jesus' deity and humanity, individual responsibility and the role of substitutionary sacrifice for sin. Most every systematic theology deals with these.[4]

In these areas we are especially confronted with mystery. Although the Bible tells us a great deal about these matters, there is much that it doesn't say, and much more that we don't understand. We should not expect to have anything like an exhaustive understanding of the nature of God, his eternal plan, and his actions in history. We should certainly expect that when God reveals himself, we will experience some residual bewilderment. When God meets with people in Scripture, they are typically overwhelmed by his greatness, not prone to analyzing him. Those who insist on precise

---

4. In my work, see especially *DG* and *SBL*.

answers to the problems noted above need to ask whether their attitude expresses an appropriate humility before their Creator and Lord.

Indeed, it would be most surprising if there were no such mysteries in God's revelation. Given God's nature, his majesty, and his transcendence, we cannot imagine that any of us could understand him exhaustively. A God who can be fully understood by human reason is not the God of the Bible.

But there is no ground for anyone to assert that these mysteries amount to error in Scripture.

The criticism of these doctrines is usually logical, the claim that these doctrines are self-contradictory: God, it is said, for example, cannot be both one and three, because that would mean that he is both one and not-one, a logical contradiction.

It may seem as though logical contradictions are easy to identify: any proposition that says X is A and not-A is contradictory. So to say that God is one and not-one is a contradiction. But logic (most any elementary logic text, at that) requires us to think harder. If someone says X is A, and then X is not-A, there is a contradiction only if in both assertions A is used in the same sense, at the same time, and in the same respect. "All men are mortal" and "Some men are not mortal" sound contradictory. But they are not contradictory unless *mortal* means the same thing in both sentences, at the same time, in the same respect. If *mortal* is used literally in one sentence, figuratively in the other, there is no contradiction.

Similarly, "God is one" does not contradict "God is not-one," in the church's Trinitarian confession. For in that confession, the church does not affirm and deny God's oneness in the same sense of oneness. We confess that God is one *substance* or *essence*, but three *persons*. There is no more contradiction here than if someone were to say that Abraham Lincoln had two arms, but only one heart.

The mystery enters when we start asking what is meant by *substance* and *person*. Theologians have proposed rough-and-ready definitions of these terms, but it is not perfectly plain how being a divine substance differs from being a divine person. Must there be precise definitions of these terms to refute the charge of contradiction? I would say not. To draw a parallel: If I say that I have two *bilbs*, but only one *glud*, there is mystery as to what I am saying, because we have no definitions of the italicized terms. But given that these terms can be defined acceptably, there is no reason to think the statement is contradictory. But if someone wants to show that it is, the burden of proof is on him.

Often when there is an appearance of contradiction, a more careful reading dispels that appearance. People often say that "God controls all things" contradicts "human beings are responsible." But that depends more precisely on what we mean by divine control and what we mean by human responsibility. Again, it is not perfectly easy to identify a logical contradiction. The same is true for all the other theological problems listed above.[5]

ETHICAL PROBLEMS

Criticisms of Scripture have been urged both against the ethical teachings of Scripture and against the actions of God and Bible characters. As for the actions of Bible characters, it should be remembered that Scripture does not endorse all the actions of the people it describes, even those with a reputation for holiness. Even the greatest people in the Bible, such as Noah, Abraham, Moses, and David, fell into grievous sin. This is only what we should expect, since Scripture teaches that "all have sinned and fall short of the glory of God" (Rom. 3:23).

The Bible teaches, of course, that God himself and Jesus Christ are sinless. Yet they, too, have received criticism. Some have asked how a God of love could send people to hell. Others have thought that Jesus was too self-centered, making eternal life depend on what people think of him. And many have taken issue with the ethical principles that God has set forth in Scripture.

A major problem with such arguments is that in the absence of a theistic foundation for ethics, ethical disagreement runs rampant in our society. People often fault the Bible for its condemnation of homosexuality, for example. But the argument gets pretty murky when someone asks why we should accept the views of modern society and reject those of Scripture. How do we determine what is right or wrong?

In the history of secular philosophy, there have been roughly three theories on how we should make ethical decisions.[6] In *existential* ethics, we judge by our inner subjectivity—feeling or conscience. But people have been able to justify even the worst atrocities by appeal to these. In *teleological* ethics, we make choices according to how much happiness they bring—to the individual or to society, the predominance of pleasure over pain. But such calculations have also led to atrocities, such as the trampling of a minority's rights so that a majority can be happier. In *deontological* ethics, people make decisions according to objective rules. But it is very difficult for one person to convince another what the objective rules are.

5. I have discussed the role of logic in more detail in *DKG*, 242–301.
6. For a fuller discussion, see *DCL*, 19–125.

In my judgment, the only basis for ethics is in the word of the absolute personal God of Scripture.[7] No impersonal principle has the ability, or the authority, to tell us what to do. Ethical conviction flows from loyalty to persons. Absolute ethical principle flows from a person who is absolute. And only in the Bible do we find a God who is truly absolute and truly personal at the same time.

But if the God of Scripture is the ultimate standard of human ethics, which he claims to be, then he is beyond criticism. He has given his personal words to us, and we dare not find fault with them. We may wrestle with how to *apply* them to this situation or that, but the principles themselves can be nothing less than law for us.

Sometimes when such questions arise, it is helpful if we try to better understand the reasons for God's behavior as he has revealed those in Scripture. For example, Scripture is not silent as to why a loving God would consign some to eternal punishment. For it also teaches that (1) God is a God of justice as well as love, (2) rebellion against the Creator of heaven and earth is a crime deserving the highest penalty, and (3) those who go to hell would not be happy in heaven, where all of life amounts to praise of God. But of course, those considerations don't answer the most fundamental question: why did God eternally plan that some would rebel against him and spend eternity without redemption? To that question, Paul can only reply, "Who are you, O man, to answer back to God?" (Rom. 9:20). When we get down to the most fundamental questions, we must choose between the mysterious wisdom of God's personal word and our own would-be autonomous thought. Only the former choice is appropriate to our covenant relationship with God.

FACTUAL PROBLEMS

Many Bible difficulties have to do with claims that the Bible is factually wrong about something. One writer has been known for opposing inerrancy by denying that the mustard seed is the smallest of all seeds, as Jesus appears to teach in Matthew 13:31–32. But in that passage Jesus is evidently referring to the seeds that Palestinian farmers sowed in their fields at the time. Certainly, nothing in the context necessitates a wider reference than that. And the mustard seed is, within that limited universe of discourse, the smallest seed.

7. I have argued this position in ibid., and in AGG, 89–118.

Many problems of this kind deal similarly with misinterpretations of biblical texts. Often the misinterpretation assumes that Scripture is making a universal statement when in fact it addresses only a narrow context. Recall again that Scripture generally speaks the way ordinary people speak, except when it deals with lofty mysteries. It is absurd to imagine that Jesus, in the parable of Matthew 13:31–32, was giving his hearers the conclusion of an exhaustive botanical taxonomy, and it is irresponsible to demand that we read the text in such a way.[8]

So the question of factual accuracy is tied into questions of interpretation. Often we think we can determine facts simply by looking and reporting. Often people refer to "brute facts" as a kind of final authority, facts that can supposedly be understood apart from any interpretation or context. But there are no such facts.[9]

Sometimes what people call "hard facts" or "brute facts" are the conclusions of various historical or scientific theories (see below for discussions of these). But whatever we may say about such assertions, a fact that needs to be buttressed by a very sophisticated theoretical framework does not deserve to be called a "brute fact."

Even worse is when the supposed fact is the result of a theory that at the outset rejects biblical authority—that is, a theory based on autonomous reasoning. For example, when Bible critics have denied that Jesus could actually walk on water, change water to wine, or rise from the dead, clearly their assertions assume that miracles cannot happen—an assumption that flatly contradicts the biblical worldview.

PROBLEMS OF FACTUAL CONSISTENCY

Many Bible problems stem from allegations that one factual assertion in Scripture contradicts another. The Bible, of course, is a large book, written by many authors. It would indeed be strong evidence for the supernatural inspiration of Scripture if all these authors were to be in perfect agreement. But Bible critics are often unwilling to concede such agreement.

8. One often hears the charge that believers in inerrancy read the Bible as a textbook of science. But certainly critics of inerrancy do the same in cases such as this one.

9. For a longer discussion of the relationship between fact and interpretation, see *DKG*, 71–73. After publication of Peter Enns' *Inspiration and Incarnation: Evangelicals and the Problem of the Old Testament* (Grand Rapids: Baker, 2005), someone invited me to sit on a panel dealing with how Christians should respond when the Bible conflicts with "hard facts." I was not able to accept that assignment for various reasons. But I've often wondered what the organizers of this panel would have thought if I had indicated my true position, that there is no such thing as a "hard fact."

On the other hand, if there were no *apparent* contradictions in Scripture's accounts of facts, critics would likely suspect collusion between the authors. So in a paradoxical way, the existence of such apparent contradictions is evidence of Scripture's truth.

But we need to get more specific. These issues typically arise in cases in which two biblical writers are dealing with the same fact or event. The four Gospel writers often discuss the same events from their different perspectives, and critics have pointed out places where their agreement is not obvious. Similar problems exist in the relationships between Kings and Chronicles in the OT, and also with regard to NT references to events in the OT.

To a large extent, questions of factual consistency are simply more complicated forms of the factual questions we discussed earlier, and they should be treated in the same way as the others. Each factual claim needs to be understood properly, with an understanding of its proper universe of discourse and its right interpretation, with an understanding of the flexibility of literary forms.

For example, Matthew (4:5–10) presents the wilderness temptations of Jesus in a different order from Luke (4:5–12). Matthew lists the temptation at the pinnacle of the temple as the second, while Luke places it third. Recall, however, from my discussion in chapter 26 that Scripture doesn't always list events in chronological order, as modern historical texts usually do. In this case, most likely Matthew records the temptations chronologically, while Luke rearranges them so as to build toward a climax in the pinnacle temptation. The terms by which Luke connects these events are less time-specific than those of Matthew.

Where logical consistency is in question, sometimes, as in my earlier discussion of theological problems, there must be discussion of the nature of logic. For example, Matthew 8:28–34 says that Jesus healed two demoniacs. But parallel passages, Mark 5:1–20 and Luke 8:26–39, mention only one. Some have claimed that these passages are factually contradictory. Many evangelical commentators, however, have replied to this objection with a simple logical point: if there were two, then there was one. There would have been a logical contradiction if Mark and Luke had added that Jesus healed *only* one and no more. But they say nothing to suggest such a thing.

Why would Mark and Luke neglect the second demoniac? There could have been any number of reasons. Perhaps they didn't know there were two, but Matthew learned of a second by additional testimony. Perhaps the one mentioned by Mark and Luke was more famous, or infamous: it was his healing that was really big news. But certainly nobody can say that there is no possible explanation for the difference. And if there is one possible explanation, then no one can say that these accounts are contradictory.

What if we cannot identify even one possible explanation? Even then, there is no way to prove that none exists. None of us was there, and it is impossible for us at our present distance to enumerate all the possible combinations of circumstances that led to the problem before us. Perhaps there is an explanation known only to God. One would have to prove that there is no such explanation in order to demonstrate that these two biblical accounts are contradictory.

So the question is this: in the face of *alleged* contradiction, whom do we believe? God, who addresses us with his personal word, or some Bible critic who believes, but cannot prove, that the text is contradictory? To those committed above all to obeying God's personal words, the answer to this question is obvious.

PROBLEMS OF QUOTATIONS AND REFERENCES

A particular area of concern in recent discussions has been the NT use of the OT. NT writers quote, refer to, and allude to the OT many times. Often these references are problematic. The OT passages do not always appear to justify their use by the NT writer.[10]

For example, Matthew, in 2:13–14, tells how Jesus and his parents escaped Herod's massacre of babies by fleeing to Egypt, then returning after Herod's death. Then in verse 15, Matthew adds:

> This was to fulfill what the Lord had spoken by the prophet, "Out of Egypt I called my son."

Here, Matthew quotes Hosea 11:1, which in its own context refers not to Jesus but to Israel's own deliverance from Egypt by the hand of God. Clearly, the event described in Matthew does not "fulfill" the Hosea passage in the straightforward way in which we often understand fulfillment. The Hosea passage is not a *prediction* of Jesus' return from Egypt. Indeed, Hosea's words are backward-looking rather than forward-looking. No clear reference is made there to a coming Messiah. So some are inclined to think that Matthew misuses the Hosea passage.

---

10. For a discussion that claims to treat all the quotations, allusions, and references to the OT in the NT, see G. K. Beale and D. A. Carson, *Commentary on the New Testament Use of the Old Testament* (Grand Rapids: Baker Academic, 2007). These authors believe that in every case the NT reference reflects a proper reading of the OT material.

But the word *fulfill* (*pleroo*) means "to fill, make full, complete." Fulfillments in Scripture are not limited to predictions that come true. In Matthew 3:15, Jesus says that the purpose of his baptism by John was to "fulfill all righteousness." Jesus undergoes baptism, even though he needs no repentance, because in God's sight it is the right thing to do. There is here no prediction to be fulfilled in a current event. In Matthew 5:17, Jesus says that he has not come to abolish the Law and the Prophets, but to "fulfill" them. Scholars have argued about the meaning of this, but certainly Jesus is not saying that the Law and the Prophets are a kind of prediction that comes true in his ministry.

I think that "fulfill" in many passages has the force of *illumine* or, more generally, *reflect* or *fit together with*. In Matthew's quotation of Hosea 11:1, he is saying that just as God delivered Israel from Egypt, so it is fully appropriate that God should deliver Jesus, the new Israel and the true Israel, from Egypt. The life of Jesus at crucial points mirrors the experience of Israel.

Of course, in many cases, the fulfillment of OT Scripture, especially prophecy, is the coming true of a prediction. When Matthew 12:17–21 cites Jesus' fulfillment of Isaiah 42:1–3, the passages are related as prediction and fulfillment. Matthew 8:17, which says that Jesus' healings fulfill Isaiah 53:4, is something of an intermediate case. Isaiah is speaking of the Messiah as having "borne our griefs and carried our sorrows," which might be understood to include his healing ministry, but its main thrust is to the overall redemptive work of the Messiah. It is not specifically a prediction that the Messiah will heal people's diseases, but it implies more generally that the Messiah's redeeming work will deal with our diseases and sorrows.

We can see, then, that the idea of fulfillment in Matthew (and I think more generally) covers a number of different relationships between prophecy and the work of Christ. There is no reason to think that Matthew's quotations of the OT are inappropriate. Indeed, they are illuminating. Jesus reflects the OT messianic expectations in a great many ways—indeed, in every way.

To note a somewhat different kind of example, consider Paul's use in Galatians 4:21–31 of the Hagar story (Gen. 16). Paul says:

> Now this may be interpreted allegorically: these women are two covenants. One is from Mount Sinai, bearing children for slavery; she is Hagar. Now Hagar is Mount Sinai in Arabia; she corresponds to the present Jerusalem, for she is in slavery with her children. But the Jerusalem above is free, and she is our mother. For it is written, "Rejoice, O barren one who does not bear; break forth and cry

aloud, you who are not in labor! For the children of the desolate one will be more than those of the one who has a husband." Now you, brothers, like Isaac, are children of promise. But just as at that time he who was born according to the flesh persecuted him who was born according to the Spirit, so also it is now. But what does the Scripture say? "Cast out the slave woman and her son, for the son of the slave woman shall not inherit with the son of the free woman." So, brothers, we are not children of the slave but of the free woman.

Generally, Protestants have condemned allegorical interpretations; but in this case Paul presents one. And most likely Moses, writing Genesis, never thought that Hagar in any sense "corresponds to" the Jerusalem of Paul's day. Is Paul imposing an interpretation on Genesis 16 that the passage will not bear?

I think not. Paul is not claiming to reproduce the original meaning of the Genesis passage, or the meaning it may have had for its original readers, or even the meaning it had in the mind of its human author. Rather, he is drawing a parallel, a "correspondence." Hagar is *similar* in significant ways to the Judaism of Paul's day, and Isaac to the Christians. Paul is saying to the Jews, physically sons of Isaac, that they really are more like Ishmael (son of Hagar) than like Isaac because they are slaves to the old order. The comparison is bold, highly offensive to some Jewish readers, but it is *appropriate*. It is similar to what a pastor does when he tells his congregation that they are like Moses, or David, or Peter.

There is much discussion today about what principles governed the NT writers in their use of the OT. Peter Enns argues that the NT writers are influenced by the interpretative methods of second-temple Judaism, methods that sometimes lead to wrong conclusions (though Enns hesitates to say that these methods actually led the NT writers to false conclusions).[11] I would not deny that second-temple interpretative methods influenced NT writers to some extent, though I doubt that any of these writers self-consciously followed a particular method of interpretation. The doctrines of inspiration and inerrancy, however, rule out the idea that the NT writers are guilty of false, inappropriate citations.

Yet I think it important to recognize that there are many reasons for citing texts, many edifying purposes to be served. The OT is valuable in many ways, not just as a book of predictions. Many OT passages are suitable also as illustrations (even allegorical ones), as pictures of NT realities, and as divine laws to be obeyed.

11. Enns, *Inspiration and Incarnation*, 113–65.

Though Enns rejects this possibility,[12] I think the term that best summarizes the many ways in which the NT writers cite the OT is the term *application*. That term includes citations to show the fulfillment of predictions, to show similarity between New and Old Testament narratives, to draw allegorical illustrations, and many others. A citation is legitimate if it is a legitimate *application* of the OT text.

HISTORICAL PROBLEMS

As I have indicated in earlier chapters, history is an important element of Scripture. Biblical religion is based on events that have taken place in space and time. It is not merely a set of timeless truths or an abstract philosophy. So it is important that God's words to us be historically accurate. To say this is not to invoke some modern notion of historical *precision* (see chap. 26). Rather, given God's decision to speak to us in ordinary language, we should expect the Scriptures to contain reliable truth about the events of redemption, including their historical backgrounds and settings.

Our approach to biblical history in general should be similar to our approach to individual factual assertions, as presented earlier in this chapter. It is important to understand the biblical context, the nature of logic, and the type of literature we are examining. But in addition to these factors, the claims of Scripture about the events of history often run up against secular theories about that history.

In these secular theories, historical claims are often based on considerations beyond the biblical text, such as archaeology, extrabiblical writings, and philosophical speculations.

Among the latter was the theory of F. C. Baur that Peter and Paul held contradictory views of Christ, views reconciled in the writings of Luke. This theory was a transparent attempt to impose on the NT a Hegelian dialectic: Peter the thesis, Paul the antithesis, and Luke the synthesis. Most of Baur's successors, conservative and liberal, agreed that there was no place for such philosophical speculation in the study of the NT.

No less speculative was the view of Julius Wellhausen and other OT scholars that Israel's religion evolved from a barbaric henotheism (Yahweh as the one God out of many that Israel happened to worship) to a lofty monotheism. They saw this as a passage from simple to complex, imitating the pattern of Darwinian evolution. But this speculation had no basis

12. Ibid., 115.

in the biblical text,[13] and it deeply contradicted the biblical account, which portrayed one God, existing from eternity to eternity, from creation throughout history, revealing himself consistently to successive generations of human beings.

Clearly, these schemes were based on philosophical presuppositions that were not only extrabiblical but opposed to the Bible's theistic worldview and epistemology.

Other historical problematics, however, are less philosophical, more focused on the discipline of history as such. Often they derive from the practice of trusting extrabiblical sources over against the Scriptures, such as Josephus over the Gospel writers. But Josephus for the most part verifies the assertions of the Gospels, and where he does not, should a believer not trust God's inspired Word over the ideas of a mere man?

Similarly, the theories of archaeologists should not be treated as self-validating. Archaeologists typically discover fragments of artifacts and tie these discoveries together to create theories about the historical background of their artifacts. This work should be respected. It has often validated assertions of Scripture, at least by showing a historical reality consistent with biblical claims. We should expect that in the end all archaeological evidence will be consistent with God's Word, and when there is apparent contradiction, we should try to relieve that appearance, either by rethinking the archaeological claims or by reconsidering our interpretations of Scripture.

But archaeology is not infallible, and to believers it does not speak the final word. If we cannot find any plausible reconciliation between the biblical text and some data or theory of archaeology, then we should say honestly, "I don't know," and trust God for the final validation of his Word.

Other Bible difficulties in the realm of history seem to be the result of simple confusion. For example, in *Inspiration and Incarnation*, Peter Enns seems to think it problematic that nations other than Israel had creation narratives, flood stories, temples, priests, and law codes. Some of these antedated the writing of Scripture. He asks how Scripture can be inspired of God if it is in these respects not "unique." I reply that uniqueness of this kind is no part of the doctrine of biblical inspiration.

---

13. Julius Wellhausen took his cue from the uses of the divine names in the books attributed to Moses. From these he developed the theory that these books actually came from multiple sources: one inclined to use the divine name *Yahweh*, another the name *Elohim*, still another who was interested in priestly matters, and a fourth who developed the Deuteronomic history; hence, "J, E, P, and D." Later scholars modified this system completely, some making it more complex (J1, J2, E1, E2, etc.), some rejecting it altogether. Today, many scholars continue to speak of the "J document," for instance, but the whole system hardly carries the conviction that it did in Wellhausen's time.

That doctrine does not require Scripture to be unique in this sense, only true.

Of course, the creation and flood stories in Scripture are different in many ways from those of other nations. This is also true for the priestly and legal institutions, though there is some similarity. But the more important point is that the epics and religious institutions from nations other than Israel honor gods other than Yahweh, and thus are vastly different from biblical revelation. If we assume that creation and flood were actual historical events, then it should not be surprising that accounts of them were passed down from generation to generation in many cultures, with some distortion along the way. And it should not be surprising for us to learn that the true God, at some later point in history, determined to give his own people a pure version of these events. The non-Israelite traditions actually validate to some extent the events described in Scripture. And where they do not, the Christian believer must choose God's Word over the extrabiblical sources. The biblical content is not unique in every respect, but it is unique among rival documents as the one true written Word of the one true God.

To demand that Scripture be absolutely unique in its content over against the traditions of other nations is confusion. Nothing in the biblical doctrine of Scripture requires uniqueness of that kind.

Similarly confused is the notion that accounts of the same event are contradictory unless they have exactly the same emphasis and perspective. It is likely true that Matthew's Gospel has a Jewish audience in mind, Mark and Luke less so. It is also true that John presents Jesus as having long debates with his Jewish opponents; the Synoptic writers (Matthew, Mark, and Luke) present less of this. But these are differences in emphasis or perspective, not differences of accuracy or truth. It is not difficult to conceive of Jesus combining in himself the qualities stressed by all the Gospel writers. Each writer certainly selected aspects of Jesus' ministry most conducive to his own purposes. None presented Jesus exhaustively; certainly no author could have, as John admits in 21:25 of his Gospel. But God gave us four Gospel documents that together give us a fuller picture of Jesus than any one of them could have. They are supplementary, not contradictory. The Bible contains no error, but many different perspectives on the truth.

Some NT scholars have actually maintained the principle that a saying ascribed to Jesus is most likely inauthentic if it addresses needs and concerns of the church in the book of Acts and after. This is sometimes called the *method of dissimilarity*. It is hard to believe that anyone could take this principle seriously. It dismisses from the outset the obvious teaching of Scripture that Jesus was the foundation of the church, that he made provision for its later needs, and that the church for the most part sought to follow his teaching.

GENRE

It would be wrong, however, to assume that every story in Scripture describes a real historical event. As an obvious example, Jesus' parables take the form of narrative, but they do not discuss events that take place in real space and time. If someone had asked Jesus the date on which the "sower went forth to sow" (Matt. 13:3), that person would have shown that he had completely misunderstood the point of the parable of the sower. Parables do communicate truth, as all Scripture does; but that truth is not the representation of historical events.

So when questions of the historicity of Scripture come up, it is important to understand the *genre*, or the type of literature under discussion. Study of the genre will enable us to better understand the *claim* being made by the text in question, whether it is claiming to be a literal historical account or something else.

It is worth considering, for example, the view that the book of Job is a dramatic fiction, not a historical account. To answer this type of question, of course, is not easy. In the discussion of Job, for example, one would have to have a good idea of the document's date and the types of literature written at that time. And to argue the question, one would have to identify criteria that could be observed in the text. My own, naive view is that the book of Job describes historical occurrences, but has been written up by one skilled in Hebrew poetry and drama who supplied the actual words of Job and his friends. But the most important thing is that this discussion should be carried out with full respect for the biblical worldview, with no trace of autonomy, no inclination to disbelieve what Scripture really asserts.

Another example is the book of Ecclesiastes, in which the author identifies himself as Solomon. Many conservative scholars, however, have thought that the book was not actually written by Solomon, but that the pseudonymous ascription was a literary device, a kind of first-person fiction. To endorse or rule out this hypothesis, one would have to investigate the literature of the time, other examples of or references to such pseudonymy, and the literary cues from the book itself that point to this conclusion. In my judgment this hypothesis is possible, but it requires more evidence and argument than I have personally seen.

Some have said that Genesis 1 has a poetic structure and therefore should not be given a literal interpretation. Most interpreters, indeed, have noticed that the six-day framework is divided into two groups of threes, with the first corresponding to the fourth, the second to the fifth, and so on. In the first three days, God creates realms (sky, land, water), and in the second three days God places inhabitants in those realms. I don't think I'd call Genesis 1 poetry, for it doesn't resemble other Hebrew poetry in Scripture, such as the psalms. Still, there is evidence in Genesis 1 of literary artifice. But does that exclude a literal interpretation? I don't think so. Yet in investigating such questions, it is important for us to know somewhat the type of literature we are dealing with.

At the extreme, some people believe that the Bible as a whole is a kind of parable or poem, which makes no claim to narrate events of real history. That I think is absurd. As I have indicated before, history, in the sense of significant events in ordinary space and time, is vitally important to Scripture. Scripture's doctrine of salvation is a doctrine about events that really took place. So if someone wants to show that a part of Scripture (such as the book of Job) does not intend to narrate history, he or she should bear the burden of proof. Such a scholar may be right; the history of Scripture does include some nonhistorical narratives. But such nonhistorical narratives are the exception, not the rule. To accept such exceptions, we must have evidence—evidence that fully assumes the biblical worldview.

SCIENTIFIC PROBLEMS

As I argued in chapter 26, the Bible is, for the most part, ordinary language, not technical or scientific language. It is not intended as a textbook of science, nor is it intended primarily to answer the types of questions we describe as scientific. Nevertheless, as I indicated in chapter 27, nothing in Scripture restricts God's words to specific subject matter. We have no right to dictate to God the subjects about which he may speak. And since Scripture is the Word of God, when Scripture touches on matters of interest to science, we must regard it as true and right.

The most widely discussed scientific problems cluster around the book of Genesis, particularly its accounts of creation and the flood. The creation account in Genesis 1 presents God's work of creation as a work of six days. Objections center not so much on the shortness of time: obviously, if God is who the Bible says he is, he can create the world in as short a time as he likes, or no time at all. But Genesis 1 raises other questions, such as the question how light could exist (v. 3) before the heavenly bodies (vv. 14–19). That question should not trouble anyone. Certainly, it is possible for an omnipotent, all-creating God to create a collection of photons that illuminate the earth independently of a particular heavenly body.

A more serious problem is that the Genesis account, coupled with genealogical material in Genesis 5 and 11, seems to assume a "young earth," one that came into existence thousands of years ago, rather than billions, as most scientists believe. Such a view entails that God created much of the universe with an "appearance of age," an appearance that made many things (stars, fossils, plants, even Adam and Eve themselves) seem older than they really were. I have defended literal six-day creation, with appearance of age,[14] and I still think this is the most reasonable way to understand Genesis 1. But other Christian exegetes have argued that the days of Genesis represent either long periods of time (amounting to the billions of years required by the scientific account) or a literary framework that makes no chronological claims whatever. I am not so certain of the literal interpretation as to judge the alternatives irresponsible.

The doctrine of biblical inerrancy does not imply that such questions are always easy to answer. Nor does it require all interpretations to be as literal as possible. It calls us, rather, to interpret texts *correctly*. And it tells us that when we have interpreted them correctly, they will convey truth to us. Remember from chapter 26 that the inerrancy of a text is its ability to make good on its *claims*. Interpretation is the process by which we discover what a text claims to be true. In the issue before us, the question is whether Genesis 1 claims that the earth is young, or that it is relatively old (allowing billions of years), or whether the text makes no chronological claims at all. The interpretative question will depend on exegetical issues: lexical, grammatical, and literary.

But none of these interpretations can be shown to contradict science. The "long days" and "literary framework" interpretations do not imply a young earth at all. The literal interpretation does. But I am not convinced that creation of a young earth with appearance of age is impossible for God.[15] And there are other possibilities. Some have suggested that God acted in a time frame different from that of human beings, so that what amounts to six days of his time appears from a created perspective to be billions of years. Given the variety of possible interpretations of the text, and the variety of scientific possibilities, is it not possible that one of them

14. *DG*, 307–10.

15. In fact, as I argue in *DG*, it is hard to imagine any creative act of God that does not involve appearance of age. Even if we assume that God's creation of the world coincides with the "big bang," it is legitimate to ask where the big bang came from, and what may have existed before it. So the big bang itself may *appear* to presuppose an aged universe.

presents the truth without error? So if this is possible, then no one has the right to say that the Bible's doctrine of creation is erroneous.

Our overview of this typical Bible-science problem suggests some principles that apply more broadly: (1) We ought to consider alternative interpretations of the texts we investigate. (2) We should also consider alternative scientific possibilities. And (3) we need to reflect on our own willingness to think God's thoughts after him, rather than demanding that he conform to some standard of our own.[16]

Science itself presupposes the absolute personal God of the Bible to validate the relative uniformity of nature and the possibility of intelligible thought about the world. If the universe is fundamentally impersonal, there is no reason why we should feel obligated to seek truth rather than error, or any reason why we should think our intellectual faculties capable of finding truth.[17]

PROBLEMS OF DATE, AUTHORSHIP, SETTING

Many debates between conservatives and liberals on biblical inerrancy have focused on matters of date, authorship, and setting. Conservative church bodies will often ask ministerial candidates whether they believe that Moses wrote the Pentateuch, or whether the eighth-century B.C. prophet Isaiah wrote all of the book that bears his name. Some have raised questions whether the book of Daniel was written before the Jews' return from exile, or after it. New Testament critics have often claimed that Paul did not write all the letters traditionally ascribed to him.

In these discussions it is important to keep in mind a point made earlier: biblical inerrancy means that the Bible measures up to its *claims*. It is not always clear what Scripture claims for itself with regard to date and authorship.

In regard to authorship, for example, many biblical books are anonymous. The book of Judges does not claim authorship by a particular person, nor does Ruth. The same may be said of the books of Samuel, Kings, and Chronicles, of Ezra through Esther, of Job. In the NT, the Gospels, Acts, and Hebrews are strictly anonymous, though passages in Luke (1:1–4), John (21:24), and Acts (1:1–3) are relevant to a determination of their authorship. Certainly, there are strong traditions from the early church relevant to these questions. But questions remain: for example, some grant that a person named John wrote

16. Among these three principles, (1) is normative, (2) situational, and (3) existential.

17. For a more comprehensive Christian analysis of science, see Vern Poythress, *Redeeming Science* (Wheaton, IL: Crossway, 2006), also available at http://www.frame -poythress.org.

the Gospel and letters attributed to John, but they claim that this person was not the same John who was Jesus' apostle.

The books of Moses do not say that Moses was the author of all their contents, and there are some passages that even the most conservative scholars ascribe to other authors, such as Numbers 12:3 ("Now the man Moses was very meek, more than all people who were on the face of the earth") and Deuteronomy 34 (which describes Moses' death and Israel's mourning). Still, the books present Moses as the one who brought God's law to Israel in written form. He even had a hand in the writing of it (Ex. 34:27–28). The speeches in Deuteronomy are presented as words of Moses, and at the end, Moses writes the words of the law in a book (Deut. 31:24–29) and arranges to have the book placed by the ark of the covenant. So it is natural to associate Moses with the writing of the first five books of Scripture.

When Jesus and the NT writers cite the books of the Pentateuch, they often refer not only to the book, but to Moses the man as the author of the words (e.g., Matt. 8:4; 19:7–8; 22:24). They do not question the Jewish tradition that Moses is the author of these books.

Is this data sufficient for us to conclude that Scripture *claims* Moses as the author of these books? The data from the Pentateuch itself do not constitute an irrefutable case, though they do provide a high level of probability. Who would more likely have written these books? The NT data is stronger, but is it possible that Jesus and the apostles were merely joining in a Jewish convention? Today we sometimes speak of the actions of Captain Ahab or Peter Rabbit without claiming that these characters actually existed.

I could perhaps be persuaded that the NT references to the books of Moses are a social convention, but I don't believe that case has been made. It seems to me that Jesus, the apostles, and the Jewish community of their time really believed that Moses was the substantial author of the Pentateuch (excluding a few portions, as we've seen). That is their *claim*. And since it is their claim, we are obligated to believe it.

This is the question that should guide us through all problems of this kind. What does Scripture *claim*? Does it claim that all of Isaiah was written in the eighth century by a single author? Does it claim that the book of Job is a historical record from the patriarchal age, or might the book be a poetic literary piece that does not claim (any more than do Jesus' parables) to be a historical narrative? Does it claim that Ecclesiastes was written by Solomon, or should we say (with some conservative scholars) that in the book an unknown author takes on a Solomonic role?

Sometimes determining what Scripture claims for a document will require some hard research. But I think it is helpful to understand the precise question that must be answered when we are dealing with such issues.

CHAPTER 29

The Clarity of Scripture

Discussions of Scripture in Reformed theology have often included reflection on certain "attributes" of Scripture, particularly necessity, authority, clarity (or perspicuity), and sufficiency. Reflecting the general plan of the Theology of Lordship series, I have tried to line these attributes up with God's lordship attributes of control, authority, and presence. It is, of course, not easy to align a fourfold distinction with a threefold one, so I have taken some liberties with the traditional list. It is not difficult to find biblically warranted attributes of Scripture beyond the traditional four. We have already looked at Scripture's authority, inspiration, inerrancy, and other categories in passing. So I will not apologize for expanding the traditional list from four to six, which enables me to have two groups of three: (1) power, authority, and clarity; and (2) necessity, comprehensiveness, and sufficiency. Each of these triads expresses, in ways I will indicate, the lordship attributes.[1] The first triad focuses on qualities of Scripture itself; the second triad focuses on how Scripture (including the first group of attributes) is important for our lives.

Of course, that distinction is not a sharp one, but one of focus or emphasis. We cannot entirely separate the qualities of Scripture from its functions in our lives. Indeed, we will see how the power, authority, and clarity of the Word are for us, and how the necessity, comprehensiveness, and sufficiency

---

1. I have also discussed these attributes in DCL, 144–75. That discussion and the one here are mutually supplementary.

of Scripture are ways of describing what Scripture is in itself as the Word of God.

In this chapter, I will focus on the first triad. The power of Scripture corresponds to God's control, its authority to his authority, and its clarity to his presence. Or, in terms of the three perspectives, the power of Scripture is situational, the authority normative, and the clarity existential. These are perspectivally related because each depends on the other two, and a full understanding of each requires a full understanding of the others.

After the earlier discussions in this book, there is little more to be said about the power and authority of Scripture. In chapter 9, I discussed the word as God's controlling *power*. Since Scripture is God's Word, it, too, conveys God's power. It is our present access to the words of the prophets and apostles, which by the Spirit's power bring upon their hearers both God's blessing and curse (Isa. 6:9–10; Matt. 13:10–17; Rom. 1:16; 16:25; 1 Cor. 2:4–5; 1 Thess. 1:5; 2:13). We should not think of the written Word as a mere object of our reflection. It is living and active (Heb. 4:12). It revives the soul, makes us wise, rejoices the heart, enlightens the eyes (Ps. 19:7–9). Scripture makes us wise to salvation (2 Tim. 2:15). Psalms 19 and 147:15–20 implicitly compare the power of the written Word to the power of God in creation.

And in chapters 16–28, I have argued that the written Word of God carries with it all the *authority* of God's divine voice and of the oral words of Jesus, the prophets, and the apostles. That authority can be nothing less than ultimate and absolute.

It is therefore the doctrine of biblical *clarity* that will occupy our attention in this chapter. The WCF formulates this doctrine as follows at 1.7:

> All things in Scripture are not alike plain in themselves, nor alike clear unto all: yet those things which are necessary to be known, believed, and observed for salvation are so clearly propounded, and opened in some place of Scripture or other, that not only the learned, but the unlearned, in a due use of the ordinary means, may attain unto a sufficient understanding of them.

This is a carefully nuanced statement, with important qualifications. It is directed against the attempts in the Roman Catholic Church of the time to keep the laity from studying Scripture on their own. The Roman church feared that if laymen were to interpret Scripture for themselves, they would come up with unorthodox, even bizarre, interpretations of it. That fear, as we can now observe, was not groundless.

But Scripture itself (as in Deut. 8:3; Pss. 19:7; 119; Matt. 4:4) says that God's written Word is for everybody. We live by it. The Confession, of course, agrees. But the Confession's statement does not encourage autonomous or lawless Bible study. It does not make every layman an expert in Scripture. It recognizes that not every part of Scripture is equally clear to everybody. Laymen, indeed all Christians, need to watch their step in studying the Bible. There are mysteries in Scripture beyond anyone's understanding, and there are many things in Scripture that we cannot understand without more knowledge of the languages of Scripture and its cultural background.

So the Confession also says that those who would study Scripture should be humble enough to seek help. The kind of Bible study it recommends is not individualistic. One should make "due use of the ordinary means." Those ordinary means include the church's preaching and teaching. That teaching is not, however, as in the Roman church, an inflexible set of conclusions with which all Bible students must agree. Rather, it seeks to guide believers into paths by which we can progress in our knowledge of God, even beyond the levels attained by our teachers.

Prayer and the Holy Spirit are also means available to every Christian in Bible study. Involvement with God himself, the author of Scripture, draws us toward a greater understanding of the truth. So our understanding of Scripture is not directly proportional to the amount of education we have. It is for "not only the learned, but the unlearned."

A further qualification is that this level of clarity does not apply to everything in Scripture. It pertains to "those things which are necessary to be known, believed, and observed for salvation." Now, in this book, I have opposed distinctions between "matters of salvation" and "matters of cosmology, history, and science" in several contexts. In chapters 24, 25, and 27, I have opposed the idea that Scripture's purpose is redemptive in a narrow sense, so that it is not authoritative on other matters, and I will make similar points in regard to the comprehensiveness and sufficiency of Scripture. I don't think Scripture's purpose can be defined that narrowly, and given the comprehensive nature of salvation in Scripture, I don't think it is possible to draw a sharp line in Scripture between "matters of salvation" and other matters.

Nevertheless, there is a legitimate distinction to be drawn within Scripture between what a person is required to *know* for salvation and what he is not.[2] Nobody would claim, for example, that a person will go to hell if

---

2. Of course, to try to draw this line raises up a great many other issues. I agree with the Confession's statement at 10.3 that "elect infants, dying in infancy, are regenerated, and saved by Christ," though they are "incapable of being outwardly called by the ministry of the Word." It lists as proof texts Luke 18:15, Acts 2:39, and some others that are less to the point. It might also have referred to Luke 1:41, 44, in which the unborn John the Baptist leaps for joy in Elizabeth's womb when she meets Mary, the mother of Jesus. His joy

he does not understand the difference between guilt offerings and trespass offerings in Leviticus. These are certainly "matters of salvation," but they are not matters that one must know in order to be saved. So the Confession is not making the sort of distinction that I have been opposing.[3] I would say that everything in Scripture is a "matter of salvation," that is, significantly related to salvation. But a person can be saved even if he does not know or understand some things in the Bible. The clarity of Scripture pertains to those fundamentals that constitute a credible profession of Christ.

My purpose in this book, however, is to expound not primarily confessions, but biblical teaching, granted the considerable overlap between these. Does Scripture itself warrant this doctrine of the clarity of God's written Word?

I will consider this question in terms of the lordship attributes. First, in relation to God's *control*: God is fully in control of his communications to human beings. When he intends to communicate with a human being, he is always able to do it successfully. But another name for successful communication is *clarity*. An unclear word is one that does not succeed, that fails to accomplish its purpose. But we know that God's word always accomplishes its purpose (Isa. 55:10–11). Therefore, his word is always clear.

Why, then, do people fail to understand God's word? The ultimate answer is that God did not intend for them to understand. Note again God's commission to Isaiah, in 6:9–10. God's word in Isaiah's mouth, oddly enough, brings dullness and a lack of understanding, not complete understanding. Jesus quotes this saying in Matthew 13:14–15 to explain why he speaks in parables. Note also verses 10–13:

> Then the disciples came and said to him, "Why do you speak to them in parables?" And he answered them, "To you it has been

---

in the presence of Christ indicates regeneration. But what do infants actually *know* about salvation? What do they *believe*? Propositionally, nothing. So in one sense if we ask what is "necessary to be known, believed, and observed for salvation," the answer is "nothing." But of course, in 1.7 the Confession is not thinking about the responsibilities of preborn infants, nor of "other elect persons who are incapable of being outwardly called by the ministry of the Word" (10.3), but of adults of normal intelligence. At 1.7, the Confession seems to have in mind the kind of "credible confession" required for church membership, what an adult needs to confess to be recognized as a member of the body of Christ. In this sense (and I think in this sense only), we may distinguish within Scripture some matters "which are necessary to be known, believed, and observed for salvation" and others that are not. Later in this chapter, I will discuss other ways in which the clarity of Scripture is person-variable.

3. Indeed, as I will argue later, the Confession's statement of the sufficiency of Scripture in 1.6 gives to the Bible unlimited scope: it is "the whole counsel of God concerning all things necessary for His own glory, man's salvation, faith and life." Here, Scripture is sufficient for everything.

given to know the secrets of the kingdom of heaven, but to them it has not been given. For to the one who has, more will be given, and he will have an abundance, but from the one who has not, even what he has will be taken away. This is why I speak to them in parables, because seeing they do not see, and hearing they do not hear, nor do they understand."

Jesus says here that he intentionally speaks in parables, which enlighten the disciples as to the mysteries of the kingdom, but hide those mysteries from those outside the circle.[4] His words are clear to one group, unclear to another. They have exactly the power he intends them to have. He intends to communicate to one group, so to them his word must be clear. To the other group, he does not intend to fully communicate; so to them the word is not clear.

The clarity of the Word, therefore, is selective. It is for some, not all. It is for those with whom God intends to fully communicate.

That selectivity has further dimensions, for even disciples of Jesus do not always find the Scriptures entirely clear. For example, a six-year-old child may believe in Jesus, but have a very rudimentary understanding of Scripture. That, too, is under God's sovereign control. It is God's decision generally to communicate with us through Scripture more and more clearly as we grow in spiritual maturity. So the Confession says that not everything in Scripture is equally clear to every Christian.

But "those things which are necessary to be known, believed, and observed for salvation," that knowledge by which we ascertain the authenticity of a person's Christian profession, is known by, or attainable by, all believers. Many have that knowledge by the age of six; others take longer. Few have such knowledge by age one or two. But those who belong to Jesus are able to attain such knowledge (sometimes over a period of years) "in a due use of the ordinary means."

Another way to speak of God's sovereign selectivity in revelation is to refer to the role of the Holy Spirit in bringing understanding and faith to the hearers of the Word. I will write later (especially in chapter 42) about

---

4. In general, the dividing line is between believers and unbelievers. But that line is imprecise. In Matthew 13, the line is between disciples and nondisciples so far as parables are concerned. But the disciples don't automatically understand everything for the first time. Indeed, they sometimes need to have the parables explained to them, as in Matthew 13:18–23. Among believers, as we will see, there are degrees of understanding. And unbelievers also vary in their understanding, as God sovereignly determines. Natural revelation is "clear" even to unbelievers (Rom. 1:20), though suppressed (see *DKG*, 49–61). And some enemies of God understand special revelation, too—enough to be offended by it. The Pharisees exhibit such knowledge in their response to Jesus' words.

his "internal testimony," by which he illumines the text of Scripture, persuades us that it is true, and enables us to apply it to the circumstances of our lives. It is the Spirit who sovereignly decides who will understand and who will not. I have already made the general argument that our ability to identify the true word of God is supernatural—by the Spirit (as in chaps. 1 and 14–16).

Second, let us consider the clarity of Scripture in relation to God's lordship attribute of *authority*. To say that God's Word has authority, as we have seen, is to say that it creates obligations in its hearers: obligations to believe what it says, to do what it commands, to write it on our hearts, and so on. The clarity of God's Word means that we have no excuse for failing to meet those obligations. To say that God's Word is clear is to say that we have no excuse for misunderstanding or disobeying it. So the clarity of Scripture has ethical implications.

In Romans 1:20, the clarity of God's revelation in nature implies that its recipients are "without excuse" for their sinful response. The same is the case with the written Word of God. Jesus says to his Jewish opponents:

> You search the Scriptures because you think that in them you have eternal life; and it is they that bear witness about me, yet you refuse to come to me that you may have life. (John 5:39–40)

The fact that they have studied the Scriptures makes it all the worse that they refuse to come to Jesus. They have no excuse. In Luke 12:47–48, Jesus says:

> And that servant who knew his master's will but did not get ready or act according to his will, will receive a severe beating. But the one who did not know, and did what deserved a beating, will receive a light beating. Everyone to whom much was given, of him much will be required, and from him to whom they entrusted much, they will demand the more.

As in modern civil law, "ignorance of the law is no excuse," but it is a mitigating circumstance. Of course, Scripture teaches that everyone knows, in general, God's requirements on their lives (Rom. 1:18–32), but there are degrees of knowledge, and those who have more knowledge incur greater obligations. So those who have studied the Scriptures ought to be more obedient than others. Of them more will be required. God has (sovereignly, as we have seen) granted them greater knowledge, and that greater knowledge has taken away their excuses.

So the clarity of Scripture is an ethical doctrine, a doctrine about our responsibilities before God, a doctrine that ought to motivate greater obedience.

The relation of God's authority to the clarity of Scripture illumines further what I have called *selectivity*, that Scripture is not equally clear to all. We can see now that the clarity of Scripture is relative to the responsibilities that God places on each person. When a person is only one year of age, he usually has no conscious knowledge of the content of Scripture; but that accords with the fact that God does not call such children to tasks of conscious discipleship. By two years old, a child can usually understand at least "Children, obey your parents" (Eph. 6:1). His understanding is commensurate with his responsibility. As he grows older, he is able to understand what it means to believe in Jesus, to refrain from stealing, to love others. Later, the child will understand much more, but at each stage his greater understanding will be parallel to a greater level of responsibility.

The six-year-old is not likely to understand the sacrificial rituals of Leviticus. But he doesn't have to. God has not given him responsibilities for which a knowledge of that material is a requisite. If he grows up to become an OT scholar, that situation will change.

I conclude this as an important principle: *Scripture is always clear enough for us to carry out our present responsibilities before God.* It is clear enough for a six-year-old to understand what God expects of him. It is also clear enough for a mature theologian to understand what God expects of him. But the clarity of Scripture (as we saw under the lordship attribute of control) is person-relative, person-specific. Scripture is not exhaustively clear to anyone. It is not clear enough to satisfy anyone who merely wants to gain a speculative knowledge of divine things. It is, rather, morally sufficient, practically sufficient, sufficient for each person to know what God desires of him.

This emphasis on the personal dimension of Scripture's clarity leads us to relate it to the third lordship attribute, God's personal *presence*. In Deuteronomy 30:11–14, God through Moses speaks thus to the people of Israel:

> For this commandment that I command you today is not too hard for you, neither is it far off. It is not in heaven, that you should say, "Who will ascend to heaven for us and bring it to us, that we may hear it and do it?" Neither is it beyond the sea, that you should say, "Who will go over the sea for us and bring it to us, that we may hear it and do it?" But the word is very near you. It is in your mouth and in your heart, so that you can do it.

God's Word is *near* to Israel, *present* to them. This is literally true, for it is located in the "Book of the Law" (v. 10), the written document to be placed by the ark of the covenant, God's literal dwelling place. The Levites are to read the law to the people in an assembly every seven years (31:9–13), so that they and their children might hear and obey (cf. 6:6–9). Thus the law is to be written on their hearts (6:6).

Figuratively, too, the Word is near. The questions of Deuteronomy 30:12–13 ("Who will ascend to heaven?" and "Who will go over the sea?") assume that the Word cannot be appropriated without great efforts, that without strenuous pilgrimage we cannot understand and obey it. God denies this assumption. To Israel, he says, you do understand. You can do it. So the clarity of Scripture is the presence, the closeness of Scripture.

The apostle Paul makes an interesting Christological application of Deuteronomy 30:11–14, in Romans 10:5–9:

> For Moses writes about the righteousness that is based on the law, that the person who does the commandments shall live by them. But the righteousness based on faith says, "Do not say in your heart, 'Who will ascend into heaven?'" (that is, to bring Christ down) or "'Who will descend into the abyss?'" (that is, to bring Christ up from the dead). But what does it say? "The word is near you, in your mouth and in your heart" (that is, the word of faith that we proclaim); because, if you confess with your mouth that Jesus is Lord and believe in your heart that God raised him from the dead, you will be saved.

Here Paul finds in Deuteronomy 30 something more than the promise of blessing through obedience to law. He notes that in that passage the *presence* of the law points to Christ. Moses' hearers had assumed that the Word could not be appropriated without great efforts. But the *nearness* of God's Word speaks of grace, not strenuous effort. In Christ, we do not need to ascend to heaven, for he has by grace come down to us. And we don't need to go down to the grave, for Christ has by grace risen from the dead. The nearness of the Word, now, is the nearness of Christ himself in the Word of faith, Paul's gospel. We meet Christ in the gospel, and as we confess and believe him, we are saved.

Here the clarity of the Word is nothing less than the presence of Christ in the Word.

Is Paul distorting the meaning of Deuteronomy 30:11–14? Superficially, it would seem that Moses' words speak of legal obedience, but Paul uses them to speak of grace. But recall that (1) the law itself proclaims the righteousness and grace of Christ (John 5:39–40).[5] And (2) Deuter-

---

5. Cf. "Preaching Christ from the Decalogue," in *DCL*, 400–401. Note also the message of grace in the historical prologue of the Decalogue, 403–4.

onomy 30 itself counsels Israel to rely, not on their own strenuous efforts, but on God's grace in bringing the Word near them, most significantly into their hearts.[6]

The lordship attributes, as always, work together. The presence of God in the Word is his sovereign choice, and it underscores the Word's authority. God draws near in the Word so that we can *do* the Word (Deut. 30:15–20). The control and authority of God in the Word bring his Word to people in his covenant presence.

---

6. Later I will discuss the work of the Spirit writing the words of God on our hearts as a form of revelation.

CHAPTER 30

The Necessity of Scripture

Let us now consider the second triad of biblical attributes: Scripture's necessity, comprehensiveness, and sufficiency. As I indicated, the first group of attributes focuses on qualities that Scripture has in itself. The second group focuses on why Scripture is important for us, the ways in which Scripture is preeminent in our lives.

Students of logic are familiar with the distinction between necessary and sufficient conditions. "A is a necessary condition of B" means that without A there can be no B. "A is a sufficient condition of B" means that if there is A, there will certainly be B. Readers may notice that if A is a necessary condition of B, then B is a sufficient condition of A, and vice versa. So Scripture is necessary to our spiritual lives, in that without trusting Scripture we have no spiritual life; and it is sufficient in that if we have trusted Scripture, we have spiritual life. I have added *comprehensiveness* to this pair, to stress that Scripture is necessary and sufficient not only to our life in general, but to every aspect of it.

As with the previous triad, I am lining these qualities up with God's lordship attributes. I must admit that here I am stretching the scheme slightly, but the following may serve at least to inform readers how I see this discussion fitting in with the rest of the book. Necessity focuses on God's authority (normative perspective) because it comes with a *must*. It tells us what must be if we are to live before God. Comprehensiveness focuses on God's power to control the situations of our life. Through his providence, God sees to it that Scripture bears on all aspects of life (situational perspec-

210

tive). Sufficiency speaks of God's intimate presence with us (existential perspective), for it is a fullness of satisfaction in our relation to God. We need not hunger or thirst for any other words of God.

The first of this group is the necessity of Scripture. To say that Scripture is necessary is simply to say that we need it. When Satan tempted Jesus in the wilderness, he taunted him to relieve his hunger by turning stones into bread. Jesus replied by quoting Deuteronomy 8:3: "Man shall not live by bread alone, but by every word that comes from the mouth of God" (Matt. 4:4).[1] Certainly, human beings need food. But our need for God's Word is of even greater importance.

Obviously, we need the word of God in a general way. For it was by the word of God that he created all things, including ourselves (Gen. 1; Ps. 33:6, 9; John 1:3), and it is by the word that he upholds our existence continually (Ps. 147:15–18; Heb. 1:3). But Deuteronomy 8:3 and Matthew 4:4 speak specifically of the *written* Word of God, for us the Bible.

The WCF deals with the necessity of Scripture in its very first statement, 1.1:

> Although the light of nature, and the works of creation and providence do so far manifest the goodness, wisdom, and power of God, as to leave men unexcusable; yet are they not sufficient to give that knowledge of God, and of His will, which is necessary unto salvation. Therefore it pleased the Lord, at sundry times, and in divers manners, to reveal Himself, and to declare that His will unto His Church; and afterwards for the better preserving and propagating of the truth, and for the more sure establishment and comfort of the Church against the corruption of the flesh, and the malice of Satan and of the world, to commit the same wholly unto writing; which makes the Holy Scripture to be most necessary; those former ways of God's revealing His will unto His people being now ceased.

The Confession here establishes the necessity of Scripture based on the insufficiency of other forms of revelation to give the knowledge of salvation. But Scripture is also necessary because of the nature of our relationship with God, the covenant.

---

1. Notice here that Jesus refers to *every* word. This (like the "all Scripture" of 2 Timothy 3:16) implies that *everything* God reveals in Scripture is necessary to our spiritual diet. This is the root of the doctrine of *plenary* inspiration, the idea that all of Scripture is inspired, not just some parts of it. It is also the background of the phrase *tota Scriptura*, "by all Scripture." That phrase is often coupled with *sola Scriptura*, "by Scripture alone," which we will consider in chapter 32, "The Sufficiency of Scripture."

The written Word is, first, necessary for our relationship with God as our covenant Lord. We have seen (chaps. 2, 24) that *covenant* is a relationship between the Lord and his servants or vassals, characterized by the Lord's control, authority, and presence. In this relationship, the Lord *speaks* to his vassals, defining the covenant relationship. The elements of his speech correspond to those of the suzerainty treaty form. He tells them his name, his previous deliverances and benefits (historical prologue), his laws (stipulations), his threats and promises (stipulations), and his rules for future administration of the covenant.

From this we see that the covenant is a *verbal* relationship, among other things. Without the Lord's words, there is no covenant authority; indeed, there is no covenant. "Obey my voice" and "keep my covenant" are parallel expressions in Exodus 19:5 (cf. Deut. 33:9; Ps. 89:34). The Ten Commandments are "the words of the covenant" (Ex. 34:28; 2 Kings 23:3; 1 Chron. 16:15; 2 Chron. 34:31); compare the expression "tablets of the covenant" (Deut. 9:9, 11; elsewhere). In Deuteronomy 4:13, the Ten Commandments are the covenant itself:

> And he declared to you his covenant, which he commanded you to perform, that is, the Ten Commandments, and he wrote them on two tablets of stone.

Cf. 1 Kings 8:21; 2 Chron. 6:11. When Israel fails to keep God's words, they "break my covenant" (Lev. 26:15), the Lord says.

So if there are no written covenant words, there is no covenant, nor is there a covenant Lord.

Similarly, Jesus says that if we love him, we will keep his commandments (John 14:15, 21, 23; 15:7, 10; cf. 1 John 2:3; 5:3; 2 John 6). Cf. Mark 8:38; John 12:48. Remember that his words are absolutely necessary for our lives (John 6:68). If we do not do as Jesus says, we may not call him Lord (Matt. 7:21–27). Since Jesus wrote no books, we must trust the writings of his apostles and disciples, the NT books, to mediate our covenant relationship with Jesus (cf. chap. 20).

People often claim to have a personal relationship to Christ, while being uncertain about the role of Scripture in that relationship. But the relationship that Christ has established with his people is a covenant relationship and therefore a verbal relationship, among other things. Jesus' words, today, are found only in Scripture. So if we are to have a covenant relationship with Jesus, we must acknowledge Scripture as his Word. No Scripture, no Lord. No Scripture, no Christ.[2]

---

2. For a short analysis of the force of these sentences, see my "No Scripture, No Christ," Appendix N in this volume.

And no Scripture, no salvation. Salvation is a work of God's covenant lordship, in which the Lord intervenes to deliver his people. Salvation in the ultimate sense, salvation from sin, is the result of Jesus' sacrificial death and resurrection. But it is also verbal. For we learn of it in a divine message, the gospel, and we receive salvation by faith in that gospel message. "So faith comes from hearing, and hearing through the word of Christ" (Rom. 10:17). Without that message, that gospel, there is no possibility of salvation.

The work of Christ is not something that human wisdom could have devised. Nor could a mere human report of Jesus' death and resurrection tell us what we need to know. The atonement comes out of the wisdom of God's eternal plan, and its meaning could be given only in divine words. It is God's promise that if we believe, we will be saved. A mere human promise to that effect could be dismissed as wishful thinking. Just as salvation is not by human works, it is not by human wisdom. In the message of the cross, God destroys the wisdom of the wise (1 Cor. 1:19), makes it foolish (v. 20). Paul describes his preaching thus:

> Yet among the mature we do impart wisdom, although it is not a wisdom of this age or of the rulers of this age, who are doomed to pass away. But we impart a secret and hidden wisdom of God, which God decreed before the ages for our glory. None of the rulers of this age understood this, for if they had, they would not have crucified the Lord of glory. But, as it is written, "What no eye has seen, nor ear heard, nor the heart of man imagined, what God has prepared for those who love him"—these things God has revealed to us through the Spirit. For the Spirit searches everything, even the depths of God. For who knows a person's thoughts except the spirit of that person, which is in him? So also no one comprehends the thoughts of God except the Spirit of God. Now we have received not the spirit of the world, but the Spirit who is from God, that we might understand the things freely given us by God. And we impart this in words not taught by human wisdom but taught by the Spirit, interpreting spiritual truths to those who are spiritual. (1 Cor. 2:6–13)

Because the gospel transcends human wisdom, it must come in words "taught by the Spirit."

Those words, today, can be based only in Scripture. So no Scripture, no salvation.

PROPOSAL FOR A REFORMATION

Nevertheless, as I indicated in chapters 3–7, modern liberal theology has largely abandoned the doctrine of Scripture as God's personal word, for to accept Scripture that way requires us to renounce our own autonomy. But if believers have no personal word from God, they lose their confidence that God really speaks to them, and they can believe in Jesus' salvation only as they might believe in any number of human theories. But why should we believe that human beings, even those with degrees in theology, can figure out how God forgives human sin? The question is so immense, and the human minds are so small. No amount of instruction in ancient culture, the history of religion, or philosophy can give one the wisdom he needs to tell people how to get right with God. Only God can do that. And if we are to receive God's wisdom, it must be expressed in words. Rejecting the very possibility of such divine words, modern liberal theology confesses its utter bankruptcy.

I keep praying that God will raise up some voice that will persuade modern theologians to renounce their autonomy and receive God's personal words. For over three centuries, the disease of liberalism has afflicted the church and robbed it of divine power. Surely it is time for a reformation.

Young theologians often picture themselves as leaders of a reformation. When they get too old to play cops and robbers or cowboys and Indians, they want to play Martin Luther and the pope. And when the real pope won't play with them, they tag somebody else, say "you're it," and go on the attack. I confess that I cringe whenever someone announces that they are leading a reformation for our time. In the 1960s and 1970s, one heard the expression "Stop the revolution; I want to get off"; I have often thought the same, substituting *reformation* for *revolution*. Contemporary reformations are often havens of sloppy thought, nasty rhetoric, and church division.

But I confess to having asked this question: If God were to send a real reformation today, what would be its target? What would be its chief doctrinal concern? My answer: the necessity of Scripture as God's personal word.

I see two periods of church history that can be described as major reformations. (Of course, reformations also occur in more localized, denominational contexts.) The first was the fourth century, in which the church broke away from a synthesis between Scripture and Greek philosophy (fostered by Origen, among others) and developed a clear understanding of the Trinity. Athanasius, bishop of Alexandria, was very similar to Luther as the leader of the Reformation: single-minded, clear-headed, courageous. The doctrine of the Trinity today has often been accused of being a philosophical imposition on the church. But for Athanasius, the important thing was not philosophical sophistication or logical rigor. It was the fundamental nature of our relationship with God, both in worship and in salvation.[3] For him, if the Son of God is not fully divine, we are (1) worshiping him idolatrously, and (2) trusting our salvation to someone less than God.

Luther's Reformation was similar. His quarrel with the pope similarly focused on worship and salvation. (1) He considered Roman Catholic worship, in which people bowed to images, saints, and the sacred host, idolatrous. And (2) he believed the Roman doctrine of justification left believers to depend on their own works. For Athanasius, the remedy was to recognize that the Son of God is fully divine. For Luther, the remedy was to recognize that human justification is also fully divine: God's work, not man's.

Here's my proposal for a reformation in our own day: The issue is again the recognition of deity. As Athanasius saw the Son of God as fully divine, and Luther saw the work of salvation as fully divine, so people today, especially the dominant theologians, need to see that the *message* of salvation is fully divine. The gospel is not the result of human wisdom. It is entirely the mind of God, delivered to be sure by means of human words. A reformation today that will get to the roots of the doctrinal ills of the church will focus on Scripture as necessary to our worship and salvation, and as nothing less than God's personal word to us.

3. Worship is, of course, our fundamental relation to God as creatures. Salvation remedies our fundamental need as sinners. Even before the fall, worship was the center (in a broad sense, the whole) of human obligation. Salvation is what human beings need after the fall, the remedy for their sin.

CHAPTER 31

The Comprehensiveness of Scripture

In several earlier chapters (especially 24–27),[1] I argued that Scripture's authoritative content is not religious as opposed to secular, not about "matters of salvation" in contrast with matters unrelated to salvation. Rather, Scripture addresses all of human life, as only God himself has a right to do. It applies to all the situations of our experience.[2] So the comprehensiveness of Scripture represents the situational perspective in our discussion of how Scripture is important to our lives before God.

Throughout Scripture, we see God speaking to all aspects of human life, issuing commands, making promises, wooing our hearts. In the Cultural Mandate of Genesis 1:28, God tells Adam to fill the earth and have dominion over it—the whole earth. Everything Adam does is part of that task, everything a response to that divine command.

In God's covenant with Israel, he rules their calendar, holidays, diet, clothing, economy, employment practices, education, marriage and divorce, and civil government, as well as their prayers and priestly sacrifices.

One who loves God from the heart will not deny him entrance into any sector of life. Israel's fundamental law is the *shema*:

1. Notice especially the five-step argument in chapter 27.
2. This issue is sometimes described, especially in Dutch and Dutch-American discussions, as the issue of the *scopus* of the Bible, the subject matter that the Bible addresses. My article "Rationality and Scripture" discusses *scopus* in the Dutch-American theological context. See Appendix B in this volume.

> Hear, O Israel: The LORD our God, the LORD is one. You shall love the LORD your God with all your heart and with all your soul and with all your might. (Deut. 6:4–5)

People who love God more than everything else will want to express that love in every situation. If we love God more than anything else, we will seek to know how to love him wherever we are, whatever we are doing. We will continually ask how my love for God makes a difference—in my relationship to my family and neighbors, on the job, in my recreation.[3] And believers will want to know how to take dominion of human culture for the lordship of God: art, literature, science, medicine, government.[4]

In the NT, the believer does not face such a heavy volume of specific laws to govern his life. This is the way of maturity, a result of the passage of God's people from childhood to mature sonship (Gal. 4:1–7). But if anything, the NT is even more explicit than the OT as to the comprehensiveness of God's rule over his people. Having completed his redemptive work, Jesus rises (and we with him, Rom. 6) to receive "all authority in heaven and on earth" (Matt. 28:18). As the Cultural Mandate sent Adam and Eve to take dominion of the whole earth in God's name, so Christ calls his disciples to do this:

> Go therefore and make disciples of all nations, baptizing them in the name of the Father and of the Son and of the Holy Spirit, teaching them to observe all that I have commanded you. And behold, I am with you always, to the end of the age. (Matt. 28:19–20)

The difference between the Cultural Mandate and the Great Commission is that the former precedes the fall and the work of Christ; the latter follows these. Otherwise, they are very much the same. Of course, it is not possible for people to subdue the earth for God until their hearts are changed by the Holy Spirit. So "taking dominion," following the resurrection, begins with evangelism and baptism. But baptism is not the end, and

---

3. Meredith G. Kline and others have argued that Scripture distinguishes two spheres, holy and common. The holy sphere is ruled by Scripture and God's saving grace. The common sphere is ruled by natural revelation ("natural law") and common grace. This is a kind of sacred/secular distinction, related, I think, to the medieval distinction between grace and nature and to Martin Luther's distinction between "two kingdoms." I have frequently argued against this type of thinking through *DCL*, especially 534–40. See also ibid., 182–92, on the related distinction between law and gospel.

4. See chapters 45–49 of *DCL*, on Christ and Culture, also Appendix E of that book, "In Defense of Christian Activism," and Appendix F, "Is Natural Revelation Sufficient to Govern Culture?" See also my discussion of the "two kingdoms" position in many places, such as *DCL*, 609–16, and my review of David VanDrunen, *A Biblical Case for Natural Law* (Grand Rapids: Acton Institute, 2006), at http://www.frame-poythress.org.

evangelism is not simply bringing people to an initial profession of faith. It is making disciples and teaching them to observe comprehensively all that Jesus has commanded, with the assurance of Jesus' continuing presence.[5] Jesus' commands deal not only with repentance, faith, and worship. They also concern our treatment of the poor, our sexual ethics, marriage and divorce, anger, love of enemies, fasting, anxiety, hypocrisy, and many other subjects.

Jesus anticipates a kingdom covering the earth, in which people love God and their neighbors from the heart. The gospel that we preach throughout the world is the good news that the kingdom of God is at hand (Matt. 3:2; 4:17, 23; 5:3; Acts 1:3; 8:12; 19:8; 20:25; 28:23, 31). In the fundamental prayer of God's people (Matt. 6:10), we ask that God's kingdom come. That kingdom will inevitably change human institutions as well. When people are converted to believe in Christ, they bring their new faith and love into their daily work. They ask how Christ bears upon their work as historians, scientists, musicians, how this new passion of theirs affects art, entertainment, medicine, the care for the poor and sick, the justice of courts, the punishment of convicts, relations between nations. All of life is different because of grace. And indeed, Christians have influenced their societies in profound ways through the centuries: adopting babies left to die, building hospitals and orphanages, working to abolish slavery.

So Paul says, "Whether you eat or drink, or whatever you do, do all to the glory of God" (1 Cor. 10:31). *Whatever* includes everything. Other *whatever* verses include Romans 14:23: "But whoever has doubts is condemned if he eats, because the eating is not from faith. For whatever does not proceed from faith is sin." Anything we do that is not motivated by our Christian faith is sin. Note also two verses in Colossians:

> And whatever you do, in word or deed, do everything in the name of the Lord Jesus, giving thanks to God the Father through him. (Col. 3:17)

And (to slaves!):

> Whatever you do, work heartily, as for the Lord and not for men. (Col. 3:23)

God's lordship, therefore, is totalitarian. He rules every aspect of our lives, and he wants his lordship recognized in every corner of the earth, over every life, every family, every nation, every field of human endeavor.

5. On the relation between the Cultural Mandate and the Great Commission, see my fuller treatment in *DCL*, 307–11.

Of course, his lordship is totalitarian in a good way, for he intends to extend the blessing of his presence throughout the earth and in every aspect of human life as his name is honored there.

Scripture constitutes the words by which God directs us in carrying out the Cultural Mandate and Great Commission. It is to Scripture we go to find "every word that comes from the mouth of God" (Matt. 4:4, quoting Deut. 8:3) and "all that I have commanded you" (Matt. 28:20). Scripture shows us how to bring Christ's words to bear over the whole earth. So its content cannot be anything other than comprehensive.

CHAPTER 32

The Sufficiency of Scripture[1]

The last of the six attributes of Scripture is sufficiency, sometimes called *sola Scriptura*, "by Scripture alone."[2] The sufficiency of Scripture is a doctrine of immense importance and a doctrine frequently misunderstood. So I will discuss it at greater length than the other attributes. My basic definition: Scripture contains all the divine words needed for any aspect of human life.

CONFESSIONAL FORMULATION

WCF 1.6 formulates the doctrine thus:

> The whole counsel of God concerning all things necessary for His own glory, man's salvation, faith and life, is either expressly set down in Scripture, or by good and necessary consequence may be

---

1. This chapter is a revision of chapter 11 of *DCL*, which has the same title. Of course, the sufficiency of Scripture is an important principle of ethics (the chief concern of *DCL*) as also of the doctrine of Scripture itself (as here). The discussion in *DCL* also deals with related topics such as *adiaphora* and the relations between strong and weak believers in Romans 14 and 1 Corinthians 8–10. I will not deal with those topics here. See also my article "In Defense of Something Close to Biblicism," Appendix O in this volume.

2. For the companion doctrine, *tota Scriptura*, "by all Scripture," see chapter 30, "The Necessity of Scripture." Combining these with the discussion in chapter 3, "The Comprehensiveness of Scripture," yields the slogan: "All Scripture, and only Scripture, for all of life."

deduced from Scripture: unto which nothing at any time is to be added, whether by new revelations of the Spirit, or traditions of men. Nevertheless, we acknowledge the inward illumination of the Spirit of God to be necessary for the saving understanding of such things as are revealed in the Word: and that there are some circumstances concerning the worship of God, and government of the Church, common to human actions and societies, which are to be ordered by the light of nature, and Christian prudence, according to the general rules of the Word, which are always to be observed.

Below is a commentary on this statement, phrase by phrase.

1. *The whole counsel of God concerning all things necessary for His own glory, man's salvation, faith and life.* The sufficiency of Scripture is comprehensive, in the way that I presented the doctrine of comprehensiveness in chapter 31 (anticipated in 24–27). Everything we need to know for God's glory is in the Bible. The same is true for our own "salvation, faith and life." The Confession does not understand these terms in the narrow ways that I argued against earlier. It sees salvation as comprehensive, as we can tell from the rest of the document. Similarly, "faith and life" is a comprehensive pair of concepts. The WSC says, "The Scriptures principally teach what man is to believe concerning God, and what duty God requires of man."[3] So it is reasonable to think that "faith and life" in WCF 1.6 refers to everything we are to believe and do, the whole content of Scripture applied to the whole content of the Christian life.

Christians sometimes say that Scripture is sufficient for religion, or preaching, or theology, but not for such things as auto repairs, plumbing, animal husbandry, and dentistry. And of course, many argue that it is not sufficient for science, philosophy, or even ethics. That is to miss an important point. Certainly, Scripture contains more specific information relevant to theology than to dentistry. But sufficiency in the present context is not sufficiency of specific information but sufficiency of divine words. Scripture contains divine words sufficient for all of life. It has all the divine words that the plumber needs, and all the divine words that the theologian needs. So it is just as sufficient for plumbing as it is for theology. And in that sense it is sufficient for science and ethics as well.

2. *Is either expressly set down in Scripture, or by good and necessary consequence may be deduced from Scripture.* The sufficient content of Scripture

3. Q and A 3.

includes not only its explicit teaching, but also what may be logically deduced from it. To be sure, logical deduction is a human activity, and it is fallible, as are all other human activities. So when someone tries to deduce something from Scripture, he may err.[4] But the WCF speaks not just of any attempt to deduce conclusions from Scripture, but of "good and necessary consequence." That phrase refers to logic done right, ideal logic. When deductive logic is done right, the conclusion of a syllogism does not add to its premises. It rather brings out content already there. In the classic syllogism "All men are mortal; Socrates is a man; therefore Socrates is mortal," the conclusion doesn't tell you anything you couldn't find out from the premises themselves. What the syllogism does is to make the implicit content explicit. Logic is a hermeneutical tool,[5] a device for bringing out meaning that is already there in the text. So (a) the "content of Scripture" includes all the logical implications of Scripture, (b) the logical implications of Scripture have the same authority as Scripture, and (c) logical deductions from Scripture do not add anything to Scripture.

3. *Unto which nothing at any time is to be added.* Covenant documents in the ancient Near East often contained an "inscriptional curse," a prohibition against adding to or subtracting from the document. Scripture, our covenant document, also contains such language (Deut. 4:2; 12:32; Prov. 30:6; Rev. 22:18–19; cf. Josh. 1:7). These passages do not forbid seeking information outside of Scripture. Rather, they insist that we will never need any *divine words* in addition to God's written words, words that are available to us only in the Bible. That means as well that we should never place any human words on the same level of authority as those in Scripture. That would be, in effect, adding to God's words.

4. *Whether by new revelations of the Spirit, or traditions of men.* Adding to God's words can be done either by falsely claiming to have new words

---

4. This liability to error should caution us to be careful in the work of logical deduction. Certainly it must be done with hermeneutical wisdom. "All men have sinned (Rom. 3:23), Jesus is a man (1 Tim. 2:5), therefore Jesus sinned" may seem like a valid syllogism, but of course it presupposes a defective Christology. (Thanks to Richard Pratt for this example.) So the right use of logic depends on many other kinds of skill and knowledge. On the other hand, the possibility of error should not lead us to abandon logical deduction. For error is not found only in logic, but also in every other activity by which we seek to understand Scripture: textual criticism, translation, interpretation, theology, preaching, and individual understanding. If our goal is to avoid making any error at all, not only should we avoid logic, but we should avoid all these other activities as well. But that would be an error of another kind.

5. See *DKG*, 242–301.

from God himself or by regarding human tradition on the same level of authority as God's Word. The Confession ascribes these errors to its two main opponents, respectively: the enthusiasts and the Roman Catholics. The enthusiasts were largely Anabaptists, who held views of continuing verbal revelation similar to those of some modern charismatics. The Roman Catholics defended their tradition as a source of revelation equal to the Bible. Roman Catholic theology has since changed its formulations somewhat,[6] but it still regards tradition as highly as it regards Scripture. Since the writing of the Confession, it has become important also for Protestants to guard their respect for their own traditions, so that it doesn't compete with the unique respect due to Scripture.[7]

5. *Nevertheless, we acknowledge the inward illumination of the Spirit of God to be necessary for the saving understanding of such things as are revealed in the Word.* To say that Scripture is sufficient is not to deny that other things may also be necessary.[8] We should always remember that the sufficiency of Scripture is a sufficiency of divine words. It is a sufficient source of such words. But we need more than divine words if we are to be saved and to live holy lives. In particular, we need the Spirit to illumine the Word, if we are to understand it. So no one should object that the doctrine of the sufficiency of Scripture leaves no place for the Holy Spirit.

6. *And that there are some circumstances concerning the worship of God, and government of the Church, common to human actions and societies, which are to be ordered by the light of nature, and Christian prudence, according to the general rules of the Word, which are always to be observed.* On the concept of "circumstances," see the discussion in *DCL* of the second commandment.[9] For now, let us note that the sufficiency of Scripture does not rule out the use of natural revelation (the "light of nature") and human reasoning ("Christian prudence")[10] in our decisions, even when those decisions concern the worship and government of the church.

---

6. Today, Roman Catholic theologians tend to speak not of "two sources" of revelation (Scripture and tradition), but of "one source," the stream of tradition of which Scripture is a part. Neither of these views, however, is compatible with the sufficiency of Scripture.

7. See my articles "In Defense of Something Close to Biblicism," Appendix O in this volume, and "Traditionalism," Appendix P.

8. Recall the discussion in chapter 30 of the logical distinction between necessary and sufficient conditions.

9. *DCL*, 464–81.

10. Note the triad: Scripture, the light of nature, and Christian prudence: normative, situational, and existential, respectively.

The reason, of course, is that Scripture doesn't speak specifically to every detail of human life, even of life in the church. We have seen that in one sense Scripture speaks of everything, for its principles are broad enough to cover all human actions. The principle of 1 Corinthians 10:31, "do all to the glory of God," speaks to every human activity and grades every human act as right or wrong.

But it is often difficult to determine in specific terms what actions will and will not bring glory to God. At that point, natural revelation and Christian prudence give us important guidance. For example, Scripture doesn't mention abortion. But natural revelation tells us that abortion is a procedure that takes innocent life. That shows us that the Bible's prohibition of murder is relevant to the matter of abortion.

Note that in this example, as the Confession says, there are "general rules of the Word" that are relevant to our decision. There are always general rules of the Word relevant to any human decision, as we have seen, at least the rule of 1 Corinthians 10:31. So to use the data of natural revelation in this way, though it is extrascriptural, is not to add to Scripture in the sense of Deuteronomy 4:2. To do this is not to add more divine words. It is, rather, a means of determining how the sufficient word of Scripture should be applied to a specific situation.

The fact that Scripture doesn't mention abortion, or nuclear war, or financial disclosure, or conflicts of interest, or parking meters, therefore, never means that we may abandon Scripture in considering these issues. A principle of Scripture is always relevant. The only question is how that principle specifically applies. Recourse to natural revelation and human prudence is an attempt to answer that question.

BIBLICAL BASIS

But is this confessional doctrine itself biblical? I believe it is. I have already cited some relevant biblical passages and principles. Let us look more closely at Scripture's teaching about its own sufficiency.

As we've seen, the covenant document contains an inscriptional curse, forbidding adding and subtracting. This is to say that God alone is to rule his people, and he will not share that rule with anyone else. If a human being presumes to add his own word to a book of divinely authoritative words, he thereby claims that his words have the authority of God himself. He claims in effect that he shares God's throne.

Nevertheless, through the history of Israel some did have the audacity to set their words alongside God's. False prophets claimed to speak in God's name, when God had not spoken to them (1 Kings 13:18; 22:5–12), a crime that deserved the death penalty (Deut. 18:20). And the people worshiped according to human commandments rather than God's:

> And the Lord said: "Because this people draw near with their mouth and honor me with their lips, while their hearts are far from me, and their fear of me is a commandment taught by men, therefore, behold, I will again do wonderful things with this people, with wonder upon wonder; and the wisdom of their wise men shall perish, and the discernment of their discerning men shall be hidden." (Isa. 29:13–14)

Jesus applies Isaiah's words to the Pharisees, and adds, "You leave the commandment of God and hold to the tradition of men" (Mark 7:8). And it is likely that some people in Paul's time wrote letters forged in Paul's name, claiming his authority for their own ideas (2 Thess. 2:2).

God's own representatives, however, fearlessly set God's word against all merely human viewpoints. Think of Moses before Pharaoh, Elijah before Ahab, Isaiah before Ahaz, Jonah before Nineveh, Paul before Agrippa, Felix, and Festus. Consider Jesus, who spoke with the same boldness before the Pharisees, Sadducees, scribes, Herod, and Pilate. Those who are armed with God's Word, the sword of the Spirit, are free from the tyranny of human opinion!

So Paul, in his famous statement about biblical inspiration, speaks of sufficiency as well:

> All Scripture is breathed out by God and profitable for teaching, for reproof, for correction, and for training in righteousness, that the man of God may be competent, equipped for every good work. (2 Tim. 3:16–17)

"Every" refers to sufficiency.

GENERAL AND PARTICULAR SUFFICIENCY

We should notice that 2 Timothy 3:16–17 ascribes sufficiency to the OT. That is an interesting point, that the OT is actually a sufficient guide for NT Christians. As we saw in chapter 20, Paul recommends the OT as the criterion Christians should use to evaluate new heresies after Paul has died. Why, then, does God give us the NT as well? That question leads to a distinction between two kinds of sufficiency.[11]

---

11. Compare here the distinction I made in connection with the closing of the canon in chapter 22.

First, *general sufficiency*. I use this phrase to refer to the principle that at any point of redemptive history, the revelation given at that time is sufficient. After Adam and Eve sinned, God revealed to them how they would be punished, and he also, remarkably, revealed to them the coming of a deliverer, a seed of the woman, who would crush the serpent's head (Gen. 3:15). This revelation, extensive as it is, is not nearly as extensive as the revelation available to us in the completed biblical canon. Was this revelation sufficient for them? Yes, it was. Had they failed to trust this revelation, they could not have used as an excuse that it wasn't full enough. In this revelation, they had all the divine words they needed to have. So that revelation was sufficient.

Nevertheless, God added to that revelation, by speaking to Noah, Abraham, and others. Why did he add to a revelation that was already sufficient? Because Noah needed to know more than Adam did. The history of redemption is progressive. In Noah's time, God planned to judge the world by a flood, and Noah had to know that. The Adamic revelation was sufficient for Adam, but not for Noah.

Recall the principle I suggested in chapter 29 regarding the clarity of Scripture: *Scripture is clear enough to make us responsible for carrying out our present responsibilities to God*. Like clarity, sufficiency is an ethical doctrine. It takes away excuses for disobedience. When we violate God's commandments, we cannot claim that they were unclear, or that they were insufficient.

So, like clarity, sufficiency is relative to our present duties before God. God's revelation to Adam was sufficient for him to carry out his present duties, but Noah needed more, for he had additional duties. He needed more in order to do God's will in his time.

Similarly, the revelation of the OT was sufficient for the first generation of Christians (2 Tim. 3:16–17). But God graciously provided them with much more, including the letters of Paul. In God's judgment, these were necessary for the ongoing life of the young church; and when they were collected and distributed, the believers recognized them as God's Word. Once the NT began to function as God's Word in the church, the OT was no longer sufficient in itself, but it continued to function as part of the canon, which was, as a whole, sufficient.

That consideration raises the question whether God will add still more revelation to the canon. Sufficiency in itself, what I am calling *general sufficiency*, does not preclude divine additions to Scripture, though it does preclude mere human additions.

But an additional principle should lead us not to expect any more divine words until the return of Christ. That is the finality of Christ's redemption, which implies what I call the *particular sufficiency* of Scripture.

When redemption is final, revelation is also final. Hebrews 1:1–4 draws this parallel:

> Long ago, at many times and in many ways, God spoke to our fathers by the prophets, but in these last days he has spoken to us by his Son, whom he appointed the heir of all things, through whom also he created the world. He is the radiance of the glory of God and the exact imprint of his nature, and he upholds the universe by the word of his power. After making purification for sins, he sat down at the right hand of the Majesty on high, having become as much superior to angels as the name he has inherited is more excellent than theirs.

Verse 3 speaks of Jesus' purification for sins as final, for when finished he sits down at God's right hand. Verse 2 speaks of God's speech through his Son as final, in comparison with the "many times and . . . many ways" of the prophetic revelation. Note the past-tense "has spoken." The revelation of the OT is continuous, that of the Son once for all. Nothing can be added to his redemptive work, and nothing can be added to the revelation of that redemptive work.

Hebrews 2:1–4 also contrasts the revelation of the old covenant with that of the new:

> Therefore we must pay much closer attention to what we have heard, lest we drift away from it. For since the message declared by angels proved to be reliable and every transgression or disobedience received a just retribution, how shall we escape if we neglect such a great salvation? It was declared at first by the Lord, and it was attested to us by those who heard, while God also bore witness by signs and wonders and various miracles and by gifts of the Holy Spirit distributed according to his will.

The "message declared by angels" is, of course, the Mosaic law. The "great salvation" in Christ is something far greater. The message of this salvation was declared first by Christ, then by the apostles ("those who heard"), and then by God himself, through signs and wonders. From the writer's standpoint, these declarations are all in the past tense. Even though part of that message (at least the Letter to the Hebrews) is still being written, the bulk of it has already been completed.

Scripture is God's testimony to the redemption he has accomplished for us. Once that redemption is finished, and the apostolic testimony to it is finished, the Scriptures are complete, and we should expect no more additions to them.

The same conclusion follows from 2 Peter 1:3–11. There, Peter notes that Jesus' "divine power has granted to us all things that pertain to life and godliness, through the knowledge of him who called us to his own glory and excellence" (v. 3). All things that pertain to life and godliness, therefore, come from Jesus' redemption. After that redemption, then, evidently, there is nothing more that could contribute anything to our spiritual life and godliness. Peter then mentions various qualities that we receive through Jesus, concluding, "For in this way there will be richly provided for you an entrance into the eternal kingdom of our Lord and Savior Jesus Christ" (v. 11). This is the language of sufficiency. The virtues that come from redemption are sufficient for us to enter the final kingdom. Nothing more is needed.

So within the concept of sufficiency, I distinguish between *general* and *particular* sufficiency. As we saw earlier, the general sufficiency of Scripture excludes human additions, but is compatible with later additions by God himself. This is the sense in which the OT is sufficient, according to 2 Timothy 3:16–17. The particular sufficiency of Scripture is the sufficiency of the present canon to present Christ and all his resources. God himself will not add to the work of Christ, and so we should not expect him to add to the message of Christ.

THE USE OF EXTRABIBLICAL DATA

If we remember that the sufficiency of Scripture is a sufficiency of divine words, that will help us to understand the role of extrabiblical data, both in ethics and in theology. People sometimes misunderstand the doctrine of sufficiency by thinking that it excludes the use of any extrabiblical information in reaching theological or ethical conclusions. But if we exclude the use of extrabiblical information, then reflection is next to impossible.

Scripture itself recognizes this point. As I said earlier, the inscriptional curses do not forbid seeking extrabiblical information. Rather, they forbid us to equate extrabiblical information with divine words. Scripture itself requires us to correlate what it says with general revelation. When God told Adam to abstain from the forbidden fruit, he assumed that Adam already had general knowledge, sufficient to apply that command to the trees that he could see and touch. God didn't need to tell Adam what a tree was, how to distinguish fruits from leaves, what it meant to eat. These things were natural knowledge. So God expected Adam to correlate the specific divine prohibition concerning one tree to his natural knowledge of the trees in the garden. This is theology as application: applying God's Word to our circumstances.

The same is true for all other divine commands in Scripture. When God tells Israel to honor their fathers and mothers, he does not bother to define *father* and *mother* and to set forth an exhaustive list of things that may honor or dishonor them. Rather, God assumes that Israel has some general knowledge of family life, and he expects them to apply his command to that knowledge.

Jesus rebukes the Pharisees not because they had no knowledge of the biblical text, but because they failed to apply that knowledge to the things that happened in their own experience. In Matthew 16:2–3, he says:

> When it is evening, you say, "It will be fair weather, for the sky is red." And in the morning, "It will be stormy today, for the sky is red and threatening." You know how to interpret the appearance of the sky, but you cannot interpret the signs of the times.

The chief deficiency in the Pharisees' application of Scripture was their failure to see Jesus as the promised Messiah, the central theme of the Hebrew Bible. In John 5:39–40, Jesus says:

> You search the Scriptures because you think that in them you have eternal life; and it is they that bear witness about me, yet you refuse to come to me that you may have life.

Against the Sadducees, who deny the resurrection, Jesus quotes an OT text that at first glance doesn't seem to speak to the point:

> "And as for the resurrection of the dead, have you not read what was said to you by God: 'I am the God of Abraham, and the God of Isaac, and the God of Jacob'? He is not God of the dead, but of the living." And when the crowd heard it, they were astonished at his teaching. (Matt. 22:31–33)

That text (Ex. 3:6) was a famous one; every Jewish expert in Scripture knew it well. The Sadducees' problem was not that they didn't know the text, but that they were unable or unwilling to apply it to the current discussion of resurrection. Jesus teaches them that to the extent that one cannot apply Scripture, he is actually ignorant of Scripture. Knowing Scripture cannot be separated from knowing its applications.[12] But that is to say that one cannot know Scripture without understanding how it applies to extrabiblical data. Here, one cannot rightly understand the normative without the situational.

So Scripture itself says that Scripture has an ethical purpose. The right way to study Scripture is to apply it to the issues that face us in our own time. In Romans 15:4, Paul says:

12. See *DKG*, 81–85, 95–98.

> For whatever was written in former days was written for our instruction, that through endurance and through the encouragement of the Scriptures we might have hope.

Unlike any other ancient book, Scripture is written with the purpose of instructing those who would live many centuries into the future, to give them instruction, endurance, encouragement, and hope. Its own authors (divine and human) intended for it to guide us in our ethical and spiritual struggles. Similarly, the familiar passage in 2 Timothy 3:16–17:

> All Scripture is breathed out by God and profitable for teaching, for reproof, for correction, and for training in righteousness, that the man of God may be competent, equipped for every good work.

Here, Paul indicates not only that Scripture is God's Word, but also that it has a practical and ethical purpose. As we saw in chapter 20, both this passage and the famous passage 2 Peter 1:19–21 are written by aged apostles, concerned about false teaching likely to enter the church after their deaths (2 Tim. 3:1–9; 2 Peter 2:1–22). Paul and Peter agree that Scripture contains the resources necessary to distinguish true from false teachers, both in their doctrine and in their character. But to use Scripture that way is, of course, to apply it to the situations that people encounter.

THE LOGIC OF APPLICATION

Let us look further at the process by which we should combine biblical knowledge with information about our situations, to generate applications of Scripture. The material below focuses specifically on ethics, but the same principles apply to theology, science, history, and any other field of human interest. Remember that ethics, considered broadly, embraces all of theology.[13] And remember that theology itself is the application of Scripture to all of human life.[14]

Much ethical reasoning can be expressed in the form of *moral syllogisms*. In a moral syllogism, the first premise states a principle, the second a fact to which the principle applies. Then the conclusion states the application.[15]

---

13. In *DCL*, 10, I define ethics as "theology, viewed as a means of determining what persons, acts, and attitudes receive God's blessing and which do not." Note: Ethics is not a part of theology, or a branch of theology. It is theology itself, viewed from a certain perspective.

14. *DCL*, 9; *DKG*, 81–85; I recapitulate this argument in this book, chapter 37.

15. Within this general structure, of course, there are usually further complications: subsidiary arguments to establish the normative premise and the situational premise. So

We might describe the first premise as normative, the second as situational, and the conclusion as existential, since it brings the principle to bear on our own ethical decision. For example:

1. Stealing is wrong (normative premise).
2. Embezzling is stealing (situational premise).
3. Therefore, embezzling is wrong (existential conclusion).

In Christian ethics, the normative premise ultimately comes from God, for only he has the authority to define ethical norms for human beings. In principle, this premise may come from any kind of divine revelation. But we must remember the primacy of Scripture, which governs our understanding and interpretation of general and existential revelation. Our interpretations of general and existential revelation must be tested by Scripture. If someone claims that God wants me, say, to move to Paris, he needs to show me from Scripture that this is indeed God's will. But then the ultimate norm is Scripture, not general or existential revelation by itself.

So we may formulate the sufficiency of Scripture for ethics as follows: Scripture is sufficient to provide all the ultimate norms, all the normative premises, that we need to make any ethical decision. Scripture contains all the words of God that we need for any area of life, and all ultimate norms come from divine words.

Then what use is general revelation? First, it is important, especially, in furnishing situational premises. Of course, the Bible, too, furnishes situational premises, as in:

1. Adultery is wrong (Ex. 20:14).
2. Lust is adultery (Matt. 5:27–28).
3. Therefore, lust is wrong.

But most of the time, we need extrabiblical data to formulate the situation that we are seeking to address, as in the following example:

1. Stealing is wrong.
2. Cheating on your income tax is stealing.
3. Therefore, cheating on your income tax is wrong.

The Bible, of course, does not mention the U.S. income tax, though it does mention taxes in general. What it says about taxes in general is relevant, of course. It is among the "general rules of the Word" mentioned in the

---

ethical arguments in practice have many premises and many twists and turns of logic. In the present discussion, I am presenting a general form that summarizes many arguments about ethics.

Confession's statement. But in order to evaluate premise 2, we need to know not only these biblical principles, but also some facts not mentioned in Scripture that tell us what the income tax is. Here is an even more obvious example:

1. Sabbath-breaking is wrong.
2. Operating a tanning salon on Sunday is Sabbath-breaking.
3. Therefore, operating a tanning salon on Sunday is wrong.

To establish premise 2, of course, we need to know some general principles of Scripture about the Sabbath. But Scripture doesn't mention tanning salons. So we need some specific information from outside the Bible to warrant the second premise.

Of course, to go "outside the Bible" is not to go outside of God's revelation. It is rather to move from the sphere of special revelation to the sphere of general revelation. So the whole syllogism utilizes general revelation, illumined and evaluated by special revelation.

Second, however, it should also be evident that even the normative premises of ethical syllogisms use extrabiblical data at some point. For all our use of Scripture depends on our knowledge of extrabiblical data. Scripture contains no lessons in Hebrew or Greek grammar. To learn that, we must study extrabiblical information. Similarly, the other means that enable us to use Scripture, such as textual criticism, text editing, translation, publication, teaching, preaching, concordances, and commentaries, all depend on extrabiblical data. So in one sense even the first premises of moral syllogisms, the normative premises, depend on extrabiblical knowledge. So without extrabiblical premises, without general revelation, we cannot *use* Scripture at all. But Scripture is emphatically a book to be used.

None of those considerations detracts from the primacy of Scripture as we have described it. Once we have a settled conviction of what Scripture teaches, that conviction must prevail over all other sources of knowledge. So Scripture must govern even the sciences that are used to analyze it: textual criticism, hermeneutics, and so on. These sciences enable us to understand Scripture, but they must themselves be carried on in accord with Scripture. There is a hermeneutical circle here that cannot be avoided, and that circle shows how the normative and situational perspectives are interdependent. But in the hierarchy of norms, Scripture must remain primary.

Certainly, it is a misunderstanding, then, to think that the sufficiency of Scripture rules out the necessity of extrabiblical information. At every stage of our use of Scripture, we should legitimately refer both to the content of Scripture and to extrabiblical revelation. But each in its proper place: when we are convinced that a teaching is the teaching of Scripture itself (even when we used extrabiblical information in reaching that conviction), that teaching must take precedence over any conclusion derived from outside Scripture.

CHALLENGES TO THE SUFFICIENCY OF SCRIPTURE

The statement earlier quoted from the WCF contrasts its doctrine of the sufficiency of Scripture with the views of its frequent opponents, the Roman Catholics and the Anabaptist enthusiasts. The Roman Catholics placed their traditions alongside Scripture as having the same authority, so the Confession condemns those who would supplement Scripture by "traditions of men." The enthusiasts, somewhat like the charismatic tradition of our day, believed that God gave new revelations, of a similar type and similar authority to that of Scripture. So the Confession forbids us to add anything to Scripture by way of "new revelations of the Spirit."

In traditional post-Reformation Roman Catholicism, Scripture and tradition are two sources of revelation, equal in authority. But again, in more recent Catholicism (especially since the Second Vatican Council of the 1960s), theologians speak of "one source" of revelation, which sounds better to Protestants. Yet the one source is tradition, and this theology considers Scripture to be only one part of this tradition. So plainly Roman Catholicism continues to differ from the Protestant doctrine of scriptural sufficiency.

The position of charismatic theology, the successor to the Anabaptist enthusiasts, is more difficult to pin down. Most charismatics agree with orthodox Protestantism that the canon is closed. Although they believe in "new revelation" in some sense, they do not believe that it should be placed on the same level as Scripture. But if these new revelations are actually God's personal words, how can they *not* be as authoritative as Scripture? Some charismatic writers distinguish Scripture, not as having greater authority than present-day revelation, but as having an official status as the governing document of the church. Certainly, it is good that they recognize the nature of Scripture as the sole official constitution of the church. But one continues to wonder why it would not be possible to add the "new" revelations to the constitutional document.

A growing development in charismatic theology is the view of Wayne Grudem that the "new" revelations do not have the same authority as

Scripture.[16] Grudem believes that prophets in the NT did not have the same authority as prophets in the OT. So although he believes that prophecy continues in our day, giving new revelations to believers, he thinks that such prophecy does not always turn out right and that we can be critical of it. I commented briefly on Grudem's view in chapter 15. It seems to me unlikely that the concept of prophecy would change so radically between Old and New Testaments. And if such prophecy constitutes a personal word of God, as I have expounded that concept, then I don't see how it could be less than ultimately authoritative and inerrant.[17]

Nevertheless, it does seem to me that there are ways in which revelation continues today, and these senses constitute talking points between Reformed and charismatic Christians.

Christians often find themselves discussing whether God will add new revelation to what we already have. In many circles the tendency is to reply to this question with a simple yes or no: In Reformed circles, the instinct is to answer no; in some charismatic circles, the instinct is to answer yes.

But books like this one are intended to raise such discussions to a higher level of reflection. So I suggest the often useful reply, "Yes in some senses, no in others."

1. God's revelation of himself in creation, *general revelation* (revelation through events), certainly continues, and we learn new things from it every day. Every time the sun rises, the heavens declare his glory in a new way. So our knowledge of God is not a fixed quantity—"static," as theologians say. Our life with God is an ongoing drama with exciting new experiences throughout our history.

   Further, we should not be intellectualistic in our understanding of how this knowledge comes to us. It may well be true that some general revelation comes to us through subconscious intuitions, through dreams, through visions, through hunches of various kinds. We simply don't know all the dimensions of human knowledge, which is to say that we don't know all the ways in which God reveals himself to us.

16. See Wayne Grudem, *Systematic Theology* (Grand Rapids: Zondervan, 1994), 1049–61. Grudem is solidly Reformed in most areas, but he takes a charismatic position on the continuance of prophecy and tongues.

17. The gift of tongues, which charismatics believe continues today, is similar to prophecy. When coupled with interpretation, tongues are equivalent to prophecy. I have nothing to add to the present discussion of tongues, except to commend the Poythress article cited below (note 20).

We should not equate such general-revelation knowledge with God's personal words in Scripture. But it is real knowledge of God, as I indicated in chapter 13. And as I indicated in chapter 12 and earlier in this chapter, we cannot understand scriptural word-revelation without general revelation, even though the authority of Scripture, once we understand it, takes precedence over anything we may think we have learned through general revelation.

So general revelation is real revelation, though it would not be appropriate for us to add it to the biblical canon. It may be that some claims to extrabiblical special revelation are really based on general revelation. When someone gets a "hunch" that turns out to be eerily correct, I'm inclined to say that that is what has happened. And when it does, God is certainly involved.[18]

2. Redemptive covenant revelation, sometimes called *special revelation*, has ceased. God will not be making new covenants with us, following the new covenant par excellence made with us in Christ. So there will be no more covenant words or covenant documents. This is only to say that Jesus' work is complete, once for all, and that therefore his revelation concerning Christ is complete as well. This is the *particular sufficiency* of biblical revelation.

3. The *application* of Scripture to the believer continues. The Christian life is a continuing conversation with the Bible, with God's revelation in the creation, and also with the Holy Spirit, who enables us to understand and use revelation. Every day, God in Scripture speaks to us in new ways. He brings to our attention teachings, commands, promises, and questions that we had not yet seen. He points out new ways in which Scripture applies to our lives. He responds to our prayers based on Scripture. Not only does he work in an intellectual way, but he works with our will, conforming it to God's commands, and with our emotions, so that we delight to hear what he says. In these ways, God the Holy Spirit teaches us. As we will see, this teaching is equated

---

18. In this connection, theologians of the charismatic movement often refer to the phrases "word of wisdom" and "word of knowledge" in 1 Corinthians 12:8 NKJV. The *New Spirit Filled Life Bible* (Nashville: Thomas Nelson, 2002), 1596 defines the first phrase as "a spiritual utterance at a given moment *through the Spirit*, supernaturally disclosing the mind, purpose, and will of God as applied to a specific situation" (emphasis theirs). The latter phrase is "a supernatural revelation of information pertaining to a person or an event, given for a specific purpose, usually having to do with an immediate need." I am not entirely convinced of these definitions. But, accepting those definitions provisionally, what is evidently happening in both cases is divine assistance in the application of Scripture. I have no reason to deny that such events take place in our own day.

with revelation in Matthew 11:27 and Ephesians 1:17. So in this sense also, revelation continues.[19]

Believers often wish that God had revealed more to them than he has revealed in Scripture. Often, Reformed writers will respond to this need by simply telling people to read their Bible more and more carefully. Charismatic writers often suggest that the troubled believer should listen for a fresh revelation of the Spirit. But both of these solutions are essentially intellectualistic. Both of them urge that we resolve our unease by seeking further propositional knowledge, either from Scripture or beyond Scripture. But Scripture itself tells us that often our need is not for more knowledge, but for spiritual growth, spiritual perception, the revelation of Ephesians 1:17.

4. The *preaching* and *teaching* of Scripture in the church continues, and this, too, is a kind of revelation, as we will see (chap. 35). Spirit-filled preaching has often been called *prophesying* in the Reformed tradition. When we pray for our pastor's sermon, we are asking God to take bad words away from him and to place good words in his mouth. The pastor's sermons are not the Word of God in the sense that the Bible is. But the Second Helvetic Confession, a Reformed confession, did not hesitate to say in a heading in chapter 1, "The Preaching of the Word of God Is the Word of God." I will discuss this idea further in chapter 35.

5. At the return of Christ will come the *apokalupsis*, the revelation par excellence, when every eye will see the Lord. This is revelation of an entirely different order. See Luke 17:30; Rom. 8:19; 1 Cor. 1:7; 2 Thess. 1:7; 1 Peter 1:7; 4:13. In this sense, revelation is yet to come.[20]

As we have seen, WCF 1.1 addresses the sufficiency of Scripture in contrast with the views of Roman Catholicism and Anabaptist enthusiasm, views I have just discussed. But our present-day situation requires me to discuss a third challenge to the sufficiency of Scripture, namely, Protestant traditionalism.

The Reformers did not dismiss all church tradition in theology and worship, but the main thrust of their work was antitraditional, as was Jesus'

---

19. I will have more to say about this continuing revelation in later chapters of this book, and also the senses in which God influences the words of pastors and teachers.

20. For a discussion by a Reformed scholar of how these forms of continuing revelation may lead to experiences significantly *analogous* to the charismatic gifts of the NT, see Vern S. Poythress, "Modern Spiritual Gifts as *Analogous* to Apostolic Gifts: Affirming Extraordinary Works of the Spirit within Cessationist Theology," *JETS* 39, 1 (1996): 71–101, also available at http://www.frame-poythress.org/poythress_articles/1996Modern.htm.

stance against the Pharisees. They used a very broad brush to eliminate from their theology and worship anything they considered contrary to Scripture or supplementary to Scripture. So the doctrine of the sufficiency of Scripture has served as a weapon against the imposition of extrabiblical notions on the conscience of the believer.

Nevertheless, nearly five hundred years have passed since the beginning of the Protestant Reformation, and during that time Protestantism itself has accumulated a large amount of tradition. Some of this is good, some bad. My present point is that it is just as important as ever to distinguish human tradition from the norms of Scripture and to fight any attempt to put the two on the same level of authority. Some cases in point:

1. In American fundamentalism, it has been common to insist on abstinence from alcoholic beverages. This insistence is understandable. Scripture itself condemns drunkenness, and in modern society the consumption of alcohol is one of the chief sources of automobile accidents. But Scripture, of course, does not teach abstinence. Indeed, Jesus and the apostles drank wine. Jesus supplied wine to the wedding at Cana (John 2:1–11). In 1 Timothy 5:23, Paul recommends wine for stomach ailments. Those who are severely tempted to abuse alcohol might well consider abstinence as a personal policy. But Scripture does not regard abstinence as a general rule, to be observed by all. Here we need to be reminded that God rules us by the Scriptures, not by the human tradition of abstinence.

2. Reformed theology rightly treasures its confessions, which are magnificent theological documents. So it is understandable that Reformed churches have often required officers, sometimes even congregations, to subscribe to these documents. It is thought that such subscription is necessary to prevent theological error from entering the church. Arguments persist, however, as to what kind of subscription is warranted. Some argue that "strict" subscription is necessary, which means either that one must not take any exceptions to the document or that one may not preach or teach in the areas where he takes exception. Others argue for a looser kind of subscription, qualified by such expressions as "subscription to the 'system of doctrine' taught in the Confession."

   Yet Scripture nowhere says that the church must be governed by human theological documents in addition to Scripture. Therefore, it is impossible to find biblical support for any particular view of subscription. I don't believe that Scripture *forbids* subscription to such documents. Subscription may indeed be a good means to a biblical goal, namely, soundness of teaching in the church. I do think, however, that "strict" subscriptionism violates the principle of *sola Scriptura*. If the formula of subscription is so strict that it is impossible for the church to correct the Confession in the light of Scripture, then it should not be employed. There ought to be freedom within the church to rethink the confessions and reevaluate and reform them according to the Word of God. That means that teachers, preachers, and members of the church must have the right on some occasions to teach contrary to the Confession. Otherwise, the church is ruled by tradition rather than by Scripture alone.[21]

3. Many traditions have also developed concerning worship and other aspects of church life. These concern the style and instrumentation of worship songs, the order of events in worship, degree of formality or informality, and so on. Many of these are not commanded by Scripture, but many are in accord with broad biblical principles. The problem is that church people will sometimes defend their particular practice as mandatory on all Christians, and they will criticize as spiritually inferior churches that use different styles and patterns. Often the criteria used are not scriptural, but aesthetic. People argue that this style of music is more dignified, that that liturgy is more ancient, and so forth. These aesthetic and historical criteria are often used in place of Scripture, leading to the condemnations of practices that Scripture permits and commanding of practices that Scripture does not command. That, too, in my judgment, violates the principle of *sola Scriptura*, the sufficiency of Scripture.[22]

---

21. For more discussion of this issue, see chapter 38.

22. For more of my critique of Protestant traditionalism, see chapter 38 of this volume; also my "In Defense of Something Close to Biblicism," *WTJ* 59 (1997): 269–318, also available at http://www.frame-poythress.org/frame_articles/Biblicism.htm (and also Appendix O in this volume); and "Traditionalism," available at http://www.frame-poythress.org/frame_articles/1999Traditionalism.htm (and also Appendix P in this volume).

CHAPTER 33

The Transmission of Scripture

In our study of God's revelation in human words, we have noticed that God usually delivers his revelation to us by a process, using human speakers and writers. He sometimes speaks in a "direct voice," though even that revelation contains a human element, since God speaks in human language. But in other forms of divine speech, God's revelation takes on even more of a human dimension. He speaks to human beings, called prophets and apostles, whom he appoints to communicate to the rest of us. And they often communicate in writing. Indeed, our only present direct access to the prophetic-apostolic revelation is through the written text of Scripture.

So the process of divine communication can be illustrated by this diagram:

the divine voice
↓
prophets and apostles
↓
the written Word

I have argued that there is no decrease in power, authority, or divine presence, as we move from the divine voice, to the prophets and apostles, and to the written Word. The written Word, for example, is no less authoritative than the oral word of the prophets, or than the divine voice.

But this is only the beginning of the process by which God's personal words come from him to us. The written Word itself passes through a number of processes before it reaches our ears, our eyes, and our hearts. Here are some additional steps in the process:

- copies
- textual criticism
- translations, editions
- teaching, preaching
- sacraments
- theology
- confessions, creeds, traditions, human reception
- interpretation, understanding
- assurance

I have not put downward arrows between the items on this list, as I did on the previous list. On this list, the order is more flexible. Confessions, for example, may be based on theology, or theology on confessions. "Human reception," even "assurance," is something that was doubtless experienced by the first readers of Scripture, before any copying or translating took place. But I want to focus on the assurance of present-day Christian readers that they are hearing and reading the Word of God. In general, I believe the list represents the sort of temporal order of events through which we usually receive the Word of God today.

A more important difference between the two lists is that on the first list, as I said, every form of the word bears the divine lordship attributes: controlling power, authority, and presence. As we pass down the first list, there is no decrease in power, authority, and divine presence. The second list, however, is a list of fallible means by which human beings hear and assimilate the Word of God. These are works and responses of human beings, not inspired in the sense that God inspired the biblical writings themselves. These cannot claim the full power, authority, and presence of God, but they are means of conveying the Word of God, which does indeed bear these lordship attributes. In these events, the interplay between divine revelation and fallible human communication will be a major subject of my discussion.[1]

I begin in this chapter with a discussion of the *copying* of Scripture. As we saw in chapter 23, God inspires not only prophets and apostles, but also written *texts*. Second Timothy 3:16 says that all *Scripture* is inspired by God. Now, evangelicals have typically limited that inspiration to the *autographs*

---

1. In chapter 12, I address the general question whether the human aspects of God's word necessarily make it fallible. I conclude that they do not.

or *autographa*, the original manuscripts produced by the inspired writer, as opposed to *copies* or *apographa*.[2] As I will explain, I think this limitation is better described as a limitation to the *autographic text*, rather than to the autograph as such. I agree with this limitation, but it does raise a number of questions that we should consider here.

WHAT IS AN AUTOGRAPH?

It may seem obvious to us that an *autograph* is simply the document written by the prophet, apostle, or other inspired writer. Any other manuscript of the same text is a *copy*. But the issue is more complicated, when you consider that the biblical writer may have written more than one draft of his book or letter, and that he might have made use of an amanuensis (secretary).[3] Is the first draft the autograph? Or is it possible that the first draft required some revisions before it was sent to its destination? What if the amanuensis made some mistakes in his first draft, and the biblical writer needed to correct the manuscript?

I agree with Greg Bahnsen that the *autograph* is "the first completed, personal, or approved transcription of a unique word-group composed by its author."[4] It is a "finished product," as Bahnsen says, not a rough draft in need of perfecting. And it is certified by the author in some way so as to assure readers that this is his inspired teaching. In the case of 1 Corinthians, Paul would have certified it by declaring that he was finished with it and by sending it to Corinth by a messenger. When the messenger brought Paul's letter to Corinth, that messenger's testimony certified to the church that it was an authentic letter of Paul.

IS THIS LIMITATION SCRIPTURAL?

Common sense tells us that the content of any book consists of what the author wrote and nothing else. If I write my own ideas in the margin

2. This limitation is not new to nineteenth- or twentieth-century evangelicalism. Greg Bahnsen cites many writers, including Augustine, John Calvin, and Richard Baxter, who made the distinction between the truth of the autograph and errors in the copies. See his "The Inerrancy of the Autographa," in *Inerrancy*, ed. Norman Geisler (Grand Rapids: Zondervan, 1979), 156–59. Bahnsen's article is one of the best recent treatments of this issue, and much in this present chapter will reflect his arguments.

3. Paul evidently used amanuenses regularly. Tertius played that role in the writing of the letter to the Romans (Rom. 16:22). In 1 Corinthians 16:21, Galatians 6:11, 2 Thessalonians 3:17, and Philemon 19, Paul writes in his "own hand" at the end of each letter, indicating that the rest of the letter was written by someone else's hand.

4. Bahnsen, "The Inerrancy of the Autographa," 190.

of Kant's *Critique of Pure Reason*, that does not make those ideas part of his book. Similarly, when Thomas Jefferson edited out many passages of the Bible that displeased him, he did not reduce the content of the Bible. The Bible is what God gave to us, not what God gave minus Jefferson's omissions. The Bible is God's own written Word, without addition or subtraction.

Scripture itself is concerned that we follow what it says, not what someone adds to it, nor a truncated version that emerged from human subtractions. So God says in Deuteronomy 4:2:

> You shall not add to the word that I command you, nor take from it, that you may keep the commandments of the LORD your God that I command you.

And:

> Everything that I command you, you shall be careful to do. You shall not add to it or take from it. (Deut. 12:32)

In Deuteronomy, the reference is specifically to the law of God given to Moses. But Proverbs 30:5–6 presents this as a general principle, applicable to all of God's words:

> Every word of God proves true; he is a shield to those who take refuge in him. Do not add to his words, lest he rebuke you and you be found a liar.

Very near the end of the NT, we read this:

> I warn everyone who hears the words of the prophecy of this book: if anyone adds to them, God will add to him the plagues described in this book, and if anyone takes away from the words of the book of this prophecy, God will take away his share in the tree of life and in the holy city, which are described in this book. (Rev. 22:18–19)[5]

These passages reflect the "inscriptional curses" that were found in the ancient suzerainty treaties to which I referred in chapters 17, 32, and else-

---

5. People sometimes ask whether this curse pertains only to the book of Revelation or to the whole Bible. I think the author intended it to apply to the book of Revelation, the book he had written; he was not thinking of a broader reference. Nevertheless, as we have seen, this text reproduces a principle that pertains to anything God says. Whenever God speaks, we should not add to it or subtract from it. So it is appropriate, and an interesting providential development, that these verses ended up nearly at the end of the Bible as the church has arranged it. It is an appropriate place to warn readers to take God's Word as it is and not try to reconstruct it.

where. Those treaties were the words of the great king, and it was important that his words not be confused with any other words. The presence of such curses in the Bible is consistent with our earlier-stated view that Scripture is very much like a suzerainty treaty between God and his people.

This principle is important to the sufficiency of Scripture, which we considered in chapter 32. Recall my references there to Isaiah 29:13–14 and Mark 7:8. Jesus quoted Isaiah 29:13–14 to show that the Pharisees were making their tradition as authoritative as Scripture, in effect adding to God's Word. He also charges them in Matthew 23:23 with neglecting "the weightier matters of the law: justice and mercy and faithfulness," in effect subtracting from God's Word.

Of course, there are various ways of adding to and subtracting from God's Word. Jesus does not tell us in Mark 7:8 that the Pharisees literally crossed out passages in Scripture, or that they wrote their traditions into the margins. But in effect they lived by a distorted canon, one that was a combination of God's Word and their own ideas.

Even more obviously, though, it would be wrong for someone to have literally crossed words out of the definitive manuscript of the law of Moses that resided in the holiest part of the temple, denying the authority of those words. And it would have been just as bad to add one's own thoughts to that document and claim that they were God's (Deut. 18:20).

So the inscriptional curse passages do distinguish between the original manuscripts of Scripture and the copies, and they forbid any copying that changes the original text.

This is not to say, however, that copies are always worse than the originals. When the copy agrees with the original, without any additions or subtractions, then it is just as true as the original, indeed just as authoritative. This observation should help us to see that what is at issue is not primarily the autographic document, but the autographic *text*.[6] The *text* is a linguistic object that can be found in any number of physical media. If I type out Lincoln's Gettysburg Address on my computer and then print it out five times, there is an original autograph and five copies, but only one *text*. That same text could be reproduced on clay tablets, or papyrus, or paper, or digital media. As long as there is no change, all these copies present a single text.

Similarly with Scripture. By divine inspiration its text is found in the autograph, and when the copy is perfect, the text is found in the copy as well. It is therefore not important whether or not the autographic *document* is preserved. It is important that the autographic *text* be available

6. Compare Bahnsen's discussion in "The Inerrancy of the Autographa," 160–62.

to us, even though that text may be found only in copies (*apographa*) of the original.

But it is *possible* that there will be errors in the copy. Why? Because God has not promised that copies will be perfect. He has not, in other words, promised to keep all copyists from error. Like all the other items in our second list of terms, the process of copying is a fallible process. Sit down for yourself and try to copy the first chapter of Genesis. Most likely, you will make a few mistakes. Even computer printouts sometimes fail to reproduce the original text accurately. (Sometimes the printer is unable to reproduce characters given to it by a word processor.) Neither any passage in Scripture nor any biblical principle promises otherwise.

So the limitation of inspiration (and hence of authority, infallibility, and inerrancy) to the autographic text is a biblical limitation.

BUT DON'T BIBLICAL WRITERS QUOTE COPIES AS GOD'S WORD?

A number of writers have argued that we should not limit divine inspiration to the autograph because Jesus and the apostles regularly quote copies, even translations and versions, as God's Word. It is true that Jesus and the apostles did not possess autographs of the texts they quote. Indeed, they often quote as God's Word the Septuagint (LXX), the Greek version of the OT commonly used among the Jews. But consider the following:

1. These quotations do not erase the fact I emphasized earlier, that Jesus and the apostles distinguished between the true Word of God and the additions and subtractions of human beings. They believed that any deviation from the original was unauthorized by God and therefore had no authority.
2. Recall that the important thing is not the autographic manuscript, but the autographic *text*. That text may exist in many copies, if those copies are accurate copies. So to cite a copy, when the copy is accurate, does not violate the sole authority of the autographic text.
3. In chapter 28, I discussed the practices of Jesus, the apostles, and the NT writers in quoting or alluding to the OT. I concluded that there is no reason to think they were quoting inaccurately or misusing the passages they quote. If that is correct, then it follows that their quotes are quotes of the autographic text. Therefore, their use of the OT is consistent with the principle that authority is limited to the autographic text.

4. Unlike the Qur'an, the Bible does not assume that God's Word is untranslatable. Rather (in keeping with the nature of Christianity as a missionary religion), the Bible itself uses multiple languages (Hebrew, Aramaic, and Greek, with further variations of style). When NT writers quote the Hebrew Bible in Greek, there is no reason to think the differences between the two languages necessarily invalidate the quotation. The same is true when they quote the LXX. Insofar as their quotation reproduces the content of the Hebrew autographic text, it is true and authoritative.

5. In chapter 26, I indicated that biblical language is, generally speaking, ordinary, rather than technical. It is not, therefore, perfectly precise. It exhibits a level of precision appropriate to its context and purpose. Now, there are always minor differences, at least in nuance or feel, between a sentence in Hebrew and a translation of that sentence into Greek. So there are often some levels of imprecision in the NT quotes of the OT. But those do not impugn the accuracy of the quotes for their purpose. They do not negate the value of those quotations as *applications* (see chap. 28) of God's Word.

6. When theologians use NT quotations of the OT to criticize the limitation of inspiration to the autographic text, they mean to say that the autographic text is not unique in authority, that it is not uniquely inspired. On this basis, texts that are contrary to the autographic text, even erroneous ones, can be just as inspired as the autographic text. If this is true, then an inspired text can contain error. But I have argued extensively in earlier chapters to show that this is not the case.

7. When Jesus and the apostles quote the OT using the LXX version, their intent is not to assert the authority of the LXX as a translation, but to quote what is said in the OT autographic text. The LXX is only a vehicle for accomplishing that, a good means of communication to people who know Scripture primarily through the LXX.

IS THIS LIMITATION AN APOLOGETIC DODGE?

Some have claimed that the limitation of inerrancy to the autographs is a "convenient dodge" to avoid dealing with Bible problems. The argument is that when evangelicals find a problem in Scripture that they can't answer, they simply respond that "there must have been some textual error," that is, an error by a copyist.

But this criticism is unfair. In the first place, as we've seen, evangelicals arrive at this principle not from apologetic motives, but because the limitation to the autographic text is implicit in Scripture's own doctrine of Scripture.

Second, evangelical responses to Bible problems very rarely appeal to the possibility of copyist error. In only a few places is copyist error a likely explanation of a difficulty. One is 1 Kings 4:26, which says that Solomon had "40,000" stalls of horses for his chariots, while 2 Chronicles 9:25 reports that he had only "4,000." Norman Geisler and Thomas Howe point out that these numbers are visually very similar in the Hebrew, and a scribe may well have miscopied.[7] This explanation is a reasonable one. Geisler and Howe are not bringing in the textual issue arbitrarily or inappropriately. They bring it up because there is a rational likelihood of textual corruption in this passage.

In general, it is not wise for evangelical apologists to bring up the possibility of textual corruption in the abstract. When an apologist discusses (as I did in chapter 28) Jesus' statement in Matthew 13:31–32 about the mustard seed's being the smallest seed, it won't help to say, "Well, the text may be corrupt at that point." That reply is not cogent or even plausible, given that there is no reason to assume textual corruption in that passage. The apologetic appeal to textual corruption is cogent only where (as in 1 Kings 4:26 and 2 Chronicles 9:25) there is good reason to expect textual corruption.[8]

But most evangelical apologists are wise in dealing with such matters. They don't recklessly appeal to copyist error whenever a problem appears.

And as I suggested in chapter 28, there is no need for evangelicals to appeal to such implausible possibilities. When we reach the end of our ability to explain, it is far better, indeed more cogent, to say honestly, "I don't know."

DOES THIS LIMITATION MAKE INERRANCY A DEAD LETTER?

Another criticism is that if we limit biblical inerrancy to the autographic text, then we must make the damaging admission that our present Bibles are not inerrant. In that case, inerrancy pertains only to documents

---

7. Norman L. Geisler and Thomas A. Howe, *When Critics Ask* (Wheaton, IL: Victor Books, 1992), 181.

8. And as I indicated in chapter 28, there is a better way to deal with the problem of the mustard seed.

(the autographs) that are now lost. It makes no difference to our use of Scripture today.

In reply:

1. Even if our present Bibles are not inerrant in any sense, the doctrine of inerrancy is still important. For the doctrine of biblical inerrancy, important as it is to us, is not primarily a doctrine facilitating our use of Scripture. It is primarily a doctrine about God's own truthfulness. What the doctrine of inerrancy does first of all is this: it enables us to confess the truthfulness of God. If there were errors in the autographs of Scripture, then God would not be truthful.

2. But in fact, inerrancy is not *only* a doctrine about God's truthfulness. It is also a doctrine that makes an immense difference in our own use of Scripture. As we have seen, inerrancy is limited to the autographic *text*, not to the autograph itself. Although the autographs are all missing (so far as we know), the autographic text has been transmitted through copies and editions through the centuries, down to our own time. That transmission has been imperfect, as we have seen. But it is possible, through the science of textual criticism, to determine where the imperfections are likely to be. Where there is no evidence of textual corruption, we are quite within our rights to assume that our present text is autographic and therefore to appeal to the text as the inerrant Word of God—just as Jesus and the apostles appealed to copies and versions of their day. So inerrancy is a practical doctrine as well as a theological one.

3. In fact, the biblical text has been far better preserved than any other ancient document. There are far more ancient manuscripts of Scripture and Scripture portions than manuscripts of the religions of Greece, Egypt, and Babylon, more than manuscripts of the Greek philosophers and poets. The manuscripts we have of Scripture are closer to the time of their original writing. And they are of higher quality. The variations among different manuscripts and manuscript families are many, but minor. They consist mainly of spelling differences, word substitutions, and minor grammatical differences that make little difference to the meaning of the passage. So WCF 1.8 rightly speaks of the "singular care and providence" by which God has preserved the biblical text.[9]

---

9. This singular care and providence does not imply, as some have argued, that one textual tradition is far more reliable than the others, which we are obligated to accept.

4. Where there are significant textual problems, as in the ending of Mark, they do not affect any doctrine of the faith. In my judgment, the "long ending" of Mark (which many Bibles include as 16:9–20) was not part of the original text. But nothing in that passage is contrary to anything elsewhere in Scripture.[10] And what Mark 16 says is found in other passages. So that textual difficulty is actually of minor importance, even though twelve verses are involved.

5. One reason why textual problems do not affect biblical doctrine is that they are almost always minor, as I've said. Another reason is that Scripture is highly redundant, in a good way. The doctrines of the Christian faith are never derived from a single text.[11] Rather, each doctrine is based on many texts, drawn together to form a consistent pattern of teaching. Scripture repeats itself over and over again, in many different literary genres, through the work of many authors, over many centuries. So when a textual problem makes it difficult to appeal to a single text, many other texts on the same subject give us assurance of the truth.

So just as Jesus and the apostles appealed to the Scriptures available to them as the Word of God, without denying biblical inerrancy, so may we.

This sort of view lies behind the argument that we must use only the KJV, or other versions based on the Byzantine textual tradition, a text family that includes the majority of the ancient manuscripts, but not necessarily the oldest or most reliable. But God may have used his singular care and providence to preserve the text by distributing it through several manuscript families.

10. In verse 18, Jesus promises believers that they will pick up serpents with their hands and be unharmed, and that drinking poison won't hurt them. Of course, I don't recommend these practices as a general rule. But Acts 28:3–5 describes Paul's shaking off a deadly viper without suffering harm, and I would not be surprised if God also in some situation allowed a believer to drink poison without suffering harm, as a witness of Christ's power. The other kinds of miracles mentioned here (exorcism, tongues, healing) are explicitly mentioned elsewhere in the NT. Mark 16:18 does not imply that God does such miracles anytime we choose to pick up serpents or drink poison; but it does teach, truly, that such miracles will *sometimes* happen, in the course of gospel proclamation. The point of Jesus' teaching here is not that such miracles will be a normal part of every believer's experience, but that miraculous signs will *accompany* those who believe, as they bring the gospel to the world (v. 15). And in fact, God did accompany the apostles' message by signs like these, the "signs of a true apostle" (2 Cor. 12:12).

11. Occasionally, somebody will try to build an elaborate doctrinal construction on a single obscure text, as in the Mormon doctrine of baptism for the dead, supposedly based on 1 Corinthians 15:29. But this sort of thing is a mark of cultic, as opposed to orthodox, exegesis.

WHY DID GOD ALLOW THE AUTOGRAPHS TO BE LOST?

I have been arguing that biblical inerrancy is limited to the inspired autographic text. There is no guarantee in Scripture that copies of the original autograph will be perfect. Nevertheless, God has remarkably preserved the biblical text so that we can appeal to our present versions of Scripture as the inerrant Word of God. But we ask, would it not have been easier if God had providentially, even miraculously, preserved the autographic manuscripts? Scripture gives us no explicit reason. But consider:

1. Many have suggested that if the original manuscripts had been preserved, they might have become objects of idolatrous worship. Given the use of relics in the history of the church, this consideration carries some weight. Recall that King Hezekiah destroyed the brass serpent that Moses had made to heal the people in the wilderness, because the people had begun to worship it (2 Kings 18:4).
2. The present existence of the autograph would not help us much with the problem of understanding and applying God's Word. We have considered many debates about the inspiration, authority, and inerrancy of the biblical text. The presence of the autograph would not have stifled those debates. Nor would it have eliminated the debates about the interpretation of texts and the doctrinal use of Scripture. Very few of those debates, if any, hinge on textual questions, and they would not be resolved by the existence of a pure text. So for God to have preserved the autographs would have been a superfluous use of his power.

WHY DID GOD NOT GIVE US PERFECT COPIES?

A similar question is this: why did God choose not to give us perfect copies, ensuring the perfect preservation of the autographic text, though not of the autographic manuscripts? If having an inerrant Bible is so important, why didn't God determine to make *all copies* of Scripture inerrant?

We should understand, first, what such divine providence would entail. It would mean that if you sat down to copy Genesis 1, you could not fail to produce a perfect replica of it. God would prevent any lapses of memory as you glanced between the original and your copy-page. He would prevent on the spot any sinful inclination you might have toward distorting the text in any way. All of that is, of course, possible for God to do. But it suggests a picture of his providence that is rather at odds with his usual ways of working among us.

More seriously, though, we need to consider this question from a larger perspective. Recall the second list of events that I presented at the beginning of this chapter: copying, textual criticism, translation, teaching, and so on, right down to understanding and assurance. These are all steps on the way for us to receive edification from Scripture. God intends that we will receive such edification, so he provides all these operations. But note that in each of those operations we may ask why God did not institute perfection. After all, he might have provided not only perfect copies, but also perfect textual criticism, perfect translations, perfect teaching, and so on. Indeed, he might have guaranteed that all our attempts to *understand* might be perfectly successful. He might even have determined to skip the steps between inspiring the Scripture and giving us understanding of it. For why should we go through the whole process of copying, translating, and teaching, if God is able to give us an immediate understanding of his Word? Why should God institute such a process? Why should he not rather give each of us an immediate, intuitive understanding of his revelation, so that we could magically understand it all, with a glance at the Hebrew or Greek text? For that matter, why did God even bother to place his revelation in a book? Why didn't he simply reveal it immediately to every human being?

God has not given us a clear answer to any of these questions. But they are all similar. If it seems unlikely that God would provide an inerrant book, but consign the publication of it to fallible copyists, then is it not equally unlikely that he would turn the work of translation, teaching, and theology over to fallible human beings?[12] And if it seems likely that God would provide infallible copies of Scripture, then it is equally likely that God would provide perfect translations, and so on. If we think that God would probably not provide a perfect translation, then it is equally unlikely that he would provide us with perfect copies.

The question then becomes: why did God inspire an inerrant Word, and then consign that Word to a fallible process of distribution and appropriation? That way of putting it may suggest an answer. I think it most likely that God wanted us to appropriate his personal words in a *communal* way. Had he given us perfect copies, perfect translations, and so on, each individual could have come to an understanding of Scripture without help from anyone else. He could have gone to the bookstore and

---

12. The gift of tongues shows that God is supernaturally able to circumvent the normally laborious process of translation in a particular situation. So, we are asking, why did he not choose to do this on every occasion?

bought for himself a perfect translation of Scripture, taught it to himself, and gained thereby a perfect understanding.[13] But that was not God's intention. He wanted the church to gather around the Word together, covenantally. He wanted each individual to benefit from the gifts of others in the body. Some would be gifted in languages; they would translate. Others would be gifted to teach, and they would instruct. Some would teach by words, others more by the example of their lives. Everyone would contribute something to the "edifying of the body," building up one another.[14] Each individual would rely on the gifts of others. Listening for God's Word would draw the body together.

Granted, the communal process of assimilating the Word often works in the opposite way. Churches are divided over Bible translations, interpretations, theological understanding, and the rest. Sin always messes things up. But at its best, the process of learning God's Word together is, even now, a precious one. It leads us not only to love God, but also to love one another, to honor one another's gifts, to grow in relationships as well as knowledge.

God may have additional, or completely different, reasons for his decision to give us fallible copies of an infallible book. But certainly he has made that decision for his own reasons, and we would be unwise to second-guess him.

ISN'T ANY LOSS A SERIOUS LOSS?

On the basis of our previous arguments, we can say that nearly all the autographic *text* of Scripture has been preserved, and through Scripture's lavish redundancy all the doctrinal teaching of Scripture is available to the church. But because the process of transmission is fallible, we must admit that *something* has been lost to us. For example, we don't know for sure how the Gospel of Mark originally ended. So it may well be that we have lost a summary paragraph, or some words of Jesus. Since we live by *every* word that comes from God's mouth (Matt. 4:4), that loss is a serious loss, even if it is the loss of a mere nuance or perspective on what we already have.

But remember that losses of the word of God are not unprecedented. John tells us that many things Jesus did (doubtless including much teaching)

---

13. That we should even seriously consider such a possibility speaks to the individualism of our culture. Most peoples of the world, including first-century Jews and Christians, take the communal approach to knowledge for granted.

14. This is a fundamental NT theme. See Rom. 14:19; 15:2; 1 Cor. 8:1; 14:3–5, 12, 17, 26; 2 Cor. 10:8; 12:19; 13:10; Eph. 4:12, 16, 29; 1 Thess. 5:11; 1 Tim. 1:4.

have not been recorded in writing (John 21:25). John says there, "Were every one of them to be written, I suppose that the world itself could not contain the books that would be written." So we have lost some of Jesus' teaching, teaching that would certainly have been helpful to us, even if it differed from the recorded teaching only by way of nuance or emphasis. The same is true of the prophets of the OT. Certainly, the prophet Obadiah received more words of God than the brief book we have that bears his name. And at least two letters of Paul have not been preserved for us (mentioned in 1 Corinthians 5:9 and 2 Corinthians 7:8).

God did not take care to preserve for us all his personal words through Jesus, prophets, and apostles. Some of them met needs of their original hearers, but God determined that they did not need to be preserved for us.

Certainly, it would be a wonderful thing if archaeologists were to unearth a lost letter that could be authenticated as coming from Paul—or an authentic fifth Gospel. But God has determined that up to now, such lost revelation is not needed by the church. We should take the "every" of Matthew 4:4 to refer to the revelation that God has provided us today, not to every word of God that has ever been uttered in history.

We should think similarly of those fragments of verbal revelation that may have been lost through the process of textual transmission. God is sovereign over this process, and he has determined what should survive and what should not. He has determined that we will have all the personal words he intends to speak to us today. In that theological sense, we have lost nothing through the process of textual transmission.

To summarize: (1) The autographic *manuscripts* of Scripture are presently lost, though we should not despair of finding at least some of them in the future. (2) The autographic *text* has been almost entirely preserved, accessible through manuscripts available to us and through the science of textual criticism. (3) The distinctive *teaching* of the Scriptures has been entirely preserved, given the beneficial redundancy of doctrinal teaching in Scripture. (4) Because of God's "singular care and providence" (WCF 1.8) over the process of transmission, we now have in Scripture all the personal words that God intends to say to us today.

CHAPTER 34

Translations and Editions of Scripture

In the last chapter, I provided a list of the events by which the Bible is usually transmitted from its original manuscripts to us modern readers. In that chapter, I discussed the first events on the list, namely, copying and textual criticism. I argued there that although the copying of Scripture is a fallible process, God provides it as a suitable means of bringing to us his authoritative personal words.

I will say similar things about the processes to be discussed here, those of translating and editing Scripture. These, too, are fallible processes, imperfect in their results. Yet by God's providence, they are suitable means of bringing his personal words to us.

First, let us consider translation. As with many other topics in this book, it is important to consider translation from a broad perspective. I argued earlier (chaps. 8–11) that the word of God is God himself, expressing himself through his lordship attributes of control, authority, and presence. In its identity with God's nature and with his eternal thought, God's word is not spoken in a human language. We don't know the language by which the Father, Son, and Spirit communicate with one another eternally, but it certainly is not a language that we have ever heard on the street.

Indeed, that language is not a language that any human being has ever heard, even in God's conversations with us. Ear has not heard it (1 Cor. 2:9). What God says to the hearers of his divine voice (chap. 14) is always a *translation* of his eternal thought, a translation from divine speech to human speech. God tells Israel in Hebrew, or in some linguistic ancestor of Hebrew, that he is their Lord (Ex. 20:1–2).

Scripture never suggests that such translation distorts the divine words. His spoken words, so translated, as we have seen, bear his ultimate authority. They are God's personal words to human beings. They are infallible and inerrant.

Compared to God's great work of translating his eternal thoughts into human language, other levels of translation are easy. From what we know of the pace of linguistic change, for example, it is likely that the Hebrew Moses spoke had changed considerably between his original writing and the manuscripts available to us. Evidently some editing was done to update Moses' language. But Scripture does not mention that process. Scripture does not consider such translation to have any importance at all to the doctrine of the word of God or to redemptive history.

Certainly, Scripture never suggests that translation itself reduces the power or authority of the word of God. In the NT, the words of Jesus may have originally been spoken in Aramaic.[1] But the texts themselves do not reflect on that possibility. More obviously, as we saw in chapter 33, Jesus and the apostles often refer to the LXX translation of the Hebrew Scriptures into Greek. Again, Scripture never suggests that such use of a translation presents a difficulty. Rather, insofar as a quotation reproduces the meaning of the autographic text, it reproduces the meaning, and therefore the authority, of the original. As I also pointed out in the previous chapter, when NT writers quote the LXX, it is not their intention to grant authority to the LXX as a translation, but to use the LXX as a vehicle by which to quote the autographic text.

What Scripture does say is that the diversity of languages in the world is a divine judgment (Gen. 11:1–9). Noah's descendants had sought to build a city to glorify their own name, not God's (v. 4), built around a tower (Babel) that would supposedly extend into heaven. They intended to stay there, rather than to obey God's command to "fill" the earth (Gen. 1:28; 9:1). When God broke up the linguistic unity of mankind, people began again to spread all over the earth. Language diversity has since been a great barrier to human unity. But it has not been a barrier for God. As God invented the division of languages, he is able to overcome it for his purposes. He is able to speak in all the languages of human beings, and there is no difference in power or authority between a divine word spoken in Hebrew, Aramaic, or Greek—or, for that matter, in English, Italian, Swahili, or Japanese.

---

1. That is by no means certain. Jesus (in his human existence) certainly knew Hebrew from the Scriptures and the Jewish liturgy from the synagogue and the temple. And he may well have known Koine Greek as well, the lingua franca of the time.

At Pentecost, God partially rolled back the curse of Babel, enabling Jews from many lands to hear the gospel in their own languages (Acts 2:1–12). God's purpose had always been a purpose for the whole world, implicit in his command to Adam and Eve to fill the earth, renewed in his promise to Abram that in him would be blessed "all the families of the earth" (Gen. 12:3). Jesus' Great Commission instructed the apostles to "make disciples of all nations" (Matt. 28:19). So it had always been God's plan to distribute his Word to all nations of the earth.

Thus, it should have been no surprise that the apostles wrote the NT in Greek, the lingua franca, rather than Hebrew or Aramaic. And throughout history, Christians have had a strong motivation to learn languages and to translate Scripture into all the languages of the world.

So the translation of Scripture is not only a practical necessity. It is rooted in the very nature of the biblical gospel, a gospel for "every . . . language" (Rev. 14:6).

Our basic stance toward Bible translation must, therefore, be affirmative. Unlike Islam, Christianity does not believe that God's Word is untranslatable. Rather, God speaks his Word into every language.

Now, we should admit that translation sometimes results in loss of content. That is, however, not always the case. The Greek word for *door*, for example, is *thura* (as in John 10:1). In its literal use, this term does not differ at all from the English word *door*. Everything that can be called *door* in English can be called *thura* in Greek, and vice versa. And although I have not made an extensive study of the matter, I would say that the two terms can be similarly used in figurative ways as well. But certainly there are some terms in each language that are not as easily commensurable with one another, and when we look beyond the individual word level, to phrases, sentences, paragraphs, and literary wholes, many problems of translation arise. There are idioms in each language that do not translate into other languages word for word. And when translators try to paraphrase idiomatic expressions, they sometimes create additional problems. So in most cases, beyond the word level, it is impossible to perfectly reproduce in the target language the meaning of the original. Between the two there will always be some difference of nuance, emphasis, or association, if not more.

For this reason, it is important for Christians of all nations to work toward better and better translations of Scripture into their own languages. The work of translation has not ended, even in the most Christianized parts of the world.[2] And as language continues to change, translations need to be revised.

---

2. I confess, however, that I don't quite see the point of the huge number of translations now available in English. I suspect that the rush to bring out more and more English translations has more to do with the financial profitability of these than the inherent need

But imperfect translations can be means of communicating God's personal words. We saw in the previous chapter that Jesus and the apostles quote the OT in copies, rather than original manuscripts. But we saw also that one can quote the autographic *text* even when one is quoting a fallible copy of that text. We noted then also that the apostles do not only quote copies; they sometimes quote the LXX *translation*. The same argument must be made in this case. Even though a translation may differ in some ways from the original text of the original language, the differences are not extensive enough to invalidate all quotations of them.

In the last chapter, I indicated that textual difficulties are of minor importance and do not invalidate any doctrinal teaching of the church. The same must be said of translation difficulties. Even the worst translation contains the basic gospel; I note that even the translations of heretical groups are not able to keep the gospel out. The best translations are imperfect; but they are usually able to capture nearly all the meaning of the original, so that one can quote them, confident that one is quoting the autographic text. In most Scripture passages, there are no translation difficulties. When there is a problem in one passage, it is usually not difficult, by virtue of Scripture's eloquent redundancy (chaps. 18, 33), to find another passage where the same subject matter exists without translation difficulty.

People often ask what translations they should use. That is a difficult question, because different translations have different goals. Some seek literal, word-for-word correspondence with the original language (such as, in English, the ASV, NASB, or, at the extreme, interlinear translations[3]). But these often sacrifice some level of readability. Others seek readability at the expense of word-for-word correspondence (such as the NIV and NLT). The word-for-word approach to translation is very useful for those who are learning Greek or Hebrew. A translation such as the KJV or the NASB actually gives the reader a feel for the way sentences are phrased in the original languages, as well as providing a direct way to compare English words with those of the original. Further, a more literal translation often provides useful correlations between parts of Scripture. Such translations prefer to use the same English word to translate the same Hebrew or Greek word, whenever possible. That enables the English reader to note parallels between passages that might get lost in a less literal translation.

---

of them. I pray that God will send more of our linguists out to translate the Scriptures into languages where translations are more needed, even though less lucrative.

3. Some Hebrew and Greek Bibles are produced with an equivalent English word under each Greek or Hebrew word, so *interlinear*. These interlinear words are in effect translations, though scarcely readable.

But for many, these literal translations do not communicate very well. And communication is, in one sense, the bottom line of translation. The very best translation would be one in which all the content of the original language is communicated in the target language, in the way the target language is actually spoken and written. But that double goal is rarely attained. A good compromise for theological teaching is the ESV, which I regularly quote in this book. But for other purposes—such as teaching children, teenagers, or people who speak regional dialects—other translations may be better.

The line between translation and paraphrase is not sharp. We apply the term *paraphrase* to translations that are pretty far toward the nonliteral side of the spectrum. We should remember, however, that the reason for nonliteral translation is to communicate more effectively with speakers of the target language. If that communication is effective, it is effective in capturing biblical meaning that would otherwise be lost. So we shouldn't think that only literal translations capture biblical meaning. Literal and nonliteral translations differ in the *kind* of meaning they convey.

And when a translation conveys biblical meaning of *any* kind, it communicates the autographic text of Scripture. To the extent that it conveys biblical meaning, it should be received as God's personal words to us.

The same is true of Bible *editions*, published versions, often with notes, maps, cross-references, and other helps. People do need to be warned to distinguish between the text, which is God's inspired Word, and the editorial additions, which have only human authority. But these are often useful, and the usefulness of an edition varies according to the purpose for which it is used. So today we have an Apologetics Study Bible, a Life Application Bible, study Bibles for different doctrinal traditions, and so on. The study helps and notes, to the extent to which they are reliable, communicate biblical truth that some readers might not learn from the text alone. In that way, they add to our knowledge of the autographic text.

CHAPTER 35

Teaching and Preaching

Over the centuries, more people have received the gospel through teaching and preaching than through reading. Many cultures influenced by the gospel have been illiterate, so in them the chief means of communicating God's Word have been oral. And of course, the oral medium preceded the written medium in time. Jesus and the apostles taught orally before any of their words were written down. So we need to consider the oral media of the communication of God's Word.

We discussed the prophetic and apostolic proclamations in chapter 15. Those oral words were directly inspired by God and were therefore supremely authoritative, infallible, and inerrant. Scripture does not promise that anyone after the apostolic period will speak words with such authority. Indeed, with the closing of the canon, Scripture is sufficient as a source of divine words (see chaps. 22, 32).

Nevertheless, the Bible does indicate that after the apostolic period, preaching and teaching will continue. Timothy is not an inspired apostle, but Paul commands him to "preach the word; be ready in season and out of season; reprove, rebuke, and exhort, with complete patience and teaching" (2 Tim. 4:2). Overseers (= bishops, elders) must be "able to teach" (1 Tim. 3:2).

There has been debate over the difference in meaning between *preaching* (*kerysso, keryx, kerygma*) and *teaching* (*didasko, didaskalia, didache*). C. H. Dodd argued that kerygma and didache were two very different forms of communication in the NT,[1] each with a distinctive subject matter, but that conclusion is too extreme. The *didasko* language and the *kerusso* language can refer to the same activity (e.g., Matt. 4:23; 9:35; 11:1; Acts 5:42; 15:35; 28:31; Rom. 2:21; Col. 1:28; 1 Tim. 2:7; 2 Tim. 4:2). The two terms differ somewhat in their connotations, so the presence of the one supplements that of the other in these passages. The *kerusso* terms represent a more dramatic form of communication, that of a herald, a proclamation. The *didasko* group refers more broadly to communication of ideas. It is fair to say that kerygma is a kind of didache, a style of didache. Preaching, *kerussein*, seems more appropriate to describe a dramatic discourse before a large group. Teaching, *didaskein*, seems to suggest a less formal, perhaps smaller, setting.

Preaching (*kerussein*) in the NT tends to be used most often for the proclamation of the gospel to a group for the first time, so it is associated with the most basic elements of the gospel. Jesus engaged in preaching, but the NT uses the term most often to refer to the apostolic proclamation, especially that of Paul. The apostles preached Christ to Jews in their synagogues (as Acts 9:20), to Samaritans (8:5), and to Gentiles in their cities (14:1–7).

Teaching occurs in all the same contexts, as we saw earlier. But as we've also seen, it is connected with the office of "overseer" as well. The *didasko* terms seem especially appropriate in a church context. The overseers are given particular responsibility for teaching, but there is also a sense in which every Christian is a teacher (Eph. 4:29; Col. 3:16; Heb. 5:12; 1 John 2:27). In Reformed theology, the official teaching is said to belong to the *special office*, while the teaching of all believers is part of the *general office*, that is, the priesthood of all believers. Special-office teaching requires special gifts of character and competence (1 Tim. 3:1–7), and (as I understand 1 Timothy 2:12) that teaching is restricted to men only.[2] Women may and do participate in general-office teaching, however, as when Priscilla (mentioned first, most likely, to indicate her prominence in this activity) with her husband Aquila instruct Apollos in the word of God (Acts 18:26), and as when Paul instructs older women to teach younger women (Titus 2:2–5).

We are accustomed to think of preaching as what takes place in our Sunday-morning sermons. But it is perhaps significant that the NT never uses *kerusso* terminology to refer to anything in the Christian worship service. As I have said, the line between preaching and teaching is not

---

1. C. H. Dodd, *The Apostolic Preaching and Its Developments* (London: Hodder and Stoughton, 1936).
2. See *DCL*, 635–44.

sharp, and that line distinguishes connotation and nuance rather than two completely distinct activities. So it is not wrong to describe teaching in worship as *preaching*. But in Reformed theology, the concept of preaching tends to be drawn from the apostolic proclamation following the ascension of Christ: a heralding, a mode of authoritative announcement rather than discussion or debate, a redemptive-historical emphasis, an address to people who are not yet committed to Christ. It would be wrong, in my judgment, to say that all those connotations necessarily carry over into the instruction that is part of Christian worship.

It is actually very difficult to find in the NT any reference to sermons as an element of Christian worship. The closest reference is in 1 Corinthians 14:26:

> What then, brothers? When you come together, each one has a hymn, a lesson, a revelation, a tongue, or an interpretation. Let all things be done for building up.

"Lesson" here is *didache*, "teaching." As we have seen, it is a broader term than *kerygma*. It does not necessarily connote a heraldic stance, an announcement mode, or a redemptive-historical emphasis. In my judgment, it does not set forth in any detail what must be said or how it should be said. Presumably, it should be Christian teaching (that is, biblical content), and it should contribute to the spiritual edification of the congregation, as should every other part of worship ("let all . . . be done for building up"). But I think it would normally be inappropriate for a teacher to take the same stance in Christian worship that he might take before unbelievers in a synagogue or marketplace. Certainly, we should not neglect the possibility that some unbelievers may be present in the worship service and may need to be addressed (as in 1 Cor. 14:23–25). But in the Christian meeting, the chief goal is not conversion, but the edification of people already converted.

The text does not specify in detail how the lesson brings edification. If we can rid ourselves of some common assumptions, we may note that 1 Corinthians 14:26 is less restrictive than many of our churches today as to the nature of teaching in worship. For example, (1) the text does not say that the lesson must be given by only one person. In fact, the pattern of 1 Corinthians 14:26, in which different members of the congregation propose worship activities, suggests that occasionally more than one member of the church might have a "lesson." (2) Nor does the passage state that only an overseer may present the lesson. The overseers should, of course, oversee. They should prevent anyone from teaching error, or from teaching matters about which he is ignorant. But as we have seen, there is a sense in which every believer is competent to teach.[3] (3) Nor does the passage say that this teaching must emulate the style and content of the apostolic sermons in Acts. The only limitation here is that the lesson ought to edify the congregation. (4) Such freedom encourages creativity. Nothing in 1 Corinthians 14:26 prevents us from considering any method or style of teaching that is consistent with biblical principles and that is educationally (i.e., edificationally) valuable, such as, perhaps: children's sermons, or sermons given to other age groups; object lessons; teaching through music or drama; visual aids; personal testimonies; fielding questions.

My purpose here, however, is not to give a detailed account of preaching and teaching in the church, but to consider the relation of these to the Word of God.

The Reformed tradition has often emphasized "the centrality of preaching." The Second Helvetic Confession, in fact, says in a heading of a section of chapter 1, "The Preaching of the Word of God Is the Word of God." That section reads:

> Wherefore when this Word of God is now preached in the church by preachers lawfully called, we believe the very Word of God is proclaimed, and received by the faithful; and that neither any other Word of God is to be invented nor is to be expected from heaven: and that now the Word itself which is preached is to be regarded, not the minister that preaches; for even if he be evil and a sinner, nevertheless the Word of God remains still true and good.

Given this exposition and the place of this paragraph in the context of the Confession's general discussion of Scripture, it is plain that "Word of God" here refers to the Scriptures, not to the preaching itself, though the heading might suggest otherwise. The Word of God is what the preacher preaches, the subject of his sermon, the content that he intends to expound. The point of the Confession here is that we should not seek the word of God in some new revelation, but rather in the old revelation, the Scriptures, to which we have access through preaching.

So the Confession is not saying that preaching is the Word of God in the same sense that Isaiah's prophecies are the Word of God. Certainly, the writers of the Confession recognized that preachers sometimes err. But the Confession asserts that even though a preacher may be wicked, and therefore likely to preach falsehood, yet insofar as his preaching is true "the Word of God remains still true and good." That is to say: the biblical

---

3. I do believe, for example, that sex should not be a barrier to such teaching. If a woman has something to say that the overseers regard as edifying, she should be permitted to say it.

revelation loses none of its power, truth, or authority from being on the lips of a fallible, even wicked, human being. When a preacher speaks the Word truly, it is just as true, and just as authoritative, as it is on the pages of Scripture itself. It is therefore a means that God uses to bring the true Word of God to his people, just as he uses copies, translations, and editions. Insofar as the preacher brings the true Word to us, the autographic text is on his lips, just as surely as it was on the lips of Jesus or Paul. If we rebel against the Word of God that we hear on Sunday morning, it is no excuse to say that "it came from a fallible man." God uses the fallible man to bring his Word to us, and we must respect it.

So theologians have often put preaching in a central place. In Karl Barth's theology, the Word of God has three forms: Christ (who alone is revelation in the fullest sense—see my chap. 7), Scripture (which for Barth is not directly the Word of God, but is its witness and instrument), and preaching (which, in turn, is the witness and instrument by which we receive Scripture). And historically, in Protestant churches, pulpits have replaced altars in the central position in the front of the sanctuary.

I agree, of course, that preaching is an important means by which God brings the message of Scripture to us. But I have some reservations about the "centrality of preaching":

1. I see no biblical reason to put preaching above teaching as a means of communicating the Word of God. In my judgment, as I indicated earlier, these concepts overlap, and their differences don't favor either one as a means of communicating God's Word. First Corinthians 14:26 speaks of teaching, not specifically of preaching.
2. Certainly, there is no reason to assume that Christian worship should be dominated by the kind of preaching defined by apostolic proclamation to unsaved Jews and Gentiles. There is no biblical evidence that that kind of preaching was part of the Christian worship service.
3. The Second Helvetic Confession implies that preaching is limited to those "lawfully called." Probably it has in mind those who hold what I have called the *special office*. Although there is wisdom in limiting the bulk of instruction in the church to those with official ordination,[4] I do not think Scripture limits teaching in the church to these. If the overseers in the church believe that an

---

4. In my understanding, ordination gives someone the right to speak in the name of the church. That is the particular kind of authority that unordained people do not have. But that does not mean that unordained people should never teach, or that their teaching is not useful.

unordained person can speak words that would edify the congregation, they should permit such a person to do so. And I see no biblical reason why the words of that unordained person might not be a communication of the Word of God, just as the words of ordained persons are.

4. Indeed, I see no reason why we should not say the same thing about the words of all believers when they testify of Christ. Insofar as they communicate biblical content, their speech is the Word of God.

5. Centrality is always relative. When someone says that X is central, we may always ask: in relation to what? If X is central, what should be decentralized? In the Reformation period, preaching became central at the expense of the sacrament. Now, I accept the Protestant critique of the Roman Mass, so I can understand why the Reformers sought to attack the Mass at its root and replace it with a preaching service. (Huldrych Zwingli took an even more extreme position, excluding music from the meeting.) But it is not obvious to me that any of the "elements" of true biblical worship is more central than any other. I have no biblical reason to think that the "lesson" (*didache*) (1 Cor. 14:26) is more central to worship than hymns, or sacraments, or prayers. And to the extent that the Reformers, in rejecting the Mass, also deemphasized the biblical sacraments, I believe they were mistaken.

Central or not, however, preaching and teaching are effective means by which God communicates his Word to us today. When these effectively communicate the meaning of Scripture, we hear Scripture. In that sense, "the preaching of the Word of God is the Word of God." Preachers sometimes get it wrong. But when they get it right, the Word of God is on their lips, as surely as it was on the lips of Jesus and Paul. When we hear such messages, we hear the autographic text of Scripture.

To be sure, much preaching and teaching consists of illustrations and applications of Scripture, rather than translation or paraphrase of the text itself. If, however, an illustration or application is a good one, one that truly conveys what Scripture teaches, requires, or promises, it is nothing less than a communication of biblical content. As such, even an illustration can be a communication of the autographic text of Scripture, a personal word from God to us.

CHAPTER 36

Sacraments

In the previous chapter, I said that the Reformed tradition has sometimes erred in its tendency to exalt preaching over the sacraments. So I would like to say here some fairly brief things about the sacraments as communications of the word of God.

In chapter 12, I distinguished three kinds of *media* by which God communicates his word to us: events, words, and persons. Chapter 13 dealt with events. Chapters 14 through the present chapter (and some chapters yet to come) have dealt with revelation in words. I have had to speak about the verbal medium far more extensively because Scripture emphasizes it, and because most controversy about the word of God has centered on the verbal medium. Later in the book, I will speak about the word of God in and through persons.

The sacraments are somewhat hard to place in this scheme. Literally, they are events, not words. But theological reflection on them focuses on them as a bearer of meaning. In the Reformation, they were sometimes called "visible words." And in one sense, they are also revelation through persons. Much discussion of the sacraments has focused on the nature of the "presence of Christ" in these events.

I am mentioning them here, in order to correlate them with preaching and teaching as parts of public worship.[1]

I hold, with the Reformed tradition, that there are only two sacraments: baptism and the Lord's Supper. Scripture has much to say about these, but it never groups these two into a larger category called *sacra-*

1. Parts of this discussion are revised from my chapter on the sacraments in *SBL*, 274–86.

ment. One wonders whether the theological world would have been more peaceful if the church had never developed the concept of sacrament. Nevertheless, there do appear to be significant similarities between baptism and the Supper that make it useful to discuss them together. Here is the WCF's definition of *sacrament*, a definition that certainly pertains to both institutions:

> Sacraments are holy signs and seals of the covenant of grace, immediately instituted by God, to represent Christ and His benefits; and to confirm our interest in Him: as also, to put a visible difference between those that belong unto the Church and the rest of the world; and solemnly to engage them to the service of God in Christ, according to His Word. (27.1)

Gathering these ideas together, we can see (I trust this isn't a surprise!) three main aspects of a sacrament, corresponding to God's lordship attributes (chap. 2) and the three perspectives based on them. The sacraments are signs, divine actions, and means of divine presence, which I assign to the categories normative, situational, and existential, respectively.

First, normatively, the sacraments are signs. That is, they are authoritative divine communications, revelations to us. They symbolize the gospel and teach us authoritatively what the gospel is. They teach us not by words, but by pictures, by actions. In baptism, not only do we hear about our cleansing, but we see and feel it, depicted dramatically. In the Supper, not only do we hear about Jesus' death for us, but we see his body given for us, and we taste, smell, and touch it. As the Reformers used to say, the sacraments are visible words. They supplement the Word of God by divinely authorized dramatic images. So the fullness of divine teaching is by Word *and* sacrament.

Second, situationally, the sacraments are God's actions on our behalf. The sacrament is not just our doing something in God's presence; it is his doing something for us. He is really there, acting. For one thing, the sacraments are not only signs, but *seals*. When we talk about a seal here, we are talking about something like the government seal on your birth certificate, which makes it official that you are a citizen of the country, with all rights and privileges appertaining. Baptism and the Lord's Supper are seals of God's covenant of grace with us in Christ, as Abraham's circumcision was a seal of his righteousness of faith (Rom. 4:11). As seals, the sacraments confirm and guarantee the covenant promises. In this respect, as I said earlier, they are visible words. As the Word of God guarantees the promises of God, so do the sacraments.

Thus, as the Confession says, they separate us from the world, locating us in the people of God.

Third, existentially, the sacraments are locations of God's presence. That is implicit in what I have already said. If God is *doing* something for us in and through the sacrament, then he is, of course, present, and that itself is a wonderful blessing. So Paul speaks of the Supper as a *communion* of the body and blood of Christ (1 Cor. 10:16). The word translated "communion" in the KJV, "participation" in the ESV, is *koinonia*, "fellowship."

In his intimate presence, God helps us to grow in faith. Roman Catholics understand this process as something automatic. It happens *ex opera operato*, that is, from the very act of participating in the sacrament. But Scripture teaches that no, our growth comes through the presence of Christ by his Spirit dealing with us personally. So the efficacy of the sacrament is by faith alone.

BAPTISM

Let us think more specifically, first about baptism, and then about the Supper. Note the confessional definition of baptism (WCF 28.1):

> Baptism is a sacrament of the New Testament, ordained by Jesus Christ, not only for the solemn admission of the party baptized into the visible Church; but also to be unto him a sign and seal of the covenant of grace, of his ingrafting into Christ, of regeneration, of remission of sins, and of his giving up unto God, through Jesus Christ, to walk in the newness of life. Which sacrament is, by Christ's own appointment, to be continued in His Church until the end of the world.

In this statement, we see that baptism is, first, the rite of entrance into the visible church. As a person takes an oath of citizenship to become an American citizen, so we undergo baptism to become members of the Christian church. It is baptism that gives us the right to be recognized as Christians, unless or until we are excommunicated. Thus, it gives us the right to be part of the great work that God is doing through his church.

As an administration of the covenant, baptism is a sign and seal, as we indicated earlier. As a sign, it represents cleansing, repentance, and union with Christ. Cleansing (Lev. 8:5–6; 14:8–9, 15), like the OT ceremonial washings, is a requirement for entering God's presence. In this case, it symbolizes cleansing from sin. Not everybody who is baptized is cleansed or forgiven from sin. But that is what baptism symbolizes, pictures. Baptism, as a sacrament, pictures the gospel; and the gospel is about the forgiveness of sins. Scripture doesn't say, as some do, that baptism is the new birth, or that our forgiveness comes through baptism. But it pictures forgiveness, so that people who are baptized as well as those who witness the ceremony will know what the gospel says, that God offers cleansing, forgiveness in Christ.

Second, baptism represents repentance, as in the early ministry of John (Matt. 3:6, 11). For we must recognize that we are in need of God's cleansing, that we are sinners. When an adult is baptized, he confesses his own sin, turns from it, and asks God's forgiveness. In churches where infants are baptized, the parents make this confession on behalf of their children.

Third, baptism symbolizes union with Christ. It is "into the name of" the Trinity (Matt. 28:19). To be baptized into the name of someone is to belong to that person (cf. 1 Cor. 1:13, 15; 10:2). In Romans 6:3–6 (cf. 1 Cor. 12:13; Gal. 3:27–28; Col. 2:11–12), Paul says that we have been baptized with Christ in his death and resurrection, dying with him to sin and rising with him to new life. So Paul many, many times speaks of Christians as being "in Christ." We are also baptized into the Spirit, as we discussed in chapter 12 (Matt. 3:11; 1 Cor. 12:13).

All the blessings of salvation are based on our union with Christ. Effectual calling is calling into union with Christ. Regeneration means being created anew in the image of Christ. Faith and repentance are in, upon, and into Christ. Justification, adoption, and sanctification are all blessings of union with Christ, our being in him.

We have been talking of baptism as a sign. It is also a seal, God's confirmation that we belong to the covenant. Again, baptism is a name-giving ceremony (Matt. 28:19), placing the name of God on us, as the high priest placed the name of God on Israel in Numbers 6:24–27. On the basis of that seal, we are admitted into the visible church. Again, baptism does not give us eternal salvation. As I indicated in our discussion of assurance in chapter 16, baptized people do sometimes betray the Lord. When they do that, they receive the curses of the covenant rather than the blessings. But baptism does entitle the baptized person to all the blessings of fellowship with God in the church and with God's people.

So I must disagree with the position ascribed to the early Swiss Reformer Huldrych Zwingli, that baptism is a *mere* symbol, a *mere* sign. Also, we must take issue with the Roman Catholic notion that baptism is the new birth, or any other idea of baptismal regeneration.

THE LORD'S SUPPER

We must now turn to the Lord's Supper. If baptism is the sacrament of initiation, given only once, the Lord's Supper is the sacrament of continuing fellowship with God, to be received over and over again.

WCF 29.1 defines it as follows:

> Our Lord Jesus, in the night wherein He was betrayed, instituted the sacrament of His body and blood, called the Lord's Supper, to be observed in His Church, unto the end of the world, for the perpetual remembrance of the sacrifice of Himself in His death; the sealing all benefits thereof unto true believers, their spiritual nourishment and growth in Him, their further engagement in and to all duties which they owe unto Him; and, to be a bond and pledge of their communion with Him, and with each other, as members of His mystical body.

Like baptism, this ordinance is instituted by Christ for us to observe perpetually until the last day. It has past, present, and future references: we look to the past, remembering his death, to the present as we receive nourishment, and to the future as we anticipate his coming, remembering "the Lord's death until he comes" (1 Cor. 11:26; cf. Rev. 19:9). Our present nourishment comes by feeding on Christ (1 Cor. 10:16–18; cf. John 6:53–58), and by a closer relationship with others in the body (1 Cor. 11:18–22; notice the Confession's reference to "communion with Him, and with each other, as members of His mystical body"). So the Lord's Supper is a means of grace, a way in which God equips us better to serve him.

One major theological controversy concerns the presence of Christ in the Supper. The Roman Catholic view is called *transubstantiation*. That means that after the priest consecrates the bread and the wine, they actually *become* the physical body and blood of Christ, though they still *appear* to be bread and wine. So the Supper is a continual sacrifice of Christ's body and blood. But Scripture never suggests anything like this. When Jesus said to his disciples, "This is my body," he cannot have meant that the bread and wine on the table were his literal body, for his literal body was *behind* the table, not on it. Rather, what he plainly meant was that the bread and wine *represent* his body and blood. It's like a professor's pointing to a map and saying, "This is France." He doesn't mean that the map is literally France, but that the picture represents France.

The most serious error in this view, however, is that it represents the Lord's Supper as a continuing sacrifice. Scripture is clear that there is no continuing sacrifice and cannot be. Jesus' atonement is final and complete.

There is no other sacrifice for sins. It needs no continuation, repetition, or supplementation.

The Lutheran view is midway between the Roman Catholic and the Reformed. Lutherans teach that in the sacrament Jesus' physical body is "in, with, and under" the bread and the wine. That is, the elements are still bread and wine, but Jesus' literal body and blood are there, too. They do deny the Roman Catholic idea of the sacrament as a continuing sacrifice, and that is good. But I do think their emphasis on a literal physical presence of Christ dilutes the biblical emphasis on receiving Christ by faith alone.

The view attributed to Zwingli, the early Swiss Reformer, is that the sacrament is *only* a sign, only a memorial. The mainstream Swiss Reformers, following John Calvin, believe, however, that the Supper is not a mere memorial, but a means of grace. Calvin said that when we take the Supper, Christ is present in the Spirit. So we "participate" in his body and blood, as Paul says in 1 Corinthians 10:16–18. We "feed on him," as Jesus teaches in John 6:53–58. These benefits come by faith alone. The physical body of Christ is in heaven, not on earth. I think this mainstream Reformed view is best: it incorporates more of the riches of Scripture than the others, and it avoids superstitions that are not based on Scripture.

But I think it unfortunate that these wonderful sacraments have become such a source of battles in the church. It seems that sometimes they are more a cause for warfare than a blessing to God's people.

Let us now focus on the richness of the blessings that God has given us in the Lord's Supper. In our church, we have the Lord's Supper every Sunday, and I am usually asked to lead it once a month. So every month I have to come up with a new devotional message focusing on the Lord's Supper. I worried about this at first, because the sacraments are not an academic specialty of mine, and I wondered how I could possibly come up with twelve communion messages per year. But as I studied the Scriptures, God showed me how rich was the background and symbolism of the Lord's Supper. We usually say that the Supper symbolizes Jesus' death for us, and it certainly does. But much more comes with this symbolism.

In Scripture, even in the OT, table fellowship with God is an important element of the covenant blessing. When two people are at odds with each other, they need to be reconciled. Reconciliation can, of course, be rather superficial. But when it is deep and profound, when it is complete reconciliation, not only do you become friends again with your former enemy, but you have him to dinner. That was often the case in the ancient Near East (see Gen. 31:52–54; 2 Sam. 9:7–13; 19:28; 1 Kings 2:7).

Now, the fall has made us enemies of God. God provided food for Adam and Eve before the fall (Gen. 1:29), but they abused that privilege by taking the one fruit that he kept from them. But through Christ, he seeks recon-ciliation with us. And that reconciliation is so deep, so complete, that he invites us to share meals with him. So after the great flood, God provided food for Noah and his family, inviting them to eat the flesh of animals as well as the fruits of the garden (Gen. 9:3). When God redeemed Israel from Egypt, he gave them a sacramental meal, the Passover, as a memorial of their salvation and their covenant with God (Ex. 12). When Israel met with God around Mount Sinai on the "Day of the Assembly," God made a covenant with them as his people and called the seventy elders up to the mountain to eat and drink with him (Ex. 24:9–11). For all the people, God provided manna, supernatural food, for them to eat on their long journey to the Promised Land (Ex. 16:1–35; cf. Ps. 78:19–20).

And the tabernacle offerings were offerings of food. Bread and flagons of wine were kept on a table in the tabernacle and again in the temple (Ex. 25:30; 37:16; Lev. 24:5–9; Num. 4:7). This food ("the bread of the Presence," Num. 4:7) is an offering to the Lord (Lev. 24:7), and it represents a covenant relation between God and Israel (Lev. 24:8). The animal sacrifices, the whole burnt offering, the sin offering, and the guilt offering focused on the idea of atone-ment. Another of the tabernacle offerings, the peace offering, reckons on that atonement already completed. It focuses on the reconciliation between God and the Israelite following atonement. The peace offering was a meal of which part was burned up for God, part eaten by the priests, and part eaten by the worshipers, celebrating reconciliation (Lev. 7:11–18; 19:5–8; Deut. 27:7).

So a first-century Jew would not have been surprised to hear that the Lord's Supper was the new covenant in Jesus' blood (Luke 22:20; 1 Cor. 11:25). Whenever we take the Supper, as when Israel took the Passover and the other meals, we renew the covenant relationship between God and ourselves.

Further, meals with God also provide continuing nourishment and fel-lowship with him. Think of how David in Psalm 23:5 speaks of God's preparing a table for him in the midst of his enemies. Think of how God's wisdom, in Proverbs 9:2, invites the young man into her home for a meal. Think of Jesus, who twice miraculously fed great multitudes (Matt. 14:13–21; 15:38). Think of how Jesus, after his resurrection, invited his disciples to eat and drink with him (Luke 24:30; John 21:9–14; Acts 10:41). This all anticipates the great meal in heaven, the messianic banquet, the wedding supper of the Lamb, in which we celebrate the consummation of redemp-tion (Luke 13:29; 14:15–24; 22:30; Rev. 19:9). As we eat and drink now, therefore, we look forward to his coming, when we will eat and drink with consummate joy (1 Cor. 11:26).

So when we take the Lord's Supper, we should reflect on the past, the present, and the future. We should remember Jesus in his death, thanking him for his complete salvation. The Supper is called a thanksgiving (Matt. 26:27; Luke 22:17, 19; 1 Cor. 11:24), hence the word *Eucharist*.

In the present, we know that we can gain spiritual nourishment only from Christ (John 6:35–59; 1 Cor. 10:16). By eating and drinking, we participate in his body and blood; we sense a greater union with him. Calvin, who emphasized that Christ is not physically present in the Supper but lives physically in heaven, thought that the Supper was not so much Christ's coming to be with us as our being caught up to heaven to be with him, as we join him in the heavenly places.

And then as we eat and drink, we look forward to the greater banquet to come (1 Cor. 11:26). We eat only little bits of bread and drink little cups of wine, for we know that our fellowship with Christ in this life cannot begin to compare with the glory that awaits us in him.

How does all this relate to the theology of the word of God? I hope it is obvious from my discussion that the symbolism of both sacraments is exceedingly rich. These two simple ceremonies portray salvation in Christ in an astonishing variety of ways. As I mentioned before, they bridge the categories of event-, word-, and person-revelation. As word-revelation, they present a large amount of biblical content. They are "visible words," as the Reformers said, but they are also words that can be touched, smelled, and tasted. All our senses are engaged, filled with biblical content.

I am not saying that the sacraments communicate the gospel apart from any words. If we had only sacraments and no verbal revelation, the meaning of the sacraments would be opaque to us. The words of Scripture provide the necessary interpretation of the sacraments, so that we can benefit from them. But if we had only words, and no sacraments, we would lose much of the force of the biblical words. God intends to communicate to us not only propositions, commands, and promises, but also visions and feelings commensurate with those words. Our participation in Christ is not merely verbal, but also visual and tactile.

And the sacraments also enliven the verbal revelation, driving its meaning into our heads and hearts. As they do so, they are a mode of verbal revelation, just as much as copies, translations, teaching, and preaching. They convey to us the teaching of Scripture in depth. So they speak to us the autographic text of Scripture, God's personal words.

I have indicated before, and will indicate again, that our appropriation of God's written words is not merely an academic task. Understanding Scripture in depth is not merely reading it with an appropriate language competence. It is a process of personal engagement with God's Spirit. That engagement comes through preaching and teaching, and also from baptism and the Lord's Supper.

CHAPTER 37

Theology

Theological reflection is an important means of appropriating the Word of God. The basic idea of *theology* is evident in the etymology of the term: a study of God. But we should seek a more precise definition.[1]

In Christianity, the study of God is a study of God's revelation of himself. Natural revelation and word-revelation illumine one another in ways that I have indicated in chapters 13–14. Scripture (our presently available form of word-revelation) is crucial to the task of theology because as a source of divine words it is sufficient for human life (chap. 32), and it has a kind of clarity not found in natural revelation (chap. 29). But natural revelation is a necessary means of interpreting Scripture. To properly understand Scripture, we need to know something about ancient languages and culture, and that information is not always available in Scripture alone. Nevertheless, once we have reached a settled interpretation as to what Scripture says, that knowledge takes precedence over any ideas supposedly derived from natural revelation.

So theology must be essentially a study of Scripture. It is not an analysis of human religious consciousness or feelings, as in the view of Friedrich Schleiermacher.[2] But we need to ask *how* theology is to study Scripture.

---

1. In this chapter, I have summarized and reworked material from *DKG*, 76–85, 206–14. That book and this one present the same view of theology. See also the summary discussion in *SBL*, 72–84.
2. Friedrich Schleiermacher, *The Christian Faith* (Edinburgh: T&T Clark, 1928). See chapter 6 of this volume.

Theology is not interested in finding the middle word in the Hebrew text of Ecclesiastes, for example.

Charles Hodge saw theology as a science that dealt with the facts of Scripture, as an astronomer deals with facts about the heavenly bodies and a geologist deals with facts about rocks. He said that theology "is the exhibition of the facts of Scripture in their proper order and relation, with the principles or general truths involved in the facts themselves, and which pervade and harmonize the whole."[3] If Schleiermacher's concept of theology is *subjectivist*, Hodge's might be called *objectivist*. To Hodge, theology seeks the objective truth about God through Scripture.

Certainly, Hodge's definition of theology is better than Schleiermacher's, because Hodge's is Bible-centered. But Hodge, like many orthodox evangelical theologians, leaves us confused about an important question: why do we need theology when we have Scripture?

Scripture itself, given Hodge's own view of Scripture and my earlier discussions in this book, gives us objective truth about God. We don't need a theological science to give us that truth. So what is the role of theology?

In the statement quoted above, Hodge says that theology is an "exhibition of the facts of Scripture." But aren't the facts of Scripture already exhibited in the biblical text itself?

He says that theology exhibits these facts "in their proper order and relation." This sounds a bit as though the order and relation of the facts in Scripture itself are somehow improper, and that theology has to put them back where they belong. People sometimes talk about the theological "system" of biblical doctrine as if that system stated the truth in a better way than Scripture itself, or even as if that "system" were the real meaning of Scripture hidden beneath all the stories, psalms, wisdom, and so on. I don't think Hodge had anything like this in mind; such ideas are inconsistent with Hodge's high view of Scripture. But his phrase "proper order and relation" doesn't guard well against such notions. And in any case, it leaves unclear the relation between theology and Scripture.

He continues by saying that theology, together with its work of putting the facts of Scripture into proper order and relation, seeks to state "the principles or general truths involved in the facts themselves, and which pervade and harmonize the whole." Certainly, this is one of the things that theologians do, and ought to do. But again we ask: hasn't Scripture done this already? And if it has, then what is left for theology to do?

---

3. Charles Hodge, *Systematic Theology* (Grand Rapids: Eerdmans, 1952), 1:19.

The answer seems to be that the theologian *restates* the facts and general truths of Scripture, for some purpose. But for what purpose? Hodge does not tell us.

In my view, the only possible answer is this: the theologian states the facts and truths of Scripture for the purpose of *edification*. Recall my emphasis on that concept when we considered the role of teaching in worship (chap. 35). Yes, theology states the objective truth. But it states that truth not for its own sake, but to build up people in Christian faith.

In this way, we align the concept of theology with the concepts of teaching and preaching in the NT. The terms for *teaching* that we considered in chapter 35, *didasko, didache*,[4] and *didaskalia*, refer not to the stating of objective truth for its own sake, but to the exposition of God's truth in order to build up God's people. Consider:

> And they devoted themselves to the apostles' *teaching* and the fellowship, to the breaking of bread and the prayers. (Acts 2:42)

> Now, brothers, if I come to you speaking in tongues, how will I benefit you unless I bring you some revelation or knowledge or prophecy or *teaching*? (1 Cor. 14:6)

> [The law is for] the sexually immoral, men who practice homosexuality, enslavers, liars, perjurers, and whatever else is contrary to sound *doctrine*. (1 Tim. 1:10)

> For this I was appointed a preacher and an apostle (I am telling the truth, I am not lying), a *teacher* of the Gentiles in faith and truth. (1 Tim. 2:7)

> If you put these things before the brothers, you will be a good servant of Christ Jesus, being trained in the words of the faith and of the good *doctrine* that you have followed. (1 Tim. 4:6)

> Keep a close watch on yourself and on the *teaching*. Persist in this, for by so doing you will save both yourself and your hearers. (1 Tim. 4:16)

> If anyone teaches a different *doctrine* and does not agree with the sound words of our Lord Jesus Christ and the teaching that accords with godliness, he is puffed up with conceit and understands nothing. He has an unhealthy craving for controversy and for quarrels

---

4. *Didaskalia* is translated *doctrine* in 1 Timothy 1:10; 2 Timothy 4:3 (KJV, NKJV, NASB, NIV; *teaching* in ESV); and Titus 1:9 and 2:1. Of course, today we often use *doctrine* as a synonym of *theology*.

about words, which produce envy, dissension, slander, [and] evil suspicions. (1 Tim. 6:3–4)

Preach the word; be ready in season and out of season; reprove, rebuke, and exhort, with complete patience and *teaching*. (2 Tim. 4:2)

[The overseer] must hold firm to the trustworthy word as taught, so that he may be able to give instruction in sound *doctrine* and also to rebuke those who contradict it. (Titus 1:9)

Everyone who goes on ahead and does not abide in the *teaching* of Christ, does not have God. Whoever abides in the *teaching* has both the Father and the Son. (2 John 9)

I have italicized the words that correspond to the *didasko* word group (*teacher*, *teaching*, *doctrine*). Notice the emphasis that teaching has the purpose of building people up in faith and obedience to God. Notice also the phrase *sound doctrine*, in which *sound* is *hygiainos*, "health-giving." The purpose of teaching is not merely to state the objective truth, but to bring the people to a state of spiritual health.

In defining theology, it is not strictly necessary to align it with a biblical term, but it is certainly an advantage when we can do this. I propose that we define theology as synonymous with the biblical concept of teaching, with all its emphasis on edification.

So theology is not subjective in Schleiermacher's sense, but it has a subjective thrust. We need theology in addition to Scripture because God has authorized teaching in the church, and because we need that teaching to mature in the faith. Why did Hodge not state this as the reason we need theology? Perhaps he wanted to encourage respect for academic theological work, so he stressed its scientific character. Perhaps he was worried that reference to our subjective edification would encourage the disciples of Schleiermacher. But such considerations are inadequate to justify a definition of theology. Scripture must be decisive even here, and Scripture commends to us a kind of teaching that has people's needs in mind.

Theology, on this basis, responds to the needs of people. It helps those who have questions, doubts, or problems with the Bible. Normally we associate theology with questions of a fairly abstract or academic sort: How can God be one in three? How can Christ be both divine and human? Does regeneration precede faith? But of course, there are other kinds of questions as well. One might be confronted with a Hebrew word, say *dabar*, and ask what it means. Or one might ask the meaning of a Bible verse, say Genesis 1:1. A child might ask whether God can see what we are doing when Mom isn't watching. I see no reason to doubt that all these sorts of questions are proper subject matter for theology.

It would not be wrong, either, to say that theology occurs in the lives of people, in their behavior. Behavior consists of a series of human decisions, and in those decisions believers seek to follow Scripture. Behavior, too, as well as speech, can be edifying or unedifying. As I indicate later in chapter 43, the imitation of godly people is an important form of Christian learning, and the behavior of these people is a form of revelation. Their application of the Word in their behavior may be called theology. So theology is not merely a means of teaching people how to live; it is life itself.

There really is no justification for restricting theology only to academic or technical questions. (*How* academic? *How* technical?) If theology is edifying teaching, theologians need to listen to everybody's questions. My point is not to divert theology from theoretical to practical questions, or to disparage in any way the theoretical work of academic theologians. But I do think that academic and technical theology should not be valued over other kinds. The professor of theology at a university or seminary is no more or less a theologian than the youth minister who seeks to deal with the doubts of college students, or the Sunday school teacher who tells OT stories to children, or a father who leads family devotions, or the person who does not teach in any obvious way but simply tries to obey Scripture. Theoretical and practical questions are equally grist for the theologian's mill.

The only term I know that is broad enough to cover all forms of biblical teaching and all the decisions that people make in their lives is *application*. To apply Scripture is to use Scripture to meet a human need, to answer a human question, to make a human decision. Questions about the text of Scripture, translations, interpretation, ethics, Christian growth—all of these are fair game for theology. To show (by word or deed) how Scripture resolves all these kinds of questions is to *apply* it. So I offer this refinement of my definition of theology: theology is *the application of Scripture, by persons, to every area of life*.[5]

Why, then, do we need theology in addition to Scripture? The only answer, I believe, is "because we need to apply Scripture."

KINDS OF THEOLOGY

Traditionally, theology has been divided into different types. *Exegetical* theology is interpreting the Bible verse by verse. That is application,

5. Note the three perspectives here: Scripture (normative), persons (existential), every area of life (situational).

because it aims to help people understand particular passages in Scripture. *Biblical* theology expounds Scripture as a history of God's dealings with us. If it is theology, it cannot be pure narrative. It must be application, dealing with the meaning that narrative has for its hearers and readers.

Systematic theology seeks to apply Scripture by asking what the *whole* Bible teaches about any subject. For example, it examines what David said about the forgiveness of sins, and Jesus, and Paul, and John, and tries to understand what it all adds up to. Another way of putting it is to say that systematic theology seeks to determine what *we today* should believe about forgiveness or any other scriptural teaching. Seen that way, systematic theology is a highly practical discipline, not abstract and arcane as it is often presented.

Sometimes systematic theologians have produced systems of theology— comprehensive attempts to summarize, analyze, and defend biblical teaching as a whole. When a writer calls his book a systematic theology, a dogmatics, a body of divinity, or a *summa*, we can expect to find in that book such a system. But (1) we should not imagine that any such system is the true meaning of Scripture, lurking, as it were, beneath the text. At best, the system is a summary of Scripture; but Scripture itself (in all its narratives, wisdom deliverances, songs, parables, letters, visions) is our true authority, the true Word of God. (2) This kind of comprehensive system- making is not the only legitimate form of systematic theology. Systematics is equally interested in studies of individual doctrines and answers to individual questions.

Historical theology is the analysis of past theological work. It is truly theology when it does this study in order better to apply biblical teaching to the church of the present day. Without this goal, it is something less than theology, a merely academic discipline among others. I define historical theology as a study of the church's past theology, for the sake of its present and future.

Practical theology is, in my understanding, a department of systematic theology. It asks a particular question of Scripture, among the other questions of systematics. That question is this: how should we *communicate* the Word of God? It therefore deals with preaching, teaching, evangelism, church planting, missions, media communications, and so on.

THEOLOGICAL METHOD

In *DKG* I discussed many aspects of theological method. Here I want to make only a single point, related to the distinct concerns of this volume.

That is that theology should be Bible-centered. That is obvious, given the definition of theology I have presented. If we are to apply the Bible, we must be in constant conversation with the Bible. If we are to argue adequately for a theological view, we must be able to show the biblical basis of that view.

There are, of course, many auxiliary disciplines that aid the work of theology. As I said earlier, natural revelation illumines Scripture, as well as the reverse. So to do theology well, we need to have some knowledge from extrabiblical sources: knowledge of ancient languages and culture, knowledge of how past theologians have dealt with issues, knowledge of the various alternatives available in the theological literature of the present. It is also helpful for us to have some knowledge of secular disciplines, such as psychology, sociology, politics, economics, philosophy, literary criticism, and the natural sciences. Some of these aid us directly in the interpretation of Scripture. Others help us to understand the situations to which we intend to apply Scripture.

Yet I think theology today has become preoccupied by these auxiliary disciplines to the extent of neglecting its primary responsibility: to apply Scripture itself. Theological literature today is focused, especially, on history of doctrine and contemporary thought. Often this literature deals with theological questions by comparing various thinkers from the past and from the present, with a very minimal interaction with Scripture itself.[6]

6. See my "In Defense of Something Close to Biblicism," Appendix O in this volume. I cannot help but mention my conviction that this problem is partly the result of our present system for training theologians. To qualify for college or seminary positions, a theologian must earn a PhD, ideally from a prestigious liberal university. But at such schools, there is no training in the kind of systematic theology I describe here. Liberal university theologians do not view Scripture as God's Word, and so they cannot encourage theology as I have defined it, as the application of God's infallible Word. Students are welcome to study historical and contemporary theology, and to relate these to auxiliary disciplines such as philosophy and literary criticism. But they are not taught to seek ways of applying Scripture for the edification of God's people. Rather, professors encourage the student to be "up-to-date" with the current academic discussion and to make "original contributions" to that discussion, out of his autonomous reasoning. So when the theologian finishes his graduate work and moves to a teaching position, even if he is personally evangelical in his convictions, he often writes and teaches as he was encouraged to do in graduate school: academic comparisons and contrasts, minimal interaction with Scripture. In my judgment, this is entirely inadequate for the needs of the church. It is one source of the doctrinal declension of evangelical churches, colleges, and seminaries in our day. Evangelical denominations and schools need to seek new methods of training people to teach theology, educational models that will force theologian candidates to mine Scripture for edifying content. To do this, they may need to cut themselves off, in some degree, from the present-day academic establishment. And to do that, they may have to cut themselves off from the present-day accreditation system. Cf. Appendix A in this volume.

It is good for readers of theology to know what Augustine thought about a particular issue, or Martin Luther, John Calvin, Jonathan Edwards, Karl Barth, Rudolf Bultmann, Jürgen Moltmann, Wolfhart Pannenberg, or someone else. And it is often interesting to see how a theologian "triangulates" among these, going beyond Barth here, avoiding the extreme of Pannenberg there.

But no theological proposal fully makes its case until it shows itself to be biblical. That means that any theologian worth his salt must interact in depth with the Bible. Such interaction is not only the work of biblical scholars or of exegetical theologians. It is the work of systematic theologians as well. In fact, the systematic theologian, since he aspires to synthesize the teaching of the *whole* Bible, must spend more time with Scripture than anybody else.

The application of Scripture is a very distinctive discipline. Although it depends to some extent on the auxiliary disciplines I have listed, none of them has the distinct purpose of applying Scripture to the edification of people. To carry out that purpose requires not only academic excellence, but a heart-knowledge of Jesus, a prayerful spirit, and an understanding of the needs of people.

THEOLOGY AS COMMUNICATION OF THE WORD OF GOD

I have identified theology with the teaching discussed in chapter 35. Since good teaching is a legitimate communication of the Word of God, good theology is also. This is not to say that any theologian is infallible or inerrant, any more than any other teacher or preacher. But like other teachers and preachers, the theologian has as his goal, when he is doing the proper work of theology, the application of Scripture.

When he does that work well, he is communicating the contents of Scripture. So theology is a means God uses to get his written Word into the minds and hearts of his people. That is to say, good theology is a communication of the autographic text of Scripture.

CHAPTER 38

Confessions, Creeds, Traditions

In this chapter, I will discuss some documents and practices that have gained various kinds of authority in the church. In most cases, churches regard their authority as somewhat less than Scripture, though in Roman Catholicism tradition is equal to Scripture in its authority.[1]

Tradition (*paradosis*) refers to words or practices "passed down" from one person or group to another. The NT distinguishes two kinds of tradition, one good and one bad. The good tradition is that revelation that God the Father "handed over to" (*paradidomi*) Jesus his Son, to be further delivered to "anyone to whom the Son chooses to reveal him" (Matt. 11:27). This tradition is the mystery of the gospel, kept secret for ages (Rom. 16:25–26), that is revealed to the apostles (1 Cor. 2:9–10). The apostles pass this tradition on to the church (1 Cor. 15:2–3), and the church has the responsibility to obey that tradition (2 Thess. 3:6; 2 Peter 2:21), to hold it firmly (2 Thess. 2:15; 2 Tim. 1:12–14), and to guard it against distortion (1 Tim. 6:20; Jude 3), as God gave to the Jews the responsibility to guard the oracles of God (Rom. 3:2). The church is then to pass the tradition on to "faithful men who will be able to teach others also" (2 Tim. 2:2). This tradition is God's revelation through Jesus and the apostles, now deposited permanently in Scripture (see chapter 16, our discussion of the permanence of God's written Word).

---

1. See my discussion of the Roman Catholic denial of the sufficiency of Scripture in chapter 32, under "Challenges to the Sufficiency of Scripture."

The bad tradition is the tradition of the Pharisees, which they placed on a level of authority equal to Scripture, thus "making void the word of God" (Mark 7:13). The Jewish tradition was a system of commentaries on Scripture and commandments that went somewhat beyond Scripture, so that no one would ever risk breaking any biblical commands. But they gave too much authority to this tradition, so Jesus says, "they tie up heavy burdens, hard to bear, and lay them on people's shoulders" (Matt. 23:4). Cf. Col. 2:8; 1 Peter 1:18.

Roman Catholic theologians often claim that there is authentic teaching from the apostles that was never recorded in Scripture, but was communicated orally and passed on through the generations of the church over the centuries. Certainly there was apostolic teaching that was not recorded in Scripture. As I said earlier, the canon does not contain everything said by the prophets, Jesus, or the apostles. It does not even contain all of Paul's letters. No doubt if I were living in A.D. 60 with my present knowledge and interests, I would not hesitate to seek out an apostle's oral teaching to settle matters not clearly resolved in the written record. I would love to have asked Paul what he thought about the mode and subjects of baptism, or about the millennium. Certainly, the apostles' oral teaching (see chap. 15) was as authoritative as their written teaching, that is, ultimately authoritative.

But in fact, as we have seen, God chose to rule his church permanently by a book, not by oral tradition. And he determined for his own reasons that not everything the apostles taught orally would survive. Further, there is no way for us today to evaluate claims supposedly based on oral tradition, especially given the breakdown of trust between Protestants and Catholics. So we must reject the notion that claims about supposed traditions are as authoritative as Scripture, or even that they are reliable guides for Christian faith and life.

Extrabiblical tradition is not necessarily bad, however, whether or not it comes from the apostles. Indeed, such tradition is unavoidable. In the nearly two thousand years since Jesus' ascension, Christians could hardly avoid accumulating many standard ways of doing things and of formulating doctrine—ways that are not strictly required by Scripture, but that are intended to facilitate the application of Scripture in various situations. For example, Scripture does not provide a liturgy, or a list of events to take place in worship. But to carry out Paul's admonition to do everything "decently and in order" (1 Cor. 14:40), many churches have agreed that worship should follow a certain standard order of events, usually allowing for variation on certain occasions. There is nothing wrong with this; it is not a violation of the sufficiency of Scripture. Since Scripture tells us to worship, but does not give us a standard liturgy, we must devise that for ourselves, trying to stay within general biblical guidelines. On the other hand, Scripture does not forbid believers to worship without a standard liturgy.

What we must not do, however, is to claim that such tradition has the same authority as Scripture, or greater authority than Scripture. In the case of liturgy, no one should presume to argue that using a different order of worship necessarily violates God's will.

Theology is filled with technical terms that come from tradition, not Scripture. Scripture never says, for example, that we should refer to God as one *substance* or as three *persons*. Those terms come from philosophy, not the Bible. But those terms have entered theology as standard ways of referring to the oneness and manyness of God's Trinitarian existence. It would not be wrong to use other terms, as long as they affirmed the biblical teaching. But it is hard to imagine any other terms that would do the job as well. Today, of course, the terms we use about the Trinity must not only communicate biblical teaching accurately, but also communicate effectively to others in the Christian community, who have adopted conventional definitions and would be misled by any unusual definitions of the standard terms.

So when the claims of a tradition are suitably modest, and that tradition facilitates the communication of the biblical Word of God, that tradition should be respected, even while being viewed with a critical eye. What we should avoid is *traditionalism*, such as (1) the view that once a tradition is established, it can never be changed, (2) the notion that some tradition is just as authoritative as Scripture, and (3) the notion that we should not test traditions by the Scriptures.[2]

Now, sometimes traditions are put into writing, into creeds, confessions, conciliar declarations, and so on. These have various purposes: (1) to instruct believers, especially to prepare them for baptism, (2) to present a witness to the world as to what Christians believe, (3) to declare the truth about a controversial matter and to warn against heresy, and (4) to enforce orthodoxy in the church by requiring subscription of teachers (or even church members) to a doctrinal statement, usually through an official examination.

The first three purposes are fairly unproblematic.[3] They are part of the normal work of teaching in the church, addressed to the church itself and to the world. The fourth, however, is controversial.

---

2. See my "Traditionalism," Appendix P in this volume.
3. Yet I would quibble a bit about purpose (1). The Apostles' Creed evidently grew out of the practice of requiring a baptismal confession of basic Christian beliefs, and it is

There are passages of Scripture that may have had a creedal function in the church. Deuteronomy 6:4–5 reads:

> Hear, O Israel: The Lord our God, the Lord is one. You shall love the Lord your God with all your heart and with all your soul and with all your might.

This passage has long been used by Jews as a confession of faith in Yahweh. Later in Deuteronomy, we hear the confession of those who settle in the Promised Land and bring their firstfruits to the priest:

> And you shall make response before the Lord your God, "A wandering Aramean was my father. And he went down into Egypt and sojourned there, few in number, and there he became a nation, great, mighty, and populous. And the Egyptians treated us harshly and humiliated us and laid on us hard labor. Then we cried to the Lord, the God of our fathers, and the Lord heard our voice and saw our affliction, our toil, and our oppression. And the Lord brought us out of Egypt with a mighty hand and an outstretched arm, with great deeds of terror, with signs and wonders. And he brought us into this place and gave us this land, a land flowing with milk and honey. And behold, now I bring the first of the fruit of the ground, which you, O Lord, have given me." And you shall set it down before the Lord your God and worship before the Lord your God. (Deut. 26:5–10)

In the NT, we can mention Romans 10:9–10, in which the confession "Jesus is Lord" (cf. 1 Cor. 12:3; Phil. 2:11), together with the heart confession that Jesus is risen, defines one as a saved person. Perhaps the summary of the gospel found in 1 Corinthians 15:3–7 was also recited by the Christians as a confession of faith:

> For I delivered to you as of first importance what I also received: that Christ died for our sins in accordance with the Scriptures, that he was buried, that he was raised on the third day in accordance with the Scriptures, and that he appeared to Cephas, then to the twelve. Then he appeared to more than five hundred brothers at one time, most of whom are still alive,

---

appropriate for that purpose. But longer documents such as the WSC should not, in my judgment, be used as "educational requirements" for baptism or confirmation. In the NT itself, people were expected to repent of their sins and confess Christ before baptism. But they were not expected to understand or articulate a complicated theology. Note how quickly converts were baptized in Acts 8:26–40 and 16:25–34.

though some have fallen asleep. Then he appeared to James, then to all the apostles.

Paul continues to speak of Christ's appearances to him. This creed speaks of the atonement ("died for our sins"), the authority of the OT prophetic Scriptures, and Jesus' burial and resurrection. Some have also speculated that Paul's rather lyrical treatment of Jesus' incarnation, death, resurrection, and ascension was an early Christian confession or hymn:

> Have this mind among yourselves, which is yours in Christ Jesus, who, though he was in the form of God, did not count equality with God a thing to be grasped, but made himself nothing, taking the form of a servant, being born in the likeness of men. And being found in human form, he humbled himself by becoming obedient to the point of death, even death on a cross. Therefore God has highly exalted him and bestowed on him the name that is above every name, so that at the name of Jesus every knee should bow, in heaven and on earth and under the earth, and every tongue confess that Jesus Christ is Lord, to the glory of God the Father. (Phil. 2:5–11)

Then there are the "trustworthy sayings" of Paul's pastoral letters (1 Tim. 1:15; 3:1; 2 Tim. 2:11–13; Titus 3:4–8), which may have been proverbial in the church. These are all well suited to the first three purposes of creeds that I mentioned earlier.

But in regard to the fourth purpose, there is no reason to believe that any of these statements were used as tests of orthodoxy among God's people. The statement "Jesus Christ has come in the flesh" certainly was a test of orthodoxy, according to 1 John 4:1–3, in a situation in which false prophets, Docetists, were disturbing the church. But even here there is no suggestion that church members or officers had to formally confess this statement in the course of an examination in order to be in good standing. Of course, those who denied it, according to John, could not have been accepted as Christians.

Scripture speaks very strongly of the need to maintain doctrinal truth within the church. It condemns false prophets, false apostles, and false teaching in the strongest terms (Deut. 18:20–22; Matt. 7:15–20; 24:11; Luke 6:26; 2 Cor. 11:13; Gal. 2:4; 1 Tim. 6:2–5; 2 Tim. 3:1–9; 2 Peter 2:1–22; 1 John 4:1; Rev. 16:13; 19:20; 20:10), and it warns believers to turn aside from them (2 Tim. 3:5). Passages such as 2 Timothy 3:1–9 and 2 Peter 2:1–22 draw a very close parallel between false teaching and other kinds of sins. As Jesus said, "You will recognize them by their fruits" (Matt.

7:16). The problem with false teaching is not merely intellectual. Where there is false teaching, there is moral turpitude.

Presumably, then, the early church dealt with false teaching as with any other sin: by confrontation leading to the scrutiny of the church (Matt. 18:15–17) and possible sanctions, including shunning and excommunication (1 Cor. 5:9–12; 2 Thess. 3:14–15; 2 John 10). This is, of course, a reactive, post facto approach. The church gives its members and teachers the benefit of the doubt until it hears something contrary to the apostolic teaching or experiences the evil fruits of such heresy.

There does not seem to be evidence of a proactive, preventive approach to false teaching, such as the modern practice of requiring people to subscribe to a confession upon entering the church or entering an office. The church may well have required a confession upon baptism, perhaps a simple "Jesus is Lord," or something like the Apostles' Creed. One who becomes an overseer (bishop, elder) must be "able to teach" (1 Tim. 3:2) and able to "preach the word" (2 Tim. 4:2), which doubtless presuppose some training and examination before the candidate receives the office. But all of that can be done, of course, informally within the church, and in the absence of any formal confessional document.

So the NT church protected its orthodoxy mainly reactively, rather than proactively. I am not convinced that this model shouldn't be followed today.

In any case, the use of creeds and confessions to maintain orthodoxy in the church must be regarded as an optional method of protecting true doctrine, not a mandatory means of it. I think this point is obvious. But the discussion in various denominations about the necessity of this or that confession, or this or that form of subscription to the confession, is remarkably intense, considering that Scripture does not even require us to have such confessions.

In my judgment, there should be no confessional requirement for church members. Certainly, the officers of a church should examine any person who asks to become a church member. The object of that examination should be simply to determine whether he or she can make a "credible profession of faith," a profession of trust in Christ as Savior and Lord, not contradicted by a pattern of sin. But when a church, in addition to this examination, requires the person to study and subscribe to a confession (such as the Westminster, Belgic, or Thirty-nine Articles), it requires more than Scripture requires, something beyond faith in Christ. Further, it limits church membership only to those who are well enough educated to understand the confession and master its teaching, guaranteeing that the church will be limited to a particular stratum of society. So it would close the door that Jesus opened.

It is different, of course, with regard to church officers. As I indicated above, overseers must be competent to teach, preach, and maintain orthodoxy in the church. Overseers should not be elected or appointed if they have not shown a detailed knowledge of Scripture and the gospel. One way to determine their orthodoxy is to prepare them to endorse a formal doctrinal statement. But there is no evidence that this was done in NT times.

Even though there was no confessional subscription during the biblical period, it is possible to argue the value of it in other situations pragmatically—that such a practice is the best method for ensuring orthodoxy in a church situation. If that argument can be made, then confessional subscription may be seen as an *application* of the biblical principle that church officers should be orthodox. But it cannot be shown, in my view, that this is the *only* way to ensure such orthodoxy.

Even today, I think, there is much to be said for the more reactive approach to these matters presented in the NT. Candidates for the office of overseer will show other overseers over a period of training and scrutiny that they love Jesus and his Word, that they are competent to teach and shepherd the flock, and that they believe the true gospel.[4] Then they will be received as officers by the laying on of hands and prayer (1 Tim. 4:14). From that point, if any charge against their orthodoxy is made, the burden of proof will be on the prosecution. This principle, sometimes called the *presumption of innocence*, is common to American civil law, and it is also biblical. In both Testaments, accusations must be verified by "two or three witnesses" (Deut. 17:6; 19:15; Matt. 18:16; 2 Cor. 13:1; 1 Tim. 5:19; Heb. 10:28), meaning that the accuser must have a cogent case. It is not the responsibility of the accused, faced by an unsubstantiated charge, to prove his innocence.

This form of discipline, even in the absence of an extrabiblical confessional test of orthodoxy, should be sufficient to maintain orthodoxy in the church, though it is not infallible, any more than confessional subscription infallibly ensures orthodoxy. Another benefit of such discipline is that it would also guard against false accusations. The test of accusations would be solid evidence of what took place, and the ultimate test of orthodoxy would be God's written Word itself, the only book that God has given to rule his church.

---

4. I do believe that the training of church officers is best done in the most personal way possible, with a minimum of academic or ecclesiastical formality. See my "Proposal for a New Seminary," available at http://www.frame-poythress.org/frame_articles/1978Proposal.htm.

Extrabiblical confessional documents such as the WCF have done the church good service as baptismal instruction, witness to the world, and warning against falsehood, to list the first three purposes of such documents that I named earlier. But the attempt to maintain orthodoxy in the church by confessional subscription has not, historically, achieved its goal. Many denominations that require subscription, even strict subscription, have fallen away into liberalism and other heresies.[5] And my experience has been that in churches that use confessions as tests of orthodoxy, much time has been wasted trying to exegete the confession that could have been spent exegeting the Bible.

So I maintain some skepticism about the very practice of confessional subscription. I admit, however, the unlikelihood that this practice will be abandoned in Presbyterian and Reformed churches anytime soon. So I have a fallback position. Granted that churches will continue to use confessional subscription to maintain orthodoxy, I would argue that the form of subscription should be loose enough to allow the confession to be reformed by the Word of God.

A few years ago there was a debate in the Presbyterian Church in America (PCA) on the nature of confessional subscription.[6] Some argued for *strict subscription*, in which an officer must subscribe to every statement in the confession. Some strict subscriptionists allow for ministers to take exceptions to minor points of the confession, but they forbid the ministers to teach or preach their exceptions. Looser forms of subscription include *system subscription*, the present formula of the PCA, in which the minister subscribes to the confession "as containing the system of doctrine taught in the Scriptures." Usually this is understood to mean that the minister need not subscribe to every statement of the confession, but must only affirm that the confession teaches the system (the main elements) of the Bible's teaching.[7] Still looser forms are used in more liberal denominations, as when the minister agrees only to "be guided by" the confession.

---

5. Arguably, the stricter the formula of subscription, the more people will be tempted to subscribe ignorantly or deceptively, keeping to themselves the parts of the confession that they don't understand, or that they doubt.

6. See, e.g., David Hall, ed., *The Practice of Confessional Subscription* (Lanham, MD: University Press of America, 1995).

7. PCA candidates for ordination are asked this question: "Do you sincerely receive and adopt the *Confession of Faith* and the *Catechisms* of this Church, as containing the system of doctrine taught in the Holy Scriptures; and do you further promise that if at any time you find yourself out of accord with any of the fundamentals of this system of doctrine, you will on your own initiative, make known to your Presbytery the change which has taken place in your views since the assumption of this ordination vow?" (*The Book of Church Order* [Office of the Stated Clerk of the General Assembly of the Presbyterian Church in America, 2008], 21.5). Note that this statement not only loosens subscription

In my judgment, strict subscription violates the sufficiency of Scripture. It prevents any teaching in the church that contradicts the confession. Thus, in effect, it recognizes no difference in authority between the confession and the Bible itself. If the sufficiency of Scripture is to have any meaning in the church, it must be possible to recognize error in the extrabiblical confessional document, bring that error to the church's attention, and revise the confession to make it agree with the Bible. But strict subscription guarantees that the confession will never be reformed according to the Word of God.

Nevertheless, it cannot be denied that God uses creeds and confessions to communicate his Word to us. We have seen in chapter 35 that all authentic teaching and preaching conveys the Word of God, and chapter 37 makes the same claim for theology. The creeds and confessions of the church are essentially theological teaching. They are not infallible, but when they agree with Scripture they communicate the teaching of Scripture.

Indeed, creeds and confessions have an authority above other teaching. For one thing, they represent a consensus of the church, and that consensus carries greater weight than the teaching of any individual. Individuals should be subject to others in the body of Christ, recognizing the gifts of others and the wisdom of the body as a whole. Further, that consensus is a consensus of people with special authority in the church: overseers, bishops, or elders. Though such people are not infallible, God has called them to exercise oversight of the church's doctrine and practice. Their authority should be honored, even after their death (Heb. 13:7, 17).

Each generation should rethink these documents, reforming them, where necessary, by the Word of God. But as "secondary standards," under Scripture, they should be respected. And insofar as these documents convey the true teaching of the Bible, they bring to us God's personal words.

---

by the phrase "system of doctrine," but also requires presbytery scrutiny only of views that (1) the minister himself identifies as problematic, and (2) he considers out of accord with what he himself considers the *fundamentals* of the system of doctrine.

CHAPTER 39

Human Reception of Scripture

In this chapter, I continue to discuss the list of events presented in chapter 33. So now we will briefly consider the human reception of Scripture. As I said before, the list is not chronological in a general way. Certainly, the human reception of Scripture began before there was theology, or teaching, or translations, or even copies. And there is human reception of Scripture in every one of these events, by the copyists, the preachers and teachers, their audiences, and others. But the list is somewhat chronological in showing the process by which the biblical Word reaches a modern reader. So today we tend to receive the biblical message through copies, translations, editions, theology, confessions, and so on. Through these means God presents Scripture to us, and we receive it through that process.

In chapter 6, I mentioned the theological controversy about whether revelation exists apart from human reception of it—indeed, whether it exists apart from a human response in faith. I argued there that we should distinguish among (1) objective revelation, (2) subjective revelation received in unbelief, and (3) subjective revelation received in faith.

1. Objective revelation is revelation that God has made *available* for human knowledge, even to people who do not actually make use of it. In that sense, both nature and Scripture contain divine revelation addressed to everyone.
2. There are many examples of revelation subjectively received in unbelief. Romans 1 speaks of the repression of natural revelation. Scripture speaks of the many times God spoke through the

prophets, Jesus, and the apostles to a response of rejection and rebellion. It is important for us to recognize that this is genuine revelation. Though its audience does not receive it in faith, it exists despite their reaction, and it takes away their excuses (Rom. 1:20).

3. Of course, God desires that people receive his revelation in faith. Some have argued that revelation received in faith is the only true revelation, because otherwise God's attempt to communicate has failed. Certainly, there are some kinds of revelation that by definition produce a faith response (Matt. 11:27; Eph. 1:17). But this fact does not invalidate the kinds of revelation listed under 1 and 2. Mysteriously, sometimes God's very purpose in communication is to harden hearts and to take away excuses (Isa. 6:9–10; Matt. 13:14–15; Acts 28:25–27).

Given this distinction, we can also make distinctions among the different kinds of recipients of the Word. Remarkably, God does speak to himself. There are communications among the persons of the Trinity (Gen. 1:26; Pss. 2:7–9; 45:6–8; 110; Matt. 11:25–27; John 4:34; 5:20; 6:38–39; 17:1–26; Acts 2:33–36).

There are also divine communications given to the natural world (Gen. 1:9, 20, 22, 24), to angels (Ex. 23:20; Dan. 3:28; etc.), and to the human race as a whole (Gen. 1:28–30; Rom. 1:18). The gospel of Jesus Christ is given to the apostles, but the Lord commissions them to bring it to everyone on earth (Matt. 28:19–20).

How does God want his Word to be received? I would distinguish three aspects that correlate with the lordship attributes and my epistemological perspectives:

Belief (normative): When God describes his mighty acts, we are expected to accept his description and interpretation. When he promises blessing or threatens judgment, we dare not call his Word into question.

Obedience (situational): What God commands must be obeyed without question.

Participation (existential): Since the Word is not exclusively propositional or imperative, God expects more from us than is easily summarized in the previous two headings (though either of them may be taken as a perspective on the whole of our response). Since the Word includes poetry, symbol, parable, exhortation, and so forth, God wants us to take his Word into our heart, to let it work upon us in all the subtle ways in which these forms of language change people. The Word thus changes our interests, our emotions, our priorities, our perspectives, our preoccupations. God wants us not only to believe him and obey him, but to be involved with him personally in a wide variety of ways.

How do we receive the Word of God? By use of the faculties that God has given us: our ability to read, hear, reason, feel. But of course, our sin makes it impossible for us to use these capacities rightly apart from his grace. What keeps us from suppressing the truth (Rom. 1:18), exchanging it for a lie (Rom. 1:25), and hardening our hearts (Isa. 6:9–10) is the Holy Spirit, who opens our eyes to perceive the full blessing of God's address to us and who enables us to rejoice in God's kindness. He opens our eyes first to see the reality of our own sin, and then to see God's forgiveness of sin for the sake of Christ.[1] So we can understand God's revelation only through the gospel. In that sense Scripture, the message of the gospel, takes primacy over all of God's revelation. It becomes the "spectacles" (John Calvin) by which we are enabled to see God's revelation in creation rightly.

---

1. I will discuss the Spirit's work in detail in chapter 42.

CHAPTER 40

The Interpretation of Scripture

Once we receive the Bible, it is our task to understand it, and to do that we must interpret it correctly. So interpretation is the next event on the list I placed in chapter 33, though of course it occurs throughout the process by which Scripture reaches us. Certainly, interpretation is involved at every step along the way: in confessions, theology, teaching, translation, and even making copies (since many copyist errors result from misinterpretations).

The literature on interpretation is vast. Jews and Christians have been interpreting Bible passages for many centuries. But far beyond that, in the modern period, the idea of interpretation has been raised to a new level of philosophical sophistication and abstraction. Such thinkers as Friedrich Schleiermacher, Wilhelm Dilthey, Martin Heidegger, Hans-Georg Gadamer, Jürgen Habermas, and Paul Ricœur have expanded the notion of interpretation (or *hermeneutics*, as they prefer) to include the philosophy of language and communication. And because philosophy is an attempt to interpret the world, many have identified philosophy itself, indeed all forms of human knowledge, as hermeneutic.

I will not be able here to discuss hermeneutics in such an exalted way. My interest is in hermeneutics in the old, modest sense, the attempt to understand texts. And I limit that in turn, for purposes of this book, to the understanding of biblical language. Further, this discussion will be quite elementary. I only hope to send my readers along the right track.[1]

1. For a much more elaborate treatment of interpretation, I recommend especially Vern Poythress, *God-Centered Biblical Interpretation* (Phillipsburg, NJ: P&R Publishing,

What is interpretation, in this context? We often say that to interpret is to find the meaning of a text. But what is meaning?

We often think of meaning as translation (see chap. 34). Here, to find the meaning of a sentence is to put it in other words that are somewhat equivalent. But why do we do that? In the case of Bible interpretation, why aren't the original words adequate?

In chapter 37, I asked a similar question about theology: why do we need theology when we have the Bible? The answer cannot be that the Bible is inadequate in some way. Rather, the inadequacy is in us: we need theology because *we* have a problem understanding Scripture. Theology is the teaching ministry of the church, addressing that need.

Human questions about Scripture are of various kinds: What does this Hebrew word mean? What does John 1:1 mean? What is a covenant? Why did Jesus have to die? Such questions expose in us a lack of ability to use Scripture as God intended. As I indicated in chapter 37, these questions can be understood as questions of *application*. We face a text, but we lack the ability to relate it to our own lives. We may lack the ability to say it in our language, or we may lack the ability to relate it to our business decisions. In all these situations, we are trying to understand how to *apply* Scripture. So I said in chapter 37 that theology is the application of Scripture. In that sense, theology is equivalent to teaching and preaching (chap. 35), and they, too, can be understood as the application of Scripture. We tend to use the term *theology* to refer to an academic discipline, and *teaching* to refer to the ministry of a church. But the two are essentially the same, though they may differ in emphasis and the kinds of questions they typically address.

So now I suggest that interpretation-hermeneutics is also application. As I asked earlier, when we look for the "meaning" of a passage, what are we looking for? I now answer that we are looking for an application.

Questions about meaning are of different kinds. When an English speaker asks, "What is the meaning of this Greek sentence?" a teacher often gives him an equivalent English sentence. John 1:1 begins, *En arche en ho logos.* The teacher tells the inquirer, "That means, 'In the beginning was the Word.'" So we are tempted to say that the English sentence is "the meaning of" the Greek sentence. But that is odd, for in a similar way a French speaker might find the meaning of the Greek in a French sentence, and

---

1999). Poythress has thought about these matters in great depth, and like me his chief interest is to be in accord with Scripture. Readers of my work will be especially interested in his threefold distinction between classificational, instantiational, and associational aspects of language, which leads to a view of meaning that balances sense, application, and import (72–74).

similarly for all the languages of the world. Is the meaning of John 1:1 to be identified with equivalent sentences from all the languages of the world?

Further, after a teacher gives the inquirer an equivalent English sentence, the inquirer may claim that he still does not know the meaning.[2] For the English itself may be as problematic as the Greek. After all, it is not obvious what it means for a *word* to exist in the "beginning." Well, then, we seek another level of meaning: perhaps a theological explanation of the original sentence. We tell the inquirer that the "beginning" is the beginning of Genesis 1:1, the original creation. And we tell him that the "Word" is Jesus Christ (as John 1:14). So Jesus Christ was already present (*en*) when God created the world.

But even then, the inquirer might say something like this: "I understand intellectually what this means, but I don't know how it is supposed to affect my life. What does it mean *to me?*" So we move to another level of meaning. The teacher may reply, "If Jesus Christ, this Jew of Galilee, existed at the very beginning of creation, he must be pretty special. We need to put our hearts into knowing more about him and understanding who he is and what he has done."

So now we have three levels of meaning: (1) an equivalent English phrase, (2) a theological explanation of the terms, and (3) a program for our lives. I know of no term that better covers all these kinds of meaning (and more) than *application*. When we ask the "meaning" of a passage, we are simply confessing that we don't know what to do with it. When we explain meaning in various ways, we are helping people learn what to do with the language, how to apply the language to themselves.[3]

Now, I used this correlation between interpretation and application in chapter 28 when I considered Bible problems. One problem was the apparent inappropriateness of NT citations of the OT. I argued there that we need to have a broader view of the purposes of such citations. They are not always citations of predictions being fulfilled in the NT age. Sometimes they have the purpose of underscoring narrative parallels (e.g., between

---

2. I've often noticed that expressions that are problematic in Greek tend to be equally problematic in English. So switching languages doesn't necessarily help to clarify meaning.

3. As I indicated in footnote 1, Poythress correlates application with sense and import. *Sense* is the meaning of an expression that remains constant through its use in multiple contexts. *Application* is "any instantiation of a passage in word or deed" (Poythress, *God-Centered Biblical Interpretation*, 73). *Import* is the connection of an expression to other expressions (its contexts), and its distinctive function within that field of expressions. Poythress understands these as perspectivally related, so it is possible (as in my discussion above) to understand all meaning as application, or as sense, or as import. My treatment thus simplifies that of Poythress. Of the categories *sense*, *import*, and *application*, I think the latter is the most "practical," the easiest for most readers to follow.

the life of Jesus and the history of Israel), of noting verbal parallels of some importance, and so on. We can have a better understanding of these cita-tions if we regard them as applications.

Now, the most common general question that people ask about biblical interpretation is how we can understand texts from times and cultures far removed from ours. At first glance, this task may seem terribly difficult. But some considerations mitigate the problem:

1. In God's providence, human cultures are never sealed off from one another. We share with people in the ancient world our com-mon humanity, and there are many ties between their languages and ours, their cultures and ours. There are differences between us and them, but also important similarities. These similarities are even greater between modern believers in Christ and ancient believers.

2. The greater cultural differences are bridged by the continuous existence of the church throughout the centuries. Since the time of Moses, God's people have studied Scripture and applied it to many of their own situations. We are part of that history, that interpretative process. We learn from the previous generation, and the generation before them, all the way back to Bible times. We are not, therefore, faced with a huge, empty cultural gap. That gap is filled with our own brothers and sisters in the Lord who have built bridges from the original composition of the Bible down to our own day. With their help, we can get back to the original cultural settings of Scripture by small steps.

3. Among the teachers whom God has provided to the church (chap. 35) are people gifted with expertise in these ancient cultures and languages. They are not infallible, but they can help us in a great many cases.

4. Scripture itself is the most important guide to its own interpreta-tion, and it is an infallible guide. As WCF 1.9 says:

> The infallible rule of interpretation of Scripture is the Scripture itself: and therefore, when there is a question about the true and full sense of any Scripture (which is not manifold, but one[4]), it must be searched and known by other places that speak more clearly.

---

4. In this parenthetical, the Confession repudiates the "fourfold sense" of the medi-eval interpreters. These interpreters (and some in the early church) thought that most Bible passages contained a literal sense, an allegorical sense, a tropological (moral-ethical) sense, and an anagogical sense (anticipating heaven and the last days). Often those who distinguished these senses took little care to relate their interpretations to the original bibli-

Scripture interprets Scripture; *Scriptura ipsius interpres*. As believers live in the Word of God, they come to see how the later parts presuppose earlier parts and how the earlier anticipate the later. They see how the Scriptures are bound together in a common worldview, a common symbolic structure, a common ethic, a common history, a common gospel of salvation. The fact that God has inspired the Scriptures means that they are consistent with one another, that they tell a common story, though they are written by many human authors over many centuries. So each part illumines other parts. As we live in God's Word, cultural differences make less difference. The unity of Scripture makes more.[5]

5. Many times in this book I have argued that the ultimate identification of the word of God is supernatural. This was true for Abraham; as we saw in chapter 1, he knew that God was talking to him because God himself gave him the assurance that God was talking. This was true when God led the church to recognize his canon (chap. 22). So I have often noted through this book that our confidence in the word of God in any form is given by God himself. We will see (chap. 42) that God, in the person of the Holy Spirit, also gives us grace to understand what God is saying to us. The Spirit illumines the Word and enables us to interpret.

So the difficulties of interpretation do not stand in the way of God's communicating his personal words to his people. We do not understand everything in Scripture,[6] but we understand much, by God's grace. And what we understand becomes the foundation of our lives, our only comfort in life and death.[7]

---

cal contexts, and their nonliteral interpretations were often arbitrary. Actually, however, they weren't always, or entirely, wrong. It is often appropriate, of course, to understand texts literally. But it can also be helpful to draw parallels to apparently unrelated matters (allegory, as Paul in Galatians 4:21–31), to indicate ethical applications ("tropological," as often in the NT; see 1 Cor. 10:6–12) and to draw trajectories ("anagogical"—typology, prophecy) to the future.

While we're looking at WCF 1.9, we should also note the Confession's emphasis that each passage has one meaning, not many. This parenthetical observation is, I think, also a rejection of the "fourfold sense" type of interpretation. It does not imply that the meaning of a passage is never complex. One look at the elaborate accounts of the Ten Commandments in the Larger Catechism makes it clear that the writers of the Confession often found very expansive levels of meaning in Scripture.

5. Compare our discussion in chapter 24 about the unity of Scripture.

6. See chapter 29, on the clarity of Scripture.

7. Alluding to the Heidelberg Catechism, Question 1.

CHAPTER 41

Assurance

It may seem that we have been on a long, strenuous journey through the steps listed in chapter 33: copying, textual criticism, translations, editions, teaching, preaching, sacraments, theology, confessions, creeds, traditions, human reception, interpretation, and understanding. It may seem that we can barely perceive the autographic text through the fog. And it may seem that with every step, we lose assurance. For at every step, errors enter the picture. Can we be sure that our Bible is based on accurate copies, a proper textual tradition, sound teaching, interpretation, and so on?

But believers understand that reading the Bible is not like this. It's not like a slog through a jungle in which we have to hack away at thousands of pieces of underbrush before we reach our destination. Rather, it is very much like listening to our Father talking to us. As in Abraham's case, we hear in Scripture a personal word from God.

If the problems of text, translation, and so on are so difficult that we can never identify the voice of God, then, of course, our faith is an illusion. Faith in Scripture is precisely hearing the voice of God, believing, obeying, and participating in his words (chap. 39). Abraham is the primary model of Christian faith in the NT (Rom. 4:1–25; cf. John 8:56; Gal. 3:6–29; Heb. 6:13–20; 11:8–22; James 2:21–23). "He believed the LORD, and [God] counted it to him as righteousness" (Gen. 15:6) is quoted three times in the NT (Rom. 4:3; Gal. 3:6; James 2:23). We, too, are to believe Christ, and our faith in the promise of his free grace is the instrument of our salvation.

It will not do to say that revelation is something nonpropositional, perhaps an occasional mystical experience. That is not the kind of revelation Abraham heard. God gave him commands, and an intelligible promise. Our own salvation is grounded in that promise. Without it, there is no hope.

In 1 Corinthians 15, Paul expresses amazement that some in the church have come to deny that the dead are raised. He replies:

> Now if Christ is proclaimed as raised from the dead, how can some of you say that there is no resurrection of the dead? But if there is no resurrection of the dead, then not even Christ has been raised. And if Christ has not been raised, then our preaching is in vain and your faith is in vain. We are even found to be misrepresenting God, because we testified about God that he raised Christ, whom he did not raise if it is true that the dead are not raised. For if the dead are not raised, not even Christ has been raised. And if Christ has not been raised, your faith is futile and you are still in your sins. Then those also who have fallen asleep in Christ have perished. If in this life only we have hoped in Christ, we are of all people most to be pitied. (1 Cor. 15:12–19)

If there is no resurrection for human beings, then not even Christ has been raised. We know that Christ has been raised, so certainly there is a resurrection for all believers. But how are the Corinthians to be sure that Jesus was actually raised from the dead? The answer is that they have learned this in a personal word from God:

> Now I would remind you, brothers, of the gospel I preached to you, which you received, in which you stand, and by which you are being saved, if you hold fast to the word I preached to you— unless you believed in vain.
>
> For I delivered to you as of first importance what I also received: that Christ died for our sins in accordance with the Scriptures, that he was buried, that he was raised on the third day in accordance with the Scriptures, and that he appeared to Cephas, then to the twelve. Then he appeared to more than five hundred brothers at one time, most of whom are still alive, though some have fallen asleep. Then he appeared to James, then to all the apostles. Last of all, as to one untimely born, he appeared also to me. For I am the least of the apostles, unworthy to be called an apostle, because I persecuted the church of God. But by the grace of God I am what I am, and his grace toward me was not in vain. On the contrary, I worked harder than any of them, though it was not I, but the

grace of God that is with me. Whether then it was I or they, so we preach and so you believed.

Now if Christ is proclaimed as raised from the dead, how can some of you say that there is no resurrection of the dead? (1 Cor. 15:1–12)

Now, apologists often quote this passage as a list of evidences for the resurrection, and it certainly is that. Paul lists resurrection appearances to apostles, even one appearance to five hundred brothers at once, some of whom are still alive and therefore, we should assume, capable of testifying. But the Corinthians, most of them, had not personally witnessed the resurrection. Nor had they individually cross-examined the witnesses. For them, the knowledge of the resurrection came from another source, namely, the preaching of Paul (vv. 1–3, 11–12). Paul's primary argument is that the resurrection of Christ was part of the apostolic preaching, the preaching God used to plant the church. To doubt that is to doubt the whole gospel. To reject the resurrection is to reject Paul's preaching as "vain" (v. 14) and faith itself as vain. And if our faith is futile, we are yet in our sins (v. 17).

Paul's preaching was like the promise to Abraham: a personal word from God. Our faith, too, is based on this personal word. If we have no personal word, our faith is futile, and we are yet in our sins. And if we cannot identify God's Word (despite the history of textual and interpretative problems), then we have no hope. Christianity is a sham.

But we have seen that God intends to speak personal words to his people. He acknowledges no barriers that can keep him from communicating with us successfully. And believers throughout the centuries have been assured that God's Word is true. They have found that Word to be trustworthy enough to build their lives upon it, to trust it as their only comfort in life or death, to believe and obey it no matter what the unbelieving world may say.

How is such assurance possible? For one thing, it is not at all difficult for God. Abraham's case was also problematic. Humanly speaking, it is hard to understand why he would accept God's word. His reason and emotions must have questioned the notion that he should leave his home to dwell in a new and strange land (Gen. 12:1). Even more, his conscience must have rebelled against the idea that God would want him to sacrifice his beloved son, the son of the covenant (22:2). Any of us would have been inclined to say that the voice asking him to do such things could not have been the voice of God. But God somehow managed to identify himself. Abraham was assured that this was the word of God. It was the highest assurance because it came from God himself.

Similarly, God gets through to believers today. The unbelieving world, the academic establishment, and our own rebellious inclinations pose a thousand reasons why we should not accept Scripture as humble servants. The problems of text, interpretation, and theology often seem insuperable. But many still believe, and their number increases. It is hard to account for this. But it is God at work.

Subjectively, it works like this. When someone believes God's Word with true faith, he or she does not accept it through autonomous reasoning, through the consensus of scholars, or through an independent examination of evidences. We do not believe God because we have subjected God to our tests and the tests of others. Rather, God's Word is the foundation of our thought.[1] God's Word is the ultimate criterion of truth and right. It is the judge of what reasoning is valid and sound. The ultimate test of a scholar is whether his work agrees with Scripture. And Scripture determines what evidences are to be believed.

It is God himself who enables us to accept his Word as our foundation, our presupposition.

To say this is not to deny that Scripture presents problems to us. Often, it is not easy to know what Scripture is saying, or to answer the objections that arise in our hearts. So there is much in the Bible of which we do *not* have assurance, even when we seek to trust God's Word as our presupposition.

But the Christian life is a journey, a movement from faith to more faith (with, to be sure, ups and downs along the way). This is a journey both toward better understanding and toward overcoming our unbelief (Mark 9:24). The latter process is called *sanctification*. The former process is also related to sanctification: our level of understanding is related to our level of trust and obedience.[2] But our lack of understanding is also related to our finitude, our inability to resolve all the questions that the phenomena of Scripture pose to us.

Yet every believer begins with certainty. When we trust in Christ, we "know" that we have eternal life (1 John 5:13), and we "know" that he hears our prayers (v. 15).[3] As I mentioned earlier, if we have faith

---

1. It should be obvious to those who know about such things that I am not asserting "foundationalism" in the sense that it is usually criticized today. For some observations on the subject, see *DKG*, 128–29, 386–87. I do not believe that all human knowledge should be deduced from Scripture, as René Descartes tried to deduce all human knowledge from his foundational argument. But I do maintain that all human knowledge must be reconcilable with Scripture.

2. See *DKG*, 40–49.

3. I am describing here the faith of normal adults. God is able to make special provision for those who are unable to understand propositional content. See WCF 10.3.

at all, we *know* that Christ has been raised from the dead. It is our fundamental confession that Jesus is the Christ, the Son of the living God (Matt. 16:16; cf. John 6:69). Such facts become our presuppositions, the foundations of knowledge.

These presuppositions are the ultimate criteria of truth for a Christian. All other ideas must be consistent with them. They form the foundation on which all our other knowledge is to be built. When someone raises an objection that conflicts with one of these presuppositional beliefs, we know that objection is false, whether or not we can otherwise refute it.

But there are things in the Bible that we do not understand well enough to affirm them with this kind of assurance. My former colleague Richard Pratt uses a diagram that he calls the "cone of certainty" to illustrate this problem. It is simply a cone with the narrow end at the top and the broader end on the bottom. At the narrow end of the cone are those beliefs we are sure of: say, the existence of God, the deity of Christ, his resurrection, salvation by grace through faith, and so on. At the bottom of the cone, there are matters in Scripture of which we are very unsure: Where did Cain get his wife (Gen. 4:17)? Why did Jephthah keep the vow to make his daughter an offering (Judg. 11:29–40)? Why was it such a serious crime for somebody to gather sticks on the Sabbath (Num. 15:32–36)? At the bottom of my cone is God's reason for bringing evil into the world, and the timing of the millennium. We may have views about such matters, but we are not sure of them.

In between the bottom and the top are matters about which we may have opinions, but we would not claim that they are absolutely certain. For me, these would include the mode and subjects of baptism, the frequency of the Lord's Supper, the biblical pattern for church government, and the nature of Jesus' ignorance (Matt. 26:36).

As we grow as believers, there is movement through the cone. Some things of which we were once very certain become uncertain. Other things of which we have been uncertain become certain. But the overall progression, I think, is toward greater certainty. Scripture values certainty; and therefore our sanctification moves toward that goal, as part of the holiness God seeks in us.

The Bible often tells us that Christians can, should, and do know God and the truths of revelation (Matt. 9:6; 11:27; 13:11; John 7:17; 8:32; 10:4–5; 14:17; 17:3; many other passages). Such passages present this knowledge not as something tentative, but as a firm basis for life and hope.

Scripture uses the language of certainty more sparingly, but that is also present. Luke wants his correspondent Theophilus to know the "certainty" (*asphaleia*) of the things he has been taught (Luke 1:4) and the "proofs" (*tekmeria*) by which Jesus showed himself alive after his death (Acts 1:3). The centurion at the cross says, "Certainly [*ontos*] this man was innocent!" (Luke 23:47).

The letter to the Hebrews says that God made a promise to Abraham, swearing by himself, for there was no one greater (Heb. 6:13). So God both made a promise and confirmed it with an oath, "two unchangeable things, in which it is impossible for God to lie" (v. 18). This is "a sure and steadfast anchor of the soul" (v. 19). Similarly, Paul (2 Tim. 3:16–17) and Peter (2 Peter 1:19–21) speak of Scripture as God's own words, which provide sure guidance in a world where false teaching abounds. God's special revelation is certain, and we ought to be certain about it.

On the other hand, the Bible presents doubt largely negatively. It is a spiritual impediment, an obstacle to doing God's work (Matt. 14:31; 21:21; 28:17; Acts 10:20; 11:12; Rom. 14:23; 1 Tim. 2:8; James 1:6). In Matthew 14:31 and Romans 14:23, it is the opposite of faith and therefore a sin. Of course, this sin, like other sins, may remain with us through our earthly life. But we should not be complacent about it. Just as the ideal for the Christian life is perfect holiness, the ideal for the Christian mind is absolute certainty about God's revelation.

We should not conclude that doubt is always sinful. Matthew 14:31 and Romans 14:23 (and indeed the others I have listed) speak of doubt in the face of clear special revelation. To doubt what God has clearly spoken to us is wrong. But in other situations, it is not wrong to doubt. In many cases, in fact, it is wrong for us to claim knowledge, much less certainty. Indeed, often the best course is to admit our ignorance (Deut. 29:29; Rom. 11:33–36). Paul is not wrong to express uncertainty about the number of people he baptized (1 Cor. 1:16). Indeed, James tells us, we are always ignorant of the future to some extent, and we ought not to pretend that we know more about it than we do (James 4:13–16). Job's friends were wrong to think they knew the reasons for his torment, and Job himself had to be humbled as God reminded him of his ignorance (Job 38–42).

So Christian epistemologist Esther Meek points out that the process of knowing through our earthly lives is a quest: following clues, noticing patterns, making commitments, respecting honest doubt. In much of life, she says, confidence, not certainty, should be our goal.[4]

I agree. But in regard to our knowledge of God's Word, certainty should be our goal. We should not be complacent with doubt, but we should use all the abilities God has given us to advance in knowledge of his Word. Besides following clues, noticing patterns, and such things, we should employ our

---

4. Esther Meek, *Longing to Know* (Grand Rapids: Brazos Press, 2003).

spiritual resources: prayer, sacrament, teaching. In all these, God comes through to us. That is to say, as we obey the revelation of which we are certain, God grants us certainty about other things.

So the process I have described since chapter 33—copying, textual criticism, translations, and so forth—is not a journey toward more and more uncertainty and confusion. To be sure, we encounter errors at each step of the human assimilation of God's Word. But each step also represents progress toward greater understanding. At each step, errors enter in, but errors are also corrected. By faith we expect that the overall trajectory of our assurance is upward. With each step, we grow in grace, knowledge, confidence, and certainty.

To speak of this journey toward certainty is to speak of the workings of the Holy Spirit, the subject of the next chapter.[5]

---

5. The present chapter may be usefully compared to my article "Certainty," available at http://www.frame-poythress.org/frame_articles/2005Certainty.htm.

CHAPTER 42

Person-Revelation: The Divine Witness

Now, at this point I need to remind you of the macro-structure of this book. Part 1, "Orientation," presented the personal-word model and the relationship between the word of God and God's lordship. Part 2, "God's Word in Modern Theology," covered how God's Word has been discussed in the liberal theological tradition. Part 3, "The Nature of God's Word," presented how Scripture itself regards the Word of God, as the Lord's controlling power, meaningful authority, and personal presence. Part 4, "How the Word Comes to Us," distinguished revelation through events, words, and persons. Chapter 13 discussed event-revelation. Then chapters 14–41 discussed word-revelation.

That long section on word-revelation might have engendered some confusion about where the book was going. But yes, we are now going to move on to the third group of media, person-revelation. I spent a very long time on word-revelation because that is the greatest emphasis of Scripture, and because it is in that area that most controversy and confusion has arisen.

But person-revelation is also important, and vitally necessary for the process of divine-human communication. It is also necessary to our proper understanding and use of word-revelation. You may wish to review chapters 11 and 12 in order to get your bearings here.

God reveals himself in events, words, and persons. That triad reflects the lordship attributes: control, authority, presence, though each of the media conveys to us all the lordship attributes. Event-revelation, for example, especially demonstrates God's powerful control. But it also carries the full authority of God, and God himself is personally present in it.

Persons are an important means of divine communication. For one thing, God, the one who reveals himself, is personal rather than impersonal (chap. 2). Indeed, as we saw in chapter 8, God's word, his communication, is identical with himself. So revelation includes manifestation of divine persons, angelic persons,[1] and human persons in the image of God.

Another consideration: If meaning is application, at least from one perspective (chaps. 37, 40), then we cannot understand language without understanding how its speakers apply it. Language is part of life. To understand language, we must see what people *do* with it, how it is *used*. So in understanding the word of God, it is important to learn how God intends that word to be used. That means, first, that we should understand how God himself makes use of his word. And second, we need to see examples of how fellow human beings use God's word—wrongly and rightly. So persons, as they speak, hear, and act out the word of God, are an important subject of our study.

In this chapter, we will consider the role of the three persons of the Trinity as person-revelation, with special emphasis on the witness of the Holy Spirit. In the next, we will look at human persons as God's image.

As we saw in chapter 8, the word is God, both as his divine attribute and as the second person of the Trinity. So wherever the word is, God is. God accompanies his word to bring it to pass. So the word is never an impersonal object or force. It is God himself drawing near to us (recall Deut. 30:11–14; Rom. 10:6–9). As we hear or read the Word, God speaks it to us. In chapter 40, we considered the chief difficulty of Bible interpretation, namely, the distance between the time and culture of the writers and of ourselves. The ultimate answer to that difficulty is that in an important sense the word of Scripture is always contemporary. God speaks it in our hearing, our time, our culture. This fact does not take away our responsibility to interpret Scripture in the context in which it was first given. But it does eliminate the possibility that the historical gap might make the Word inaccessible to us.

Let us consider now some forms of divine person-revelation.

THEOPHANY

In theophany, God appears in the form of something created, often as an angel or man. The "angel of the LORD" appears as an angel, but at

---

1. I will not consider angelic persons here, mainly because of my lack of insight into their role as revelation. Generally, they are messengers of God, as their names *malak* and *aggelos* suggest. But how does the *person* of the angel reveal God? I have nothing much to offer on that subject. For some reflection on the role of angels in the Christian life, however, see *DCL*, 253–57.

some point in the context identifies himself as God (e.g., Gen. 16:7–14; 21:17–21). In Genesis 32:22–32, Jacob wrestles with "a man" (v. 24), who turns out to be God (v. 30). Similarly, the "men" who met with Abraham in Genesis 18:1–33 are related in a mysterious way to "the LORD."

Most often the theophany takes the form of a "glory cloud,"[2] in which God is surrounded by heavenly beings and the light of his glory. This is the cloud and pillar of fire by which God led Israel through the wilderness. In that cloud was God himself (Ex. 16:6–10). Here revelation has a strongly visual aspect. Although God is invisible, he voluntarily takes on visible forms that impress people with his terrifying power and magnificent glory.

But Jesus Christ is also a theophany. When Philip asked him, "Show us the Father," Jesus replied:

> Have I been with you so long, and you still do not know me, Philip? Whoever has seen me has seen the Father. How can you say, "Show us the Father"? (John 14:9)

Of course, Jesus is more than a theophany, for he is himself God, the second person of the Trinity. And he is not only a visible representation of the Father; he actually became a man. And that manhood is itself a profound revelation of God, since man himself is God's image, and Jesus was unfallen man, the most perfect of men. Against the Docetists, who thought Jesus only seemed to have a human body, John says:

> That which was from the beginning, which we have heard, which we have seen with our eyes, which we looked upon and have touched with our hands, concerning the word of life—the life was made manifest, and we have seen it, and testify to it and proclaim to you the eternal life, which was with the Father and was made manifest to us—that which we have seen and heard we proclaim also to you, so that you too may have fellowship with us; and indeed our fellowship is with the Father and with his Son Jesus Christ. (1 John 1:1–3)

Note the excited, eloquent sensory language about the disciples' knowledge of Jesus.

Theophany is also connected in Scripture with the Holy Spirit, the third person of the Trinity. Kline believes that the hovering of the Spirit over creation in Genesis 1:2 is the theophanic glory cloud. So he regularly calls this theophany the glory-Spirit.

---

2. See Meredith G. Kline, *Images of the Spirit* (Grand Rapids: Baker, 1980). See also *DG*, 585–87, 592–95.

CHRIST, THE MEDIATOR OF ALL REVELATION

We have considered Jesus Christ in his divine identity with the word of God (chaps. 7, 8, 11) and, as man, the chief theophany of God. We have also looked at him as the chief speaker of God's authoritative word (chap. 10), and as the divine voice incarnate (chap. 14).

Here we will note that Christ speaks through all forms of revelation. This statement follows from the fact that he and the Father are both involved in all of God's works in the world. He does everything the Father does (John 5:19).

Like the Father, then, he is Creator (John 1:1–3; Col. 1:15–16; Heb. 1:2–3) and the author of providence (Col. 1:17; Heb. 1:3). So natural revelation, the revelation of God through creation, is a revelation of Christ. It is not only God who speaks to us in creation; it is specifically Jesus.

He is also the Redeemer, who, not only in his own atoning death and resurrection, but also in all the events preparatory to these, accomplishes salvation for his people. So he is the chief theme of the Scriptures (Luke 24:25–27; John 5:45–47; 1 Cor. 10:4).

He is also the chief prophet, who interprets these events (John 3:34–36; 6:63; 7:16; 8:28; 12:47–49; 17:8; 19:24, 31). His Father sent him into the world to utter the word of God, giving him the Spirit without measure (3:34). So his words are of utmost importance to the believer, as Peter understood when he said, "Lord, to whom shall we go? You have the words of eternal life" (6:68). So the words of the apostles, whom Jesus commissions to pass his words on to others, are also of utmost importance to us.

We will see in the next chapter that human example is an important form of revelation, for as I said, it is important to see how exemplary persons use the word of God. God's revelation comes to us in both word and deed. Jesus is the chief example (e.g., Matt. 11:29; 16:24; John 13:35; 1 Cor. 11:1; Phil. 2:5–11; 1 Peter 2:21; 1 John 3:16).

God, Word of God, theophany, divine voice, Creator, provider, Redeemer, prophet, example. Jesus is all of these, and in all these ways, Jesus is the mediator of all revelation. And Jesus' use of the word of God shows us how we should use it.

THE WORK OF THE HOLY SPIRIT

As with Jesus the Son of God, the Spirit does everything that God does. He, too, is active in creation and providence (Gen. 1:2; Ps. 104:30). He gives life, both physical and spiritual (Job 33:4; Ps. 104:30; John 3:5–8;

6:63; Rom. 8:11). Through him we are washed, sanctified, and justified (1 Cor. 6:11). So God's Word is a word about the works of the Spirit, as it is about the works of Christ and the Father.

The Spirit is also the teacher of the church, the Spirit of the prophets and apostles (Num. 11:25; Matt. 10:20; 1 John 2:27). In Hebrews 10:15–17, the writer quotes words ascribed to God in Jeremiah 31:33 and ascribes them to the Spirit. The prophets speak their word by the authority of the Spirit (Gen. 41:38; Num. 24:2; 1 Sam. 10:6; Isa. 61:1; Luke 1:17; 1 Peter 1:11). So do Jesus and the apostles (Matt. 10:20; Luke 4:14; John 3:34; 14:16–17; 15:26; 16:13; Acts 2:4; 1 Cor. 2:4; 12:3). So the Spirit is the one who *inspires* the words of people, making those words identical with the word of God (see chap. 23). And he inspires the written Word as well. In 2 Timothy 3:16, as we have seen, all Scripture is God-breathed. The *breathed* in that expression refers to the work of the Spirit. Both Hebrew and Greek terms for *spirit* refer to *breath* or *wind*. The Spirit is God's breath. By him, God breathes out his words. So the Spirit is the author of the Bible.

Not only does the Spirit *inspire* the Bible, he also *illumines* it to its readers. Scripture teaches that apart from God's grace it is impossible for us to appropriate God's Word for our salvation. As with natural revelation in Romans 1, our sinful inclination is to suppress the truth, to exchange it for a lie. So Paul says that when the Jews read the law of Moses without Christ, "a veil lies over their hearts" (2 Cor. 3:15). In such darkness, we need God's light to see his Word properly. John Murray defines illumination as "regeneration on its noetic side."[3] The Spirit gives new birth (John 3:5), and that new life includes change in our noetic faculties, our ways of gaining knowledge (Col. 3:10). So he enables us to understand the Scriptures (Ps. 119:18; 1 Cor. 2:12–15; Eph. 1:17–19). Without him, we cannot gain spiritual knowledge from the Bible.[4]

John Murray believes that we should make a further distinction in the Spirit's work:

> The question may properly be raised, however, whether or not the notion of illumination is fully adequate as an interpretation of the nature of the [Spirit's] testimony. On the view that it consists merely in illumination, the testimony, most strictly considered, resides

3. John Murray, "The Attestation of Scripture," in *The Infallible Word*, ed. Ned Stonehouse and Paul Woolley (Philadelphia: Presbyterian and Reformed, 1946), 51.

4. Scripture never suggests that the Spirit's illumination *makes* the Bible into the word of God, as many modern theologians have suggested. Even less does it suggest that the Spirit causes a momentary or transitory union between the Scripture and God's word, so that Scripture "becomes" God's word from time to time. The Bible is objectively God's word. The work of the Spirit is to make us understand and apply it.

entirely in the Scripture itself and not at all in the ever-present activity of the Spirit. And the question is, may we not properly regard the present work of the Spirit as not only imparting to us an understanding to perceive the evidence inhering in the Scripture but also as imparting what is of the nature of positive testimony?[5]

Murray answers yes, and finds that positive testimony in the "power and demonstration" of which Paul speaks in 1 Thessalonians 1:5:

> Our gospel came to you not only in word, but also in power and in the Holy Spirit and with full conviction. You know what kind of men we proved to be among you for your sake.

Compare 1 Corinthians 2:4–5:

> My speech and my message were not in plausible words of wisdom, but in demonstration of the Spirit and of power, that your faith might not rest in the wisdom of men but in the power of God.

This demonstration and power leads to firm conviction. Paul's hearers accepted his message as the word of God (1 Thess. 2:13). This "demonstration" (*apodeixis*) does not convey truth content in addition to that of Scripture itself. Rather, it persuades us to embrace the content of the word itself. Cf. 1 John 2:20–27.

Frequently through this book I have argued that our identification of God's word is supernatural. Only in this way could Abraham have been sure that God was talking to him, despite his natural resistance to the commands he heard (chap. 1). Only in this way could God's people identify the divine voice (chap. 14). Only this way, in the final analysis, can God's people identify true prophets and distinguish them from false (chap. 15). The same is true of the church's recognition of the canon (chap. 22), the right interpretation of Scripture (chap. 40), and our final assurance of the truth (chap. 41). The work of the Holy Spirit in illumination and demonstration is the supernatural factor that enables us to hear the words of Scripture as God's personal words to us. Here the author of the text opens the text to us.[6]

The *indwelling* of the Spirit is also revelatory. We are the temple of the Spirit (1 Cor. 3:16), and the Spirit dwells in us. The Spirit's intimate presence motivates our holiness, the only kind of character appropriate in the Spirit's temple. So Paul admonishes:

5. Murray, "The Attestation of Scripture," 51.
6. And in this case the author, and only the author, has the absolute right to explain his writing to us, contrary to some postmodern literary theory.

> But I say, walk by the Spirit, and you will not gratify the desires of the flesh. For the desires of the flesh are against the Spirit, and the desires of the Spirit are against the flesh, for these are opposed to each other, to keep you from doing the things you want to do. But if you are led by the Spirit, you are not under the law. Now the works of the flesh are evident: sexual immorality, impurity, sensuality, idolatry, sorcery, enmity, strife, jealousy, fits of anger, rivalries, dissensions, divisions, envy, drunkenness, orgies, and things like these. I warn you, as I warned you before, that those who do such things will not inherit the kingdom of God. But the fruit of the Spirit is love, joy, peace, patience, kindness, goodness, faithfulness, gentleness, self-control; against such things there is no law. And those who belong to Christ Jesus have crucified the flesh with its passions and desires.
>
> If we live by the Spirit, let us also walk by the Spirit. (Gal. 5:16–25)

So the Spirit not only inspires, illumines, and demonstrates the word. He also takes residence in our lives as a person. And when we recognize the promptings of the Spirit, the kind of life he urges upon us, we seek to live in that way, to encourage the growth of his fruits in our lives.

For these reasons, the Spirit and the word, God's breath and speech, are always together (Gen. 1:2; Ps. 33:6; Isa. 34:16; 59:21; John 6:63; 16:13; Acts 2:1–4; 1 Thess. 1:5; 2 Tim. 3:16; 2 Peter 1:21).[7] The Spirit inspires, illumines, and demonstrates the content of God's word, and his indwelling presence motivates us to obey that word.

So in the long trail of events we have considered from the initial copying of the text to our present-day reception of Scripture, God himself walks with us. He never leaves us alone. He continues to speak his personal words to us through the biblical text. Hearing and learning Scripture are not impersonal, academic tasks. They are a person-to-person interaction with God as he teaches us his personal words.

EPISTEMOLOGY AND THE SPIRIT'S WITNESS

In chapter 41, I suggested a basis for our assurance of the truth of God's Word. That discussion concluded with a general reference to God's own witness. In this chapter, we have seen that that divine witness is especially

---

7. When Paul refers to counterfeit revelation in 2 Thessalonians 2:2, interestingly, he refers to a counterfeit spirit, as well as a counterfeit word.

connected with the testimony of the Holy Spirit. At this point I will try to show the relation between the Spirit's witness and the witness of Scripture itself that we discussed in chapter 41. Many questions have been raised, for example, as to how the witness of the Spirit relates to evidence and arguments for Scripture's authority.

In *DKG*[8] I argued that human knowledge is triperspectival. It is an application of God's revealed norms for thought (normative) to the facts of God's creation (situational) by a person qualified to make such applications (existential). How, then, do we know that Scripture is the Word of God? By its self-witness (normative), as I described it in chapter 41, by facts and evidences (situational), and by the Spirit's working subjectively in our hearts (existential), enabling us to see the Bible's claims and the evidences in their proper light.

When we ask why someone (S) believes a proposition (p), there are several possible answers. One type of answer sets forth the *causes* of this belief. They may be psychological (e.g., "S believes it because he is delusional"), sociological (e.g., "S believes it because he was raised in a community where everyone believes it"), or of some other kind. Another type of answer sets forth the *reasons* for the belief ("S believes p because he thinks that p is rationally necessary"; or "S believes p because of items of evidence a, b, c"). The distinction between causes and reasons is often important. Thinkers such as Karl Marx, Ludwig Feuerbach, and Sigmund Freud argued that religious belief is illegitimate because of its *cause* (for Marx, economic; for Feuerbach, projection; for Freud, wish-fulfillment). I reject these views of the origin of religious faith. But even if one or more of them are true, the causes of a belief never disprove the reasons for it. Frank may believe that the world is round because he has a psychological preference for circles. That preference could be described as a cause of his belief. But the existence of that cause does not disprove his belief that the world is round. Nor does it disprove the reasons he might offer for holding that belief. Applied to the religious case: even if Christians are motivated to believe in God by, say, wish-fulfillment, that doesn't prove God doesn't exist, nor does it disprove any reasons we may give for believing in God.

The previous paragraph may sound as though causes of beliefs are irrelevant and don't play any role in epistemology. That is not the case. Reasons for beliefs are important, but causes are as well. Unless something causes me to believe something, I won't believe it.[9]

---

8. See especially the section in *DKG* on epistemological justification, 104–64.

9. I am not taking account here of the issue of free will. If we are free in a libertarian sense (see *DG*, chaps. 4, 8), then the cause of my belief may be a libertarian free choice to

In general, the internal testimony of the Spirit is a cause of faith, rather than a reason. That is to say, if someone asks my reasons for believing Scripture to be God's Word, I should not refer to the witness of the Spirit. I would say, rather, that I believe because the evidences available to me (situational) interpreted according to the laws of thought (logic, but ultimately God's revelation) yield that conclusion. The Holy Spirit's witness (existential[10]) is not a reason for faith, but a cause of faith.[11] The Spirit is the one who opens my eyes to see the evidence in the proper light, and to evaluate it by God's laws of thought. He *makes* me believe. Because of him, I cannot help believing.

I hope this discussion clarifies some debates about the relation of the Holy Spirit's witness to evidence and arguments. Consider this passage from WCF 1.5:

> We may be moved and induced by the testimony of the Church to an high and reverent esteem of the Holy Scripture. And the heavenliness of the matter, the efficacy of the doctrine, the majesty of the style, the consent of all the parts, the scope of the whole (which is, to give all glory to God), the full discovery it makes of the only way of man's salvation, the many other incomparable excellencies, and the entire perfection thereof, are arguments whereby it doth abundantly evidence itself to be the Word of God: yet notwithstanding, our full persuasion and assurance of the infallible truth and divine authority thereof, is from the inward work of the Holy Spirit bearing witness by and with the Word in our hearts.

This statement begins by listing various evidences, reasons why we should accept Scripture as God's Word. The Confession regards these evidences as substantial: they "abundantly evidence" the divine character of Scripture. This sentence does not quite say that these evidences warrant certainty that Scripture is God's Word, nor does it quite deny that idea.

---

believe, but that is still a cause. So libertarianism does not eliminate causality at this level. I do, however, reject the libertarian theory, as I indicate in chapter 8 of *DG*.

10. But note distinctions in the following footnote.

11. We should not conclude that the existential perspective in general deals with causes rather than reasons. The existential perspective includes the other two perspectives. A mind that is renewed by the Spirit (existential) is one that will accept true evidences (situational) interpreted by the true laws of thought (normative). Such a mind draws its conclusions on the basis of what it subjectively prefers. But what it subjectively prefers is God's objective truth and God's laws of thought. So the existential perspective describes a way of reasoning as well as causes of that reasoning. Within this perspective, the Holy Spirit's witness is the chief cause. And since the Spirit enables us to choose proper evidence and true laws of thought, the Spirit's witness is relevant to the other two perspectives as well.

But then it mentions the inward work of the Spirit as the basis for "our full persuasion and assurance of the infallible truth and divine authority" of Scripture. "Full" seems to be something more than "abundant evidence." The impression left is that the evidences take us maybe 90 percent of the way to full assurance, but we need the work of the Spirit to reach 100 percent assurance. The evidences give us partial persuasion, but the Spirit gives us full persuasion.

In my view, this statement (which is similar to many other statements in Reformed theological literature) needs refinement. First, the evidences in Scripture of its own divine authority are not merely probable. They are certain. They are not 90 percent cogent, but 100 percent cogent. I showed in chapter 41 that Scripture adequately attests itself as God's Word. When Scripture is read according to scriptural presuppositions,[12] it provides certain evidence that it is God's Word.

Further, the work of the Spirit is not to add 10 percent to the probability of the argument, as if we could go 90 percent of the way without the Spirit, but we needed the inner work of the Spirit to go the rest of the way. Rather, without the Spirit's illuminating and demonstrating the truth of Scripture, we cannot even go 1 percent of the way. If the Spirit does not regenerate and guide us, we are blind to the truth; we suppress it (Rom. 1:18). We may know it well enough to use it for our own purposes, as the Pharisees in the Gospels; but we will not be able to use any piece of Scripture as God intended.

So the Spirit does not present more evidence or argument to us. His role is not to add another piece of evidence, or another argument to the case for faith. Nor does he miraculously turn uncertain evidence into certain evidence. Rather, he witnesses to the evidence for the truth that is objectively present in Scripture. He witnesses to what is certainly true. His role is to *cause* faith. His role is to take away our blindness so that we can rightly see Scripture's self-attestation and be convinced by it. He enables us to see the evidence for what it is: God's clear and certain revelation of himself. He makes us accept Scripture's self-attestation.[13]

---

12. Again, I acknowledge a kind of circularity here. See my defenses of this circularity in chapter 1 and *DKG*, 130–33.

13. Some may ask about the relationship between Scripture's self-attestation and evidences external to Scripture. On this, see *DKG*, 104–64. Scripture itself testifies that the whole world speaks of God (Ps. 19:1; Rom. 1:18–20) and thus constitutes evidence of his reality. The firmness of God's control over the world testifies to the truth of his spoken word: note the relationships between Psalm 19:1–6 and verses 7–11, and between Psalm 147:1–18 and verses 19–20. So Scripture warrants the use of extrabiblical evidence. But that evidence must be used as Scripture requires, not offered as a rival to Scripture's self-witness. In this way, extrabiblical evidence becomes part of Scripture's self-authentication. It is evidence that Scripture itself authorizes.

So the work of the Spirit is the cause of faith; the self-witness of Scripture is the reason for faith. We need both in order to be assured of the truth of Scripture. It is in this way that God comes with his personal words to attest them to our minds and hearts.[14]

THE SPIRIT AND THE SUFFICIENCY OF SCRIPTURE

If we see the Spirit's work in this way, we will not find a tension between the work of the Spirit and the sufficiency of Scripture. The sufficiency of Scripture, as I indicated in chapter 32, means that Scripture contains all the divine words that we will ever need for any area of life. Sufficiency in this sense, however, does not deny that the work of the Spirit is also necessary. Indeed, the Spirit's work is indispensable if we are to properly understand Scripture and make use of it.

Nor does the continuing work of the Spirit mean that the canon is still open. Following the completion of Jesus' work, the Spirit is no longer inspiring books to be added to the Bible (see chap. 22).

Nevertheless, the Spirit continues to illumine the Word of God in all its forms—copies, texts, and editions, in preaching, teaching, theology, confession, and so on.

When we pray for our pastor, that he will preach a good sermon, we are praying that the Spirit will influence his speech. We pray that the Spirit will take away from the pastor any words that mislead or detract from the gospel, and that the Spirit will give him instead words that edify. Often God answers such prayers affirmatively. And when he does so, the Spirit does a verbal work, purifying our pastor's words. This is not inspiration. But it is something *like* inspiration. The Spirit is taking away the errors that the pastor may intend to make, and he is replacing those errors with sound, edifying, biblical teaching. The sermon will not be fully identical with God's own speech, as were the sermons of Isaiah and Paul. There may be errors in it. But in that sermon, the Word of God will be on our pastor's lips. And insofar as the biblical Word is on his lips, it is as authoritative as if it were on the pages of Scripture itself (recall chap. 35).

This is a distinctively Reformed view, but it gives us some talking points to use with our brothers and sisters from the charismatic tradition. When they speak of "continuing revelation," they do not generally

---

14. For more discussion of the testimony of the Spirit, compared with the views of modern theologians Karl Barth and G. C. Berkouwer, see my article "The Spirit and the Scriptures," Appendix Q in this volume.

want to say that such revelation has the same status as Scripture. But it is often hard for them to define just how this revelation is different from Scripture. Sometimes (not always) they seem to be describing "continuing prophecy" as something very much like what Reformed people call "Spirit-filled preaching," as I have described that concept above. It is something *like* inspired words, but also *unlike* the revelation given to Isaiah and Paul. We can be thankful that although the canon is closed, the Spirit continues to influence the words of believers, particularly the preaching and teaching of the Word of God.[15]

15. For more important talking points in the discussion over continuing revelation, see Vern Poythress, "Modern Spiritual Gifts as *Analogous* to Apostolic Gifts: Affirming Extraordinary Works of the Spirit within Cessationist Theology," *JETS* 39, 1 (1996): 71–101, also available at http://www.frame-poythress.org/poythress_articles/1996Modern.htm.

CHAPTER 43

Human Beings as Revelation

Finite persons are also a means of God's revelation. We are made in the image of God (Gen. 1:26–27), meaning that everything we were created to be reflects God in some way.[1] Our bodies, minds, personalities reflect God, both individually and corporately.[2] That image continues after the fall, contrary to some theological traditions (Gen. 5:1; 9:6; 1 Cor. 11:7; James 3:9). Sin does counteract the knowledge, righteousness, and holiness of the image (Eph. 4:24; Col. 3:10), but it does not entirely erase the image of God. Even sin, in one sense, images God, for sin is basically an attempt to *be* God, to replace God on the throne.[3]

When a person comes to trust Jesus as Savior and Lord, the distortions of sin begin to fade, and the believer images God in a deeper sense. So Scripture says that by grace we are "renewed in knowledge after the image of [our] creator" (Col. 3:10; cf. Eph. 4:24).

So we are created as images of God's nature, and in salvation God re-creates us as images, revelations, of his grace. People ought to be able to see the nature of the gospel by seeing how it changes us. We ought not only to obey God, but to be examples to others of such obedience (1 Thess. 1:7).

---

1. I would add that each of us reflects all of God in some way. How can different persons each reflect "all of God"? By reflecting him from different perspectives!

2. For longer discussions of man in the image of God, see *SBL*, 85–99, and *DCL*, 318–23, 623–30.

3. The way in which sin images God is analogous to a mirror image: it reflects every aspect of him, but is lacking in two ways: (1) it reverses the reality of God, and (2) it is all image, no substance.

Imitation of other persons is an important means of learning in general, and specifically an important means of learning the Word of God. As I indicated in the last chapter, understanding the Word is applying it, and there is no better way to learn the application of the Word than by seeing it applied by others who understand it well. So God himself is the norm for our life, as he says "be holy, for I am holy" (Lev. 11:44; 1 Peter 1:15–16; cf. Matt. 5:48).[4] And the life of Jesus, as God and man, is an example to us, as are all the lives of people who follow him.

The *imitatio Christi* is a major theme of the NT. We are to be like Jesus.[5] We do that by obeying his teaching, but also by watching how he interacts with people in his earthly ministry.[6] We should copy not only what Jesus says, but the way he says it. But the most profound form of imitation is the imitation of Jesus' atonement.

We might think that we can imitate Jesus in many ways, but not in his atoning love. After all, none of us can bring about the salvation of others by giving our lives. But remarkably, in the NT, it is the atonement that is the main point of comparison between the love of Christ and the love of the Christian. The love of God that we are to imitate is most fully displayed in the atonement (John 3:16; 15:13; Rom. 5:8; 8:39 [in context]; Eph. 2:4–5; 2 Thess. 2:16; 1 John 3:16; Rev. 1:5; cf. Mark 10:45; Phil. 2:1–11; 1 Peter 2:18–25). We are to love one another, specifically as Jesus first loved us, by dying for our sins (John 13:34–35; 1 John 4:9–11).

God's love to us in the atonement is beyond measure (Eph. 3:18–19), in the depth of Jesus' suffering, including his estrangement from his Father, in the greatness of the blessing he bought for us, and also in our total lack of fitness for this blessing. As recipients of God's grace, we are supremely unattractive to him. We are the tax collectors and sinners (Matt. 9:9–13), the "poor and crippled and blind and lame" (Luke 14:21), those who were "still sinners" (Rom. 5:8) when Jesus came to die for us.

Truly, no sacrifice of ours can atone for the sins of someone else. But these passages make abundantly clear that our obligation is nothing less than to lay down our lives for one another, as Jesus did for us.[7]

---

4. See the discussion of God as norm in *DCL*, chapter 9.

5. The liberal tradition often tried to reduce the atoning work of Christ to "moral influence." Evangelicals were perfectly right to reject this conception. Jesus' atonement was also a sacrifice, expiation, and propitiation. Nevertheless, Scripture does present Christ over and over again as someone we should imitate.

6. In chapter 42, I spoke of the centrality of Christ in revelation, summarizing that concept by referring to him as God, Word of God, theophany, divine voice, Creator, provider, Redeemer, prophet, example. Here I expound the latter category further.

7. See examples of moral heroism in *DCL*, chapter 12.

In a lesser and derivative sense, we can also find examples for imitation in godly people described in Scripture. The apostles, particularly, call on believers to imitate them (as they imitate Christ).

The apostles place great weight on themselves as person-revelation. We can see this idea in the passages where they express their desires to visit the churches personally, rather than merely to write letters to them. In other passages, they commend the personal visits of other church leaders and look forward to visits from those leaders. These passages are sometimes described as looking forward to the *apostolic parousia*, somewhat analogous to the return of Christ. See in this regard Rom. 1:8–17; 15:22–29; 1 Cor. 4:14–21; 5:1–5; 2 Cor. 7:5–16; 12:14; 13:10; Gal. 4:12–20; Eph. 6:21–22; Col. 4:7–9; 1 Tim. 3:14–15; 2 Tim. 4:6–8; Titus 3:12–14; Heb. 13:23; 2 John 12; 3 John 13–14. In 2 John 12, the apostle says that he would rather visit the "elect lady" personally than with "paper and ink," so that "our joy may be complete." Other references to apostolic parousia are more threatening, such as those in 1 Corinthians.

There is evidently something about a personal visit that goes beyond what can be achieved in a letter. Certainly, mutual expressions of love are more meaningful when presented face-to-face. The exercise of apostolic authority, too, is easier accomplished in the flesh. Paul does exercise discipline against a sinner in the Corinthian church, in 1 Corinthians 5:3, by letter. But he has to remind the church that "though absent in body, I am present in spirit." Another important element of the apostolic presence, however, is that then the church is better able to observe the apostle's life, the way he puts the word into practice. In 2 Timothy 3:10–11, Paul commends his own lifestyle to Timothy as a model for Timothy's own ministry:

> You, however, have followed my teaching, my conduct, my aim in life, my faith, my patience, my love, my steadfastness, my persecutions and sufferings that happened to me at Antioch, at Iconium, and at Lystra—which persecutions I endured; yet from them all the Lord rescued me.

So he calls the Corinthians to "be imitators of me, as I am of Christ" (1 Cor. 11:1; cf. 4:16; Phil. 3:17; 4:9; 1 Thess. 1:6; 2 Thess. 3:9). Paul's character is a revelation of Paul's gospel. It shows how Jesus' people should live. Paul is not perfect. But he is a mature believer, who has endured much suffering for Christ, and we should study his life as well as his doctrine.

And person-revelation continues beyond the generation of the apostles. A major qualification of leaders in the church is that they are to be examples of the Lord's saving work (1 Tim. 4:12; Titus 2:7; 1 Peter 5:3). An overseer must be above reproach, the husband of one wife, sober-minded, self-controlled, respectable, hospitable, able to teach, not a drunkard, not violent but gentle, not quarrelsome, not a lover of money. He must manage his own household well, with all dignity keeping his children submissive, for if someone does not know how to manage his own household, how will he care for God's church? He must not be a recent convert, or he may become puffed up with conceit and fall into the condemnation of the devil. Moreover, he must be well thought of by outsiders, so that he may not fall into disgrace, into a snare of the devil. (1 Tim. 3:2–7; cf. Titus 1:5–9)

Similarly for deacons (1 Tim. 3:8–13) and women teachers (Titus 2:3–5).

Learning by imitation is an important means of sanctification, a vital means of appropriating the Word of God. We should imitate God, Jesus, the apostles, and other exemplary characters in Scripture. Scripture often refers to such exemplary people. See Rom. 4:16–25; 1 Cor. 10:1–12; Heb. 6:11–12; 11:1–12:2; 13:7; James 5:17–18. For this reason I oppose the notion that preaching should merely expound the redemptive narrative of Scripture and should never appeal to biblical characters as examples. In expounding past revelation, the Bible itself appeals to such examples, and we are not preaching the Word as we should if we omit such references.

And we should ourselves seek to be examples that can be imitated by our fellow believers. Human life, redeemed and matured, is a profound form of revelation. We and others need to have it in order to rightly apply God's Word.

CHAPTER 44

Writing on the Heart

Person-revelation manifests God's lordship attribute of covenant presence (chap. 2). In person-revelation, God himself comes into our midst (chap. 42) and makes human persons into media of his revelation (chap. 43). But the most intimate way in which God's revelation is present with us is his saving revelation on the hearts of his people.

There may be some anticipation of this idea in the many passages that speak of God's placing his *name* on his people, identifying himself with them. In the ancient Near East, names had significance. Today, we often give children names mainly for their sound or a family connection. But in Bible times, a person's name reflected events surrounding his birth, his parents' hopes for him, or some other meaning. The name always said something about the person.

In some passages, God gives new names to people to signify their place in his redemptive plan (Gen. 17:5; 32:28). The redemptive promise is a promise of a new name (Isa. 62:2; Rev. 2:17). Further, God knows his people by name (Isa. 43:1) (i.e., intimately and completely), and he calls on them by name (Isa. 45:3–4) to serve his purposes.

In Scripture, "name of the Lord" is used both for various terms such as *Yahweh*, *Elohim*, and *Adon* that apply to him, and for God's whole revelation of himself.[1] So God's name is a virtual synonym for his *word*. God

---

1. For a longer discussion of God's name and names, see *DG*, 21–35, 343–61. See also my treatment of the third commandment in *DCL*, 487–97. Much of the material in the following paragraphs is taken from *DG*.

vindicates his name, for it represents his reputation (1 Sam. 12:22), as we refer to a man's "good name" (Prov. 22:1). As with *word* (chaps. 8–11), God's name is God himself.

As we sing praise to God, we sing praise to his name (Pss. 7:17; 9:2; 18:49; many other passages); we give the glory due to his name (Ps. 29:2); we exalt the name (34:3) and fear it (61:5). God's name is an object of worship. Since in Scripture God alone is the proper object of worship, this language equates the name and the Lord himself.

Similarly, the name of God defends us (Ps. 20:1). We trust in the name for deliverance (33:21). God's name endures forever (72:17; 135:13). It "reaches to the ends of the earth" (48:10). It is holy and awesome (111:9). God saves us by his name (54:1). He guides us "for his name's sake" (23:3). In Isaiah 30:27, it is the "name of the LORD" itself that comes to bring judgment on the nations and blessings on his people. So God's name has divine attributes and performs divine acts. In short, Scripture says about the name of God virtually everything it says about God.[2]

So when God chooses to make his "name" dwell in a place (Deut. 12:5, 11, 21; 14:23–24; 1 Kings 8:29; 9:3; 2 Kings 23:27), that place becomes a location of his special presence. To say that God's name dwells in that place is to say that God himself dwells there. God's name is his *glory*: when Moses asks to see his glory, he expounds his name (Ex. 33:18–19). (Note also parallels between the name and the glory in Psalm 102:15 and Isaiah 59:19.) To say that God's "name" is in an angel is to say that the angel has the authority of God (Ex. 23:21).

It is not surprising, then, that the third commandment of the Decalogue tells us not to misuse God's name. We should speak the name of God with the reverence we should have in his personal presence.

One of the most remarkable proofs of the deity of Christ, then, is that the NT uses his name just as the OT used the name of Yahweh. When the Jewish rulers ask Peter and John "by what power or by what name" they had healed a crippled man, Peter replies that it was "by the name of Jesus Christ of Nazareth" (Acts 4:7, 10). He concludes, "There is salvation in no one else, for there is no other name under heaven given among men by which we must be saved" (v. 12; cf. v. 17). In 5:41, we read that the apostles "left the presence of the council, rejoicing that they were counted worthy to suffer dishonor for the name." Cf. 9:21; 22:16. We see that *name* can be used as a substitute for *Jesus*, as it substitutes for *Yahweh* in the OT, and that the name of Jesus has the same powers as the name of Yahweh.

2. Compare the discussion of the word of God as God himself, chapters 8, 11.

In Isaiah 45:23, Yahweh says, "To me every knee shall bow, every tongue shall swear allegiance." In Romans 14:11, Paul applies this passage to God (*Theos*); but in Philippians 2:10–11, he applies it to Christ:

> At the name of Jesus every knee should bow, in heaven and on earth and under the earth, and every tongue confess that Jesus Christ is Lord, to the glory of God the Father.

In Romans 10:13, Paul quotes Joel 2:32: "Everyone who calls on the name of the Lord will be saved." Joel spoke of the name of Yahweh; Paul speaks specifically of the name of Jesus. In Genesis 4:26, the family of Seth begins to "call upon the name of the LORD," an indication of the beginnings of corporate worship. In 1 Corinthians 1:2, Paul describes the Christian church as "those who in every place call upon the name of our Lord Jesus Christ." We call on the name of Christ for salvation and to praise him. We pray for healing "in the name of the Lord" (James 5:14, certainly again a reference to Jesus).

According to Matthew 28:19, we are to baptize "in the name of the Father and of the Son and of the Holy Spirit." One name, threefold. *Son* is on the same level as *Father*. Baptism is initiation to discipleship, and it places upon us the name that brings together Father, Son, and Spirit.

The reference to baptism indicates that we also, as well as the Father and the Son, are bearers of the holy name of God. In our case, the name is not ours by nature; it does not make us objects of worship. Rather, God's name dwells in us as it dwelled in the tabernacle. God places his name upon us, as he placed his name in the tabernacle and in the Holy Land (Deut. 12:5). In the Aaronic benediction of Numbers 6:24–26, the priests, says Yahweh, "shall put my name upon the people of Israel, and I will bless them" (v. 27). Certainly, the Trinitarian apostolic benediction of 2 Corinthians 13:14 has the same significance. So God's people are "called by" his name (Jer. 14:9; cf. Isa. 43:7) and on this basis pray to God for their deliverance (Jer. 14:21). We are temples of God's Spirit and thus bearers of his name.[3]

Once he has chosen a people for himself, he will not forsake them, for the sake of his own name, which he has identified with theirs (1 Sam. 12:22). In Amos 9:11–12, the Lord promises:

> "In that day I will raise up the booth of David that is fallen and repair its breaches, and raise up its ruins and rebuild it as in the days of old, that they may possess the remnant of Edom

3. Cf. Rev. 3:12; 14:1; 22:4.

and all the nations who are called by my name," declares the
LORD who does this.

God's word to Amos says that not only Israel is called by God's name, but
other nations as well, speaking (see the quotation in Acts 15:17–18) of
the outreach of the gospel of Christ to all the nations of the world. New
believers are to be baptized into that one "name of the Father and of the
Son and of the Holy Spirit" (Matt. 28:19). God's new name will be on the
"foreheads" of the people of God in the last day (Rev. 22:4).

In a still broader sense, all creation bears the name of the Lord. As we
saw earlier, God's covenant lordship is over all the earth. He has made the
world to be his temple, and of course his name must dwell in his temple. I
believe that Jesus implies the presence of God's name in creation in Matthew 5:33–37 (cf. 23:16–22), his exposition of the third commandment.
There he addresses those who tried to avoid the force of oaths by not using
particular names of God. Rather than swearing by Yahweh or by God, they
would swear by heaven, earth, Jerusalem, or even their own heads. Jesus'
answer is that heaven, earth, Jerusalem, and, yes, our heads are subject to
God's sovereignty, so that to invoke anything in creation is to invoke God
himself. If we swear, "May the heavens collapse if I fail to do this," only
God can bring about that collapse or prevent it. If I swear, "May my hair
turn white if I am lying," only God can enforce that oath. So when we
swear by created things, we are implicitly swearing by God himself, by his
own name. That means that everything in creation is a dwelling place for
God's name, a place of God's presence.

My application of this rich vein of biblical theology is that God sets his
own name, a revelation of himself, indeed his own presence, upon every
believer. He places upon us a seal that says we belong to him and he belongs
to us. That is a word of God that defines who he is and who we are in relation to him. It says that our deepest nature is to be his covenant servants.
We can be intelligibly described only as God's people, and as the people in
whom he himself has chosen to dwell. We are, by our very nature, God's
people, and therefore we are revelations of him.

Some of God's people, to be sure, rebel against him. But they, too, reveal
God, even in their rebellion, as I indicated in chapter 43. These people are
members of God's covenant, but they receive the curses of the covenant
rather than the blessings. Even in their case, their deepest nature is to be
covenant servants of God, but in their case rebellious servants.[4]

---

4. Here, of course, I am using *servant* to describe the covenant status of the rebels, not
their heart-allegiance, which I will discuss in the following pages. In terms of *DG*, chap-

Another expression in Scripture that shows the deep penetration of God's revelation into our being is the writing of God's word on our hearts. The heart is the inner core of a person, the basic direction of his life (for good or ill), the person as God sees him. The heart is what we really are, when all our masks are off. Jesus taught:

> The good person out of the good treasure of his heart produces good, and the evil person out of his evil treasure produces evil, for out of the abundance of the heart his mouth speaks. (Luke 6:45)

When God revealed his law to Israel, he intended it to reside not only on tablets of stone, but also on their hearts (Deut. 6:6). That means that it was to govern their deepest thoughts and motives, to control all their actions, in all areas of life. They were to live a life surrounded, saturated, by his words:

> You shall teach them diligently to your children, and shall talk of them when you sit in your house, and when you walk by the way, and when you lie down, and when you rise. You shall bind them as a sign on your hand, and they shall be as frontlets between your eyes. You shall write them on the doorposts of your house and on your gates. (Deut. 6:7–9; cf. Rev. 22:4)

God's word was to be everywhere. The people were to know it so well that it would direct their decisions even when they had no time to think about it. They were to be a people for whom obeying God's word was second nature.

So the psalmist says, "I have stored up your word in my heart, that I might not sin against you" (Ps. 119:11). And the wisdom teacher tells his pupil, "Let not steadfast love and faithfulness forsake you; bind them around your neck; write them on the tablet of your heart" (Prov. 3:3; cf. 7:1–3). The righteous man is one who has the word in his heart (Ps. 37:31). In Psalm 40:7–8, the redeemed man who delights to do God's will has God's word in his heart.[5]

Not all Israel had God's word in their heart. But some did. God says through Isaiah:

> Listen to me, you who know righteousness, the people in whose heart is my law; fear not the reproach of man, nor be dismayed at their revilings. (Isa. 51:7)

---

ter 16, these people are historically elect, not eternally elect. These two types of election are vastly different, though Scripture describes them in similar terms.

5. The writer of Hebrews quotes this passage at 10:5–7 in his letter as applying to Christ. He doesn't refer to the writing of the word on his heart, doubtless because that was obvious in the case of Jesus, whose deepest inclination was to do the Father's will.

These people are the remnant, the believers within Israel, as opposed to those who rejected God. But God looks forward to a time when all his people will have a new heart, and a new spirit (Ezek. 11:19; 18:31). Their new heart will be a gift of God's sheer grace (Jer. 24:7; Ezek. 36:26; 37:23). The gift of a new heart is part of a new covenant that God will make with his people:

> Behold, the days are coming, declares the LORD, when I will make a new covenant with the house of Israel and the house of Judah, not like the covenant that I made with their fathers on the day when I took them by the hand to bring them out of the land of Egypt, my covenant that they broke, though I was their husband, declares the LORD. But this is the covenant that I will make with the house of Israel after those days, declares the LORD: I will put my law within them, and I will write it on their hearts. And I will be their God, and they shall be my people. And no longer shall each one teach his neighbor and each his brother, saying, "Know the LORD," for they shall all know me, from the least of them to the greatest, declares the LORD. For I will forgive their iniquity, and I will remember their sin no more. (Jer. 31:31–34)

In this covenant, God will write his word not on stone tablets, but on the hearts of his people. Those hearts will be the covenant document (chap. 17). They will all know God, and he will forgive their sins. God himself will be their teacher (cf. John 6:45; 1 Thess. 4:9; 1 John 2:27).

The writer to the Hebrews says that the new covenant was established by the new priesthood of Jesus, rendering the Mosaic covenant obsolete (Heb. 8:1–13). Through Christ, God has written his word on the hearts of his people. The people of God in the OT, the righteous remnant, were saved not by their works, but by looking forward to the promise of God to redeem his people through Christ. And those who had the word written on their hearts back then (as Pss. 37:31; 40:7–8) were righteous because of Christ, just as "Abraham believed God, and it was counted to him for righteousness" (Rom. 4:3, quoting Gen. 15:6). By anticipation, the old covenant saints were members of the new covenant, though it was yet to be sealed by the shedding of Jesus' blood.

So we who believe in Christ have the word of God written on our hearts. Though we often fail, our deepest inclinations are to follow Jesus and to obey his Father. Paul is even able to say of the Corinthian church:

> You yourselves are our letter of recommendation, written on our hearts, to be known and read by all. And you show that you are a

letter from Christ delivered by us, written not with ink but with the Spirit of the living God, not on tablets of stone but on tablets of human hearts. (2 Cor. 3:2–3)

The church at Corinth had many problems; Paul rebukes them about many things. But God knew their hearts, and Paul knew also that their hearts were with Jesus. So they serve as person-revelation. They themselves are a letter recommending the ministry of Paul.

We have seen through this book that revelation begins in God's own heart, and that it typically follows a very indirect process between his speech and our hearts. In nature and Scripture, his word is objective. But the destination of revelation is deeply subjective. For as I indicated in chapter 6, the ultimate purpose of God's word is to communicate with his creatures, and that purpose is incomplete until the word resides within his hearers. So Scripture speaks of revelation in both objective terms and subjective terms (cf. also chap. 39). In this book, I have focused on the objective. God's word exists in creation and in Scripture, regardless of what anyone thinks of that. But Scripture also speaks of revelation as something subjective.

In Isaiah 53:1, God through Isaiah asks the rhetorical question, "Who has believed what he has heard from us? And to whom has the arm of the LORD been revealed?" By the parallelism of these two questions, we can tell that here God's arm (his power) has been revealed only to those who have believed. This verse does not speak of a revelation given to everyone as an objective datum, but as a revelation given to those who have heard and believed the prophecy.

Similarly, Jesus, in Matthew 11:27, says:

> All things have been handed over to me by my Father, and no one knows the Son except the Father, and no one knows the Father except the Son and anyone to whom the Son chooses to reveal him.

Reveal here refers neither to natural or general revelation nor to the biblical canon. It is rather an event in the heart of the recipient. Jesus does not merely make the knowledge of the Father available objectively in case we might like to consider it. Rather, he gives us actual *knowledge* of the Father, as a gift.

A similar use of *revelation* appears in Ephesians 1:17, where Paul prays

> that the God of our Lord Jesus Christ, the Father of glory, may give you a spirit of wisdom and of revelation in the knowledge of him.

This revelation is not additional natural revelation. Nor is Paul asking that God will give to the Ephesians some new books to be included in the canon. Rather, he is praying that in all the objective revelation God has given, the Spirit will actually reveal God so that the Ephesian Christians will subjectively know God better.

For other references to such subjective revelation, see John 3:3; Rom. 1:17; 2 Cor. 4:6; Gal. 1:15–16; Phil. 3:15; 1 John 2:27.

Our hearts, then, are the destination of God's revelation. In us the process of communication reaches its terminus. In our hearts we receive God's personal words to us in such a profound way that they become the foundation of all our thinking and living. We look forward to the consummation of this knowledge in the last day, when God will tear away from us our sinful inclinations to disobey and devalue this wonderful word. God has accompanied his word through all the vicissitudes of history, the problems of Scripture, and the spiritual battles of our lives,[6] so that we might receive it with joy. And he will continue to accompany it until he receives us into glory.

---

6. After writing this sentence, I noticed that it contained a covenantal triad.

CHAPTER 45

Summary and Organizational Reflections

I have presented the doctrine of the word of God according to what I call the *personal-word model* (chap. 1). This model is developed by analogy with God's speech to people such as Adam, Noah, and Abraham, in which God identified himself as God and talked with them as one man talks to another. Through that conversation, they learn of their relationship to God, his promises, and his directions for their lives. If God had not spoken to them, they would not know how to trust or obey him. If God has not spoken to us in a comparable way, all our talk about him is speculation at best, wish-fulfillment at worst.

Through his word, we learn the nature of our personal relationship with him. He is our covenant Lord (chap. 2). So his word to us reflects his lordship attributes of control, authority, and presence. His word has a power that controls all things. It has supreme authority, so that it creates obligations in its hearers: obligations to believe, obey, and otherwise participate in what he presents to us (cf. chap. 39). And the word is also the location of God's very presence with us.

In chapters 3–7, I discuss modern liberal views of revelation, since around 1650. What distinguishes the liberal tradition from orthodox theology is that liberals seek to study God by autonomous reason—reason subject to no authority outside itself. By that autonomous reason they reach conclusions contrary to Scripture's own account of revelation. On these views, God cannot speak to us in personal words. But if he cannot, then our faith is only speculation or wish-fulfillment. We have no way to know God's promises or commands, and we have no basis for faith in Christ.

In chapters 8–44, I describe Scripture's own view of divine-human communication. Chapters 8–11 show that the word of God is nothing less than God himself, in his controlling power, meaningful authority, and personal presence.

The *media* by which God brings his word to us (chap. 12) reflect, therefore, his lordship attributes. They fall into the general categories of events, words, and persons (roughly corresponding to control, authority, and presence). In *event-revelation* (chap. 13), God reveals himself in creation, general history, and redemptive history.

In *word-revelation* (chaps. 14–41), God identifies his word with human words, spoken or written. There is the *divine voice* (chap. 14) in which God speaks without any human mediation. Then there is revelation through prophets and apostles (chap. 15). Although these speakers are human, Scripture always identifies their words with the very words of God.

God also identifies certain written words as his own. These have the same power, authority, and divine presence as every other form of the word. They have no less power, authority, or divine presence than the divine voice or the prophets and apostles. God identifies those words for us as the words of the Old and New Testaments (chaps. 16–22).

In the following chapters, I investigate features of Scripture as a whole: its inspiration (chap. 23), content (chap. 24), scope (chap. 25), inerrancy (chap. 26), phenomena (chap. 27), problems (chap. 28), clarity (chap. 29), necessity (chap. 30), comprehensiveness (chap. 31), and sufficiency (chap. 32).

In chapter 33, I begin a discussion of how Scripture comes from its original writing into our minds and hearts. This is a journey of many steps, beginning with copying (chap. 33), and continuing with translating and editing (chap. 34), teaching and preaching (chap. 35), sacraments (understood as a means by which we receive the word) (chap. 36), theology (chap. 37), confessions, creeds, and traditions (chap. 38), our reception of the text (chap. 39), our interpretation of it (chap. 40), and our assurance of its truth (chap. 41).

Chapters 42–44 explore the third mode of revelation, following event-revelation and word-revelation. That mode is *person-revelation*. Chapter 42 discusses God himself as revelation, when he enters our history as Father, Son, and Spirit. The discussion of the Spirit brings in the concept of the "internal testimony of the Holy Spirit." Scripture attests itself, but we need the Spirit to illumine that self-attestation and to convince us that that self-attestation is true. In chapter 43, I discuss human persons as revelation:

biblical characters, church officers, and individual Christians as examples for others, vehicles of the word of God.

Chapter 44 describes the culmination of revelation, when it rests in the heart of the believer, transforming him so that his very nature is inclined to hear God's word and do it.

GENERAL, SPECIAL, AND EXISTENTIAL REVELATION

The structure of revelation as I have presented it here suggests the value of rethinking the traditional distinction between general and special revelation. In fact, as we have seen, there are many forms of revelation, and there is some peril in trying to group them under general categories. But some may want to know why I have chosen the distinction event/word/persons over the traditional general/special ordering.

The distinction between general and special revelation has always been a bit unclear. General revelation has usually been understood as follows:

1. Revelation by events (nature, history), rather than words.
2. Revelation given to all mankind.
3. Revelation that does not present the way of salvation.

Special revelation is:

1. Revelation by word.
2. Revelation not given to all mankind, but to people chosen by God to hear it.
3. Revelation about salvation.

This leads to trivial questions, such as the status of secular writings, like Charles Dickens's novels. They are words, and they are revelation (since everything is God's revelation in one sense or another). But since they are verbal, they don't seem to fit under the category of general revelation; and since they do not present God's plan of salvation, they don't fit under the category of special revelation either.

And I have given reasons in this book not to distinguish sharply between "matters of salvation" and other matters. See chapters 24, 25, 27, 29, 31, and 32. At least we ought to revise the third qualification of special revelation to read "revelation about salvation and other matters."

More seriously, some have asked whether there was special revelation in Eden, before the fall of our first parents. We are inclined to say yes, because God spoke to them verbally. But that speech was not about salvation, because it was not until later that Adam and Eve needed salvation. Some have called these divine words "pre-redemptive special revelation," emphasizing the first characteristic of special revelation. Others have denied that there is any such thing, because of the third qualification. But it also seems quite awkward to fit this revelation under the "general" category.

This discussion, I think, like many other theological discussions, takes extrabiblical theological concepts too seriously. The terms *general* and *special revelation* are not found in Scripture. They are an attempt by theologians to summarize some of the variety in the ways in which God communicates with us. If they create problems, we should not be embarrassed about redefining them or abandoning them. Generally, it would have been better, I think, for theology to distinguish events, words, and persons, as I have here, and then to make further distinctions within these categories.

If we wish to maintain the old *general/special* terminology, I suggest that we reconstruct it as follows.

> General: Revelation in all objects of human knowledge (situational).

> Special: Revelation in word, setting forth God's standards for human life (normative).[1]

Then I would add:

> Existential: God's revelation in our person [chaps. 43–44], by which we appropriate the other forms of revelation. This kind of revelation is mentioned in Scripture at Isaiah 53:1; Matthew 11:27; Ephesians 1:17; etc. [chap. 44].

These three forms are perspectival, in that you cannot have one without having the others.

---

1. This would include, of course, both *law* and *gospel*, however those are defined. For my thoughts, see *DCL*, 182–92. My point here is that special revelation should be defined as those "spectacles" (John Calvin) that God has given us, to enable us to rightly understand and use general revelation.

CHAPTER 46

Epilogue

At the end of what is likely the last volume in the Lordship series, perhaps I will be permitted some reflections of a more personal nature.

In my rather conservative Reformed circles, I am known as fairly progressive. The reasons for that can be found in my multiperspectivalism, my critique of denominations,[1] my suggested revisions of Cornelius Van Til's work,[2] my sympathy with contemporary worship,[3] my advocacy of a biblical rather than a confessional-historical approach to theology,[4] my concern to avoid traditionalism,[5] and my somewhat negative evaluation of the doctrinal battles in my denominational circles.[6]

The present volume, however, will probably not be seen as progressive. It is not much in accord with the current trend among evangelicals, which is to find value in the liberal tradition and to discuss these subjects not from Scripture itself, but by surveying historical and contemporary options. My book is a regression to an older way of treating the doctrines of revelation and Scripture, mainly by reading what Scripture has to say about them.

1. ER.
2. CVT.
3. *Worship in Spirit and Truth* (Phillipsburg, NJ: P&R Publishing, 1996); CWM.
4. DKG, 76–88, 165–346; "In Defense of Something Close to Biblicism," available at http://www.frame-poythress.org/frame_articles/Biblicism.htm.
5. "Traditionalism," available at http://www.frame-poythress.org/frame_articles/1999 Traditionalism.htm.
6. "Machen's Warrior Children," in *Alister E. McGrath and Evangelical Theology*, ed. Sung Wook Chung (Grand Rapids: Baker, 2003), also available at http://www.frame -poythress.org/frame_articles/2003Machen.htm.

This is the way in which B. B. Warfield typically dealt with these issues, not to mention my teachers at Westminster Seminary: Edward J. Young, Meredith G. Kline, Ned Stonehouse, Cornelius Van Til, John Murray, and Edmund Clowney.

I do not condemn studies focused on the history and contemporary expressions of these doctrines. Those have their usefulness. But what we need most is to hear God's voice, even when we try to understand what God's voice is. It may seem circular to go to Scripture to learn what Scripture is. Here I invoke my frequently expressed defense: circularity of a kind is required when we are defending an ultimate standard of truth (chaps. 1, 4, 8, 16, 42; Appendices C and E in this volume; *DKG*, 130–33). But more important is the fact that Scripture is where we must go to establish any doctrine. In the fields of theology proper, anthropology, Christology, and soteriology, everyone who seeks to be orthodox recognizes Scripture as our ultimate source of knowledge. The same is true in bibliology, the doctrine of Scripture.

One gets the impression these days that many Christians, even evangelicals, even those with Reformed convictions, think there is no doctrine of Scripture in Scripture. They profess Christ as the resurrected Lord, and they seek to honor him. But even when they confess some idea of inspiration, they see the Bible, practically speaking, as nothing much more than some human reflections on Jesus' work that Christians revere as a primary source. But of course, every historian knows that even primary sources are often faulty.[7] So on this view we can expect faults in Scripture that can be evaluated and corrected by—what? Autonomous reason (see chaps. 3–7). But if this is the case, then there are two lords: Jesus and autonomous reason. We trust Jesus as our Lord, but we accept as our ultimate authority the dictates of our own minds. Jesus is Lord, but we are our own lords. That is an intolerable contradiction.

On this issue, I cannot be progressive. If I lost some conservative friends through my progressive ideas, I will now probably lose some progressive ones on publication of this book. It may be called fundamentalist. If so,

---

7. So many evangelical writers today think inerrancy is dispensable or at least highly questionable. For some of those writers, see my reviews of books by Wright, McGowan, and Enns, included as appendices in this volume. And other evangelicals seem to think inerrancy is a theological nuisance. They think we should rather ponder the great realities of Christ and salvation than defend the inerrancy of biblical details. I sympathize with this latter concern. I trust that in this book I have buried the chapters on inerrancy and Bible problems so deeply in the text that nobody will accuse me of overemphasizing them. But Scripture is God's Word; God tells only the truth; and inerrancy means only that his Word in Scripture is true. When that conviction is questioned, it needs to be defended, concisely at least.

fine. I realize that *fundamentalist* is a term of derision, and for many reasons I would rather not be called by it. But I know through experience that name-calling is a staple of theological debate, and I have a thick skin. For all their frequent literalism, dispensationalism, and anti-intellectualism, the fundamentalists were stalwart in defending Scripture as God's Word, in the face of attacks on all sides.[8] Many of them will be closer to Jesus in heaven than many of us who seek to be more respectable.

I do think that, reactionary as it is, this book introduces some new ideas into the discussion—the *personal-word model*, an emphasis on divine lordship, some triperspectival distinctions, an attempt to delineate the process of God's word from his mouth to our hearts, new understandings of *general*, *special*, and *existential* revelation. I have tried to present the argument as concisely as possible, getting down to the crucial issues as quickly as possible. I have tried to keep in mind the epistemological questions that always come up when people consider the doctrines of revelation and Scripture. The question "How can I be sure?" has always been at the forefront of my thinking.

Most important, the book takes absolutely seriously the reality of God as "the one with whom we have to do," the Lord, the real, personal absolute who is active in all of history and our experience. The doctrine of the word of God in this book is unintelligible apart from the role that God plays every moment to vouch for his word and to accompany it to its destination. He is not a God who has gone away and left us with a book.[9] He is the God who brings his book to us each day, each minute. And that fact makes that book all the more precious to us. It is his personal words to us, not only delivered by him, but spoken to our hearts whenever we hear or read them.

8. For my tribute to one of them, see "Remembering Donald B. Fullerton," available at http://www.frame-poythress.org/frame_articles/Remembering_fullerton.htm.

9. Some Reformed writers, I have thought, in effect represent the closing of the canon in this way. I have referred to this tendency as *Reformed deism*. In Reformed deism, the Christian life is an academic study of Scripture. Talk of personal experience or personal friendship with Christ is decried as evangelical, charismatic, or pietistic as opposed to Reformed.

ANTITHESIS AND THE DOCTRINE OF SCRIPTURE

Note: This essay was my Inaugural Address at Reformed Theological Seminary, upon my assumption of the J. D. Trimble Chair of Systematic Theology and Philosophy. It discusses the relationship between the biblical doctrine of Scripture and its alternatives. It compares the biblical doctrine with those of liberal theology and of evangelicals who compromise with liberalism. This discussion supplements chapters 3–7 of the present book.

The Bible often divides people into two classes, antithetically related. There are the sons of Cain and of Seth (Gen. 4–6), Israel and the nations (Ex. 19:5–6), the righteous and the wicked (Ps. 1), the wise and the foolish (Prov. 1:7), the saved and the lost (Matt. 18:11), the children of Abraham and those of the devil (John 8:39–44), the elect and the nonelect (Rom. 9), practitioners of the wisdom of the world and of the wisdom of God (1 Cor. 1–2), believers and unbelievers (1 Cor. 6:6), those who walk in light and those who walk in darkness (1 John 1:5–10), and the church and the world (1 John 2:15–17).

These antitheses aren't all equivalent. That is to say that they are not simply alternative names for the same two groups. The distinction between elect and nonelect, for example, is not the same as the distinction between believer and unbeliever. There are elect people among the current group of unbelievers, and that fact motivates missions and evangelism. So in Acts 18:10, the Lord assured Paul that "I have many in this city who are my people"—many elect who had not yet embraced the gospel.

Similarly, under the old covenant there were Gentiles such as Melchizedek, Rahab, and Ruth who entered the people of God; and as Paul says in Romans 9:6, "not all who are descended from Israel belong to Israel." Some Gentiles, then, belong to God's people, and some Jews, in their hearts, do not. So the distinction between elect and nonelect is different from the distinction between Jew and Gentile, between Israel and the Nations.

Furthermore, the antithesis between wise and foolish, for example, is a division within the body of professing believers. Nevertheless, wisdom and not foolishness is the mentality proper to believers in the Lord. Foolishness really belongs outside of God's people. In a believer, foolishness contradicts his belief in God. In the consummation glory, all believers will be wise, not foolish. The distinction between the antitheses of belief/unbelief and elect/nonelect is also a distinction destined for dissolution. In the end, all the elect will be believers, just as even now all the nonelect are unbelievers.

In that way, given these nuances and qualifications, the antitheses actually coalesce. There is a great big ugly ditch, to abuse the metaphor of Lessing, that runs through the human community. Some are on one side, some on the other. Although the location of that ditch is not always plain today, God will make it plain in his final judgment. Eventually, the inconsistencies of believers and of unbelievers will be erased, everyone will show their true colors, and the antithesis will be fully manifest.

Now, Christians have often used these antitheses in the interest of theological polemics. Let me quote from one: "Whoever wills to be in a state of salvation, before all things it is necessary that he hold the catholic faith, which except everyone shall have kept whole and undefiled without doubt he will perish eternally." So begins the so-called Athanasian Creed,[1] which continues by summarizing Nicene Trinitarianism and Chalcedonian Christology, and then concludes, "This is the catholic faith, which except a man shall have believed faithfully and firmly he cannot be in a state of salvation." You see, what this creed does is to align the antithesis of saved and lost with the antithesis of orthodox and unorthodox. You can't be saved unless you profess orthodox doctrine.

That alignment, of course, doesn't take account of people who are too young, for example, to intelligently profess these doctrines, or of those who do not have sufficient mental capacity or education. I don't know the extent to which the writers or the original readers of the creed understood these qualifications, but of course they must be made.

---

1. Most likely not by Athanasius, the famous bishop of Alexandria. It is usually thought to be from western Europe, around A.D. 500.

Nevertheless, it is not wrong to define Christian belief in terms of a definite content. That content certainly includes the full deity and humanity of Christ, as the creed says. Although I think one can be devoted to Christ without intelligently confessing the formulae of the creed, surely the church should not recognize as a Christian anyone who understands these doctrines and *denies* them. Denial of them is the spirit of antichrist, as John puts it in 1 John 4:3. Or, as Paul puts it in Galatians 1:6–9, if anyone preaches a different gospel, contrary to that of the apostles, he is under a divine curse.

We find the same antithetical language in the polemics of the Protestant Reformation, which identifies the pope as Antichrist and his doctrine as devilish. And often in the following centuries, with varying degrees of justification, theologians have invoked the biblical antitheses against rival theologies.

The most significant, and to my mind most justifiable, recent use of these antitheses has been in the controversy between liberalism and orthodoxy. Liberalism is a movement that developed in the seventeenth century, came to flourish in the so-called Enlightenment of the eighteenth century, dominated the academic theological world in the nineteenth century, and came to rule many major denominations of the church in the twentieth. Liberalism's distinctive position is that the Bible is not the inspired Word of God, but a group of human reflections about God. That view of the Bible led many to contradict the teachings of the Bible, such as prophecy, miracle, the deity of Christ, his blood atonement, his physical resurrection, and his second coming.

Many who disagreed with the liberals nevertheless regarded them as a legitimate faction within the church, just as U.S. political parties, even when they strongly disagree, recognize the right of their opponents to participate in the political process. In this model, opponents see one another as holding different positions on the "spectrum of opinion." Many in the church today continue to hold such a view of liberalism. But in 1924, in his great book *Christianity and Liberalism*,[2] J. Gresham Machen evaluated the situation very differently:

> In the sphere of religion, in particular, the present time is a time of conflict; the great redemptive religion which has always been known as Christianity is battling against a totally diverse type of religious belief, which is only the more destructive of the Christian faith because it makes use of traditional Christian

2. J. Gresham Machen, *Christianity and Liberalism* (Grand Rapids: Eerdmans, 1923).

terminology. This modern non-redemptive religion is called "modernism" or "liberalism."[3]

In Machen's view, liberalism was not a faction or party within Christianity, a position along the Christian "spectrum." It was a different religion entirely.[4] In his book, Machen shows that the two religions hold exact opposite positions on everything of importance: doctrine, God, man, the Bible, Christ, salvation, and the church. Machen's approach is antithetic. Liberalism is by its very nature non-Christian, unbelieving. We may extrapolate that on this view liberalism is also foolish, not wise, wicked, not righteous, in darkness, not light, worldly, not churchly.

Machen's antithetic evaluation of liberalism led him eventually to leave Princeton Seminary, and later the Presbyterian Church USA, to found new institutions that would maintain the biblical gospel against unbelief. Others followed his example. Significantly, this year we celebrate the fortieth anniversary of Reformed Theological Seminary, which was also formed by men deeply convinced that existing seminaries in the Southern Presbyterian Church compromised the gospel itself by liberal teaching.

Antithesis was also a major element in the thought of Machen's disciple Cornelius Van Til. Occasionally, he made joking reference to it, as when he announced on the first day of class that the human race consisted of two distinct groups, Dutchmen and non-Dutchmen. But most of the time, he was deadly serious. As Machen had written *Christianity and Liberalism*, so Van Til wrote *Christianity and Barthianism*.[5] As Machen regarded liberalism as a different religion entirely from Christianity, so Van Til had the same view of the theology of Barth, Brunner, Hordern, Hendry, Dowey, and others in the so-called neoorthodox camp.

Van Til's apologetics also traded heavily on the concept of an antithesis between believer and unbeliever. I have criticized him for overstating the antithesis, as when he says that "the unbeliever can know nothing truly,"[6] and for other unclarities in his particular formulation. I have also objected to the fact that he sometimes used antithesis language to refer not only

---

3. Ibid., 2.

4. Many followed Machen in this analysis, although it never became a majority view. Jan Karel Van Baalen, in his *The Chaos of Cults* (Grand Rapids: Eerdmans, 1938), 283–317, identified modernism as a cult. On page 303, he quotes liberal Charles Clayton Morrison, longtime editor of *Christian Century*, as agreeing with Machen in 1924 that fundamentalism (as he preferred to call it) and modernism are indeed two different religions. On page 314, Van Baalen quotes Morrison again and liberal theologian Wilhelm Pauck as agreeing with Van Til's similar assessment of neoorthodoxy.

5. Cornelius Van Til, *Christianity and Barthianism* (Philadelphia: Presbyterian and Reformed, 1962).

6. CVT, 187–213.

to believer and unbeliever, but also to Reformed and non-Reformed, and even to Van Tillian and non–Van Tillian apologists within the Reformed community. But his basic insight wears well: the difference between faith and unbelief is relevant to human thinking and reasoning, not merely to some narrowly defined "religious" dimension of life. Religious antithesis generates epistemological antithesis. Christians *think* differently from non-Christians; and when they don't, they should.

In describing the difference between Christian and non-Christian thinking, Van Til argued that the two groups of people held different *presuppositions*. A presupposition, for Van Til, was the most fundamental commitment of the heart, a commitment that governed human life. Some people are committed to Jesus Christ and seek to "take every thought captive" to him (2 Cor. 10:5). The rest are committed to something else, either another religion, a philosophy, a political movement, or their own reason. There is no neutrality. To paraphrase Bob Dylan, "you gotta serve somebody." Our presuppositional commitments govern all our life decisions, indeed all our thinking. And in the end there are only two presuppositions: the supremacy of God and the supremacy of something in creation, which Scripture calls idolatry.

To be committed to Jesus Christ is to honor his word, above all other words. Van Til, together with all other orthodox believers, held that the word of Christ, the word of God, is to be found in the Holy Scriptures, indeed that the Bible *is* the Word of God. So a short way of setting forth the content of the believer's presupposition is to say that it is the content of the Bible. Of course, believers vary in the degree to which they know and understand Scripture, and therefore in the degree to which they can apply that presupposition. But they seek a greater and greater understanding, so that more and more aspects of their lives can be subject to God's Word.

Van Til therefore maintained that a strong doctrine of Scripture, such as the first chapter of the WCF, is an indispensable element of Christian theology. To deny the ultimate authority of God's written Word is to adopt a different authority, one that must in the nature of the case be allied with Satan.

For several years during the 1950s and 1960s, as I recall, Van Til's OT colleague Edward J. Young reviewed books for *Christianity Today*, often publishing a yearly roundup of writings in the OT field. Although Young reviewed books by liberal and orthodox writers equally, he made a very sharp distinction between them. When there was a book that was hard to classify in these categories, he took careful note of the book's orthodox elements and of its liberal elements. Like Van Til, Young saw biblical scholarship in an antithetical pattern. Either OT scholars honored the Bible as God's Word or they didn't, or they wavered unstably between the two positions. And for Young, the most important element of a review was to identify where the author stood in terms of these two positions.

Today, Young's reviews look very old-fashioned, though one cannot deny his expertise and analytical perception. In the years since the 1960s, it has become more and more difficult to classify works of scholarship in the antithetical pattern of Machen, Van Til, and Young. "Liberal" writings and "orthodox" writings are getting harder and harder to tell apart, and many evidently think that it's something of a waste of time even to make this distinction. Those who come from the liberal traditions of the academic mainstream have (with exceptions, such as the so-called Jesus Seminar) tended to come to more and more conservative conclusions concerning the dates, authorship, and historical accuracy of biblical texts. Those who come from the evangelical traditions, on the other hand, have come more and more to obtain doctorates from institutions in the academic mainstream. They have therefore gotten into the habit of carrying out their scholarship using the methods, and sometimes the assumptions, of that mainstream. So as the two parties have come closer and closer together, there has come about a unity among biblical scholars unprecedented since the 1700s. This is a most remarkable event that has taken place in our time.

As an example, consider the book *The Last Word* by N. T. Wright,[7] which I recently reviewed in the *Penpoint* newsletter.[8] The subtitle of the book promises that this book will lead us "beyond the Bible wars to a new understanding of the authority of Scripture." I should mention that the title and subtitle are found in the American edition only, not the original British edition. Evidently, the author or publisher wanted to address battles over biblical inerrancy, which European Christians tend to regard as American and therefore unimportant. In fact, however, the book does not address those issues at all. Rather, Wright provides his readers with a context for biblical authority in which, he thinks, questions about biblical inerrancy and the like do not arise.

Wright is considered conservative in his evaluation of biblical history. He displays no bias against the idea of the miraculous, and elsewhere he has staunchly defended belief in the resurrection of Jesus. He regards the hyperliberal scholarship of the Jesus Seminar with ill-disguised con-

---

7. N. T. Wright, *The Last Word: Beyond the Bible Wars to a New Understanding of the Authority of Scripture* (San Francisco: HarperCollins, 2005). The book was published in Great Britain under the title *Scripture and the Authority of God*, by the Society for Promoting Christian Knowledge.

8. *Penpoint* 17, 4 (August 2006). The review is included as Appendix K of the present volume.

tempt. But he does not follow the old American evangelical pattern of declaring Scripture to be inerrant, or of painting a picture of antithesis between belief and unbelief in Scripture. Rather, he gives the impression that those questions don't even arise if we understand Scripture in its proper context.

That context is that of God's own authority. Wright tells us that

> the phrase "authority of Scripture" can make Christian sense only if it is shorthand for "the authority of the triune God, exercised somehow *through* scripture."[9]

What is the force of that *through*? *How* does God exercise his authority through Scripture? God's authority, Wright says, "is his sovereign power accomplishing the renewal of all creation."[10] Scripture is an instrument of that authority. Specifically, Scripture is the story, the narrative, of that sovereign power. So we should not read Scripture as a "list of rules" or a "compendium of true doctrines," although both doctrines and rules can be found in the text.[11] Although he does not quite say so, I think that the narrative character of Scripture is what, to his mind, should keep us from raising the kinds of questions distinctive of the Bible wars. He seems to think that as long as we regard Scripture as story or narrative, we don't need to worry about the infallibility of its doctrinal or ethical teaching, much less the inerrancy of its statements on other subjects.

Wright is, of course, not the first scholar to opt for narrative as the basic form of divine revelation in Scripture. The literature advocating "narrative theology" and "story theology" is enormous, and the discussion of it has been going on for several decades.

And we should trace this development back much earlier than the birth of narrative theology in the 1980s. The Ritschlian quest for the historical Jesus sought to turn theology away from a focus on Scripture as an inspired text to a neutral investigation of the history of the origins of Christianity, from which it was thought that value judgments would arise that would guide our theological reflection.

The post-Bultmannian "new quest of the historical Jesus" of Ernst Käsemann, Ernst Fuchs, Gerhard Ebeling, and others tried to trace the roots of Bultmann's existentialist gospel, somehow, to Jesus. The so-called "third quest" of the 1990s disavowed theological agendas and tried to place Jesus in his Jewish environment. The name of N. T. Wright has

9. Wright, *Last Word*, 23.
10. Ibid., 29.
11. Ibid., 25–26.

been associated with this movement, as well as with the movement of narrative theology.

To go back to the early and middle twentieth century, we should note Karl Barth, who also identified revelation with history of a sort. Barth and his associates despised the Ritschlian program and emphasized that God speaks to us from above, not through our autonomous historical research. But Barth, like Ritschl, denied that revelation was to be identified with the text of Scripture. Rather, in the Barthian circle, as in Ritschl's, revelation was event, a kind of history (a *Geschichte*). I will not try to unpack Barth's difficult concept here, but to summarize, it seems to me that for Barth revelation is the event in which God opens his mouth to speak—as he once put it, *Dei loquentis persona*. What God actually says when he opens his mouth cannot be translated into human words or sentences; these are only pointers to the event of his utterance, a word of power by which he overturns our self-righteousness. Barth did also defend the literal historicity (*historisch*) of some supernatural events, such as the virgin birth and resurrection of Christ, but the relation of these events to our actual salvation was highly obscure. When Barth said that God accomplished our salvation by historical events, he seems to have meant not events that happened in time and space but events within God's own inner life.

The "acts of God" theology of the mid-twentieth century, advocated by G. Ernest Wright and others, also located revelation in history. In Wright's view, the events in question may have been unremarkable in themselves, but they became revelation when interpreted by faith. Wolfhart Pannenberg and his circle criticized this kind of subjectivism, and opted to build faith on the objective foundation of rational historical inquiry, carrying us back, in some respects, to the Ritschlian project.

So we should see narrative theology as one of many attempts to locate God's revelation in historical events. This project is not without a biblical basis. Scripture has much to say about God's mighty acts—his signs and wonders, the events of history by which our salvation comes. These events are revelatory. God says of the events of the exodus that through them "the Egyptians shall know that I am the LORD" (Ex. 7:5; cf. v. 17). Similar expressions are found often in Scripture.

But it would be wrong to think that God in Scripture reveals himself *only* in events and actions and not also by words and sentences. James Barr in his 1966 book *Old and New in Interpretation*[12] took his fellow liberals to task for this assumption. As modern men we can, he said, deny the idea

12. James Barr, *Old and New in Interpretation* (London: SCM Press, 1966).

of God's speaking to people in authoritative propositions, but we cannot deny that the biblical writers affirmed such a concept. And surely we must be blind indeed not to note that verbal communication from God to human beings is a pervasive biblical theme, from the garden of Eden to the consummation of redemption. Indeed, that verbal revelation often takes written form, as when God writes the Ten Commandments with his own finger (Ex. 31:18).

If we are to deny that this can take place, it can only be because of a general skepticism about the supernatural, which is in the end a skepticism about the reality of God. If we allow the possibility but deny the actuality of such revelation, it can only be because of a general skepticism about the claims of the Bible itself. Neither skepticism is worthy of people who profess to be Christians.

Why, then, has such skepticism come to dominate the supposedly Christian discipline of theology? Certainly, no church council has authorized it. Certainly, there is no argument for it from Scripture or the main body of church tradition. The only explanation that makes any sense is that theologians are no longer willing to think according to biblical and Christian presuppositions. They want, like their colleagues in other fields, to think autonomously or neutrally.

N. T. Wright is not, in my view, a neutralist. He defends biblical supernaturalism, and very effectively. But in his book *The Last Word*, he says nothing about the Bible as a verbal revelation of God. He says that the Bible is a narrative of God's saving power. He also says at one point[13] that God's providence gathered together the books that belong to our canon. But there are other books that narrate the coming of God's kingdom, some written by Wright himself. And God's providence has placed some of them in my library. Does that make them Scripture? Surely not. To be Scripture, a book must be more than a narrative, and more than a providential collection of books. It must be authored by God, written by God's finger, God-breathed. Of that, Wright tells us nothing, and apparently he hopes the question won't arise, lest we get back into the Bible wars.

I have no nostalgia for the fundamentalist-modernist controversy; indeed, I would prefer that there be as little controversy in the church as possible. But the question of a divinely authored text will not go away. And it remains a major point of dispute between orthodox Christians and the mainstream of biblical and theological scholarship today.

Wright's book, I think, is symptomatic of many titles in theology and biblical studies that seek to avoid, disguise, or suppress the antithesis

13. Wright, *Last Word*, 37.

between Christianity and liberalism. We can be thankful to God for what Wright and others have taught us. In other forums, I would gladly commend Wright's picture of Scripture as a tool of God's advancing kingdom. Those who seek, for example, to avoid the political implications of the gospel need to deal seriously with Wright's model. That model is a necessary one for our understanding of the place of Scripture. But it is not *sufficient*. Scripture is a narrative about God's kingdom, but it is not *merely* that. It is God's own account of that kingdom, and it is that kingdom's written constitution.

It is, therefore, not only narrative. It is also doctrine, the teachings by which God governs his church. The narrative involves the doctrine, and the doctrine involves the narrative. The narrative shows us how God redeems all aspects of human life and rules us through his word, spoken by prophets and apostles, incarnate in Jesus, written in the Bible. The doctrine tells us that we are saved by God through his mighty acts in Christ. Scripture is both situational, telling us about events of history, and normative, ruling our beliefs and our lives.

The situational and normative sides of Scripture are perspectives—ways of looking at Scripture that necessitate and imply one another. Neither can be itself without the other. Those familiar with my writings will expect a third perspective, and I will not disappoint them: Scripture is also existential—a message from God to the human heart.

When Wright expresses reservations about using Scripture as a "court of appeal," he is questioning the normative perspective. When he criticizes its use as a *lectio divina*,[14] he is questioning the existential perspective. His lack of balance is therefore due in part to monoperspectival thinking.

In any case, the attempt of Wright and many others to isolate the situational perspective and to negate the others is biblically indefensible, and it obscures a crucial antithesis.

There are lessons here also for Reformed people, especially for those who are self-consciously orthodox in their thinking. We have our own reasons for putting much emphasis on the situational perspective, for we of all people want to insist that God saves his people through historical events, most particularly through the incarnation, sacrificial death, resurrection, ascension, and return of Jesus Christ. As with all historical events, these must be seen in the context of other historical events, especially, in this case, the history of God's covenants with Adam, Noah, Abraham, Moses, and David, through the history of Israel. Hence the emphasis in our circles upon redemptive history.[15] We should remember, however, that

---

14. Ibid., 64–65.

15. A redemptive-historical approach to theology is sometimes called "biblical theology," but that is a misnomer. All theology is biblical, if it is sound theology.

the best advocates of a redemptive-historical method, such as Vos, Gaffin, Clowney, and Kline (and to an extent Herman Ridderbos), also insist on the normative dimension: we learn of this history through a divinely authored Bible.

For the same reasons, there are dangers in drawing too close a relation between theology and history, as, I believe, Richard Muller does in his *The Study of Theology*.[16] I have also drawn attention to the dangers in approaches to theology that emphasize church history over biblical exegesis.[17] Over the last thirty years it has been common for evangelical and Reformed theologians to earn PhDs in church history or historical theology, for in these disciplines there appear to be fewer conflicts between evangelical convictions and the liberal academic mainstream. This is understandable, and it may be necessary. But in this atmosphere, it is all too easy for young theologians to forget the indispensable normativity of theology. Theology is the discipline of going to the Scriptures and reporting its teaching as a norm, saying, "Thus says the Lord." One cannot say this in a secular university graduate program without being laughed at. That kind of theology won't earn you a doctorate. But after the doctorate, it is important for the young theologian to recover his roots and return to the normative exposition of Scripture as the infallible Word of God.

In the past I have often urged Reformed theologians to put more emphasis on the existential perspective—to avoid pseudo-intellectualism and to put a genuinely biblical emphasis on human feelings—the subjective side of knowing God. I still think that, too, is an important need in our circles. But in this paper I am urging that we accentuate the normative. Historically, Reformed theology has had a good record on this score; perhaps it has even been guilty of an overemphasis at times. Some may even think that in this paper I am bringing coals to Newcastle. But today the pendulum has shifted to the point where I sense the need to warn us again to see the vast difference between those who understand Scripture as the Word of God and those who do not.

---

16. Richard A. Muller, *The Study of Theology: From Biblical Interpretation to Contemporary Formulation*, Foundations of Contemporary Interpretation 7 (Grand Rapids: Zondervan, 1991). My review of this book was published in *WTJ* 56, 1 (Spring 1994): 438–42, and is now available at http://www.frame-poythress.org/frame_articles/1994Muller.htm and as Appendix C of the present volume.

17. "In Defense of Something Close to Biblicism," *WTJ* 59 (1997): 269–318, also available at http://www.frame-poythress.org/frame_articles/Biblicism.htm and as Appendix O of the present volume. Also see my article "Traditionalism and Sola Scriptura," *Chalcedon Report* (October 2001): 15–19 (November 2001): 434–35, which is available at http://www.frame-poythress.org/frame_articles/1999Traditionalism.htm and as Appendix P of the present volume.

I don't want to go back to the days when we spent inordinate amounts of time debating the historicity of every little thing in the Bible. Theology should be focused where the Bible is—on the gospel of Christ. Nor do I want to simply reject scholarship written from a liberal point of view. That scholarship has much to teach us, as even Cornelius Van Til and Edward J. Young knew well. But it is important to draw a line here, and where the line is fuzzy to describe how and why. In assessing a liberal theologian, there should be a point where we say not merely that this or that detail of his thought is false, or that this theme is overemphasized or that theme underemphasized, but that the overall theological method is wrongheaded. We should be gentler, more gracious, and more nuanced in making these judgments than were some of the old fundamentalists. But those judgments must be made. In the end, the doctrine of Scripture creates an antithesis, and we mislead our readers to the extent that we fail to acknowledge it.

And in our own theological work, we should make clear that the Bible is our sole ultimate authority. That is, we should not give the impression that we are merely triangulating—positioning ourselves between Barth over here, Pannenberg over there, perhaps Vos or Ridderbos in some other direction. The theologian, like the preacher, must be willing to say, "Thus says the Lord." May he give us the perception and the courage to do that, whatever the cost.

RATIONALITY AND SCRIPTURE[1]

Stimulus paragraph: We all take the Bible to be the Word of God inscripturated. Consequently, the Bible presents Christian philosophers with the supreme standard for all of human life. Is our understanding of Scripture in faith a rule for human analysis? In what sense do the canons of inference hold for our understanding of the Bible? If our intercourse with Scripture involves more than propositions and intellectual operations, how can this "more" be defined and what is its importance relative to propositions and intellectual operations? Given the traditional view of the autonomy of reason, is our confession of Scripture as the Word of God compatible with our views of the nature of inference?

Note: The organizers of the conference "Rationality in the Calvinian Tradition" formulated the paragraph above as a stimulus to our thinking concerning the relationship of Scripture to rationality. As such, I have found it excellent, and I will try to respond to all its questions in this paper, though not necessarily in the order presented. The first two sentences of the paragraph are evidently presented as convictions to be presupposed, not argued, and I gladly accept them as such.

---

1. This was a paper delivered at a conference, later published in Hendrik Hart, Johan Van Der Hoeven, and Nicholas Wolterstorff, eds., *Rationality in the Calvinian Tradition* (Lanham, MD: University Press of America, 1983), 293–317. I was asked to comment critically on the opening paragraph, which was given to me by the conference organizers. This essay supplements the discussion of revelation and reason in chapter 4 of the present volume, and the discussions of the content of Scripture in chapters 24–25 and 31–32. Indeed, it is in many ways an anticipation of *DKG*, which I would publish four years later.

The paper will deal, first, with the rule of Scripture over the Christian life as a whole. I will then seek to show, at least in broad terms, how this rule applies specifically to our use of reason, concluding with a discussion of how reason, so understood, functions in our interpretation of Scripture itself. Obviously, these discussions are interdependent: for as I seek to interpret Scripture's teachings at the beginning of the paper, I will be presupposing the hermeneutical points made at the end, as well as the epistemological points made in the middle, and naturally, the middle and end also presuppose the beginning. Such circularity is common in theology and philosophy, and I know of no way to avoid it. God's truth is an organism.

I. SCRIPTURE AS OUR RULE OF FAITH AND LIFE

I think it is important for us to recognize that reasoning is one of many human activities, one of many aspects of human life. Scripture therefore governs our reasoning, first of all, as it governs life as a whole. We ought, therefore, to give some attention to the way in which Scripture is intended by God to rule human life in general. I will assume, here, with the "stimulus paragraph," that "the Bible [is] the Word of God inscripturated" and thus is "the supreme standard for all of human life." But some reflection is needed as to how Scripture functions as "supreme standard."

A. Scripture and the Organism of Revelation

First, although Scripture is the Word of God, it is not the whole of God's revelation to us. It has often been pointed out (especially, in recent years, by thinkers oriented to the cosmonomic idea philosophy)[2] that in Scripture, "word of God" applies not only to spoken and written revelation, but also to that divine speech that created[3] and directs[4] the world, and to Jesus Christ himself[5] as the supreme self-expression of the Father. Thus, God makes himself known to us not only through the Bible but through every-

---

2. Note, e.g., James H. Olthuis and Bernard Zylstra, "Confessing Christ in Education," *IRB* 42 (Summer 1970): 41f.; Bernard Zylstra, "Thy Word Our Life," *IRB* 49–50 (Spring/ Summer 1972): 57–68. On page 68, Zylstra says that "a number of leaders in the orthodox protestant community have lately insisted that the Scriptures are the Word of God, only and exclusively." If this means that these leaders deny the existence of the other forms of divine speech we have noted, then I am at a loss as to what leaders Zylstra is referring to.

3. Ps. 33:6 (cf. Gen. 1:3, 6, 9, etc.); John 1:1–3; 2 Peter 3:5.

4. Pss. 119:89–92; 147:15–18; 148:8.

5. John 1:1–14; 1 John 1:1; Rev. 19:13.

thing in creation.[6] We ourselves, made in God's "image,"[7] constitute an especially important form of God's self-disclosure.[8]

God never intended that any of these forms of revelation should function without the others. From the very beginning of Adam's existence, he was confronted by a world that revealed God, a spoken word that defined his nature and task,[9] and his own nature as God's image. Clearly, God intended Adam to interpret the world and himself consistently with the spoken revelation: Adam was to accept his status as the image of God and to regard the world as properly subject to his godly dominion. Thus, the spoken word was to determine Adam's interpretation of the revelation of God in creation.

But on the other hand, Adam's knowledge of the creation surely also influenced his understanding of and response to God's spoken words. It is hard to imagine Adam understanding the spoken revelation of Genesis 1:28–30 without some understanding of the world independent of that particular revelation. For him to understand that word of God, he had to understand the language in which it was spoken; he had to have some idea what it meant to "be fruitful and multiply," to "replenish and subdue"; he had to know what the "earth" was. Possibly, some of that information was given to him by additional verbal revelations, but to assume this would be gratuitous. Surely such additional revelation does not occur today, at least when the need for it would seem to be identical. And it is in any case impossible to teach anyone language through words alone; the words must be tied to the world about which they speak.[10]

6. Ps. 19:1ff.; Rom. 1:18ff. Note also that the Bible does not exhaust even the total of oral and written revelation that God has given to men. There were prophecies, words of Jesus, and probably even Pauline Epistles that in God's providence did not find their way into the canon of Scripture. Since, however, I believe that oral and written revelation (with the status of covenant law) has ceased, I would maintain that Scripture contains all the revelation of that type available to us. So, for simplicity, I will speak as though "Scripture" is equivalent to "oral and written revelation."

7. Gen. 1:26f.

8. The assertions of this paragraph have always been central to Reformed (or "Calvinian," if you will) theology. Calvin, more than any of the other Reformers, was impressed by the stamp of God upon the whole creation, and with man as a reflection of God's glory. Note the remarkable first pages of the *Institutes* where he correlates the knowledge of God with self-knowledge, and then (contrary to what we might expect from a Calvinist) tells us that he doesn't know which comes first.

9. Gen. 1:28–30; see also 2:16f., 19.

10. If one does not know English, for example, it will not help him to define one English word by means of synonyms or definitions in English. The teacher must, at some point, speak a language that the student knows. You cannot learn a language (through verbal teaching, at least) unless you already know one. So I assume that God did not teach language to Adam merely by speaking to him. There must have been some other means.

Furthermore, it is also the case that Adam could not *obey* the command of Genesis 1:28–30 without some additional knowledge of himself and the world. How, after all, does one go about "subduing the earth"? Surely this is a technological feat of enormous complexity, requiring a careful study both of the earth and of one's own capacities. Such study was essential if Adam and his descendants were to learn *concretely* and *specifically* what it meant to replenish and subdue the earth. And surely we must ask: if we understand God's word only in general terms and not in its specific requirements, can we claim to understand it at all?

The same situation exists today. To understand and apply Scripture, we must know something about the world and about ourselves. Understanding Scripture is never merely a matter of memorizing words and locations of verses. A parrot—or a computer—could be taught to do that. The Jews of Jesus' day had a good rote knowledge of Scripture, but Jesus accused them of ignorance of the Word of God, since they failed to see the *relationships* between the old covenant documents and the crucial redemptive events of their own time.[11] To understand Scripture is to understand its bearing on our lives, upon our world. But if this is so, then we cannot claim to understand Scripture unless we also understand things other than Scripture. Not even theology may restrict its attention to Scripture alone, for theology aims not to reproduce the Bible, but to put Scripture into different words—words designed to communicate its truth into a new context. Theology seeks to answer people's questions about the Bible—to meet people's needs from the Bible. Thus, it must understand those needs, those questions, that present context into which the truth must be spoken.[12]

Thus, revelation is an organism. Revelations in Scripture, world, and self presuppose and supplement one another; one cannot understand one of them without reference to the others. However, we may not stop with such observations. From what I have said so far, the distinctive role of Scripture within this organism is not apparent. Until now, I have communicated no sense of the *prominence* of Scripture in the believer's life. Indeed, at this point it may seem as though Scripture is just one of a number of sources for revelation to be considered on an equal basis, so that when apparent conflicts arise, for example, between my understanding of Scripture and

---

Thus, when Adam received the verbal revelation, he understood it partly in reference to what he already knew.

11. Matt. 22:29–32; John 5:39f.; cf. Luke 24:25.

12. For more considerations as to why general and special revelation presuppose and supplement one another, see Cornelius Van Til, "Nature and Scripture," in *The Infallible Word*, ed. Ned Bernard Stonehouse and Paul Woolley (Grand Rapids: Eerdmans, 1946), 255–93.

my understanding of the natural world, I might, with an equal sense of responsibility before God, go either way. Such an attitude, however, would scarcely do justice to the sharp distinctions in Scripture itself between the word of God on the one hand and the word of man on the other. On such a view, what practical distinction could be drawn between the word of God and my own wisdom, imagination, reasoning? Why wouldn't Abraham have had the option of acting on the evidence of his eyes, rather than of the promise (Rom. 4:18–21)?

The question, then, of Scripture's *distinctive* role within the "organism" must be faced. I suggest that Scripture is distinctive in at least three ways.

1. *Subject Matter.* Scripture is distinctive, first of all, in that it is a story that would not otherwise be available to us—the story of Jesus Christ and how he saved his people from their sins. The purpose of Scripture, then, is not to give us miscellaneous information on all sorts of subjects. It has a specific focus—a direction. It is directed toward a particular human need—the need for redemption—rather than other needs, such as the need for a cancer cure or the need for an adequate theory of geologic strata. This focus is reflected in the *style* of Scripture: it is written, generally, in the language of everyday life, rather than in the technical style of scientists and philosophers.

Much has been written by Reformed authors in recent years concerning this focus (*scopus*) of Scripture.[13] Essentially, the same point has been made in various terminologies that Scripture is a "book of faith,"[14] that it is "confessionally qualified,"[15] and that it is "Christologically theocentric."[16] In itself, the point is neither new[17] nor controversial. Controversy does arise, however, concerning certain conclusions that have been drawn from

13. Important in this development has been G. C. Berkouwer, *Holy Scripture* (Grand Rapids: Eerdmans, 1975). Cf. also the study committee report, *The Nature and Extent of Biblical Authority* (Grand Rapids: Board of Publications of the Christian Reformed Church, 1972).

14. Herman Dooyeweerd, *In the Twilight of Western Thought* (Nutley, NJ: Craig Press, 1968), 132–56.

15. Gordon J. Spykman, "A Confessional Hermeneutic," *RESTB* 1, 3 (December 1973): 9.

16. P. Klooster, "Toward a Reformed Hermeneutic," *RESTB* 2, 1 (May 1974): 5.

17. In response to the charge that such theologians as the Hodges and B. B. Warfield neglected this truth, Norman Shepherd (in an unpublished lecture, "The Nature of Biblical Authority") cites Warfield, *The Inspiration and Authority of the Bible* (Philadelphia: Presbyterian and Reformed, 1948), 161: "If the 'inspiration' by which Scripture is produced renders it trustworthy and authoritative, it renders it trustworthy and authoritative only that it may the better serve to make men wise unto salvation." Cf. also Cornelius Van Til's response to Jack B. Rogers in E. R. Geehan, ed., *Jerusalem and Athens* (Nutley, NJ: Presbyterian and Reformed, 1971), 165–71.

this principle. Jack B. Rogers, for instance, takes issue with Van Til's statement that "the Bible has much to say about the universe," giving as his sole argument the redemptive focus of Scripture.[18] Quite a large logical jump here. The focus on redemption proves that Scripture does *not* say anything much about the universe? Why? Does Christ have nothing to do with the universe? Does redemption? Even if redemption has nothing to do with the universe, does a "focus" on such redemption exclude incidental reference to things in the universe? The universe, you know, is a big place, and the Bible is a big book. It's a bit hard to conceive of the latter while avoiding the former to the extent that Rogers conceives. Similarly, Arnold De Graaff and Calvin Seerveld reflect on the soteriological focus of Scripture and, again from that fact alone, conclude

> that the references to God's creating do not answer our scientific, biological or geological questions, just as little as the Bible answers the questions of the historian or the anthropologist. The Bible is just not that kind of a book.[19]

Again, it sounds as though redemption takes place somewhere other than in the world. De Graaff and Seerveld write as though it were perfectly obvious that a focus on redemption excludes *anything* of interest to the sciences. And Dooyeweerd tells us that since Scripture deals with concepts of faith, it can have no interest in the chronological relations among the days of creation.[20]

The question of *scopus* is, of course, a serious one—not to be ridiculed. But it ought to be plain that arguments on the issue need to be constructed with more care than has been common to this point. We need particularly to take into account (a) that the gospel message is a message about events that took place in time-space history—the incarnation, crucifixion, resurrection, and ascension of Jesus, and the filling of the church with the Spirit. These events are crucial to any account of history, "scientific" or otherwise.[21] And also (b) that the gospel message is a message of cosmic

18. Jack Rogers, "Van Til and Warfield on Scripture in the Westminster Confession," in Geehan, *Jerusalem and Athens*, 162f.

19. Arnold H. De Graaff and Calvin Seerveld, *Understanding the Scriptures* (Toronto: Association for the Advancement of Christian Scholarship, 1968), 12. Earlier in the paragraph, however, the authors say that "the creation story serves as the religious basis and directive for the Christian biologist's and geologist's theorizing." Thus, apparently, Scripture does, after all, answer biological and geological questions—namely, questions about the religious basis of those disciplines. Possibly De Graaff and Seerveld are working with some highly precise concept of a "biological or geological question," but if so, why do they not tell us about it?

20. Dooyeweerd, *In the Twilight of Western Thought*, 149ff.

21. Shepherd, "The Nature of Biblical Authority"; J. I. Packer, *Beyond the Battle for the Bible* (Westchester, IL: Cornerstone Books, 1980), 54f.

importance about the creation, fall, and redemption not only of man, but of all things,[22] and that it makes a demand upon all areas of human life,[23] including, of course, his science. And if Scripture is the Word of God written (stimulus paragraph), then surely what God teaches us therein must be accepted not only in its central thrust but also in its *obiter dicta*. It is blasphemous for us to tell God that we will honor only what we regard as the "main drift" of his words.

Having said all of this, I still would not expect to find in Ezekiel predictions of the invention of the airplane, or in Proverbs a formula for converting mass into energy. But I do expect to find in Scripture those religious assumptions about the cosmos that Christians ought to hold and with which they ought to bring their scientific theories into conformity.[24] And especially in regard to biblical teachings about creation, miracle, and resurrection, I would not be at all surprised to find in Scripture *some* detailed factual assertions that would conflict with *some* assertions of *some* scientists. On specific questions (e.g., whether Genesis 5 contradicts the common scientific view of the antiquity of mankind), I know of no a priori theological or philosophical principle by which an answer can be found by way of deduction from the *scopus* of Scripture as a whole. Rather, the passage in question must be studied individually to determine its own *particular scopus*, that *scopus* being consistent, to be sure, with what 2 Timothy 3:16f. and other passages say about the purpose of Scripture as a whole. The fact that Scripture has a redemptive focus gives us a rough-and-ready guide, a general rule as to what we should expect to find in Scripture, but it does not answer all detailed questions about Scripture's contents; it does not make exegesis unnecessary; it does not immunize us against the power of God's Word to surprise.[25]

22. Cf., e.g., Gen. 3:17ff.; Rom. 8:18–22; Col. 1:20.

23. Rom. 14:23; 1 Cor. 10:31; Col. 3:17, 23; cf. our stimulus paragraph. Note also Van Til in Geehan, *Jerusalem and Athens*, 165ff. (vs. Rogers) and Norman Shepherd, "Bible, Church and Proclamation (Response to Prof. Johan A. Heyns)," *IRB* 54 (Summer 1973): 60f.

24. De Graaff seems to recognize this (above, note 19), but I cannot regard this recognition as consistent with his later statement that Scripture answers no scientific questions. For one thing, I see no reason to say that questions about the religious direction of a science are not "scientific." Furthermore, if this religious direction exists, then surely it influences in some way the specific assertions of that science. Thus, if one challenges that religious direction, one simultaneously challenges some of the specific assertions of the science in question. Thus, if Scripture answers the question about religious direction, it answers at least some specific questions as well.

25. The same must be said about statements to the effect that Scripture is a "naive" or "pretheoretical" book, as opposed to a "theoretical" book. I have criticized the common naive/theoretical distinction as taught by the cosmonomic philosophy in my pamphlet *The*

Thus, it will be understood that for purposes of this paper, the chief importance of *scopus* is not that it limits the subjects that Scripture may address, although it does set some rough limits of this sort. Rather, the importance of *scopus* is that it gives Scripture a centrality for all thought and life. Since Scripture contains the message of redemption, we must have continual recourse to it in all areas of life. As sinners saved by grace, struggling with the remnants of sin in all our thinking and living, we must hunger and thirst constantly for the written Word of God, seeking in it the means by which God wishes to sanctify each area of life. First in importance for every part of life must be the implications of the biblical message. And since it is in Scripture, not nature in general, that this saving message is to be found, this principle necessarily gives to Scripture a certain primacy within the total organism of revelation. It is Scripture that shows us how to use the other revelation obediently, how to repent of sin in our use of creation. Scripture must be allowed to *correct* that thinking, which is based on natural revelation. But how can Scripture have such primacy without destroying the organic character of revelation? How can Scripture correct our understanding of creation when, as we mentioned earlier, creation also often helps us to correct our understanding of Scripture? Be patient; I must first move on to other aspects of Scripture's "distinctive role" within the organism.

2. *Soteric Function.* Scripture not only contains a distinctive subject matter, but also has a distinctive kind of *power.* As the apostle says, the gospel, the message of Scripture, is "the power of God for salvation."[26] In Scripture we not only find the *information* needed to reform, to sanctify our lives, but also find there the *ability* to do so, for the Holy Spirit of God works in and with the Word, and he works in saving power.[27] Thus, we have an additional motive to return again and again to Scripture. It is there that we find the strength to change, to reform our ideas and life decisions in obedience to

---

Amsterdam Philosophy (Phillipsburg, NJ: Harmony Press, 1972), 6–14. I find the distinction unclearly defined, its persuasiveness built upon vivid but unexplained metaphors. I find no justification for the apparent denial of any continuum between the "naive" category and the "theoretical," especially since each seems able to include elements of the other. I see no basis for saying that naive thinking is somehow beyond the scope of philosophical or scientific criticism or that theoretical thought must be strictly limited to the cosmos. Thus, I do not find it helpful to discuss Scripture in terms of such a dichotomy. Certainly Scripture is generally written in the language of ordinary life as opposed to that of the academic world. But there are large diversities of language within Scripture itself (e.g., between Psalms and Romans). Again, I don't expect to find $E = MC^2$ in the Bible. The connection of that with redemption is remote, and I don't think Scripture gets to be *that* theoretical. But to say that "Scripture speaks the language of ordinary life" gives me, again, only a rough, general guide to Scripture's contents. It gives me no a priori basis for excluding any exegetical possibilities.

26. Rom. 1:16; cf. John 6:63; 2 Tim. 3:15; etc.

27. 1 Thess. 1:5. For more discussion of this point, see I.B, below.

God. The words of Scripture and the Spirit therein work together (not, of course, independently). Thus, by the Spirit's work, the words "captivate" us, "grip" us.[28] We find them memorable, penetrating, profoundly true. We find that we cannot avoid taking them into account.

It is often pointed out that the soteric "grip" of Scripture upon us is not to be equated with theoretical insight.[29] It is a "heart knowledge."[30] Indeed, the regenerating and sanctifying power of the Word operates on children as well as adults, upon ordinary people as much as scholars. That much truth, at least, may be found in the assertion that this knowledge of God is "beyond . . . scientific problems" and "not a question of theoretical reflection."[31] Furthermore, it is right to point out that the product of this saving power is knowledge of God, not a mere knowledge of miscellaneous facts, theological or otherwise. Such observations, however, ought more often to be balanced by the following considerations. (a) The power of the Spirit energizes *all* of Scripture, for all of Scripture is God's redemptive message, God's gospel.[32] The Spirit drives home to God's people, therefore, all of Scripture's implications—its applications for our lives.[33] As observed earlier, our responsibility to Scripture is not merely to its "general drift" but to its full range of meaning—"every word that comes from the mouth of God," "*all* Scripture."[34] Thus, the implications of Scripture for theoretical work come under the empowering, illuminating ministry of the Spirit, although the work of the Spirit is certainly not limited to that. (b) Therefore, although every Christian is in the "grip" of the Word, not every Christian has experienced illumination with respect to the same scriptural contents. A theologian may be convicted by the Spirit as to the relevance of Romans 6 to the doctrine of sanctification, while his ten-year-old son may have no idea even as to what the questions are. To summarize: the *scopus* of the Spirit's work in and with Scripture is as broad as the *scopus* of Scripture itself (see I.A.1).

28. The metaphors of "gripping" and so forth introduce a helpful vividness into our formulations. We must be careful, though, that we do not regard the power of the Word as a kind of "blind force" that influences us apart from the linguistic meanings of scriptural words and sentences. "Being gripped" by the Word must involve a conviction as to its truth and a desire to obey.

29. Dooyeweerd, *In the Twilight of Western Thought*, 115, 120, 125.

30. Klooster, "Toward a Reformed Hermeneutic," 4.

31. Dooyeweerd, *In the Twilight of Western Thought*, 125.

32. 2 Tim. 3:16f.

33. For the correlation between meaning, implication, and application, recall what was said above in the second and third paragraphs of section I.A.

34. Matt. 4:4; 2 Tim. 3:16.

So as we return to the question of the place of Scripture in the organism of revelation, we find that the importance of the Spirit's work does not lie in any limitation of the *scopus* of Scripture, in addition to those limits noted earlier. Rather, the soteric function of Scripture is important in that it shows us how Scripture can have a primacy among the other forms of revelation, even while being in some ways dependent upon them. We must have continual recourse to Scripture, not only that we might be rightly informed of God's truth, but so that we may gain power to reform our ways of thinking and living. Scripture, rightly understood (with the inevitable help of general revelation!), can cut through our falsehood in a way that nothing else (even general revelation seen in the light of Scripture) can.

3. *Covenantal Status.* Scripture is also distinctive in that it is the constitution of the covenant between ourselves and God. Suzerainty covenants in the ancient Near East were governed by written documents. The document was authored by the "great king" and laid down as law before the "vassal king," the lesser king who became, by covenant, the servant of the great king. Kline[35] argues persuasively that written divine revelation should be viewed as falling under that genre, that Scripture is a "covenant document." As such, it is by Scripture, by the covenant document, that our faithfulness to the covenant is to be tested. To disobey the document is to violate the covenant, and vice versa. When God, through the prophets, conducts his "covenant lawsuit" against Israel, it is the treaty, the covenant document, that serves as the standard of judgment. Thus, the document has a special status: it is placed in the ark of the covenant, the holiest place in Israel. It is to be read publicly, to be taught to children, to govern all areas of community life.

Fundamental to the covenantal status of Scripture is its divine authorship. The covenant document, we recall, was authored by the great king himself, written in the first person. The same pattern is found in the Decalogue, which is, according to Kline, the first covenant document in Israel. So strongly does Scripture emphasize the divine authorship of the Decalogue that it is said to be "written with the finger of God."[36]

Whatever we may think of the details of Kline's argument, it certainly presents a useful model of scriptural revelation, emphasizing concerns that Reformed theology has always had about the divine authorship of Scripture and its unique office as the "supreme standard" of faith and life (stimulus paragraph). Nature does not have this kind of status. Although created and directed by God, it does not consist of words divinely authored. (Nature

---

35. Meredith G. Kline, *The Structure of Biblical Authority* (Grand Rapids: Eerdmans, 1972).

36. Ex. 31:18; cf. 24:12.

is governed by God's word, but it is not the word.) And nature is not our covenant document; Scripture is.

All our thought and life, therefore, must be tested by Scripture. Although general revelation aids us in interpreting Scripture, once we are assured of Scripture's teaching, that assurance ought to take precedence over any opinions gained from any other source.

Thus, the fact that general revelation helps us interpret Scripture, indeed that it often moves us to correct our interpretations of Scripture, does not make the two forms of revelation equivalent in function. To put the matter somewhat schematically: (a) Scripture does not correct general revelation, nor vice versa; the two are equally authoritative, equally true. (b) Scripture does often correct our *interpretation* of general revelation, but the reverse is also true. All our interpretations are subordinate to every form of divine revelation. (c) But there is also an important asymmetry: we must believe Scripture, even when it appears to contradict information available from other sources. We are not to accept information apparently derived from other sources that seem to us to contradict Scripture. Or, to put it more concisely: what we interpret as the teaching of Scripture must prevail, in event of conflict, over what we interpret as the teaching of general revelation. I am, of course, talking about *settled* interpretations. Certainly, information derived from general revelation can correct our interpretation of Scripture, as I have said earlier. But once we are convinced that Scripture teaches *x*, we must believe it, even if general revelation appears to teach *not-x*. This formulation is only an attempt to systematize the teaching of Romans 4 regarding the faith of Abraham. So far as Abraham could tell, the data of natural revelation (his great age, the condition of Sarah) rendered the divine promise impossible. Yet he believed the promise and was commended for his faith.

If, therefore, we try to maintain (a) and (b) without (c), we can make no meaningful distinction between walking by faith and walking by sight. Without (c), Scripture and general revelation are equivalent in function, and Scripture is in no unique sense the covenant document of the people of God. No distinction, then, becomes possible between the Word of God and the opinions of men, so far as their practical authority is concerned.

Therefore, when we formulate the doctrine of the sufficiency of Scripture, it is important to say that it contains all the divine norms we need for any area of life. This is not to say that Scripture contains all truth or all of God's revelation; it does not.[37] It is to say that only Scripture stands in this particular relation to our decisions.

---

37. I would say that the doctrine entails that every human obligation is an application of Scripture. Otherwise, no distinction could be made between divine doctrine and "commandments of men" (Matt. 15:9; see also Col. 2:22). This does not mean, however, that

The first point, then, regarding how Scripture rules human life in general, is that it functions interdependently with other forms of God's revelation, but with a primacy among them necessitated by the nature of God's redemptive covenant with his people.

B. Scripture and Sanctification

We noted earlier (I.A.2) that one aspect of Scripture's rule over us is its role as a locus of soteric power: we go to Scripture not only to gain information concerning God's will but also to receive strength to obey. But there is also another, seemingly opposite fact that must be noted about the relation between Scripture and sanctification: not only is Scripture necessary to our sanctification, but sanctification is necessary for a right use of Scripture. For a person to "prove what is the will of God," not only does he need the intellectual ability to relate the biblical message to his situation (I, above), but he also needs to offer his body as a living sacrifice, to be transformed by the renewing of his mind,[38] to live as a child of light,[39] to *love* in a way that abounds in knowledge.[40] According to Hebrews 5:11–14, the deeper truths of Scripture (in context, the Melchizedek priesthood) are available only to the spiritually mature "who by constant use have trained themselves to distinguish good from evil."[41] To properly apply Scripture, then, requires not only intellectual capacities, but moral and spiritual maturity as well. There is an inevitable circularity here: we go to Scripture in order to become more obedient, and as we become more obedient we come to understand Scripture better. How do we break into this circle? We don't; we enter the circle by the grace of regeneration, by the power of the Holy Spirit.[42]

C. The Richness of Scripture's Pedagogy

We have discussed the rule of Scripture in relation to other forms of revelation and in relationship to our growth in grace. At this point, we

---

our duty is exhausted by the specific, explicit injunctions of Scripture. As we have seen, application involves both scriptural and extrascriptural premises, since it seeks to relate Scripture to our situations.

38. Cf. Rom. 12:1f.

39. Cf. Eph. 5:8.

40. Cf. Phil. 1:9f.

41. Heb. 5:14 NIV.

42. Hence another good reason for saying that "heart knowledge" of God transcends theoretical problems (Dooyeweerd, *In the Twilight of Western Thought*, 120, 125). But none of this implies that theoretical knowledge of Scripture is irrelevant to, or unhelpful for, becoming obedient.

will focus more sharply on the language of Scripture to learn something of the *methods* by which God in Scripture instructs his people.

There has often been, I think, a tendency among us—both as theologians and as simple believers—to think of Scripture as containing only one type of language. We tend sometimes to read the Bible as if it consisted exclusively of propositional truths—bits of true information. (And yet we are not consistent: when in a different mood, we tend to read Scripture as a collection of ethical commands!) We know, of course, that Scripture does not consist only of one kind of language, but the usual goals of Bible study ([a.] ascertaining doctrinal truths, [b.] finding ethical principles) often lead us to read *as if* Scripture were all of one or two sorts. And our tendency to see theology exclusively as an academic or "theoretical" discipline has certainly not helped matters in this respect.[43]

In fact, of course, the variety of language in Scripture is rich indeed. Its grammatical moods include not only indicative and imperative, but also significant interrogatives[44] and exclamations.[45] Our God teaches us not only by informing, but also ("Socratically") by asking penetrating questions and by shouting us out of our complacency. The "illocutionary" and "perlocutionary" functions[46] of biblical language are manifold: asserting, commanding, but also questioning, expressing, promising,[47] praising, cursing, lamenting, confessing, instructing, edifying, comforting, amusing, and convicting. The literary genres, too, are varied: historical narrative, law, prophecy, poetry, proverb, romance, letter, and apocalypse. And many more specific things could be said under the category of *Formgeschichte*. We should also note what David Kelsey says about the many different ways in which Scripture may function in a theological argument.[48]

To speak of Scripture, therefore, as "propositional revelation" is misleading, although against the mystical concepts of revelation prevalent in our day it is important to stress that Scripture does have *some* propositional

43. My own (radical) suggestion is that we define theology simply as "the application of Scripture to all of life." Broad as this notion may be, I think it is virtually equivalent to the *didache*, *didaskalia* of the Pastoral Epistles.

44. Cf. Gen. 3:9; John 21:15; Rom. 6:1, 15; 7:1, 7, 13; etc.

45. Cf. Rom. 6:2: *me genoito!*

46. For this terminology, see J. L. Austin, *How to Do Things with Words* (Cambridge, MA: Harvard University Press, 1962).

47. Austin (see previous note) argues that a promise is not the same as an assertion. An assertion may predict that something will happen in the future, but a promise commits the speaker to accomplish what is promised.

48. David H. Kelsey, *The Uses of Scripture in Recent Theology* (Philadelphia: Fortress Press, 1975). My review of this book appears in *WTJ* 39, 2 (Spring 1977): 328–53, and as Appendix H of the present volume.

content.[49] And since we must consult the whole Bible to determine the propositional content of God's revelation, it is legitimate to say that all of Scripture is propositional in that it all has a propositional function; it all serves to inform us. But we should remember that the same can be said of the imperative, interrogative, and exclamatory functions: all Scripture binds our conduct, questions us, awakens us. All Scripture is a hymn of praise to our great God and Savior; all Scripture is the faithful response of redeemed sinners. All is law; all is prophecy; all is wisdom. Thus, although all Scripture is propositional in a sense, Scripture is far *more* than propositional.[50]

It will be important for evangelical theologians in the future to work out a concept of scriptural authority that does justice to this variety in biblical pedagogy. Too often our formulations make it sound as if acceptance of scriptural authority simply amounts to believing a certain set of propositions taught by Scripture. It is important for us to consider how not only the propositional function, but also the other functions of Scripture serve as "authority" for us. For instance, what does it mean to say that a poem or a psalm, let us say, is authoritative? Certainly, not merely that we should accept whatever propositional teaching can be extracted from an analysis of it. Somehow, there is a difference between an authoritative *poem* (a *canonical* poem) and other poems. Surely, the

49. Dooyeweerd rightly emphasizes the variety of content communicable in language (in Geehan, *Jerusalem and Athens*, 84f.). But I fail to understand why he finds it necessary to deny the existence in Scripture of "conceptual thought-contents." Or does he have some technical definition of *conceptual* that he has failed to share with the uninitiated reader? Clearly, in the usual sense, Scripture is quite full of "conceptual thought-contents."

50. The suzerainty-treaty pattern (above, I.A.3) illuminates this unity-in-diversity. Kline (*The Structure of Biblical Authority*) shows how the covenant structure necessarily includes history, law, curse, blessing, and administrative regulation. If Scripture is a covenant of this sort, we should expect such many-facetedness. Note also WCF 16.2, which stresses the different kinds of language in Scripture and the consequent variety in the human response solicited by it.

The other major criticism of "propositional revelation" in our circles is found, for example, in Zylstra, "Thy Word Our Life," 67. There, Zylstra argues against "*rationalistic propositionalism*" (emphasis his), which holds, he says, that Scripture contains "*verbal statements that are true in and of themselves.*" As often, Zylstra's language is a bit too obscure to do his point justice. (One wants to know: is "Washington is the capital of the United States" such a statement? If not, what is? Are there any? If the Washington statement is the type of thing that Zylstra is speaking of, what prevents statements of this kind from being in the Bible?) The discussion is clarified somewhat when Zylstra quotes from Zuidema, who argues against "prying off a text from the whole." Apparently, "rationalistic propositionalism" is the view that biblical sentences can be adequately interpreted with no regard to their context. Well, perhaps there is some danger of this among us; the reader can judge for himself.

authoritative poems are to become the songs of our hearts, are to rule our inner life in some peculiar way. Much more work needs to be done on this kind of question.

II. SCRIPTURE AS A RULE FOR HUMAN REASONING

To avoid trespassing on ground to be covered by other papers in this series (and to avoid getting beyond my depth!), let me define *reason* in a simple, quasi-dictionary fashion: "A person's capacity for forming judgments, conclusions, and inferences." *Reasoning*, then, will be the process of forming those judgments, conclusions, and inferences. So understood, reasoning is a part of life, and therefore we have been talking about it implicitly all along in this paper. What remains is to make explicit the applications of the preceding generalities to the specific topic of human reason.

The word *reason*, as defined above, does not appear in English translations of Scripture (any more than does the word *Trinity* or phrases such as *personal God* and *Christian labor union*). Yet it is evident that Scripture addresses the subject. First, as we have argued, Scripture addresses, redemptively, all of human life, and reason is part of that.[51] Second, Scripture has much to say about human qualities and activities that presuppose and involve the ability to reason: wisdom, teaching, discernment, and so forth.[52] Third, Scripture commands actions that involve making judgments, conclusions, and inferences: obeying, understanding the word, loving others as Jesus loved us, and so on.[53] Fourth, Scripture itself contains any number of judgments, conclusions, and inferences that it calls us to accept.[54] To accept these is in itself a rational activity—a forming of a judgment, conclusion, and inference. To say these things is *not* to say that Scripture is *primarily* concerned with reasoning, or that the "rationality" of Scripture is its most important quality. Scripture is not "qualified by the analytical aspect," to use Dooyeweerdian language.[55] But it is concerned with human

51. Cf. the discussion of *scopus* above, I.A.1.

52. These qualities are not merely rational; they involve elements other than reason, but they do involve reason.

53. See II.A, below.

54. Thus, in a sense, we are called to "think God's thoughts after him." Why Dooyeweerd objects to this idea is utterly beyond me. See Geehan, *Jerusalem and Athens*, 84.

55. I get the impression that when someone says, for example, that Scripture is "rational," those trained in the cosmonomic philosophy immediately assume that he is asserting what they would call an "analytic qualification" to Scripture. This is the only assumption by which I can make any sense at all out of Dooyeweerd's and Knudsen's articles in

reasoning, as it is concerned with everything we do before God. Let me summarize some of the important applications of Scripture to the rational enterprise under two headings: first, the status, and second, the practice, of human reasoning.

A. The Status of Reason

1. *Its Importance.*

(a) Reasoning pervades human life. The forming of judgments, conclusions, and inferences is not limited to academic or theoretical activities.[56] It does not occur only when we are composing syllogisms, nor is it limited to *thinking,* if by the term we mean puzzling ourselves about some problem or other. For example, we often form judgments, unconsciously or subconsciously. A woman sees a military officer coming toward her front door with a solemn expression on his face, and she concludes immediately that he has brought bad news about her soldier husband. This is reasoning—drawing a conclusion by inference from data. It may very well be excellent reasoning, but there is no period of inward dialogue, no making of a syllogism. A football quarterback sees a telltale movement in the defensive backfield, and he moves instinctively to avoid the defensive play that he knows is coming. This, too, is reasoning. He has formed a conclusion by inference. But there is nothing academic about it; it is more like a reflex mechanism, but a mechanism inwrought by much training and study of the game. We call such a person an "intelligent" quarterback, but such intelligence is different from the intelligence one hears in a lecture hall.[57]

Reasoning, therefore, is something that everyone does, in every area of life. It is certainly not limited to those who have studied logic or epistemology. Those disciplines seek to map only *some* of the conditions that distinguish good from bad reasoning.[58] Reasoning is so pervasive because it

---

Geehan, *Jerusalem and Athens,* or out of John C. Vander Stelt's *Philosophy and Scripture* (Marlton, NJ: Mack Publishing, 1978). But if so, then the cosmonomic thinkers are guilty of enormous and culpable misunderstanding. No one except a Dooyeweerdian would ever dream of using a mere adjective to express a "modal qualification." In fact, no one but a Dooyeweerdian would believe that there are such things as modal qualifications. It is totally without justification for cosmonomists to read their own idiosyncratic technical meanings into the words of people who obviously hadn't the slightest intent of using them that way.

56. Cf. J. M. Spier, *An Introduction to Christian Philosophy* (Philadelphia: Presbyterian and Reformed, 1954), 71ff.

57. One could argue that a lecture-hall type of intelligence presupposes the ability to react to stimuli intelligently.

58. Some, not all. See below, II.A.2.e.

is involved every time we respond voluntarily to a situation in our experience. Thus, our response to Scripture inevitably involves reasoning. When I seek to obey Scripture, for example, by showing more love to Christian brothers and sisters in my church, I do this because (consciously or not) I have reached the *conclusion* that such activity is a proper application of Scripture. (Scripture does not tell me specifically to love Mr. Jones; my obligation to love Mr. Jones is a conclusion based on inference.[59])

(b) Scripture demands a rational response.[60] Since *any* voluntary response to Scripture involves reasoning (good or bad), we must say that Scripture requires a rational response. The alternative is to claim that Scripture requires no voluntary response at all. Furthermore, since Scripture demands a *proper* response, we conclude that it requires of us not only reasoning, but good reasoning. Reasoning is a crucial aspect of our responsibility before God. God *cares* that we make the right judgments, conclusions, and inferences; he cares about this because he cares about our *obedience.* Reason has its limitations and its dangers, as we will see, and from those dangers some have concluded that it is somehow impious to apply human reason to the things of God.[61] Surely our use of reason must be responsible—subject to God's lordship. But to deny altogether the legitimacy of reasoning from scriptural data is to deny the legitimacy of obedience, for it is to deny the application of Scripture to the world in which we seek to obey the Lord. Irrationalism is not pious; it is ungodly, satanic. God *commands* us to apply his Word to our world;[62] and in doing so he commands us to reason and to reason well. That is the basic point: reasoning is part of obedience.

In addition, it is also worth noting that Scripture contains a great many arguments, reasonings, that it expects us to appreciate. But it is not only these that demand a rational response; it is the whole Bible. Thus, the position of WCF 1.6, which finds the "whole counsel of God" not only in the express statements of Scripture, but also in what may be deduced from Scripture by "good and necessary consequence," is

59. We saw earlier (I.A) how every application of Scripture, every act of obedience, involves some extrascriptural knowledge.

60. Again, the response is "rational," but not "merely rational" or "primarily rational."

61. It is interesting that Van Til, criticized in cosmonomic circles for being something of a rationalist, is also applauded in other circles for being opposed to the use of reason in religious matters. See my review of William White Jr., *Van Til, Defender of the Faith* (Nashville: Thomas Nelson, 1979), in *WTJ* 42, 1 (Fall 1979): 198–203. But neither rationalism nor fideism is to be applauded. We must seek to avoid both through a careful and biblical delineation of the powers and limits of reason. And for that task, Van Til's writings are immensely helpful.

62. We saw earlier (I.A) how every application of Scripture, every act of obedience, involves some extrascriptural knowledge.

inescapable. Our obligation before God consists not of the bare words of Scripture, but of the *bearing*, the *application* that these words have upon our decisions.

If anyone objects that this principle exalts human wisdom (e.g., humanly formulated laws of logic) to the status of divine revelation, I would repeat what I said earlier,[63] that *every* obedient response to Scripture involves a knowledge of creation and of self, as well as a knowledge of Scripture. This fact does not erase the "primacy" of Scripture.[64] Scripture retains the prerogative to judge any system of logic that we use to interpret it. But we must face the fact that whenever we use the Bible, some human reasoning is involved.

2. *Its Limitations.* Since reasoning is part of life, part of our total responsibility before God, it is never something "neutral." As a part of human life, reasoning is something that we can do in a godly or an ungodly way, obediently or disobediently, competently or incompetently. Such sciences as logic, mathematics, and epistemology may usefully be classified as "ethical" sciences,[65] for they seek to help us determine what we *ought* (ethical *ought*) to believe, granted certain data or certain other beliefs. But we must also say that not only the conclusions, but also the premises, the presuppositions, the starting points of these sciences are subject to ethical—ultimately religious—evaluation.

The idea that human reason, or at least the "laws of logic," is a neutral, even infallible basis for human decision-making is an idea that dies hard. Doubtless, it will be discussed and criticized often in this series of papers. Here, however, it would be wise to remind ourselves briefly of various specific limits on the ultimacy, the powers, and the reliability of reason in general and logic in particular. (a) The law of noncontradiction is "necessary" only to those who acknowledge a practical ("ethical") necessity to think logically.[66] (b) Logic presupposes that those using it are able to agree on the nature of and criteria for truth and falsity, but these concepts are controversial, and religiously so. The agreement to say that "*p* may not be both true and false in the same respect and at the same time" is a formal (and thus in an important sense meaningless) agreement unless there is agreement on the meaning of *true* and *false*. (c) The disciplines of mathematics and logic, far from consisting of tru-

---

63. Above, I.A.
64. Above, I.A.3.
65. Of course, this is not the only helpful or legitimate way to classify them.
66. Cf. Arthur Frank Holmes, *All Truth Is God's Truth* (Grand Rapids: Eerdmans, 1977), 87f.

isms, are riddled with controversy.[67] (d) No one has succeeded in justifying induction from within the discipline of logic, yet all nondeductive reasoning presupposes it.[68] (e) We do not know all the "laws of logic." In fact our systems fail to account for many everyday forms of inference (such as the examples above under II.A.1[a].[69] (f) The discovery of one fact apparently contrary to one's belief, or even an apparent contradiction within that belief, does not serve to refute it. When faced with such a challenge, one may simply treat it as a "problem" to be worked out within one's already-existing system of thought. One cannot specify in precise terms *how much* unresolved discrepancy will, or ought to, cause someone to reject a belief. The point at which "refutation" occurs will depend greatly upon practical, personal—even religious—factors.[70] And generally, such discrepancy will produce modifications in one's position rather than abandonment of it. (g) The conclusion of a syllogism is true only if its premises are true; thus, logical rigor in itself never guarantees truth. And our knowledge of the truth of premises is always conditioned by our fallibility.[71] (h) The principle of noncontradiction states that "A is A and not non-A *at the same time and in the same respect.*" Thus, it is limited in its application to aspects of reality that are unchanging.[72] (i) Logical syllogisms generally require some restatement of an argument, some translation from ordinary language into the technical language of logic. There are acknowledged discrepancies that enter here: the logical *if-then* (material implication), for example, is generally not equivalent to the use of *if-then* in ordinary language. Thus, an otherwise adequate argument may fail by inadequately translating the ordinary language that it purports to test.

Thus, it is evident that we do not find in human reason alone, even in logic, an infallible criterion of truth that might compete with Scripture as our ultimate covenant rule. Scripture, indeed, must be seen to rule over our reasoning, as over every other aspect of life.

67. Ibid., 92. Cf. Vern Poythress, "A Biblical View of Mathematics," in *Foundations of Christian Scholarship*, ed. Gary North (Vallecito, CA: Ross House, 1976), 159–88. See also his treatment of logic in *Philosophy, Science and the Sovereignty of God* (Nutley, NJ: Presbyterian and Reformed, 1976), 199–205.

68. Cf. Nicholas Wolterstorff, *Reason within the Bounds of Religion* (Grand Rapids: Eerdmans, 1976), 34–36.

69. Cf. Gilbert Ryle, "Formal and Informal Logic," in his *Dilemmas* (Cambridge: Cambridge University Press, 1954), 111–29.

70. Cf. Thomas S. Kuhn, *The Structure of Scientific Revolutions* (Chicago: University of Chicago Press, 1970).

71. Holmes, *All Truth Is God's Truth*, 90f.

72. Ibid., 89f.

B. The Practice of Reason

How does Scripture rule our reasoning? As it rules all of life. Let us refer back to the principles discussed under I above.

1. *The Organism of Revelation*. We get the premises of our argument, as well as the principles of reasoning, by a godly, obedient correlation between Scripture, the world, and ourselves, with Scripture having "covenantal primacy." The triad "Scripture, world, and self" corresponds roughly, not perfectly, to the epistemological triad "law, object, and subject."[73] The correlation is imperfect because, as we have seen, we discover laws (of thought and life) by *correlating* Scripture, world, and self, and we learn of objects and subjects similarly. Indeed, every item of experience functions in all three ways, as law, object, and subject. Everything has a law-function, since any such item may be involved in an application of Scripture to a situation (God expects us to take account of, and thus to be governed by, all that is, to the extent that this is possible for us). Everything has an object-function, since everything (in experience, again) is a possible object of knowledge. And everything in experience has a subject-function, because it is *my* experience, part of my inner life. Items of experience, then, can be seen from what I would call "normative, situational, and existential perspectives." But no item functions in only one or two perspectives; each functions in all three.[74] Without normativity, an item cannot be understood; without objectivity, it cannot be real; without subjectivity, it cannot be known.

This triadic scheme illuminates some ways in which epistemologists have tried to justify the holding of a belief: (a) by showing that that belief follows from a sound application of the laws governing reasoning, (b) by showing that the belief "corresponds to reality" (often conceived in empirical terms), (c) by showing that the belief is subjectively satisfactory, that it leaves one at peace, with no further inclination to question. Some have attempted to reduce two of these to the third. (a) It can be argued that law is fundamental, since "correspondence" and "satisfaction" presuppose *criteria* for correspondence and satisfaction. (b) It can be argued that correspondence is fundamental, since "law" and "satisfaction" are suitable criteria only to the extent that they are grounded in *reality*. (c) It can be

---

73. Spier, *Introduction to Christian Philosophy*, 125ff. His argument that knowing involves not only subject and object but also law I find cogent and important. Cf. my previous comments on knowing as an ethico-religious response to revelation.

74. Thus, we are saved from various philosophical dilemmas, such as the tendency in secular philosophy either to absorb all reality into the self or to lose the self altogether in a quest for "objectivity."

argued that satisfaction is primary, since we *acknowledge* only those "laws" and alleged "correspondences" that leave us satisfied.

But if we assume the teaching of Scripture and of Calvin concerning the interdependence between our knowledge of God's law, the creation, and ourselves, we do not need to elevate any of the three perspectives above the others. Since God has established all three and established them in a coherent, wise order, we can start with any perspective, as long as we do not neglect the principles emphasized by the others. We can justify our beliefs by reference to God's laws for thought, as long as we recognize that these must be applied to the creation and to ourselves. We can justify our beliefs by reference to the objectivity of creation, as long as we accept God's criteria for objectivity and recognize the problematics of approaching that objective world through a fallible subjectivity. And we can justify our beliefs subjectively, as long as we recognize God's criteria for legitimate subjective satisfaction and the fact that we are not alone in God's world.

Thus, our reasoning, as all of life, is founded on the full richness of God's organic revelation: law, object, and subject interpenetrate and interpret one another. But we should also note that here, as in the rest of life, Scripture is primary. From one point of view, Scripture is a rather small "item." From the normative perspective, it is only part of the "organism of revelation" by which we determine our obligations. From the situational perspective, it is only one part of creation. From the existential perspective, it is only one item of our subjective experience. Yet it is, in each case, the definitive part. As I said earlier, our settled beliefs about Scripture's teaching (however influenced those beliefs may be by extrascriptural knowledge) must prevail, in the event of conflict, over beliefs drawn from any other source. As this is the case in all of life, it is the case in the area of reasoning. And so when Scripture teaches that human reasoning is subject to God's law, that it is subject to the fallibilities of sin and finitude, that God and his plan are incomprehensible, then it is to be believed. Scripture is not a textbook of logic any more than it is a textbook of biology or geology, but what it says about logic and reasoning in general must be respected.

2. *Sanctification.* The subjective basis of reasoning ("existential perspective," above) underscores the important fact that one cannot reason or understand unless he has the capacity to do so. One cannot see unless he has "eyes to see." One cannot, therefore, make adequate use of the organism of revelation unless he is subjectively qualified by virtue of regeneration and sanctification. And growth in sanctification leads to a more adequate use of revelation. What of the unregenerate? Are they unable to reason at

all? Scripture speaks of them both as "knowing God"[75] and as "not knowing God."[76] To distinguish adequately between their "knowledge" and their "ignorance" would take up too much space here. Their knowledge, at least, is an ironic, paradoxical sort of knowledge-in-ignorance that exists only by virtue of God's common grace, which restrains the effects of sin. We are, however, considering reason as it *ought* to operate, that is, regenerately.

I should, however, address this question: are the most sanctified people always the best reasoners? No. (a) Because sanctification is not the only factor bearing upon reason. A person's intelligence, his access to data, his education and training, his experience in reasoning all play a role as well. (b) Because sanctification bears on all areas of human life, not only reasoning. And it affects these areas of life sometimes unevenly; a person may show his holiness by helping the poor, while not being as faithful in other areas of life. Yet sanctification *can* be an epistemological advantage because it opens our eyes to relate our experience to God.

3. *Richness of Pedagogy.* Scripture teaches us about reason by describing (at least implicitly) the importance, limits, and practice of reason (above), by providing examples of godly reasoning to govern our thought, and in many other ways. Remember the examples of "informal logic" cited earlier (II.A.1[a]): the woman observing the soldier and the quarterback observing the defensive players. In Scripture, not only does God want us to draw conclusions from arguments, from propositional teaching; he also wants us to respond rationally to poems, to parables, to the events described in the narratives. And he wants us to recognize the multiplicity of uses to which Scripture can (rationally) be put. This point is of hermeneutical importance. The allegory of Hagar and Sarah (Gal. 4:21–31) is baffling if we believe the OT story is written only to inform us of a significant event. But no; God also gave us that story as an illustration of NT truth. That, too, is a legitimate use of Scripture, a use by which people can be taught, by which their understanding can be illumined.

The richness of Scripture's pedagogy also implies that to apprehend what Scripture teaches, we need *all* our faculties—not only logical skills, but imagination, emotional empathy with the text, the will to obey, and so forth. We need these faculties if we are to respond rightly (and therefore "rationally") to all the richness of Scripture.[77]

75. Rom. 1:21.
76. 2 Thess. 1:8.
77. "Emotion" and "intellect" are mutually dependent—for example, if I had no emotional reactions to the issues about which I am writing, it is unlikely that I would form any

III. REASONING ABOUT SCRIPTURE

Having discussed some points about Scripture and about reasoning, I will now state a few conclusions of a "hermeneutical" sort concerning the role of reason in the use of Scripture. Much of this has been said already, but it ought to be stated here so that all the questions in the "stimulus paragraph" will be explicitly addressed, if not adequately answered. The outline will parallel that in II.

First, there can be no question that reason has a legitimate application to Scripture. To say that there is something wrong about drawing inferences from Scripture is to deny that Scripture can be *used*, that it can be *applied* to our situations, that it can be *obeyed*. Obedience always involves (consciously or unconsciously) a rational correlation between the words of Scripture and some present human decision.

Still, we must remember that human reason is limited, fallible. We do make mistakes in our use of Scripture as well as in everything else. And in one sense the limits of reasoning are especially evident when we seek to apply it to Scripture, for God is incomprehensible; his thoughts are not our thoughts; his understanding is unsearchable.[78] I assume that the papers on the subject "Thinking about God" will consider the problems involved here, so I will say little more. We should recognize, however, that historically theologians have found it difficult to speak of God without at least "apparent contradiction."

My own conclusion (argued more fully elsewhere[79]) is that we must simply "hang loose" to our current standards of what is logical or rational, that we must, in reasoning about God, be especially sensitive to the limitations of our logic, opening ourselves even more than usual to catch the practical "informal logic" of Scripture's teachings. When our logical deductions lead to more and more flagrant "apparent contradictions," when they lead us to deny things that are plainly taught in Scripture, then we should "back off," acknowledge an unresolved "problem,"[80] and direct our thinking elsewhere until we get a new insight. But such problems must

opinions or even think the project worth spending time on.

78. Cf. Isa. 55:8; Rom. 11:33.

79. Cf. my "The Problem of Theological Paradox," in North, *Foundations of Christian Scholarship*, 295–330. Also published as a pamphlet, *Van Til: The Theologian* (Phillipsburg, NJ: Pilgrim, 1976).

80. Cf. above, II.A.2(f). An apparent contradiction does not always render a doctrinal formulation useless. It is useful to note the "informal logic" by which the biblical writers use doctrines (such as divine sovereignty and human responsibility) that often seem contradictory to us. We may seek to employ, e.g., the doctrine of divine sovereignty in contexts similar to those in which the biblical writers used it without necessarily being able to reconcile

never lead us to abandon (if such a thing were even possible) the use of logic altogether in the appropriation of Scripture. To abandon logic is to abandon our responsibility before God.

We gain a rational understanding of Scripture in the same way we gain a rational understanding of anything else: by correlating Scripture, world, and self (and thus law, object, and subject); by receiving from the Holy Spirit the grace to understand; and by recognizing the richness of scriptural pedagogy and the corresponding richness of the response demanded (a response of the whole person, involving all his capacities).[81] Scripture has the primacy even here, even in its own interpretation (*Scriptura ipsius interpres*). But this primacy is not threatened by the use of reason if our reasoning is carried out in a godly way.

---

it with human responsibility. A contextually limited use may be a possible answer (either temporarily or permanently) in such cases.

81. Note above under 11.3.3 for a hermeneutical application of this point.

REVIEW OF RICHARD MULLER, *THE STUDY OF THEOLOGY*[1]

Note: In this review, I interact with Richard Muller's view of theology. Muller is a prominent Reformed historian of doctrine whose work in that field I respect greatly. But I think his view of theology is inadequate in that he tries to assimilate it to a concept of history that itself is not fully biblical. This discussion will supplement chapter 5 of the present volume, which deals with revelation and history, and chapter 37, which deals with theology.

Richard Muller is certainly one of the most impressive scholars writing today in the fields of history of doctrine and systematic theology. Therefore, news that he has addressed the question of theological method properly arouses our expectations. In some respects, this book did not disappoint me: it is learned and erudite; it provides a useful compendium of much ancient and recent wisdom on the subject; and there is very little in it with which I literally disagree. On the whole, however, I found the book deeply unsatisfactory, for reasons that will appear later.

The book is important, both in its achievements and in its shortcomings. Positively, it formulates, more concisely and clearly than ever before, the thinking that underlies much (possibly most) evangelical and Reformed theology in our time—a pattern of thinking that is arguably very different

1. Richard A. Muller, *The Study of Theology: From Biblical Interpretation to Contemporary Formulation*, Foundations of Contemporary Interpretation 7 (Grand Rapids: Zondervan, 1991). This review originally appeared in *WTJ* 56, 1 (Spring 1994): 438–42. Used by permission. For stylistic purposes, this appendix has been copyedited for inclusion in this volume.

from the pattern that was dominant fifty years ago. Negatively, the book's weaknesses reveal potentially fatal flaws in that theological mentality and therefore hard questions that every contemporary Reformed or evangelical theologian must ask.

But first, we must see what Muller wants to tell us. He begins by posing the much-discussed question of the relation of theory to practice in preparation for the ministry. As a foil, he presents the extreme view of one unnamed recent DMin graduate (I will call him "Elmer," for I want to refer to him from time to time) who scorned all theoretical, academic study, and who complimented his DMin program because it required "no theological speculation, no ivory-tower critical thinking, no retreat from the nitty-gritty of daily ministry" (p. vii). In contrast, Muller notes his own seven-year experience in the pastorate, in which "everything I had learned both in seminary and in graduate school had been of use to me in my ministry" (p. viii). How, then, can we show that the traditional academic disciplines really are relevant to the pastoral ministry? Or should we simply abandon those disciplines, as Elmer would prefer?

Muller thinks we can best answer these questions by carefully reviewing the nature of the traditional fourfold theological curriculum: biblical, historical, systematic, and practical theology. Like E. D. Hirsch, Allan Bloom, and others in the field of general education, Muller advocates in theological education a renewed appreciation of traditional models and content, not only to create a better-informed clergy, but also as a means of forming character (pp. xiii–xiv).

Elmer might be rather scandalized at the suggestion that academic theological study builds character. We will have to follow the argument; but first more questions. Muller points out that the traditional curriculum is also under stress in our time because of the proliferation of subdisciplines and because of wide differences (especially since the Enlightenment) about history, hermeneutics, and method, as well as doctrine. Those problems, too, are on his agenda.

Some potential solutions exist in recent volumes on theology written by Gerhard Ebeling, Edward Farley, and Wolfhart Pannenberg. Ebeling, according to Muller, sacrifices the unity of theology because of his unwillingness to exclude options that he deems to be open questions in the present discussion (p. 45). Farley finds the unity of theology only in the student, and the goal of theology not in the impartation of a definite content, but in the "shaping of human beings under an ideal" (p. 50). Pannenberg, however, reminds us of the importance of objective historical content and scientific method. Muller's response to these positions is to seek a balance between objective study and subjective character formation, without sacrificing the unity of the discipline (pp. 40–41, 60). We will see that his theological method is, as we might expect from his past writings, strongly influenced by the method of historical study. It is this kind of careful study, he believes, that generates the best in contemporary theological formulation and pastoral character.[2]

He analyzes, in turn, the four major theological disciplines in order to show the path "from biblical interpretation to contemporary formulation" (to cite his subtitle). In biblical studies (where he considers himself only a "dabbler at best" [p. xvii]) he emphasizes the importance of reading the text in its original setting "to place us as readers of the text into the milieu of its authors" (p. 68). This principle forbids us, for example, to assume that the monogenēs of John 1:14, 18 "stands as a direct reference" to inter-Trinitarian relationships, or to read "image of God" in Genesis 1:27 as a reference to Christ or to human virtues (p. 66), at least in the "basic interpretation" or "primary exegetical reading" (p. 74) of the text. It is also wrong, he says, to read Psalm 2:7 "in terms of an inter-Trinitarian begetting or even in terms of the New Testament application of the text to Christ (Heb. 1:5) if done at a primary level of interpretation" (p. 66).[3] Such interpretations would not, he says, have occurred to the original authors or readers, and therefore they are not historically responsible. Further, such interpretations fail to allow the Scriptures to speak for themselves, to rule over our dogmatic formulations (p. 81).

Therefore, if we want a right understanding of the NT, we must read the OT "separately" (p. 71), not as if it were "interpretatively subordinate in all its statements to the New Testament" (p. 73). Indeed, it must be studied "critically as a pre-Christian and, therefore, to a certain extent non-Christian body of literature" (ibid.). Nor should the NT be "understood as the second of two books that God once wrote." Rather, it should be understood as part of an "unbroken stream of writings extending from the Old Testament through the so-called Intertestamental Period, and followed historically by an unbroken stream of writings extending from the last book of the New Testament down to the present" (p. 79). Muller does affirm the canonical status of our Bible, distinct in that respect from the rest of the "unbroken stream" of

---

2. I would advise the reader to look first at the appendix (pp. 41–60), which analyzes the books of Ebeling, Farley, and Pannenberg, and only after that to read the main body of chapter 1 (pp. 19–41). That way, one can make more sense out of the references to the three theologians in the main body of the chapter. If Muller were to rewrite the book, I would suggest to him that the material in the appendix be integrated with the main body of the chapter, toward the beginning.

3. For some other examples, see discussions beginning on pages 132 and 190.

writings (pp. 81–82). But that status is justified by objective historical analysis of the entire stream.

Biblical theology as such considers "the unity and larger implication" of the biblical materials and thus "joins biblical study to the other theological disciplines" (p. 85). Over against systematic theology, it addresses "the religion of the Bible on its own terms" (p. 86), "free from the encumbrances of later dogmatic language" (p. 92). Such study can "point critically and constructively toward contemporary systematic and practical theology *precisely because* it is constructed biblically and historically without reference to the structures of churchly dogmatics" (pp. 94–95).

Church history and the history of doctrine also, in Muller's view, should be seen as in some sense independent of dogmatics: "at least for our times, the historical investigation must precede the doctrinal statement and in fact supply the information from which the doctrinal statement takes its shape and on which it rests" (p. 99). His example: It is doctrinally arguable to attribute the accurate preservation of the text of Scripture to divine providence. Historical investigation cannot, however, rest content with the doctrinal explanation but must look to the process of the transmission of the text and examine the techniques and procedures of the Masoretes, the monastic calligraphers of the church, and the scholarly editors of later centuries, and find in the actual practice of these people the historical grounds for arguing whether or not the text has been accurately preserved.

The historian of doctrine is not to "evaluate in any ultimate sense the rightness or wrongness of Arius' views" (ibid.). "A dogmatic reading of the materials that assumes the rightness of Nicea on the basis of some contemporary orthodoxy will entirely miss the full significance of the council" (p. 100). Some of the church fathers, ignoring this rule, produced "incredibly theologically biased interpretations" (p. 102), such as the triumphalism of Eusebius of Caesarea and Augustine's identification of the institutional church with the "city of God." Objective historical study corrects such bias.

Objective history also helps us to see the differences between biblical content and later formulations. Presbyterian church government, says Muller, owes more to the structure of Swiss cantons than to the NT, from which little of a definitive nature can be gathered on that subject (p. 104). And the formulations of Anselm and the Reformers concerning the atonement owe much to the doctrinal concerns of the later church. Although substitutionary atonement is "firmly rooted in Scripture," there are other "equally biblical" views ("ransom from bondage to the powers of the world," "the free gift of reconciling love through the loving example of Christ"). The Protestant churches adopted the penal substitutionary view because it was "a perfect corollary of the doctrine of justification through faith alone" (p. 107). Thus we learn how doctrines are formulated, and we learn how to participate in the process. Character is developed as we understand and come to join the unfinished task, as we come to understand our "roots" (pp. 107–8).

Such historical study extends to the history of religions. Although specialists in the history of religion tend to relativize the claims of Christianity, the discipline can perform useful service for Christian theology. For instance, the triumph of Christianity in the ancient world can be better understood once we understand the mystery religions and other rivals that Christianity had to overcome (p. 115).

Systematic theology is "the broadest usage for the contemporary task of gathering together the elements of our faith into a coherent whole" (p. 124). It is "oriented to the question of contemporary validity," and therefore must consider philosophical and apologetic issues (p. 125). Dogmatic theology is a subdivision of systematics, which is "the contemporary exposition of the great doctrines of the church" (p. 127). Again, Muller emphasizes the unilateral priority of biblical and historical theology to systematics: the latter "is a result, not a premise of the other disciplines" (p. 129). Nevertheless, there is a "churchly hermeneutical circle" (ibid.) that finds "closure" in dogmatics and therefore "returns, via the tradition, to the text and provides a set of theological boundary-concepts for the continuing work of theology" (p. 130). Nevertheless, we must not use a doctrinal construction as "a key" to Scripture so that "the scriptural Word becomes stifled by a human a priori" (ibid.). In this connection he takes to task the many "centrisms" of theology: Barth's Christomonism, the modernists' use of "God is love" to the exclusion of other divine attributes, and so on.

Philosophy is useful to the work of systematic theology. "Philosophical theology can be defined as the philosophical discussion of topics held in common by theology and philosophy" (p. 138). This discipline, "in order to be true to itself, must not utilize Scripture or churchly standards of truth: it rests on the truths of logic and reason—and occupies the ground of what has typically been called 'natural theology'" (p. 139).[4] Nevertheless, philosophical theology, "so long as it stands within the circle of the theological encyclopedia, must be a Christian discipline, no matter how philosophically determined its contents" (p. 141). Christian without Christian "standards of truth"? Yes, in the sense that it is limited to topics of concern to Christian theology.

---

4. Cf. p. 140: "Philosophical theology . . . is the only one of the subdisciplines grouped together as 'systematic theology' the structure of which is determined by a nontheological discipline."

Philosophy of religion is distinct from philosophical theology, though there is overlap. Philosophical theology "provides a logical and rational check on dogmatic formulation. Philosophy of religion, by way of contrast, considers the nature of religion itself a focus that it shares with the phenomenology of religion" (p. 139).[5]

Ethics is "the translation of the materials of Christian teaching . . . into the contemporary life situation of the community of belief, first as principles and then as enactments" (p. 147). As such, Muller thinks, it is distinct from doctrinal theology (p. 146).

In his discussion of apologetics, he recognizes with the presuppositional school that that discipline "rests on the presupposition of faith or belief,"[6] while "its actual content must be dictated as much by the circumstances of the argument as by the content of the message." And as it rests on faith, it in turn influences theological formulation (p. 151).

As we might expect, Muller's interest in practical theology is mainly to emphasize its theological character. While it is not the case that theory "absolutely precedes practice" (p. 156), nevertheless practical theology must refer back to theological truths. Unlike secular psychology, for example, pastoral counseling must ask about the "soul" (p. 158).

Contemporary formulations of theology, then, must be aware of the whole sweep of history from the biblical period down to the present. Muller's example here is the distinction between natural and supernatural (particularly natural and supernatural revelation). Comparative religion shows that in many faiths God is manifested everywhere, not merely in supernatural interventions (pp. 166–67). The progress of science also indicates the futility of limiting God's activity to the miraculous, for many things that once seemed miraculous can be given natural explanations (pp. 167–68). We can, nevertheless, distinguish "between an original, generalized revelation of the divine, grounded in the divine presence in and through all things, and a subsequent, special and gracious revelation of the divine, specific to a single religion, distinguishing it from all others, and understood as the completion and fulfillment of the original revelation, in and for a particular community of belief" (p. 169). Thus, we can recognize truth in all religions without sacrificing the distinctiveness of the Christian gospel.

5. I suspect that in this quote there should be a comma or colon following "itself." I have quoted it as it is in the book.

6. Cf. his later comment, "there is no question that the 'presuppositional' approach to theology carries the day against a purely 'evidential' approach" (p. 213). While there are rational proofs and evidences, "the rational proofs and the historical or empirical evidences are seldom if ever the reason for belief" (p. 214).

The fourth and final chapter of the book deals with "The Unity of Theological Discourse." There is unity, first, between "objectivity and subjectivity." Here Muller points out that "theology has never been a purely academic discipline" (p. 174). The major theologians have always been active in the work of the church. The very looseness with which they sometimes cite Scripture indicates that they were less interested in academic precision than in *using* the text practically (pp. 176–77). Further, the enormous difficulties involved in defining theology as a "science"[7] suggest that we should pay closer attention to the "subjective side of theology," which "arises in an individual in community," and note "that the ongoing historical life of the community is necessary to the mediation of objective statements of doctrine, as significant statements, to individuals" (pp. 183–84). He emphasizes that "theology arises and becomes significant in this corporate context of belief and interpretation" (p. 184). This emphasis on subjectivity need not compromise the scientific character of theology, for science in general "has long since set aside the illusion of 'detached objectivity' in scientific inquiry." Indeed, "there is arguably a prejudgment concerning significance in the initial identification and selection of data." There are no "brute facts" (p. 185).

This discussion of the interpenetration of objectivity and subjectivity prepares us for Muller's more extended treatment of "hermeneutical circles." Circularity exists between subject and object, and between whole and part. We should come to an individual Scripture passage with an understanding of the whole, specifically of the "genre" of the book to which it belongs (pp. 188–89). Further, we must bring to exegesis all our understanding of the book's linguistic, historical, cultural, and social context (p. 190), and the "restraints" of "source, form, redaction, rhetorical, and canon criticism," recognizing, of course, that "each of these critical approaches supplements the others and provides some checks on them" (p. 194). And despite its perils, there is no way to escape an element of "personal involvement," which influences our use of a text (p. 196).

Muller notes that although at an earlier point, in considering the Johannine prologue, he rejected the assumption "of the Nicene language as a presupposition to interpretation," nevertheless, there are historical reasons why this passage played a significant role in the later Trinitarian discussion, not the least "that logos-language was crucial to the contextualization of the gospel in the second century" (p. 200). That historical development "becomes an important element in the subsequent interpretative work of

---

7. His critique of Hodge here on pages 179–81 parallels my own in some respects. See my *DKG*, 77–81.

understanding the text in our present context" (p. 201). Thus, the Nicene Trinitarian doctrine does after all, in some ways, properly influence our understanding of John 1.

Thus, the interpretative "whole" includes "contextualization," bringing the Christian message to bear upon the various cultural situations of the present day. Contextualization has always occurred, but in recent times it has, for historical reasons, been done with greater self-consciousness. Again, Muller refers to "atonement theory" for examples. The various "approaches to atonement" in the NT are "not to be viewed as mutually exclusive, nor are they to be viewed as easily harmonizable into a single theory" (p. 205). The theorizing of Irenaeus, Anselm, and others represents contextualizations understandable in the light of their historical situations. Contextualization is "the completion of the hermeneutical circle in our own persons and in the context of present-day existence" (p. 211).

The book concludes with an "epilogue" describing the beneficial effects of theological study upon human character. Such education is "spiritually uplifting"; it inculcates "wisdom concerning human nature"; it is "a way of life as well as a pattern of thought" (p. 215). The study of theology communicates "values—values to be believed and values to be acted upon" (p. 216). Further, study of the doctrinal materials of the church reveals "the cultural and social relativity of the documents," which serves "to press us toward our own statement of these corporately held values, insofar as we recognize both the limitation of the particular cultural form and the ultimacy of the values expressed under it" (p. 217).

Elmer must learn that his anti-intellectualism is counterproductive in the church's effort to proclaim the truth relevantly and practically. Facile invocations of the supposed absolute contrasts between "Hebrew and Greek thought" and between "heart and head" in opposition to academic learning are untenable (p. 217). A pastor must be "a bearer of culture," not merely, as Elmer sought to be, a "technician or operations manager." Otherwise, his people will be "spiritually impoverished" (p. 219).

In book reviews, I do not usually exposit a text in such detail, but in view of the importance of the book, and in view of the nature of my criticisms, I wanted the reader in this case to hear Muller, as much as possible, in his own words. Muller seeks to achieve some very delicate balances of emphasis, which need to be heard. In view of those delicate balances, it is indeed possible that my criticism will misread him. In fact, I think that any critic will find this book a minefield (as well as a treasure field!). As I read, I found that most of the criticisms that occurred to me were answered, at least in passing, at some point in the book. I suspect that critics who attack this book in a superficial way will often experience backfire—the critique reflecting unfavorably upon the critic.

With this caveat I must, nevertheless, proceed to evaluation. I would first reiterate that in many ways this is a fine book, and one can learn from it a great deal about the history and method of theology. Doubtless there is much here, too, that will encourage those who are swimming against the tide of modern culture, trying to maintain the traditional disciplines of theological learning. However, I find the book to be confused, or at least confusing, in three important areas represented by the following distinctions: priority/circularity, description/normativity, and theory/practice.

1. PRIORITY AND CIRCULARITY

I must say that until my reading reached about page 127, I was fully prepared to give Muller an introductory lecture on hermeneutical circularity! Until that point, his entire emphasis is on the unilateral priority of one discipline over another. There is the unilateral priority of synchronic exegesis over diachronic: we must not read inter-Trinitarian relationships into Psalm 2 or Christ into Genesis 1:27, because exegesis must restrict itself to what would have occurred to the original readers. Indeed, the OT must be read as a "pre-Christian" or even "non-Christian" text (p. 73). And there is the unilateral priority of biblical theology to systematics: biblical theology must never be encumbered with dogmatic language (p. 92). We must not find Trinitarian distinctions in John 1, any more than in Psalm 2. And there is the priority of historical theology to dogmatics: church history must not proceed with doctrinal preconceptions; it may not even evaluate the rightness or wrongness of the theological views it describes (p. 99). Systematics is a result, not a premise, of the other disciplines (p. 129). Even philosophical theology has a unilateral priority over systematics in one respect: it "must not utilize Scripture or churchly standards of truth: it rests on the truths of logic and reason" (p. 139).[8] Certainly, there is some truth in these statements: most theologians can supply additional examples of exegesis distorted by the "reading in" of later dogmatic concepts, or where truth is stifled by the imposition of a "human a priori." But is it not going a bit far to say that the OT must be read as a "pre-Christian" or "non-Christian" book? Perhaps Muller understands the connotations of these phrases differently from the way that I do, but I find them entirely

8. He also says that philosophical theology is a "Christian discipline," but only (so far as I can determine in context) in the limitation of its subject matter to Christian concerns.

inappropriate. Are we to say that the early Christians and the early church misread the OT when they claimed it testified of Christ? Was Athanasius wrong about John 1? Was Calvin wrong about substitutionary atonement? Must philosophical theology really be religiously neutral?

These, of course, are only "preliminary criticisms." For we must immediately note Muller's attempts at balance. For one thing, the above priorities are guarded by some rather vague qualifications. The monogenēs of John 1 does not stand "as a direct reference" to inter-Trinitarian relationships (p. 66). Well, might it possibly stand as an *indirect* reference? And what, precisely, is the difference between a direct and an indirect reference? We suspect that this distinction is important, for through some such distinction we may be able to account for the church's traditional Christological use of the text. But Muller doesn't explain it. Similarly, Genesis 1:27 does not refer to Christ or to human virtues as its "basic interpretation" or on a "primary exegetical reading." Well, what about nonbasic interpretations, or secondary exegetical readings? And what are those? Or what about the implicit distinction between "primary" and "secondary" "levels of interpretation" on page 66? And if the OT may not be "interpretatively subordinate in all its statements to the New Testament," may it, perhaps, be interpretatively subordinate in *some* of its statements?

But of course Muller does, from about page 127 on,[9] bring the concept of a hermeneutical circle to central prominence. Indeed, he does say that once hermeneutics issues in dogmatic formulations, it "returns, via the tradition, to the text and provides a set of theological boundary-concepts for the continuing work of theology" (p. 130). We may, for example, at some level in our exegesis, make use of the fact that the Johannine prologue led to Nicea through various historical circumstances (p. 201). To use one of Muller's favorite terms, there is a historical "trajectory"[10] linking John to Nicea.

But that is still awfully vague. Just how is this fact to be used in exegesis, without violating Muller's earlier strictures? We have a fairly clear idea what is to be done at level one, but what of level two? This is tremendously important, for preaching and theological writing are generally not level-one enterprises. Historically (and this begins in the NT), the church has preached Christ from OT texts, and has defended its dogmatic statements from both Testaments. Muller doesn't seem to want to say that this was all

9. There are a few earlier hints (see pp. xvi–xvii, 33, 61, where he emphasizes that the four theological disciplines are interdependent, not neatly separable), but most of his detailed discussion belies this claim; systematics, for example, seems to be dependent on exegesis, but not at all the reverse.

10. Cf. pp. 62, 79, 82, 85, 96, 108.

a mistake. But if it is not a mistake, how is it to be justified, and how is it to be done? If Muller's approach provides us no way to do this, and if through that failure it in effect calls such preaching and teaching into question, perhaps we will have to conclude that it is not the church's practice but Muller's metatheology that is flawed at a fundamental level.

One might try to find an answer in Muller's concept of the circular relation between "whole and part": since the OT is part of a larger whole, the Christian canon, we may legitimately read Psalm 2 Christologically. But that is to misconstrue Muller's position. His concept of "whole" does not seem to be applied to the canon as a totality. He coordinates "whole" with "genre" (pp. 188–89), and of course, the entire canon doesn't fit into any particular genre. His "wholes" would seem to be particular books of the Bible, or at most groups of books with common genre. Nor does it seem that we can relate John 1 to the Nicene Trinitarianism by any kind of whole-part relation.

Or is the circularity between "object and subject" more relevant to our question? On that basis we might say that the interpreter, who is himself a believer in the Trinity, cannot, finally, forget that belief when he is exegeting Psalm 2. Nor can he forget that the NT itself reads Psalm 2 Christologically. Thus, he is constrained to find an interpretation of Psalm 2 that is consistent with that NT usage. I would accept that justification for Christological exegesis of the OT; but I cannot imagine that Muller would, after all he has said against that sort of procedure. Similarly with John 1.

What Muller seems to have in mind in the case of John 1 (although here I am especially unsure that I am rightly interpreting him; I am somewhat reading between the lines, expanding his "hints") is something like this (cf. pp. 200–201): John 1 refers only to Jesus' filial consciousness in relation to God as Father and has no Trinitarian implication. However, the second-century apologists used the *logos* terminology to account for universal divine revelation, and they needed then to make a distinction between God immanent and God transcendent, God in himself and God in his revelation. Thus we have a God who is one, yet diverse in some way. Since *logos* is identified with Christ in John 1, it was natural for Christ's relationship with the Father to be understood in this pattern. Thus the text was read as teaching the Nicene Trinitarian relationships. We cannot really turn back the clock by reversing the church's decision, so we should simply accept the Nicene episode as part of our own history and try to build on it.

Now, certainly the church did use *logos* as Muller says, and his explanation for the prominence of this text in Trinitarian theology is plausible. But was the church *right*? That is a very important question. I think it was, because I disagree with Muller's "first level" exegesis. John 1 makes an equation between God, the creative Word of Genesis 1, and Jesus Christ, and also distinguishes God from the Word. The church's Trinitarian use of the passage was not only justifiable in the light of historical circumstances; it was *right*. What is Muller's verdict? Perhaps he will feel that I am asking the wrong question, but I honestly think my question is the most important one that can be asked at this point. Was the church *right*? From what I can make of Muller's analysis, he would have to say, respectfully, that it was wrong, though what it did was somehow historically justifiable. Should we continue to honor its mistake simply to avoid trying to "turn back the clock"? Muller seems to say yes. But the Reformers became famous for correcting mistakes made by earlier theologians; can we do less? It does seem to me that the logic of Muller's view, adding a bit of the Reformers' zeal for truth, is that we should abandon the use of John 1 to prove the doctrine of the Trinity, if indeed we are to maintain the doctrine of the Trinity at all. And if I am confused, I believe it is Muller who has confused me.

I prefer a method that is more self-consciously circular. Certainly, the possible legitimate uses[11] of Psalm 2 or John 1 were not all known to the original authors, and of course, it is a useful exercise to ask how the original authors might have explained the passages. But they were known to the divine author (about which more must be said later). And what the human authors wrote had legitimate implications, interpretations, and applications beyond what they were able to grasp. Those applications fully justified the uses of those texts by later biblical writers and by the ecumenical councils. The goal of exegesis is to find not "how the original authors would have expounded their writings," but rather "the applications which are justified by the texts." When exegesis observes that norm, it is saved both from eisegesis and from triviality.

In other ways, too, Muller seems to be unclear on the implications of hermeneutical circularity. His statement that philosophical theology "must not utilize Scripture or churchly standards of truth: it rests on the truths of logic and reason" (p. 139) is horrendous. I am amazed that such an intelligent writer can pen a sentence like that while endorsing presuppositional apologetics! The whole point of presuppositional apologetics, a biblical point in my view, is that in *all* areas of life we must "utilize Scripture [and] churchly standards of truth." There are no other legitimate standards. Nor is there any legitimate use of "logic and reason" that is not itself subject to

---

11. Here the correlation of *meaning* and *use* or *application* becomes useful; see my *DKG*, 81–85, 93–100.

scriptural standards of rationality. Indeed, this statement (together with his general approach to "first level exegesis") is inconsistent with his emphasis on page 185 that there is no "detached objectivity" or "brute facts." But so far as I can tell, Muller is not even a little bit aware of the tension (to say the least) in his book between unilateral priorities and hermeneutical circularity. I confess I can only express bafflement.

2. DESCRIPTION AND NORMATIVITY

David Hume taught that you cannot deduce *ought* from *is*. Now, in a Christian epistemology, the matter is not quite that simple. The very fact of God's existence is a normative (as well as a descriptive) fact. The fact that God commands something implies that those addressed are obliged to carry out that command. The reason is that God, simply because he is God, is worthy of all obedience. And since God reveals himself in creation as well as Scripture, one may gain normative (Rom. 1:32) as well as descriptive data from the creation.

That having been said, it is nevertheless important for the theologian to account for the normative force of his teachings. It certainly cannot be assumed, for example, that a description of various historic events or views will yield normative conclusions. We cannot decide our theology by counting noses among the Puritans, or the Reformers, or the nineteenth-century American Presbyterians, or some other favored group. Nor can we assume that because some view has been endorsed by a church council or has otherwise gained a following among Christians, we have an obligation to agree with it. *Sola Scriptura* means that the only ultimate norm for theology is the teaching of Scripture. Other norms must justify themselves by their faithfulness to the inspired Word.

Theologians such as Muller who put a heavy emphasis on historical method run the risk of jumping from description to norm without adequate justification. When reading G. C. Berkouwer, I have often found myself lost among the citations and historical comparisons, wondering exactly what he is recommending as normative content and why. We have already seen this problem in Muller, for the question of circularity in theological method is ultimately the question of authority, of norm. The ultimate presupposition of the Christian interpreter, as he enters the hermeneutical circle, is the presupposition of God's revealed norms. But if that presupposition is compromised by supposed norms that are not themselves given by divine revelation—Muller's "logic and reason," for instance—then the relation of description to norm becomes confused. As we have seen, for example, Muller refuses or neglects to ask the important normative question, whether the early church was *right* in its Trinitarian exegesis.

Muller seems at least to assimilate the whole work of theology to a historical-descriptive model. His "first level" exegesis is essentially a work of historical investigation. Studying the NT is a study of that "unbroken stream of writings extending from the OT through the so-called Intertestamental Period, and followed historically by an unbroken stream of writings down to the present" (p. 79). It requires study of the culture of the times, the different religious groupings that competed with Christianity, the various tendencies in the early church, and so on. This study essentially continues the "historical model introduced in our discussion of the Old Testament" (ibid.).

Now, Muller does not ignore the fact that the canon is unique and authoritative. This is one example of the "delicate balance" of the book. He notes that "these historical issues and the problems they raise for interpretation stand in a constant tension with the doctrinally and dogmatically precise canon of the New Testament in which we have the closest and clearest witness to Jesus Christ as Savior and Redeemer" (p. 81). But how is this "tension" to be resolved? The answer seems to be through reiteration of the historical model. It is "historical understanding" that, though it does not "give us the canon of the New Testament," nevertheless "does offer a basis for grasping first historically and then theologically the significance of the canon" (p. 82). Remember his principle that "without historical and critical understanding, the tendency to overlook differences of approach [among the Synoptics] and to find a theological common denominator— typical of later orthodox dogmatics—becomes all too easily the norm for interpretation, and the New Testament can no longer critique our theology" (ibid.).

Historical study is the "first level" of exegesis, and everything else (I assume, without consideration of the hermeneutical circle, for Muller tends to emphasize unilateral priority in such contexts) must be based on that. So we begin with a historiography that is religiously *neutral* (this is not his term, but I do not see how we can avoid using it as the clearest way to characterize his view), not based on Christian presuppositions. On that basis, we establish the significance of the canon. Then we can make theological use of it. But why should we assume that this objective, neutral historiography is normative? Why should that be the bedrock upon which we must build our exegesis and theology, indeed upon which Scripture itself as canon is built?

Muller does affirm the unique authority of Scripture. I state this point with some vagueness, as he does. Whether he would affirm "inerrancy" in some sense, I do not know. He tends to take the issue of biblical authority rather casually—far too much so in view of its intrinsic importance and in view of the present theological climate. He says rather flippantly concerning the NT, "Nor can it be understood as the second of two books that God once wrote" (p. 79). I will assume in charity that addition of the word *merely* to this sentence would better reflect his thought.[12]

In response to Farley, who rejects the traditional fourfold curriculum on the ground that it presupposes biblical inspiration, Muller says that "we do not have to invoke classic orthodox doctrines like the inspiration, infallibility, and divine authority of Scripture at this point: in the context of the question, such doctrines do not amount to proofs in any case" (p. 97). Rather, all we need is to point out that the books of the canon have a "qualitatively different effect" on the Christian community than do noncanonical documents. Well, maybe so. But should not something more be said, lest the reader gain the impression that these doctrines are entirely inconsequential?

He does invoke the Scripture principle of the Reformation—without notable enthusiasm (pp. 131, 172; but cf. vii)—and he does, as we have seen, present his history-oriented methodology as a means of allowing Scripture (so interpreted) to "rule" our theology. On the other hand, he recommends source, form, redaction, rhetorical, and canon criticism (p. 194) without any critique of how these disciplines are commonly practiced today. His discussions of Farley, Ebeling, and Pannenberg, too, reflect no sense at all of Kuyperian "antithesis." He never even hints in the direction of the great gulf that Machen and Van Til found between the orthodox Reformed faith and the dominant forces in modern theology. He makes it plain that, although he may differ with modern theologians in this or that detail or emphasis, he is essentially playing the same game that they are.

It is hard to sort all of this out, amid Muller's careful balancing of motifs. But the sum of it seems to be something like this: yes, Scripture is uniquely normative, but that really does not make much difference to the concrete work of theology. Scriptural authority is our dogmatic confession, but we must not allow it to interfere with the purely historical work of theological

---

12. The same casual attitude toward Christian doctrine is reflected in his treatment of divine providence on pages 99 and 117–18. Yes, he says in effect, divine providence does guide history, but what the historian wants to know are the specific natural causes of events. I do not doubt that historians want and need to know the latter, but I do not think we should use this consideration virtually to make providence a historical irrelevancy. But Muller has nothing positive and specific to say about providence as a factor with which the historian must deal in his work.

understanding and formulation. That norm must, in any case, be discovered and justified by neutral, objective history. Therefore, that neutral historical method is our actual *working* norm.

If indeed this is his view, and I find nothing in the book to contradict it, then I must say that I think it is seriously wrong. "Neutral, objective history" is a totally illegitimate notion within the context of a Christian epistemology. Thus, it certainly is not the basis of biblical authority. Scripture is authoritative because it is inspired by God. On page 186, Muller mentions inspiration as the source of biblical authority, but characteristically rather shrugs it off:

> The reason that Scripture is authoritative—apart from our traditional doctrinal statements concerning its divine inspiration and its authority as a doctrinal norm—is that its contents are mirrored in the life of the church and that, in this historical process of reflection, the believing community has gradually identified as canon the books that rightly guide and reflect its faith while setting aside those books that fail to reflect its faith adequately.

That seems to be his regular stance toward matters of biblical inspiration and authority: yes, fine; but other things are more important for theological method. Nowhere in the book does he suggest that the inspiration of Scripture, its uniquely divine authorship, has any implications at all for the work of theology.

Again, I am appalled. The inspiration of Scripture is not an incidental matter, nor is it a mere confessional datum that we can set aside in the practical work of theological formulation. If indeed we have a divinely inspired Bible, then that is a fact of overwhelming importance for theology and for every other area of life. It is more important than any other fact that Muller brings to bear upon the work of theology. That fact implies that we cannot exegete Scripture in the same way that we exegete other texts (even when the general rules of exegesis have been reformed by the Word). Not only the intention of the human author, but (especially!) the intention of the divine author must guide our interpretation.[13] And our concepts of history, culture, logic, reason, and critical thought must all be reconsidered in the light of scriptural teachings. With sadness, I must say that there is not a trace of this emphasis in Muller's book.

And as to his use of Ebeling and others, let me say that I can sympathize with evangelical theologians who do not want to be marginalized,

---

13. *God-Centered Biblical Interpretation* (Phillipsburg, NJ: P&R Publishing, 1999), by Vern Poythress, provides wonderful insight into these matters.

who do not want to be stigmatized as "fundamentalists" and therefore excluded from the mainstream of modern theological discussion. In charity, I will credit them with the motive of wanting to be "salt and light," not of coveting "academic respectability" for its own sake. Nor do I think that we have to disagree with every sentence that Ebeling, for example, writes. On the other hand, although the lines seem fuzzier today than when Machen and Van Til wrote, their critique is far from irrelevant to the theologians of the 1990s. There is still an enormous difference between theologians who submit their reasoning to the Word of God and so-called theologians (however prominent) who do the reverse. It may be that to bear the offense of the cross today, Bible-believing theologians will have to accept marginalization as part of the (relatively small in our day) cost of discipleship. I do hope not. But at least this is not the time to confuse readers about the nature of our stance. Those who are confused or confusing about this matter will not be salt and light, but will have to accept partial responsibility for the continued drift of modern thought away from biblical norms.

3. THEORY AND PRACTICE

As I read the book, I tried to put myself in Elmer's shoes. Would Elmer have been persuaded or helped by Muller's argument? Of course, Muller portrays Elmer as being rather oafish; perhaps the real Elmer was unteachable. But he was at least intelligent enough to earn a DMin degree at a school that had Richard Muller on the faculty, so he cannot have been brain-dead. And in any case, I know of others who are intelligent enough, and who have some knowledge of culture and historical theology, who nevertheless echo Elmer's sentiments.

There is a real problem today as to the applicability of the "traditional fourfold curriculum" to the pastorate, and we must not brush that problem aside as mere anti-intellectual laziness. We can, of course, understand why Muller himself, in his seven-year pastoral experience, found his studies so useful. He is a very gifted scholar and communicator. He has the eyes to see the present relevance of historical events and the words to teach that relevance vividly to others. And he ministers in a denomination that has traditionally cultivated a large appreciation for gifts of that sort. But there are others, not necessarily stupid or culturally ignorant, who have had very different experiences.

There is a lot of Elmer in me. Muller would probably recognize me as a "bearer of culture," from my general education at Princeton and Yale and my very traditional theological studies at Westminster Seminary in Philadelphia (1961–64). I have never been the full-time pastor of a church, but I have done much preaching, teaching, and counseling over the years, and much of that has been disappointing in its effects. When I returned to Westminster in a teaching capacity in 1968, Jay Adams had been added to the faculty and was developing his concept of "nouthetic counseling." Without getting into detailed evaluation of this concept, I must say that I was delighted (and a bit envious) to see how students like me, without great gifts for interpersonal ministry, nevertheless found themselves "competent to counsel" by following Adams' methods. Nouthetic counseling is a theological concept, but it is also a set of techniques. And it has seemed to me that students at Westminster have needed to learn more, not fewer, "techniques." I have known a good number of bright, well-educated, cultured men who have been shipwrecked in the pastorate because they never learned "how-to's." And I have known others who have turned failure into success by learning a few techniques.

Muller tends to deplore the modern emphasis on "technique" at the expense of classical learning. My view is that both are valuable for pastors. Therefore, hard choices have to be made. Ideally, I have often thought, a seminary degree should require four or even five years. But the economics of the situation will not permit that. So how do we seek balance? I do not get much help from Muller in answering that question. He is so busy fighting for the maintenance of classical learning that he does not bother to wrestle with the hard questions of curriculum design. He is like a congressman fighting for the needs of his own district who has no time—or heart—for considering the overall national welfare.

Nor will I try to answer those questions here. But surely here, as in every other perplexity, we need to seek God's wisdom. What does the Bible say about the nature of training for the pastorate? Scripture does, after all, have much to say about wisdom, the knowledge of God, revelation, and the office of pastor-teacher. My own view is that while Scripture values the special gifts of intellectuals such as Isaiah, Luke, and Paul, it does not require such gifts of all teaching elders. The biblical qualifications for elders are mainly ethical and spiritual, with some emphasis on the ability to teach. Certainly, the latter requires some "head knowledge." But the heavy emphasis of Muller on being a "bearer of culture" seems oddly out of sync with the NT.[14]

14. It is rather amusing, too, that although Muller tells us to be "bearers of culture," he also echoes the fashionable "contextualization" rhetoric about how we must not, in missions, seek to impose Western culture on the rest of the world (p. 202). Well, what culture

In my view, the church ought to encourage a "learned ministry," up to a point. But there is danger here. Was the Presbyterian Church correct, in the early nineteenth century, to insist upon an educated ministry, thereby in effect conceding the frontier to the Methodists and Baptists (not to mention others, including secularists)? Should the churches of the Third World be denied pastors from among their own people until some of their number complete a university education? Consideration of such questions, along with the biblical data noted earlier, shows, I think, that however desirable a cultured ministry may be (especially in some situations), that goal must in general be secondary to others. There are people without Muller's kind of learning (or at least without a great deal of it) who are nevertheless biblically qualified for the pastorate.

Certainly, hard, careful academic study can build character (though it does not always do this). But any kind of disciplined activity can build character (even the mastery of techniques). And it would be slanderous to claim that no one can have a good pastoral character without the experience of classical learning. Even if there are character traits that can be acquired *only* through classical learning, is it self-evident that these particular traits are required for the Christian ministry? So the "character-building" standard does not automatically answer the hard curricular question.

Again, Muller's approach greatly disappoints me. He does not even touch upon the question of biblical qualifications for eldership, nor upon the biblical doctrines of knowledge and wisdom. He comes across as a cultural conservative, nostalgic for the good old days, recalling (I imagine) the time when ministers could sit around smoking pipes and discussing Chaucer, Aristotle, or Duns Scotus, reassuring their people that they had a certain intellectual depth that overshadowed any mere technical incompetence. Some people do find that an appealing scene. But such cultural conservatism is a frail reed. As we have seen in Muller's case, it easily makes common cause with cultural and theological liberalism; for academic scholarly types, even those of conservative temperament, tend to want to follow all the latest intellectual trends. Whatever happened to the Calvinist *semper reformanda*—the passion to reform all of life under the Word of God? How can that be reconciled with a merely conservative defense of the status quo?

And people such as Elmer, who, however uncultured they may be, have a passion for the care of souls, will not find the arguments of such conservatism very weighty. What *ought* to move Elmer (note how we keep returning

---

does he expect Western missionaries to be "bearers" of? Chinese? And if we are to be bearers of our own Western culture, how can we avoid being accused of "imposing" it on others?

to the issue of normativity) is a biblical analysis of covenant wisdom and a theological exposition of how God uses extraordinary intellectual and spiritual gifts.[15]

I wish I did not have to be so negative about this book. I approached it with very positive anticipations. But I have reluctantly come to see it, for all its wealth of information, balance, and general cogency, as part of the problem, rather than as part of the solution. Some initial readers of this review article have suggested that my positive comments on the book sound rather hollow in the light of my severe criticisms, but those positive comments are quite sincere. This is an erudite and informative book, and, point by point, there is little that I can literally disagree with. I have quoted the few statements that are very disagreeable to me. But even where I have criticized Muller, I find some value in the points he is trying to make. Certainly, for example, we should not naively read OT concepts as if they were NT concepts, or NT teachings as if they were identical to the statements of the later creeds. On all of that, Muller is right. There are both continuities and discontinuities throughout the history of redemption, and these must be sorted out. But Muller's book is less than the sum of its parts. He overstates the discontinuities and then brings in the continuities (too little, too late) without intelligibly relating them to what he has said before.

Similarly, he is right that classical learning can develop character. But he presents this point without any reasonable sense of proportion, so that the reader will tend to write off this potentially valuable point as the expression of hidebound intellectualism.

Thus, the faults of the book are largely (but not entirely) faults of omission and emphasis. I usually discount criticism based on omission and emphasis, since no author can be expected to say and emphasize everything relevant to his subject. But there are always some things that must be said and said loudly, lest the entire picture be falsified. Omitting the vast implications of biblical inspiration in a book dealing with theological method, of all things, is no small error.[16]

---

15. Some of my own thoughts on the nature of ministerial preparation can be found in "Proposal for a New Seminary," *JPP* 2, 1 (Winter 1978): 10–17. This article was republished with some revision as "Case Study: Proposals for a New North American Mode," in *Missions and Theological Education in World Perspective*, ed. Harvie M. Conn and Samuel F. Rowen (Farmington, MI: Associates of Urbanus, 1984), 369–86. It is also available, under its original title, at http://www.frame-poythress.org.

16. My reaction to Muller's book mirrors my reaction to Hessel Bouma et al., *Christian Faith, Health and Medical Practice* (Grand Rapids: Eerdmans, 1989), a book that arises from the same cultural and theological milieu. My review of it was published in *Christian Renewal* (June 18, 1990): 16–17 (now available at www.frame-poythress.org). I must say that these

I hope that readers will also learn some broader lessons from this encounter with Muller. (1) There are dangers in traditionalism as well as in liberalism, and many of those dangers are the same in both cases. (2) "History," unless carefully defined in the light of Scripture, is not a suitable master-model for theological method. (3) We should overcome objections to "techniques" that are based mainly on snobbish or traditionalist prejudices.[17] One great theological challenge of our time is to bring the new ecclesiastical techniques captive to Christ's word.

---

and other writings (recall my earlier reference to Berkouwer) seem to indicate a trend, rather than peculiarities of individual authors. That trend in my view is unfortunate.

17. Nor should we object to "techniques" simply because of the sovereignty of God. In Scripture, divine sovereignty and human responsibility are not opposed. God accomplishes his great work through our faithful service, and in that service we must seek to use the best methods available.

DOOYEWEERD AND THE WORD OF GOD

Note: In the early 1970s, I was involved in some theological battles with disciples of the great Dutch Christian philosopher Herman Dooyeweerd. These disciples had founded the Institute for Christian Studies (ICS) in Toronto, Canada. They held conferences throughout North America and published books and papers. Under the influence of this movement, a number of our students at Westminster Seminary, Philadelphia, where I taught at the time, attacked traditional Reformed theology as "scholastic," "dualist," and so on, especially because of our teaching concerning the Bible. Other ICS-influenced zealots tried to influence other Christian organizations (schools, churches, seminaries) to follow their lead.

I took issue with the ICS teaching, particularly about the word of God, but also more broadly.[1] The following four articles deal with various aspects of this controversy. "The Word of God in the Cosmonomic Philosophy" was published in the *Presbyterian Guardian* in 1972. The second article, also from the *Guardian*, consists of notes taken by the *Guardian*'s editor, the Rev. John Mitchell, of a lecture I gave; the notes are accurate. In that lecture, I was trying to present a positive view of Scripture, as I interacted with Association for the Advancement of Christian Scholarship (AACS) formulations.

1. See my booklet *The Amsterdam Philosophy*, available at http://www.frame-poythress .org/frame_books/1972Amsterdam.htm.

392

Dr. Bernard Zylstra of the ICS was gracious enough to respond to me, and so the third article here is my reply to him. The fourth article, "Toronto, Reformed Orthodoxy, and the Word of God," appeared in *Vanguard*, the publication of the AACS, which supported the ICS position. After that paper, there was a kind of truce: we more or less agreed to disagree. They toned down their militant rhetoric, as did I, and the atmosphere quieted. There were not many attempts after that by the ICS people to disrupt institutions that were committed to traditional Reformed views. This discussion supplements the discussions in the present volume on the nature of the word of God (chap. 8), its relation to God (chaps. 8–11), and its relationship to Scripture (chaps. 14–41).

"THE WORD OF GOD IN THE COSMONOMIC PHILOSOPHY"—PART ONE[2]

The "philosophy of the cosmonomic idea," first formulated in the 1920s by Herman Dooyeweerd and his associates at the Free University of Amsterdam, has in the last few years become a popular movement in Reformed circles in North America.

Organizations such as the Association for the Advancement of Christian Scholarship (AACS), the Institute for Christian Studies in Toronto, and the National Association for Christian Political Action (NACPA) have been formed to study, revise, and apply the insights of this philosophy to various areas of human life. This movement has also become influential in older Christian organizations, such as the National Union of Christian Schools, and has attracted some enthusiastic followers in the Christian Reformed Church and the Orthodox Presbyterian Church.

Serious criticisms, however, have been raised against many of the distinctive teachings of this philosophy, and perhaps the most serious have been directed toward the "cosmonomic" view of the word of God.

2. This paper was published in two parts in *Guardian* (October 1972): 123–25, and (November 1972): 140–42. Used by permission. For stylistic purposes, this appendix has been copyedited for inclusion in this volume.

This article will attempt to discuss some of these issues in a popular, though hopefully not oversimplified, way. We should keep in mind at the outset that not everyone in the AACS, for example, would accept all the views here attributed to the cosmonomic philosophy. Nevertheless, it is clear that a general consensus has developed in the movement. Published works from members of the circle never deviate very far from the position I will attempt to describe.

THE WORD AS EVENT

Dooyeweerd is fond of emphasizing "the distinction between the word of God in its full and actual reality and in its restricted sense as the object of theoretical thought."[3] We must ask first of all, what is that "word of God in its full and actual reality"? This concept is not altogether clear to me, but certain things may be said about it.

1. The Word to Man's Heart

The word in its "full" sense is addressed to the *heart* of man, not merely to his intellect, senses, aesthetic sensitivity, or any other "aspect" of man's nature.[4] It strikes the very core of one's being and determines the overall direction of one's life. Paul Schrotenboer, one of the leading American "cosmonomists," says:

> God does not just give us rules for this and that; He gives us a law word that directs the entire life of man. God's word does not direct itself to one or other action or situation but it directs itself to man's heart and it takes in the entire creation.[5]

It is certainly scriptural to say, as these men do, that the word addresses man's *heart* and effects *comprehensive change* in our life-direction. I doubt very much, however, whether the Bible justifies such a severe split between comprehensive direction and "rules for this and that," as Schrotenboer envisages.

3. Herman Dooyeweerd, *In the Twilight of Western Thought* (Nutley, NJ: Craig Press, 1968), 143.

4. Ibid., 136; cf. 42, 125.

5. Paul G. Schrotenboer, "Orthodoxy and the Bible," *CalCon* (February 21, 28, 1972): 1, 3. Cf. Arnold H. De Graaf and Calvin Seerveld, *Understanding the Scriptures* (Toronto: Association for the Advancement of Christian Scholarship, 1968), 98, 29, passim.

God's speech, according to Scripture, does make a comprehensive demand on human life (e.g., Deut. 6:4f.; 1 Cor. 10:31). But it also makes many *detailed* demands (e.g., Ex. 21–23; 1 Cor. 16:1f.). These detailed demands are not in conflict with the comprehensive demand; on the contrary, they are manifestations of it. It is true enough, of course, that "God does not *just* give us rules for this and that"; but to say that "God's word does not direct itself to one or other action or situation" is going too far and places an arbitrary restriction upon the relevance of God's word.

2. THE WORD AS PROCESS

The word in its "full" sense is an *event, a process*—the total process by which God's word reaches the heart of man.[6] Prophetic utterance, biblical inscripturation, preaching, the testimony of the natural world—all of these are *elements* in the process, but none is the *complete* process. These, therefore, are the "word of God" only in a secondary and derivative sense.[7]

Again, I must question the scripturality of this construction. It is true, no doubt, that such a "process" of revelation exists. But Scripture rarely puts any particular emphasis on it, and it rarely if ever designates such a process as "word of God," let alone making this process the word par excellence.

In Scripture, we should remember, the term *revelation* is rarely used to describe divine-human communication. In general, the God of Scripture is not a God who "reveals himself"; he is a God who *speaks*. He is a God who speaks *words*, and those words may be heard or not heard, obeyed or ignored, by man. Therefore, when God speaks to man, there may or may not be a "process of revelation" by which God's words take root in the human heart. If man ignores or rejects the word, there is no "revelation-event"; but in such a case the word remains the word! The word remains powerful to judge the rebellion of that man.

The point is that Scripture does not elevate any "event of revelation" to the position of word par excellence. God's words are God's words, whether they are part of a total "process" or not. His spoken

6. Schrotenboer, "Orthodoxy and the Bible," in *CalCon*, 1, 4; 2, 3. ("We will not understand the many thousands of words in the Bible unless we see the One Word, God-in-his-coming-to-me." In an unpublished discussion paper, "The Bible as the Word of God," 17ff., Schrotenboer expounds on the proposition that "revelation is process.")

7. Schrotenboer, "The Bible as the Word of God," 6, 178.

words, written words, prophetic words—all have an equal status on a scriptural view. It is true that these words all point "beyond themselves" in a sense to the one who speaks them and to their divinely ordained purpose. But that fact does not make them the word in a "secondary or derivative" sense.

3. THE WORD AS POWER

Further, on the cosmonomic view this "word-as-event" is conceived of as a "power."[8] This is understandable, for it is precisely the event by which *changes* are wrought in the heart of man (and the rest of creation, too). Members of this school of thought do not often refer to Christians as those who "believe" or "obey" the Word of God; they prefer to speak of them as those "in the grip of"[9] or "directed by"[10] the word.

These latter expressions are more indicative of the "powerful" character of the word. The emphasis is a scriptural one. But in this philosophy it is often not properly balanced by a corresponding emphasis upon the *meaning* of the word. The word of God according to Scripture, after all, is not a *blind* power. The power of the word is the power of God's *language*: its "effects" are the effects of language.

God's creatures obey his *commands*, believe his *statements*, trust his *promises*, rebel against his *directives*, reject his *expressions* of love, and so on (cf. Ps. 119). Christians, furthermore, are not "gripped" by the Word as if by some irrational force. They *hear* the Word, *believe* it, *trust* it, *obey* it.

These are scriptural ways of talking, and the lack of emphasis upon them in the cosmonomic philosophy is disturbing. In many liberal theological movements today, there is the tendency precisely to see God's word as a "blind power"—a power that "affects" us, even when the language itself may be false. We could wish that the cosmonomic thinkers would use language better calculated to avoid confusion with such false modernistic teachings.

8. Dooyeweerd, *In the Twilight of Western Thought*, 42, 125, 136, 144; Schrotenboer, "Orthodoxy and the Bible," in *CalCon*, 2, 3 ("not so much information and rules but Power"); Frederik Hendrik Von Meyenfeldt, *The Meaning of Ethos* (Hamilton, ON: Guardian Press, 1964), 278; H. Evan Runner, *The Relation of the Bible to Learning* (Pella, IA: Pella Publishing, 1960), 36, passim.

9. Dooyeweerd, *In the Twilight of Western Thought*, 125; Schrotenboer, "Orthodoxy and the Bible," in *CalCon*, 1, 4.

10. Schrotenboer, "Orthodoxy and the Bible," in *CalCon*, 2, 3.

4. The Word, beyond Analysis

In the "full" sense, on the cosmonomic view, the word may not be *theoretically analyzed.*[11] Why?

a. Dooyeweerd tells us that the word in this "full" sense is "a matter of life and death to us, and not a question of theoretical reflection."[12] I must say that this argument rather perplexes me. I have never been able to see why a "matter of life and death" cannot also be a "matter of theoretical reflection." The present ecological crisis is in one sense a "matter of life and death"; but surely no one would argue that this makes the ecological crisis incapable of scientific investigation. On the contrary, that fact makes the scientific study of ecology all the more urgent.

The word of God, of course, is a "matter of life and death" in a much stronger sense. But it surely is not evident that this fact makes it any less capable of analysis. Indeed, that fact should make analysis all the more urgent.

b. There are other arguments made by these thinkers on this point. The "central theme" of Scripture—creation, fall, and redemption—"cannot become the theoretical object of theological thought, since it is the very starting point of the latter, insofar as theology is really biblical."[13]

I do not doubt, of course, that the word must be our "starting point." It furnishes the basic presuppositions of all thinking that is truly Christian. And, to be sure, there seems to be something paradoxical about the idea of "analyzing one's presuppositions." After all, how can we analyze them except on the basis that those very presuppositions supply? But that paradox is only on the surface. In fact, "examining presuppositions" is something we do all the time in theology, and *should* do. These presuppositions (insofar as we hold them consistently) will indeed supply the basis for their own analysis; but that does not invalidate the analysis. To put it in simpler terms, each of us tries to *understand* his basic commitments in order to understand himself better and to carry out those commitments more effectively. To say that this can't be done is absurd.

c. Schrotenboer argues: "In the sense of that one central, multiform Word of God, the Word is not the object that we investigate, any more

---

11. Dooyeweerd, *In the Twilight of Western Thought*, 42, 125, 136, 143f.; Schrotenboer, "The Bible as the Word of God," 16ff.

12. Dooyeweerd, *In the Twilight of Western Thought*, 125.

13. Ibid., 144.

than we investigate God."[14] Here he seems to be saying that the word-as-event partakes of God's own incomprehensibility, so that to "investigate" the word is an act of presumption, an undue exaltation of the human mind against the mystery of God.

Now, it is certainly true that God's thoughts are not our thoughts, that God cannot be comprehended by any human "investigation." But we must also keep in mind that God has *spoken* to us, and has spoken *clearly.* Because God has taken the initiative, we can understand the word and can understand him through it. In one sense, therefore, "investigation" of the word—and of God himself!—is our divinely given privilege and duty. We *must* search the Scriptures so as to understand God's self-revelation to the best of our God-given ability.

But why, then, should that "searching" exclude the use of sophisticated theoretical equipment? Surely such exclusion is arbitrary. We may not, to be sure, go beyond the bounds of what God has revealed. That indeed would be presumption. But we *must* "study" the word with all the "scientific" and "nonscientific" tools at our disposal. To forbid such study is not an act of pious humility; it is a denial of the clarity of God's self-expression, and an arbitrary limitation upon the believer's understanding of (and obedience to!) that revelation.

5. The Word as Basic Theme

Although these thinkers insist that the word-as-event cannot be theoretically analyzed, they do believe that it can be *characterized* in various (presumably "nontheoretical") ways. Dooyeweerd describes the word in this sense as "the basic theme of Holy Scripture, namely that of creation, fall into sin, and redemption by Jesus Christ in the communion of the Holy Spirit."[15]

Note also the following in which, as I understand it, Dooyeweerd is expounding again the "basic meaning" of the word-as-event, but here in terms of its *normative* force: "The entire divine Law for God's creation displays its radical unity in the central commandment of Love, addressed to the heart, i.e., religious center of human life."[16]

14. Schrotenboer, "Orthodoxy and the Bible," in *CalCon*, 1, 4; cf. Dooyeweerd, *In the Twilight of Western Thought,* 136.
15. Dooyeweerd, *In the Twilight of Western Thought,* 136; cf. 41f., 125, 144.
16. Ibid., 123; cf. Schrotenboer, "Orthodoxy and the Bible," in *CalCon*, 1, 3; De Graaff and Seerveld, *Understanding the Scriptures,* 24, 35, 37f.; Von Meyenfeldt, *The Meaning of Ethos,* 41ff.; Bernard Zylstra, "Thy Word Our Life," *IRB* 49–50 (Spring/Summer 1972): 60f.

I have no quarrel with these as *general* descriptions of the content of the word of God. We will see later (in part 2) how these descriptions can be used in unwholesome ways. Remember also the danger noted earlier (in 1 above) of thinking that the word supplies comprehensive, but not specific direction to us. The emphasis on general descriptions of the contents of the word is that such an emphasis may encourage such thinking.

"THE WORD OF GOD IN THE COSMONOMIC PHILOSOPHY"—PART TWO: THE FORMS OF THE WORD[17]

We have seen how the cosmonomic thinkers speak of the word of God in the sense of the total process of God's making himself known to the heart of man. We have seen that in their view the word in that sense is essentially a "power," incapable of theoretical analysis, characterized as a message of creation, fall, redemption, and love. We must recall,

17. Note by *Guardian* Editor. John Frame is a professor in systematic theology at Westminster Theological Seminary. In the second portion of this article he discusses the "forms" in which the Word of God can become an "object of theoretical thought," according to the cosmonomic thinkers. Of particular interest is the relation of the word of God to and in creation and the word of God in Scripture and their normativity for us today.

Note by *Guardian* Editor. Serious criticisms have been directed against various teachings of those, particularly in North America, who have followed and developed the "philosophy of the cosmonomic idea," first formulated in the 1920s by Herman Dooyeweerd in the Netherlands. Perhaps the most serious criticism is that leveled at the "cosmonomic" view of the "Word of God."

In the first portion of this article, appearing in the October issue of the *Guardian*, Professor Frame pointed out the distinction made by many of the "cosmonomists" between "the Word of God in its full and actual reality and in its restricted sense as the object of theoretical thought." In the "full" sense, God's word is seen as a power or process directed to the heart of man, and not subject to theoretical analysis.

In this concluding portion of the article, the focus is on the "restricted sense" of God's word, particularly on the various "forms" in which that word is said to come to us. (As in the first portion, we have not capitalized *God's word* except when quoting others, or when it is used as a title for Scripture.) The material in this article has been prepared and published not to "put down" any of the writers mentioned in it. It is only just to point out that much of what has been written on the "Word of God" by " cosmonomists" lacks the consistency of a carefully developed formulation. Frankly, however, the tendencies visible in what has been written would lead to dangerous and unacceptable conclusions if consistently developed. It is our hope that open discussion—before this developing approach becomes rigid—will serve to clarify and improve the understanding of the vitally crucial importance for a right view of Scripture.

however, that Dooyeweerd distinguishes sharply between the word in this "full" sense and the word as "object of theoretical thought." We must therefore discuss the views of the cosmonomic thinkers concerning the word in this second sense.

THE "MEDIA" OF REVELATION

In the "process" of revelation, God makes use of certain *media:* the created world, prophets, apostles, written Scripture.[18] Even Christ is a "medium" of revelation in one sense, for he "relays" words from the Father to his disciples (e.g., John 17:8). These are ways in which the divine speech gets from God's mouth into the human heart.

As we have seen, on the cosmonomic view none of these media is equivalent to the whole process, and therefore each must be sharply distinguished from the "full" word. These media are, after all, *created* things (except, presumably, Christ in his divine nature), and therefore point beyond themselves to God who speaks through them, and to other elements in the "process."[19] Further, these particular created things (unlike the "full" word), because they are created and experienced in space and time, may properly be studied in a theoretical way.[20]

On the other hand, the *message conveyed* by these media is the word of God itself. Therefore, the media are not only media; they are "forms" of the word.[21] The *message* of a prophet or of the written Bible is the very word of God. What they say, God says.[22] Therefore, the

18. There is no fixed number of media recognized in the movement. The most common list is simply "creation, Christ, Scripture"; cf. James H. Olthuis and Bernard Zylstra, "Confessing Christ in Education," *IRB* 42 (Summer 1970): 41f. (reprinted in *Guardian* [October 1972]: 120). Others add "preaching"; cf. Schrotenboer, "The Bible as the Word of God," 7, 10f.

19. Cf. especially Paul G. Schrotenboer, "The Bible, Word of Power," *IRB* 32–33 (January–April 1968): 1–4.

20. Dooyeweerd, *In the Twilight of Western Thought*, 136, 143; Schrotenboer, "Theology, Its Nature and Task" (a mimeographed paper), 4f.

21. See the references in notes 18 and 19 above on the concept of "form."

22. Members of this school do not say very much about biblical inspiration, and sometimes (as we will see in subsequent discussion) they almost seem to have forgotten about it. There are, however, occasional affirmations to the effect that the Bible is the Word of God. So De Graaff, in the preface to *Understanding the Scriptures*, affirms, by citing the Belgic Confession, that he believes "without doubt all things contained in the holy Scriptures." Note also Zylstra, "Thy Word Our Life," 66f.; James H. Olthuis, "Ambiguity Is the Key," *IRB* (July 1969): 8; Olthuis and Zylstra, "Confessing Christ in Education," 41 (p. 120 in the *Guardian* reprinting).

cosmonomic thinkers often attribute to the *forms* of the word those qualities belonging to the "word-as-event," for in a real sense those forms *are* the word. The forms constitute the process that Dooyeweerd calls the word.

Thus, to hear the "form" is to hear the word of God; to disregard it is to disregard the word. Not only the word-as-event, but also the written Bible is addressed to the "heart."[23] Scripture, like the "full word," is a "word of power."[24] It, too, is in one sense incapable of scientific analysis. It, too, is a message of creation, fall, redemption, and love.[25]

The cosmonomic thinkers say nothing unusual about Christ as the Word of God. But we should look a bit more closely at their treatment of two other "forms."

1. The Word in Creation

This form of the word is very important to the cosmonomic philosophy. That philosophy speaks often of the "law-word,"[26] the word spoken *to* creation and *through* creation to man.[27]

"General revelation," of course, is not a new idea. What is unusual in the cosmonomic construction (in comparison with traditional Reformed thinking) is the use of general revelation to discover divine commandments or norms beyond those in Scripture—divine commands by which the human conscience may be bound. J. M. Spier, for instance, tells us that a study of art will reveal aesthetic "norms."[28] To transgress such a "norm" is sin. Examples of "sins" against aesthetic norms are the building of "churches in the Roman style" or the writing of "a book in the language of the 17th century."[29]

23. Schrotenboer, "Orthodoxy and the Bible," in *CalCon*,1, 3.

24. Ibid.; cf. Schrotenboer, "The Bible, Word of Power."

25. Dooyeweerd, *In the Twilight of Western Thought*, 136; cf. 41f., 125, 144, noting how the Bible is mentioned.

26. Olthuis and Zylstra, "Confessing Christ in Education," 41 (p. 120 in the *Guardian*), seem to be saying that the "law-word" is the most basic "form" of the word of God. It is, however, hard to distinguish in this article (and in other cosmonomic literature) between the "law-word" and the "word-as-event." They do appear to define the word of God as "the very law-order of creation," but later they speak of creation as one of three "forms" of the word. It is at least clear that Olthuis and Zylstra think that the "law-word" is the most neglected "form" of the word today, and that it is the form most in need of publicity. Cf. also Olthuis, "Ambiguity," 15f.

27. Schrotenboer, "The Bible, Word of Power," 9f.

28. J. M. Spier, *An Introduction to Christian Philosophy* (Philadelphia: Presbyterian and Reformed, 1954), 88.

29. Ibid., 119f.

As I see it, the Bible does not speak of any "word of God in creation." It is true that according to Scripture God speaks *to* creation and creation obeys (Ps. 147:15ff., etc.). It is also true that God reveals himself *through* creation (Ps. 19; Rom. 1:20). But that revelation through creation is not in words and sentences, and it is dangerous to pretend that it is. You cannot "read" a tree as you read a book. The revelation in creation is *indirect*. Furthermore, the idea that the human conscience may be bound by extrascriptural "commandments" is in direct contradiction to 2 Timothy 3:17, and is repugnant to all Christians who have struggled against the bondage of human theories and traditions.

2. THE WORD IN SCRIPTURE

As we have seen, for the cosmonomic philosophers Scripture is both a form of the word of God and a created "human artifact."[30] Its "basic theme" of creation, fall, and redemption may not be scientifically analyzed. That theme affects the heart of man by the pure sovereign action of the Holy Spirit.[31]

As a created "human artifact," however, as an object in time and space, Scripture *can* be studied theoretically. And the first thing such study teaches us is the basic character of this Bible-artifact—it is a "book for faith."[32] The point seems clear enough on the surface. What is the Bible? Not a science text, not a mere literary creation, not a mere history, not a book of mere ethical lessons. Its purpose has to do with our faith—our primary assurances of life.

So far the view seems uncontroversial. But the implications derived from it are a bit shocking. Dooyeweerd, for instance, tells us that because the Bible is a faith-book, the "days" of Genesis 1 *cannot* be chronological. They must be *faith*-days, whatever that might mean.[33] Schrotenboer, too, tells us that because the Bible is a faith-book, its doctrine of election

30. Schrotenboer, "Orthodoxy and the Bible," in *CalCon*, 1, 4.

31. Dooyeweerd, *In the Twilight of Western Thought*, 42. I must confess, however, that I do not see how this distinction between the "basic theme" of Scripture and (presumably) the details of Scripture can be maintained. How does Dooyeweerd know that the Spirit brings only the "basic theme" of Scripture to bear upon our heart? Why is it only the "basic theme" that is incapable of theoretical analysis? If the whole Bible is God's Word, then why not say that the "message" of Scripture cannot be analyzed at all? Then the only "sciences" involved with Scripture would be those sciences studying the human environs into which the message came.

32. Dooyeweerd, *In the Twilight of Western Thought*, 143; Schrotenboer, "Theology and the Bible," in *CalCon*, 1, 4.

33. Dooyeweerd, *In the Twilight of Western Thought*, 149ff.

cannot be "causal." And for good measure, he adds that the numbers "three" and "one" in the doctrine of the Trinity are in some sense non-mathematical numbers![34]

It certainly seems that to call the Bible a "faith-book" in this scheme is to adopt a most unusual system of Bible interpretation. I must say that the concepts of "faith-days" and "faith-numbers" are virtually unintelligible to me.[35] In any case, the cosmonomic thinkers at this point appear to be imposing a philosophical scheme on Scripture that has no basis in Scripture itself and that has very little to do with the biblical meaning of faith. Few of us, surely, ever dreamed that such a scheme was involved in our simple confession of the Bible as a "book for faith."

A SHARPLY CURTAILED SCRIPTURE

This approach that would see the Bible as only a "faith-book" permits the sciences and philosophy to work in relative autonomy. Since the Bible contains only "faith-concepts," or since at least all biblical statements about God must be read as "faith-statements" in the peculiar cosmonomic sense, the Bible as "artifact" can say nothing much of direct interest to scientists and philosophers.

Dooyeweerd often says, to be sure, that scientists and philosophers must respect the "central basic motive" of Scripture[36] (i.e., creation, fall, redemption), but he seems to regard the detailed teachings of Scripture as of little interest to nontheologians. It thus seems that scientists and philosophers in their theoretical work can pretty much ignore the Bible, except for an occasional nod toward the "basic motive." The cosmonomic movement, which once appeared to many of us as a movement *opening* the Bible to all fields of learning, now appears rather to be closing the Bible.

34. Schrotenboer, "Theology and the Bible," in *CalCon*, 1, 6. Note also De Graaff and Seerveld, *Understanding the Scriptures*, 10, who say that to ask whether the events described in Scripture "actually happened in every detail and in the order in which they are presented is to ask the wrong question." De Graaff and Seerveld don't say so, but I presume they would elaborate by saying that such questions are not "faith-questions" in some sense. At any rate, De Graaff and Seerveld also rather severely, in my view, restrict those subjects concerning which Scripture can "speak to us," and such restrictions seem fairly typical of the cosmonomic movement.

35. At a meeting we both attended, Paul Schrotenboer once asked me to accompany him to his hotel room while he retrieved something he had forgotten. As we went through the halls, he could not find his room number. The series of numbers seemed to stop and pick up again elsewhere. As our frustration increased, I remarked to him, "Paul, maybe these are faith-numbers." As I recall, he was not amused.

36. Dooyeweerd, *In the Twilight of Western Thought*, 145, 148.

Furthermore, the Bible is even more "closed" by those cosmonomic thinkers who regard Scripture as directed almost exclusively to a past age. Schrotenboer, for instance, discusses some of the problems we face in applying biblical commandments to the modern cultural situation, and comes to the conclusion that even the Ten Commandments

> are not normative for us in the same way that they were normative for the people of Moses' day. No, the Decalogue is not the absolute changeless law, it is rather an *adaptation* or expression of God's law for a particular time and place.[37]

But if the Decalogue is only an "adaptation" of law, where do we go to find *the law itself*? Schrotenboer answers: "The great and only comprehensive commandment is the love commandment, both to God and to our fellows." How do we decide, however, *how* God wants us to "love" in *our* particular time and place? Schrotenboer says that the particular injunctions of Scripture are "illustrations of how we should do it." Imitating the biblical writers, therefore, "the church today must do for its age what the apostles did for theirs."[38]

Scripture, in other words, does not tell us what God wants us to do, except in those passages where the love command is stated. Outside of those passages, the Bible presents only examples of how ancient man applied the love command to his circumstances with God's help. The Bible gave to *ancient man* the definitive interpretation of the love command, but it does not give *us* such an interpretation. To get the latter, we must write *our own* Bible! It may, of course, be an uninspired Bible, in comparison with the original Bible, which was inspired. But it must be a Bible, in the sense that it will replace the old one in determining God's specific will for *us*. We must, like Moses and Paul, derive specific commandments from the law of love, but *we* must do so without benefit of inspiration.

THE "LAW-WORD"—MOST BASIC FORM

Arnold De Graaff and Calvin Seerveld, who hold the same view, try to be a bit more helpful. They say that we have something to help us today besides the love commandment and the biblical "illustrations." We also have the "law-word."[39] It appears that both for De Graaff and

---

37. Schrotenboer, "Orthodoxy and the Bible," in *CalCon*, 1, 3 (emphasis his).
38. Ibid.
39. De Graaff and Seerveld, *Understanding the Scriptures*, 37.

Seerveld and for Schrotenboer, the "law-word," the creation-word, is the most basic form of revelation. After all, even the law of love can be found in creation.[40]

Scripture, therefore, tells us nothing that the "law-word" doesn't tell us. Scripture is merely an application and illustration of general revelation! Some might object, indeed, that Scripture at least goes beyond general revelation in that it contains the gospel of salvation. But think about that in relation to what Schrotenboer and De Graaff and Seerveld have said. What is the gospel? It is the offer of eternal life conditioned upon a *command* to repent and believe in Christ. But Schrotenboer and De Graaff and Seerveld have told us that all biblical commands are merely applications of the law of love. Thus it would seem that even the command to repent and believe in Christ is an application of the law of love for a particular time and place. Even the gospel, then, if this cosmonomic view is carried out consistently, becomes a mere adaptation of general revelation. And Scripture loses all uniqueness of content.

In my view, this is a horrendous distortion of the truth. Just think: On this scheme, everything except the law of love is culturally relative! Everything except the law of love could lose its validity as the result of cultural change! At some future date, murder might be a *good* thing to do! Perhaps by the year 2020, it will no longer be in accord with the law of love to command all men everywhere to repent and believe in Christ! Perhaps by the year 2500, the law of love might require us to worship four or five gods instead of the one God who spoke and is spoken of in the ancient Decalogue.

NO! TO THIS DETRACTION OF SCRIPTURE

To all of this, the orthodox Christian can only answer "No!" To be sure, there are difficulties in applying biblical commands to the modern age. No one ought to be so naive as to say that we apply these commands in all cases precisely the way the ancient Israelites did. But difficult as these problems may be, these difficulties do not justify the absurd suggestion that only the law of love is permanently valid. The law of love holds a central place in Scripture, but nothing in Scripture even remotely suggests that this command is the only permanent one. We need not fear that God will require us to commit adultery at some time in the future. We need not fear that someday there will be two ways of salvation.

40. Dooyeweerd, *In the Twilight of Western Thought*, 123.

The cosmonomic scheme, in summary, detracts from Scripture in two ways: (1) It detracts from the *sufficiency* of Scripture by binding us to extrascriptural norms derived from the "law-word." (2) It detracts from the *authority* of Scripture by accepting only the love command as permanently authoritative, and by restricting that scriptural authority to the so-called "realm of faith." This philosophy, therefore, turns us away from Scripture where God *has* spoken, and turns us toward an alleged "law-word" full of human speculations.

It may be that these thinkers are not aware of the implications of their scheme. They may not see the seriousness of the problem. I do not question the heart commitment of any of these men. But a philosophy that turns men away from the written Word of God and that binds them to human philosophical speculations is a philosophy that should be decisively rejected by the Reformed community.

"WHAT IS GOD'S WORD?"[41]

The ten propositions set forth here are intended to contribute to the ongoing dialogue with the men from Toronto, and are presented as a kind of outline of a Christian philosophy of revelation.

1. THE WORD OF GOD IS DIVINE

The basic ontological (i.e., referring to whatever basically exists) distinction in Scripture is between Creator and creature; everything that is has been created except for God himself. There are no in-betweens, no half-divine or semicreated beings.

This is not to say that there may not be cases where you have both in close proximity. Certainly, you have that in the incarnate Christ, who is fully God and fully man. But it is to say that there are no missing links, no *tertium quid*, no chain of being between God and his creation.

Is the word of God a creature, Creator, or both? Well, if by the word of God the heavens were made (Ps. 33:6), then the word is not itself created

41. Note by *Guardian* editor: Originally published in *The Presbyterian Guardian* (November 1973): 142–43. This is a very condensed summary of a paper presented by Professor Frame of Westminster Theological Seminary at a conference in April 1973 that was sponsored by the Westminster Student Association. It was greeted as a helpful approach in the "dialogue" between Professor Frame and others at Westminster and representatives of the Association for the Advancement of Christian Scholarship. The summary has been made by the *Guardian*'s editor, and he should be held responsible for any unfortunate expressions in it.

but is Creator. It is coeternal with God (John 1:1ff.); the word of God *was* God; the word of God is divine.

So then, to obey the word is to obey God; to disobey it is to disobey God. But the Word in *Scripture is God come in human form*; it is an incarnation. The Bible is *both* Creator and creature, as Jesus is both God and man.

2. THE WORD REFLECTS GOD'S PLURALITY

Not only is the word identified with God, it is distinguished from God (John 1:2). It is *by* the word that the heavens were made, so that the word is a tool. There is a unity *and* a distinction that we cannot fully account for. There is a mystery here like that of the Trinity, the one God in three persons.

It should not surprise us to learn that there is also a unity and a plurality in God's speaking, even as there is in God himself. God speaks *one* word; God also speaks *many* words. The word reflects the unity of God's speaking. All of nature and history is governed by a single unified plan of God. But within this unity there is a richness of detail, a vast diversity. There is one word and many words.

3. THE WORD ADDRESSES MAN IN ITS UNITY AND PLURALITY

When God speaks to man, we hear one word and we hear many words. God's word has a single unified theme—call it the theme of creation-fall-redemption, if you will. But Scripture presents that theme in a multitude of stories, songs, prophecies, letters, and so on. God's word imposes on us the single command of love; but that command is presented in a variety of commands on many issues covering the whole of human life.

Both the unity and diversity of God's word are binding upon us; they are equally powerful, equally true, equally authoritative. The one central message of God's word grips man's heart; the many details of God's word also grip the heart.

4. THE WORD ADDRESSES MAN IN HIS UNITY AND PLURALITY

Man in God's image is also one and many, even as God is one and many. The word of God grips man's heart, but it also grips all his faculties. The one central message grips all of man's faculties, gifts, concerns, cares, worries, and fears; but the details of the word also grasp all our fears, needs, heartaches, questions, and concerns.

Both the central message and the details of God's word address both the heart of man and all of man's functions and concerns. The word of God is comprehensive and specific—to the heart of man and all his faculties, to the whole person in all areas of his life.

5. THE WORD IS ACCESSIBLE TO ALL HUMAN FACULTIES

God's word, in its central meaning and in its detail, is addressed to all our faculties. God expects that word to be appropriated, accepted, and obeyed by the heart and by the faculties. We cannot begin to comprehend the word of God exhaustively, but the word is to be understood, accepted, and obeyed. We are obligated to mobilize all our gifts in appropriating the word—to use our senses, feelings, rationality, historical sense, lingual capacity, economic skills, aesthetic sensitivity, moral sense, unity, and whatever else there may be. To withhold any faculty is unbelief.

What God wants us to know—the norms that God commands us to obey—is clear and accessible. These norms can be understood and appreciated and obeyed. To say that the word is beyond our faculties may sound humble, but it is actually a form of disobedience and arrogance. God spoke clearly in human language, accommodating his revelation to us. We can therefore speak the word, study and analyze it, apply and obey it. To limit the word's freedom to speak to us is to limit the authority of the word over us.

6. GOD'S WORD AS BOTH POWER AND MEANING

The gospel is the power of God unto salvation. But it is not a bare power or raw force. The power of the word reflects God's wisdom, knowledge, and understanding. It *communicates* these to us. God's word is a word, is language, having not only power but meaning. The power of the word saves us when the meaning is believed and obeyed.

Now, the power of the word is not something more basic than its meaning. God's word is powerful because its meaning is truth. God's word is true and means what it says because it has the power to do what it sets out to do. Because God's word is not a blind force upon our heart, it can and does engage all our faculties as we approach the meaning of God's word.

7. SCRIPTURE EMBODIES THE UNITY OF GOD'S WORD

The Scriptures are a kind of incarnation of the word of God. Scripture is God's Word, but it is also the words of men. It has a human and a divine nature. It has all the truth, power, holiness, and majesty of God; yet it conveys also the personalities of the human writers, speaking their language, their experience, faith, hopes, questions, and concerns.

Nevertheless, in this incarnate form the Word of God loses none of its truth and perfection. It is God's Word with supreme authority for us. It cannot be tested by anything else; it is not subordinate to some other word of God. The words of the Bible do not merely witness to some other law, nor are they applicable to one cultural setting in contrast to some other word that is valid for other times and places. No, Scripture is law, and has the authority of the one Word of God. It brings God's demand and God's promise to bear on man's heart and upon all areas of man's life.

8. SCRIPTURE EMBODIES THE DIVERSITY OF GOD'S WORD

Scripture carries to us the full force of the one Word of God. At the same time, it is one word of God among many. It does not contain everything God said. Instead, Scripture conveys a special message. It is necessary for a particular purpose that is not fulfilled by God's revelation in nature. It brings to us a message not found elsewhere—the message of redemption in Christ.

Thus, Scripture is not revelation in general, but is specifically the gospel, the power of God unto salvation. The Gentiles were not left to natural revelation alone. But God has spoken a particular Word that they must have, the Word that names the name of Christ by which alone men can be saved.

9. SCRIPTURE IS SUFFICIENT FOR ALL GOOD WORKS

As the one Word of God, Scripture conveys the *whole will of God* to us. It needs no supplementation (2 Tim. 3:15–17). Scripture is profitable for the man of God that he may be thoroughly furnished unto *every* good work.

But obviously the Bible does not contain everything we need to know. How can we say it is sufficient for all good works? Put it this way: Scripture does not contain all the *knowledge* we need, but all the *commandments*.

Scripture does not tell us how many kinds of trees there are, but it tells us to use the trees to God's glory.

When I obey the speed law, I obey Scripture, for Scripture tells me to obey the ordinances of men (Rom. 13:1; 1 Peter 2:13). Scripture requires me to obey that speed limit. I do not discover that this is God's Word from some other source. When I apply Scripture to my present situation—and obey the speed law—I have truly appropriated the teaching of Scripture.

Since Scripture conveys God's whole will for us, it covers all areas of our lives (1 Cor. 10:31). Scripture certainly does have a focus—the message of salvation. But that focus does not limit Scripture's message to some single area of man's life. The message of salvation is of salvation for *all of life*, for history, philosophy, aesthetics, psychology. Scripture corrects our ideas in all these areas, both the naive and the theoretical. It is the height of presumption to claim that Scripture cannot speak on any matter of human life or concern.

10. SCRIPTURE HAS A DISTINCTIVE FUNCTION IN REVELATION

As one word of God among many, Scripture has its distinctive function in the process of God's revelation of himself to us. Not only should we make use of God's Word in Scripture, but we should also make use of God's word in nature and history. The scientist will study God's world as well as the Scriptures. He will realize that the world is controlled by God's plan and reflects God's wisdom and power.

Then when we come to the Scriptures, we bring many things from our study of the world. We bring all sorts of ideas we have learned elsewhere— from ordinary experience, from philosophy, theological systems, or history. We bring our world- and life views to bear upon our study of Scripture.

Yet we must remember that God has given us Scripture because without it we are blind to God's revelation in the world. Scripture was given to save us from our sinful wisdom, to correct our sinful ideas. The words of Scripture must take unconditional precedence over any ideas that we have gained from other sources. We must bring our philosophies, sciences, and world- and life views all to the Scripture.

We must use all these in interpreting the Bible. But we must hold such things loosely. We must allow Scripture to resist our attempts to interpret it through those means. We must allow Scripture to question our worldviews, scientific views, naive ideas, theoretical ideas, and philosophies.

This is not to say that Scripture is more authoritative than the words of God in creation, or than the living Word, Jesus Christ. It is simply to admit that one distinctive function of Scripture, as one word of God among many, is to correct sinful misconceptions of God's general revelation. Scripture must be allowed to surprise us, to be what it is, to be the Word of God himself.

In other words, Scripture must be allowed to be God's Word in all its meaning and power, its unity and plurality, its power and authority and justice and holiness and purity and wisdom and truth.

REPLY TO PROFESSOR ZYLSTRA[42]

First, I wish to express my sincere thanks to Dr. Bernard Zylstra for his article "The Word of God, the Bible, and the AACS: In Defense of a Reformational Movement." Although I find much to disagree with in the article (as will be evident shortly), I am pleased with its constructive spirit and with its potential value as a contribution to a continuing dialogue. Although I have been making rather serious criticisms of the AACS for about four or five years now, Dr. Zylstra is the first adherent of that movement, to my knowledge, who has given my arguments any kind of serious scrutiny.

I did not come to Westminster Theological Seminary with the idea of becoming a militant anti-AACS polemicist. I had hoped, originally, that I could get to know some of the AACS people and learn from them while they learned from me. My attempts at such dialogue, however, proved almost entirely futile. Doubtless, this futility was partly my own fault. But the situation was certainly not helped when my arguments were met with Gnostic replies ("you don't understand") and even with gratuitous attacks on my character. And the arguments themselves were never seriously discussed.

It is generally such breakdown of communication that turns brotherly disagreement into heresy-hunting. The most distinctive characteristic of a heretic is his *unteachableness*, his unwillingness to participate in serious discussion with brethren of a different mind on an issue. When dialogue breaks down, our only recourse is to *warn* the church about the errors that concern us. And that means heresy-hunting; that means polemics. I would much rather discuss than polemicize any day, and if Dr. Zylstra's article opens up again the channels of brotherly communication, I can only praise God.

Now a few comments on the content of the article.

42. Originally published in *Guardian* 42, 3 (March 1973): 40–43.

1. THE "THIRD CATEGORY"

The following quote from Dr. Zylstra's article pinpoints one of the crucial issues.

> In this booklet Frame asks the fundamental question: What is the relation of law to God? Before he answers this question he formulates the frame of reference within which the answer can be given: "The Scriptures teach that God is creator, the world is his creature, and that there is nothing in between, no third category." (p. 29).
>
> Here, we submit, Frame departs from the teaching of the Bible, which clearly posits a "third category," namely the Creator's law for creation, the statutes, ordinances, and words that creatures must obey and do. The absence of this "third category" in Frame's conception makes it extremely difficult for him to understand the Bible on this score, as we will see later.

It seems that the issue is pretty clear-cut: Zylstra says there is a "third category"; Frame says there is none. But perhaps we need to be clearer on what we mean by "category." Now, there is a sense in which you can have as many "categories" as you like, for instance: God, the world, God's law, God's love, God's justice, and God's eternity. None of these phrases is synonymous with another; each says something a little "different." Each, therefore, might be a "category" all its own; thus you might have nine, twelve, twenty-five, or a hundred and two categories if you like. Obviously, however, I wasn't saying there are "two" categories in *that* sense of "category." In my usage, "two categories" does *not* mean "two non-synonymous designations." Why did I say there were only two? Simply because "Creator" and "creature" exhaust the universe. *Everything* is either Creator or creature. By Jesus Christ *all* things were created, in heaven and earth (Col. 1:16f). Christ created *all* things except himself. All things are divinely creative or created. There is nothing outside of these categories.

Many heresies in the history of the church have tried to posit some intermediary between God and his creation. It seemed to them that God could not create or redeem the world directly, that there must be some "link." The Gnostics had a great ladder of mediators between God and man. None of them were exactly divine, but none of them were creatures, either. Rather, they were "emanations" from God. The Arians thought that Christ was such a mediator—neither fully divine nor really a creature. In contrast with these heretical views, the Bible boldly proclaims that there is only *one* mediator between God and man. And that mediator, rather than being some half-divine "link" between God and creation, is fully God and fully man—both

Creator *and* creature. In Scripture, God does not need some "third category" in order to create, redeem, and govern; he comes into *direct contact* with his world. He speaks *clearly* to his people, acts with direct and personal *power*. Any other view removes God from his world and calls into question the clarity of his revelation and the personal power of his sovereignty.

Now, what about "law"? Is law Creator or creature? Well, that's easy, isn't it? Law is that word of God by which all things were made (Gen. 1:3; Ps. 33:6; John 1:1–3; Heb. 11:3; 2 Peter 3:5). The law has divine attributes (Pss. 19:4–9; 119:89, 160; etc.). To obey law is to obey God; to disobey law is to disobey God. God's law, God's word, is God himself (John 1:1). The law is divine in the same way that God's justice, love, grace, and eternity are divine. In fact, in some mysterious way, the divinity of the word *is* the divinity of the Son of God himself (John 1:1–14). To make the law a "third category" in Dr. Zylstra's sense is to place upon that law an unbiblically low estimate. To make law a "third category" in this way is to place a mediator between God and man, other than the one mediator who is *fully* divine and *fully* human.

True, John 1:1 also asserts a *distinction* between the word and God, but not such a distinction as to compromise the deity of the word. Such unity and distinction brings us to the heart of the mystery of the Trinity; it does not require (as Gnostics and Arians supposed) that the word be something less than God.

2. THE WORD OF GOD AS "LINGUISTIC COMMUNICATION"

I have said that "word of God" in the Bible may be understood as a kind of "linguistic communication." Professor Zylstra thinks that this is a "reductionist" view. I must say that I am entirely baffled. What is a "word"? A word *is* a "linguistic communication." "Words" and "linguistic communication" are *synonyms*; in fact, they are so closely synonymous that to define one in terms of the other doesn't tell you very much. If you don't know what a word is, chances are you won't know what a "linguistic communication" is, either. Honestly, I never thought I was saying anything momentous in defining the word of God "linguistically"! I certainly never thought that I was saying anything controversial, let alone offering a "reductionist" view. Now, of course, I know that God's "word" is more than mere *human* language; that is to say, God's language is not our language. But the Bible presents God's language as *language*—as *word*. In the Bible, God has *conversations* with people. Can we find any *better* way to describe the word of God than as God's linguistic communications?

Or put it this way: how, in Dr. Zylstra's view, is God's word *more* than "language"? In what way is "God's word" more than "God's language"? That seems a bit like asking, "How is Peter more than Cephas?" But Dr. Zylstra has several answers. At one point, by what is at best a bizarre exegesis, he suggests that "word" refers to manna and clothing in Matthew 4:4 and Deuteronomy 8:3. I confess that I find it rather difficult to take such a suggestion seriously. However, his most serious answer to our question runs as follows: the word is more than language because it is God's *power*, God's *decree* that governs and upholds all things. God's word is power, and therefore more than language. Here we must make some observations. (a) Language itself is powerful; it accomplishes great things in the world. The president declares war, thousands are killed. Scripture abounds in reference to the power of language (cf. Gen. 11:6; Rom. 1:16; James 3:1–8). One cannot argue "power, therefore more than language," for language itself is a power. (b) The power of God's word is presented in Scripture as the power of divine *language*. God is the great King who *speaks*, and his subjects *obey* (Pss. 33:9; 147:15; 148:5–8; etc.). Scripture never suggests that we must think of God's decree as something supralinguistic. It is more than *man's* language, to be sure, but (again) Scripture persists in calling it language, and I can't see any reason to reject the scriptural usage.

But why does Scripture so regularly speak of God's power as a kind of language? Obviously, some will insist, this usage is metaphorical; for God does not have a mouth; his speech need not be limited to the utterance of sounds. Why, then, is the "linguistic" terminology so important? It is important (and I wish this point were occasionally acknowledged in the AACS literature) because the power of God is never a *blind* power. It is never a *raw force*. In all situations, it reflects God's *wisdom* and *understanding*. Thus, his power (like language!) is a *revelation* of his mind. God's word, that is, is not *merely* "power"; it is also *meaning*. It is interpretation, communication, revelation; it is *language*. God's power does not come upon us as an ineffable, indescribable, unanalyzable "experience." Rather, it clearly *reveals* God to us (Rom. 1:20) so that we *know* God and *know* his requirements (Rom. 1:32). This is why God's word is a *word*. It is not merely power; it is powerful *language*. Dr. Zylstra's argument "power, therefore more than language" confuses this important biblical truth.

Incidentally, let me clear up a minor misunderstanding at this point. I have defined God's word as "God's linguistic communication." I have never defined it (as Dr. Zylstra seems to think at one point in his paper) as "God's linguistic communication to *man*." Obviously, on a scriptural view God's word is not addressed solely to *man*. God's word is also the conversations between Father, Son, and Spirit within the Trinity. And it is God's commands to the natural world, as in Genesis 1.

3. "WORD" AND "BIBLE"

It shouldn't be necessary to make the following point, but for some reason our AACS brethren keep expecting us to make it again and again. Let me say as clearly as possible that I do *not* "simply" identify "word of God" and "Bible." Nor do I "reduce" the word to the Bible. The Bible is a particular utterance of the word of God, but it is not the only such utterance. Many words of God are not found in the Bible. Jesus said many things that are not recorded in Scripture; God says many things to the sun, moon, and stars that are not recorded in Scripture; the persons of the Trinity speak to one another in eternal communication—a communication that no human language, not even Scripture, can exhaust. I have never "reduced" the word to Scripture in Zylstra's sense, nor has Norman Shepherd, nor has any other critic of the AACS so far as I know. We do, however, want to insist on certain important *continuities* between "word" and "Bible," such as these: (a) The words of the Bible *are* words of God, not merely words of men. (b) Therefore, the words of the Bible are *law* for us; they are not merely (as is suggested in some AACS literature) "applications" of God's law to a particular cultural situation. (c) Scripture need not be supplemented by other divine commandments, for it contains all that we need to be "complete, thoroughly furnished unto every good work" (2 Tim. 3:17). (Again, it is not clear to me that the AACS enthusiasts recognize this crucial scriptural principle.) (d) Because it is the Word of God, Scripture is self-interpreting and self-attesting; it is not in need of a philosophical system to tell us what it is about. (e) Because it is the Word of God, *all* of Scripture (not merely the "basic motives") must be studied and applied to *all* areas of human life.

To me these "continuities" between word and Bible are terribly important. And in my view, the AACS witness to these continuities is at best unclear. Therefore, when I write about Dooyeweerd, the AACS, and others, I generally focus on these "continuities." Perhaps, therefore, I have given some the impression that I "reduce" the word to Scripture in Dr. Zylstra's sense. I hope Dr. Zylstra and his colleagues will accept my word that I don't *intend* any such "reductionism." But at the same time, I would like to have some clear testimony from them that they affirm the "continuities" about which I am so concerned.

The issues between us are still quite large. I trust, however, that we are coming to understand one another better. Thank you again, Dr. Zylstra, for speaking to the central questions.

TORONTO, REFORMED ORTHODOXY, AND THE WORD OF GOD: WHERE DO WE GO FROM HERE?[43]

Well, I guess if Nixon can visit China, then Frame can write for *Vanguard*! Why not?! Seriously, it's good to note something of a thaw in the cold war between the AACS and the more traditional Reformed theology. Honestly, brethren, I did not originally come to Westminster Theological Seminary with the idea of becoming a militant anti-AACS polemicist. In fact, heresy-hunting is one phase of theological work that I would prefer to leave to other people. I had hoped, when I began teaching five years ago, that I could get to know some of the AACS people and learn from them while they learned from me. My attempts at such dialogue, however, proved largely futile. Doubtless, that futility was partly my own fault, but the situation was certainly not helped when my arguments were met with Gnostic replies ("you don't understand") and even with gratuitous attacks upon my character, and when the arguments themselves were never seriously considered. Things have changed lately, however. I've had some helpful discussions with Bernard Zylstra, James Olthuis, and others during the past year. I've had some Toronto-oriented students who actually made helpful contributions in class, rather than simply writing me off as an enemy (relieving my apprehensions that the latter approach had been the official AACS policy). And now I'm writing for *Vanguard*! Well, praise the Lord! When Christian brothers can sit around a table and talk to one another, the need for warning the church about one another diminishes substantially.

Now where do we stand in the discussion concerning the word of God? That's rather hard to say at the moment. My present bafflement chiefly derives from a rather paradoxical feature of the "Toronto approach." On the one hand, the rhetoric of the movement suggests that the AACS is urging upon the church an exciting, new view of the word of God—a view that though taught in Scripture itself has been buried under centuries of rationalistic, scholastic, nature-grace dichotomizing theology and has recently been rediscovered through the monumental intellectual energies of Dooyeweerd and his disciples, thus liberating the Christian community from the shackles of the past. On this view, the contemporary villains are the orthodox Reformed theologians who do not appreciate these great AACS rediscoveries and thus are perpetuating a traditionalism that in the

---

43. This article originally appeared in *Vanguard* (January–February 1975): 6–8. The editorial note at the beginning of the article reads: "In this letter addressed to *Vanguard* readers, Professor Frame demands that the members of the Institute for Christian Studies explain exactly how their view of the word of God differs from the neoorthodox view."

present context is counter-Reformational. Such rhetoric fires the hearts of young zealots. Students go off to weekend conferences and come back prepared to subject the whole theological tradition to a "radical transcendental critique." Their ministers, parents, and seminary professors, of course, are incapable of understanding these new insights: how could they possibly understand, caught up as they are in the chains of nature-grace thinking?

On the other hand, on at least three different occasions when I have presented what I considered to be sharp criticisms of the Toronto approach and have presented my own positive view (which I consider fairly traditional), I have been told by rather prominent AACS people (Peter J. Steen, James Olthuis, Paul G. Schrotenboer) that my views did not differ substantially from theirs, that in fact they "agreed" with me.

Now, brethren, where do we really stand vis-à-vis one another? Do you really "agree" with me, or do you insist that my approach is hopelessly mired in nature-grace thinking and in need of some sort of radical reformation? If your view really is radically different from the tradition, how is it new? And don't tell me that the AACS has discovered general revelation! A few others have beaten you to it. And don't say that you have discovered the "power" of the Word, for most any "traditional" Bible commentary on John 1 or Psalm 33 or Romans 1:16 will show you that. And don't say that you have discovered that the Bible ought to be interpreted in terms of its central message, because that point, too, though important, is a theological commonplace. On the other hand, if you really "agree" with us traditionalists, if our differences are merely differences of detail or of emphasis, then why not cool the rhetoric? You've no idea, I suspect, of how much trouble has been caused by this bombast in churches, Christian organizations, and seminary classrooms. Why divide the body of Christ over details? Why the "Red Guard" tactics among the young, AACS fanatics? Why not teach them to behave themselves?

Well, for what it's worth, here's where I stand at the moment. Despite your professions of "agreement" with me, I still suspect that we disagree on some pretty important matters. At the same time, I am becoming more impressed by the ambiguities in the discussion, and feel that once all of us gain more clarity on the issues, we may find ourselves closer together than we had expected. Particularly, I would like some help in the following areas.

I. THE WORD AND GOD

I still find Toronto people (especially Bernard Zylstra) writing in a way that suggests that the word of God is some kind of intermediate reality between God and the creation: a *tertium quid*—neither fully divine nor created, neither Lord nor servant.

Now, I realize that in certain contexts it is helpful (for specific purposes) to use a scheme God-word-creation. Sometimes it is helpful also to speak of God-Christ-man-universe to indicate spheres of kingdom authority. One gets the impression, however, that for Zylstra the God-word-creation scheme is more than a convenient device for making certain points. Rather, he seems to wish to deny to the word full divine authority, dignity, and capacity. When I point out the scriptural teaching concerning these "divine attributes" of the word, I am told that there are also distinctions to be made between God and the word, and the whole matter is left up in the air. I insist, however, that these divine attributes be acknowledged and stressed, else we fall into the error of the Gnostics, Arians, and all "chain-of-being" thinkers—the error of supposing that God's involvement with us is less than direct and personal, that God needs semidivine mediators of various sorts to carry out his business, and that there is something in the universe other than God that does not serve him as his creature (contra, e.g., Rev. 4:1).

II. THE WORD AND THE BIBLE

First, let me freely acknowledge that there is more to the word of God than what is written in the Bible (cf. Ps. 147:15; John 20:30f.; Acts 1:3; etc.). On this point, the traditional Reformed theology has given me perfectly adequate guidance with no need of help from the Toronto Institute. The real question, however, is: what is the "word of God" and what is its relation to the Bible? I still hear the Toronto people saying that the word is first and foremost a kind of "power." Although I agree that the "power of the word" is an important biblical concept, I think that this is a most inadequate way of describing the basic character of the word. The word in Scripture has many other qualities besides power, and one of the most crucial in my view is "meaning." The word is something that can be obeyed, believed, and understood. (Even when spoken to inanimate things, it reflects God's own understanding, wisdom, and knowledge.) Toronto has a strange aversion to emphasizing the meaning of the word. This aversion is further underlined by the Toronto insistence that the word is something other than language. This insistence is bafflingly paradoxical to one unacquainted with Dooyeweerd's philosophical scheme, for how can a "word" be nonlinguistic? (And, in my opinion, Dooyeweerd's scheme only muddies the waters further.)

Now, when people emphasize the "power" of the word with no corresponding emphasis on meaning, and when they fiercely deny the "linguistic" character of the word, then the relation between the word and the text of Scripture becomes problematic in the extreme. How can nonlanguage be recorded in language? How can a "power" (and of course, we are given the impression that this is an inarticulate "power") be recorded on paper? I grant, of course, that God has said more than there is in the Bible. Yet I would maintain that part of God's word has actually been set down on paper. God's utterances, I maintain, can be written down because they are language. But in the Toronto view, it seems, none of the word is language. If the word is not really a word, not really language, then how can it be written down in words and sentences? How can we understand it, obey it, take it on our lips? Scripture is not the whole word of God—on that we agree. But is Scripture the word of God at all? I know that Toronto wants to say that it is, in some sense. All things considered, however, I am still unable to distinguish the Toronto position from neoorthodoxy, "new hermeneutics," and so on. I await your help. Surely, though, brethren, you must admit at least that this is a confusing way to talk about the Bible.

III. THE BIBLE AND US

To reaffirm my credentials as a traditional Reformed scholastic, let me structure this discussion in terms of the traditional "attributes of Scripture."

1. THE NECESSITY OF SCRIPTURE

James Olthuis likes to talk about the Bible as a "republication" of natural revelation. Well, fine; but the Bible is not merely a "republication." It also contains a distinctive message, one not available to men through a mere study of nature. To be saved from sin, one must hear the preaching of Christ. It is this distinctive message, especially, that makes Scripture necessary for us. Now, I think James Olthuis agrees with this, but I would like to have him write to this effect and to be more joyful and less grudging about it.

2. THE AUTHORITY OF SCRIPTURE

First, why is it that the Toronto literature says so little about biblical infallibility and inerrancy? If you don't accept these concepts, of course, then there is a great gulf between you and me. If, however, you do accept them, then you have surely committed a major tactical blunder in not emphasizing them, clarifying them, expounding them in an age when they are being challenged even in conservative Reformed communions. How can a Christian talk about the word of God in Scripture without stressing the infallibility of its authority? But further: not only does the AACS literature fail to stress these concepts, its positive teachings tend to call them into question. When, for instance, Arnold De Graaff and Calvin Seerveld (*Understanding the Scriptures*, p. 10) tell us that historical questions about the Bible are "wrong" questions, do they mean that biblical authority does not necessitate historical reliability? When they say (ibid., 35) that the love commandment "relativizes" all other biblical commandments and that the Ten Commandments are positivizations of the love command for "a particular culture in a particular period of history," do they mean that in some cultures or some periods of history the love commandment might require adultery or murder, instead of forbidding them? If they do not mean these things, why don't they or someone at Toronto say so? This sort of language certainly does little other than confuse the flock of Christ. I think myself that this confusing use of neoorthodox slogans, together with the customary belittling of the orthodox tradition, would fade away if some of the Toronto experts in the "word" would actually read some of the traditional stuff and if they would apply to the neoorthodox slogans the same critical zeal that they customarily reserve for "nature-grace" thought.

3. The Sufficiency of Scripture

Does Toronto really believe that Scripture is enough so that "the man of God may be complete, thoroughly furnished unto every good work" (2 Tim. 3:17)? I certainly hope so.

The church has undergone a lot of grief through the years at the hands of those who would bind our consciences with extrascriptural norms. Extrascriptural knowledge, of course, is often needed for the proper application of scriptural commands; but like Luther, we must never permit ourselves to be tyrannized by human expertise. Now, when I read that passage in J. M. Spier's *Introduction to Christian Philosophy* (p. 88) where he suggests that it is sinful to "build churches in Roman style, or write a book in the literary style of the 17th century," I still bristle. Where does the Bible say that I can't do that if I want to? Jim Olthuis once tried to convince me that Spier is operating on the basis of biblical norms (e.g., don't give offense), but the argument there is precarious, to say the least, both exegetically and logically. The key question, though, is this: Is Toronto willing boldly and forthrightly (again, not grudgingly!), alongside its strong concern for general revelation, to proclaim the liberty of the Christian man from all alleged divine commands that cannot be validated through Scripture? For if Toronto is out to entangle me in a yoke of bondage (even if that bondage be called the "word for creation"), then I must stand with Paul, Luther, and the partisans of Christian freedom.

4. The Perspicuity of Scripture

Now, I know that in theory, at least, the Toronto position is that Scripture does not need philosophy to make it clear. That theory, however, sometimes appears to be compromised when other aspects of the Toronto approach are taken into account. For one thing, that approach does insist that all of us read Scripture through the spectacles of a "life view," and the proper life view (by which Scripture can be correctly understood) always comes out sounding like the cosmonomic idea philosophy, at least in general outline. It is, in any case, a life view against which philosophical objections may be urged.

Further, the insistence that Scripture is a "naive" book and in no degree or measure "theoretical" is an insistence that no one but a "cosmonomic" philosopher would dream of making (and, I might add, this is one of the least plausible features of the cosmonomic philosophy, in my opinion). Further, the insistence in Dooyeweerd that Scripture is a "book of faith" and the related assertion of Olthuis that Scripture is "confessionally qualified" utilize concepts of "faith" and "confession" that are part and parcel of a distinctive philosophical outlook. It is therefore clear to me that in the Toronto view, Scripture cannot be rightly understood unless the reader accepts at least certain important elements of the cosmonomic-idea philosophy. In Dooyeweerd and others, this hermeneutic leads to some rather gross distortions of scriptural teaching. Olthuis's "confessional qualification" appears to me much less likely to cause such distortions. The fact remains, however, that for all these men philosophy governs exegesis to one extent or another. Philosophy determines what Scripture can and cannot say. In my view, this philosophic imperialism seriously compromises the clarity of Scripture—the power of Scripture to speak for itself and thereby to correct our wayward philosophizing.

I am not committed to maintaining any of these criticisms down to my dying day. I'm willing to be taught if I have misunderstood or misjudged. I trust, however, that respondents to this article will try to tell me not only that I am wrong, but also how and why. And if you Toronto people "agree" with me, would you please implement that agreement by a softening of the rhetoric, by clarifying these matters in your own writing, by working to alleviate the confusion that some of your previous writings have wrought in the church of Christ?

GOD AND BIBLICAL LANGUAGE: TRANSCENDENCE AND IMMANENCE[1]

Note: In this early essay, I address the objection that human language is in some general way unfit to speak of God. I address this issue in general linguistic terms, and also the form this objection often took in the 1970s—that language about God is "unverifiable" and therefore "cognitively meaningless." This essay will supplement chapters 14–23 of the present volume, which deal with Scripture's teaching that God's word comes to us in human language. It will also address the views of Karl Barth and other liberal theologians, which I criticized in more general terms in chapters 3–7 of this book, and the issue of circular argument, which comes up several times in the main text.

One of the most persuasive and frequent contemporary objections to the orthodox view of biblical authority goes like this: the Bible cannot be the word of God because no human language can be the word of God. On this view, not only the Bible but human language *in general* is an unfit vehicle—unfit to convey infallibly a message from God to man.

1. This article was originally published in John W. Montgomery, ed., *God's Inerrant Word* (Minneapolis: Bethany Fellowship, 1974), 159–77. Used by permission of Bethany House, a division of Baker Publishing Group, copyright 2005. All rights to this material are reserved. Materials are not to be distributed to other Web locations for retrieval, published in other media, or mirrored at other sites without written permission from Baker Publishing Group. Available at http://bakerbooks.com, http://www.BakerPublishingGroup.com. For stylistic purposes, this appendix has been copyedited for inclusion in this volume.

This objection takes various forms, three of which I will discuss.

1. Some linguists and philosophers of language have suggested that language is never completely true—that the undeniable discrepancy that always exists between symbol and reality (the word *desk* is not a desk, for instance) injects falsehood into every utterance. This contention is sometimes buttressed by the further assertion that all language is metaphorical, figurative, and thus can never convey the "literal" truth. There is, however, something odd about any view that attributes falsehood to all language. For one thing, the assertion that "all sentences are false" is self-refuting if taken literally; and if we don't take it literally, what does it mean? Perhaps the real point is that language never conveys the "*whole* truth"—that it never conveys the truth with absolute precision or absolute comprehensiveness. But consider the following. (a) Some sentences are, in one sense, perfectly precise and comprehensive. Take "Washington is the capital of the United States"; could that fact be stated more precisely? more comprehensively? (b) Of course, even the aforementioned sentence is not comprehensive in the sense of "saying everything there is to say" about Washington and the United States. But no human being ever *tries* to say all that. Nor does the Bible claim to say "everything" about God. The claim to infallibility does not entail a claim to comprehensiveness in this sense. And where no claim to comprehensiveness is made, lack of comprehensiveness does not refute infallibility. (c) Nor is imprecision necessarily a fault. "Pittsburgh is about three hundred miles from Philadelphia" is imprecise in a sense, but it is a perfectly good sentence and is in no usual sense untrue. An "infallible" book might contain many imprecise-but-true statements of this sort. Granting, then, that there is a sense in which language never conveys the "whole truth," we need not renounce on that account any element of the orthodox view of biblical authority.

More might be said about this first form of the objection that we are discussing—its reliance upon the discredited referential theory of meaning, its strangely generalized concept of "metaphor," its dubious presuppositions about the origin and development of language, its ultimate theological roots. These topics, however, have been adequately discussed elsewhere,[2] and my own interests and aptitudes demand that I press on immediately to other aspects of the problem. The following discussion will raise some basic issues that I trust will shed further light on this first area of concern.

2. If the first form of our objection was raised primarily by linguists, philosophers of language, and their entourage, the second form (though

---

2. One helpful discussion of these matters from an orthodox Christian perspective can be found in Gordon H. Clark, *Religion, Reason and Revelation* (Philadelphia: Presbyterian and Reformed, 1961), 111–50.

similarly focused on language) arises out of broader epistemological and metaphysical concerns. In the 1920s and 1930s, the philosophy of logical positivism attempted to divide all philosophically important language into three categories: (a) tautologies ("A book is a book"; "Either it is raining or it is not raining"), (b) contradictions ("It is raining and it is not raining"; "The table is square and it is not square"), and (c) assertions of empirical fact ("There is a bird on the roof"; "The President has put price controls on beef"). Tautologies, on this view, were said to be true purely by virtue of the meanings of the terms, and contradictions false on the same account. Empirical assertions could be either true or false, and their truth or falsity was said to be ascertainable by something like the methods of natural science. When someone claims to state a fact, but upon examination it turns out that this "fact" cannot be verified or falsified by such methods, then, said the positivists, this utterance is not a statement of fact at all; it is not an "empirical assertion," so it is neither true nor false. Such an unverifiable utterance may have a use as poetry, expression of feeling, or the like, but it does not state any fact about the world; it is (to use the positivists' technical term) "cognitively meaningless"; it does not measure up to the "verification criterion of meaning." On such grounds, the positivists dismissed metaphysical statements ("Mind is the absolute coming to self-consciousness") and theological statements ("God is love") as cognitively meaningless. Ethical statements ("Stealing is wrong") were also seen not as statements of fact but as expressions of attitude, commands, or some other noninformative type of language.[3]

As a general theory of meaningfulness, logical positivism was too crude to last very long. Disputes quickly arose over what methods of verification were to be tolerated, how conclusive the verification or falsification must be, and other matters too technical to discuss here. Many felt that the whole project was to some extent a rationalization of prejudice—not an objective analysis of what constitutes "meaningfulness," but an attempt to get rid of language distasteful to various philosophers by constructing a "principle" arbitrarily designed for that purpose.[4]

---

3. The classical exposition of logical positivism in the English language is A. J. Ayer, *Language, Truth and Logic* (New York: Dover, 1946).

4. One of the sharpest debates was over the status of the verification principle itself. Surely it was not to be regarded as a tautology; but it did not seem to be "verifiable" either in any quasi-scientific sense. Was it then to be dismissed as "cognitively meaningless"? Ayer himself (see previous note) came to the view that the verification principle was a "convention" (see his introduction to the anthology *Logical Positivism* [Glencoe, IL: Free Press, 1959], 15). He maintained that this "convention" had some basis in ordinary usage, but admitted that it went beyond ordinary usage in crucial respects.

No thinker of any consequence today subscribes to the "verification principle" as a general criterion of meaningfulness. One aspect of the positivists' concern, however, is very much with us. Although we do not buy the whole logical positivist theory, many of us are quite impressed with the basic notion that *a fact ought to make a difference*. This concern is vividly presented in the oft-quoted parable of Antony Flew:

> Once upon a time two explorers came upon a clearing in the jungle. In the clearing were growing many flowers and many weeds. One explorer says, "Some gardener must tend this plot." So they pitch their tents and set a watch. No gardener is ever seen. "But perhaps he is an invisible gardener." So they set up a barbed-wire fence. They electrify it. They patrol with bloodhounds. (For they remember how H. G. Wells's *The Invisible Man* could be both smelt and touched though he could not be seen.) But no shrieks ever suggest that some intruder has received a shock. No movements of the wire ever betray an invisible climber. The bloodhounds never give cry. Yet still the Believer is not convinced. "But there is a gardener, invisible, intangible, insensible to electric shocks, a gardener who has no scent and makes no sound, a gardener who comes secretly to look after the garden which he loves." At last the Sceptic despairs, "But what remains of your original assertion? Just how does what you call an invisible, intangible, eternally elusive gardener differ from an imaginary gardener or even from no gardener at all?"[5]

If there is *no difference* between "invisible gardener" and "no gardener," then surely the dispute between Believer and Sceptic is not about facts. If there is no difference, then talk of an "invisible gardener" may be a useful way of expressing an attitude toward the world, but it cannot make any empirical assertion about the world. Flew is not asking the Believer to verify his view in some quasi-scientific way (although one suspects that is what would make him most happy); he is simply asking him to state what *difference* his belief makes.

As we might suspect, Flew thinks that much language about God makes "no difference." Believers say that "God is love," even though the world is full of cruelty and hatred. How does such a God differ from a devil or from no God at all? And if "God is love" makes no difference, how can it be a fact? How can it be, as the positivists liked to say, "cognitively meaningful"?

5. Antony Flew et al., "Theology and Falsification," in *New Essays in Philosophical Theology*, ed. Antony Flew and Alasdair C. MacIntyre (London: SCM Press, 1955), 96.

Flew does not suggest that *all* religious language succumbs to this difficulty, or even that all language about God is in jeopardy. He seems to be thinking mainly of what "often" happens in the thought of "sophisticated religious people."[6] Still, his knife cuts deep. Can any Christian believer offer a straightforward answer to Flew's concluding question, "What would have to occur or to have occurred to constitute for you a disproof of the love of, or of the existence of, God?"[7] Our first impulse is to say with the apostle Paul, "If Christ be not risen, then is our preaching vain, and your faith is also vain."[8] The resurrection shows that God does make a difference! Disprove the resurrection, and you disprove God. The resurrection (but of course not only the resurrection!) demonstrates the great difference between God and no-God.

But push the argument back another step: what would have to occur or to have occurred to constitute for you a disproof of the *resurrection*? Do we have a clear idea of how the resurrection may be falsified? Paul appeals to witnesses,[9] but the witnesses are dead. What if a collection of manuscripts were unearthed containing refutations of the Christian message by first-century Palestinian Jews? And what if these manuscripts contained elaborate critiques of the Pauline claim in 1 Corinthians 15, critiques backed up with massive documentation, interviews with alleged witnesses, and so on? And then: what if the twenty-five most important NT scholars claimed on the basis of this discovery that belief in the physical resurrection of Christ was untenable? Would that be sufficient to destroy our faith in the resurrection? It would be hard to imagine any stronger sort of "falsification" for any event of past history. And I don't doubt that many would be swayed by it. But many would not be. I for one would entertain all sorts of questions about the biases of these documents and those of the scholars who interpreted them. I would want to check out the whole question myself before conceding the point of doctrine. And what if I did check it out and found no way of refuting the antiresurrection position? Would that constitute a disproof? Not for me, and I think not for very many professing Christians. We all know how abstruse scholarly argument can be; there are so many things that can go wrong. In such a situation, it is not difficult to say, "Well, I can't prove the scholars wrong, but they may be wrong nonetheless." And if the love of Christ has become precious to me, and if I have been strongly convinced that the Bible is his Word, I am more likely to believe what he says in 1 Corinthians 15 than to believe what a lot of scholars say on the basis of extrabiblical evidence. Could we *ever* be persuaded that the resurrection was a hoax? Perhaps; but such a change would be more than a change in opinion; it would be a loss of faith. In terms of

---

6. Ibid., 98.
7. Ibid., 99.
8. 1 Cor. 15:14. All quotations of Scripture in this appendix are from the kjv.
9. 1 Cor. 15:5–8.

Scripture, such a change would be a yielding to temptation. For our God calls us to believe his word even when the evidence appears against it. Sarah will bear a son, even though she is ninety and her husband is a hundred![10] God is just, even though righteous Job must suffer! The heroes of the faith believed the word of God *without* the corroboration of other evidence: they walked by faith, not by sight.[11] As long as we remain faithful, God's word takes precedence over other evidence.

Flew's objection, therefore, is not to be lightly dismissed. There is a sense in which not only the language of "sophisticated religious people" but even the language of simple Christian believers fails to measure up to his challenge. God-language *resists* falsification. It is difficult to say what would refute a faith assertion, for faith requires us to resist all temptation to doubt within the faith language. No terms can be specified for renouncing faith assertions, for faith *excludes, prohibits,* such renouncement.

Does this, then, mean that the resurrection "makes no difference"? We hope not! We certainly want to say that it *does* make a difference. Yet we find it difficult to say what would refute our belief in the resurrection. We find it difficult to conceive of any state of affairs in which we would abandon our belief. We find it difficult to say what the resurrection rules out. And thus we find it difficult to state *what difference it makes.* Perhaps, then, talk of the resurrection does not really concern any empirical fact. Perhaps all God-talk is cognitively meaningless. And perhaps, then, God cannot be spoken of at all in human language. And if that is true, all talk of Scripture as the Word of God is clearly nonsense.

This, then, is the second form of the objection that I stated at the beginning of the paper, the second way in which human language is said to be disqualified as a medium of divine speech. Let us briefly examine the third form of the objection before I present my response:

3. The third form of our objection is more distinctively theological. Karl Barth, for example, suggests on theological grounds that human language is unfit to convey truth about God:

> The pictures in which we view God, the thoughts in which we think Him, the words with which we can define Him, are in themselves unfitted to this object and thus inappropriate to express and affirm the knowledge of Him.[12]

10. Gen. 17:16–17.

11. Heb. 11. The contrast between faith and sight alludes to 2 Corinthians 5:7.

12. Karl Barth, *Church Dogmatics,* vol. 2, *The Doctrine of God,* ed. G. W. Bromiley and T. F. Torrance, trans. T. H. L. Parker, W. B. Johnston, H. Knight, and J. L. M. Haire (New York: Scribner, 1957), 1:188.

> The Bible, further, is not itself and in itself God's past revelation, but by becoming God's Word it attests God's past revelation and is God's past revelation in the form of attestation. . . . Attestation is, therefore, the service of this something else, in which the witness answers for the truth of this something else.[13]

This sort of point, which is very common in twentieth-century theology, is essentially a religious appeal to the divine transcendence. God is the Lord, the Creator, the Redeemer. To him belong all praise and glory. How can any human language ever be "fitted" to the conveyance of his word? Surely human language, like everything else human and finite, can be only a servant, confessing its own unfitness, its own inadequacy. The Bible cannot *be* revelation; it can only *serve* revelation. To claim anything more for human language, for the Bible, is to dishonor God—to elevate something finite and human to divine status. To claim anything more is to think of revelation "in abstraction from" God himself and from Jesus Christ.[14] It is not just a mistake; it is an impiety.

At the same time, Barth does insist that the words of revelation have an importance:

> Thus God reveals Himself in propositions by means of language, and human language at that, to the effect that from time to time such and such a word, spoken by the prophets and apostles and proclaimed in the Church, becomes His Word. Thus the personality of the Word of God is not to be played off against its verbal character and spirituality.
>
> The personification of the concept of the Word of God . . . does not signify any lessening of its verbal character.[15]

The words are still unfit; they are not themselves revelation; they are not necessarily true themselves, but they witness to the truth of "something else." Nevertheless, the words are important, because from time to time God may use them to communicate with man. Even when they are false, they are God's instruments. God uses them, however, not as true propositional representations of his message, but as the instruments for an encounter that no human language is fit to describe.

Barth, therefore, like Flew, argues that God cannot be truly spoken of in human language. Here, it would seem, the resemblance between Barth and Flew ceases; for Barth argues "from above," Flew "from below." Barth

13. Karl Barth, *Church Dogmatics*, vol. 1, *The Doctrine of the Word of God*, ed. G. W. Bromiley and T. F. Torrance, trans. G. T. Thomson (New York: Scribner, 1936), 1:125.
14. Ibid., 155ff.
15. Ibid., 156f.

argues that God is too great for language; Flew argues that language cannot speak meaningfully of God. But are the two positions really that far apart? Thomas McPherson suggests that an alliance is possible between the logical positivist philosophers and theologians such as Rudolph Otto (McPherson might also have cited Karl Barth in this connection) who stress the transcendence of God over language:

> Perhaps positivistic philosophy has done a service to religion. By showing, in their own way, the absurdity of what theologians try to utter, positivists have helped to suggest that religion belongs to the sphere of the unutterable. And this may be true. And it is what Otto, too, in his way, wanted to point out. Positivists may be the enemies of theology, but the friends of religion.[16]

Enemies of *some* theology—not of Otto's theology, nor of Barth's, nor of Buber's (to which McPherson refers in a footnote), nor (I would judge) of the broad tradition of dialectical and existential theologies of the twentieth century. In positivism and in these modern theologies, God belongs to the sphere of the unutterable, and human language (when "cognitively meaningful") belongs to the sphere of the humanly verifiable. Let us then consider the Flew problem and the Barth problem as one.

RESPONSE

Religious language is "odd" in a great number of ways. Not only does it tend to resist falsification, as Flew has pointed out, it also tends to claim certainty for itself, as opposed to mere possibility or probability.[17] It also tends to be connected with *moral* predicates—as if disbelief in it were a *sin*, rather than a mere mistake.[18] It is frequently spoken with great passion; with Kierkegaard we tend to be suspicious of allegedly religious language that seems detached or uncommitted.

16. Thomas McPherson, "Religion as the Inexpressible," in *New Essays in Philosophical Theology*, ed. Antony Flew and Alasdair C. MacIntyre (London: SCM Press, 1955), 140f. In a footnote, McPherson notes a similar view in Martin Buber, *I and Thou*, 2nd ed. (New York: Scribner, 1958).

17. Note Ludwig Wittgenstein's interesting discussion of this point in *Lectures and Conversations on Aesthetics, Psychology and Religious Belief: Compiled from Notes Taken by Yorick Smythies, Rush Rhees and James Taylor*, ed. Cyril Barrett (Oxford: Blackwell, 1966), 53–59. Wittgenstein seems to make the extreme suggestion that religious belief *never* is "probable" in character. Wittgenstein obviously never spent much time around seminary students and academic theologians.

18. Cf. ibid., 59.

On the other hand, religious language is in some respects very "ordinary," very similar to other language. It is not a technical, academic language like that of physics or philosophy; it is the language of ordinary people. It is not restricted to some limited and distinctive compartment of human life; rather, it enters into all human activities and concerns. We pray for the healing of a loved one, for help in a business crisis; we seek to eat and drink to the glory of God.[19] We believe that our faith "makes a difference" in the real world, that God can enter into all the affairs of our life and make his presence felt. In this respect, the "action of God in history" is like the action of *anyone* in history. God can change things, can make them different. And what he does does not occur unless he chooses to do it. God makes a difference, and in that sense he is *verifiable*—much as the existence of any person is verifiable (or so, at least, it appears to the simple believer!). Few religious people would claim that their faith is a blind leap in the dark. They have "reasons for faith." These reasons may be the technical theistic arguments of the philosophers, or simply the childlike appeal to experience—"He lives within my heart." One who really believes (as opposed to one who merely drifts along in a religious tradition) believes for a *reason*, because he thinks God has somehow made his presence felt, because God now *makes a difference*—to him.

Religious language, then, is "odd" and it is "ordinary." If an analysis of religious language is to be adequate, it must take *both* features into account, not just one of them. Flew and Barth do not reflect very much upon the "ordinariness" of religious language. They seem to imply that it is a sort of delusion, for it makes a claim to verifiability that cannot on analysis be sustained, or because it betrays a spirit of human pride, bringing God down to man's level. For Barth at least, we gather that the "ordinariness" of religious language is a mark of its *humanity*, a mark of its *unfitness* to convey the word of God. There is, however, another interpretation of the data—one that does not write off the "ordinariness" of religious language as a delusion, one that accounts both for the verifiability of religious statements and for their tendency to resist verification, one that illumines the ways in which Scripture itself speaks of God.

Religious language is language of *basic conviction*. It is the language by which we state, invoke, honor, advocate (and otherwise "bring to bear") those things of which we are most certain, those things that are most important to us, those things that we will cling to even though we must lose all else. Not all language of "basic conviction" is religious in the usual sense. Many people who consider themselves irreligious have "basic convictions"

19. 1 Cor. 10:31.

of some sort. In fact, it may well be disputed whether anyone can avoid having *some* basic conviction—whether it be a faith in reason, in material success, in a philosophical absolute, or in a god. But all language that is religious in the usual sense is language of basic conviction.

Someone may object that for many people their religion is *not* their most basic commitment. A man may mumble through the church liturgy every Sunday while devoting his existence almost exclusively to acquiring political power. For him, surely, the liturgy does not express his "basic commitment." True, but that is because there is something wrong. We call such a man a hypocrite, for the liturgy is *intended* to express basic conviction, and our fanatical politician utters the words deceitfully. He does not *really* "believe in God, the Father almighty" in the sense of biblical faith, though he says he does. His real faith is in something else. The man is a liar. But his lying use of the language does not change the meaning of it, which is to confess true faith in God.

All of us have basic convictions, unless possibly we are just confused. Positivists do, too—and Barthians. And insofar as we try to be consistent, we try to bring all of life and thought into accord with our basic conviction.[20] Nothing inconsistent with that conviction is to be tolerated. An inconsistency of that sort amounts to a divided loyalty, a confusion of life direction. Most of us, at least, try to avoid such confusion. The conviction becomes the paradigm of reality, of truth, and of right, to which all other examples of reality, truth, and right must measure up. As such, it is the cornerstone of our metaphysics, epistemology, and ethics. It is not, be it noted, the *only* factor in the development of a system of thought. Two people may have virtually identical "basic commitments" while differing

20. Some readers may be helped here by the observation that there are many different degrees of "basicness" among our convictions. All our convictions govern life to some degree. When someone disagrees with one of our opinions, we naturally tend to try to defend it—either to refute our opponent's argument or to show that his position is compatible with ours. The learning process is such that we always try to interpret new knowledge in such a way as to minimize disturbance to past opinions. Some opinions we hold more tenaciously than others. It is fairly easy to convince me that I am wrong about, say, the team batting average of the Pittsburgh Pirates. It is much more difficult to persuade me that the earth is flat. In the first instance, citation of one presumably competent authority is enough. In the second instance, the intrinsic unlikelihood of a flat earth would bring into question the competence of any "presumably competent authority" who held such a position. Nevertheless, if there were a full-scale revolution among scientists over systems of measurement, and cogent reasons could be given for reverting to a flat-earth view, I might be persuaded to reconsider. Some convictions, then, we relinquish less easily than others, and the "most basic convictions" (which we focus upon in the text of the article) are relinquished least easily of all. In fact, we never relinquish those unless at the same time we change in our basic concept of rationality.

greatly in their systems of thought. The two will both try to develop systems according with their common presupposition, but because of differences in experience, ability, secondary commitments, and the like, they may seek such consistency in opposite directions. But though the "basic commitment" is not the only factor in the development of thought (and life), it is (by definition) the most important factor.

We have suggested that religious language is a subdivision of "basic-commitment language." The next point is that basic-commitment language in general displays the same kinds of "oddness" and "ordinariness" that we have noted in religious language. We state our basic commitments as certainties, not merely as possibilities or probabilities, because our basic commitments are the things of which we are most sure—the paradigms of certainty against which all other certainties are measured. Basic commitments are paradigms, too, of *righteousness*; challenges to those commitments invariably seem to us unjust because such challenges, if successful, will deny our whole reason for living. And basic-commitment language is (almost tautologically) the language of *commitment*, not of detached objectivity. And to these "oddnesses" we must add the oddness of resistance to falsification.

Take a man whose basic commitment in life is the earning of money. To him, the legitimacy of that goal is a *certainty* beyond all question. When that goal conflicts with other goals, the basic goal must prevail. Questions and doubts, indeed, may enter his mind, but these questions and doubts are much like religious temptations. Insofar as he takes them seriously, he compromises his commitment; he becomes to that extent double-minded, unstable. He faces then a crisis wherein he is challenged to change his basic commitment. Under such pressure he may do so. But then the new commitment will demand the same kind of loyalty as the old one. Challenges *must* be resisted. Evidence against the legitimacy of the commitment must somehow be ignored, suppressed, or accounted for in a way that leaves the commitment intact. "Are people starving in India? We must be compassionate, of course, but the best means of helping the poor is by teaching them the virtues of free enterprise and self-help. If everyone were truly dedicated to earning money, there would be no poverty. We do them no favor by compromising our commitment!" A rationalization? It might not seem so to one so committed, especially if no other answer to the poverty question lies close at hand.

Let us rephrase Flew's question as it might be addressed to the mammon-worshiper: what would have to occur or to have occurred to constitute for you a disproof of the primacy of moneymaking? What would have to happen to cause him to abandon his faith? Well, one simply cannot say in advance! Committed as he is, he devoutly hopes that *nothing* will bring about such a change. He not only hopes, but *knows* (or so he thinks), because he interprets all reality so as to accord with that commitment. Some event, indeed (we can't say what), may cause him to change—if he yields to the temptation of regarding that event from a non-mammon perspective. He changes then because he has already compromised; it is like a change in religious faith.

The basic-commitment language is "odd," indeed, but it is also "ordinary." It is not something strange or esoteric; we use it all the time. It enters into every area of life, simply because it is so basic, so important. It is important because it "makes a difference"—more difference than anything else. Without it nothing would make sense. All of experience, then, "verifies" the validity of the commitment. We can "prove" our commitment true in any number of ways. The evidence is there.

But how can a commitment be verifiable and nonverifiable at the same time? How can it present proof and at the same time resist falsification by contrary evidence? The resolution of this paradox gets us to the heart of the matter. Think of a philosopher who is committed to establishing all truth by the evidence of his senses. Sense experience is his criterion of truth. What evidence would disprove that criterion? In one sense none, for if sense experience is truly his criterion, then all objections to the criterion will have to be verified through sense experience. They will have to be tested by the criterion they oppose. "Disproof," as with other basic commitments, will come only when there is something like a crisis of faith. At the same time, all evidence proves the criterion. The philosopher will argue very learnedly to establish his conviction. He will refute contrary claims; he will produce carefully constructed arguments.

The arguments, of course, will be "circular." Arguments for the sense criterion must be verified by the sense criterion itself. The philosopher must argue for sense experience by appealing to sense experience. What choice does he have? If he appeals to something else as his final authority, he is simply being inconsistent. But this is the case with any "basic commitment." When we are arguing on behalf of an absolute authority, then our final appeal must be to that authority and to no other. A proof of the primacy of reason must appeal to reason; a proof of the necessity of logic must appeal to logic; a proof of the primacy of mammon must itself be part of an attempt to earn more money; and a proof of the existence of God must appeal in the final analysis to God.

Such arguments are circular, but they are also arguments. A "proof" of, say, the primacy of reason can be highly persuasive and logically sound, even though, at one level, circular. The circularity is rarely blatant; it lurks in the background. One never says, "Reason is true because reason says it is." One says instead, "Reason is true because one must presuppose it even to deny it." The second argument is just as circular as the first. Both presuppose the validity of reason. But in the second argument, the presupposition is implicit rather than explicit. And the second one is highly persuasive. The irrationalist cannot help but note that he is (in many cases) presenting his irrationalism in a highly rational way. He is trying to be more rational than the rationalists—a contradictory way to be. He must decide either to be a more consistent irrationalist (but note the paradox of that!) or to abandon his irrationalism. Of course, he might renounce consistency altogether, thus renouncing the presupposition of the argument. But the argument shows him vividly how *hard* it is to live without rationality. The argument is circular, but it draws some important facts to his attention. The argument is persuasive, though circular, because down deep in our hearts we know that we cannot live without reason.[21]

21. *How* do we know? That's hard to say, but we do. Some circular arguments simply are more plausible than others. "Truth is a giant onion, for all true statements are onion shoots in disguise." That argument is best interpreted as a circular one, the conclusion being presupposed in the reason offered. But there is something *absurd* about it. "Reason is necessary, for one must use reason even in order to deny it." That, too, is circular, but it seems much more plausible. A skeptic might say that the second argument seems plausible because it is our argument, while the first is not.

Knowledge itself is dreadfully hard to define. Logicians, epistemologists, and scientists have devoted countless hours to the task of finding criteria for genuine knowledge. Yet *knowledge* may not be defined as the observance of any such criteria. Knowledge occurred in human life long before there was any science of logic or epistemology or biology, and people still gain knowledge without referring to such disciplines. These disciplines try to conceptualize, define, and understand a phenomenon that exists independently of those disciplines. They do not make knowledge possible. And their concepts of knowledge change rather frequently. It would be presumptuous indeed to suppose that these disciplines have succeeded at last in defining everything that constitutes "knowledge." Thus, if the recognition of plausibility in a circular argument does not fit any existing technical criteria of "knowledge," then so much the worse for those criteria.

The fact is that recognition of such plausibility is a type of knowledge that epistemologists are obligated to note and account for. "Basic convictions" cannot be avoided, and such convictions may be proved only through circular argument. Therefore, circular argument is unavoidable at the level of basic conviction. This sort of circularity is not a defect in one system as opposed to others. It is an element of all systems. It is part of the human condition. It is altogether natural, then, that the term *knowledge* be applied to basic convictions, and if no technical account has yet been given of this sort of knowledge, then such an account is overdue.

Within a particular system, the basic convictions are not only truths, but the most certain of truths—the criteria of other truths. If we deny the term *knowledge* to these greatest of all certainties, then no lesser certainty can be called *knowledge* either. And no epistemologist may adopt a view that by doing away with all knowledge does away with his job. Knowledge is not an ideal; it is not something that we strive for and never attain. It is a commonplace

Some circular arguments are persuasive to us, others not. Those circular arguments that verify the most basic commitments of our lives are by definition the *most* persuasive to us. And because we believe those commitments true, we believe that those arguments ought to be persuasive to others, too. A Christian theist, while conceding that the argument for God's existence is circular, nevertheless will claim that the argument is sound and persuasive. For he devoutly believes that his position is true, and he believes that it can be clearly recognized as such. He believes that God made men to think in terms of *this* circularity, rather than in terms of some competing circularity.[22]

Basic-commitment language, therefore, is both "odd" and "ordinary." It resists falsification; it refuses to be judged by some antithetical commitment; yet it accepts the responsibility to verify itself. It accepts the responsibility of displaying whatever rationality and consistency it may claim.

What is Antony Flew's "basic commitment"? To reason? To "academic integrity" of some sort? To a secular ethic? To religious agnosticism? I don't know, but I would assume that he has one, since he does not seem like the sort of person who accepts values unreflectively. And more can be said: if with the Bible we divide the human race into Christian and non-Christian, those who know God and those who don't, those who love God and those who oppose him, clearly Flew by his writings has identified himself with the God-opposing group. If this self-identification truly represents his heart commitment, then according to Scripture Flew is committed to "hindering the truth" of God, exchanging the truth of God for a lie.[23] According to Scripture, he is committed at a basic level to opposing, contradicting, and resisting the truth of God that in some sense he nevertheless "knows."[24] This commitment, too, will be unfalsifiable and yet self-verifying, for it is a basic commitment; and for all its irreligiosity, it is logically like a religious commitment. Let us illustrate by a parody on Flew's parable:

> Once upon a time two explorers came upon a clearing in the jungle. A man was there, pulling weeds, applying fertilizer, trimming branches. The man turned to the explorers and introduced himself

---

of everyday life. It is the job of epistemologists to account for that commonplace, not to define it out of existence. One may not define *knowledge* in such a way as to require us to transcend our humanity in order to know. One must defer to the commonplace. And "knowledge of basic principles" is part of that commonplace.

22. These are the terms in which the matter must be phrased. The controversy is between competing circularities, not between circularity and noncircularity.

23. Rom. 1:18–25.

24. Rom. 1:19–21a; note the phrase *gnontes ton theon*, "knowing God."

as the royal gardener. One explorer shook his hand and exchanged pleasantries. The other ignored the gardener and turned away: "There can be no gardener in this part of the jungle," he said; "this must be some trick. Someone is trying to discredit our previous findings." They pitch camp. Every day the gardener arrives, tends the plot. Soon the plot is bursting with perfectly arranged blooms. "He's only doing it because we're here—to fool us into thinking this is a royal garden." The gardener takes them to a royal palace, introduces the explorers to a score of officials who verify the gardener's status. Then the sceptic tries a last resort: "Our senses are deceiving us. There is no gardener, no blooms, no palace, no officials. It's still a hoax!" Finally the believer despairs: "But what remains of your original assertion? Just how does this mirage, as you call it, differ from a real gardener?"

A garden indeed! How convenient that we should be talking about gardens—for that is where the Bible's own story begins. Adam and Eve lived in a garden, and they knew the divine Gardener. He talked to them, worked with them, lived with them, until one day Eve—and Adam—denied that he was there. Irrational it was, for sin is at its root irrational. And Scripture tells us that ever since that day, sinners have been guilty of the same irrationality. God is verifiable, knowable, "clearly seen" in his works;[25] but men still—"irrationally" because sinfully—deny him. To the Christian, the denials lapse into cognitive meaninglessness—an attempt to evade God by using atheistic language to describe a patently theistic world.

From a "neutral" point of view, both Flew and the Christian are in the same boat. Both have beliefs that are "odd" and "ordinary"—resistant to falsification, yet verifiable on their own terms. But of course, there is no "neutral" point of view. You are either for God or against him. You must place yourself in one circle or the other. Logically, both systems face the difficulties of circularity. But one is true and the other is false. And if man is made to know such things, then you can tell the difference. You *know* you can!

Our response to Flew, in short, is this: (1) He has told only half the story. Religious language does resist falsification, as he says—but it also often claims to be verifiable in terms of its own presuppositions. (2) These epistemological peculiarities attach to all "basic-commitment language," not just to religious or Christian language, and thus they attach to unbelieving language as well. Therefore, these considerations may not be urged as a criticism of Christianity. They are simply descriptive of the human epistemological condition. (3) Scripture pictures the *unbeliever* as the truly

25. Rom. 1:20.

ridiculous figure, who ignores patent evidence and makes mockery of reason, on whose basis no knowledge is possible. To the Christian, the unbelieving circle is, or ought to be, absurd: something like "Truth is a giant onion; therefore truth is a giant onion."

Flew, therefore, does not succeed in showing religious language to be "cognitively meaningless," and therefore he fails to show that human language cannot speak of God. But what of the third form of our objection? What of Karl Barth? Should we simply leave him behind?

Let us go back to the "oddness" and "ordinariness" of religious language, and Christian language in particular. The oddness of Christian language derives from the transcendence of God, and the ordinariness of it derives from God's immanence. Christian language is odd because it is the language of basic commitment, and the transcendence of God's lordship demands that our commitment be basic. This language is odd because it expresses our most ultimate presuppositions, and these presuppositions are the demands that God makes upon us—nothing less. It is odd because it attempts to convey God's demands—his demands for all of life. It will not be "falsified" by some secular philosophical criterion, because God will not be judged by such a criterion. "Let God be true, but every man a liar."[26] God's own Word, the paradigm of all Christian language, is therefore *supremely* odd.

Christian language is "ordinary," verifiable, because not only is God the transcendent Lord, he is also "with us," close to us. These two attributes do not conflict with one another. God is close to us *because* he is Lord. He is Lord, and thus free to make his power felt everywhere we go. He is Lord, and thus able to reveal himself clearly to us, distinguishing himself from all mere creatures. He is Lord, and therefore the most central fact of our experience—the least avoidable, the most verifiable.

And because God's own Word is supremely odd, it is supremely ordinary. Because it is supremely authoritative, it is supremely verifiable. Because it furnishes the ultimate presuppositions of thought, it furnishes the ultimate *truths* of thought.

Barth's argument essentially reverses this picture (derived from Scripture) of God's transcendence and immanence. To Barth, God's transcendence implies that he *cannot* be clearly revealed to men, clearly represented by human words and concepts. This view of God's transcendence contradicts the view of God's immanence that we presented. Similarly, Barth has a view of God's immanence that contradicts the view of transcendence that we presented. To Barth, the immanence of God implies that words of merely human authority, words that are fallible, may from time to time "become"

26. Rom. 3:4.

the word of God. Thus, the only authority we have, in the final analysis, is a fallible one. The only "word of God" we have is a fallible human word. God does not make authoritative demands that require unconditional belief; he does not determine the presuppositions of our thought; he does not resist all falsification—rather, he endorses falsehood and sanctifies it.

Well, who is right? Does God's transcendence include or exclude an authoritative verbal revelation of himself to men? Note that this question must be faced squarely. It is not enough to say that revelation must be seen in the context of God's transcendence, for that transcendence has been understood in different ways, and one must therefore defend his particular view of it. One does not get into the heart of the matter by saying that one view sees revelation "in abstraction from" God's lordship, for the two sides do not agree on the nature of this lordship or the relation that revelation is supposed to sustain to that lordship.

Both views claim scriptural support. Barth can appeal to the basic Creator-creature relationship as presented in Scripture: man is a creature; his ultimate trust must rest solely in God. To put ultimate confidence in something finite is idolatry. Human words are finite. Therefore, to put ultimate confidence in Scripture is idolatry. And in a fallen world, such confidence is all the more foolish, for human words are sinful as well as finite. Sinful speech can never perfectly honor God. The gospel precisely requires us to *disown* any claim to perfection, to confess the *inadequacy* of all human works, to cast all our hope on the mercy of God. How can we put ultimate trust in human words and in God's mercy at the same time?

Barth's view can be stated very persuasively, as long as it focuses on the general facts of creation and redemption. Scripture *does* condemn idolatry; it *does* condemn reliance on merely human means of salvation. But when this view turns specifically to the concept of revelation, its unbiblical character becomes obvious. For Scripture itself never deduces from God's transcendence the inadequacy and fallibility of all verbal revelation. Quite to the contrary: in Scripture, verbal revelation is to be obeyed without question, *because* of the divine transcendence:

> Hear, O Israel: The LORD our God is one LORD: and thou shalt love the LORD thy God with all thine heart, and with all thy soul, and with all thy might. And these words, which I command thee this day, shall be in thine heart: and thou shalt teach them diligently unto thy children, and shalt talk of them when thou sittest in thine house, and when thou walkest by the way, and when thou liest down, and when thou risest up. . . . Ye shall diligently keep

> the commandments of the LORD your God, and his testimonies,
> and his statutes, which he hath commanded thee.[27]

One who serves God as Lord will obey his verbal revelation without question. One who loves Christ as Lord will keep his commandments.[28] God's lordship—transcendence—demands unconditional belief in and obedience to the words of revelation; it *never* relativizes or softens the authority of these words. But how can that be? Is Scripture itself guilty of idolizing human words? The answer is simply that Scripture does not regard verbal revelation as merely human words. Verbal revelation, according to Scripture, is the Word of *God*, as well as the word of man. As with the incarnate Christ, verbal revelation has divine qualities as well as human qualities. Most particularly, it is divine as to its *authority*. To obey God's Word is to obey *him*; to disobey God's Word is to disobey *him*. Unconditional obedience to verbal revelation is not idolatry of human words; it is simply a recognition of the divinity of God's own words. It is the deference that we owe to God as our Creator and Redeemer.

Dishonoring the divine is just as sinful as idolizing the creature. The two are inseparable. To disobey God is to obey something less than God. When we turn from God's words, we idolize human words. If Scripture is right, if verbal revelation does have divine authority, then it is Barth's view that encourages idolatry. For Barth's view would turn us away from proper deference to God's words, and would have us instead make a "basic commitment" to the truth of some other words—our own, perhaps, or those of scientists, or those of theologians.

These considerations do not prove that Scripture is the Word of God. They do show, however, that the biblical doctrine of divine transcendence does not compromise the authority of verbal revelation. One may, indeed, prefer Barth's concept of transcendence to the biblical one, but such a view may not be paraded and displayed as the authentic Christian position.

We conclude, then, that the "objection" before us is unsound in all its three forms. Human language may convey the infallible word of God, because God is *Lord*—even of human language.

---

27. Deut. 6:4–7, 17.
28. John 14:15, 21, 23; 15:10. On these matters, compare my other essay in this collection—Appendix F in this volume.

SCRIPTURE SPEAKS FOR ITSELF[1]

Note: In this early essay, I summarize Scripture's teaching about itself in a somewhat different way from my treatment in this book. The essay interacts somewhat with Barth, Brunner, and other recent theologians. This discussion supplements the account of Scripture's self-testimony in the present volume, chapters 14–41 and the accounts of modern theology, especially in chapter 7.

What does Scripture say about itself'? The question is both momentous and commonplace.

It is momentous: the self-witness of Scripture has been for centuries the cornerstone of the orthodox Christian argument for biblical authority. For one thing, there would never be any such argument unless there were reason to believe that Scripture *claimed* authority. If Scripture renounced all claim to authority, or even remained neutral on the subject, there would not be much reason for Christians today to claim authority *for* Scripture. But if Scripture *does* claim authority over us, then we are faced with a momentous challenge indeed. Acceptance or rejection of that claim will influence every aspect of Christian doctrine and life.

1. This article was originally published in John W. Montgomery, ed., *God's Inerrant Word* (Minneapolis: Bethany Fellowship, 1974). Used by permission of Bethany House, a division of Baker Publishing Group, copyright 2005. All rights to this material are reserved. Materials are not to be distributed to other Web locations for retrieval, published in other media, or mirrored at other sites without written permission from Baker Publishing Group. Available at http://bakerbooks.com, http://www.BakerPublishingGroup.com. For stylistic purposes, this appendix has been copyedited for inclusion in this volume.

Furthermore, the authority of Scripture is a doctrine of the Christian faith—a doctrine like other doctrines—like the deity of Christ, justification by faith, and sacrificial atonement. To prove such doctrines, Christians go to Scripture. Where else can we find information on God's redemptive purposes? But what of the doctrine of the authority of Scripture? Must we not, to be consistent, also prove that doctrine by Scripture? If so, then the self-witness of Scripture not only must be the *first* consideration in the argument, but must also be the final and decisive consideration.

Now, of course, someone may object that that claim is not competent to establish itself. If the Bible *claims* to be God's Word, that does not prove that it is God's Word. That is true in a sense. Many documents claim to be the word of some god or other. The Qur'an, the Book of Mormon, and countless other books have made such claims. In no case does the claim in itself establish the authority of the book. The claim must be compared with the evidence—evidence furnished through the presuppositions that come from, among other things, our religious convictions. A Christian must look at the evidence with Christian assumptions; a rationalist must look at the evidence with rationalistic assumptions. And the Christian finds his most basic assumptions in the Bible.

As I have argued elsewhere,[2] it is impossible to avoid circularity of a sort when one is arguing on behalf of an *ultimate criterion*. One may not argue for one ultimate criterion by appealing to another. And the argument over scriptural authority is precisely an argument over ultimate criterion.

We must not, of course, simply urge non-Christians to accept the Bible because the Bible says so. Although there is much truth in that simplicity, it can be misleading if stated in that form without further explanation. A non-Christian must start where he is. Perhaps he believes that Scripture is a fairly reliable source, though not infallible. He should then be urged to study Scripture as a historical source for Christian doctrine, as the *original* "source." He will be confronted with the claims of Scripture—about God, about Christ, about man, about itself. He will compare the biblical way of looking at things with his own way. And if God wills, he will see the wisdom of looking at things Scripture's way. But we must not mislead him about the demand of Scripture. He must not be allowed to think that he can become a Christian and go on thinking the same old way. He must be told that Christ demands a *total* repentance—of heart, mind, will, emotions—the whole man. He must learn that Christ demands a change in "ultimate criterion." And thus he must learn that even the evidentiary procedures he uses to establish biblical authority must be reformed by the Bible. He must

---

2. See Appendix E, "God and Biblical Language."

learn that "evidence" is at bottom an elaboration of God's self-witness, that "proving" God is the same as hearing and obeying him.

So the question[3] of the biblical self-witness is a momentous one indeed. In a sense it is the *only* question. If by "self-witness" we mean not merely the texts in which the Bible explicitly claims authority but the whole character of the Bible as it confronts us, then the question of biblical authority is purely and simply the question of biblical self-witness.

On the other hand, the question is also commonplace: simply because it is so important, the question has been discussed over and over again by theologians. Although I feel greatly honored by the invitation to speak and write on such a basic question, I must confess also to a slight feeling of numbness. What can I say that hasn't been said already? What can I say that Gaussen, Warfield, Kuyper, Murray, Young, Van Til, Kline, Ridderbos, Pache, Wenham, Packer, Montgomery, Pinnock, and Gerstner haven't said? Even in this collection, some of the other papers will overlap this topic. No doubt, in a collection of papers of this sort, someone ought to summarize the basic material. But I can't help thinking that it might be best just to quote snatches from other authors whose scholarship and eloquence are far superior to my own. It *might* be, but I won't follow that

---

3. We will cite some of the most helpful sources, in these questions. The classic nineteenth-century work on the subject, still useful, is Louis Gaussen, *The Inspiration of the Holy Scriptures*, trans. D. D. Scott (Chicago: Moody Press, 1949). The most impressive piece of scholarly work in this area to date remains Benjamin Breckinridge Warfield, *The Inspiration and Authority of the Bible*, ed. S. G. Craig (Philadelphia: Presbyterian and Reformed, 1948). In relating the doctrine of inspiration to a comprehensive Christian world- and life view, Abraham Kuyper's *Principles of Sacred Theology*, trans. J. H. De Vries (Grand Rapids: Eerdmans, 1965), is unsurpassed. Almost the only new things that have been said in the last few years about the doctrine have been said by Meredith G. Kline in his *Structure of Biblical Authority* (Grand Rapids: Eerdmans, 1972). A helpful guide through the issues raised by NT biblical scholarship is Herman Ridderbos, *The Authority of the New Testament Scriptures*, ed. J. M. Kik, trans. H. de Jongste (Philadelphia: Presbyterian and Reformed, 1963). The soundest overall guide to the theological controversies (in my opinion) is Cornelius Van Til, *A Christian Theory of Knowledge* (Philadelphia: Presbyterian and Reformed, 1969); cf. his "unpublished" syllabus, "The Doctrine of Scripture" (Ripon, CA: Den Dulk Foundation, 1967). For general summaries of the issues, see: Ned Bernard Stonehouse and Paul Woolley, eds., *The Infallible Word*, 3rd rev. ed. (Philadelphia: Presbyterian and Reformed, 1967)—the article by John Murray is especially helpful; Carl F. H. Henry, ed., *Revelation and the Bible* (Grand Rapids: Baker, 1958); and, on the more popular level, but most eloquent and cogent, Edward J. Young, *Thy Word Is Truth* (Grand Rapids: Eerdmans, 1957). Other recent works useful to resolving the question of the Bible's self-witness are René Pache, *The Inspiration and Authority of Scripture*, trans. Helen I. Needham (Chicago: Moody Press, 1969); Clark Pinnock, *Biblical Revelation* (Chicago: Moody Press, 1971); and John William Wenham, *Christ and the Bible* (Chicago: InterVarsity Press, 1973).

course here, because I do have a few reasons for attempting an individual, if not independent, study.

Past orthodox Christian discussions of this matter have, in my opinion, done a very adequate job, on the whole. As in all human endeavors, however, there is room for improvement here. The improvements I have in mind are chiefly two.

1. There needs to be a greater emphasis upon the *pervasiveness* throughout Scripture of the biblical self-witness. As we suggested earlier, there is a sense in which the entire Bible is self-witness. Whatever the Bible says, in a sense, it says about itself. Even the genealogies of the kings tell us about the content, and therefore the character, of Scripture. The way in which the Bible speaks of kings and vineyards and wilderness journeys and God and man and Christ—its *manner* is a testimony to its character. More specifically, the overall doctrinal structure of Scripture is an important element of the biblical self-witness. For when the Bible speaks of atonement, reconciliation, justification, and glorification, it speaks of these in such a way as to presuppose a crucial role for itself. Or, to look at redemption from a more historical perspective, from the beginning of God's dealings with men, God has taught them to give his words a particular role in their lives—a lesson that is taught again and again throughout the thousands of years of redemptive history. Now, when we neglect this emphasis on the pervasiveness of the biblical self-witness, at least two bad things happen. (a) People can get the idea that the concept of biblical authority is based largely on a few texts scattered throughout the Bible, texts that may not be very important in the overall biblical scheme of things. They might even get the idea that the doctrine of inspiration is based largely upon a *couple* of texts (2 Tim. 3:16; 2 Peter 1:21), which liberal scholars dismiss as being late and legalistic. Thus, it may seem as though the doctrine of biblical authority is a rather peripheral doctrine, rather easily dispensable for anyone who has even the slightest inclination to dispense with unpalatable doctrines. (b) People can get the idea that Christ and the Bible are separable, that you can believe in and obey Christ without believing in and obeying the Bible. They may think that Scripture is unimportant to the Christian message of redemption.

2. If, as orthodox people maintain, the biblical self-witness to its authority and infallibility is *obvious*, *clear*—and certainly if it is "pervasive"!—then we must face more squarely the question of why not-so-orthodox people see the matter differently. At one level, of course, it is legitimate to say that they fail to see the truth because of their unbelief: the god of

this world has blinded their minds.[4] Sin is "irrational"—it turns away from the obvious. But sinners, when they are scholars, at least, generally do things for a *reason*, perverse as that reason may be. And perverse or not, such reasoning is often highly plausible. If orthodox people can identify that reasoning, explain its surface plausibility, and expose its deeper error, then the orthodox view of the biblical self-witness will be stated much more cogently.

In the remaining portion of this essay, I will present an essentially traditional argument concerning the character of the biblical self-witness, but I will structure the discussion in such a way as to implement the above two concerns—not comprehensively, to be sure, probably not adequately, but to a greater degree than one might expect in a paper of this length.[5] The first section will examine the role of verbal revelation in the biblical understanding of salvation. The second will discuss the relationship of that verbal revelation to Scripture, and the third will analyze what I take to be the most common and plausible objection to the previous line of reasoning.

I. REVEALED WORDS AND SALVATION

We have suggested that the whole Bible is self-witness, but the Bible is not *only* or *primarily* self-witness. It is first and foremost not a book about a book, but a book about God, about Christ, about the salvation of man from sin. But that message of salvation includes a message about the Bible. For this salvation requires *verbal revelation*. In saving man, God *speaks* to him.

A. Lord and Servant

God spoke to man even *before* man fell into sin. The first human experience mentioned in Scripture is the hearing of God's word. Immediately after the account of man's creation, we read:

> And God blessed them, and God said unto them, Be fruitful, and multiply, and replenish the earth, and subdue it: and have dominion over the fish of the sea, and over the fowl of the air, and over every living thing that moveth upon the earth.[6]

4. 2 Cor. 4:4.
5. Therefore, the paper will also fail to do justice to other legitimate concerns.
6. Gen. 1:28. All quotations of Scripture in this appendix are from the KJV, unless otherwise noted.

It is appropriate that the hearing of these words be presented in Scripture as man's first experience. For this was the experience by which the whole course of man's life was determined. When man heard these words of God, he heard God's own definition of man. God was telling man who man was, what his task was. Everything else that man did was to be in obedience to this command. Whether a shepherd, a farmer, a miner, a businessman, a teacher, or a homemaker—his main job was to replenish and subdue the earth in obedience to this command. The command covered *all* of life, not just some compartments of it. The command was not to be questioned; it was God's sovereign determination of man's responsibility. The command asserted God's claim to *ultimate* authority, for, paradoxically, while the command declared man to have dominion over the earth, it also declared God's dominion over man. Whatever dominion man enjoys, he receives from God; he enjoys it at God's pleasure; he enjoys it out of obedience to God's command.

Why? Simply because God is God, and man is man. God is Lord; man is servant. God commands; man must obey. To have a Lord is to be under authority. A servant is responsible to obey the *commands* of another. What kind of lordship would there be without commands? The very idea is absurd. Without commands, no obedience; without obedience, no responsibility; without responsibility, no authority; without authority, no lordship.

Man was created in obedience; he fell through disobedience—disobedience to another command, this time the command concerning the forbidden tree.[7] The simplest biblical definition of *sin* is "lawlessness"[8]—rejection of, disobedience to God's commands. Therefore, just as the Word of God defines our status as God's creatures and servants, it also defines our status as *fallen* creatures, as sinners.

Redemption, according to Scripture, involves a reassertion of God's lordship. The fall, of course, did not annul God's lordship; God's lordship over fallen man is vividly expressed in divine judgment against sin. But if man is to be saved, he must be brought to realize again that God is Lord and demands man's unconditional obedience. When God saved Israel from Egypt, he called himself by the mysterious name Jehovah, which, although its exact meaning is uncertain, clearly asserts his claim to unconditional lordship.[9] And throughout the history of redemption, God continually asserted this claim by making *absolute demands* upon his people.

7. Gen. 2:17; 3:6, 11f.
8. 1 John 3:4 NASB.
9. Ex. 3:14; note context. In later years, when this sacred name was considered too sacred to be pronounced, the Jews read the word *Adonai*, "Lord," in its place.

God's demands are absolute in at least three senses. (1) They *cannot be questioned*. The Lord God has the right to demand unwavering, unflinching obedience. God blessed Abraham because he "obeyed my voice, and kept my charge, my commandments, my statutes, and my laws."[10] He did not waver,[11] even when God commanded him to sacrifice his son Isaac, the son of the promise.[12] To waver—even in that horrible situation—would have been sin. (2) God's demand is absolute also in the sense that it *transcends all other loyalties*, all other demands. The Lord God will not tolerate competition; he demands *exclusive* loyalty.[13] The servant must love his Lord with all his heart, soul, and strength.[14] One cannot serve two masters.[15] One of the most remarkable proofs of the deity of Christ in the NT is that there Jesus Christ demands—and receives—precisely this kind of loyalty from his followers, the same sort of loyalty that Jehovah demanded of Israel.[16] The Lord demands *first* place. (3) God's demand is also absolute in that it *governs all areas of life*. In the OT period, God regulated not only Israel's worship but also the diet, political life, sex life, economic life, family life, travel, and calendar of his people. No area of life was immune to God's involvement. To be sure, the NT gives us more freedom in a certain sense: the detailed dietary restrictions, uncleanness rituals, animal sacrifices, and other elements of the old order are no longer literally binding. But the NT, if anything, is *more* explicit than the OT on the comprehensiveness of God's demand: *whatsoever* we do, even eating and drinking, must be done to the glory of God.[17] We must never shut the Lord out of any compartment of our lives; there must be no areas kept to ourselves. God's lordship involves such *absolute demands*.

B. Savior and Sinner

But salvation is more than a reassertion of God's lordship. If God merely reasserted his lordship, we would be without hope, for we have turned against him and deserve death at his hand.[18] If God merely spoke to us absolute demands, we would perish, for we have not obeyed these demands. Yet our God is not only Lord, but also *Savior*. And he speaks to us not only demands, not only law, but also *gospel*—the good news of Jesus Christ. But we must empha-

---

10. Gen. 26:5.
11. Rom. 4:20.
12. Gen. 22:18.
13. Ex. 20:3, "Thou shalt have no other gods before me."
14. Deut. 6:4f.; cf. Matt. 22:37ff. and parallels in the other Gospels.
15. Matt. 6:22ff.
16. Matt. 19:16–30; cf. 8:19–22, 10–37; Phil. 3:8.
17. 1 Cor. 10:31—a NT dietary law! Cf. Rom. 14:23; 2 Cor. 10:5; Col. 3:17.
18. Rom. 3:23; 6:23.

size that he *speaks* the gospel. The gospel is a *message*, a revelation in words. How can we know that the death of Christ is sufficient to save us from sin? No human wisdom could have figured that out. Only God can declare sinners to be forgiven; only God has the right to promise salvation to those who believe. The same Lord who speaks to demand obedience also speaks to promise salvation. As Abraham,[19] we are called to believe the gospel simply because it is God's own promise. We know that believers in Christ are saved because Jesus has told us they are.[20] Only the Lord can speak the word of forgiveness, the word that declares sinners to be forgiven and that promises eternal life.

Just as there can be no lordship without an absolute demand, so there is no salvation without a gracious and certain promise. Therefore, the whole biblical message presupposes the *necessity of verbal revelation*. Without revealed words, there is neither lordship nor salvation. To "accept Christ as Savior and Lord" is to accept from the heart Christ's demand and promise. Let there be no misunderstanding: you *cannot* "accept Christ" without accepting his words. Christ himself emphasizes this point over and over again.[21] If we set aside the words of Christ in favor of a vague, undefined "personal relationship" to Christ, we simply lose the biblical Christ and substitute a Christ of our own imagination.

And not just any words will do. They must be *God's* words—words of divine (not merely human) authority, words that cannot be questioned, that transcend all other loyalties, and that govern all areas of life. They must be words that cannot be contradicted by human philosophies or theologies—or even by the "assured results of modern scholarship." Without words like *that*, we have no Lord and we have no Savior.

But where can we find words like *that*? No mere philosopher or theologian or scholar speaks such words. Many religions, indeed, claim to have such words, but how are we to judge among these many claims? How do we distinguish the voice of God from the voice of devils and the imaginations of our own hearts?

II. REVEALED WORDS AND SCRIPTURE

Scripture tells us to go to Scripture. Or, rather, the God of Scripture tells us in Scripture to go to Scripture.

---

19. Rom. 4:19f.
20. John 5:24.
21. Matt. 7:24–29; Mark 8:38; Luke 8:21; 9:26; John 8:31, 47, 51; 10:27; 12:47–50; 14:15, 21, 23f.; 15:7, 10, 14; 17:6, 8, 17. The relationship between Christ and his words is essentially the same as that between God and his words in the OT.

Of course, we must note at the outset that the Bible is not the *only* word that God has spoken. God has spoken words to and by his apostles and prophets that are not recorded in the Bible. He has also spoken, in a sense, to the earth, to the storms, to the winds and waves.[22] And in a mysterious sense, the word of God may also be identified with God himself[23] and particularly with Jesus Christ.[24] But God does not always tell us what he says to the winds and waves, and he has not always provided us with prophets at a handy distance. Rather, he has directed us to a *book*. That is where we are to go for daily, regular guidance. That is where we may always find the demands of the Lord and the promise of the Savior.

Writing goes back a long way in the history of redemption. The book of Genesis appears to be derived largely from "books of generations."[25] We don't know much about the origin of these books, but it is significant that (1) they include inspired prophecies,[26] and (2) they were eventually included among Israel's authoritative writings. From a very early time, God's people began to *record* the history of redemption for their posterity. It was important from the beginning that God's covenants, his demands and his promises, be written down, lest they be forgotten. The first explicit reference, however, to a divinely authorized book occurs in connection with the war between Israel and Amalek shortly after the exodus:

> And Joshua discomfited Amalek and his people with the edge of the sword. And the LORD said unto Moses, Write this for a memorial in a book, and rehearse it in the ears of Joshua: for I will utterly put out the remembrance of Amalek from under heaven. And Moses built an altar, and called the name of it Jehovah-nissi: For he said, Because the LORD hath sworn that the LORD will have war with Amalek from generation to generation.[27]

Not only does the Lord authorize the writing of the book, the content of it is God's own oath, his pledge. It is the Word of God, a word of absolute authority and sure promise. Because God has spoken it, it will surely happen.

22. Gen. 1:3; Pss. 33:6, 9; 119:90f.; 147:15–18; 148:5f.; cf. Matt. 8:27.
23. John 1:1.
24. John 1:14.
25. Gen. 5:1; cf. 2:4; 6:9; 10:1; 11:10, 27; 25:12, 19; 36:9; 37:2.
26. Gen. 9:25–27. Though Noah is speaking, he is administering covenantal blessing and curse, which can take effect only under divine sanction. The fulfillment of these words at a much later period shows that these words were in essence the words of God. Cf. Gen. 25:23; 27:27–29; etc.
27. Ex. 17:13–16. The language here suggests a parallel with the divine "book of life," as though this earthly book were a kind of copy of the divine original.

But an even more important example of divine writing occurs a few chapters later. In Exodus 20, God speaks the Ten Commandments to the people of Israel. The people are terrified, and they ask Moses to act as mediator between themselves and God. From Exodus 20:22 to 23:33, God presents to Moses further commandments, in addition to the ten, that Moses is to convey to the people. In Exodus 24:4, we learn that Moses wrote down all these words, and in verse 7 that he read them to the people. The people received these words as the word of God himself: "All that the LORD hath spoken will we do, and be obedient."[28] They accepted these *written* words as words of absolute demand. But something even more remarkable occurs a few verses later. The Lord calls Moses alone to ascend the mountain, "and I will give thee tables of stone, and a law, and commandments which I have written; that thou mayest teach them."[29] Note the pronouns in the first-person singular. *God* did the writing. In fact, the implication of the tenses is that God had completed the writing before Moses ascended the mountain. Moses was to go up the mountain to receive a completed, divinely written manuscript. Nor is this the only passage that stresses divine authorship of the law. Elsewhere, too, we learn that the tables were "written with the finger of God";[30] they were "the work of God, and the writing was the writing of God, graven upon the tables."[31]

What was going on here? Why the sustained emphasis on divine writing? Meredith G. Kline[32] suggests that this emphasis arises out of the nature of covenant-making in the ancient Near East. When a great king entered a "suzerainty covenant relation" with a lesser king, the great king would produce *a document* setting forth the terms of the covenant. The great king was the author because he was the lord, the sovereign. He set the terms. The lesser king was to read and obey, for he was the servant, the vassal. The covenant document was the law; it set forth the commands of the great king, and the servant was bound to obey. To disobey the document was to disobey the great king; to obey it was to obey him. Now, in Exodus 20

---

28. Ex. 24:7.

29. Ex. 24:12.

30. Ex. 31:18.

31. Ex. 32:16; cf. also 34:1; Deut. 4:13; 9:10f.; 10:2–4. In Exodus 34:27f., Moses, too, is said to have done some writing—probably portions of the law other than the Ten Commandments. And yet the written work of Moses is no less authoritative than that of the Lord himself—cf. Ex. 34:32. Moses was the mediator of the covenant, and as such was a prophet conveying God's word to the people. Cf. Ex. 4:10–17; Deut. 18:15–19. Therefore, the unique "finger of God" writing is not necessary to the authority of the documents; humanly *written* documents may be equally authoritative, as long as the words are God's. But the "finger of God" picture places awesome emphasis on the authority of the words.

32. Kline, *Structure of Biblical Authority*.

and succeeding chapters, God is making a kind of "suzerainty treaty" with Israel. As part of the treaty relation, he authors a document that is to serve as the official record of his absolute demand. Without the document there would be no covenant.

Later, more words were added to the document. We read in Deuteronomy that Moses put all these words in the ark of the covenant, the dwelling place of God, the holiest place in Israel, "that it may be there for a witness against thee."[33] The covenant document is not man's witness concerning God; it is God's witness *against* man. Man may not add to or subtract anything from the document,[34] for the document is God's word, and must not be confused with any mere human authority.

This divine authority takes many forms. In the extrabiblical suzerainty covenants, certain distinct elements have been discovered:[35] the self-identification of the lord (the giving of his name), the "historical prologue" (proclaiming the benevolent acts of the lord to the vassal), the basic demand for exclusive loyalty (called "love"), the detailed demands of the lord, the curses upon the disobedient, the blessings upon the obedient, and finally the details of covenant administration, use of the document, and so on. In the law of God, all these elements are present. God tells who he is;[36] he proclaims his grace through his acts in history;[37] he demands love;[38] he sets forth his detailed demands;[39] he declares the curses and blessings contingent on covenant obedience;[40] and he sets up the machinery for

33. Deut. 31:26.

34. Deut. 4:2; 12:32; cf. Prov. 30:6; Rev. 22:18f. How, then, could any additions be made to the document? For some additions were clearly made (Josh. 24:26, etc.). Since no man could add or subtract, the addition of a book to the covenant canon carries with it the claim that the addition has *divine* sanction.

35. Kline, *Structure of Biblical Authority*; we are listing the elements Kline finds in treaties of the second millennium B.C. He regards the Decalogue and the book of Deuteronomy as having this basic structure (thus implying a second-millennium date for Deuteronomy!), and he regards the entire OT canon as an outgrowth of these "treaties."

36. Ex. 20:2, "I am the LORD thy God"; cf. 3:14, etc.

37. Ex. 20:2, "which have brought thee out of the land of Egypt, out of the house of bondage."

38. Ex. 20:3, "Thou shalt have no other gods before me." Compare Deuteronomy 6:4f., where "love" is actually used to denote this exclusive covenant loyalty. The demand for love follows the account of God's gracious acts in history, and is regarded as the vassal's response of gratitude for the Lord's benevolence. Cf. the NT emphasis, "We love him, because he first loved us" (1 John 4:19).

39. Ex. 20:12–17. Though the division cannot be sharply made, the first four commandments might be said to represent the fundamental love requirement, while the last six describe some of its detailed outworkings.

40. Ex. 20:5f., 12. We have been tracing these covenant elements through the Decalogue, but we could have used many other parts of Scripture as well.

continuing covenant administration, laying particular emphasis on the use of the covenant book.[41] All these elements of the covenant are authoritative; all are words of God.

Theologians generally oversimplify the concept of biblical authority. To some theologians, it is God's personal self-manifestation (as in the giving of the divine name) that is authoritative. To others, it is the account of historical events. To others, the demand for love is the central thing. To others, it is the divine self-commitment to bless. But the covenantal structure of revelation has room for all these elements—and, what's more, places them in proper relation to one another. There is both love and law, both grace and demand, both *kerygma* and *didache*, both personal disclosure (stated in "I-thou" form) and objective declarations of facts, both a concept of history and a concept of inspired words. The covenant document contains authoritative *propositions* about history (the servant has no right to contradict the lord's account of the history of the covenant), authoritative commands to be obeyed, authoritative *questions* (demanding the vassal's pledge to covenant allegiance), and authoritative *performatives* (God's self-commitment to bless and curse).[42] The propositions are infallible, but infallibility is only part of biblical authority. This authority includes the authority of nonpropositional language as well.

We have seen that the idea of a "canon," an authoritative written Word of God, goes back to the very beginning of Israel's history, back to its very creation as a nation. The Scripture is the constitution of Israel, the basis for its existence. The idea of a written Word of God did *not* arise in twentieth-century fundamentalism, nor in seventeenth-century orthodoxy, nor in the postapostolic church, nor in 2 Timothy, nor in postexilic Judaism. The idea of a written Word of God is at the very foundation of biblical faith. Throughout the history of redemption, therefore, God continually calls his people back to the written Word. Over and over again, he calls them to keep "the commandments of the LORD your God, and his testimonies, and his statutes, which he hath commanded thee."[43] These are the words

---

41. This emphasis is not found in the Decalogue, but it is a major emphasis of Deuteronomy (see 31:24–29), which Kline also identifies as a covenant document.

42. Performatives ("I pronounce you man and wife"; "You are under arrest"; "Cursed be all who do not obey") do not merely state facts, but "perform" various sorts of actions. When spoken by one in authority, they "accomplish" what they set out to do. Performatives of the Lord in Scripture are uniquely authoritative, but their authority is not adequately characterized by the term *infallibility*. Infallibility is important, but it is only part of the meaning of biblical authority. *Infallibility* is not too strong, but too *weak* a term to adequately characterize biblical authority.

43. Deut. 6:17; cf. 4:1–8; 5:29–33; 6:24f.; 7:9–11; 8:11; 10:12f.; 11:1, 13, 18ff., 27f.; 12:1, 28; 13:4. In Deuteronomy, almost every page contains exhortations to obey God's

of absolute demand and sure promise, the words of the Lord. These were the words that made the difference between life and death. These were the words that could not be questioned, that transcended all other demands, that governed all areas of life. When Israel sinned and returned to the Lord, she returned also to the law of God.[44]

From time to time there were new words of God. Joshua added to the words that Moses had placed in the ark.[45] How could a mere man add to the words of God, in view of the command of Deuteronomy 4:2? The only answer can be that Joshua's words were also recognized as God's words. The prophets also came speaking God's words,[46] and some of them were written down.[47]

Thus the "Old Testament" grew. By the time of Jesus, there was a well-defined body of writings that was generally recognized as God's Word, and that was quoted as supreme authority, as Holy Scripture. Jesus and the apostles did not challenge but rather accepted this view. Not only did they accept it; they actively testified to it by word and deed. The role of Scripture in the life of Jesus is really remarkable: although Jesus was and is the Son of God, the second person of the Trinity, during his earthly ministry he subjected himself completely to the OT Scripture. Over and over again, he performed various actions, "that the scripture might be fulfilled."[48] The whole point of his life—his sacrificial death and resurrection—was determined beforehand by Scripture.[49] Jesus' testimony to Scripture, then, is not occasional but pervasive. His whole life was a witness to biblical authority. But listen particularly to what Christ and the apostles say concerning the OT. Listen to the way in which they

---

commandments and statutes and ordinances. But not only in Deuteronomy. Cf. Josh. 1:8; 8:25–28; 2 Kings 18:6; Pss. 1:1–3; 12:6f.; 19:7–11; 33:4, 11; 119:1–176; Isa. 8:16–20; Dan. 9:3ff. Read over these and the many similar passages and let the message sink into your heart. The conclusion concerning the authority of the written Word is simply inescapable.

44. 2 Kings 23:2f., 21, 25; Neh. 8. The whole OT history is a history of obedience and disobedience: obedience and disobedience to what? To God's commands; and after Exodus 20, to God's written Word. The self-witness of the OT is therefore present on every page. "Pervasive," as we said.

45. Josh. 24:26.

46. Deut. 18:15–19; Isa. 59:21; Jer. 1:6–19; Ezek. 13:2f., 17. The mark of the prophet was the phrase "Thus saith the Lord," which is found over and over again in the prophetic literature. Many theologians hostile to the orthodox view of biblical authority recognize that the prophets *claimed* an identity between their words and God's. See, e.g., Emil Brunner, *Dogmatics*, vol. 1, *The Christian Doctrine of God*, trans. Olive Wyon (Philadelphia: Westminster Press, 1950), 18, 27, 31f.

47. Isa. 8:1; 34:16ff.; Jer. 25:13; 30:2; 36:1–32; 51:60ff.; Dan. 9:1f.

48. John 19:28; see also Matt. 4:14; 5:17; 8:17; 12:17; 13:35; 21:4; 26:54–56; Luke 21:22; 24:44.

49. Luke 24:26 RSV: "*Was it not necessary that?*" Scripture imposes a *necessity* upon Christ!

cite Scripture, even in the face of Satan, to "clinch" an argument, to silence objections.[50] Listen to the titles by which they describe the OT: "Scripture," "holy Scripture," "law," "prophets," "royal law of liberty . . . the oracles of God."[51] Listen to the formulae by which they cite Scripture: "It is written"; "it says"; "the Holy Spirit says"; "Scripture says."[52] All these phrases and titles denoted to the people of Jesus' day something far more than a mere human document. These terms denoted nothing less than inspired, authoritative words of God. As Warfield pointed out, "Scripture says" and "God says" are interchangeable.[53]

And consider further the explicit *teaching* of Jesus and the apostles concerning biblical authority.

> 1. Think not that I am come to destroy the law, or the prophets: I am not come to destroy, but to fulfil. For verily I say unto you, Till heaven and earth pass, one jot or one tittle shall in no wise pass from the law; till all be fulfilled. Whosoever therefore shall break one of these least commandments, and shall teach men so, he shall be called the least in the kingdom of heaven: but whosoever shall do and teach them, the same shall be called great in the kingdom of heaven.[54]

Jots and tittles were among the smallest marks used in the written Hebrew language. Jesus is saying that *everything* in the Law and the Prophets (equals the OT) carries divine authority. And obedience to that law is the criterion of greatness in the kingdom of heaven.

> 2. Do not think that I will accuse you to the Father: there is one that accuseth you, even Moses, in whom ye trust. For had ye believed Moses, ye would have believed me: for he wrote of me. But if ye believe not his writings, how shall ye believe my words?[55]

The Jews claimed to believe Moses' writings, but they rejected Christ. Jesus replies that they do not *really* believe Moses, and he urges them to a *greater* trust in the OT. He urges them to believe *all* the law and thus come to accept his messiahship. We see here that Jesus did not merely quote

50. Matt. 4; 22:29–33; etc.
51. See Warfield, *The Inspiration and Authority of the Bible*, esp. 229–41, 361–407.
52. Ibid., 229–348.
53. Ibid.
54. Matt. 5:17–19. For detailed exegesis, see John Murray, *Principles of Conduct* (Grand Rapids: Eerdmans, 1957), 149–57. Cf. also his essay "The Attestation of Scripture," in Stonehouse and Woolley, *The Infallible Word*, 15–17, 20–24.
55. John 5:45–47.

Scripture because it was customary among the Jews. Rather, he *criticized* the prevailing custom because it was insufficiently loyal to Scripture. Jesus' view of Scripture was *stronger* than that of the Pharisees and scribes. Jesus sees Moses justly accusing the Jews because of their unbelief in Scripture. Believing Moses is the prerequisite to believing Christ.

> 3. The Jews answered him, saying, For a good work we stone thee not; but for blasphemy; and because that thou, being a man, makest thyself God. Jesus answered them, Is it not written in your law, I said, Ye are gods? If he called them gods, unto whom the word of God came, and the scripture cannot be broken; say ye of him, whom the Father hath sanctified, and sent into the world, Thou blasphemest; because I said, I am the Son of God?[56]

A difficult passage, this, but note the parenthetical language. Concerning a fairly obscure psalm, Jesus says that "the scripture cannot be broken." It cannot be wrong; it cannot fail; it cannot be rejected as we reject human words.

> 4. For whatsoever things were written aforetime were written for our learning, that we through patience and comfort of the scriptures might have hope.[57]

Here, the apostle Paul tells us that the OT is relevant not only for the people of the OT period but for us as well. It teaches us, and gives us patience, comfort, and hope. And most remarkably, the *whole* OT is relevant. None of it is dated; none of it is invalidated by more recent thought. Of what human documents may *that* be said?

> 5. We have also a more sure word of prophecy; whereunto ye do well that ye take heed, as unto a light that shineth in a dark place, until the day dawn, and the day star arise in your hearts: knowing this first, that no prophecy of the scripture is of any private interpretation. For the prophecy came not in old time by the will of man: but holy men of God spake as they were moved by the Holy Ghost.[58]

Note the context of this passage: Peter expects to die soon, and he wishes to assure his readers of the truth of the gospel.[59] He knows that

---

56. John 10:33–36; cf. Warfield, *The Inspiration and Authority of the Bible*, 138–41.
57. Rom. 15:4.
58. 2 Peter 1:19–21; cf. Warfield, *The Inspiration and Authority of the Bible*, 135–38.
59. 2 Peter 1:12–15.

false teachers will attack the church, deceiving the flock.[60] He insists that the gospel is not myth or legend, but the account of events that he himself had witnessed.[61] Yet even when the eyewitnesses have left the scene, the believers will still have a source of sure truth. They have the "word of prophecy"—the OT Scriptures—a word that is "more sure."[62] They are to "take heed" to that word, and forsake all conflicting teaching; for the word is light, and all the rest is darkness. Moreover, it did not originate through the human interpretative process; it is not a set of human opinions about God; nor did it originate in any human volition. Rather, the Holy Spirit carried the biblical writers along as they spoke for him! The Holy Spirit determined their course and their destination. The Bible consists of human writings, but its authority is no mere human authority.

> 6. All scripture is given by inspiration of God, and is profitable for doctrine, for reproof, for correction, for instruction in righteousness: that the man of God may be perfect, thoroughly furnished unto all good works.[63]

Note again the context, for it is similar to that of the last passage. Paul in this chapter paints a gloomy picture of deceivers leading people astray. How can we know the truth in all this confusion? Paul tells Timothy to hang on to the truth as he learned it from Paul,[64] but also to the "holy scriptures"[65] (which, we note, are available even to us who have not been taught personally by Paul). This Scripture is "given by inspiration of God," as the KJV says, or more literally "God-breathed"—*breathed out by God*. In less picturesque language, we might say simply "spoken by God"; but the more picturesque language also suggests the activity of the Holy Spirit in the process, the words for "spirit" and "breath" being closely related in the original Greek. Scripture is *spoken* by God; it is *his Word*; and as such it is *all* profitable, and it is *all* that we need to be equipped for good works.

---

60. 2 Peter 2.

61. 2 Peter 1:16–18. In the current theological scene, it is worth noting that Peter denies any mythological character to the message. It is not *mythos*.

62. Is the word "more sure" in the sense of being confirmed by eyewitness testimony? Or is it, as Warfield suggests (see note 58), "more sure" than eyewitness testimony? In either case, the passage places a strong emphasis upon the *certainty* of the word.

63. 2 Tim. 3:16f. For detailed exegesis, see Warfield, *The Inspiration and Authority of the Bible*, 133–35, and also 245–96 (a comprehensive treatment of the meaning of "God-breathed," another translation of "given by inspiration of God").

64. 2 Tim. 3:14.

65. 2 Tim. 3:15.

Both Old and New Testaments, then, pervasively claim authority for the OT Scriptures. But what about the NT Scriptures? Can we say that they, also, are the Word of God?

We have seen the importance of verbal revelation in both Old and New Testaments. Both Testaments insist over and over again that such words are a necessity of God's plan of salvation. As we have seen, the concepts of lordship and salvation presuppose the existence of revealed words. And in the NT, Jesus Christ is Lord and Savior. It would be surprising indeed if Jehovah, the Lord of the OT people of God, gave a written record of his demand and promise, while Jesus, the Lord incarnate of whom the NT speaks, left no such record. Jesus told his disciples over and over again that obedience to *his words* was an absolute necessity for kingdom service and a criterion for true discipleship.[66] We *need* the words of Jesus. But where are they? If there is no written record, no NT "covenant document," then has Jesus simply left us to grope in the dark?

Praise God that he has not. Jesus promised to send the Holy Spirit to lead his disciples into all truth.[67] After the Holy Spirit was poured out on the day of Pentecost, the disciples began to preach with great power and conviction.[68] The pattern remains remarkably consistent throughout the book of Acts: the disciples are filled with the Spirit, and *then* they speak of Jesus.[69] They do not speak in their own strength. Further, they constantly insist that the source of their message is God, not man.[70] Their words have absolute, not merely relative, authority.[71] And this authority attaches not only to their spoken words but also to their written words.[72] Peter classes the letters of Paul together with the "other scriptures."[73] Paul's letters are "Scripture," and we recall that "Scripture" is "God-breathed."[74]

---

66. Matt. 7:21ff., 24, 28f.; Mark 8:38; Luke 8:21; 9:26; John 8:47; 10:27; 12:47; 14:15, 21, 23f.; 15:7, 10, 14; 17:6, 8, 17; 18:37; cf. 1 Tim. 6:3; 1 John 2:3–5; 3:22; 5:2f.; 2 John 6; Rev. 12:17; 14:12. Again, look these up, and allow yourself to be impressed by the *pervasiveness* of this emphasis.

67. John 16:13, cf.; Acts 1:8.

68. Acts 2.

69. Acts 2:4; 4:8, 31; 6:10 (cf. vv. 3, 5); 7:55; 9:17–20; 13:9f., 52ff.

70. Rom. 16:25; 1 Cor. 2:10–13; 4:1; 7:40; 2 Cor. 4:1–6; 12:1, 7; Gal. 1:1, 11f., 16; 2:2; Eph. 3:3; 2 Thess. 2:2.

71. Rom. 2:16; 1 Thess. 4:2; Jude 17f.; and cf. the passages listed in the preceding and following notes.

72. 1 Cor. 14:37; Col. 4:16; 1 Thess. 5:27; 2 Thess. 3:14.

73. 2 Peter 3:16. Compare 1 Timothy 5:18, which appears to couple a quotation from Luke with a quotation from the law of Moses under the heading "Scripture."

74. The question of what books are to be regarded as NT Scripture is beyond the scope of this paper, since no actual list can be found as part of the NT's self-witness. We may certainly assume, however, on the basis of what has been said, that if revealed words are

We conclude, then, that the witness of Scripture to its own authority is *pervasive*. (1) The whole biblical message of salvation presupposes and necessitates the existence of revealed words—words of absolute demand and sure promise; without such words, we have no Lord, no Savior, no hope. (2) Throughout the history of redemption, God directs his people to find these words in written form, in those books that we know as the Old and New Testaments.

III. REVEALED WORDS AND MODERN THEOLOGIANS

Our conclusion, however, raises a serious problem. If the witness of Scripture to its own authority is *pervasive*, then why have so many biblical scholars and theologians failed to see it?

We are not asking why it is that these theologians fail to *believe* the claim of Scripture. The unbelief of theologians is at bottom rather uninteresting; it is not much different from the unbelief of anyone else. Yet it is surely possible to disbelieve Scripture's claim while at the same time admitting that Scripture makes such a claim. And some liberal theologians have indeed accepted this option: the Bible *claims* inspiration and authority, but modern men cannot accept such a claim.[75] But others have refused to admit even that Scripture makes that claim. Or more often: they have recognized this claim in some parts of Scripture, but they have judged this claim to be inconsistent with other, more important scriptural teachings, and thus have felt that Scripture "as a whole" opposes the notion of authoritative Scripture in our sense.

Putting the same question differently: is it possible to construct a sound *biblical* argument for biblical *fallibility*? Some theologians, amazingly enough,

---

a *necessary* ingredient of biblical salvation, and if specifically the words of the incarnate Christ and his apostles have such necessity, our sovereign God will "somehow" find a way to enable us to find those words. And surely he has. Although there have been disputes among different churches concerning the *Old Testament* canon, there have never been any church-dividing disputes over the *New Testament* canon. Through history, of course, some NT books have been questioned. But once all the facts have gotten before the Christian public, it seems, the questions have always melted away. This is rather amazing, for the Christian church has always been, to its shame, a very contentious body. And yet no serious contentions have ever arisen over the matter of canonicity, a matter that many have found baffling. Try an experiment: read Paul's letter to the Corinthians (canonical), and then read Clement's (noncanonical) letter. *Think* about it; *pray* about it. Is there not an *obvious* difference? Christ's sheep hear his voice.

75. Cf. Warfield, *The Inspiration and Authority of the Bible*, 115, 175ff., 423f. More recently, F. C. Grant admits that the NT writers assume Scripture to be "trustworthy, infallible, and inerrant." *Introduction to New Testament Thought* (Nashville: Abingdon Press, 1950), 75.

have said yes, despite the evidence to the contrary that we and others have adduced. Is this simply a wresting of Scripture in the interest of a heresy? Is it at bottom simply another form of modern unbelief (and therefore as "uninteresting" as the unbelief alluded to earlier)? In the final analysis, I would say that the answer is yes. But some analysis, final or not, is called for. The argument must be scrutinized, lest we miss something important in the biblical self-witness.

We are not here going to argue specific points of exegesis. Some thinkers would question our interpretation of Matthew 5:17–19, arguing that in the Sermon on the Mount and elsewhere Jesus makes "critical distinctions" among the OT precepts. Some, too, would question our reading of the phrase "inspiration of God" or "God-breathed" in 2 Timothy 3:16. And indeed, some would argue from 2 Peter 1:21 (but in defiance of 2 Timothy 3:16) that inspiration pertains only to the writers of Scripture and not to the books that they have written. For enlightenment on these controversies, see the references in the footnotes. In general, we may say that even if it is possible to question a few points of our exegesis, the evidence is so *massive* that the general conclusion is still difficult to avoid:

> The effort to explain away the Bible's witness to its plenary inspiration reminds one of a man standing safely in his laboratory and elaborately expounding—possibly by the aid of diagrams and mathematical formulae—how every stone in an avalanche has a defined pathway and may easily be dodged by one of some presence of mind. We may fancy such an elaborate trifler's triumph as he would analyze the avalanche into its constituent stones, and demonstrate of stone after stone that its pathway is definite, limited, and may easily be avoided. But avalanches, unfortunately, do not come upon us, stone by stone, one at a time, courteously leaving us opportunity to withdraw from the pathway of each in turn, but all at once, in a roaring mass of destruction. Just so we may explain away a text or two which teach plenary inspiration, to our own closet satisfaction, dealing with them each without reference to the others: but these texts of ours, again, unfortunately do not come upon us in this artificial isolation; neither are they few in number. There are scores, hundreds, of them, and they come bursting upon us in one solid mass. Explain them away? We should have to explain away the whole New Testament. What a pity it is that we cannot see and feel the avalanche of texts beneath which

we may lie hopelessly buried, as clearly as we may see and feel an avalanche of stones![76]

Not even the cleverest exegete can "explain away" the biblical concepts of lordship and salvation and the necessary connection of these concepts with the revealed words of Scripture. No exegete can explain away *all* the verses that call God's people to obey "the commandments, statutes, testimonies, ordinances" of the Lord; *all* the "it is written" formulae; all the commands delivered by apostles and prophets in authoritative tone.

Rather than such detailed questions, therefore, we will confine our attention to broader considerations that have carried considerable weight in contemporary theological discussion. For just as we have argued that the biblical concepts of lordship and salvation *require* the existence of revealed words, so others have argued that certain basic biblical concepts *exclude the possibility of* such words.

The primary appeal of these theological views is to the divine transcendence, as the following quotes from Karl Barth and Emil Brunner, respectively, will indicate:

> Again it is quite impossible that there should be a direct identity between the human word of Holy Scripture and the Word of God, and therefore between the creaturely reality in itself and as such and the reality of God the creator.[77]

> It is therefore impossible to equate any human words, any "speech-about-Him" with the divine self-communication.[78]

Such statements have a kind of primitive religious appeal. God alone is God, and nothing else may be "equated with him." To "equate" or "directly identify" something else with God is idolatry. Now, surely we must agree that Scripture endorses this sentiment, for Scripture clearly opposes idolatry and exalts God above all other things. And if this is the case, then it seems that Scripture requires us to distinguish sharply between God himself on the one hand and language about him on the other; the transcendence of God is surely a central biblical concept. And if transcendence requires us to eliminate all thought of "revealed words," even though other biblical doctrines suggest otherwise, then perhaps we ought to give serious thought to this issue.

---

76. Warfield, *The Inspiration and Authority of the Bible*, 119f.

77. Karl Barth, *Church Dogmatics*, vol. 1, *The Doctrine of the Word of God*, ed. G. W. Bromiley and T. F. Torrance, trans. G. T. Thomson and Harold Knight (New York: Scribner, 1956), 2:499.

78. Brunner, *The Christian Doctrine of God*, 15.

However, Barth's concept of "direct identity" is a difficult one, as is Brunner's reference to "equating." What does it mean to assert—or deny—a "direct identity" or "equation" between God and language? Clearly, no one wants to say that *God* and *language about God* are synonymous terms. Nor has anyone in recent memory suggested that we bow down before words and sentences. Even the most orthodox defenders of biblical infallibility maintain that there is *some* distinction to be made between God and language. Further, even the most orthodox agree that the words of Scripture are in some sense creaturely, and thus specifically because of their creatureliness to be distinguished from God. On the other hand, if such words are *God's* words, and not *merely* human, then they are closely related to him, at least as closely as in words that are related to me. If God has spoken them, then their truth is his truth; their authority is his authority; their power is his power. Barth is willing to say that from time to time Scripture *becomes* the word of God; therefore, he admits that some close relation between God and Scripture is essential. The question then becomes: in what way is God "distinct" from this language, and in what way is he "related" to it? A pious appeal to God's transcendence, eloquent though it may be, does not really answer this sort of question. Both the orthodox and the Barthian would like to avoid being charged with idolatry. But *what kind* of distinction between God and language is required by the divine transcendence?

Barth is most reluctant to give any positive description of this relationship. Commenting upon 2 Timothy 3:16, he says:

> At the centre of the passage a statement is made about the relationship between God and Scripture, which can be understood only as a disposing act and decision of God Himself, which cannot therefore be expanded but to which only a—necessarily brief—reference can be made. At the decisive point all that we have to say about it can consist only in an underlining and delimiting of the inaccessible mystery of the free grace in which the Spirit of God is present and active before and above and in the Bible.[79]

Inspiration, says Barth, is a mystery, because it is an act of God's grace. We cannot define what it is; we can only assert the graciousness of the process. At another point, however, he does venture to describe inspiration, alluding to the term used in 2 Timothy 3:16:

> *Theopneustia* in the bounds of biblical thinking cannot mean anything but the special attitude of obedience in those [biblical writers] who are elected and called to this obviously special

79. Barth, *The Doctrine of the Word of God*, 2:504.

service. . . . But in nature and bearing their attitude of obedience was of itself—both outwardly and inwardly—only that of true and upright men.[80]

Inspiration is an act of God to create in men a special attitude of human obedience. It does not give them more than ordinary human powers. Therefore:

> The Bible is not a book of oracles; it is not an instrument of direct impartation. It is genuine witness. And how can it be witness of divine revelation, if the actual purpose, act and decision of God in His only-begotten Son, as seen and heard by the prophets and apostles in that Son, is dissolved in the Bible into a sum total of truths abstracted from that decision and those truths are then propounded to us as truths of faith, salvation and revelation? If it tries to be more than witness, to be direct impartation, will it not keep from us the best, the one real thing, which God intends to tell and give us and which we ourselves need?[81]

The question, of course, is rhetorical. Barth is appealing to something he thinks his reader will concede as obvious. And this much we will concede: that if the Bible tries to be more than it is, if it exceeds its rightful prerogatives and usurps those of God himself, then it will indeed hide from us the real message of God's transcendence. But what *are* the "rightful prerogatives" of Scripture? That must be established before the rhetoric of divine transcendence can have force. The rhetoric of transcendence does not itself determine what those prerogatives are.

It is clear from the last quoted section, at least, that Barth denies to Scripture one particular prerogative—the prerogative of presenting "truths of revelation in abstraction from" God's saving act in Christ. But what does "in abstraction from" mean in this context? An abstraction is always some sort of distinction or separation, but what kind of distinction or separation? An orthodox theologian will insist that the biblical "truths of revelation" are *not* "in abstraction from" God's act in Christ. On the contrary, we learn about this act, we come to adore this act, because the Bible gives us a true account of it.

I think that in the back of Barth's mind—perhaps in the front of it—is a concern of many academic people. When we teachers see students cramming for theological exams, stuffing truths into their heads, we sometimes

---

80. Ibid., 505. In my view and Warfield's, Barth offers here a most inadequate exegesis of the "God-breathed" of 2 Timothy 3:16.
81. Barth, *The Doctrine of the Word of God*, 2:507.

wonder what all of this has to do with the kingdom of God. And the students wonder, too! The whole business of "mastering truths" somehow seems "abstract." It almost trivializes the message. Often there is here no real sense of the presence of God, no real spirit of prayer and thankfulness; it seems as if we are taking God's Word and making a *game* of it.

Well, theology examinations, theological study *can* be a spiritual trial. But surely if we lose touch with God in studying his truths, it is our fault, not his for providing the truths. And sometimes, at least, the study of truths can be downright inspiring; sometimes, even in the academy, the law of the Lord purifies the soul. The evil in Barth's mind (as I understand him) is not an evil that can be remedied by eliminating the concept of revealed truth. It would be nice if such personal sinfulness could be eliminated by such a conceptual shift. But the sin of trivializing God's Word is one of which we are all guilty—Barthians as much as anyone. We cannot eliminate that in Barth's way, nor ought we to try to construct a doctrine of Scripture that will make such trivialization impossible. That is the wrong way to go about constructing doctrinal formulations. Doctrines must not be arbitrarily constructed to counteract current abuses; they must be constructed on the basis of God's revelation.

"Abstraction," then, can't be avoided by renouncing the idea of revealed truths or revealed words. Nor can it be avoided by renouncing biblical infallibility. And in the absence of any other clearly stated threat to God's transcendence in the doctrine we have advocated, we are compelled to stand our ground. The orthodox view does *not* "abstract revelation from God's act," and it does not compromise the greatness and majesty of God. On the contrary, the true greatness of God, his lordship and saviorhood as described in Scripture, *requires* the existence of revealed truths. Without such truths, we have no Lord, no Savior, no basis for piety. Without such truths, all that we say, think, and do will be hopelessly "abstracted" from the reality of God. Without such truths, we have no hope. A Barthian or liberal or "neoliberal" theology can provide no such words; it can locate no words of absolute demands and sure promise. Rather, such a theology retains the right to judge the truth or falsity of *all* words with no divinely authorized criterion. Such theologies must be decisively rejected by the church of Christ if she is to have any power, any saving message for our time. When Scripture speaks for itself, it claims to be no less than God's own Word, and the claim is pervasive and unavoidable. Insofar as we deny that claim, we deny the Lord.[82] Insofar as we honor that Word, we honor Christ.[83]

---

82. Mark 8:38.
83. John 8:31, and those passages cited above in note 66.

REVIEW OF JOHN WENHAM, *CHRIST AND THE BIBLE*[1]

Note: This book review supplements the treatment of biblical inspiration in the present volume, chapters 16–26.

Mr. Wenham has been following in the footsteps of James I. Packer, first in becoming warden of Latimer House, Oxford, and now in writing a most helpful book on biblical authority. Like Packer, Wenham is both a capable scholar and a skillful popular writer. I am amazed, for example, that Wenham chose in a popular volume to include a highly complicated discussion of textual criticism (pp. 164ff.) and a lot of argument generally classed as "technical"; yet he brings it off quite beautifully, packing an enormous amount of information into a twenty-three-page chapter, yet keeping it clear and interesting enough to be genuinely helpful (perhaps even memorable) to an intelligent nonspecialist. Specialists as well as non-specialists, moreover, will frequently find herein ideas that, if not exactly new, are yet phrased so strikingly as almost to compel thoughtful reflection. Some examples that I found personally helpful: page 19 (the OT as the *highest* law), page 39 (the "eccentricity" of the Jesus fabricated by radical biblical critics), page 93 (free quotation of a source as a sign of mastery of it rather than a sign of ignorance), page 102 (defense of Paul's use of "seed"

---

1. John William Wenham, *Christ and the Bible* (Downers Grove, IL: InterVarsity Press, 1973). This review originally appeared in *Banner of Truth* (July–August 1973): 39–41. Used by permission. For stylistic purposes, this appendix has been copyedited for inclusion in this volume.

in Galatians 3:16 ᴋᴊᴠ), and page 173 (the sense in which the over 100,000 textual variants in the NT are an "embarrassment of riches").

This is the first volume of a projected tetralogy in defense of the ortho-dox view of Scripture. As Wenham explains, "This first book tries to show what Christ's view of Scripture was, why we should regard his view as authoritative, and what books and texts should be regarded as Scripture. The second looks at the moral difficulties of the Bible. The third proposed book would deal with the main problems arising from OT criticism. The fourth proposed book is concerned with the problem of harmonizing the Gospels" (p. 8). As this prospectus suggests, Wenham's approach is more exegetical in focus than Packer's, and less concerned with broadly dogmatic and epistemological matters. Both types of emphasis are needed, but both also risk certain perils. The peril in Wenham's approach, which because he has not escaped it is also the chief weakness of his book, is a lack of adequate epistemological self-consciousness.

To be sure, Wenham is explicit as to the presuppositions of his argument: (1) that "Jesus was God incarnate, the supreme revelation of god," and (2) that the Gospels are "substantially true" (p. 9). And he is explicit as to what he does *not* presuppose, namely, biblical infallibility (ibid.; cf. back cover). In this book, infallibility is to be *proved*; thus it must not be *assumed* lest the argument be caught in a vicious circle. This method of avoiding the vicious circle is the one aspect of the book for which Wenham claims originality (ibid.).

In the first place, there is nothing new about this sort of point; it is found in a host of authors, including Warfield, to whom Wenham often refers (cf. Warfield's *Inspiration and Authority of the Bible*, pp. 210–14).[2] More important, unless this point is carefully qualified, it tends to give the impression that there is, after all, *one* area of the Christian life where the Bible need *not* be taken as authoritative, that is, when one is *arguing for* biblical authority. Further, this approach tends often to leave the reader up in the air, for Wenham constantly makes judgments about possibilities and probabilities—controversial judgments in the context of contemporary theology—without telling us how he arrives at them. I think, frankly, that Scripture itself plays a large role in determining what he regards as "prob-able"; but he doesn't tell us this, since it might seem "circular."

In my view, circular argument of a sort is inevitable when one is argu-ing on behalf of an *absolute authority*. This is true of Christian as well as non-Christian arguments. One cannot abandon one's basic authority in

---

2. Benjamin Breckinridge Warfield, *The Inspiration and Authority of the Bible* (Phila-delphia: Presbyterian and Reformed, 1948; repr., Grand Rapids: Baker, 1970).

the course of arguing for it. The problems created by this circularity can be mitigated by bringing in data from various sources, but they cannot be totally avoided.

Though space forbids any further analysis, I believe that these problems generate some difficulties in other parts of the book also. The section on canon, rather good as a historical study, contains a rather confused account of the inward work of the Spirit (pp. 125f.), and presents a rather distorted picture of Warfield's view of the NT canon (pp. 153–57)—I think in part because the author has failed adequately to think through the basic question "How do we know?" In this respect, Packer's book *Fundamentalism and the Word of God*,[3] though thinner in the exegetical and historical areas, presents a more satisfying argument, buttressed as it is by a careful and scriptural discussion of faith and reason. Nevertheless, all things considered, Wenham's book is a worthwhile contribution. Particularly as a layman's introduction to questions of text and canon, it is *uniquely* valuable.

---

3. J. I. Packer, *Fundamentalism and the Word of God* (Grand Rapids: Eerdmans, 1958).

APPENDIX H

REVIEW OF DAVID KELSEY, *THE USES OF SCRIPTURE IN RECENT THEOLOGY*[1]

Note: This review discusses a very important book in which David H. Kelsey argues that a theologian's *use* of Scripture is as important as his *doctrine* of Scripture in evaluating his claim to do theology according to Scripture. It supplements chapters 23–25 in the present volume.

Although the authority of Scripture has been one of the chief preoccupations of twentieth-century theology, it is surprising that there has been so little genuine progress in understanding the subject. On the conservative side, following the Warfield corpus, I count only Meredith G. Kline's *The Structure of Biblical Authority*, Cornelius Van Til's *A Christian Theory of Knowledge*, and possibly Herman Ridderbos's *The Authority of the New Testament Scriptures* as providing significant new light on biblical authority.[2] The more fashionable theological schools have produced, on the whole, more sophisticated studies than the orthodox; and the seminal works of

1. David H. Kelsey, *The Uses of Scripture in Recent Theology* (Philadelphia: Fortress Press, 1975). This review originally appeared in *WTJ* 39, 2 (Spring 1977): 328–53. Used by permission. For stylistic purposes, this appendix has been copyedited for inclusion in this volume.
2. G. C. Berkouwer, *Holy Scripture* (Grand Rapids: Eerdmans, 1975), recently made available in English, is a work of prodigious scholarship, amazing subtlety, and infectious spirituality. Berkouwer is eloquent in urging attention to difficult questions, and he is helpful in pointing out "contexts" in which the answers to such questions will be found. Yet he does not provide much fresh clarification of the questions or very adequate answers to them, and many of his attempts to do so are, in my opinion, counterproductive. For more discussion of Berkouwer's book, see Appendix Q in this volume.

Karl Barth, Emil Brunner, Rudolf Bultmann, Gerhard Ebeling, Austin Farrer, Paul Tillich, and others must be praised at least for raising important issues. Most liberal theology, however, like most orthodox theology, merely echoes a few paradigmatic treatments, and even the leading thinkers in the academic theological mainstream have often been bogged down in the tiresome business of reconstructing the historic doctrine to make it agree with modern science and/or philosophy. This accommodationism not only produces doctrines of Scripture devoid of all relevant offensiveness, Christian distinctiveness, and practical impact, but also sidetracks these theologians from the really useful task of thinking through what is at issue in controversies over Scripture.

There is promise, however, of better things to come. The challenge of analytic philosophy has, since the late 1950s, caused theology itself to become more analytic, more interested in clarifying issues, less satisfied with merely advocating positions. On the question of biblical authority, the work of James Barr, Langdon Gilkey, F. Gerald Downing, and others in the early 1960s has pioneered in implementing this sort of concern, and others have followed since that time. In the last ten years, several important contributions of this sort have emanated from Yale Divinity School, specifically from Professors Brevard Childs, George Lindbeck, Hans W. Frei, and Paul L. Holmer.

David H. Kelsey, the author of the work before us, is also a professor at Yale and an analytically minded theologian, but he very nearly transcends the young tradition of which he is a part. In shedding fresh light on the subject of biblical authority, his book is the most helpful volume of the group, and possibly the most significant writing on the subject since Warfield.

The kind of work Kelsey does precludes him from easily achieving the sort of popular fame that attaches to some theologians, yet he has become a most important figure in the theological field and ought to be recognized as such, at least by those fellow scholars who have done some thinking about the issues with which he deals. His first book, *The Fabric of Paul Tillich's Theology,*[3] is, in my view, the best introduction to Tillich's thought, and one of the most accurate and incisive critiques of it. The volume here under review, an expansion of his article "Appeals to Scripture in Theology" (*Journal of Religion* 48 [1968]: 1–21), discusses biblical authority from an entirely new angle, using important new analytical tools and categories (unfortunately, but perhaps necessarily, producing a new jargon), and makes significant new suggestions. Although the book is open to serious criticisms, anyone concerned in a scholarly way with the question of

3. New York and London: Yale University Press, 1967.

biblical authority must do some hard thinking about it. Therefore, the book merits a "major review."[4]

The freshness of Kelsey's approach derives largely from the fact that he is concerned not with what theologians have said *about* biblical authority (their "doctrines of Scripture"), but with how they actually *use* Scripture to "authorize" their theological proposals (pp. 2, 3, 4, 152, 210). As far as I know, except for Kelsey's earlier article, this is the first time that such an approach has ever been attempted. The inquiry raises an immensely broad range of new questions and topics for discussion. Kelsey wisely restricts the scope of the present book; he does not attempt to survey all the theological uses of Scripture, but simply to examine several different kinds of use and to discuss certain significant questions about them (p. 4).

We will discuss the following theses, which summarize the argument of the book: (1) that it is useful and in some respects necessary to consider these issues from a "theological position neutral" standpoint; (2) that the theological uses of Scripture are far more diverse than is usually supposed; (3) that one's use of Scripture is logically dependent upon his conception of Christianity and vice versa; (4) that "authority" refers to *functions* that Scripture performs in the church; (5) that Scripture performs its functions only when God himself enables it to do so; and (6) that theologians ought to and do decide how to use Scripture on the basis of an "imaginative construal" of Scripture and of Christianity as a whole.

1. THEOLOGICAL POSITION NEUTRALITY

Kelsey wishes to study theologians' uses of Scripture without theological bias. He does not wish to favor one doctrine (or use) of Scripture above another (p. 2), and he even denies that he makes any historical, exegetical, or theological claims (p. 9). He calls the book an essay "*about* theologies" (ibid.). Some might describe it as "metatheology" or "prolegomena," but Kelsey himself does not. Even these terms, however, do not adequately connote the sort of neutrality to which Kelsey aspires, for they might be understood as involving an argument for a particular "theological method."

---

4. In writing this review, I acknowledge the help of Miss Tiina Allik, a former student of mine and presently a student of Kelsey, who has shared with me at length some of her well-thought-out critical reflections on the book. I have also consulted a manuscript of Dr. Carl F. H. Henry (unpublished at the time I received it) dealing with Kelsey's approach to Warfield. I have profited from both accounts. My remarks on the "translation metaphor" owe some indebtedness to Professors Poythress and Dillard of Westminster. I am myself, however, solely responsible for any inadequacies in this review.

Kelsey denies any such purpose: the book "is a study of theologians' methods, not an exercise in 'theological methodology' " (p. 7). Does he wish, we might ask, to make any proposals at all, to commit himself on any question? Indeed, but he insists that his proposals are "purely formal" (p. 194), and he even concludes his essay by drawing "purely formal morals" (p. 207).

It is hard to imagine anyone being so enthusiastic about formality. Why? There are, I gather, three reasons: First, Kelsey believes that such neutrality is virtually necessary for a fair representation of the different viewpoints and approaches under discussion (pp. 2, 8, 191, 195). Second, he wishes to develop a theory that is generally applicable (pp. 191, 209f.), meaning, apparently, a theory that could not be objected to on any theological grounds whatever. Third, he wishes to avoid begging questions about the proper use of Scripture and about the nature of theology and Christianity (pp. 8, 194).

As far as I can tell, Kelsey never asks in the book whether such neutrality is *possible*. This question is controversial enough in contemporary theology and crucial enough for Kelsey's argument to have deserved some explicit consideration. Yet, ironically, that question is, precisely, begged.

The general argument against the possibility of such neutrality is available in such diverse sources as Van Til, Barth, and Kuhn. The office of the book reviewer, however, warrants a more *ad hominem* approach. Whether or not neutrality is possible, Kelsey has not achieved it, for he begs a number of theological questions in addition to the question about neutrality itself. Theological judgments abound in the book. Kelsey's critiques of significant theological arguments are among the book's most interesting and useful features. Some of these, to be sure, do not violate the book's basic neutrality, for Kelsey argues in some cases that even if the critique fails, his basic metatheological argument can be sustained (pp. 29, 209ff.). In these cases, then, the metatheological point does not prejudice the particular theological issue in view, nor vice versa. But there are other cases where the claim to neutrality is open to more serious challenge, particularly those cases where Kelsey charges theologians themselves with inadequate neutrality. He argues, for instance, that "most doctrines about 'the authority of Scripture' are very misleading about the sense in which Scripture is 'authority' precisely *for theology*" (p. 2). This sort of criticism would be telling if the theologians in question were engaged in the same task as Kelsey, the analysis of how theologians actually use Scripture, and were producing analyses distorted by theological bias. But theologians other than Kelsey have never engaged in this sort of task before, to my knowledge, and they certainly do not engage in it when they are formulating "doctrines about 'the authority of Scripture.'" Instead, such doctrines attempt to show how Scripture *ought* to be used in theology, regardless of how this or that theologian actually uses it, and it is difficult to see how such a doctrine could be challenged by a "theological position neutral" analysis without that analysis abandoning its neutrality. (For further examples of this problem, see discussions beginning on pages 152, 191, 209.)

Even if unacceptable, it is understandable that Kelsey would advocate neutrality for a metatheological analysis, but why does he want to require the same neutrality of theologians? How can theology itself be "theological position neutral"? Clearly it cannot be, nor can Kelsey himself be neutral insofar as he takes positions on theological doctrines. There are no "purely formal morals for doctrines about Scripture." The only morals for doctrines are doctrinal morals. The problem is that Kelsey wants to have it both ways: he wants not only to maintain a neutral stance, but also to make an impact upon *doctrinal* discussion. He wants to criticize theologies, but he refuses at the outset to allow the relevance of theological criticisms against his own work (p. 9). Such a double standard is inadmissible. If Kelsey has the right to charge the doctrines of Scripture with being misleading, then a theologian has an equal right to argue, for example, that Kelsey is demanding consideration for certain "uses" of Scripture that are theologically illegitimate uses, and thus misuses. We cannot credit Kelsey, therefore, with having achieved the neutrality he seeks; moreover, we find it difficult to imagine how one ever could achieve such neutrality on an issue of such theological import.

Nor is it evident that neutrality is really necessary to accomplish the task. Regarding the three reasons listed earlier: First, it is not *necessarily* the case that fairness in analysis demands neutrality. Kelsey himself claims only that a nonneutral approach runs a "risk" of being unfair. I would concede that theologians often distort one another's positions in order to make theological points, and Kelsey is right in urging us to guard against that danger. However, a perfectly "neutral" approach, were it possible, would certainly distort the positions under analysis by failing to bring to bear on those positions the relevant theological judgments.

Second, it is not evident that any analysis can be "generally applicable" in Kelsey's sense. It is legitimate and useful, of course, to attempt an analysis that will adequately deal both with good and with bad uses of Scripture. Nor can there be any objection to categories that express features common to both kinds of use. In these senses, an analysis of the uses of Scripture in theology may be, and sometimes ought to be, "generally applicable." But it is neither desirable nor possible to produce an analysis "generally applicable" in the sense of "unobjectionable on any theological position."

Again, if Kelsey wants to object to theologies, he must allow them to object to him.

Third, as we have seen, it is not as easy as Kelsey thinks to avoid "begging questions." In my view, to avoid begging theological questions entirely, one would have to refrain from all value judgments and even from description. But clearly there is no need to carry on this study with a theological *tabula rasa*. One may, or ought to, postpone certain questions until after he has dealt with others. But to postpone all theological questions until one has dealt with matters under "neutral analysis" is unnecessary, impossible, and prejudicial. If the authority of Scripture is *comprehensive*—if it must be heard on all matters of human faith and life—then it must be heard even in the analysis of theological uses of Scripture, and that imperative puts an end to neutrality in this realm. In this sense, metatheology of all sorts must be part of, or at least subject to, theology. No doubt theology must also take account of the facts of contemporary life, including the way theologians use the Bible. Thus, there is surely a legitimate reciprocity between theology in the traditional sense and the sort of analysis Kelsey proposes—reciprocity, but not neutrality. If scriptural authority is *not* "comprehensive" in the above sense, then neutrality becomes religiously and methodologically, if not psychologically, possible. But to deny the comprehensiveness of Scripture's authority at the outset—is that not itself "prejudicial"?

2. THE DIVERSITY OF THE THEOLOGICAL USES OF SCRIPTURE

It was a serious mistake for Kelsey to attempt and claim neutrality, yet that mistake did not prevent him from making some important observations about the uses of Scripture in theology. To that positive analysis we must now turn. Kelsey argues that the uses of Scripture are much more numerous and diverse than generally thought. To establish this point, he presents "case studies," analyzing certain selected uses of Scripture by seven theologians—B. B. Warfield, Hans-Werner Bartsch, G. Ernest Wright, Karl Barth, Lionel Thornton, Paul Tillich, and Rudolf Bultmann. In regard to each case, he poses the following "diagnostic questions": (1) What aspect (s) of Scripture is (are) taken to be authoritative? (2) What is it about this aspect of Scripture that makes it authoritative? (3) What sort of logical force is ascribed to the Scripture to which appeal is made? (4) How is the Scripture that is cited brought to bear on theological proposals so as to authorize them? (pp. 2,

3).[5] He finds that the cases studied present a wide variety of answers to the questions, and thus reveal substantial diversities in the theological uses of Scripture. For various reasons, I will postpone consideration of question (2) to a later point in the review, discuss (1), (3), and (4) here, and also consider a fifth question that Kelsey treats in a different section of the book: What uses of the cited Scriptures in the church are being advocated by the theologians considered? (pp. 147ff.).

(a) Diversities in authoritative aspects. Kelsey argues, first, that there is a diversity in the *aspects* of Scripture taken to be authoritative. For Warfield, he argues, it is doctrinal content that is authoritative (p. 21); for Bartsch, the authoritative aspect is "biblical concepts" (p. 26); for Wright and Barth, "narrative" (pp. 32ff.); for Thornton, Tillich, and Bultmann, "images," "symbols," and "myths," respectively (p. 56). These correlations, Kelsey reminds us, pertain only to the particular cases studied, and do not constitute analyses of any theologian's position taken as a whole. For example, it would clearly be unfair to say that for Bultmann all revelation is mythical in character or that for Warfield revelation is exclusively propositional.[6]

Here and elsewhere Kelsey is a bit inclined, I think, to exaggerate diversities. Clearly, for instance, one who appeals to biblical "doctrines" will not be able to do so without at the same time making appeal to biblical concepts and narratives. Kelsey's analysis of Warfield shows just that. In formulating the "doctrine" of Scripture, Warfield appeals to biblical concepts (*theopneustos, pherein*) and to biblical narrative (John 10). Kelsey's suggestion that Warfield appeals to "eternal truths" (p. 100)—as opposed to what? truths about historical events?—strikes me as entirely gratuitous. Warfield does appeal to doctrine, but in doing so appeals to many aspects of Scripture. The case is somewhat more convincing in regard to the other theologians, but even in those instances I think Kelsey would have been better advised to state his point as a difference in emphasis rather than as a radical difference in approach.

5. Cf. p. 15. There appears to be an error on page 15, where the chapter numbers are correlated with the different "authoritative aspects." I believe that chapter numbers 4, 5, and 6 are wrong and should be replaced by 2, 3, and 4.

6. One of Kelsey's own quotes from Warfield suggests that Warfield advocates (if he does not actually employ) appeal to more than merely "doctrinal" aspects of Scripture (at least as the term *doctrinal* is commonly used today). Christians, says Warfield, "receive its statements of fact, bow before its enunciations of duty, tremble before its threatenings and rest on its promises" (p. 17, quoting Benjamin Breckinridge Warfield, *The Inspiration and Authority of the Bible* [Philadelphia: Presbyterian and Reformed, 1948], 107. Warfield's language, in turn, reflects that of WCF 14.2, which recognizes quite explicitly the diverse functions of different "aspects" of authoritative Scripture.

Nevertheless, the basic point is sound. There is a difference between appealing to doctrine and appealing to concepts. Even though the latter is generally involved in the former and vice versa, one may appeal to concepts as an *alternative* to doctrine (possibly, as James Barr has argued, out of distaste for "propositional revelation"). The same holds for the other categories. These differences, furthermore, are important. When two theologians appeal to the same Scripture passage to support opposing theological positions, diversities of this sort may sometimes underlie the confusion. One theologian may be appealing, for example, to the doctrinal teaching of the passage, another to its juxtapositions of symbols. Even those who, like this reviewer, wish to take *all* aspects of Scripture as authoritative must do further thinking about how the different aspects ought to function in theological discussion. For they do function "differently."

(b) *Diversities in logical force.* Furthermore, argues Kelsey, there are differences in the ways theologians interpret the aspects of Scripture to which they appeal. Two theologians who agree in appealing to the *narrative* aspects of Scripture (Kelsey's examples are Wright and Barth) may nevertheless disagree on how that narrative is to be "construed." Wright, according to Kelsey, takes biblical narrative as description of a segment of world history from which redemptive truths may be inferred. Barth, however, takes the narrative as a story describing an agent (Jesus Christ, p. 50). And although Thornton, Bultmann, and Tillich agree in appealing to "non-informative *force* as expression" (p. 85),[7] they disagree in their "construals" of that expressive symbolism, Thornton taking it to symbolize cosmic processes, Bultmann radically private, inward subjective transformations, and Tillich a subtle mixture of both (pp. 83ff.). Again, these differences are important, and they do indicate significantly different ways in which Scripture may be appealed to as "authority."

(c) *Diversities in mode of authorization.* Even if two theologians agree in citing the same "aspect" of Scripture and in "construing" that aspect in the same way, they may still differ in the way that they use that Scripture in a theological argument, in the way that they use that Scripture to "authorize" a theological conclusion. Here Kelsey employs a schematism borrowed from

7. Cf. pp. 100, 148. I question Kelsey's use of "non-informative" here. If I understand him correctly, he himself modifies this characterization in regard to Bultmann (p. 100), but I am not sure of its aptness in regard to the others. The question is difficult, of course, and I doubt if these theologians have achieved complete consistency on the point. Many theologians, of course, have wanted to eliminate or at least de-emphasize the "informative" aspect of revelation, yet if one appeals to revelation in any sense to "authorize" a (necessarily propositional) theological view, it is hard to avoid (at least implicitly) a claim to have received revealed information.

Stephen Toulmin's *The Uses of Argument*,[8] which distinguishes various types of propositions used in arguments and the functions played by each type in the establishment of a conclusion. In this schematism, an argument consists of a conclusion (C) derived from various data (D). The move from D to C is justified by a warrant (W), which, in turn, is justified (if justification is needed) by backing (B). The conclusion may have various qualifiers (Q) attached ("presumably," "possibly," "probably," etc.), and may be left open to rebuttal if certain "conditions of rebuttal" (R) are established. Kelsey argues (i) that Scripture may function in theological argument[9] as D, W, B, Q, R, or C or in various combinations of these ways; (ii) that extrascriptural propositions are also frequently found at each of these points in the argument, though it is logically possible for an argument to consist entirely of scriptural references (p. 145); (iii) that within a single argument, therefore, there are many possible combinations of scriptural and extrascriptural premises; and (iv) that even the "scriptural premises" in an argument may be of many sorts—direct quotations, generalizations about patterns of scriptural material construed in different ways (above, [a], [b]), and so on.

(d) *Diversities in church function.* Kelsey regards the theological use of Scripture as one phase of the general use of Scripture in the church. The theological use, therefore, reflects the diversities found in the more general uses. In the church, (i) Scripture is seen as having various *functions*, asserting (doctrines), proposing (concepts), rendering (an agent), expressing (redemptive events in symbols), occasioning (new redemptive events in the present) (p. 147; see [a] above); (ii) these functions solicit different sorts of *responses* from their bearers (belief, decision, worship, etc.; p. 148); (iii) the functions are open to different sorts of *assessment* (logical consistency, factuality, felicity in expression, and so on (1, p. 148); and (iv) Scripture in its various functions serves as authority *over* diverse sorts of *phenomena* (theological formulations, belief, inner subjectivity, etc.; pp. 148ff.).

(e) *Conclusions regarding the diversities.* Evidently, then, "authorizing a theological proposal on the basis of Scripture" may refer to a great many different sorts of arguments. From this diversity, Kelsey draws two more specific conclusions. First, he argues that Scripture is generally brought to bear on theological proposals "indirectly rather than directly" (p. 139). Of

8. Stephen E. Toulmin, *The Uses of Argument* (Cambridge: Cambridge University Press, 1958).

9. Kelsey also acknowledges theological uses of Scripture other than as premises in "arguments," as defined by Toulmin (pp. 123f.). These "nonargumentative" uses may, of course, influence the structure and conclusions of arguments in various (sometimes subtle) ways. The existence of such uses, then, complicates the picture still further, adding yet more "diversity" to the theological employment of Scripture.

the many sorts of possible arguments, he recognizes only two as "directly" authorizing the conclusion by Scripture: when the W is a Scripture quotation, and when the D are Scripture quotations and the W self-evident (p. 140). Only in these two cases does Kelsey find it appropriate to speak metaphorically of the theological conclusion as a "translation" of Scripture (pp. 122, 143, elsewhere). In other cases, Kelsey finds the metaphor inappropriate because (i) in those cases, one is not simply conveying biblical concepts in different words as a translation would do, but *redescribing* the biblical subject matter in *different* concepts (pp. 187ff.); (ii) in those cases, the use of the translation metaphor begs the question whether the text has contemporary meaning (p. 190); and (iii) where Scripture is indirectly used to establish a conclusion, the translation metaphor misleadingly suggests a direct use (pp. 190f.).

Kelsey's concept of "directness" is not entirely clear. Notice that it depends heavily on the notion of scriptural "quotation," as opposed to general claims about biblical teaching. But quotation from what? The original manuscripts, which are now lost? Modern critical editions of the original-language texts? English translations? Paraphrases? If the first of these is required, then there is no "direct" use of Scripture after all. But if other possibilities are admitted, then the "direct" use of Scripture may involve appeal to texts and/or versions that are in part the product of much sophisticated linguistic, historical, and theological research. And if appeal to such sources constitutes "direct" use of Scripture, why should we then exclude appeal to theological generalizations about scriptural teaching— generalizations that presuppose no more (and often less) extrascriptural reasoning than do translations and textual editions? Furthermore, Kelsey accepts certain arguments of Warfield and Bartsch as constituting "direct" uses of Scripture (pp. 23–28); but on Kelsey's own account, neither of these men bases any conclusions simply upon isolated Scripture quotations. Both appeal to "patterns"—of doctrinal teaching in Warfield's case (p. 23), and of biblical concepts in the case of Bartsch (pp. 27ff.). If, then, it is possible to draw a sharp line between "indirect" and "direct" uses of Scripture in theology, Kelsey has not succeeded in drawing it. This failure in turn raises questions about his critique of the "translation" metaphor. His argument ([iii], above) assumes the sharp distinction that he has failed to establish. Argument (ii) assumes the necessity of "theological position neutrality" (again, even for theology!) that we rejected in section 1 of the review. Argument (i) betrays (as does Kelsey's direct/indirect distinction) a somewhat naive conception of what translation is all about. If someone translated "white as snow" into the phrase "white as the swan" (for a culture that has no knowledge of snow), has he conveyed the same concept in different words, or has he redescribed the subject matter using different concepts? Again, it would seem that no sharp lines can be drawn. Translation, like theology, is a highly sophisticated business, presupposing not only knowledge of the words in the original language, but also much knowledge of the linguistic background of those words, their uses in other literature, the uses of such words in the original culture, the linguistic equipment of the "target-language," the culture and history of the speakers of that language, and so forth. Where Scripture is concerned, there can be no sharp line drawn between "translating" on the one hand and "teaching," "applying to the cultural situation," or "theologizing" on the other, which suggests that "translation," in all its diversity, may be a more appropriate metaphor for theologizing than Kelsey supposes. Had he been as aware of the diversity of factors in the translation process as he is of the diversities in theology, he would have recognized that.

Nevertheless, Kelsey has provided a valuable service in showing that theology is generally much more than the metaphor "translation" suggests, *when that metaphor is viewed naively.* Theology is merely a restatement of Scripture into fresh terminology. As Kelsey puts it, theology is "practical," "critical," "reformist" (p. 159)—a means of applying Scripture to the concrete needs of church and society. And of course, even on the broadest interpretation, "translation" can only be a metaphor; for theology may, and must, range far beyond the language of Scripture in performing its task, far beyond any formulation that would be acceptable as a "translation." Although there are no sharp lines, there are enormous differences of degree.

Kelsey's second conclusion from the diversities in the theological uses of Scripture is that it is "meaningless" to contrast authorization of a conclusion by Scripture with authorization by something other than Scripture (pp. 135, 145). All arguments in which Scripture is used "indirectly," Kelsey argues, employ extrascriptural material at some significant point. Can we say that an argument using Scripture as D and, for example, ontological analysis as B is "more scriptural" than one that uses, for example, historical research as D and Scripture as B?

Kelsey's point here is also somewhat overstated, but it is most important when pared down to size. For one thing, there is clearly a difference between arguments that use Scripture and arguments that make no use of Scripture at all. Now, B propositions ("backing") function to justify warrants (W). One who offers ontological analysis as B (Tillich is Kelsey's example, p. 132) is essentially presenting a nonscriptural argument for a warrant, unless he justifies the ontology, in turn, with an argument employing Scripture. If the passage from B to W may be viewed as a distinct argument (and there is no reason why it cannot be), then there is a significant sense in which we may describe it as a nonscriptural argument. And clearly these abound in theological writing. They may be inevitable, but it is not meaningless to distinguish them. For another thing, although we reject Kelsey's *sharp* distinction between "direct" and "indirect" uses of Scripture, we cannot deny that some uses are "more direct" than others. And it is not meaningless to point out that in some theologies the appeal to Scripture is very indirect indeed.

Despite these qualifications, however, Kelsey's basic point still stands: Most theological arguments employ both scriptural and extrascriptural premises, and those that employ scriptural premises use them in widely different ways. If theology is "application" rather than "translation" in some narrow sense, this is what we would expect. If theology must bring Scripture to bear on the world, then it must speak of the world. Clearly, we may not condemn an argument as "unscriptural" merely because it makes use of extrascriptural premises. Whatever *sola Scriptura* may mean, it does not require the exclusive use of Scripture quotations in arguments.[10] Even translation, as we have seen, presupposes extrascriptural knowledge. In general, none of us is able to understand the "meaning" of any Scripture text without some such knowledge (the structure of English, for example). Thus, caution is needed in evaluating whether or to what degree or in what way the conclusion of a theological argument is "based on Scripture." We must be more aware of the variety of ways in which Scripture can be used in argument, and to this end nothing is more helpful than Kelsey's analysis.

3. THE LOGICAL INTERDEPENDENCE OF "SCRIPTURE" AND "CHRISTIANITY"

Granted all the diversities, is it possible to find any *unity* among the theological uses of Scripture? Kelsey addresses this question by analyzing the role of biblical authority in the life of the church. That argument will claim our attention in this and the next two sections of the review. In this section, we will consider Kelsey's argument that one's concept of "Scripture" is largely determined by his view of Christianity as a whole.

Scripture is "Scripture," Kelsey suggests, only insofar as it is necessary to the establishment and preservation of the Christian community (p. 89).

---

10. What it does mean, I think, is that "only Scripture" has ultimate authority, and that the theologian's use of extrascriptural as well as scriptural material ought to have the goal of proclaiming *Scripture* (including its application), not some other message. Cf. my *Van Til: The Theologian* (Phillipsburg, NJ: Pilgrim, 1976), 24ff.

This function is part of the *meaning* of "Scripture." On the other hand, the use of Scripture to nurture, criticize, and reform itself is part of the definition of "church" (pp. 93f.). "Church" and "Scripture," then, are defined in terms of one another (p. 94). Kelsey finds this correlation to obtain in all the cases investigated in the book.

"Authority," furthermore, says Kelsey, is "part of the meaning of Scripture," and "authoritative for theology" is "analytic in" "authoritative for the life of the church" (p. 97). Theology and church, moreover, both are defined by the structure of Christianity as a whole (pp. 8, 164f.). In the course of this argument, Kelsey makes some interesting comments about "tradition" and "canon" that we cannot discuss here except to say that he defines these also in terms of the church-Scripture-Christianity complex.

There is not much to criticize in this discussion as such. The interdependences among Christian doctrines are important, and Kelsey is right to call our attention to them in this context (cf. my *Van Til: The Theologian*, 10ff., passim). I wish he were a bit more guarded in his use of the expressions "part of the meaning of" and "analytic in," in view of the criticisms of this language by such as J. L. Austin and W. V. Quine, though I do not regard those criticisms as fatal for the kind of point Kelsey is making. More seriously, the discussion at points seems insensitive to the implications of the *reciprocal* character of these relationships (see next section). Further, Kelsey does not in my mind adequately justify his *selection* of relationships for analysis. He argues, as we have seen, that the concepts "Scripture" and "church" are mutually dependent, and then concludes from that fact (and others) that the discussion of scriptural authority belongs in the locus "practical theology" (pp. 208f.), rather than in the context of a doctrine of "revelation" or "Word of God." The idea is actually rather attractive to me, but I do not believe Kelsey has established it. In order to establish such a conclusion, it seems to me, Kelsey must argue not only that "Scripture" and "church" are mutually dependent but that "Scripture" and "revelation" are not. At one point, he does suggest that "revelation" is not a singular or even coherent concept (p. 209), but to avoid compromising his neutrality (p. 210), refuses to press that point; rather, he argues that such legitimate theological questions are "begged" by the assimilation of Scripture to a doctrine of revelation. But the assimilation of "Scripture" and "church" also assumes the coherence (and to some extent the singularity) of the concepts under discussion. If the one assumption violates "neutrality," then the other does, too (showing, again, how difficult it is to maintain neutrality!). The point is that Kelsey's argument shows the "logical home" of bibliology to be ecclesiology only if the same sort of argument cannot be made for other loci. And he has not shown that a case for other loci cannot be made.

Yet I tend to regard questions of theological encyclopedia as of no great moment, and thus I do not regard the above issue as being very important, though apparently Kelsey does. The general argument is sound, and the point is valuable: our view of Scripture is determined not only by our perception of Scripture but by our general understanding of Christianity. Warfield was right in saying that the doctrine of Scripture is not a doctrine from which the rest of theology is unilaterally deduced; rather, on the contrary, our doctrine and use of Scripture are deeply influenced by our understanding and experience of the whole gospel.

4. AUTHORITY AS FUNCTION

From the interdependence of Scripture and church, Kelsey concludes that the authority of Scripture is "a function of the role played by biblical writings in the life of the church when it serves as the means by which we are related to revelation" (1, p. 30). To call Scripture authority always means "that the texts ought to be *used* in certain ways" (p. 152). To acknowledge the authority of Scripture is to adopt a policy, to commit oneself to using Scripture in these ways (pp. 109, 151, 177). To understand authority as "function," Kelsey argues, is not to lose sight of the *normativity* of Scripture. The "functions" of Scripture are precisely to govern, to rule the church and its theology in various ways. And these functions are not conferred upon Scripture by our "policy decision" to use it in those ways; rather, Scripture *deserves* to rule, whether we choose to use it or not (p. 152).

The main problem here is Kelsey's unclarity as to what the alternative is and as to why that alternative should be rejected. Evidently, the alternative to a "functionalist" view of authority is one that connects authority in some way or other with "properties" of Scripture. Sometimes he describes the alternative as a view that regards authority itself as a "property" of Scripture, which regards authority as the name of a property (pp. 30, 108). Elsewhere, he describes the view he opposes as one that ascribes authority to Scripture "in virtue of" some property (pp. 29, 47, 91, 211; cf. 109). Kelsey's arguments are fairly persuasive on the first interpretation, rather unpersuasive on the second. It would certainly be odd to *define* authority as a "property" of Scripture (taking "property" not as "characteristic," which authority certainly is, but as a sensory phenomenon on the order of "red" or "heavy").[11] Even here, I doubt that the lines are as sharp as they have

---

11. It is equally odd to define *inspiration* as a "property," as Kelsey does on page 91. Surely inspiration is essentially a fact about the *genesis* of Scripture, no more easily assimilable to "redness" and "heaviness" than is authority.

sometimes been taken to be.[12] Certainly, though, Kelsey is right if he means that "authority" must be defined not only in terms of the Scripture itself but in terms of its function in God's economy and in human life. However, it is another matter to deny that Scripture is authoritative "by virtue of" one or more properties. Certainly, to use Kelsey's own illustration, the functions of a ball in a game are determined in part by the properties of the ball. If the ball is not elastic, then it cannot be used, for example, for dribbling. Some properties, clearly, are necessary (though not sufficient) conditions of some functions. And where there are such relations between properties and functions, there can be no objection to saying that something has a function at least partly "in virtue of" a property. Now, in the case of Scripture, clearly properties such as doctrinal truth, edifying conceptual and symbolic structure, and so forth are *relevant* to its authority, and would be regarded by the theologians in Kelsey's "cases" as necessary, though not sufficient, conditions of that authority. And if x is a necessary condition of y, does not y exist (at least in part) "in virtue of" x? Conclusion: we may accept, with some qualification and definition, Kelsey's argument that "authority" is not the *name* of a "property" of Scripture; but we cannot accept his view that authority is in no sense based upon such properties.[13]

I suspect that Kelsey is led into this mistake through a misunderstanding of the church-Scripture relation (his analysis of which we discussed in the last section). Although Kelsey acknowledges that "church" and "Scripture" are "reciprocal," in the sense of being definable in terms of one another, in some of his arguments he makes the relation appear more unilateral than reciprocal. It seems sometimes as though the concept "Scripture" is wholly determined by the concept "church," and not at all vice versa (pp. 98, 109, 165f.). Here, Scripture's church-function is not only "part of the meaning" of "Scripture"; it is the *whole* meaning, and that whole meaning then turns out to have little or nothing to do with the properties of Scripture, curious as that may seem. I would argue on the contrary that even if "church func-

12. We cannot simply take for granted the old philosophical distinctions between "sensation and reason . . . impressions and ideas," "things, properties and relations," or the more recent "observations and theory." This question is closely related to that regarding analyticity, concerning which we have remarked (section 3) on the need of a more sophisticated treatment in the book under review.

13. Sometimes Kelsey writes as though the point were a matter of emphasis: one claiming authority for Scripture does not "*so much* offer a descriptive claim" (p. 89 [emphasis mine]). Notice also his frequent phrase "part of the meaning," which suggests that perhaps *some* of the meaning of "authority" may have to do with "properties" of Scripture. At other times, however, it seems to be a question of black or white: "authority," he says, "turned out not to be drawing attention to a property . . . but rather . . ." (p. 109). I would be more sympathetic to his conclusion if it were clearly stated as a matter of emphasis. But even then, the treatment would require explicit reference to balancing considerations.

tion" is the *whole* meaning of "Scripture," the properties of Scripture as a book must be taken into account in defining the nature of the church itself and of Scripture's function within the church, and hence those properties must also be taken account of in definitions of Scripture's "authority." And "church function" ought not to be regarded as the *whole* meaning of "Scripture," in any case.

But there is nothing wrong with saying that "authority" names function(s) of Scripture in the church (including the church's ministry to the world, p. 92). The fact that these functions are highly diverse (or, put differently, that the function is highly complex) does not render "authority" an incoherent or useless concept. The complexities can be charted, interrelated, and seen in their unity, as well as their diversity. Kelsey's book does that to some extent, and Kline's *Structure of Biblical Authority*[14] shows the unity among the diversities in great depth. Such analysis will never be *exhaustive*, but it may be adequate for the needs of the church.

5. GOD AS PRESENT IN THE "RIGHT" USE OF SCRIPTURE

Kelsey argues that theological proposals are not assessed on the basis of Scripture alone, but on the basis of a complex "*discrimen.*" Following R. C. Johnson, Kelsey defines *discrimen* as "a configuration of criteria that are in some way organically related to one another as reciprocal coefficients" (p. 160, quoting Johnson's *Authority in Protestant Theology*, 15).[15] In this case, the *discrimen* is "the conjunction of certain uses of Scripture and the presence of God" (p. 160; cf. 193, 215). The definition of *discrimen* is inexcusably, almost ludicrously, vague, making Kelsey's point most difficult to evaluate. Note first that Kelsey's identification of the *discrimen* is supposed to do justice to the views of all the theologians discussed, from Warfield to Bultmann. In Warfield, Kelsey finds his *discrimen* exemplified as follows: "When heard by minds illuminated by the presence of the Holy Spirit, the texts may be said to teach revealed truths" (p. 94). Now, it is true that for Warfield one does not *learn* the truth of Scripture apart from the Spirit, and so it could be said, albeit with some awkwardness, that Scripture does not "teach" truth apart from the illuminating work of the Spirit (although Warfield would say that Scripture is true apart

14. Meredith G. Kline, *The Structure of Biblical Authority* (Grand Rapids: Eerdmans, 1972).
15. Robert Clyde Johnson, *Authority in Protestant Theology* (Philadelphia: Westminster Press, 1959).

from any present, continuing work of the Spirit). Nothing in Warfield's writings, however, even remotely suggests that the presence of the Spirit is a second "criterion" in addition to Scripture, as the description of the *discrimen* implies. The apparent implication that in assessing a theological proposal we add one factor (Scripture) to another (God) and somehow calculate the result is *anathema* to Warfield. And although such a method may be implicit in the views of the other theologians studied, we cannot feel that even they would be happy with this way of putting it. There is something very odd about describing the Holy Spirit as a "criterion." For criteria are generally principles, not persons, unless they are persons who tell us what to do by speaking to us. Few theologians, moreover, want to regard the Spirit either as a principle or as a person who speaks to us outside the Bible. Further, a criterion is usually something that we employ at our own discretion, knowing how to "use" it with the confidence that when rightly "used" it will produce proper evaluations. Is God-as-criterion subject to such manipulation? Kelsey is rightly critical of this sort of notion in a related context (pp. 214ff.), but without some such idea, how can we describe the Spirit as a "criterion" at all? Is the criterion here, perhaps, not God himself but our assessment of how God is acting in the world today? If so, then Kelsey ought to say so, for clarity's sake, and then admit that the analysis simply does not apply to Warfield, and that on that account its theological neutrality breaks down at this point. Thus, the *discrimen* is unclearly described, and however interpreted it is difficult to see how it applies to all the theologians discussed.

However one interprets this principle, it does appear that "criterion" is being used in a fairly eccentric sense. If we simply give up any attempt to understand it, another possible interpretation emerges. If we begin with Warfield's doctrine of illumination (which Kelsey feels is consistent with his principle) and also with Kelsey's own discussion of the Scripture-tradition relation (pp. 94ff.), we might understand the *discrimen* as follows: Scripture alone is criterion (using "criterion" straightforwardly), and the presence of God is needed for that criterion to be rightly used. This understanding of the *discrimen* is, at least, intelligible, and not obviously at odds with theological positions under discussion.

Now, at the end of the book, Kelsey argues for a lowering of our expectations with regard to doctrines of Scripture. He says that in the past doctrines of Scripture have been thought necessary so that we may be "sure of developing theological proposals that are *truly* in accord with Scripture" (pp. 214f.). However, he replies, no doctrine of Scripture can assure us that our positions will conform to Scripture, for the divine presence is part of the *discrimen*, and no doctrine can map in advance the workings of God.

Now, there is some confusion here. So far as I know, doctrines of Scripture have not often, if ever, claimed to guarantee the truthfulness of theological proposals consistent with them. It would surely have come as no shock to B. B. Warfield that there are errors in theologies with sound doctrines of Scripture, and truths in theologies that teach erroneous doctrines of Scripture. It has been felt, however, that a sound doctrine of Scripture is needed if one is to be properly and fully motivated to seek scripturality in doctrine. That latter contention seems to me to be unexceptionable. It has also been asserted, I think with justification, that Scripture itself teaches us some things about the divine working with the Word, and that there is nothing arrogant about trusting God's promise to be present with the Word under certain circumstances. To that extent, a doctrine of Scripture may indeed "map in advance" the workings of God, since God has graciously mapped them himself beforehand in Scripture.

Yet there are plenty of things that a doctrine of Scripture cannot do, and our reformulation of Kelsey's *discrimen* may help us to see these more clearly. "Scripture is criterion, but we cannot use the criterion rightly apart from the divine presence." A doctrine of Scripture, first, is limited in the extent to which it can formulate the nature of Scripture's "authority." We have seen that there is enormous diversity in the workings of this authority, and we cannot hope to formulate them exhaustively; rather, we must always be ready to be surprised as Scripture takes on unexpected functions in governing our lives and theologies. Second, no matter how fully the authoritative functions of Scripture are set forth, no doctrine will guarantee that we will make right use of them (using "right" either for conceptual or for moral-religious adequacy). Yet if Scripture is "sufficient" with respect to any doctrine at all, it clearly must be "sufficient" in setting forth the norms for its own use. Even if we cannot set forth those norms exhaustively, somehow they must be there. We cannot accept Kelsey's apparent position that these norms are indeterminate, or that they are communicated through some divine influence apart from (though "organically related to"?!) Scripture. And certainly we cannot accept any claim that such a view is "theological position neutral!"

One more point about the *discrimen*: Kelsey is quite right that one's view of and use of Scripture is deeply influenced by his conception of the mode of God's presence among the faithful (pp. 160ff.). See my "God and Biblical Language," in *God's Inerrant Word*[16] (Appendix E in this volume), for another approach to this relationship. Kelsey's typology of modes is

---

16. John W. Montgomery, ed., *God's Inerrant Word* (Minneapolis: Bethany Fellowship, 1974), 159–77.

interesting and helpful (pp. 161ff.). But this influence results not because God's presence is a second criterion found along with Scripture in these theologies, but because these theologies want to regard Scripture itself as a mode of God's presence.

6. IMAGINATION AS GROUND FOR CONSTRUAL

In section 2 above, we saw that Scripture is used to authorize thought and life in the church in a wide variety of ways. How do we decide which uses are legitimate? Do we make *that* decision on the basis of Scripture? If so, we are caught in a form of circularity. For in order to use Scripture to make that decision, we must have already made it.

Kelsey wants to acknowledge a certain circularity here: the biblical texts do influence our understanding of their function (in his term, our "construal" of Scripture), and our construal influences our reading of the texts. But Kelsey wants to avoid any vicious circularity; as we have already seen, he does not like to "beg questions." So in discussing Warfield, he rejects a fully circular relation between believing in scriptural authority and believing in plenary inspiration. We believe in plenary inspiration, says Warfield, because plenary inspiration is taught in Scripture, and we believe Scripture to be authoritative. "But why is scripture authoritative?" asks Kelsey. "Surely, the answer cannot be, 'Because the doctrine of plenary inspiration so teaches.' That would beg the issue" (p. 24). On Kelsey's interpretation, Warfield does not beg the issue; rather, he accepts biblical authority, essentially, on the basis of his experience of Scripture as a "holy object" (pp. 17f., 24).

Kelsey wants all of us to do what he thinks Warfield did. Biblical texts are "relevant" to our "construal" of Scripture, but not "decisive" (pp. 159, 166f., 197ff., 201, 206). Were the texts decisive for the construal, he seems to think, the question would be "begged," the circularity would be vicious. What is decisive, then? "An act of the imagination that a theologian must necessarily make prior to doing theology at all" (p. 170). This imaginative act involves a decision about the "point" of doing theology, about the "subject matter of theology" (p. 159). It involves an "imaginative characterization of the central reality of Christianity, 'What it is finally all about'" (p. 205); it involves an "imaginative characterization of the mode of God's presence" (p. 170). It also seems to me, because of the general structure of Kelsey's argument, that it is in this act of imaginative judgment that we accept Christianity as true, that we accept whatever justification we acknowledge (if any) for the whole complex of Christian ideas, activities, and so forth. Kelsey does not quite say this, but I think it follows from a comparison of his language about "imaginative construal" with his language about the justification of Christianity (pp. 6, 153f., 165ff.). Furthermore, most relevantly to our present discussion, the imaginative construal determines his view of how Scripture's authority ought to function in theology and church (p. 151).

Where does this imaginative construal come from? Out of thin air? Kelsey says that "the only 'explanation' that can be given is genetic" (p. 183). This seems to mean that there is no logical or rational necessity for making one particular construal rather than another. One may describe how a particular construal comes about, what "shapes" it, what influences it (pp. 183, 205); but one may not adduce grounds, evidence, or argument at least as "decisive" considerations. The construal has causes, but not reasons.

Scripture, then, influences the construal not by providing grounds for one rather than another, but by genetically "shaping" our imaginative process. Even so, Kelsey is willing to speak of Scripture as exercising "controls" over the imaginative process or as setting "limits" for it (pp. 170ff., 196f.). The "patterns" in Scripture exclude some outrageous construals and positively provide a "limited range of determinate possibilities" (p. 196). Furthermore, for those who accept the idea of Scripture as "canon," Scripture further limits the imagination by requiring the various patterns to be related to one another so as to exhibit the "wholeness" of the canon (pp. 196f.). Kelsey also urges that theological imagination is limited not only by the *text* of Scripture but also by the use of Scripture in the common life of the church (1). p. 205). This use requires that imaginative construals of Scripture be capable of rational assessment, though they are not themselves the products of reasoned argument (pp. 1, 171); the construal must also be "seriously imaginable" by people in the community, though Kelsey grants the legitimacy of a theologian's trying to stretch the limits of what is seriously imaginable in a particular situation (pp. 172f.). Furthermore, the imaginative judgment must be responsible to the whole range of church tradition (pp. 174f.).

But now we must ask: do these factors limit the imaginative construal *decisively*? Kelsey's descriptions of them suggest that they do: a construal that conceives of God's presence as "demonic," he says, is beyond the "outside limit" of possible construals (p. 196). Yet his general principle is that the imaginative act is "logically prior" to any decisive limitation on theological thinking (pp. 151, 170, 201). The imaginative act is creative, free, and for that reason Scripture (and presumably tradition) can have no decisive bearing upon it (1). p. 206). Kelsey is not clear here, but it would seem that even the "outside limits" imposed by Scripture upon imagination are only relative guidelines. The criterion of rational assessability presents a special problem here. Not only is this "limit" relativized by Kelsey's general principle, but further: if imaginative construals were capable of rational vindication, it would be hard to escape the conclusion that they can be rationally necessary, that is, subject to other than "genetic" explanation. Thus, it appears as though the alleged "controls" on imagination are at most only advisory in character, and probably pragmatic, as if Kelsey were saying, "These are the sorts of proposals most likely to gain general acceptance in the church." If one is not swayed by such considerations, he may ignore them with no rational or religious penalties. Imagination in essence is autonomous.

This from a writer who claims to be "theological position neutral"! But the notion of an autonomous theological imagination is theologically intolerable, to this reviewer, to B. B. Warfield, and, I suspect, to most other theologians when it is stated in such straightforward terms. Here, Kelsey's interpretation of Warfield is somewhat in error, though it does reveal some unsettling truth about Warfield. It is true that in Warfield's view plenary inspiration is not the one doctrine upon which all other doctrines are built; the other doctrines might well be true even if the Bible were not plenarily inspired (pp. 21f.). It is also true that Warfield appeals to "experience" of a sort to support his view of plenary inspiration: both the corporate experience of the church in affirming this view throughout its history and the individual experience of the believer who has heard Scripture used this way at his mother's knee (pp. 17f.). We may further grant, with Kelsey, that Warfield was not fond of circular argument, and when asked why we ought to receive the teaching of Scripture concerning itself, he tended to resort to what we might call a "theological position neutral" apologetic. Thus, Kelsey's construction of Warfield's view—that it appeals ultimately to our experience of Scripture as a "holy object"—is not as far from the truth as it might initially appear.[17] But, however inconsistently, Warfield clearly makes the argument from experience subordinate to the argument from exegesis, and in a passage quoted by Kelsey himself: "The church doctrine of inspiration was the Bible doctrine before it was the church doctrine and the church

17. So far as I can tell, Warfield never speaks of Scripture as a "holy" or "numinous" object, and that terminology carries connotations inconsistent with Warfield's general position. This point, however, is not of great importance in evaluating Kelsey's basic argument. On the whole, Kelsey's treatment of Warfield is one of the most careful, balanced, and fair analyses I have read from one who does not hold to plenary inspiration. It is good to see a scholar from the theological mainstream who describes Warfield so fairly and who, moreover, takes Warfield's theological position so seriously—as one that must be "done justice" by any metatheological scheme.

doctrine only because it was the Bible doctrine" (p. 18, quoting Warfield, *The Inspiration and Authority of the Bible*, 114). Kelsey denies to Warfield the right to make the experiential-historical argument secondary to the exegetical, and granted Kelsey's neutralism, this is understandable. This procedure also produces a more consistent position than Warfield's own, but it is one that Warfield himself did not hold. Warfield held both to a form of neutralism and to the subordination of experience to exegesis. This is inconsistent, to be sure, and Kelsey has the right to try to achieve greater consistency, but he does not have the right to make Warfield more consistent than he actually was. The basic point: Warfield did not, and could not, allow for the kind of autonomous theological imagination that Kelsey advocates. To Warfield, Scripture was the supreme rule for all human activities, including those of the imagination. Warfield had much to say, particularly in his writings on perfectionism and in his shorter writings, about the believer's subjective experience, and he constantly asserted the authority of Scripture as judge of such experience.

To assert the autonomy of imagination, then, is to abandon any claim to theological neutrality. Warfield denies the autonomy of imagination on theological grounds, and so does Scripture (note the phrase "vain imaginations").

What about circular argument? Well, I have argued ("God and Biblical Language," Appendix E in this volume), together with Van Til and others, that circularity of a sort is inevitable when one is giving reasons for an ultimate criterion. Even Kelsey's appeal to imagination as ultimate must, in the end, be based on his own "imaginative construal" of what Christianity is all about. For his view of theology is, as we have seen, very different from Warfield's, and may not, therefore, be urged as a neutral starting point acceptable to all positions. Imagination is not unilaterally "prior to" theology; even our most basic imaginative construals of Scripture are governed by theological considerations, and vice versa. (Note the importance in insisting upon *reciprocities* in the Scripture-church-Christianity relation; cf. section 4 above.)

Yet Kelsey has performed a service in showing the extent to which, and some of the ways in which, imagination is involved in theology. We must never assume that *sola Scriptura* excludes the use of imagination, any more than it excludes the use of extrascriptural premises. Imagination is needed if we are to achieve anything more than a mere repetition of Scripture. Only by imagination can we discern the best ways of summarizing, applying, and communicating Scripture. Only through imagination may we discover those metaphors by which the whole sweep of the message can be visualized.

7. MORALS

The morals I draw from my study are not the same as those Kelsey recommends, and mine make no claim to being "purely formal." First, this study reinforces my previous conviction that attempts at theological neutrality are futile, that we cannot find some supratheological common ground on which to carry on metatheological discussion, and that we ought not to try. Second, "authority" is a much more complicated concept than has been dreamt by most writers. There is an enormous field here for future research, and theologians ought to get busy on it, rather than merely repeating the standard arguments for various positions. Third, one's view of biblical authority is indeed a function of his basic religious commitment, an aspect of his commitment to Christianity as a whole. It is precisely for this reason that it *cannot* be discussed from a neutral standpoint. And one's metatheological views of Scripture are determined by his commitment as much as are his theological views. But the relationship is also reciprocal: one's view of Scripture also influences the shape of his general commitment. Circularity here, too, is unavoidable. Fourth, authority is a complex of functions by which Scripture rules the church (and through the church, the world); but this authority exists in part because of the objective properties of Scripture, and because of its origin in inspiration. Fifth, the presence of God, though not a second criterion in addition to Scripture, is indispensable to the right functioning of Scripture in the church. Sixth, imagination is no autonomous (neutral!) basis for theology; rather, imagination and theology influence one another in many subtle, complicated ways.[18] Yet imagination is absolutely crucial to the proper functioning of Scripture as "authority" in the church.

Now, this review has been largely negative, but it has also attempted to show in detail the interesting issues raised by this book. In raising those issues, Kelsey has done something of immense importance. In

---

18. Kelsey is generally most sensitive to complications and rightly suspicious of oversimplification. Why is it that on the question of neutrality, the Scripture-church relation, and the imagination-theology relation he has jumped at such easy answers? Is it, after all, desire for a "starting point" (cf. his criticism of this notion, 135ff.)? Is he searching for something that exists in a logically safe realm, beyond the possibility of criticism, now that "criticism" has allegedly made Scripture itself so problematic? If so, the search is all the more forlorn: not only is it hopeless, it is an idolatry. It is an attempt to find a replacement for Scripture as Word of God. Or is his problem merely a too-rigid attachment to the analytic/synthetic distinction, or a determination to avoid "circularity" at all costs, without regard to the evidently circular way in which many arguments actually function? Wherever the problem lies, we hope that it will not continue to blemish his otherwise perceptive work.

struggling so valiantly with those issues, Kelsey has done his job well, despite our objections. My overall feeling about the book, despite the criticisms, is highly positive. Kelsey has written something that *deserves* to be criticized at this length. He has elevated discussion of these matters to a new height of sophistication. His insights are indispensable, and his mistakes eminently worth thinking about. My concluding advice is for you to buy this book, even at the outrageous price. Anyone who does not at least read it will, I expect, have nothing theologically interesting to say about biblical authority.

APPENDIX I

REVIEW OF *THE NATURE AND EXTENT OF BIBLICAL AUTHORITY: CHRISTIAN REFORMED CHURCH, REPORT 44*[1]

Note: I reviewed this report for the students in a course I taught at Westminster Seminary California. I include it here to supplement the discussion of the "content and purpose" of Scripture in chapter 25 of this book.

This document is the report of a study committee to the Synod of 1972. It was in response to a request from the Reformed Ecumenical Synod that, in turn, was prompted by a request for joint discussion by the Gereformeerde Kerken in Nederland. The GKN later produced as the result of its study the document *God with Us*. The RES (and the CRC also) had made earlier declarations about the authority of Scripture, but the GKN questioned whether these documents were adequate to deal with the issues of today. In particular, they failed to discuss the "connection between the content and purpose of Scripture as the saving revelation of God in Jesus Christ *and* the consequent and deducible authority of Scripture" (p. 16 [emphasis theirs]).

To accept the GKN's formulation of the problem at this point, of course, is to prejudice significantly the sort of answer one will arrive at. We have seen this "content/authority" issue in Berkouwer and *God with Us*, and

---

1. Committee on Biblical Authority of the Christian Reformed Church, *The Nature and Extent of Biblical Authority* (Grand Rapids: Board of Publications of the Christian Reformed Church, 1972). Used by permission. For stylistic purposes, this appendix has been copyedited for inclusion in this volume.

490

we have seen how it can lead us into danger. Certainly, in some senses, authority is derivable from content:

1. Most of us come to know Jesus first, the authority of Scripture second. We are attracted to Scripture because it tells us of Christ.
2. And indeed, the authority of Scripture is, in the final analysis, the authority of Scripture's content (what else?). It is the authority of the gospel of Jesus Christ.
3. It is not just any book that could be the inspired Word of God; only a book with truly divine *content* could have such a nature.
4. The specific nature of God's authoritative will, what he wants us to believe and to do, is a function of the content of Scripture. We find it through applicatory exegesis.

Therein lies the plausibility of the GKN's formulation. But without further elucidation it can lead us into error. One might mistakenly accept ideas such as the following:

1. That our belief in Scripture is not based on Scripture's self-attestation, but upon our autonomous value judgment concerning the significance of Scripture's message.
2. That some parts of Scripture are somewhat irrelevant to the central message and therefore can be treated as merely human words.

The fact is that *content* and *authority* are not related to one another in some simple causal way. The content of Scripture is, usually, the means by which human beings come to *recognize* the authority of Scripture. But the content is not the efficient cause of scriptural authority; it is not what makes Scripture the Word of God. What makes Scripture the Word of God is simply the fact that God has spoken it. Furthermore, Scripture makes plain that all of it is God's Word (2 Tim. 3:16; 2 Peter 1:20f.), not just those parts that modern scholars deem to best reflect the "message." The fact is that God gave us his message within a rather large context of history, poetry, prophecy, Gospel, Epistle, apocalyptic. None of this is dispensable. In the largest sense, all of it is his message. All of it is his Word.

Now, I wish that the CRC statement (henceforth *NEBA*) had analyzed the GKN formulation forthrightly as I have tried to do above. On page 16, indeed, *NEBA* does reject the possibility of a "canon within the canon" or "kernel and husk." It affirms that the whole Bible is the inspired Word of God. Yet it also affirms the need "to make some distinctions in interpreting the concrete expressions of Scripture's authority." The example they give is the "traditional distinction between historical and normative authority," a distinction that I approve of, but that I doubt is relevant to the GKN type of thinking. Anyhow, they go on to say that form and content are not to be separated "in a *dualistic* fashion" (emphasis theirs). I note the hand of committee chairman Gordon Spykman here; he often talks about "dualisms," drawing as he does upon Dooyeweerd. But what is a *dualistic* separation as opposed to some other kind of separation? I find this rather confusing. Are we allowed to separate the two, if only we don't do it dualistically? What sort of line does this distinction draw for us? What does it rule in? What does it rule out?

The statement goes on to proscribe separations (now it appears to be all separations, not just dualistic ones!) between "formal and material aspects of Scripture," between "Jesus Christ as the content of Scripture" and "the garment of Scripture in which he comes to us." *NEBA* rejects the idea that "certain aspects" (?) can be "removed or isolated from" scriptural authority. Scripture is a "single, unified, authoritative Word of God," an "integrated whole."

This is one problem that rather pervades *NEBA*. Terms such as *separate, isolate, dualism, apart from, in relationship to, in terms of, holding together, division, divorce, atomism, cutting loose,* and *dichotomy* are thrown around rather recklessly, as if they had some obvious meaning. In fact, this language is very vague, and without explanation it is quite unsuitable for theological purposes, common though it is in theological literature. It is not at all clear what is meant, for example, by "separating form and content." There are many different relations between form and content that might be described by some people (usually not all) as "separations." It is far more interesting and important to describe precisely what kind of relation we are talking about (as, e.g., I have tried to do above), rather than to talk vaguely about "separations" and so forth. These terms, used by themselves, are usually counterproductive. They paint various images in the mind of the reader so that some readers think they understand the issues when they really don't. Many (like Spykman, evidently) think that these terms give them an extraordinarily "deep" insight that more precise terms would not give. I consider that feeling of depth quite illusory.

I have described this problem elsewhere (in *DKG* and in my lecture outline *Studies in Modern Theology*) as "anti-abstractionism" (*abstract* being a common synonym for *separate, isolate, divide,* though, to be fair, I was unable to find it used in *NEBA*). This sort of language is one source of the plausibility and apparent "depth" of Barth's theology and that of Berkouwer especially, and to a lesser extent of many others. But when this language is analyzed, it proves highly vague. I am disappointed to note such a *heavy* reliance on this sort of vague rhetoric in a document of the CRC.

Interestingly, however, after its preliminary analysis, *NEBA* determines not to focus any longer on the GKN's content/authority distinction, but rather to explore a different, though related, problem: the problem of relating divine to human aspects of Scripture (pp. 16f.). Or, to put it differently, "Is the authority of Scripture in any way influenced or qualified by its historical character?" (p. 17). In my view, this latter sentence is, like the aforementioned anti-abstractionism, a very vague way to formulate the problem. Obviously, the historical character of Scripture does have *some* influence on the nature of its authority. The true question is *what* influence? In other words, and here I continue my critique of anti-abstractionism, it is not enough to say that history and authority are related; we must also show what that relation is.

The question of divine/human aspects of Scripture was posed at the Synod of Apeldoorn of the GKN in 1961, which was the fountainhead of the discussions in the RES and CRC that led to *NEBA*. Another "subsidiary" (p. 17) concern at Apeldoorn was "the desire to avoid an atomistic approach to the concept of inspiration and authority (i.e., one that views each word or verse as being inspired and authoritative in and by itself)" (p. 17). Cutting through the anti-abstractionist rhetoric, I take this to be a plea to interpret Scripture in its proper contexts, especially the context of the saving message of Christ. This concern is a proper one, but can also, if abused, lead to the two errors mentioned earlier in connection with the content/authority issue.

NEBA then moves on to the main body of its discussion. First it surveys the confessions' teaching on biblical authority. I have no serious debate with the document here, though I think the sentence "We can never adequately define but only acknowledge and confess God's authority" smacks of an irrationalism that I believe is typical of much Dutch theology today. How do we acknowledge and confess something that we cannot define at all? What is meant by definition here?

Page 20 begins a discussion of what *NEBA* said it would not be focusing on, namely, the relation between content and authority. If one ignores some anti-abstractionist vagueness, the discussion is pretty good. It emphasizes that Scripture's authority is *divine*, its extent *pervasive*, that it is *plenary* and *verbal*. It brings "content" into the discussion only by saying that "when the entire Scripture speaks with divine authority, this divine authority is understood concretely and specifically only when one takes account of what God said, how he spoke, to whom he spoke, etc." In other words, all of Scripture is authoritative, but the only way to discover what specifically God is saying authoritatively is by looking at the content, that is, through contextual exegesis. That is a fairly obvious point, but one that ought to motivate us toward serious study of Scripture. Page 22, then, excludes the positions of Roman Catholicism, liberalism, Barth, Bultmann, Ebeling, Fuchs. That is good; certainly these exclusions mark *NEBA* as a far more conservative document than either Berkouwer's *Holy Scripture* or *God with Us*.

In section C (p. 22), *NEBA* makes the point that an understanding of Scripture's purpose is necessary for good exegesis. True and important. On page 24 they speak of progressive revelation and the fact that "not all the words or commandments of Scripture apply to us in the same manner in which they were applied to those to whom they were first spoken," though all those words remain divinely authoritative. Quite right. Then they affirm that the human purposes of the authors are important for understanding and applying the texts. Again, I have no problem. (I would not endorse the distinction on page 26, taken from Krister Stendahl, between "what it meant originally" and "what it continues to mean." There are dangers there. Meaning is potential use, and all the potential uses are in the words as originally given, though not all uses are appropriate to every situation.)

Page 27 begins *NEBA*'s evaluation of "Current Methods of Interpreting Scripture," topic IV, and probably the topic of greatest interest to the church. I will review it following their outline.

A. BIBLICAL INTERPRETATION AND SCIENTIFIC FINDINGS (PP. 27FF.)

NEBA recognizes the danger here to the principle of *Scriptura ipsius interpres* ("Scripture is its own interpreter"). It points out that this principle was mostly used against allegorical and spiritualistic forms of interpretation, and in favor of the alternative, namely, grammatico-historical interpretation. But the latter requires some knowledge of language, archaeology, and so on. The operative principle is that "these findings may not dictate an interpretation of Scripture contrary to its own intent, but certainly these findings may, and in fact, must, be used to help to understand the intended meaning of Scripture" (pp. 28f.).

What of new scientific theories? *NEBA* points out that Calvin did not oppose Copernicanism. Science may not dictate the interpretation of the Bible, as in liberal teaching concerning miracle (p. 30). Without naming the culprits, *NEBA* also criticizes some (presumably this gets closer to home than nineteenth-century liberalism) who may assert "that science makes it impossible to believe any longer that there was historically an original man and woman who were the ancestors of the human race" (ibid.). In this case, "the principle that Scripture is its own interpreter is no longer being maintained" (ibid.). "However, scientific discovery does compel us to ask whether a traditional interpretation reflects the intent of the Bible, or whether it is a reading of the Bible in the light of out-dated scientific conceptions" (p. 29). "Although scientific evidence may become the *occasion* for a reexamination of a traditional interpretation, any reinterpretation must be based on principles germane to and garnered from Scripture itself" (p. 30).

These formulations are pretty good; I wouldn't actually disagree with any. I do wish, however, they had said something about the enormous extent to which science (much more in our day than in Calvin's) has bought into dogmatically anti-Christian presuppositions, making it necessary for us to engage in some radical critique before using any of its conclusions. The principle of *antithesis* is entirely missing from *NEBA*. There is no suggestion that we are fighting a spiritual battle in the area of science. Rather, *NEBA* seems to assume that science and Christian thought are simply looking at the world from different perspectives, which hinders communication somewhat, even though the two disciplines are basically headed in the same direction.

B. THE USE OF THE HISTORICAL METHOD

NEBA disavows the old liberal form of what is sometimes called the *historical-critical* or merely *historical*[2] method that operated explicitly on non-Christian presuppositions—closed universe and so forth (p. 30). Still, they affirm the need to make use of the discipline of history in order to understand, say, the Synoptic problem. Illustrations:

1. THE HISTORICITY OF THE GOSPELS

NEBA makes the point common among evangelicals that the Gospel writers did not adhere to modern criteria of "notarial precision" in writing their books. But then *NEBA* says this point is "no longer considered

---

2. I prefer not to use *historical*, as *NEBA* does, synonymously with *historical-critical*. The latter term is generally associated with naturalistic presuppositions—presuppositions that are masked when we shorten it to *historical*. *NEBA* does seem to think that there is a kind of historical-critical method (top of p. 31) that is acceptable for Christians. If there is, I would prefer to find some other label for it than *historical-critical*. But of course, these are only verbal questions.

adequate" (p. 32). Why not? Because, *NEBA* says, it doesn't answer all the questions as to how the writers report events, and so on. That doesn't seem to me to indicate any inadequacy in the point about notarial precision, only a desire to supplement it with further analysis.

NEBA goes on to say that many differences in the Synoptic Gospels may be traced to differences not in the incidents reported but in the purposes of the individual writers. This is not, they insist, to "divide" event from report, but only to "distinguish." (In my estimation, this and other language in the last paragraph on page 33 is anti-abstractionist gobbledygook.) It is not, they say, ground for speaking of the "unreliability" of Scripture (p. 34). For the writers were simply doing what all historians do, mixing fact and interpretation.

I agree with the broad point. Were I writing *NEBA*, however, I would have included a warning about how this principle can be abused.

2. The Historical Jesus

NEBA is critical of both old and new "quests." The latter reduces our knowledge of Jesus to five or six basic facts, because it dismisses much Gospel material as biased by the faith of its authors. *NEBA* considers this restriction wrong, illegitimately dictating "the limits of historical possibility" (p. 35). The New Questers claim that much of the Gospels represent postresurrection thinking. Jesus could not have claimed messiahship or deity before the resurrection. Thus, much of the Gospels' Christology is the creation of the early church—fabrication rather than history. *NEBA* rejects this extreme approach, while maintaining a legitimate role for form criticism (pp. 37f.). They conclude that "any view that allows the actual creation of events for the sake of the message calls into question the reliability of the gospels" (p. 38). I agree with their treatment, on the whole.

3. The Resurrection of Jesus Christ

NEBA says that "no one associated with the new theology in the Reformed community denies the factuality of the resurrection of Jesus Christ. The question under discussion is only what the historian can say concerning the fact of the resurrection as recorded in the gospels" (p. 38).

There is first the assertion that the historian "as historian" can say nothing about the resurrection as such, for he cannot speak about anything unique (p. 38). *NEBA* disavows this concept of history. Certainly, they say, the *Christian* historian at least should be able to include the resurrection on the list of historical events, even if it is in some way a matter of faith (p. 39).

And what basis do these people have for saying that the resurrection even took place? Clearly they are not basing their thinking on Scripture, and the authority of Scripture has been compromised. I agree with NEBA.

C. THE FIRST CHAPTERS OF GENESIS

NEBA affirms the historicity of Genesis 1–11, while recognizing there the presence of selectivity, reflection of the later time of Moses, and figurative and symbolical language. It insists that those who claim that various things are figurative must argue their case "by means of careful exegesis and sound biblical exposition. No one may make such claims simply because he thinks that modern science has made it impossible to understand Scripture in the traditional Reformed way" (p. 42). Still, we should be open to hear the scriptural rationale for new interpretations (p. 43). Well said.

The Reformed Confessions insist that creation and historical fall are events at the beginning of human history (p. 43). However, they allow some flexibility on details. They do not contain any official position on the length of the creation days, in NEBA's view. NEBA does not criticize theistic evolution as such, but it exhorts those who study it to avoid the temptation to let science dictate biblical interpretation (pp. 44f.). Those who deal with that matter should "do so with a clear and unambiguous adherence to Scripture as the authoritative Word of God, and in agreement with our Reformed Confessions which are subordinate to that Word" (p. 45). True, but I wish they had said something very specific against theistic evolution.

Genesis 3, they say, is not a mere "teaching model." People who say that it is either make science dictate interpretation or else misconstrue "rabbinic" tendencies in Paul, who affirms the Genesis 3 account in Romans 5. Romans 5 does not include any rabbinic-type stories, only Genesis 3 itself, which the rabbis clearly considered historical. Good point, good argument.

On page 46 is a brief excursus saying that the Christocentric character of Scripture does nothing to undermine its historicity. Christ himself is related to creation and history, and the basic gospel does not eliminate the legitimacy of asking other sorts of questions. I like to see the Berkouwer type of rhetoric ("you avoid the serious questions") used against the Berkouwer type of message-monism.

NEBA concludes with pastoral advice offered to the church at large. There is a bit too much heart searching about this for my taste; the actual advice is not very controversial. There is a certain amount of anti-abstractionist blather ("divorce" on p. 53, several phrases on the bottom of p. 58). The rather technical terms "event-character" and "revelational meaning" are used on page 55 without nearly enough explanation. But for the most part, the pastoral advice and its explanations merely restate the positions of the preceding report.

I wish myself that *NEBA* had been more specific, addressing theologians by name and critically analyzing their proposals. The "Dutch family" atmosphere in the CRC seems to prevent any such mutual criticism, however. Failing that, the overall position is good, though at times it is stated too vaguely and the anti-abstractionism should be replaced by some serious analysis. I would have written it very differently, and I would have given the GKN a clearer answer on the content/authority issue. But I don't disagree with most of the positions actually taken by *NEBA*.

APPENDIX J

REVIEW OF PETER ENNS, *INSPIRATION AND INCARNATION*[1]

Note: I reviewed this book in 2008 at the request of some friends. I publish it here to supplement the discussion of inerrancy in chapter 26 of this book, and the discussions of Bible problems in chapter 28.

A couple of my friends in the Westminster Seminary constituency have urged me to make some comments on Professor Peter Enns' book. I had skimmed it some time ago, but my friends wanted me to look at it in a more serious way. I have done that now. My review may be somewhat redundant, given the recent reviews of Paul Helm,[2] Greg Beale,[3] and Donald Carson.[4] I agree with these reviews more than I disagree with them, but mine is more of a blow-by-blow account.

I protest that I cannot give a definitive evaluation, since I am not an OT scholar, as Enns is. Nor am I any kind of expert on ancient Near Eastern history

1. Peter Enns, *Inspiration and Incarnation: Evangelicals and the Problem of the Old Testament* (Grand Rapids: Baker, 2005).

2. Available at http://www.reformation21.org/Past_Issues/2006_Issues_1_16_/2006_Issues_1_16_Shelf_LIfe/April_2006/April_2006/166/vobId__2795/pm__392/, discussion continuing at http://peterennsonline.com/ii/a-response-to-paul-helms-review-of-inspiration-and-incarnation/ and http://paulhelmsdeep.blogspot.com/2008/01/analysis-extra-inspiration-and.html.

3. Available at http://findarticles.com/p/articles/mi_qa3817/is_200606/ai_n17176285, discussion continued at locations noted at http://theologica.blogspot.com/2008/01/enns-vs-helm-vs-beale.html.

4. Available at http://www.reformation21.org/Past_Issues/2006_Issues_1_16_/2006_Issues_1_16_Shelf_LIfe/May_2006/May_2006/181/vobId__2926/pm__434/.

or second-temple biblical exegesis, major topics in the book. But I have given some attention in my career to the doctrine of the authority of Scripture. So perhaps my observations will not be considered entirely irrelevant.

Given the advance warnings of some about the book, I was surprised at how much I liked it and profited from it. I especially liked its emphasis that we need to be more humble in our exegetical and theological claims. That certainly is a problem in our evangelical/Reformed context. On the other hand, I didn't get from the book much help toward a more confident proclamation of the biblical message.

Humility and confidence have always been somewhat at odds. In preaching classes, we tell students to be confident and authoritative in the pulpit, to say "thus saith the Lord," not to merely share what they feel. At the same time, we tell them to be humble, to realize that they are finite and sinful, that they should shed all pretense and affectation. I don't know of any general solution to this tension. In practice, what we try to do is to become certain enough of the meaning of Scripture so that we can ascribe that meaning to the Lord, while admitting from time to time that we can and often do get it wrong. Enns' book is good for my humility, but it does not encourage me to proclaim the Word authoritatively.

He divides the book into three major sections, each dealing with a problem: (1) the non-uniqueness of the OT in its cultural setting, (2) theological diversity in the OT, and (3) the use of the OT in the NT.

NON-UNIQUENESS

In the first section, I have a hard time seeing where the problem lies. Enns' point is that OT Israel spoke languages and had institutions (temples, prophets, priests, kings, legal codes) that were in some ways like the other nations of its time. He admits that the fact that the OT uses human languages such as Hebrew, Aramaic, and Greek "hardly poses a theological problem" (p. 19), except for a few people who once thought that NT Greek was a special "Holy Spirit language." Nor, certainly, is there anything particularly odd or challenging about the fact that nations other than Israel had temples, priests, and so on. That these nations had such institutions is plain in the OT narrative. In fifty years of studying the issues of biblical authority, I have never once heard or read anybody who said that the existence of such parallel institutions was any kind of problem for the Bible's inspiration or authority.

I have heard and read a lot of reflection about the parallels between Israel's laws and narratives and those outside Israel. Israel's laws are somewhat like those of the Code of Hammurabi; non-Israelite nations have their own creation stories and flood stories, and their own wisdom literatures, which are both like and unlike those in the Bible. Perhaps there have been some evangelicals who have found these parallels problematic, but I think not very many. The fact that non-Israelite traditions are different, even older, does not prove or even suggest that there are any defects in the biblical versions.

God wanted his people to have a well-functioning legal system, geared to its life in its ancient environment. For this purpose, there was no need to reinvent the wheel. The Code of Hammurabi and other ancient codes addressed that same need, in similar cultures, and so it should be no surprise that God's laws reflected the legal tradition of which Hammurabi's Code was an instance. Moses, or some source he made use of, may well have found in a preexisting set of laws certain statutes that would fit Israel's situation. The traditional doctrine of organic inspiration says that there is no contradiction between divine inspiration and human efforts to determine the right thing to say. The former often makes use of the latter.

Similarly, God wanted Israel to know something about the creation and flood. If we assume that these events actually happened, it is not surprising that the literature of non-Israelite nations bears witness to them. And it is not surprising that God would inspire Moses to give Israel true accounts, or that these accounts are like the others in some respects. These accounts are similar not only because they presuppose similar literary conventions, but also because they are describing the same event. Here, too, it would not be contrary to the doctrine of organic inspiration to believe that Moses depended on preexisting sources from other nations.

Enns asks, "If the Bible reflects these ancient customs and practices, in what sense can we speak of it as revelation?" (p. 31). I reply, why not? It is revelation because it's God's Word and therefore true. It's like asking, "Luke and Josephus both speak of Jesus, so how can Luke be revelation?" Easy. Luke is an inspired apostle and Josephus is not. Is Enns attributing to some the view that a book cannot be revelation unless it reveals an entirely unique culture? I know nobody who says that, and such a view would be so implausible as to be undeserving of refutation. Maybe this is Enns' own point—that a document can be God's Word even if it doesn't reflect or establish a unique culture. But I can't imagine why he thought this needed to be argued.

We do often refer to Scripture as unique. Yet we don't call it unique because it reflects a unique culture, but rather because it is the written Word of God and bears a unique witness to Christ.[5]

---

5. "Uniqueness" is a fairly vague concept. In one sense, everything is unique. Nothing is absolutely identical to anything else, for if it were, there would be not two objects, but one. But there are various levels of relative uniqueness. Clearly, OT Israel is like other nations

Enns asks, "What does it mean for other cultures to have an influence on the Bible that we believe is revealed by God?" (p. 38). Again, it's hard for me to imagine where this question comes from. Most everyone in the Reformed camp confesses organic inspiration, the view that divine inspiration makes use of both human and divine causes to bring about the biblical text. Why would anybody imagine that God cannot use the influence of other cultures to do this, along with all the other historical causes that brought the Scriptures into being?

On the flood accounts, Enns says, "The problem raised by these Akkadian texts is whether the biblical stories are historical: how can we say logically that the biblical stories are true and the Akkadian stories are false, when they both look so much alike?" (p. 40). Again, the answer is easy: (1) the Akkadian account is not simply false, but contains some false claims; (2) we know that the biblical stories are true because God inspired them.[6]

I kept waiting for Enns to draw some correlation between inspiration and truth, and I couldn't find it. On page 43 he says that we should not "reason backward from the historical evidence of the monarchic account, *for which there is some evidence*, to the primeval and ancestral stories, *for which evidence is lacking*." But does not divine inspiration constitute evidence? On page 44 he says:

> One would expect a more accurate, blow-by-blow account of Israel's history during this monarchic period, when it began to develop a more "historical self-consciousness," as it were. It is precisely the evidence *missing* from the previous periods of Israel's history that raises the problem of the essential historicity of that period.

What this seems to mean is that we should suspect Genesis, for example, of lacking historicity because it lacks detail (i.e., "blow-by-blow" accounts). I'm not sure what this means. Surely the stories of Genesis (including those of chaps. 1–3) include quite a lot of detail. But even if the detail is insufficient for some scholars, does not divine inspiration outweigh that? Is it impossible for us to imagine that God might have chosen to give us a narrative with relatively little detail?

---

in a great many ways—too much so, according to Scripture. But it also differs with them in important ways: they worship a different God, they anticipate different promises from God, and so on. It would be wise to avoid talking about "uniqueness" in a general way and rather to talk about the ways in which Israel is, and is not, unique. Then we should ask how Israel *ought* to be unique if it is to be considered a recipient of revelation. Enns does not make such distinctions to my satisfaction.

6. I would reply similarly to the considerations he raises on pages 41–43.

On page 47 Enns does respond to conservatives who appeal to divine inspiration:

> The conservatives' reaction was also problematic in that it implicitly assumed what their opponents also assumed: the Bible, being the word of God, ought to be historically accurate in all its details (since God would not lie or make errors) and unique in its own setting (since God's word is revealed, which implies a specific type of uniqueness).

The "uniqueness" criterion is quite unclear, as I have said before, and it has never been a part of any conservative position that I am aware of. It is true that many conservatives have argued that inspiration entails historical accuracy, for the reasons Enns mentions. But the wisest conservatives have acknowledged that not every genre of literature makes historical claims, certainly not in details. The question, then, is whether Genesis makes any claims relevant to its historicity. I am willing to listen to arguments for the negative, but I have not heard any plausible ones, certainly not in the present volume.

On page 40 Enns suggests that "myth" might be a good description of the biblical stories, since it is a common way of referring to the non-Israelite flood stories. He defines myth as "*an ancient, premodern, prescientific way of addressing questions of ultimate origins and meaning in the form of stories: Who are we? Where do we come from?*" (p. 40). This is rather different from many definitions of myth, but I will let that pass. In this definition and in its context, Enns intentionally avoids the question whether these stories relate what "really happened." But that is, of course, the issue. Certainly, the biblical stories fit this definition of myth. Indeed, if you drop the term "origins" from the definition, *all* the stories of the Bible fit this definition. The resurrection of Jesus addresses the question of our ultimate meaning in the form of a story. But the Bible itself insists that the resurrection story, in addition to addressing the question of our ultimate meaning, tells us something that really happened. Indeed, the resurrection would not be effective in declaring our ultimate meaning if it had not really happened. Enns' definition of myth avoids the question whether these stories narrate real history, and in doing so it avoids the most important problem raised in this connection.

The major problem is not the word *myth*, though the apostolic comment in 2 Peter 1:16 (and the general perception that, contrary to Enns' definition, myth excludes historicity) should lead us at least to hesitate in using it. The problem is that to call the Genesis flood a myth and then to adopt Enns' definition of myth is to gloss over one of the main questions people have in examining that story. He raises a nonissue (How can a revealed book be culturally conditioned?) and avoids a real issue (Did the flood actually take place?).

Now, on page 49 he suggests that the second question is not legitimate. "It presupposes . . . that what is historical, in a modern sense of the word, is more real, of more value, more like something God would do, than myth." He denies that presupposition. Again, I would not claim that every genre of Scripture is "historical" in the disputed sense. And I don't deny that there may be some things in the Bible that fit Enns' definition of myth. But I do think that ancients, as well as moderns, understood the difference between a story that really happened and one that is merely a kind of parable. And sometimes, not all the time, that distinction is important. The resurrection really happened. The exodus really happened. God created the world, not Marduc.

Jesus' parables do not narrate historical events in this sense, and I certainly would not claim that they are of less value on that account. But the parables, like all the rest of Scripture, are embedded in the context of a narrative that clearly makes historical claims, claims that various events really took place in geographical space and calendar time.

In making historical claims, biblical faith is, if I may say so, unique among the religions. What historical claims there are in Hinduism and Buddhism are largely irrelevant to the substance of their teachings. But biblical religion is different. I remember Professor Norman Cantor, a Jewish Medieval historian at Princeton, saying that the reason Christianity succeeded in attracting followers while the mystery religions did not was its "historical claim." It really is important to biblical faith that God acts and speaks. It is wrong to suggest that the distinction between myth and history in this sense is a "modern invention" (p. 49).[7]

On pages 50–56 Enns uses a number of arguments to show that the ancient non-Israelite mythology is older than the Bible. This may or may not be true, but I don't understand its relevance. There are a

7. Enns himself says on page 55 that "the biblical account, along with its ancient Near Eastern counterparts, assumes the factual nature of what it reports," but he distinguishes this from a concept of truth derived from modern science. He needs to distinguish, then, (1) the truth that we can gain from myth, (2) the kind of "factual truth" assumed by the biblical documents, and (3) the truth given in modern scientific historiography. Really, (2) and (3) are the only concepts that need to be distinguished; Enns' talk about (1) is really a red herring. If there are significant differences between (2) and (3), they ought to be discussed. I am certainly open to that. But I don't think that either (2) or (3) can do without the concept of "what really happened," as Enns sometimes seems to suggest. Only after such a discussion will we be in a position to evaluate the "factuality" of Genesis 1–3, which Enns completely dismisses as a "modern" concern on pages 55–56.

number of possibilities here. (1) Certain events took place that were later recorded by non-Israelite ancient literatures. Later God inspired Moses, having read these, to present a more adequate version. (2) These events were first recorded by oral tradition, later in non-Israelite writings. Later God inspired Moses to write a more adequate version, based on the oral tradition. (3) These events were recorded in books from the very beginning (note the phrase "book of the generations" in Genesis 5:1). Perhaps those books themselves were inspired texts. These books were passed down to Moses, who used them (perhaps with some editing) in his own writings. Before this, non-Israelite cultures produced their own accounts, based (or not) on the early books. In none of these cases does the antiquity of non-Israelite mythology cast any doubt on the authenticity of the scriptural account. None of these possibilities deny that Israel's documents were like the non-Israelite documents in significant ways.

Enns rejects all these possibilities. The only argument I can find for this rejection is on page 52: "it would be very difficult for someone holding such a view to have a meaningful conversation with linguists and historians of the ancient world." I cannot see this as anything but a desire for academic respectability. Enns, like many evangelicals, wants to be invited to the table with the mainstream scholars. I don't condemn that motive, but it does not provide any kind of argument for his hypothesis.

On page 56 he returns to the uniqueness issue. Israel's laws (pp. 56–58) are much like those of its neighbors. He says that "what makes Israel's laws revelatory is not that they are new—a moral about-face vis-à-vis the surrounding nations—but that *these* are the laws that were to be obeyed in order to form Israel into a godlike community." This formulation is fine with me. And again I wonder who it is who ever embraced the other alternative. Same for Proverbs (pp. 58–59).

On the question of bias in historical writing (pp. 59–66), I largely agree with Enns. I agree that "there really is no such thing as objective historiography" (p. 66). It is certainly true that often Scripture doesn't present narratives in chronological order (pp. 65f.). The standards of "historical" writing in the ancient world were different from our own. Evangelicals have generally recognized this.

My conclusion is that in this first section of the book, Enns fails to present any thesis distinct from the traditional evangelical view of organic inspiration, though he seems to think he has done so. He confuses issues, however, by unclear uses of the concepts "evidence," "myth," and "uniqueness," and by failing to present the relation of inspiration to historicity in any clear way.

THEOLOGICAL DIVERSITY

In the second section, he argues that there is "theological diversity" in the OT, but his concept of "diversity" is as confusing as was his concept of "uniqueness" in the first section. *Diversity* is a very general term. In a broad sense, everything we say is diverse from everything else we say—that is, everything we say is different from everything else. (Another way of putting this is that everything we say is "unique.") And when we get down to more specific uses of the term, there are many diverse kinds of diversity: diversity of perspective (two authors looking at a subject from different angles),[8] diversity of emphasis, diversity of disagreement. The traditional evangelical doctrine of Scripture has never had a problem with diversities of perspective or of emphasis. It does have a problem with the idea that one part of Scripture disagrees with another; for if two assertions disagree, only one of them (at most) can be correct. If we are to discuss the doctrine of Scripture, it is very important, therefore, to define specifically the kind of diversity we find in the Bible. But Enns typically speaks of diversity in a very general way, leaving the reader confused.[9] Or he speaks of diversities that no evangelical would have a problem with, then uses that agreement to suggest that we should also agree to other kinds of diversity.

But obviously we should not accept diversity of just *any* kind in Scripture. Our view of what the Bible is clearly excludes some kinds of diversity. Scripture does not recommend faith in Yahweh and also faith in Baal. It does not tell us to trust Jesus for our salvation and also the traditions of the Hindus. It does not tell us to be saved by faith alone and also by works. It does not say that Jesus is risen and also not risen. Enns' vague use of "diversity" enables him to move easily between one kind of diversity and another, when wisdom would call us to stop moving and look where we are going.

He then mentions some specific examples of diversity. The first is Proverbs, which sometimes tells us apparently contradictory things: answer a fool according to his folly, and don't answer him according to his folly. Here I largely agree with Enns' treatment, but it's not very different from what evangelicals have traditionally said. Proverbs is poetic, ironic. It doesn't

8. On page 73 Enns defines diversity as "the Old Testament's different perspectives or points of view on the same topic." "Different perspectives" raises no problem with the evangelical tradition. "Points of view" might mean the same thing, or it might suggest disagreement, as when we refer to the conservative or liberal "point of view." Later on the same page, he speaks of "diversity at the level of factual content," an awkward phrase that seems to indicate disagreement as to what really happened in the biblical history.

9. Note how he speaks simply of "the fact of diversity" on page 108, as if all his examples exhibited the same kind of phenomenon.

claim to provide prescriptions that can individually be followed in every situation. Rather, it tells us that sometimes we should do this, other times that. As he says, "it takes wisdom to know *how* this Proverb applies to *this* situation, which means an intimate knowledge of the circumstances." Sometimes wealth is a blessing, sometimes a snare, and so forth. Wisdom literature, as a genre, works like this. God gives it to us so that we can work through the situations of our lives in this way. This is diversity of perspective. It raises no questions about the traditional doctrine of inspiration.

When Enns moves to Ecclesiastes, he points out that in the latter book there is an even deeper tension. Proverbs suggests that wisdom always works; Ecclesiastes points out that even wisdom is not consistently rewarded, and that we will all die anyway (pp. 76–77). Here Enns seems to think he has uncovered something more than a "perspectival" diversity. He says that we should not try to "iron out" the differences. Does this mean that Proverbs and Ecclesiastes disagree? I would have thought that the difference between Proverbs and Ecclesiastes could be handled like the differences within Proverbs: as wealth is sometimes a blessing, sometimes a snare, so wisdom sometimes helps and sometimes doesn't. But Enns' "diversity" language leaves the nature of the problem fairly murky. I just don't know what kind of problem I'm being asked to solve. If this is a perspectival difference, no problem at all. Otherwise, we have some conceptual work to do, even though Enns tells us (p. 80) that we really shouldn't worry about it.

In the case of Job, Enns notes that Job's friends espouse a theology of covenant blessings and curses similar to Deuteronomy, but they are rebuked. There are various ways of looking at this. One is to note that in fact Job's good deeds are rewarded, just as Deuteronomy says, but it takes some time. Deuteronomy doesn't say that good deeds are rewarded immediately, or that evil is punished immediately, though some might have that mistaken impression. Job then counteracts that mistaken impression. In the book of Job itself, the rewards come at the end of Job's life. But if the reader considers that even that doesn't happen in every case, the problem leads us inevitably to consider the afterlife (however rarely this is mentioned in the OT itself) as the time when Deuteronomic justice is consummated.

Enns is right to say that the error of Job's friends is that they appealed to the principle of covenant blessing "*superficially*, without sufficient knowledge of the *particulars of the situation*" (p. 82). But this certainly raises no problem for the traditional doctrine of Scripture, at least in its most mature formulations.

Then he goes to the differences between Samuel-Kings and Chronicles. Here, "diversity" seems to mean a difference in *emphasis*, stemming from a difference in *purpose*. Nevertheless, Enns talks about this as a "tension" (p. 85) that should be "allowed to stand," even though we "struggle" with it. This language suggests some kind of deeper problem than a mere difference in emphasis, though I suppose there are people who struggle because they construe the difference as something other than one of emphasis.

Then he suggests that there is diversity even in the Ten Commandments, illustrated by the differences between the Exodus and Deuteronomic versions. Well, the two are different in some details. They do not contradict one another. The differences are easily accounted for: the Exodus version comes from the original stone tablets, written by the finger of God (Ex. 31:18; 34:1). The Deuteronomic version is taken from Moses' oral exhortation to Israel as they prepare to enter the Promised Land. Enns' accounts of these differences (p. 87) are generally right, and he is right to say that it is important for each generation to apply the existing law to new situations. Again, I think there is nothing here that threatens, or should be seen to threaten, the traditional doctrine of Scripture.[10]

On Enns' treatment of the apparent contradiction between Exodus 20:5–6 and Ezekiel 18:19–20 (pp. 88–89), I think it should be added that Exodus does not literally say that sons are punished just because the fathers have sinned. The sons, like the fathers, are members of a generation who hate God. But of course, the fathers are especially to blame, since the cycle begins with them. Nevertheless, Enns' point that Ezekiel tells us not to "hide behind the law" (a law that the returning exiles may have misunderstood) is also a point worth making.

Most of Enns' other examples in this section are similarly unthreatening to the tradition, even when Enns seems to think that they are. I will not go over all these in detail; in most cases they deal, like those above, with the application of a revealed principle to a new situation. However, there are a few arguments of his that seem to point in a different direction.

1. If he is right on the exegesis of Exodus 12:8–9; Deuteronomy 16:6–7; and 2 Chronicles 35:13 (pp. 91–93), there is at least an apparent contradiction as to whether the Passover lamb should be roasted or boiled. This is not just the application of an old law to a new situation; it is rather a contradiction between two biblical laws. I won't try to criticize his exegesis here or to resolve the apparent contradiction.[11] But this is different from the other examples Enns has mentioned, and he should have warned us. It is as if he sneaks up on us, giving us bland, noncontroversial cases of

10. I think that here Enns is saying the same thing I have often said in reference to the "situational perspective" in ethics and epistemology.

11. My OT colleague Bruce Waltke does find fault with Enns' construal of the Hebrew terminology here.

"diversity," so that we will not be alert or alarmed when he suggests an actual contradiction in Scripture.

2. Enns suggests (p. 96) that the marriages of Ruth, first to Mahlon, then to Boaz, literally violate the stricture of Deuteronomy. 23:3 that Moabites may not enter the assembly of the Lord.[12] Perhaps they did, but this is not a contradiction in the law itself. If they violated the law, that should not be considered strange; we all violate the law. And it is significant that Scripture tells stories of a number of people who sinned greatly (such as Rahab and David) who by God's grace became progenitors of the Messiah. I don't understand why Enns considers this a problem or a tension. He says there is a coherence here that "transcends the level of simple statements or propositions." Sure, there is; but there is also a coherence among the statements and propositions.

The transcendent coherence Enns observes here is a movement in the OT from emphases on separation from Gentiles to emphasis on integration. The stories of Ruth and Jonah are part of this, and it is certainly related to the ultimate purpose of God as presented in Genesis 12:3; Isaiah 49:6; and Galatians 3:26–29. The rules mandating separation of Jews from Gentiles were temporary and for a specific purpose. It is right and important to keep this in mind when we read stories such as that of Ruth. But it raises no problems for the traditional doctrine of Scripture.

3. Enns (pp. 97–102) mentions passages where it seems that the gods, other than Yahweh, are nothing, and other passages in which they seem to have some kind of existence. The traditional view is that although there are evil supernatural beings, beings that receive worship and claim to be gods, they do not deserve to be called that. This fact can be expressed either by saying that no gods (that is, beings that deserve to be worshiped as God) exist besides Yahweh, or by saying that those popularly described as gods do really exist, but Yahweh will certainly defeat them. I see nothing in Enns' discussion that requires any reconsideration of that traditional view.

4. Enns (pp. 103–7) tells us that some passages of Scripture suggest that God cannot change his mind, and others suggest that he does. Of course, this issue has often been discussed in the literature dealing with open theism, including my book on the subject, *NOG*, and my *DG*. I think the Reformed tradition is comfortable with the view that God's eternal plan is unchanging, but that when he enters the historical narrative he is a changing protagonist. (He does one thing on Monday, another thing on Tuesday.) These changes, like all changes in the created world, are

12. I think Deuteronomy 7:3 is more relevant here, since it specifically mentions intermarriage.

governed by his unchanging eternal plan. I think that deals with the difficulties Enns alleges.

Now, on page 106 he urges us not to ask whether God can or cannot change his mind "as some abstract discussion." He is not interested in what God is like "behind the scenes" or "what God is *really* like." He admits that these are good questions, but he feels "bound to talk about God *in the ways the Bible does*, even if I am not comfortable with it." I am very sympathetic with his concern here, as with his statement "There is no part [of Scripture] that gets it 'more right' than others. Rather, they get at different sides of God." I think we should be able to tell biblical stories without always having to make theological qualifications. There is nothing wrong with saying that God went down to Sodom to learn about the sins being committed there. The text doesn't interrupt itself to point out that this event was part of God's changeless plan, and there is no reason why a pastor or Sunday school teacher should have to interrupt his exposition to explain that. But the question does come up, and when it does, Christian teachers have an obligation to point out higher-level explanations.

The question, though, is whether the Bible presents these two sides of God (unchanging and changing) as a kind of contradiction in which we affirm two sides without having any idea how they fit together, or whether it represents these in ways that we can at least begin to fit together. Enns doesn't quite deny that we can fit them together, and at times he seems merely to be siding with simple Christians who are unable to reconcile these "sides of God" but who faithfully accept both. But other times he seems to suggest that it is wrong to try to explain the apparent contradiction, even if we leave the impression that it is a logical contradiction. I think there are serious dangers down that path.

With his concluding observations (pp. 107–11) about God's accommodating himself to human understanding, as a kind of "incarnation" of his word in history, I have no complaints. Reformed theology since Calvin has emphasized divine accommodation, and incarnation is a legitimate way of putting that. Incarnation here is a metaphor, however, and in this sort of context we have to be more careful than Enns is about the implications we draw from that metaphor. I agree that the ultimate unity of Scripture is to be found in Christ, "not simply the words on the page" (p. 110). But the question of the doctrine of Scripture is precisely *how* its overall unity in Christ is or is not reflected in the words on the page. Since Scripture is language, the doctrine of Scripture is a doctrine about language. Scripture in fact says quite a lot about its own character as language, and it is not wrong for us to take that teaching seriously.

THE USE OF THE OLD TESTAMENT IN THE NEW

The third problem Enns discusses is the way NT writers interpret the OT. Many of us have been perplexed at some of these interpretations. For example, Enns points out that in Luke 20:34–38 Jesus quotes Exodus 3:6, "I am the God of Abraham, and the God of Isaac, and the God of Jacob," and uses it to prove the resurrection from the dead. But Enns says, "No one reading Exodus and coming across 3:6 would think that resurrection was suddenly the topic of conversation. There God is simply announcing himself to Moses as the God of his ancestors" (p. 114).[13]

Enns summarizes his conclusions about the NT use of the OT:

1. The NT authors were not engaging the OT in an effort to remain consistent with the original context and intention of the OT author.
2. They were indeed commenting on what the text *meant*.
3. The hermeneutical attitude they embodied should be embraced and followed in the church today.

To put it succinctly, the NT authors were explaining what the OT means *in light of Christ's coming* (pp. 115–16).

Number 1 indicates that for Enns the NT writers were not engaged in what we today call "grammatical-historical" interpretation. How, then, should we describe their method and procedure? He believes that the apostles largely followed a type of hermeneutic characteristic of second-temple Judaism and anticipated in the OT itself. He gives examples from noncanonical texts. In the apocryphal Wisdom of Solomon, for example, he points out some interpretations of OT passages that we would now consider erroneous,[14] but that seem to come from traditional understandings existing in Israel at the time (pp. 121–28). In the Qumran community a similar kind of hermeneutic operated, but it was geared to showing that "the Bible has its ultimate and final meaning in the events surrounding the Qumran community" (p. 129). Enns draws parallels between this approach and the NT procedure of showing that Christ is the meaning of the OT (cf. Luke 24:13–35).

---

13. It is odd that Enns, in discussing Luke 20:34–38, does not take account of Jesus' own reasoning: "Now he is not God of the dead, but of the living, for all live to him" (v. 38). Jesus does not claim that Exodus 3:6 is intended to *teach* resurrection; rather, he argues that it *implies* resurrection. Certainly that makes a difference as we seek to answer Enns' question whether Jesus' reference to Exodus 3:6 was appropriate.

14. I think Enns is a bit quick to accuse pseudo-Solomon of error. I think that its treatment of Adam, Cain, Abraham, Jacob, and Joseph can be read in more favorable ways. But I don't dispute Enns' larger point that pseudo-Solomon's reading of the OT contains some errors and some additions to the biblical text.

He then points out some examples of NT use of the OT that don't conform to our notions of grammatical-historical interpretation, such as the use of Hosea 11:1–3 by Matthew in 2:12–15. In each case, he argues that the NT use of the OT would be considered wrong by grammatical-historical standards, but it is justified because (1) it is similar to common uses of the OT texts during the second-temple period, and (2) it aims to present Christ as the pervasive theme of the OT. I will not discuss each of these examples,[15] for Enns' argument is clear enough without that kind of interaction.

Enns sums up his approach somewhat by saying, "The New Testament authors take the Old Testament out of *one* context, that of the original human author, and place it into *another* context, the one that represents the final goal to which Israel's story has been moving" (p. 153). I think that even on a more conservative reading of the specific examples (such as Beale's), we can see that something like this is going on. Still, we should also note (perhaps Enns does this at some point) that the original author (whether it be Moses, David, or Hosea) is also part of the Jesus context. So the NT writer is not really taking the OT passage *out of* the original writer's context. He is, rather, moving from one part of the original context to another. It is not that the OT writer is completely removed from the "trajectory" that leads to Christ; he is part of that trajectory, but at an earlier stage. If we understand that, we are not able to say that Matthew's treatment of Hosea 11:1 "did not speak of Jesus of Nazareth" in its original context, as Enns does on page 153. Christ was inseparable even from Hosea's "original context."

How should we read the OT today? Enns takes the position that we should "acknowledge the Second Temple setting of apostolic hermeneutics but discern carefully what sorts of things can and cannot carry over to

---

15. I do think there are better ways of dealing with these examples. They have been discussed in Christian literature for many centuries, and it is certainly not obvious to me that Enns' treatments are unexceptionable. Gregory Beale and Donald Carson have recently done a great service to the church by publishing *A Commentary on the New Testament Use of the Old Testament* (Grand Rapids: Baker Academic, 2007), which attempts to comment on every NT quote, reference, or allusion to the OT. They distinguish between prophecy and typology (Hos. 11:1 is the latter), and in general maintain that the NT uses of the OT are grammatical-historically, not just Christologically, appropriate. My own approach is one that Enns specifically rejects (p. 115, approach number 2; I do not accept the variant described in number 3), namely, that the word *application* is the best to cover the wide variety of ways in which NT authors cite the OT. Note also the overall theological context of biblical interpretation found in Vern Poythress, *God-Centered Biblical Interpretation* (Phillipsburg, NJ: P&R Publishing, 1999), and in Vern Poythress, "The Presence of God Qualifying Our Notions of Grammatical-Historical Interpretation: Genesis 3:15 as a Test Case," *JETS* 50, 1 (2007): 87–103, also available at http://www.frame-poythress.org/poythress_articles/2007Presence.htm.

today" (p. 158). We must, then, follow the apostles in their hermeneutical goal, to show that the OT speaks of Christ. But "we cannot be limited to following them where they treat the Old Testament in a more literal fashion . . . since the literal (first) reading will not lead the reader to the Christotelic (second) reading" (ibid.). He continues, "We do not live in the Second Temple world. What made sense back then would not necessarily make sense now." But how do we maintain the apostles' Christotelic approach while renouncing their second-temple methods?

Enns offers several answers. One is that we should not make so much of "method" as many do today (p. 160). But that is simply to reject the question as inappropriate. It would imply, I suppose, that it would be legitimate to read Scripture without any method, or with a method so loose that we could freely depart from it, which is the same thing. Then anything goes. Nobody could evaluate any interpretation as better than any other. And why would we need to have seminary professors to teach biblical interpretation?

But Enns shies away from that kind of relativism. He tries to give us guidance, for example, by telling us that interpretation is "at least as much art as science" (p. 161), urging us to be open to "multiple layers of meaning" so that "no one person, school, or tradition can exhaust the depth of God's word." Our interpretation should be "as much community oriented as it is individually oriented" (ibid.), the community working with "the direct involvement of the Spirit of God" (p. 162). And "perhaps we should think of biblical interpretation more as a path to walk than a fortress to be defended. Of course there are times when defense is necessary, but the church's task of biblical interpretation should not be defined as such" (ibid.).

Actually, I agree entirely with the points made in the above paragraph (repeated in various ways on pp. 170–71). Yes, interpretation is an art, a communal walk, a fellowship with the Spirit.[16] And yes, there are depths

16. I find it helpful to point out that interpretation is something that goes on all the time, in our conversations with one another and in our experience of reading. Few of us who do this have been trained in "methods of interpretation," but we know to some extent the languages we are hearing and reading. That knowledge of language includes an intuition or subjective sense of how words are to be taken. Hermeneutical methods are secondary to this activity. They attempt to chart the ways in which our linguistic intuition directs us. Thus, it is correct to say that interpretation is an art before it is a science, and that for believers the presence of the Spirit makes a decisive contribution to our understanding. But it is only after two people experience common ground in these intuitions that they can meaningfully develop hermeneutical theories and debate which ones are best. Now, the interpreters of second-temple Judaism may, despite their faulty method, have at times had reliable intuitions about the meanings of texts. What is crucial to modern believers is that however an interpretation came to be in Scripture, we must regard it as a good interpretation, because it is inspired by God.

of meaning in Scripture.[17] But Enns concedes that sometimes defense is necessary—defense of one interpretation over another. And I don't find in Enns' account any help for those who are called to make such defenses.

In the concluding chapter, he says that "the Bible sets trajectories, not rules, for a good many issues that confront the church" (p. 170). Frankly, I cringe at that word *trajectories*. William Webb's book *Slaves, Women and Homosexuals*[18] argues that on the titular subjects we have no direct guidance from Scripture, only "trajectories," and those trajectories permit us to espouse a rather different and better ethic than that presented in the NT itself. I consider that a violation of *sola Scriptura*, even of biblical authority.[19] On such a basis, our judgments about where the biblical trajectory is moving, rather than Scripture itself, become our ethical criteria. I don't know whether Enns buys Webb's entire argument. I hope that he does not.

I do agree with Enns' exhortations about "learning to listen" (pp. 171–73). I've published similar exhortations in a number of places. We should not deal with Enns, or any other controversial theologian, by a response motivated chiefly by fear, and that fails to really hear what the person is saying. I trust that, although I disagree with Enns more than I agree with him, I have listened hard to what he is saying and have tried to deal with him fairly. And, as he urges, with humility, love, and patience (p. 172).

CONCLUSIONS

I commend Enns for writing a very stimulating book, packed with useful, digestible information about Scripture and the literature of the ancient Near East. His motive is to help the church to move away from a sort of

17. There has been some talk lately about how this and other kinds of interpretation are consistent with WCF 1.9, which says that the sense of Scripture "is not manifold, but one." The Confession here refers to the fourfold exegesis of the medieval period, and it speaks against arbitrary interpretations not grounded in the text being expounded. But I cannot imagine that the Westminster divines intended to deny that the meanings of Scripture texts are often complex, especially given the "rules for the right understanding of the ten commandments" found in WLC 99, and the vastly complex expositions of the commandments in WLC 102–48. Generally, I think that it is unhelpful to bring the Confession into hermeneutical discussions such as the present one. The divines did not address the specific problems of modern hermeneutics. They did maintain, however, the infallibility of Scripture, and any hermeneutical theory that calls biblical infallibility into question must deal with that.

18. Downers Grove, IL: InterVarsity Press, 2001.

19. See Wayne Grudem, "Shall We Move beyond the New Testament to a Better Ethic?" *JETS* 47 (2004): 299–346.

overdefensive treatment of Scripture, rigidly defined by a grammatical-historical method that Scripture itself doesn't endorse. I applaud that as well. I do nevertheless disagree with the book more than I agree with it.

1. In regard to the "non-uniqueness" of biblical laws, institutions, and literary genres, I think the "problems" are artificially created by Enns. Most sophisticated readers of the Bible understand that it is not unique in these ways, but to my knowledge very few of these, if any, see that as posing a problem for biblical authority or interpretation. So I could simply agree with Enns on the data and then move on.

But in this section he shows an unwillingness, curious for an evangelical, to say anything about the relation of inspiration to historical factuality. When he speaks about "evidence" for this or that event, the evidence is always inductive, never an appeal to divine inspiration as evidence. Perhaps Enns thinks that inspiration is such an event that we may never appeal to it as evidence. I think that position is inconsistent with Scripture's own view of itself.[20]

2. When he discusses "theological diversity" in his oddly undifferentiated way, he mostly speaks of diversities of perspective and of emphasis, diversities that ought to be entirely uncontroversial. But from time to time he slides into discussing diversities that could amount to actual disagreements between one passage and another. He refuses to discuss the implications of this for the doctrine of biblical infallibility and inerrancy. Rather, he suggests that to deal with such matters would be an "abstract discussion" that we should avoid. On the contrary, I believe that these questions are the real heart of the issue.

3. In dealing with the use of the OT in the NT, Enns presents a number of examples that appear to be "*eisegesis*" (his word)—reading into the texts. He discusses second-temple hermeneutics and Christotelic exegesis to indicate what the NT writers were doing. But the discussion quite falls apart when he gets to the question of how we today should read the OT. We should not follow a method, he says, but should walk with our community under the guidance of the Spirit. This is fine as far as it goes. But Scripture itself implies that our proclamation of the gospel should be clear and certain, distinct from and antithetical to false teaching. That is to say that the Spirit witnesses to the Word, and we find the truth through his "speaking in the Scripture" (WCF 1.10). Enns certainly agrees. But he leaves us up in the air as to how in practice we should judge between true

---

20. It is curious that in a book entitled *Inspiration and Incarnation* there is not even a summary treatment of the concept of biblical inspiration, even in the single reference to 2 Timothy 3:16 (p. 107). One asks again and again throughout the book, "How is this idea compatible with the doctrine of biblical inspiration?" Enns *never* deals with this kind of issue.

and false readings of Scripture. How can we agree *communally* on what the Spirit is saying to us in the Scripture, when so many sects and denominations disagree as to what he is saying?

So though I find much to agree with in this book, in the end I would not recommend it as a basic text on biblical inspiration to a seminary-level reader (let alone for the less mature). Seminarians need to study biblical inspiration in a way that motivates *both* humility *and* confidence in God's Word. The present volume says much (both legitimately and illegitimately) to motivate humility. It says nothing to promote confidence in the truth of the biblical text. That, I think, is a serious criticism.

REVIEW OF N. T. WRIGHT, *THE LAST WORD*[1]

Note: N. T. Wright's views on a number of subjects have great influence today. In this review, I discuss his view of Scripture, supplementing many discussions in my book, including the discussion of inerrancy in chapter 26.

N. T. Wright, Bishop of Durham, England, is widely recognized as a brilliant and prolific NT scholar, with a deep concern for the church and its theology. He is best known for his development of the "New Perspective on Paul," of James D. G. Dunn and E. P. Sanders, which has made him controversial in many circles. But beyond this controversy, Wright is considered conservative. He believes that Scripture is substantially historical, and he has no bias against the supernatural as such. Indeed, he has published the most comprehensive and powerful recent defense of the resurrection of Jesus, setting forth its historicity, centrality, and saving power.[2]

For Wright, the Bible is the story of the coming of God's kingdom in power, a political event that from its beginning challenged the Roman empire. He is therefore an opponent of privatized religion, an advocate of a Christian faith that seeks with God's help to bring all things subject to Christ. He recognizes the centrality of the *lordship* of Christ.

---

1. N. T. Wright, *The Last Word: Beyond the Bible Wars to a New Understanding of the Authority of Scripture* (San Francisco: HarperCollins, 2005). This review originally appeared in *Penpoint* 17, 4 (August 2006) and is used here by permission. For stylistic purposes, this appendix has been copyedited for inclusion in this volume.

2. N. T. Wright, *The Resurrection of the Son of God* (Minneapolis: Fortress Press, 2003).

So one is naturally curious how a scholar with such commitments for-mulates the doctrine of biblical authority. The present volume answers this question. It is one of Wright's shorter books (146 pp.) and one of his less technical ones, though not exactly "popular." He seems here primarily to be addressing church leadership, rather than the academic community. The book is full of insight, but there are many questions that it omits—questions that many readers will consider important.

In part, these omissions are intentional. Wright here seeks to transcend the old "battle for the Bible" by putting the question of biblical authority in a larger context. The subtitle is: *Beyond the Bible Wars to a New Understanding of the Authority of Scripture.* This approach reminds me of recent books that have tried to transcend the "worship wars" by formulating "broader principles" and "common criteria." These books are sometimes interesting in their own right, but they usually fail to answer the questions that generated the worship wars in the first place.[3] Or they answer them in such a question-begging way that nobody is persuaded. *The Last Word* is better than these worship books. But those who are wrestling with issues such as inerrancy and infallibility will find it unsatisfying. Wright may hope that his approach will keep people from raising these issues, but I think that hope is unrealistic.

We should, however, examine the larger context in which Wright seeks to locate the authority of Scripture. He identifies as "the central claim of this book" the thesis "that the phrase 'authority of Scripture' can make Christian sense only if it is shorthand for 'the authority of the triune God, exercised somehow *through* scripture'" (p. 23). This implies

> that scripture itself points—authoritatively, if it does indeed pos-sess authority!—away from itself and to the fact that final and true authority belongs to God himself, now delegated to Jesus Christ. It is Jesus, according to John 8:39–40, who speaks the truth because he has heard from God. (P. 24)

The idea that Scripture "points away from itself" reminds us of the the-ologies of Karl Barth and Emil Brunner. For their followers, this implies that we should look at the Bible only as a human text, erring as humans do. But inerrantists also believe that Scripture "points away": to the God who saves and who *speaks* to us the word of Scripture. This is to say that the metaphor of "pointing away from itself" is a truism that theologians of very different views appeal to.

So we must follow Wright's argument further. Wright holds with many scholars today that the Bible, despite its many literary genres, can as a

---

3. See my "Above the Battle?" available at http://www.frame-poythress.org.

whole be described as "story," or narrative (pp. 25–26). It is neither a "list of rules" nor a "compendium of true doctrines," though the texts do include rules and doctrines. But how can a story be authoritative? Rules tell us what to do; doctrines tell us what to believe. But what does a story do? Stories, Wright points out, can be cautionary, can provide historical background to explain a command, and can shake up a reader's mindset so that he will make different decisions (pp. 26–27). In Scripture, the story is about God's kingdom coming in power. Jesus' teaching and healings carry the authority of the kingdom. So God's authority "is his sovereign power accomplishing the renewal of all creation" (p. 29). The authority of Scripture is an aspect of this kingdom power, and therefore, Wright reiterates, not merely the authority of doctrine or commands. So it is insufficient to think of Scripture merely as "revelation" or as a "devotional manual" (pp. 31–33). Rather, Scripture is God's kingdom instrument for bringing us divine speech, transformation of mind, and power for mission (p. 34).[4]

Wright then embarks on a survey of history from the Old and New Testaments, through church history, down to the present. Like Geerhardus Vos, Wright views the kingdom not only as God's general sovereignty, but as his breaking into history to defeat evil (pp. 35–37). Scripture equipped Israel for this warfare (p. 37). God's giving these books to Israel may be called "inspiration," which is "a shorthand way of talking about the belief that by his Spirit God guided the very different writers and editors, so that the books they produced were the books God intended his people to have" (ibid.). Wright believes that Scripture itself takes for granted such divine inspiration. Behind such inspiration is "the word of God," which is "not . . . a synonym for the written scriptures, but . . . a strange personal presence, creating, judging, healing, recreating" (p. 38).

Jesus is the Word made flesh and the true Israel, thus fulfilling the Scriptures. So "Jesus insists on scripture's authority" (p. 44). But according to Wright, Jesus fulfills the Scriptures, enforcing some teachings of the OT over against Jewish traditions, but also rejecting some OT provisions as no longer applicable, such as dietary laws and God's exclusive relation with Israel (p. 45). In Wright's view, the authority of Scripture does not free it from what he calls "tensions" (p. 40), as between the idea that virtue is rewarded in this life (Deut.) and the idea that it is not (Job).[5] Jesus' use of Scripture brings out such tensions in ways that

---

4. Some readers of my own writings will see this as a covenantal triad, the three functions being normative, existential, and situational, respectively.

5. Wright doesn't quite say that these themes are actually contradictory, but he does not attempt to reconcile them here. I will assume that he regards them as most orthodox

initially puzzle many readers (p. 45). But Wright says that these tensions are aspects of a rich, "narratival" kind of fulfillment (pp. 45–46).

In the apostolic church, again we meet the powerful "word of God," now the vehicle of the Spirit's authority renewing and equipping people for kingdom service. As with Jesus' teaching, there are tensions in the apostles' appeal to the OT: continuities and discontinuities with the gospel. Wright compares the OT to a ship that has brought travelers to their destination. Once they arrive, "they leave the ship behind and continue over land, not because the ship was no good, or because their voyage has been misguided, but precisely because both ship and voyage had accomplished their purpose" (p. 57).

The apostles' teaching, then, recorded in the NT books, becomes the "new covenant charter" (p. 59), guiding the church in its encounter with the cultures of the world.

Wright then discusses the understanding of Scripture in later church history. Did the church give authority to Scripture? To Wright, this view is a mistake like "that of a soldier who, receiving orders through the mail, concludes that the letter carrier is his commanding officer" (p. 63). Rather, the church recognized as canonical those books that carried on the larger narrative of the kingdom. Wright notes insightfully that the church's martyrs were "normally those who were reading Matthew, Mark, Luke, John, Paul and the rest" (ibid.), not those who read, for example, the Gospel of Thomas. For the latter was "non-narrational, deliberately avoiding the option of placing [Jesus'] sayings within the overarching framework of the story of Israel" (pp. 63–64). So, far from making the church more comfortable, as some have charged, the canonical books sustained the church's "energetic mission" (p. 64).

Nevertheless, Wright believes that in the early centuries there was in the church a "diminishing focus" on narrative, corresponding to an increasing use of Scripture as a "court of appeal," or rule book, and as a "*lectio divina*," a book of private devotions (pp. 64–65). This development also leads to allegorical exegesis and the medieval fourfold sense, about which I must pass over Wright's interesting observations (pp. 65–70).

In the Reformation, *sola Scriptura* is a protest not against tradition as such, but against the notion that anything beyond Scripture needs to be believed "in order for one to be saved" (p. 72; cf. his discussion of tradition on pp. 117–19). The Reformers also insisted on the "literal sense" of Scripture, in contrast with the medieval fourfold scheme. In this, they did not intend to exclude figures of speech (as later literalists

---

Christians do, as aspects of a larger truth.

would do), but to advocate what the actual words meant according to the original authors. If the meaning of a passage is figurative, the literal sense, according to the Reformers, requires us to take it figuratively (p. 73; cf. pp. 92–94).

In the debates between Protestant and Catholic, both parties, Wright says, devalued the narrative character of Scripture, thinking of authority as "the place where you could go to find an authoritative ruling" (p. 75).

In the Enlightenment, *reason*, which to Richard Hooker meant a responsible way of using the Bible (pp. 79–80; cf. pp. 119–20), was redefined as something authoritative in itself, supreme over Scripture.[6] Thus, the Enlightenment adopted a different narrative from Scripture, one of human progress, leading to the eschatology of a fully rational society (pp. 87–88). Reason alone will deal with the problem of evil. This leads to "the muddled debates of modern biblical scholarship" (p. 89), which try to synthesize the Bible with rationalist themes. The best response, Wright says, is not to dismiss all biblical scholarship (as we are often tempted to do) but to "make fresh and rejuvenated efforts to understand scripture more fully and live by it more thoroughly, even if that means cutting across cherished traditions" (p. 91). That, he argues, is what the authority of Scripture should mean for us today.

Wright understands well that no exegesis, whether modernist, fundamentalist, or otherwise, is without presuppositions. So the task of understanding the Bible continues. Modernism was wrong to claim "assured results." And literalists, too, should be open to rethinking their assurances, though Wright says that this "does not mean that I am indifferent to the question of whether the events written about in the gospels actually took place. Far from it" (p. 95; cf. pp. 112–13). He poses the question:

> Which is the bottom line: "proving the Bible to be true" (often with the effect of saying, "so we can go on thinking what we've always thought"), or taking it so seriously that we allow it to tell us things we'd never heard before and didn't particularly want to hear? (p. 95)

This question challenges the complacent Christian, but it does pose an apples/oranges alternative. Can we not take an interest in proving the Bible true without curbing its freedom to challenge us?

In chapter 7, Wright deals with some examples of "misreadings" of Scripture from the left and the right. Generally his critiques of these are

6. Compare his similar discussion of *experience* at pp. 100–105.

on target. In chapter 8, he argues that to get "back on track," we need to return to the original kingdom context of biblical authority. We should read Scripture, he says, to be equipped for mission.

> "The authority of scripture" refers not least to God's work *through* scripture to reveal Jesus, to speak in life-changing power to the hearts and minds of individuals, and to transform them by the Spirit's healing love. (P. 116)

As we use Scripture, then, it is important for us to see our role within the "five acts" of the narrative (creation, fall, Israel, Christ, the church) (pp. 121–27). Our reading of Scripture should be "totally contextual," "liturgically guided, "privately studied," "refreshed by appropriate scholarship," and "taught by the church's accredited leaders" (pp. 128–42). An appendix suggests resources for such Bible study (pp. 143–46).

By way of evaluation: So far as I am aware, there is no statement in the book that I simply disagree with. And the book contains some excellent insights about Scripture, on its kingdom context, the canon, and Scripture's relations with tradition, reason, and experience. Wright also has valuable things to say here about biblical interpretation: on how the New Testament fulfills the Old, and on what a "literal" interpretation ought to mean.

But there is a major problem of omission. If one is to deal seriously with the "Bible wars," even somehow to transcend them, one must ask whether and how inspiration affects the *text* of Scripture. Wright defines inspiration by saying that "by his Spirit God guided the very different writers and editors, so that the books they produced were the books God intended his people to have" (p. 37). But the same can be said about the books in my library: that God moved writers, editors, publishers, and others, so that the books in my library are the ones God wants me to have. Nevertheless, there are some horrible books in my library (which I keep for various good reasons). So it is important to ask whether inspiration is simply divine providence, or whether it carries God's endorsement. Is God, in any sense, the *author* of inspired books?

Wright doesn't discuss this question, but Scripture itself does. The Decalogue was the writing of God's finger (Ex. 31:18). The prophets identified the source of their preaching by the phrase "thus says the LORD." Jesus attributes David's words to the Spirit (Matt. 22:43). Paul says that the OT Scriptures were God-breathed, that is, spoken by God (2 Tim. 3:16). And Paul connects this God-breathed quality with the authority of Scripture, indicating that biblical authority is the authority not only of divine power, but also of divine speech.

Or look at it this way: "Word of God" in Scripture is not merely "a strange personal presence, creating, judging, healing, recreating" (p. 38). It is all these things, but it is also, obviously, divine speech (as Wright himself recognizes on p. 34). When God creates, for example, he creates by speech, by commanding the world to exist. Prophecy and Scripture are "word of God," not only in their power, but also as speech and language: not only power, but also meaning.

Wright is right to say that God's word, and specifically Scripture, is more than doctrines and commands. But if inspiration confers divine authorship, and if God's word is true speech, then it becomes very important, within the context of the kingdom narrative, to believe God's doctrines and to obey God's commands. Indeed, as Wright notes, the very nature of narrative poses the question whether the events described "really happened"—that is, what we should believe about them, and how we should act in response. But then narrative itself implies doctrines to be believed and commandments to obey.[7]

That is what the Bible wars are about. One can believe everything Wright says about the narrative context of biblical authority and still ask responsibly whether the words of Scripture are God's words to us. Wright's book does not speak helpfully to this question, nor does it succeed (if this was Wright's purpose) in persuading us not to ask it. So, like the worship books mentioned earlier, *The Last Word* does not discuss what is most relevant to the controversy. It proposes a context, but a context is not enough. Two people who accept Wright's proposal may nevertheless differ radically on the question whether the Bible is the Word of God.

Many of us would like to get away from the debates of the liberal/fundamentalist controversy. But if Scripture is God's very Word, then we cannot be indifferent to its doctrinal and ethical authority, or silent against attacks on that authority. Wright has done some great work in

7. Wright's title, *The Last Word,* is perplexing in this respect. He reproves some early Christians for regarding the Bible as a mere "court of appeal" (p. 65; cf. p. 75), a final test of doctrine and ethics. He seems to be reproving a certain *emphasis* here, which is fine. But then the question arises: if the Bible is not *merely* a court of appeal, is it at least that, along with other things? Wright has little if anything to say about how the Bible should be used as a court of appeal; he wants to steer us toward other issues. But the question will not go away. The very title, *The Last Word,* alludes to Scripture as a court of appeal (unless Wright means *last* in a merely temporal sense, which I doubt). I realize, of course, that titles are usually chosen by publishers, rather than authors. In this case, the title was chosen by the American publisher, not the original British publisher. The title of the original 2005 British version was *Scripture and the Authority of God.* Still, Wright must have had some input into the American title and subtitle, and it is surprising that he accepted a title that misleads readers about the emphasis of the book.

defending the truth of Scripture, and it is evident in the present volume that he has scant regard for the scholarship of Enlightenment skeptics such as those of the Jesus Seminar. So he has himself entered into the Bible wars. But are these wars merely contests to see who is the better scholar, or is the Word of God itself at issue? If the latter, much more must be said and done.

APPENDIX L

<hr />

REVIEW OF ANDREW McGOWAN, *THE DIVINE
SPIRATION OF SCRIPTURE*[1]

Note: This heretofore unpublished review of Andrew McGowan's
book supplements my discussion of inerrancy in chapter 26 of the
present volume.

I have long appreciated McGowan as a theologian who seeks to combine
Reformed orthodoxy with a forward-looking perspective.[2] The present volume exhibits his knowledge and creativity. I have prayed for his ministry
as Principal of Highland Theological College, Dingwall, Scotland. There,
he is well situated to play an important role in the re-evangelization of
Britain, Europe, and America. I count him as a friend.

Yet I must find some fault with the book under review. I trust that he
will receive my comments as "the wounds of a friend" (Prov. 27:6), as "iron
sharpening iron" (27:17).

He develops here a number of theses about the doctrine of Scripture. In
good sandwich fashion, he begins with some points (on encyclopedia and
vocabulary) unlikely to raise serious controversy, and he concludes with
more of the same (on confessions and preaching). But in between comes

<hr />

1. A. T. B. McGowan, *The Divine Spiration of Scripture: Challenging Evangelical Perspec-
tives* (Nottingham, UK: Apollos, 2007). The title of the American version is *The Divine
Authenticity of Scripture: Retrieving an Evangelical Heritage* (Downers Grove, IL: InterVarsity
Press, 2008).

2. See, e.g., A. T. B. McGowan, ed., *Always Reforming* (Downers Grove, IL: Inter-
Varsity Press, 2006).

the hard part, an argument against the idea of biblical inerrancy, seeking to replace it with a certain concept of infallibility.

ENCYCLOPEDIA

I will follow his discussion more or less in the order in which he presents it. First his argument on *encyclopedia*, the place of the doctrine of Scripture in the traditional order of topics (loci) in systematic theology. Here he argues that in a systematic theology the doctrine of Scripture should not be placed first, but rather should follow the doctrine of God. If it precedes the doctrine of God, it "takes the primary focus away from God" (p. 28).[3] McGowan thinks the tradition of placing the doctrine of Scripture first arises out of the belief that Scripture is in some sense the epistemological foundation of everything to follow. In McGowan's view, it is an error "to imply that the Scriptures can stand alone as a source of epistemological certainty, quite apart from the work of God the Holy Spirit" (p. 29).

At one level, the issue McGowan brings up here does not have much interest except for people who are writing complete systematic theologies. If you are writing on only one locus, the question of where that locus should be placed in relation to others is somewhat moot. For most ordinary Christians who are not writers of theology at all, this question is even more irrelevant.

But perhaps we can look at this issue from a more helpful angle. When we write and talk about, say, sanctification, we do have to be aware of the relation of that doctrine to justification, adoption, atonement, resurrection, and so on, whether or not we seek to produce a systematic theology. Similarly with other doctrines, including the doctrine of Scripture. This is the real value of McGowan's discussion: reminding us to consider how the doctrine of Scripture is related to other doctrines.

I think that point is clearer when it is removed from the question of encyclopedic order. In my view, the order of topics is largely a question of pedagogy, rather than theology. A bad doctrine of Scripture does not

---

3. As I have argued elsewhere, I don't find much value in theological arguments about emphasis or focus. For one thing, it is impossible for a theological writing to reproduce the focus or emphasis of Scripture. Theology is not Scripture. It varies from Scripture in word, structure, and emphasis, in order better to communicate scriptural truth. For another thing, it is odd to say that God must be mentioned first if we are to place proper emphasis on him. The book of Genesis does begin, of course, with a reference to God, at least to an action of his. The book of Exodus, however, doesn't mention God until 1:21. Does this fact betray an improper emphasis? The book of Esther doesn't mention God at all. Is there some evil in that? There is, I think, a certain woodenness in McGowan's theological methodology at this point.

become good simply by better positioning, by being made chapter 2 instead of chapter 1. Nor does a good doctrine become bad by any similar change. But McGowan is certainly right to say that a good doctrine of Scripture must be clear on the important relationships between the written Word and the Holy Spirit.

I am not convinced, however, that implying "that the Scriptures can stand alone as a source of epistemological certainty, quite apart from the work of God the Holy Spirit" (p. 29), is a pressing danger for evangelical theology. Of the many theologies of revelation and Scripture that I have read, I cannot recall even one that failed to include discussion of the Spirit's work—in inspiration, illumination, and persuasion. It is good, of course, to remind Christians in a practical way that we should read Scripture as a gift of God, indeed as an encounter with God himself. We are often tempted otherwise. But that temptation, I think, is more emotional than theological. It is not that we are often tempted to a theological denial of God's involvement, or a theoretical dismissal of its importance. Rather, the problem is that we often read Scripture without a conscious dependence on God. But not every temptation can be overcome by a theological formulation. In the present context, the temptation will certainly exist whether the doctrine of inspiration comes first or second in our theology texts.

On page 31, McGowan assures us that he does not, however, regard concerns for epistemological certainty as illegitimate. Our persuasion and assurance that Scripture is the Word of God comes through the work of the Spirit. This is not "blind fideism" (p. 32), for we can show (following Cornelius Van Til) that "reason, logic and evidence have their place in our thinking only because we live in a world God has created, which is therefore inherently rational" (ibid.). He goes on to discuss other apologetic issues, noting the defectiveness of natural theology and traditional evidentialism.

Certainly, I applaud McGowan's embrace of a Van Tillian epistemology and apologetic. And I am grateful for his mentions of my work in this connection. In view of what comes later, however, I remind the reader that Van Til had no hesitations about the inerrancy of Scripture. And Van Til often emphasized the self-attesting authority of the *text* of Scripture, while acknowledging the necessity of the Spirit's work for our subjective *appropriation* of the text. For him, neither the objective side (the biblical text itself) nor the subjective side (the Spirit's inward witness) can function without the other. That double emphasis does not come through clearly in McGowan's account, but it pervades Van Til's work.[4] And we should not

4. This emphasis is particularly evident in Van Til's *A Christian Theory of Knowledge* (Philadelphia: Presbyterian and Reformed, 1969), *An Introduction to Systematic Theology*

miss this implication: for Van Til, the text of Scripture (however much we need the Spirit to illumine it) is the ultimate source of epistemological certainty, God's ultimate standard for human thought and life.[5] So perhaps there are, after all, some good reasons for putting the doctrine of Scripture first in our theological systems.[6]

VOCABULARY

1. Spiration

McGowan's first vocabulary suggestion is that we replace *inspiration* with *spiration*. *Inspiration*, he says, is too easily confused with poetic inspiration, and in connection with Scripture it suggests that God breathed something *into* the book. Actually, *theopneustos*, the word translated "inspired by God" in 2 Timothy 3:16 (NASB), the only occurrence of that term in Scripture, means "breathed out by God." Here, McGowan accepts B. B. Warfield's well-known analysis, though at later points he is critical of Warfield. The idea of a word "breathed out by God" suggests that *expiration*, rather than *inspiration*, would be a good translation. Unfortunately, *expiration* in English often refers to death! So McGowan, following another suggestion of Warfield, proposes *spiration*.[7] Combining, then, the teaching of 2 Timothy 3:16 with that of 2 Peter 1:16–21, he provides a long definition of *spiration*, which I summarize: "God the Holy Spirit caused men to write books . . . such that although these books are truly the work of human beings, they are also the Word of God" (p. 43). These books have "a unique authority." But he adds, "In order to avoid misunderstanding, however, it is better to reside the authority in God rather than in the Scriptures themselves."

I have no objection to this vocabulary change, and I also have no confidence that the church will adopt it. *Inspiration* is problematic, but it is probably best at this time to make the word conform in meaning to *theopneustos*, rather than to try to persuade the church to adopt another term.

(Nutley, NJ: Presbyterian and Reformed, 1974), and *The Protestant Doctrine of Scripture* (Philadelphia: Presbyterian and Reformed, 1967).

5. Van Til also, contrary to McGowan, defends the view that the ultimate authoritative text is to be found in the *autographa* or original manuscripts of Scripture. See Van Til, *Introduction to Systematic Theology*, 153.

6. I have, however, chosen the same procedure as McGowan in my *SBL* and in my seminary systematics course. But I justify my approach for its pedagogical value, not because of any theological necessity.

7. I'm reminded of the jest of George Gobel: "I can't say that I was overwhelmed. And I really can't say that I was underwhelmed, either. Let's just say I was whelmed."

McGowan is right, further, to "reside the authority in God rather than in the Scriptures themselves." I presume that "themselves" here means "apart from God"[8] or some such thing. But even though in one sense the authority does not reside in "the Scriptures themselves," it certainly does reside in the Scriptures. Readers should not be misled into thinking that God cannot represent his authoritative words in writing. Scripture teaches that he does exactly that, so that we may refer to the *text* of Scripture as the very authoritative speech of God. There is no biblical reason to think that God's oral speech is more authoritative than his written speech. Quite the contrary.

I think McGowan slips too quickly past the assertion of 2 Timothy 3:16 that the *Scripture*, the written text, is breathed out by God and therefore authoritative. He mentions that, but then jumps immediately to 2 Peter 1:16–21 to speak of the human writers. Certainly, we dare not ignore Peter's description of the role of the human authors. But however we understand that role, the net result of it justifies the assertion that the *written Word*, the *graphe*, is God-breathed. What 2 Timothy 3:16 says is no less true simply because 1 Peter 1:19–21 describes spiration from a different perspective.

And what does *God-breathed* mean, anyway? McGowan's long definition identifies the writing with the Word of God, and that is correct. But we need to understand how literally Paul understands this in 2 Timothy 3:16. *Word of God* is a bit too much of a theological commonplace. The language of 2 Timothy 3:16 is more striking: For God to "breathe out" words is simply for him to speak. The text of Scripture consists of words that God *has spoken*. To say that Scripture is spirated, to say that it is the Word of God, means that God has spoken it. All of it.

2. RECOGNITION

McGowan's second terminological proposal is that we substitute *recognition* for the common theological term *illumination* (pp. 45–46). His point is that the latter term suggests a problem in Scripture (that they are dark and need light), whereas the only problem is a problem in ourselves due to sin.[9] Here he discusses Romans 1; 8:5–7; 12:1–2; 2 Corinthians 4:4; and

---

8. "Apart from," "in abstraction from," "separated from," and so forth are favorite expressions of theologians but usually too vague to shed any clarity on a discussion. Here, I guess the expression would mean that Scripture would have no authority unless God had chosen to inspire it and to move believers to recognize it.

9. He thinks that *illumination* usually means an illumination of the text of Scripture. In my judgment, the theological literature more often uses the term to refer to an illumination of the mind. But I would agree that McGowan's term *recognition* is less ambiguous.

Colossians 1, which speak of the noetic effects of sin and the need of the Spirit's grace to renew our minds, so that we can recognize God's Word for what it is.[10] Certainly in this discussion McGowan makes an important point: we do need supernaturally given ability to use God's Word rightly.

But we should remind ourselves that the event traditionally called *illumination*, which McGowan calls *recognition*, requires both objective and subjective elements. The Spirit acts on the mind, but he does this specifically in an encounter with the word of God (in written or some other form). It is right to say that the problem to be remedied by illumination/recognition is in ourselves, not in the text. But we should not give the impression that this divine assistance can take place without a text. The Spirit witnesses to the Word. There is no "recognition" unless both are present. The text is not the problem to be resolved, but it is a necessary element of the transaction.

I suggested in my discussion of *spiration* that McGowan seems reluctant to discuss any unique qualities of the *text* that spiration creates. Similarly here. Certainly, it is right to consider our own need as sinners. But it is also important to recognize that the Holy Spirit meets this need *through a text*. It is the text of Scripture that brings us the gospel message that corrects our sinful distortion of the truth. So it is important in this connection to say not only that the Spirit meets our own need, but also that there are qualities of Scripture, given by spiration, that make it a suitable vehicle of the Spirit's activity.[11]

How should we refer to these qualities? *Illumination* is not appropriate, so I would agree with McGowan that we don't need it in this connection. Perhaps it is appropriate here to refer with the tradition to the *power* of the written Word (Isa. 55:11; Rom. 1:16), which operates in conjunction with the Spirit's witness. And of course, the *authority* and *sufficiency* of Scripture are also relevant in this context.

3. COMPREHENSION

McGowan's next vocabulary suggestion (pp. 46–48) is that we substitute *comprehension* for *perspicuity*.[12] He says, "If illumination as traditionally understood has to do with recognizing the Scriptures as the Word of

---

10. On page 46 he opposes truth to emotion in a way that I would dispute, but to discuss this issue would take us too far afield.

11. I think this is especially important in our present theological context. Modern theologians often reject the idea that inspiration/spiration confers any special qualities on the biblical text.

12. *Perspicuity*, of course, is a ten-dollar word for *clarity*.

God, perspicuity has to do with understanding what the Scriptures mean" (p. 47). So, as he proposed replacing *illumination* with *recognition*, he here would replace *perspicuity* with *comprehension*. His argument is that *perspicuity* "can be understood to imply an access to the Scriptures that is entirely human and natural." He grants the traditional concern of the doctrine of perspicuity, that the gospel of Scripture can be understood by untrained believers. But as with *spiration* and *recognition*, McGowan wants to emphasize that our knowledge of Scripture comes through the Spirit's work, not by some merely natural process. That is, again, something that happens in us, not something inherent in the text.

As with *recognition*, I agree with McGowan's description of the human need and of the deeply personal way in which God meets that need. But I don't see that this divine work can be fully understood without reference to the qualities of the biblical *text*. Granted its deficiencies, *perspicuity* at least focuses our attention on the text, that it is the kind of text that is capable of yielding a clear understanding of the truth under the Spirit's ministry to us. If we replace *perspicuity* with *comprehension*, the discussion becomes more subjective, about a change that takes place in us, but not about the biblical text itself. But that is misleading. The Spirit witnesses to the *Word*. There is an objective and a subjective side to our growth in the knowledge of God. We need the Spirit, but we also need an objective word of God that tells us what we need to know. The Spirit gives us a clear recognition of the truth, because he witnesses to a clear message.

To stress the objective clarity of Scripture is not, of course, to say that access to it is "entirely human and natural." I can't think of a single writer except McGowan who has drawn such an implication from this use of *perspicuity*. In any case, no human knowledge is "merely" or "entirely" human. We always need God to guide us. But the distortions of revelation are our fault, not God's, as McGowan surely agrees. And that is to say that revelation as God gives it is not distorted. It is objectively clear, perspicuous.

INERRANCY

McGowan continues his discussion of vocabulary by referring to *inerrancy* and *infallibility*, but plainly he intends this discussion to be more than terminological. His proposal that we replace *inerrancy* with *infallibility* is in fact the centerpiece of the volume. His discussion of it constitutes most of the remainder of the book, from pages 48 to 164.

Much of this section analyzes the history of the controversy and the views of individual theologians. I will cover the historical discussions in less detail than I have employed up to this point in the review. I think that, as in many recent theological writings, the discussion of historical and contemporary alternatives sometimes illumines McGowan's fundamental argument, but often obscures it. I wish (as I often wish with books on this subject) that McGowan had spent much less time expounding the views of others, and much more time formulating and arguing for his own position. For the most part, I think the history of the controversy is not controversial. And anyone who argues a theological position based on history alone is guilty of the genetic fallacy. So why should we be asked to dwell on history for over fifty pages?

If McGowan ever defines the word *inerrancy*, I have not been able to locate his definition. That is, I think, a major omission, since he invests so much of the book in his critique of the idea. He does say on pages 48–49 that the term "has represented a turn towards a somewhat mechanical and even rationalistic approach to Scripture, basing its authority on a set of inerrant manuscripts." But that is a critique of the concept, not a definition. And to say that believers in inerrancy base the authority of Scripture "on a set of inerrant manuscripts" is simply inaccurate. Although inerrant autographs play a major role in inerrantist thinking, they are never the *basis* of biblical authority. For an inerrantist (as, I think, for McGowan), the authority of Scripture is based on its inspiration/spiration.

He does quote Donald Bloesch on page 98:

> Scriptural inerrancy can be affirmed if it means the conformity of what is written to the dictates of the Spirit regarding the will and purpose of God. But it cannot be held if it is taken to mean the conformity of everything that is written in Scripture to the facts of world history and science.[13]

But it is not clear in context that McGowan accepts either of Bloesch's two definitions. He mentions these only in passing while discussing Jack Rogers and Donald McKim. And I will mention later that McGowan rejects the "form/content" distinction that lies behind Bloesch's distinction of two kinds of inerrancy.

James Orr, with whose position McGowan shows some sympathy, defines *inerrancy* as "hard and fast literality in minute matters of historical, geographical, and scientific detail."[14] Orr rejects the concept of inerrancy so defined. But so far as I know, no advocate of inerrancy has ever employed

---

13. McGowan here quotes Donald Bloesch, *Holy Scripture: Revelation, Inspiration and Interpretation* (Downers Grove, IL: InterVarsity Press, 1994), 107.

14. James Orr, *Revelation and Inspiration* (New York: Scribner's, 1910; repr., Grand Rapids: Baker, 1969), 199.

such a definition. Indeed, this definition is quite wrongheaded. Inerrancy is not about literality or nonliterality. It is about truthfulness. And inerrancy is not a claim about "detail," as opposed to the broader structures of biblical language, though to be sure claims about detail may be implicit in the larger picture.

I know this is a stretch for theologians, but it might not hurt to go to the dictionary. *The American Heritage College Dictionary*[15] defines *inerrancy* as "freedom from error or untruths."[16] I believe that definition captures the basic idea behind the theological use of the term. I could wish myself that we could get rid of the term *inerrancy* (and most all other technical theological terms as well) and simply speak of *truth*. That God's word is true is easily established from Scripture (Pss. 19:9; 119:160; John 17:17). Of course, there is a need to discuss how that truth can be seen in different genres, parts, and aspects of Scripture.

Why, then, should anyone want to use the term *inerrancy*, when the simpler, more attractive word *truth* is available? Because theologians have preferred to use *truth* in more exalted senses: Christological (John 14:6), metaphysical (Heb. 8:2), and ethical (1 John 1:6). These senses are perfectly scriptural, but they have tempted theologians to devalue truth in a "merely propositional" sense. And some have entirely rejected the notion of "objective" truth, in favor of some kind of relativism. I think these theologians have missed something important. But confusion over the nature of truth is one reason why theologians have searched for other terms to describe the truth of Scripture.

Another term, hallowed by its use in the WCF (1.5, 9), is *infallibility*. This is the term McGowan would substitute for *inerrancy*, although to be sure *infallibility* has been commonly used in the Reformed churches much longer than the other term. The dictionary quoted above defines *infallible* as follows:

> 1. Incapable of erring. 2. Incapable of failing; certain. 3. *Rom. Cath. Ch.* Incapable of error in expounding doctrine on faith or morals.[17]

On the first of these three definitions, *infallibility* is a stronger term than *inerrancy*. As suggested by the etymologies of the two terms, *inerrant* means that there *are* no errors; *infallible* means that there *can be* no errors. *Inerrant*

---

15. 3rd ed. (Boston and New York: Houghton Mifflin Co., 2000).
16. Ibid., 695.
17. Ibid. Something like the second definition is sometimes invoked in discussions of Scripture. Taken literally, it encompasses the first, since erring is a kind of failure. Certainly it cannot be invoked as an alternative to the first, as some may want to do.

is about actuality, *infallible* about possibility. It is what philosophers call a "modal" expression. *Infallible* not only says that there are no errors in Scripture, but adds that there *cannot be* any errors in it.

The same dictionary defines *inerrant* as follows:

1. Incapable of erring; infallible. 2. Containing no errors.[18]

On the first definition, *inerrant* and *infallible* are synonyms. It is therefore linguistically responsible either to use these terms interchangeably or (as in the previous paragraph) to distinguish them, focusing on the modal significance of *infallible*.

McGowan does offer something like a definition of *infallibility*, though it is a description of an argument rather than a formal definition:

The argument for "infallibility" is that the final authority for the Christian is the authority of God speaking in and through his Word and that the Holy Spirit infallibly uses God's Word to achieve all he intends to achieve. (P. 49)

The last clause comes close to the second dictionary definition of *infallible*, above. As for the first clause, however, one wonders (given the focus of the various dictionary definitions) whether McGowan thinks that when God speaks "in and through his Word," he can utter errors. McGowan doesn't exactly say so here, but if he doesn't believe that, then it is hard to distinguish his concept of *infallible* from *inerrant*. If he does believe that God can utter errors, I don't see how he can embrace any of the dictionary definitions of *infallible* that we have considered. We will consider this matter again at a later point.

Now, of course, theologians rarely allow themselves to be bound to the dictionary. In theology as in many other disciplines, technical definitions abound. There is nothing inherently wrong with this. We can define terms any way we like, as long as we do not thereby confuse one another. And of course, there have been definitions of *infallible* that actually make it a *weaker* term than *inerrant*, contrary to all the dictionary definitions we have considered. Perhaps McGowan is thinking in terms of one of those, although these usually depend on a distinction of subject matter, such as in Bloesch's definition of *inerrancy* quoted earlier. But McGowan says later (pp. 105–6) that he rejects this distinction.

As I said earlier, I do not intend to address McGowan's historical account in any detail, but I should summarize it. He tells the story of Enlightenment philosophy, rationalist and empiricist traditions brought together

18. Ibid.

in Immanuel Kant (pp. 52–53).[19] Liberal theology followed Kant, dismissing the possibility of supernatural interference in nature, reconstructing the concept of revelation in terms of God-consciousness (Friedrich Schleiermacher, p. 54) or value-judgments (Albrecht Ritschl, p. 56). Ernst Troeltsch questioned the uniqueness of Scripture among the religions of the world (ibid.). John Barton and others treated Scripture as any other human book (pp. 58–61).

Others reacted against liberal theology. McGowan notes that among the neoorthodox who rejected the earlier liberalism, there was significant discussion about inspiration, verbal inspiration, inerrancy, and so on. J. K. S. Reid thought that inerrantism was a new position in church history. He considered it bibliolatrous (p. 64). Reid argues that John Calvin did not believe in verbal inspiration or inerrancy (pp. 65–66).[20] He thinks later Lutherans and Calvinists reduced the Reformation doctrine to a "literalist and rigid inerrantist position" (p. 68). McGowan, however, observes in a footnote that Richard Muller has "effectively demonstrated the weakness and inadequacy of this view." McGowan also expounds T. F. Torrance's position (pp. 68–73) on science and Christianity, but it is not clear to me what this discussion contributes to the overall argument. Perhaps McGowan thinks that Torrance's theology of science presents a significant Christian alternative to the pre-Einsteinian (and anti-supernaturalistic) views of liberalism.

Next in the historical discussion comes American conservative evangelicalism, particularly J. Gresham Machen and Cornelius Van Til (pp. 74–82). I'm happy, again, to see Van Til included, though I disagree with McGowan at a few points.[21]

19. I have a few disagreements with his account here and there. I'm inclined to think, for example, that he exaggerates David Hume's skepticism. Hume did not think of himself as rejecting cause and effect (p. 52), but only as denying the "necessary connection" between them. And it is probably not best to equate Kant's phenomenal realm with the "real" world (p. 53). The phenomenal world is, after all, only phenomenal, for Kant, and the noumenal is the realm of things in themselves.

20. Again, I am not going to take much time with this historical account of the inerrancy discussion, but I should say that some of Reid's arguments, as McGowan presents them, make no sense to me. To say, for example, that Calvin does not "identify the Holy Spirit with the Word of God" (p. 66) certainly has no bearing on whether or not Calvin believed in inerrancy. Does Reid honestly think that the fundamentalist, or any party to the discussion, *identifies* the Spirit with the Word?

21. I don't think it is accurate to say that Van Til rejected "any point of contact in the natural man" (p. 79). Van Til said that there is indeed a point of contact, namely, the knowledge of God that unregenerate man has, but suppresses. Further, although McGowan's parallels between Van Til and Torrance are interesting, it is also important to point out the vast differences between Van Til's theology of Scripture and Torrance's Barthian understanding.

McGowan then summarizes the history of American fundamentalism and its view of biblical inerrancy. He is accurate, on the whole, in his account of B. B. Warfield and Charles Hodge, of the fundamentalist movement, and of the postwar neoevangelicalism of Carl Henry, E. J. Carnell, and others. Under "the modern inerrancy debate" (p. 97), he discusses the Rogers-McKim critique of Warfield, including the debate over the influence of Scottish Common-Sense Realism. McGowan also mentions John Woodbridge's critique of the Rogers-McKim position and the view of Ligon Duncan and others that Scottish Realism had little influence on the Old Princeton view of Scripture.

In McGowan's view, the Chicago Statement on Biblical Inerrancy (1978) was a somewhat definitive formulation, mature in its rejection of divine dictation and its embrace of textual criticism (p. 103).

Then McGowan summarizes the three most common arguments against inerrancy among biblical scholars. (1) Some hold to the "critical paradigm," which implies that it is "intellectually impossible to believe in inerrancy" (p. 105). McGowan replies that this paradigm is based on "Enlightenment presuppositions" that we should not accept today. (2) Others accept inerrancy for "matters of doctrine and ethics," but believe Scripture contains "mistakes in matters of history, science, and so on, even in the *autographa*" (pp. 105–6). McGowan does not support this distinction (essentially that of Bloesch that I quoted earlier), citing "the difficulty of maintaining a distinction between form and content, or between those parts of Scripture without error and those not" (p. 106). (3) Some reject the word *inerrancy*, as a term of recent origin, and "mistaken theologically." Significantly, of the three arguments, McGowan endorses only the third.

So we should ask how, in his view, biblical inerrancy is "mistaken theologically." McGowan lists several arguments.

1. *Too many qualifications.* In McGowan's view, the doctrine of inerrancy requires too many qualifications to be useful. Many of these qualifications are spelled out in the Chicago Statement. One qualification often made is that inerrancy does not require precise numbers, for example, in enumerating Israel's troops. But McGowan asks, "If numbers can be inaccurate but not affect the claim to inerrancy, then when is an error an error?" (p. 106). He adds:

> One gets the clear impression that no matter what objection might be brought against the inerrantist position, it would simply be argued that this is an exception quite permissible within the terms of the definition. (Ibid.)

Here I think we need to go back to the fundamental intuition underlying the inerrantist position: Scripture is *true*. Now, truth and precision are not the same thing, though there is some overlap between them. A certain amount of precision is often required for truth, but that amount varies from one context to another. In mathematics and science, truth often requires considerable precision. If a student says that 6 + 5 = 10, he has not told the truth. He has committed an error. If a scientist makes a measurement within .0004 cm of an actual length, he may describe that as an "error," as in the phrase *margin of error*.

But outside of science and mathematics, truth and precision are often much more distinct. If you ask someone's age, the person's conventional response (at least if the questioner is entitled to such information!) is to tell how old he was on his most recent birthday. But this is, of course, imprecise. It would be more precise to tell one's age down to the day, hour, minute, and second.[22] But would that convey more *truth*? And if one fails to give that much precision, has he made an error? I think not, as we use the terms *truth* and *error* in ordinary language. If someone seeks to tell his age down to the second, we usually say that he has told us more than we want to know. The question "What is your age?" does not demand that level of precision. Indeed, when someone gives excess information in an attempt to be more precise, he actually frustrates the process of communication, hindering rather than communicating truth. He buries his real age under a torrent of irrelevant words.

Similarly, when I stand before a class and a student asks me how large the textbook is, say that I reply, "400 pages," but the actual length is 398. Have I committed an error, or told the truth? I think the latter, for the following reasons: (a) In context, nobody expects more precision than I have given in my answer. I have met all the legitimate demands of the questioner. (b) 400, in this example, actually conveys more truth than 398 would have. Most likely, 398 would leave the student with the impression of some number around 300, but 400 presents the size of the book more accurately.[23]

So the relation between precision and error is more complicated than McGowan pictures it. "When is an error an error?" seems to him like a very straightforward question, as if errors are always perfectly easy to identify. In fact, identifying an error requires some understanding of the linguistic

22. Even that would be somewhat imprecise. What of milliseconds and nanoseconds? Of course, when one tries to give his age that precisely, he finds that his age has changed before he gets the words out of his mouth! So in this case, absolute precision is impossible *in principle*.

23. One notes that grocery and department stores often take advantage of this psychological quirk in their shoppers, by pricing goods at $3.98 or $398, rather than at $4.00 or $400. The first digit of the number makes a far greater impression than the others.

context, and that in turn requires an understanding of the cultural context.[24] A child who says in his math class that 6 + 5 = 10 may not expect the same tolerance as a person who gives a rough estimate of his age or a professor who exaggerates the size of a book by two pages.

We should always remember that Scripture is, for the most part,[25] ordinary language rather than technical language.[26] Certainly, it is not of the modern scientific genre. In Scripture, God intends to speak to everybody. To do that most efficiently, he (through the human writers) engages in all the shortcuts that we commonly use among ourselves to facilitate conversation: imprecisions, metaphors, hyperbole, parables, and so on. Not all of these convey *literal* truth, or truth with a precision expected in specialized contexts; but they all convey truth, and in the Bible there is no reason to charge them with error.

Another qualification to the doctrine of inerrancy that McGowan opposes is the assertion that inerrancy is consistent with the (inerrant!) citation of erroneous sources (pp. 107–8). This qualification is controversial among defenders of inerrancy. I think that in most cases where a biblical writer cites, uses, or incorporates an extracanonical text, he makes a truth claim for that text,[27] and I think that claim must be respected. I agree, then, with McGowan that this sort of qualification should not be made in defense of inerrancy. When it is, it deserves to be criticized.

Finally, McGowan mentions the common distinction among inerrantists between *historical* (or *descriptive*) and *normative* authority. To define this distinction, he quotes John Feinberg:

> Historical or descriptive authority applies equally to every word of an inerrant Bible. It merely means that whatever was said or done was in fact said or done. No judgment is passed as to whether it should or should not have been said or done. Normative authority,

24. In debates about Scripture, those who oppose inerrancy often charge those who defend it with ignorance of culture and the dynamics of language. In this case, however, the shoe is clearly on the other foot.

25. I qualify this statement merely out of abstract scholarly caution, not because I have any actual exceptions in mind.

26. It is interesting that liberals often complain that conservatives read the Bible as a "textbook of science," imagining it to address the technical issues of modern life. Sometimes that sort of criticism is fair. But both parties should recognize that it is the genius of the inerrantist position to see the Bible as *ordinary* language, subject to *ordinary*, not technical, standards of truth. So here, as in the matter mentioned in note 24, the shoe is on the other foot.

27. There are some obvious exceptions, such as Paul's citations from letters sent to him by the Corinthians or the letter possibly alluded to in 2 Thessalonians 2:2. But in these contexts, the apostle clearly tells us the truth value of these documents.

on the other hand, not only means that what was said or done was actually so but also that it should or should not have been said or done. (P. 107)[28]

Oddly, McGowan does not specifically address the issue of historical versus normative authority, but rather turns back (p. 108) to the earlier issue of inerrant citation of erroneous sources. I can see why someone would think that this issue illustrates the historical/normative distinction: the erroneous sources would be historically, though not normatively, authoritative. But I agreed earlier with McGowan that this is not persuasive as a qualification of inerrancy. Does that do away with the historical/normative distinction altogether?

I think not, because that distinction is relevant to many questions other than that of possible erroneous sources. In many contexts the Bible utters language that is not actually normative. Think of the serpent's words to Eve in Genesis 3:1–5; Lamech's song of vengeance in Genesis 4:23–24; the fool's words "there is no God" (Ps. 14:1); the boasts of the king of Babylon in Isaiah 14:13–14. When we deal with such language, it is not a superfluous qualification on inerrancy to ask, "Does the biblical writer actually intend us to believe what this character is saying?" and sometimes to answer no. To answer no is to put the language in the category of historical, but not normative, authority. The same is true in regard to actions of biblical characters. Sometimes Scripture exhorts us to imitate Paul (as 1 Cor. 11:1) or Jesus (as Phil. 2:5). But Scripture also describes many sinful actions (even of otherwise admirable characters, such as David and Peter), and it does not exhort us to imitate those. Descriptions of sinful acts may be called historically, but not normatively, authoritative.

Certainly, this distinction can be abused, as a too-easy resolution of Bible problems. But it is not wrong, when a biblical writer refers to a "three story universe,"[29] to ask whether he actually wants his readers to believe that cosmology. This, too, is part of understanding ordinary language. Today, we speak regularly of the sun rising and setting, without dreaming (let alone desiring) that any of our hearers will adopt a geocentric cosmology. These are legitimate questions, not superfluous qualifications.[30]

28. McGowan quotes Feinberg's article in Norman L. Geisler, ed., *Inerrancy* (Grand Rapids: Zondervan, 1979), 297–98. Interestingly, Herman Bavinck, whom McGowan places before us as an advocate of his view, clearly distinguishes between "descriptive and prescriptive authority," though he warns against abuses of this distinction. See Bavinck, *Reformed Dogmatics*, vol. 1 (Grand Rapids: Baker, 2003), 459–61.

29. Note McGowan's reference to John Gerstner on page 107.

30. Again, I think it evident that it is McGowan, not his inerrantist opponents, who has the less sophisticated understanding of how language operates.

So the "qualifications" of inerrancy in McGowan's list are not ad hoc and arbitrary ways of resolving Bible difficulties, though they can be abused in that way. Rather, these qualifications are merely analysis of what it means to communicate *truly* in the *ordinary language* of human beings.[31] Inerrancy claims that the Bible speaks *truth*, when understood in terms of such everyday language. There is nothing esoteric or technical about it. These are the criteria by which we evaluate one another's speech all the time, and McGowan is wrong to find fault with them.

2. *The autographs.* Inerrantists have often said that only the original manuscript of a Scripture text, the *autograph*, is perfectly inerrant. Everyone, of course, admits that there are errors in the copies of these texts. McGowan considers this a fatal admission:

> If textual inerrancy is so vital to the doctrine of Scripture, why did God not preserve the *autographa* or precise copies of the same? Indeed, if inerrancy only applies to the *autographa* (which we do not possess), then surely it is a somewhat pointless affirmation? (pp. 109)

Several questions arise here.

a. What is the biblical basis for limiting inerrancy to the *autographa*? As I pointed out earlier (and as McGowan neglected to say), 2 Timothy 3:16 requires the existence of a God-breathed *document*. Spiration applies not only to prophets, apostles, and biblical writers, but also, in 2 Timothy 3:16 (the only biblical reference to spiration), to a *text*. A text created by divine spiration is necessarily a *true* text, a perfectly true text. And as we have seen, *inerrancy* can be used as a synonym for *truth* in such contexts.

But then we must ask where that true text is to be found. Certainly, at least what Exodus 31:18 describes as "the two tablets of the testimony, tables of stone, written with the finger of God" would qualify. Few would doubt that those tablets constitute an autograph, unambiguously perfect. But does God promise us that copies of those tablets will also be perfectly true? I don't believe he does. Indeed, in Deuteronomy 4:2 and 12:32, Moses contemplates that people will be tempted to add to or subtract from the autograph, corrupting the revelation of God.[32]

---

31. Critics regularly castigate inerrantists for neglecting the "human side" of Scripture, the contribution of the human writers. In this case, it is the inerrantists who better understand the humanity of Scripture. And once we have understood the human side in this way, we discover that it fits together with the divine nature of Scripture very comfortably indeed. When we construe Scripture as ordinary human language, we discover that it is at the same time divinely true.

32. Now, of course, there are many ways of "adding to" and "subtracting from" God's Word. Usually we use these expressions in regard to teaching: for example, some teachers, such as the Pharisees in Matthew 15:6–9, add to the Word of God by claiming ultimate

The point is not, of course, that only the autograph has any truth or authority. Good copies should also be respected. But if one asks the technical question what manuscripts of Scripture are 100 percent inerrant, the answer has to be the autograph.

b. What constitutes an autograph? McGowan asks:

> In any case, what do we mean by *autographa*? Even if we affirm that Moses was the author of Deuteronomy, he clearly did not write the last chapter concerning the account of his death! In that case at least, an editor or scribe added something. Could not other books have received similar treatment? If so, which is the autographic text? Could further changes have been made to Deuteronomy much later? If so, do these scribal additions or emendations affect the status of these books as Scripture? What is the relationship between the autographic text and the versions admitted to the canon? As these questions demonstrate, a simple appeal to *autographa*, as made by some scholars, does not solve all of the difficulties. (P. 109)

Good questions! One could also ask about early drafts of the four Gospels, possible first drafts of Paul's letters by amanuenses, and so forth. A review such as this one is not the best place to try to answer these questions, but here are some points to keep in mind: First, because of its great importance, every inspired book required some attestation to its original audience. In the case of the Ten Commandments, the tablets were attested by the prophet Moses and placed by the ark of the covenant. Later parts of the Books of Moses (largely by Moses, but including, as McGowan says, some editorial additions) were warranted by Moses' prior authorization, and the Levites put them by the ark as God's witness (Deut. 31:24–26). Paul's letters were attested by his distinctive signature (2 Thess. 3:17) and by Paul's coworkers who were charged to deliver each letter. Similarly with other parts of Scripture. In some cases (especially the poetic literature in Scripture), it is difficult for us to say what kind of original certification was involved. But on any view of the matter, there must have been some event or process by which the writing impressed hearers that it was the word of God. So by *autograph*, we mean the original document certified as authentic to its original readers. On this basis, at any rate, *autograph* is not

---

authority for their traditions. But it is also possible to add to the Word by adding our own ideas to a manuscript of Scripture, or to subtract from it by removing something, that is, by corrupting the text. Often, of course, textual corruption is not intentional. But Deuteronomy 4:2 and 12:32 are clear that the authority of God resides in the text as God has given it, not in any changes made by human copiers.

a meaningless concept, invoked to salvage a flawed theological position. It is simply a term for the document that first brought God's message to his people.

c. "Why did God not preserve the *autographa* or precise copies of the same?" The answer is that God has not told us why he chose not to do this. He is not obligated to tell us. But the following thoughts are, to my mind, not contrary to Scripture, and they may illuminate the question.

I think this question is a specific part of a larger question, namely, why God didn't choose to give each individual an exhaustive, immediate, and perfect understanding of his revelation. Certainly he could have done this, overcoming the limitations of our finitude and sin. And we may understand, if not condone, the complaint that the lack of such revelation makes the Christian life more difficult. Had God given us immediate revelation of this type, we would not need to teach one another or to make long journeys to foreign countries to preach the gospel. The whole apparatus of biblical and theological scholarship need never have been created. But somehow, for his own reasons, God determined that hearing, understanding, and growing in his Word would not be that easy. He determined that we would have to do some hard thinking at times, that some scholarship would be helpful.

Perhaps a large part of God's rationale was that he intended our growth in knowledge to be a communal affair, not merely individual: fathers and mothers would teach their children; pastors would teach their congregations; scholars would teach the pastors. Our knowledge of God would be a public enterprise, not merely private.

To put it in biblical terms, this is to say that our knowledge of God is *covenantal*. It is the knowledge of a family, a nation, set apart to God. This covenant community is governed by written texts, as the United States is governed by a written constitution. But ascertaining the meaning of those texts is a communal venture.

To say this is to say that there must be a divinely authoritative text, but that there also must be a human process (Spirit-illumined, but not Spirit-inspired) to appropriate that text. Where does the divine text end and the human appropriation begin? God might have provided us with not only a perfect autograph, but also perfect copies in Hebrew and Greek, leaving to godly scribes the work of translation. Or he might have given us perfect translations in every language and left it to godly human teachers to teach these translations to us. Or he might have given a perfect understanding of the text to every duly ordained pastor, but not to every church member. God might have chosen any of these methods to create a combination of divinely authoritative revelation and finite human appropriation. But what he actually chose was to give us an inerrant autograph and to begin the finite, fallible human appropriation at that point. Will anyone fault him for making that choice?

If it is implausible to imagine God spirating an autograph, but leaving the copies to human labor under the supervision of ordinary providence, then why would it not be equally implausible to imagine God spirating all the copies of the autograph, but leaving it to human beings to translate, publish, preach, and teach them? This objection would make sense on the hypothesis that divine revelation must eliminate every trace of a human factor in God's communication with us. But nobody would claim that God intends to eliminate the human factor altogether. To suggest that he intends this, or that he ought to intend this, would violate the entire biblical picture of the relation between God's action and human action.[33]

d. "What is the point of insisting that there once existed (very briefly) perfect versions of these texts, if we no longer possess them?" (p. 109). (i) The most fundamental answer is that this doctrine honors the truth of God. If we say that God spirated a text that contains errors, we charge God himself with error. McGowan quotes Greg Bahnsen as saying that in this matter "God's veracity is at stake" (ibid.), but in the following discussion he does not address this point specifically. (ii) Scripture teaches, in 2 Timothy 3:16 and elsewhere, that God inspired a *text*.[34] We have seen that this text is, first of all, the autograph. So we should insist on the existence of perfect autographs because Scripture tells us they existed. (iii) That is to say, Scripture says that it was God's intention to provide us with an inerrant autograph and then to invite us communally to identify and appropriate it. We should acknowledge that divine plan as a good thing. (iv) The imperfections in the manuscripts we have, as many writers have observed, are very few compared with other ancient texts, are of slight importance, and do not affect any point of doctrine. So excellent are these manuscripts that it is not wrong to refer to them (as biblical writers do) as the Word of God. The excellences of these texts can be traced to the original inspiration of the autograph, and because of that we should praise God for giving us the inspired autograph.

3. *Textual issues.* McGowan's third reason for saying that biblical inerrancy is "theologically mistaken" is that it forces on us inappropriate ways

---

33. As in previous comments, I point out that here it is the inerrantists, not their opponents, who have a clearer and more biblical grasp of the nature of the human factor in the revelatory process.

34. Readers should notice a continuing theme in this review of emphasis on the *text*. I believe it is McGowan's chief error to ignore the bearing of inspiration/spiration on the *text* of Scripture.

of addressing problems in the biblical text. Faced with an apparent contradiction in the text, McGowan says:

> Either they [the inerrantists] will argue that this is only an antinomy, an apparent but not real contradiction, or they will argue that if we had the *autographa* we would see that the problem does not exist there, only in errant manuscripts, because of errors in the copying over the centuries. (P. 112)

McGowan ignores a third possibility, that we set the problem aside and postpone our search for an answer. We have no obligation to answer all these problems. Certainly, one can affirm biblical authority and inerrancy without having such solutions. We confess the Bible as God's Word not because we have solved all the difficulties, but because God himself (in the text) and the Spirit (in our hearts) has so identified it. McGowan appeals to the Spirit and the Word on behalf of his own view, so why should he object when the inerrantist does the same thing?

Of course, no Christian should deny that such problems exist, and for the benefit of God's people we should do what we can to resolve these problems, as God gives us the calling and gifts to do so. McGowan mentions two types of solutions that he considers illegitimate, but I can easily think of cases in which they would be entirely proper. (a) Sometimes, certainly, the problematic texts are indeed apparent but not real contradictions—as when Paul in Galatians 6:2 says, "Bear one another's burdens," and then in verse 5 says that "each will have to bear his own load."[35] (b) It is certainly not impossible that some problems in our present texts are the result of textual corruption. If a passage says A and B, and these appear to contradict, it is always *possible* that the original text contained A, but not B, or vice versa.

These strategies of resolution are used not only by inerrantists, but by many others who try to interpret the Bible responsibly. The alternatives would seem to be (a) accepting every apparent contradiction as a real contradiction and (b) denying that textual criticism ever sheds light on a problem. It is hard to believe that McGowan or anyone else would recommend such irrational and self-defeating methodology.

Of course, both of these methods can be abused. Sometimes attempts to reconcile apparent discrepancies are hugely implausible (one thinks of

---

35. As McGowan implies, it is certainly true that on the inerrantist view there are no real contradictions. Nobody should be surprised, then, that when an inerrantist deals with an apparent contradiction, he concludes that it is only apparent. Why does McGowan imagine that there is something wrong with this? Evidently, he here begins with the assumption that Scripture is not inerrant. On that assumption, but only on that assumption, it would be wrong to conclude that all contradictions are apparent.

the assertion of some that Peter must have denied Jesus six times), and appeals to textual corruption can be an asylum of ignorance, unless actual evidence of textual corruption exists. Often it is better to leave these problems unanswered. And it is almost always wrong to dogmatically insist on a particular reconciliation. But it is equally wrong to insist dogmatically that an error exists, granting that there are always *possible* ways in which the problem could be solved, if we had more information.[36]

On the whole, I believe that evangelicals have discussed such matters responsibly, willing to admit when they have been uncertain. McGowan evidently disagrees. But I don't believe he has shown, or can show, that failures to resolve such problems prove inerrancy to be theologically mistaken. Inerrantism is not based on the claim that all apparent discrepancies can be resolved. It is based on the biblical teaching that God has given us an inspired text.

4. *The inerrantist position is rationalistic.* Judging from the style of outline and typeface he employs, McGowan evidently considers this argument to be more fundamental than those treated above. He says:

> The inerrantists make an unwarranted assumption about God. The assumption is that, given the nature and character of God, the only kind of Scripture he could "breathe out" was Scripture that is textually inerrant. (P. 113)

McGowan grants that God is *able* to deliver an inerrant text, but he refuses to accept the notion that God "is *unable* to produce anything other than an inerrant autographic text" (ibid.).

He argues first that inerrancy is "not a biblical doctrine, but rather an implication from another doctrine" (p. 115)—I presume the doctrine that God cannot speak untruth. That inerrancy is an implication of other doctrines should not be a problem for one who subscribes to WCF 1.6:

> The whole counsel of God concerning all things necessary for His own glory, man's salvation, faith and life, is either expressly set down in Scripture, or by good and necessary consequence may be deduced from Scripture.

36. Inerrantists have often made the claim that nobody has succeeded in proving the existence of an error in Scripture. Of course, to some extent this is a circular claim: once we assume inerrancy, we must logically believe that no errors have been proved to exist. But to an extent this claim is also based on the great difficulty of proving error in Scripture: to do that, one must prove the negative proposition that *no* solution can possibly be found. McGowan acknowledges the validity of this point at the top of page 137.

In the minds of the Westminster divines, the deductions or implications of biblical doctrines have the same authority as those doctrines themselves. Of course, the deduction must be correct (i.e., "good and necessary"). There is room for error here. But there is also room for error in formulating those doctrines that are explicitly scriptural. If inerrancy is indeed an inference from other doctrines, that is not in itself a criticism of it.

I indicated earlier, however, that inerrancy is not *merely* an inference. For *inerrancy* is only another word for *truth*. And that God's word is always *true* or *truth* is not merely an inference. It is an explicit teaching of the Bible.

But McGowan's complaint is not only that inerrancy is an inference. The point of his concern is that it is an inference from a false premise, namely, that God *cannot* inspire an erroneous text.

He thinks this premise comes from the rationalistic mind-set of such writers as Hodge and Warfield. I agree with McGowan that Hodge carried the analogy between science and theology too far, and that he stressed the propositional character of Scripture at the expense of its other functions of its language (address, challenge, encouragement, etc.) (p. 116). I think McGowan goes too far, however, when he says that Hodge made Scripture "into something cold and clinical, which *we* possess and which *we* manipulate" (p. 117).[37] Thankfully, McGowan admits that not all inerrantists do this.

He does say that inerrancy "limits God" by assuming that God "must conform to the canons of human reason" (p. 118). How, then, did God inspire the Scriptures? The following sentence is central to the position of McGowan's book:

> God the Holy Spirit breathed out the Scriptures. The instruments of this divine spiration were certain human beings. The resulting Scriptures are as God intended them to be. Having chosen, however, to use human beings rather than a more direct approach (e.g., writing the words supernaturally on stone without human involvement, as with the Ten Commandments), God did not overrule their humanity. (Ibid.)

37. The "possess" and "manipulate" rhetoric comes from Barth, Rudolf Bultmann, and other dialectical theologians. Frankly, I think it amounts to a slander against evangelicals. In any case, I think the dialectical theologians are as guilty of trying to possess and manipulate Scripture to suit their purposes as any evangelicals have been. Trying to possess or manipulate Scripture is a moral and spiritual issue. It is a heart attitude affecting our use of Scripture. I do not believe we should charge someone with such a sinful attitude simply because of his doctrinal formulations. People can be guilty of this sin no matter what view of Scripture they hold. I do think, however, that inerrantism discourages this sin, as no other view does. For it exhorts us to place ourselves fully under God's written Word, not to find fault with it or try to master it.

Then on the next page:

> We might sum this up by saying that the *autographa* (if we could view them) might very well look just like our existing manuscripts, including all of the difficulties, synoptic issues, discrepancies and apparent contradictions, because that is what God intended. (P. 119)

McGowan's central thesis, then, is that God can and does "breathe out" errors as well as truths. To say he cannot do this, McGowan thinks, is rationalistic. He asks, if God can communicate through preaching without making the preacher inerrant, why can't he do the same with Scripture? (p. 118).

Here I must sharply disagree. Please note the following.

1. To breathe out words is to speak. To say that God breathes out errors is to say that he speaks errors. That is biblically impossible. God does not lie (Titus 1:2), and he does not make mistakes (Heb. 4:12). So he speaks only truth.

2. As we have seen, inerrancy is not just an inference, certainly not a rationalistic inference, but an explicit teaching of Scripture: for to say that Scripture is inerrant is to say that it is true.

3. So inerrancy is not a human judgment about what God cannot do. It rather accepts God's own judgment that he cannot lie or err, and it accepts God's own account of what he has given us in Scripture.

4. God can communicate with us in noninerrant ways, such as preaching: indeed, not only preaching (as McGowan says on p. 118), but also through teaching, songs, drama, and many other ways.[38] But Christians have always admitted that Scripture has an authority greater than any of these, including preaching. Scripture is the standard that governs preaching.

5. If there are errors in the *autographa*, then we can no longer claim that there is such a thing as a text breathed out by God.

6. If there are errors in the *autographa*, then it is unclear why we should look to Scripture as our supreme divine authority, rather than preaching or some other form of communication that God providentially directs.

7. The notion that the written Word contains errors is incompatible not only with 2 Timothy 3:16, but with a vast amount of other

---

38. We should add general revelation to this list. God can communicate with us through the starry heavens and the grassy fields, and through our own nature as the image of God.

biblical data: consider the authority of the (written) statutes and ordinances in Deuteronomy, the praise of the written Word in Psalm 19:7–11 and Psalm 119, the ways in which Jesus and the apostles cited the OT, and the claims of the apostles for their own written words, as 1 Corinthians 14:37. These and other data have been explored in great depth in the inerrantist literature. It is unfortunate that McGowan largely ignores it.

8. McGowan evidently regards his position as more conservative than Rogers/McKim, because he rejects their distinction between infallible religious content and noninfallible secular content. I am happy that he rejects that distinction. But in one sense, he is less conservative than they. Rogers/McKim believed at least that the religious content of Scripture was inerrant. McGowan rejects inerrancy in both religious and secular subject matter. For him, we should always remember, there is no inerrancy at all, not even in religious, theological, or doctrinal areas. In my view, this leaves the church at sea.

INFALLIBILITY[39]

McGowan wants to present to us a positive view of Scripture, not only a critique of inerrancy. His positive view he associates with the term *infallibility*. The term *infallibility* has a longer history than the term *inerrancy*, and McGowan offers it to us as designating "an older and better way to defend a 'high' view of Scripture" (p. 123).

As I pointed out earlier, McGowan never presents a definition of *infallibility* or precisely distinguishes the meaning of the word from that of *inerrancy*. Certainly, he does not defer to the dictionary definitions of these terms that I discussed earlier. As I mentioned then, he does formulate an "argument" for infallibility that may imply a definition:

> The argument for "infallibility" is that the final authority for the Christian is the authority of God speaking in and through his Word and that the Holy Spirit infallibly uses God's Word to achieve all he intends to achieve. (P. 49)

39. I pass over McGowan's discussion of the "incarnational analogy" (pp. 119–21), evidently motivated by the controversy over Peter Enns' *Inspiration and Incarnation* (Grand Rapids: Baker, 2005). There is not much difference between McGowan's position and mine in this regard. My own review of Enns' book can be found at http://www.frame-poythress.org/frame_articles/2008Enns.htm. That review is Appendix J of the present volume.

But in view of our discussion of inerrancy, we must understand that "the authority of God speaking in and through his Word" may include his speaking errors, according to McGowan. As to the clause about the Holy Spirit, I certainly agree with McGowan that the Spirit does use the Word in that way. But the Spirit uses *everything* "to achieve all he intends to achieve," so this statement does not say anything distinctive about Scripture. Again, McGowan's view seems to be that the Spirit's work in Scripture is one of ordinary divine providence. There are no special qualities in the text.

McGowan should have considered more carefully the differences between spiration and general providence. Van Til's *Christian Apologetics* is a book I respect deeply, and I think McGowan does, too. I don't think it is wrong to say that God speaks to me through that book. That book is general revelation, like all of God's creation, and it also conveys the truth of Christ, which is something more than general revelation. And certainly the Holy Spirit is involved when I read Van Til's book. He certainly, infallibly, uses the book to achieve all he intends to achieve. Do these facts make Van Til's book infallible, in McGowan's definition? What of other books, such as Aristotle's *Nicomachean Ethics*? The fact is that McGowan's quasi-definition of *infallible* fails to make any distinction between Scripture and other books.

Other theologians have had similar problems identifying what is distinctive to Scripture. I could make the same criticism of Barth, Jürgen Moltmann, G. C. Berkouwer, N. T. Wright,[40] and Peter Enns.[41] But McGowan claims to have a "higher" view of Scripture than such authors, and so his failure to adequately present the uniqueness of Scripture is especially disappointing.

In his discussion of "Infallibility," McGowan does not add anything much to the clarity of his proposal. Here he reverts to historical analysis, comparing his position to that of various theologians. As we have seen, he is critical of Berkouwer and Rogers/McKim (pp. 124–25) and of the Old Princeton tradition (pp. 125–26). He believes that his own view is different from both, akin to the views of James Orr and Herman Bavinck.

I don't quite understand why he brings Orr into it, except perhaps to honor a fellow Scot. He disagrees with Orr on the content/form distinction, which he also criticizes in Berkouwer and in Rogers/McKim (p. 136). He also disagrees (as I do) with Orr's view of "degrees of inspiration." What positive idea does Orr contribute to the discussion? Most likely the following is foremost in McGowan's mind:

40. See my review of his *The Last Word*, http://www.frame-poythress.org/frame_articles/2006Wright.html. This review is Appendix K of the present volume.

41. See my review of his *Inspiration and Incarnation*, http://www.frame-poythress.org/frame_articles/2008Enns.htm. This review is Appendix J of the present volume.

> Like Orr, I think it is wrong to prejudge the nature of the Scriptures through some deductivist approach, based on what we believe inspiration must mean, given God's character. (Ibid.)

McGowan thinks inerrantism is deductivist; earlier in this review, I argued otherwise. Inerrantism judges the nature of the Scriptures from what Scripture says about itself and from what it says about God's character.

McGowan's main hero, however, is Herman Bavinck. McGowan thinks that Bavinck rejected inerrancy and embraced what McGowan calls infallibility. But in all of McGowan's long discussion, he does not in my view point out anything in Bavinck that Warfield would have disagreed with. There are differences of emphasis, but I think nothing of substance.

McGowan points out that (1) Bavinck rejected natural theology while embracing general revelation, (2) Bavinck held to an "organic" relation between word and fact in revelation, (3) Bavinck acknowledged both divine and human authorship of Scripture,[42] (4) Bavinck emphasized the testimony of the Holy Spirit, (5) Bavinck placed inspiration within the broader context of revelation, (6) organic inspiration is God's using all the human qualities of the writers in his spirating of Scripture, (7) inspiration (contra Berkouwer) is not limited to doctrine and ethics, as opposed to other areas of science. Again, I would say that no inerrantist would object to anything here.

It is significant that McGowan produces no evidence in Bavinck of agreement with McGowan's own most distinctive positions. Bavinck never says that God can speak errors, or that there can be errors in the Bible.

McGowan does quote Bavinck in a way that suggests otherwise:

> He [Bavinck] goes so far as to say that "the guidance of the Holy Spirit promised to the church does not exclude the possibility of human error." Such a claim could never be made by an inerrantist. (P. 158)[43]

This appeal to Bavinck is terribly misleading, bordering on slander. In the context quoted, Bavinck is not talking about biblical inspiration at all, but

---

42. Here McGowan points out that for Bavinck, "if we find passages that are in apparent contradiction, we must not try to force them into some artificial agreement" (p. 149). Evidently McGowan thinks that inerrancy requires us to force texts to agree in this way. In my view, some inerrantists (and some noninerrantists) have been guilty of this, but this is by no means required by the doctrine of inerrancy. Compare my earlier discussion to the effect that it is perfectly legitimate for an inerrantist to set such problems aside until a nonartificial resolution becomes apparent.

43. Quoting Bavinck, *Reformed Dogmatics*, 1:32.

rather about God's guidance of the church in the formulation of dogma. His point is familiar to Protestants, that church theologians, even councils and synods, sometimes err. It has nothing to do with the question of how God inspires Scripture.

It is true that Bavinck does not speak directly of biblical inerrancy (so far as I can tell), and that he does not distinguish in authority between *autographa* and copies. In part, this difference owes to the fact that Bavinck worked in a Continental theological context and was not familiar with American developments. And it is not irrelevant that he wrote his *Dogmatics* in Dutch, while Hodge and Warfield wrote in English. But I know of no passage in Bavinck that contradicts the doctrine of autographal inerrancy. I think McGowan would have shown us such a passage if it existed, and he has not. And my own study does not reveal anything like this either.

I think the main issues related to McGowan's view of biblical "infallibility" are now on the table. I will not take the time here to discuss his views of Calvin, Kuyper, Berkouwer, and others.

SCRIPTURE AND CONFESSION

We have discussed the main thrust of McGowan's view of Scripture. I will not spend as much time on the last two chapters, on confession and preaching. I consider them less controversial. Indeed, I agree with them in large measure.

McGowan opposes those who reject confessions altogether in the name of "Scripture alone" (pp. 166–68), and those who use the vagueness of confessional subscription formulae to reject basic principles of the Reformed faith (pp. 168–71). He also rejects the "strong confessionalism" that makes the confessions equal to Scripture (pp. 173–75). Then he argues the need for a more sophisticated understanding of the relation of Scripture and tradition (pp. 175–87).

The only troubling thing to me in this discussion is McGowan's reference toward the end (p. 187) to Barth's *The Theology of the Reformed Confessions*.[44] McGowan says that he was

> challenged by [Barth's] argument that the Westminster Confession of Faith heralds a departure from earlier creedal and confessional statements in that its main preoccupation is not with God but with personal salvation and the doctrine of assurance. Barth goes

44. Louisville: Westminster John Knox Press, 2002.

so far as to suggest that it represents an attempt "to make Reformed theology into anthropology." Whether or not one agrees with his whole argument, it clearly deserves serious consideration.

"Not with God"? Makes "Reformed theology into anthropology"? I am not one who regards the WCF as infallible, or as the final word on anything. But in my judgment, these statements of Barth are preposterous. Certainly, they do not deserve "serious consideration." I hope there aren't too many of us who will be "challenged" by Barth's argument.

PREACHING SCRIPTURE

The final section of McGowan's book deals with preaching. We recall that earlier in the book (p. 118), McGowan used preaching as an example of a word of God that is not inerrant.[45] Here, he favors preaching that is based on Scripture, systematic, doctrinal, applied to the needs of people. Hard to argue against that.

CONCLUSION

McGowan concludes with a summary of his argument and discusses three possible objections to his position. The last two of these I have already discussed. The first I find perplexing: The question arises, "If the Bible is not inerrant, how can we believe what it says?" (p. 210). He replies that this question is inappropriate. He opposes inerrancy, but he is not arguing for biblical *errancy*. "We can," he says, "believe what the Bible says because God gave us the Scriptures and he does not deceive." But if God speaks erroneous words, how can we escape the conclusion that he deceives us?

That pretty much sums up my own problems with McGowan's view of spiration. McGowan clearly implies that God's speech, his spiration, includes errors. But this is contrary to Scripture's evaluation of God's character and of his word. God is truth. He never deceives nor is deceived. The written Word is his own speech, and that Word is also true.

45. In my judgment, when the Second Helvetic Confession I says that "the preaching of the Word of God is the Word of God," it means not that the sermon as a sermon is divinely inspired, but rather that what the sermon preaches, the Scripture, does not cease in that context to be the Word of God. It says, "The Word itself which is preached is to be regarded, not the minister that preaches; for even if he be evil and a sinner, nevertheless the Word of God remains still true and good."

I would recommend that McGowan give much more attention to the effects of divine spiration on the *text* of Scripture. So far as I can tell, McGowan regards that text as like any other human book. It is spirated, but that spiration does not make it true. I confess that this absence of attention to the nature of the text seems to be a trend in evangelical theology these days. The same serious flaw, in my judgment, occurs in N. T. Wright's *The Last Word*[46] and in Peter Enns' *Inspiration and Incarnation*.[47] I hope future writings in this field will discuss this important issue.

46. See my review of his *The Last Word*, http://www.frame-poythress.org/frame _articles/2006Wright.html (Appendix K).

47. See my review of his *Inspiration and Incarnation*, http://www.frame-poythress .org/frame_articles/2008Enns.htm (Appendix J).

REVIEW OF NORMAN GEISLER, ED., *BIBLICAL ERRANCY*[1]

Note: This review supplements the discussion of inerrancy in chapter 26 of the present volume, and also the discussions of modern theology in chapters 3–7.

This book is the latest of a series of volumes sponsored by the International Council on Biblical Inerrancy. If I may begin with a quibble, the book is not about "biblical errancy," for the editor and essay-writers all believe that there is no such thing. Rather, they seek to examine the view (erran*tism*, perhaps?) of some who hold that Scripture *does* err. Further, the book does not contain what one might expect—extensive discussions of contemporary errantist theologians—except in parenthetical sections here and there and in the last chapter (to my mind the worst chapter of the book). Instead, the book consists mostly of discussions about philosophers, philosophers thought to "influence" contemporary errantists.

There is a thesis implicit here, which Geisler states as follows: "Hence, the rise of an errant [*sic*] view of Scripture did not result from a discovery of factual evidence that made belief in an inerrant Scripture untenable. Rather, it resulted from the unnecessary acceptance of philosophical premises that undermined the historic belief in an infallible and inerrant Bible"

1. Norman Geisler, ed., *Biblical Errancy: An Analysis of Its Philosophical Roots* (Grand Rapids: Zondervan, 1981). This review was originally published in *WTJ* 45, 2 (Fall 1983): 433–41. It is used here by permission. For stylistic purposes, this appendix has been copyedited for inclusion in this volume.

(p. 10). I find this an attractive and useful thesis, one that for many years I have instinctively believed to be true. Yet there are difficulties inherent in this idea that we should note at the outset.

1. It is not easy to demonstrate patterns of historical "influence." To show, for example, that David Hume influenced G. C. Berkouwer, one must present a careful study of Berkouwer, analyzing his questionable views and his reasons for adopting them. Geisler's admission (pp. 7ff.) that this influence may be indirect and unconscious does not make the task of demonstrating it any easier; quite to the contrary. The present volume, in my view, greatly underestimates this task. As mentioned earlier, it presents few discussions of those contemporary theologians thought to be influenced by the philosophers, and those discussions are rather inadequate. On the other hand, the discussions of the philosophers themselves are too broad in scope to aid much in supporting Geisler's thesis. The writers seem to assume no knowledge of philosophy on the part of the reader, and so they present general surveys of each philosopher's thought such as one might find in a history of philosophy. As surveys, these are generally well done, but they deal in only a cursory way with the specific issues surrounding inerrancy. At best they show how the philosophies *might* influence discussions of inerrancy (cf. John Feinberg's comment, p. 166), not how they have influenced or do influence such discussions.

2. Next, to establish Geisler's thesis, one would have to show that the philosophical influences in question were the *chief* or *determinative* influences on a particular theologian. After all, theological views have many "roots," both philosophical and nonphilosophical, academic and nonacademic. I would observe that very few theologians admit to being mere camp followers of a particular philosophy. Most theologians, even those in most obvious bondage to philosophical systems, go to great lengths to show that their philosophical commitments are warranted by, or at least permitted by, Scripture, Christian tradition, or both. These would claim that their most fundamental commitments are theological, not philosophical. (This is most certainly the case in regard to the noninerrantist evangelicals whose views are most focally at issue here.) Now, this claim may be false, but to demonstrate that falsity may be difficult. In the final analysis, it may require psychological or spiritual insight into the motives of these theologians, and

nothing is harder than achieving that. Certainly, this book does not even attempt such an analysis.

3. Then it ought to be noted that even if we do establish the primacy of philosophical influences on errantism, we have not thereby shown errantism to be false. Even if we reject the philosophical arguments for errantism, the theological-exegetical arguments remain. But the present volume doesn't deal with theological-exegetical arguments.

What good, then, does this book do for us? What good does it do to trace patterns of philosophical influence when those patterns are not persuasively established and when, even if established, they would not necessitate any theological conclusions? Well, the book does take a few steps *toward* a definitive study, and we can be thankful for that. And it contains enough good arguments against philosophical positions still fashionable among theologians that it does much to shatter errantism's pretense of *obviousness*. Rudolf Bultmann, for example, makes it sound very obvious that no modern man can possibly believe in a miracle. But once we see our way out of Baruch Spinoza's determinism and David Hume's empiricism, Bultmann's view doesn't seem so obvious at all. Does he have arguments other than those of Spinoza and Hume? If so, we think, he had better produce them. Much that passes for "common sense" is really obsolete philosophy, and recognition of that fact is one path to wisdom. The real value of this book is to teach us wisdom of that sort; it would have been a better book if it were more sharply focused on that goal.

As a critical history of some philosophical views, the book is pretty good. The subjects are well chosen. After the initial chapter, which deals with Francis Bacon, Thomas Hobbes, and Baruch Spinoza, each essay treats one philosopher: David Hume, Immanuel Kant, Georg Hegel, Søren Kierkegaard, Friedrich Nietzsche, Ludwig Wittgenstein, Martin Heidegger. An epilogue by the editor seeks to link these figures with contemporary errantist theologians G. C. Berkouwer, Jack Rogers, and Stephen T. Davis. Each essay is preceded by a summary and (as mentioned earlier) does not presume philosophical training, though it is definitely written for college level and up. The text is clear, as philosophical writing goes. I noted unclarities on pages 29, 77, 196ff., and 208ff.; in most books of this sort, I would have noted many more. The authors were largely unfamiliar to me. Their *curricula vitae* contain references to such schools as Dallas Theological Seminary, Detroit Bible College, Liberty Baptist College, and Western Conservative Baptist Seminary; but these also indicate training at such institutions as Oxford University, Boston University, University of Chicago, Claremont School of Theology, USC, and UCLA. These are, in other words, philosophers of fundamentalist[2] background and connection, but with first-rate training and competence. (Here I use the term *fundamentalist* not as synonymous with *evangelical*, but as a distinctive party within the evangelical orbit distinct from, say, confessional Lutheran or Reformed groups. There is some overlap. Howard Ducharme, who wrote the essay on Heidegger, is a member of the Christian Reformed Church, but also lists Trinity Divinity School and Campus Crusade for Christ among his past involvements.) There was a time when fundamentalism was easily equated with anti-intellectualism, especially in regard to philosophical matters, just as it was once thought to have renounced involvement in social issues. Today, however, we have seen a renaissance of fundamentalist social action and also, now, of fundamentalist philosophical activity.

Some of the essays are very fine indeed. W. David Beck's article on Kant is superb. He summarizes all the critiques and *Religion* very ably while carefully focusing our attention on the main issue, human autonomy. John Feinberg's essay on Wittgenstein is very skillfully done and may be the best short introduction to Wittgenstein by an evangelical. (But John: surely you don't mean that the early Wittgenstein objected to *if-then* statements, as you suggest on page 177!) Most of the others are good, too, so that I would not hesitate to recommend them to students who want introductory material on the thinkers discussed. I could have wished for more profundity (see below), but lack of that was inevitable when the decision was made to gear these essays to the introductory level.

The authors attack their philosophers from many angles, but we ought to note the three accusations that constitute the major themes of the book.

1. *Anti-Supernatural Bias.* The authors find this, not surprisingly, in most of the secular thinkers discussed (pp. 18, 21f., 39ff., 232, etc.). The discussion of Hume and positivism is especially helpful (though in the Hume article Gary Habermas resorts to an unbiblical definition of miracle for apologetic purposes, p. 45).

2. *Science/Scripture Compartmentalizing.* As one reads through the book, one is struck again by the pervasiveness in secular philosophy of the idea that Scripture and theology speak to some realm other than science, leaving science to function autonomously.

---

2. After this review was first published, Geisler wrote that he would prefer to be called *evangelical* rather than *fundamentalist.* I appreciate that preference and will adhere to it in future references to him. But here I am using the term in a nondisparaging way, seeking to make a distinction *within* the evangelical movement that would be hard to make without using the term *fundamentalist* as I have here.

Thus religion and reason, faith and science, pertain to two distinct realms. "This is called *separationism*" (p. 21), says Geisler. (Well, maybe so; or is that only what he calls it? If this is a common technical term, it is a new one on me!) Anyhow, the book contains some helpful discussions of this phenomenon in Bacon (p. 13), Hobbes (p. 16), Spinoza (pp. 17, 21), Kant (p. 73), Gotthold Ephraim Lessing (p. 108), and Kierkegaard (p. 117). Feinberg points out an interesting contradiction in Wittgenstein on this matter: though wanting to make "language games" (such as science and theology) sharply distinct, he also wanted to avoid defining "essences" (pp. 199ff.); but if essences cannot be defined, then differences between language games cannot be sharply defined either. Geisler somewhat confusingly tries to exempt Thomas Aquinas from the charge of "separationism" (p. 13) by saying that Aquinas made a "distinction" between the two realms but not an "actual separation." What Geisler does not say (and his sympathy with Thomism is well known) is that Thomas held "natural reason" to function independently of divine revelation, thus becoming a very significant figure in the development of "separationism." These and other interesting discussions stimulate the reader's constructive thinking concerning the attempt in modern theology (not least in errantist evangelicalism) to remove science from the realm of biblical authority.

3. *Denial of "Objective Truth" in Religion.* The authors of this volume not only are unanimous in their inerrantism and in their evangelicalism, but also display a rare degree of unity on epistemology. Crucial to that epistemology is the concept of "objective fact," which, according to Winfried Corduan, is "the unquestionable bedrock on which knowledge must be based" (p. 99). Ducharme speaks of this view as "metaphysical realism" (p. 221), corollaries of which are "epistemological dualism" and the "correspondence theory of truth." There are, in other words, real facts out there in the world, independent of us, the knowers. We come to know those facts by means of "representative ideas" (p. 223), ideas that represent or correspond to the facts. Truth, then, is the correspondence between our ideas and the facts. Ducharme adds to this a hermeneutical corollary: there is "one correct meaning of a text that resides in the original author's intention, which is cemented into propositional statements" (p. 222). To this realist epistemology is contrasted the viewpoints of the philosophers under discussion. Hegel, says Corduan, denied the existence of

"objective, ontological truth" (p. 98). That is true, I think, only if we take that phrase to denote the entire position of metaphysical realism described above. Otherwise, Corduan's charge would seem to be wildly overstated, as is his statement that (for Hegel, I presume) "something may be true or false simply because an individual wants it to be that way" (p. 99). Naturally, this sort of critique is extended to Kierkegaard (pp. 128f.), who thought Hegel was too much of an objectivist, Nietzsche (pp. 133, 143), Kant (p. 74), and Heidegger (pp. 221ff.). Since these thinkers have drawn a sharp line between religion and science, understandably they ascribe unique, nonscientific, and therefore "nonobjective" characteristics to religious truth or truth about human existence. To our essay-writers, however, abandonment of "objective truth" in religion leaves skepticism or relativism as the only alternative.

There is truth in metaphysical realism. From a Christian perspective, reality is independent of us because it is ultimately dependent on God. In that sense there is "objective truth." Learning that truth, however, is far more than merely comparing thoughts with reality, as the authors suggest it is by their talk of correspondence. What about the thoughts by which we compare thoughts with reality? How do we know that they correspond? By thoughts about thoughts about thoughts? Clearly, this process can go on to infinity or, put differently, can never reach its termination, can never attain final certainty. And then there are all sorts of questions about criteria: on what basis do we know when an idea of ours "fits the facts"? Wittgenstein agonized over the notion that something like a photographic resemblance was involved between idea and fact; but most of us (I think including Feinberg) are grateful to Wittgenstein for showing us why that notion won't work. It seems clear to me, at least, that knowledge is never mere knowledge of "facts" (except in a broad sense); it is always at the same time a knowledge of criteria, norms, law (cf. Rom. 1:32). And those norms are of value only to one with sufficient personal integrity to apply them rightly, to embrace the truth rather than suppressing it (Rom. 1:18–32). By oversimplifying these difficult epistemological issues, our authors are at a great disadvantage in evaluating thinkers such as Kierkegaard, Heidegger, and Wittgenstein, who, erroneous as their views may be, have at least thought these matters through.

A more balanced epistemology would also have helped our writers to see more clearly that skepticism and relativism are not our only enemies or even, necessarily, our chief enemies. The book itself points out that modern philosophers are not mere relativists; these philosophers have their own absolutes that they prefer to the Christian absolutes: Bacon's scientific method, Spinoza's mathematical reason, Kant's personal autonomy, Hegel's absolute Spirit. The argument, then, is not over whether or not there is an absolute, but over what that absolute is, whether the God of Scripture or an idol of the philosopher's imagination. So today, some question inerrancy because of skepticism or relativism, but others (such as Dewey Beegle and Daniel Fuller, I think) are led to it by a kind of "objectivism" not terribly different from the metaphysical realism described by Ducharme—a resolution to adopt a pure inductive method apart from any theological presuppositions and to follow that inductive method wherever it leads. As Cornelius Van Til would say, the problem is not only a problem with irrationalism, but a problem with rationalism as well.

A word now about Ducharme's "hermeneutical corollary." Is there "one correct meaning of a text that resides in the original author's intention, which is cemented into propositional statements"? Well, in a sense. Genesis 1:1 reads, "In the beginning God created the heavens and the earth." What is the correct meaning of that? The correct meaning (assuming the accuracy of the translation) is, "In the beginning God created the heavens and the earth." The authors (divine and human) intended, we believe, to say exactly that, in that propositional form. But generally, when someone asks about meaning, he is not asking to have the text repeated to him. He wants a paraphrase, a definition, an illustration, an application; he wants help in understanding. Can we say that there is only one correct way of giving such help, which must be expressed propositionally? Certainly not. We can teach the meaning of any statement in an indefinite number of ways. Not every way will do; in that sense, there is still an objective limit. Each text (and ultimately, in one sense, the author's intention; but do note Feinberg's wise remarks on this, pp. 194f.) determines the rightness and wrongness of its uses. But those uses are not susceptible to enumeration. We should also note that since not all texts are propositional (many are questions, commands, promises, emotive expressions, or combinations of these), not all meanings are propositional in any sense. Even in the sense of "meaning" most conducive to Ducharme's thesis: the meaning of "Peter, do you love me?" is "Peter, do you love me?"—a question, not a proposition.

Thus, I think the book's defense of "objective truth," while making some useful points, is rather naive epistemologically, on the whole. The best observations in this area are made by W. David Beck, who, having asked about the "final basis" of Kant's view of revelation and ethics, finds the answer in "his doctrine of the autonomy of reason" (p. 76). That, I think, is the real issue: not whether knowledge is "objective" or "subjective," but whether the object and subject of knowledge are bound by God's authority.

What most sharply separates errantists from inerrantists is the view that human reason may function independently of God's revelation. On that crucial issue, *Biblical Errancy* gives an uncertain sound. We need a book on this subject that is unambiguous in this area and that makes this question, rather than the vague question of "objectivity," its main focus.

Finally, I must comment on Geisler's "Epilogue," in which he seeks to apply the philosophical critiques to contemporary "errantist" evangelicals, Berkouwer, Rogers, and Davis. In my view, this chapter is by far the weakest in the volume. It is only six pages long, yet it attempts to deal with Berkouwer, one of the subtlest thinkers in theology, plus two others who are also worthy of far more consideration. In general, I agree with Geisler's negative evaluation of the views of these men; yet I am embarrassed by the way in which this evaluation is defended.

Geisler begins by informing us that Berkouwer changed his view of Scripture after reading Karl Barth, and that since Barth was influenced by Kierkegaard, therefore Berkouwer is influenced by Kierkegaard (p. 231). This sort of argument should alert us to the deep ambiguities in the concept of "influence." Even if we grant that Berkouwer changed his view after reading Barth, and even if we grant (by no means the same thing) that he changed his view *as a result of* reading Barth, we may in no way conclude that Berkouwer is a Barthian. Doubtless anyone who reads Barth carefully and reflectively will come away from this experience asking new questions, seeking new terminology, formulating his view of Scripture differently. Any such reader will be "influenced" by Barth in a sense, but will not necessarily be a Barthian; he may in fact be more strongly opposed to Barth than before. My own view is that although Berkouwer's second book on Barth was far more sympathetic than the first, it still included some severe criticism. And though there are many inadequacies in Berkouwer's *Holy Scripture*, these are not very well explained as the result of Barthian influence. There is in that book some terminology reminiscent of Barth (Scripture as "witness," as "taken into service"); but the overall thrust of the book is only obscured by assimilating it to Barthianism, let alone to Kierkegaard.

Then Geisler links Berkouwer to Hume, of all people, because Berkouwer criticizes "supernaturalistic" and "miraculous" accounts of inspiration (p. 232). In fact, anyone with the slightest understanding of Berkouwer knows that he does not have any general prejudice against the supernatural, and the Humean arguments play no role in his thinking whatsoever. Berkouwer does not doubt the virgin birth or the feeding of the five thousand or the resurrection. He is, however, reluctant to describe biblical inspiration as a miracle because, in his view, Scripture does not at all downplay the "natural" role of the human authors in the writing of biblical books. I think Berkouwer is somewhat confused here (his own account of the nature of miracle in *The Providence of God* would have turned him in a more useful direction). But the thing to note is that Berkouwer's argument is a *theological* argument, an *exegetical* one. Geisler's point about Hume is entirely irrelevant. Here, compare my prefatory comment 2 at the beginning of this review. Geisler seems to ignore the possibility that Berkouwer's construction has any "roots" other than the philosophical roots he has uncovered. But in ignoring the theological motivations of Berkouwer, he robs his argument of all force.

Then Geisler tells us that Berkouwer denies verbal inspiration (p. 232), ignoring all the discussion in Berkouwer on the ambiguities of the concept (*Holy Scripture*, 156–61, and passim). He quotes Berkouwer's denial that Paul taught "timeless propositions concerning womanhood" (p. 233) and concludes from this that Berkouwer denied the divine authority of Paul's utterance. Then he tells us that Berkouwer "retreats to both a relativistic and an intentionalistic view of truth," evidently finding him insufficiently in tune with "metaphysical realism." In all of this, he ignores all of Berkouwer's subtle distinctions and all the difficulties we mentioned earlier that complicate the question of metaphysical realism.

Most of the rest of the Epilogue is similarly objectionable. There is no evidence of careful analysis, no recognition of important distinctions, no anticipation of objections to Geisler's evaluations. He treats all three subjects as if they were mere philosophers, ignoring their theological and exegetical arguments, the arguments upon which these men themselves put the most weight.

Geisler is a well-trained philosopher and a zealous Christian. But this Epilogue certainly does not do him justice.

I recommend the book, therefore, with much reservation. Buy it for the essays that introduce you to important modern philosophers. But don't regard it as an adequate account of biblical epistemology or as a definitive critique of errantism. Use it to shatter errantism's pretense of "obviousness" and to chart the sad effects of the principle of rational autonomy.

NO SCRIPTURE, NO CHRIST[1]

Note: This article is one of my earliest formulations of the doctrine of Scripture (1972). It focuses on the concept of the *necessity* of Scripture and therefore supplements chapter 30 of the present book.

Why is it so important to believe in an inspired, infallible, inerrant Bible? Because of Jesus Christ.

We are not here making the usual point about the relation between Christ and Scripture. The usual point is that Christ endorsed the authority of the Old Testament and endorsed in advance the authority of the New. That point is perfectly valid (cf. Matt. 5:17–19; John 5:45–47; 10:33–36; 14:26; 15:26f.; 16:13); but we are now making a different one, namely, that unless we have a fully authoritative Scripture, it is meaningless for us to confess Christ as Lord and Savior.

I. CHRIST THE LORD

What does it mean to confess Christ as Lord? Among other things, it means confessing ourselves to be servants. In the Bible, the servant is one who has no claim upon the Lord God. He knows that his Lord owns (Ps. 24:1) and controls (Eph. 1:11) all things, and therefore owes

1. This article was originally published in *Synapse* II 1, 1 (January 1972). It was reprinted in *Guardian* (January 1979): 10–11. Used by permission. For stylistic purposes, this appendix has been copyedited for inclusion in this volume.

no goods or services to anyone (Deut. 10:14–17). He owes nothing—and has a right to demand everything. The servant has no claim upon God, but God has an absolute claim upon him. Absolute, that is, in three senses: (1) It is a claim that cannot be questioned. The Lord God has a right to demand unwavering, unflinching obedience. God blesses Abraham because he "obeyed my voice, and kept my charge, my commandments, my statutes, and my laws" (Gen. 26:5 KJV). He did not waver (Rom. 4:20), even when God commanded the sacrifice of Abraham's son Isaac (Gen. 22:18). To waver would have been sin. (2) The claim of the Lord is absolute also in the sense that it transcends all other claims, all other loyalties. The Lord God will not tolerate competition; he demands exclusive loyalty. The servant must love the Lord with all his heart, soul, and strength (Deut. 6:5; cf. Matt. 22:37). One cannot serve two masters (Matt. 6:22ff.). In the NT, Jesus Christ demands—and receives—precisely this kind of loyalty from his followers (Matt. 8:19–22; 10:37; 19:16–30; Phil. 3:8). The Lord demands first place. (3) The claim of God is therefore also absolute in the sense that it governs all areas of life. Whatsoever we do, even eating and drinking, must be done to the glory of God (1 Cor. 10:31; cf. Rom. 14:23; 2 Cor. 10:5; Col. 3:17). There may be no compartments in our lives where the Lord is left out, where he is forbidden to exercise his authority.

II. CHRIST THE SAVIOR

Even if we were not sinners, we would still have a Lord; we are called to be servants of God simply because we are his creatures. But in fact, we are not only creatures but also sinners. We need not only a Lord, but also a Savior; we need not only authority, but also forgiveness for disobeying that authority (Rom. 3:23; 1 John 3:4). Scripture tells us that Jesus Christ, the eternal Son of God, died on the cross to save his people from their sins (Rom. 5:8). But how can we know that this is enough? We know because God has told us. Who else could pronounce our sins to be forgiven? Who else could promise salvation to those who believe in Christ? The Lord, who speaks to demand obedience, also speaks to promise salvation. He who speaks the law speaks also the gospel. As Abraham (Rom. 4:19f.), we are called to believe the gospel simply because it is God's own promise. We know that believers are saved because Jesus has told us they are (John 5:24). Only the Lord can speak the word of forgiveness, the word that declares sinners to be righteous, the word that promises eternal life.

III. CHRIST THE AUTHOR OF SCRIPTURE

But where can we find such a word? Where can we find a word that makes an absolute claim upon us and makes an absolute promise of forgiveness? We must have it, or there is no hope. We must have it; else we have no knowledge of our Lord's demand or our Savior's forgiveness. Without such a word, truly we have no Lord, and we have no Savior.

Liberal or neoorthodox theologians can provide no such word. They know of no words in our experience that can demand unquestioning obedience, transcend all other claims, govern all areas of human life. They know of no words that can unambiguously communicate the "sure promise of God." Where, then, can we go? Others suggest that God gives each of us a private, individual revelation; but those who make that suggestion differ widely on what God has in fact said. If they are all right, then God contradicts himself frequently. What test is there to determine when God is in fact speaking and when he is not? How do we distinguish the voice of God from the voices of devils and the imaginations of our hearts?

The God of the Bible directs his people to a book. To be sure, he does speak to some men individually—Abraham, Moses, Isaiah, Paul—but he instructs his people as a whole to find his will in a book.

When God first led his people out of bondage in Egypt, he gave them a book (Ex. 24:12). It was a book that he had written himself; the words of the book were his own words (31:18; 32:16). Indeed, he permitted Moses to help with the writing (34:27); but the authority of those written words was a divine authority, not a mere human authority (Deut. 4:1–8; 5:29–33; 6:4–25; Pss. 19; 119; Matt. 5:17–20; John 5:45–47). Later, others wrote books at God's behest, completing what we know as the Old Testament—books that Jesus endorsed both in word (above, second paragraph) and in deed (for Jesus submitted himself entirely to Scripture, living in such a way "that the Scripture may be fulfilled"). The NT church turned to those books as the definitive transcript of God's law and promise. The books of the OT were "God-breathed" (2 Tim. 3:16, literal translation)—that is, words actually spoken by God. Also, these early Christians came to recognize further writings, the writings of apostles and others, as having the same sort of divine authority as the OT (1 Cor. 14:37; 2 Thess. 3:14; 2 Peter 3:16). It is to such divine writings that the believer must turn to avoid confusion (2 Tim. 3; 2 Peter 1:12–2:22). It is those writings that pronounce the word of supreme authority and certain forgiveness. It is those writings that utter God's absolute claim and his sure promise, his law and his gospel. It is those writings by which he speaks to us as Lord and Savior.

Without such a word, there can be neither lordship nor salvation. Without such a word, we have no basis for confessing Christ as Lord and Savior. Lordship and Saviorhood, without authoritative Scripture, are meaningless concepts. That is why the authority of Scripture is so important. That is why we cannot say that we love Christ while disowning the Bible (cf. John 14:15, 21, 23; 15:10; 1 John 5:3).

And that is why, when we present the gospel, we must present it as a word of authority and sure promise—a word that demands precedence over all other words, a word that will not be judged by the criteria of modern philosophy and science, but that demands the authority to judge all the thoughts of men (John 12:48–50). To present it as anything less is to detract from the very lordship of Christ and from the greatness of his salvation. As our Lord and Savior, Christ is the author of Scripture.

Appendix O

IN DEFENSE OF SOMETHING CLOSE TO BIBLICISM: REFLECTIONS ON *SOLA SCRIPTURA* AND HISTORY IN THEOLOGICAL METHOD[1]

Note: In this essay, I formulate and defend important aspects of *sola Scriptura* and their relevance to theology. It grows out of my earlier discussion with Richard Muller, published here as Appendix C. This essay supplements chapter 5 of this volume on revelation and history, chapter 32 on the sufficiency of Scripture, and chapter 37 on theological method.

Over the years I have sometimes engaged in playful banter with colleagues concerning the relative importance of church history and systematic theology. In these arguments, I was, of course, on the side of systematics, mocking the tendency of many of us academics to magnify the importance of our own fields of specialization. That was, of course, all in the spirit of good fun. I think that fair readers of my *DKG* will grant that I have a high regard for church historians and the contributions they can make toward our understanding of God's Word. Indeed, I tend rather to stand in awe of scholars in that field. My impression, which I have, of course, never tried to verify, is that writers in that discipline have typically mastered far more data and organized it more impressively than most of those (including myself) in the fields of systematics and apologetics.

---

1. This article is reprinted from *WTJ* 59 (1997): 269–318, and is used with permission. For stylistic purposes, this appendix has been copyedited for inclusion in this volume.

Nevertheless, I do believe that the present situation in evangelical and Reformed theology demands a more careful look at the relationships between the disciplines of history and systematic theology. The need is such that the playful banter will now have to give way, for a moment, to a more serious consideration of the issues.

I am here writing primarily to the orthodox Reformed community of theological scholarship that I inhabit. For that reason I will give little attention to some options that are important to the general theological community but not specifically to those addressed here. I recognize, of course, the importance for Reformed scholars to address the broader society, and I hope this essay will, among other things, enable us to do that better. But sometimes we must huddle together to think about what we should be saying to the larger world, before we actually say it.

My overall purpose here is to reiterate the Reformation doctrine of *sola Scriptura*, the doctrine that Scripture alone gives us ultimate norms for doctrine and life, and to apply that doctrine to the work of theology itself, including both historical and systematic disciplines. That point may seem obvious to many of us, but I am convinced that there are applications of this doctrine that need to be reemphasized in the present situation.

1. HISTORY

The term *history* can be used in both objective and subjective senses. Objectively, it refers to the actual facts of past time, or to that portion of them that is significant for human beings. Subjectively, it refers to human recollections, descriptions, interpretations, and reconstructions of those facts. In that subjective category, this article will consider especially the historical disciplines that contribute to the work of theology: history of the ancient Near East, church history, and history of doctrine.

Systematic theology is that discipline that "seeks to apply Scripture *as a whole*."[2] In my understanding, it is perspectivally related to exegetical theology (which focuses on individual passages) and biblical theology (which focuses on the historical-narrative aspects of the biblical text, on Scripture as a history of redemption).[3] By *perspectivally* I mean that these three disciplines examine the same subject matter with different foci or emphasis, rather than examining three different subject matters. All three examine the totality of the biblical revelation, and all three aim to make

2. *DKG*, 212.
3. Ibid., 206–12.

significant applications of that revelation to our doctrine and life. The question before us concerns the relation between *systematic theology*, so defined, and *historical theology*, which in my definition "applies the Word to the church's past for the sake of the church's present edification."[4]

Since Scripture, and the biblical way of salvation, is profoundly historical, theology must always be interested in history. Hence the important discipline of redemptive history (biblical theology). Other forms of historical study are also important: the history of the ancient Near East, the history of the church, the general history of mankind. The history of the biblical period enables us far better to understand the Scriptures, and the postbiblical history helps us far better to apply the Word to our own times. The latter helps us both to avoid the mistakes of the past and to build on the foundations laid by those who have gone before.

Nevertheless, history-oriented theologies have sometimes been snares and delusions for the church. This has happened whenever theologians have adopted an autonomous[5] historical method and have replaced biblical authority with history in the subjective sense as the ultimate theological norm. This happened in the late nineteenth century when, on the one hand, the Ritschlians and, on the other, the History of Religions School sought through historical study to overcome Gotthold Ephraim Lessing's "big, ugly ditch" between history and faith. Albrecht Ritschl sought to return to the historical Jesus by way of Martin Luther and the Reformation (a twofold use of historical science). But Cornelius Van Til says of his effort:

> Ritschl therefore cannot be said to have overcome the mysticism and the rationalism that he sought to overcome by his appeal to the historic Jesus. His "historic Jesus" is an utterly ambiguous figure. To the extent that he is said to be known, he is nothing more than another human personality. To the extent that he is more than human personality, that is to the extent that he is God, he is nothing but the projected ideal of would-be autonomous man, and is therefore wholly unknown.[6]

Ritschl's historical method is the method of secular historiography, which begins with the assumption that Scripture is a merely human book and that its truth is subject to the assessment of merely human criteria. The

---

4. Ibid., 310.

5. An autonomous historical method is one that is not itself subject to the ultimate authority of Scripture.

6. Cornelius Van Til, *The Triumph of Grace* (Philadelphia: Westminster Theological Seminary, 1958), 64.

result is an account in which Jesus is a mere man. Ritschl does, of course, go on to say that Jesus is divine in a sense, because as we encounter this man in history we come to value him as God. But to do this, says Van Til, is to make Jesus subject to our standards of evaluation and thus to deny his deity altogether.

The History of Religions School, of which Ernst Troeltsch was the systematic theologian, adopted historical relativism as its central concept, so that its adherents denied the uniqueness of Christianity among the religions of the world. As with Ritschl, these thinkers evaluated biblical history according to the standards of one kind of secular historical science.

The influential currents of twentieth-century theology have tried to restore some positive significance to the idea of revelation in history. The chief concept of Karl Barth's theology was *Geschichte*, history in its fullest revelational meaning. But Barth failed to locate *Geschichte* in calendar time and concrete historical space, creating more confusion than ever about "what actually happened" and how those happenings were related to human salvation.

Oscar Cullmann, C. H. Dodd, G. Ernest Wright, and others seized upon J. A. Bengel's concept of *Heilsgeschichte* and sought to present Scripture as "the book of the acts of God." For them, revelation was in event, rather than word, and therefore, importantly, "historical." Unlike Barth, Cullmann emphasized this history taking place along a timeline. Revelation occurred when a historical event was perceived by faith. But the declaration that only event, never word, could function as revelation was plainly unbiblical, as demonstrated by many, such as the liberal scholar James Barr.[7] And that proposition is incapable of any other defense except one that presupposes rational autonomy, the disease of the older liberalism that these thinkers sought to overcome.

Nevertheless, many influential recent theologians, such as Jürgen Moltmann, Wolfhart Pannenberg, and the theologians of liberation, have sought to make "history" the unique locus of revelation: history, again, as opposed to word. For Pannenberg especially, revelatory history is discovered by the criteria of secular rationality, by autonomous reflection not itself subject to the revelation.

Now, I presume that these particular history-centered approaches are not live options for orthodox Reformed theologians; hence my relatively brief treatment of them. It should at least be plain from our survey that an emphasis on "history" is not sufficient to justify a theological method. It is important also to ask what history means to the theolo-

---

7. James Barr, *Old and New in Interpretation* (London: SCM Press, 1966).

gians in question, whether they are right about the relation of history to revelation, and how they justify their descriptions, interpretations, and evaluations of history. And we should answer those questions in ways that are consistent with Scripture itself.[8] Therefore, Scripture, not a concept of history developed independently of Scripture, must be the ultimate standard in theology generally and, indeed, in the formulation of a theological method.

2. BIBLICISM

The term *biblicism* is usually derogatory. It is commonly applied to the views of (1) someone who has no appreciation for the importance of extrabiblical truth in theology, who denies the value of general or natural revelation, (2) those suspected of believing that Scripture is a "textbook" of science, or philosophy, politics, ethics, economics, aesthetics, church government, and so forth, (3) those who have no respect for confessions, creeds, and past theologians, who insist on ignoring these and going back to the Bible to build up their doctrinal formulations from scratch, (4) those who employ a "proof-texting" method, rather than trying to see Scripture texts in their historical, cultural, logical, and literary contexts.

I wish to disavow biblicism in these senses. Nevertheless, I also want to indicate how difficult it is to draw the line between these biblicisms and an authentic Reformation doctrine of *sola Scriptura*. Consider, first, that (1) *sola Scriptura* is the doctrine that Scripture, and only Scripture, has the final word on everything, all our doctrine, and all our life. Thus, it has the final word even on our interpretation of Scripture, even in our theological method.

It is common to draw a sharp line between the interpretation of Scripture and the use of Scripture to guide us in matters of philosophy, politics, economics, and so on. This is sometimes described as a line between finding *meaning* and making *application*. I have elsewhere given reasons for questioning the sharpness of this distinction.[9] For now, let me simply point out that neither interpretation nor application is a mere reading of Scripture. In both cases, the scholar asks questions of the text and answers them using some scriptural and some extrascriptural data. This activity

---

8. To do this, of course, is to introduce a kind of circularity into our process of thought: Scripture must judge our way of reading Scripture. But circularity of a kind is inevitable when we are seeking to justify our ultimate standard of truth and falsity. I have dealt with this question most recently in *CVT*, 299–309.

9. *DKG*, 81–85, 93–98, 140.

takes place even at the most fundamental levels of Bible interpretation: the study of words and syntax, the work of translation, the attempt to paraphrase. So what we call *interpretation* is a species of application: in it, scholars ask their own questions of the text and apply the text to those questions. Questions of Bible interpretation and questions of, say, Christian political theory are, of course, different in their subject matter, though there is some overlap. And the questions of interpretation certainly precede the questions of, for example, application to contemporary politics in any well-ordered study. Even so, sometimes our conclusions about politics present analogies applicable to other fields and therefore of broader hermeneutical significance. Thus, conclusions about politics can in some ways be "prior to" hermeneutics as well as the other way around, illustrating further the broad circularity of the theological enterprise. But my main point here is that both types of study involve asking contemporary questions of the text, and thus they are usefully grouped together under the general category of application. In both types of cases, we apply Scripture to extrascriptural questions and data.

There is therefore an epistemological unity among all the different forms of Christian reflection. In all cases we address extrascriptural data, and in all cases we consider that data under the *sola Scriptura* principle. That principle applies to Christian politics as much as to the doctrine of justification. In both cases, Scripture, and Scripture alone, provides the ultimate norms for our analysis and evaluation of the problematic data before us.

It is important both to distinguish and to recognize the important relations between Scripture itself and the extrascriptural data to which we seek to apply biblical principles. Scripture is something different from extrabiblical data. But what we know of the extrabiblical data we know by scriptural principles, scriptural norms, the permission of Scripture. In one sense, then, all our knowledge is scriptural knowledge. In everything we know, we know Scripture. To confess anything as true is to acknowledge a biblical requirement upon us. In that sense, although there is extrabiblical *data*, there is no extrabiblical *knowledge*. All knowledge is knowledge of what Scripture requires of us.

At this point, we may well be suspected of biblicism, for the biblicist, as we have seen, also disparages extrabiblical knowledge. But unlike the biblicist, we have recognized the importance of extrabiblical *data* in the work of theology and in all Christian reflection.

Which brings us to (2) among the distinctives of biblicism: From a viewpoint governed by *sola Scriptura*, the "scope"[10] of Scripture, the range

---

10. Or *scopus*, if you prefer.

of subject matter to which it may be applied, is unlimited. As Van Til says, there is a sense in which Scripture "speaks of everything":

> We do not mean that it speaks of football games, or atoms, etc., directly, but we do mean that it speaks of everything either directly or indirectly. It tells us not only of the Christ and his work but it also tells us who God is and whence the universe has come. It gives us a philosophy of history as well as history. Moreover, the information on these subjects is woven into an inextricable whole. It is only if you reject the Bible as the Word of God that you can separate its so-called religious and moral instruction from what it says, e.g., about the physical universe.[11]

Here we hear Abraham Kuyper's claim that all areas of human thought and life must bow before the Word of God. We also begin to smell the odor of biblicism: Scripture speaks of football games, atoms, cosmology, philosophy. But there is a difference. Van Til is not saying that Scripture is a "textbook" of all these matters. Hence his distinction between "direct" and "indirect." Nor did Van Til deny, as biblicists have sometimes been accused of doing, that Scripture is a "centered" book. As a faithful disciple of Geerhardus Vos, he understood that Scripture is concerned to tell a particular "story," the story of God's redemption of his people through Jesus. The direct/ indirect distinction should be taken to make this point as well: that Christ is central to the biblical message in a way that football games and atoms are not. But like the biblicist, Van Til believed that every human thought must be answerable to God's word in Scripture. To many, this affirmation will sound biblicistic in the present context of theological discussion.

Distinctive (3) of biblicism raises the question of the relation between Scripture and the traditions of the church. *Sola Scriptura* has historically been a powerful housecleaning tool. By this principle the Reformers gained the freedom to question the deliverances of popes, synods, and councils, as well as those of learned and respected past theologians. They did respect tradition, particularly the early fathers and Augustine. But what was distinctive about the Reformation was its differences, rather than its continuities, with the past.

Certainly, the Reformers did not, however, try to rebuild the faith from the ground up. They saw themselves as reforming, not rejecting, the teachings of their church. They saw the Protestant churches not as new churches, but as the old church purified of works-righteousness, sacerdotalism, papal

---

11. Cornelius Van Til, *The Defense of the Faith* (Philadelphia: Presbyterian and Reformed, 1963), 8.

tyranny, and the idolatry of the Mass. So they were not biblicists in that sense (3). But they came close to it. In present-day Roman Catholic criticism of *sola Scriptura*, we are reminded of how close Protestantism does come to biblicism on this score.

Sola Scriptura actually provides support to theology against (4), the last kind of biblicism. For it places the *whole* Bible as authority over any specific exegetical proposal. Hence *Scriptura ipsius interpres*. This demands attention to contexts, narrow and remote. For an interpretation falsified by a relevant context is not an interpretation of *Scriptura*. Interpretations must also be consistent with what we know about the literary genres and historical backgrounds of the texts under consideration. Thus, as we saw under (1), theology requires consideration of extrabiblical data. This is not so that we can be in line with secular fashions of thought. Quite the opposite: we do this to learn the true meaning of the Bible and thus to be accountable to it.

But for all this attention to contexts both scriptural and extrascriptural, *sola Scriptura* also demands that theological proposals be accountable to Scripture in a specific way. It is not enough for theologians to claim that an idea is biblical; they must be prepared to show in Scripture where that idea can be found. The idea may be based on a general principle rather than a specific text; but a principle is not general unless it is first particular, unless that principle can be shown to be exemplified in particular texts. So a theology worth its salt must always be prepared to show specifically where in Scripture its ideas come from. And showing that always boils down in the final analysis to citations of particular texts. This is why, for all that can be said about the abuses of proof-texting, proof texts have played a large role in the history of Protestant thought. And there is something very right about that.

I conclude that although Protestant theology under the *sola Scriptura* principle is not biblicistic, it is not always easy to distinguish it from biblicism. We should expect that those who hold an authentic view of *sola Scriptura* will sometimes be confused with biblicists. Indeed, if we are not occasionally accused of biblicism, we should be concerned about the accuracy of our teaching in this area.

3. *SOLA SCRIPTURA* AT WESTMINSTER

Born out of the fundamentalist-modernist controversy, Westminster Theological Seminary (both Philadelphia and California campuses) has always sought above all to deliver to its students "the whole counsel of

God." It has remained firm on the doctrine of biblical inerrancy while other evangelicals have wavered, without falling into hermeneutical naiveté. The seminary has published four faculty symposia over its history, and all four of them have dealt in some way with biblical authority, sufficiency, and interpretation.[12]

Not only has the seminary taught an authentic Reformation theology of Scripture, but it has shown a particular zeal about teaching Scripture to its students. Westminster has emphasized the teaching of original biblical languages when such an emphasis has fallen into disfavor among evangelicals. It has provided very thorough instruction in the various parts of Scripture, and in the disciplines of exegetical, biblical, and systematic theology. In homiletics, it has stressed the use of biblical theology and, in general, the responsibility of the preacher to preach not himself but the Word. In apologetics and Christian philosophy, it has continued Van Til's emphasis that Scripture has the right to rule every area of human thought and life.

But it is John Murray's view of method in systematic theology that I would consider at greater length. Murray taught at Westminster from 1930 to 1966 and left an indelible imprint upon the seminary. In his article "Systematic Theology,"[13] Murray reviews the history of dogmatics, mentioning names such as Athanasius, Augustine, and John Calvin.[14] He then comments:

> However epochal have been the advances made at certain periods and however great the contributions of particular men we may not suppose that theological construction ever reaches definitive finality. There is the danger of a stagnant traditionalism and we must be alert to this danger, on the one hand, as to that of discarding our historical moorings, on the other.[15]

He cites Calvin's own encounter with "stagnant traditionalism," when the Reformer dared to take issue with the view of Athanasius and others that the Son of God "*derived* his deity from the Father and that the Son was not therefore "αὐτόθεος."[16] He continues:

---

12. Paul Woolley and Ned Bernard Stonehouse, eds., *The Infallible Word* (Grand Rapids: Eerdmans, 1946); John H. Skilton, ed., *Scripture and Confession* (Nutley, NJ: Presbyterian and Reformed, 1973); Harvie M. Conn, ed., *Inerrancy and Hermeneutic* (Grand Rapids: Baker, 1988); William S. Barker and W. Robert Godfrey, eds., *Theonomy: A Reformed Critique* (Grand Rapids: Zondervan, 1990).
13. In *Collected Writings of John Murray* (Edinburgh: Banner of Truth, 1982), 4:1–21.
14. Ibid., 5.
15. Ibid., 7–8.
16. Ibid., 8.

> When any generation is content to rely upon its theological heri-
> tage and refuses to explore for itself the riches of divine revelation,
> then declension is already under way and heterodoxy will be the lot
> of the succeeding generation. . . . A theology that does not build
> on the past ignores our debt to history and naively overlooks the
> fact that the present is conditioned by history. A theology that
> relies on the past evades the demands of the present.[17]

Murray here recognizes the importance of church history in the work of
systematic theology, but he cautions us not to remain content with even
the best formulations of past theologians. For the rest of the article, Murray drops the subject of historical theology entirely and focuses on the
centrality of exegesis and biblical theology to the work of systematics.[18]
Murray's actual theological writing consists almost entirely of the exegesis
of particular texts: the proof texts of the doctrines under consideration.

There have been Reformed theologians (Berkouwer is the example
that comes most readily to mind) who construct their theological writings as dialogue with past and contemporary theological texts. In these
theologies, Scripture plays an important role, to be sure; but the exegesis
is often somewhat sketchy and often seems like an addendum to the
pages of historical analysis. Murray avoided that model of theology very
self-consciously.

I remember many years ago helping to collate the results of a survey
of Westminster alumni about the teaching they had received in seminary. One alumnus regretted that Westminster did not have any "real
systematic theology." In his view, Murray's courses were not true systematics courses, but mere courses in exegesis. I disagree radically with that
alumnus's evaluation of Murray, but I grant that the alumnus observed a
genuine and important difference between Murray's teaching and other
systematic theologians.

My own observation as a student was that Murray's approach was a
wonderful breath of fresh air, despite his often opaque, archaic language
and his insistence on the students' reproducing his lectures nearly verbatim on examinations. My fundamentalist friends at college criticized
Reformed thinkers for relying on their traditions rather than the Bible.
Murray showed me that the Reformed faith was purely and simply the

---

17. Ibid., 8–9.
18. Compare B. B. Warfield, who in "The Idea of Systematic Theology," in *Studies in
Theology* (Grand Rapids: Baker, 1981), spoke of the relationship of systematics to historical
theology as "far less close" than its relation to exegetical theology (p. 65). Note also his
remarks about tradition on page 101.

teaching of Scripture. Thus, he presented Reformed doctrine in the way most persuasive to Christian minds and hearts. This is the proper answer to anyone who considers Murray's method to be biblicistic.

In short, a Westminster education trained students to ask first of all, about any subject matter whatever, what Scripture had to say about it. And it prepared students to expect Scripture to address every possible question in one way or another.

4. WESTMINSTER'S THEOLOGICAL CREATIVITY

The notion that Scripture addresses, to some extent, every important human question produced at Westminster a high quality of theological creativity. We often associate orthodoxy with stagnancy and traditionalism. But at Westminster, the commitment to *sola Scriptura* propelled it in the opposite direction.

I have mentioned the independence of Murray's theology. He self-consciously followed the example of Calvin's struggle for the αὐτόθεος—"A theology that relies on the past evades the demands of the present." And so Murray's theology impresses the reader both with its faithfulness to Scripture and with the independence and creativity of its formulations.

The same is even more obviously true with the thought of Cornelius Van Til: strongly insistent upon biblical authority and sufficiency, boldly innovative in epistemology, in apologetics, and even in some theological formulations. Other examples, too, are not difficult to find, such as the redemptive-historical emphasis of R. B. Kuiper, Ned Stonehouse, Edmund Clowney, Meredith Kline, and Richard Gaffin, building on the work of Geerhardus Vos. I should mention also the nouthetic counseling of Jay Adams, building on the insight that Scripture has much to say about human problems, and that indeed it contains all the ultimate norms for resolving them.

Even Westminster's teaching of church history has been creative. I remember Paul Woolley as a brilliant and urbane teacher, more like a Princeton professor than were any of his Westminster colleagues. We joked that Woolley was living proof that one need not have a PhD to know everything. His independence of mind was legendary: in faculty meetings and church courts, he was often a minority of one, and it was rare that anybody could guess in advance on which side Woolley would come down. As a teacher, he had a rare ability (very much like that of J. Gresham Machen) to get inside the skins of historical figures whose ideas were very different from his own. Most of us emerged from his classes convinced that the Reformed way was best. But if we paid attention, we could not avoid a genuine sympathy for those in other traditions.

At times the creativity of Westminster has been problematic. Theonomy, for example, is certainly a child of Westminster. Its founder, Rousas J. Rushdoony, has seen himself as applying Van Til's insights to the areas of politics, economics, and social ethics. Both Gary North and the late Greg Bahnsen studied at Westminster. The two Westminster seminaries have not been hospitable to theonomy,[19] but the movement has certainly introduced some new approaches in the use of Scripture and has challenged Reformed scholars to take more seriously the legal elements of God's Word.

I will not speak of Norman Shepherd's rethinking of the doctrine of justification, or of the "multiperspectivalism" of John Frame and Vern Poythress, concerning which different readers will have different opinions, except to say that in these cases as well, students of the early Westminster faculty were moved to reconsider traditional ideas by going back to Scripture. The important thing is that this creativity has not been at the expense of *sola Scriptura*; it has not been a movement away from Scripture to accommodate secular modes of thought, even though that is what *creativity* usually means in a theological context. Rather, as was the case with the first Protestant Reformers, it has been a creativity motivated by Scripture itself.

One might also raise questions concerning the relative absence at Westminster (again, I think mainly of the early 1960s when I was a student) of a confessional or traditional focus. I must be careful here in my formulation. But I felt as a student that we were being stimulated to originality more than we were being indoctrinated into a tradition. That may be a surprising comment, and I must immediately qualify it. All professors subscribed ex animo to the Westminster Confession and Catechisms, and the subscription formula was more detailed and forceful than most ordination vows in Presbyterian denominations. Our professors loved the great teachers of past ages: Augustine, Luther, Calvin, and the many others since their time. But Westminster was independent of denominational control, and students came from many denominational backgrounds, Reformed and non-Reformed. Students were not expected to subscribe to Reformed doctrine in order to matriculate or to graduate. There was, in my experience, an atmosphere of openness. We were encouraged to ask hard questions, and our professors generally sympathized with the questions, if not with our answers.

19. See Barker and Godfrey, *Theonomy*.

During my student years, I was never asked to read any of the Reformed confessions, or Calvin's *Institutes*, except in small bits. I never read any official standards of church government or discipline, not to mention Robert's Rules of Order. We used Charles Hodge and Louis Berkhof in our systematics classes, but for the most part we were graded not on our reading but on our knowledge of Murray's lectures. After graduation I became ordained in the Orthodox Presbyterian Church, and I confess that I was rather surprised at the seriousness with which my fellow ministers took the confessional standards and Presbyterian traditions. Eventually I became more like my fellow Orthodox Presbyterian (and later Presbyterian Church in America) elders, but not without some nostalgia for the openness of theological discussion during my seminary years.

It is legitimate to criticize this openness in some respects. In my own theology courses, I always assign relevant portions of the confessions, and I try to make sure that every student understands the traditional formulations, even when I seek to improve on them. Surely one important function of a seminary is to perpetuate and recommend the confessional traditions. Students seeking to be ordained in Reformed churches must understand fully what they are being asked to subscribe to. The Westminster of the early 1960s did not do a thorough enough job in that aspect of its teaching; I do believe it has improved since that time.

But as an academic theological community, seeking to encourage students how to do careful and hard thinking about theological issues, Westminster of the early 1960s was superb. I was not entirely ready for the Orthodox Presbyterian Church, but I was more than ready to do graduate study at Yale. Some students, I think, responded to this combination of freedom and orthodoxy in the wrong way: by taking the original insights of, say, Van Til, Kline, or Adams and trying to make them tests of orthodoxy.[20] But that was, I think, more the fault of the students than of the professors. Clearly, at any rate, Westminster's particular understanding of *sola Scriptura* did not lead to a stagnant traditionalism, but to a flourishing of original and impressive theological thought.

5. SOME EPISTEMOLOGICAL OBSERVATIONS

Westminster's use of *sola Scriptura* in theology is quite inescapable if we understand correctly the relationship between norm and fact in human

---

20. Compare my observations on the "movement mentality" among some of Van Til's followers in my *CVT*, 8–14, 17–18, passim.

knowledge. A description of church historical facts does not in itself tell us what we ought to believe. In and of itself, description does not determine prescription; *is* does not imply *ought*. To suppose that it does has been called the *naturalistic fallacy*. To assume that the historical genesis of an idea determines the proper evaluation of it is called the *genetic fallacy*. To avoid these fallacies, our formulations of doctrines must always appeal to something beyond church history, to the biblical norm.

It is this insistence that distinguishes the Protestant *sola Scriptura* from the Roman Catholic view of tradition. And indeed, this principle itself is ultimately based on scriptural warrant. For Scripture itself condemns any appeal to tradition that places that tradition on the same level of authority as itself (Isa. 29:13; Matt. 15:8–9; Mark 7:6–7; Col. 2:22).

6. *SOLA SCRIPTURA* AND EVANGELICAL INTELLECTUALISM

Protestantism at its best has typically avoided opposing *sola Scriptura* to human reason as such. Reason is the God-given faculty that applies the norms of Scripture to the data of experience.[21] Therefore, the Reformers saw no conflict between *sola Scriptura* and high standards of scholarship. Luther and Calvin were scholars, and their theological distinctives were the result of careful scholarly exegesis. Indeed, in Protestantism to some extent even worship emulated the model of academic teaching. Huldrych Zwingli excluded music entirely from the worship of the church in Zurich, and made the church service into a teaching meeting. For this he has been accused of rationalism.[22] His policy was not followed by other Reformers, but there was among leaders of the Reformed churches a very cautious attitude about music. Following Book Three of Plato's *Republic*, they recognized a great emotional power in music that could, if not tightly controlled, elicit unruly emotions and lead the worshipers away from the pure teaching of the Word. The early Reformed churches excluded musical instruments, and many excluded most hymns other than psalm settings. There were theological reasons for these decisions,[23] but the net

21. I am not here defining reason, but rather describing one of its important functions in theology.

22. See Klaas Runia, "The Reformed Liturgy in the Dutch Tradition," in *Worship: Adoration and Action*, ed. D. A. Carson (Grand Rapids: Baker, 1993), 99; Carlos M. N. Eire, *War against the Idols* (Cambridge: Cambridge University Press, 1988).

23. Reasons that I have discussed and rejected in *Worship in Spirit and Truth* (Phillipsburg, NJ: P&R Publishing, 1996), chap. 11.

effect of them was to make worship much more an intellectual than an aesthetic experience.

Some Reformed scholars argued for the "primacy of the intellect," the doctrine that the intellect does or should unilaterally rule the will, emotions, and other aspects of human personality.[24] I reject this concept as well as the academic model of worship, and therefore I believe that Protestants have carried their intellectualism rather too far.

More serious, however, was the later modernist appeal to academic standards as a justification for the virtual abandonment of biblical authority. The theological modernists thought that a consistent respect for the intellect required them to accept the conclusions of the latest university scholarship. Protestantism affirms reason; why should it not accept the conclusions of recognized scholarship?

A proper answer to that question requires a distinction between the intellect itself and the norms that the intellect must follow in reaching its conclusions. Calvin affirmed the intellect, but he believed that the intellect should operate in subjection to the norms of God's Word. The modernists substituted for those norms the norms of secular scholarship, particularly the historical disciplines. As Van Til emphasized, the intellect, like a buzz saw, can function very well while pointing in the wrong direction. To make the right cut, not only must the saw turn efficiently; it must also be governed by a norm that points it the right way.

American evangelicalism inherited many of the ideas of the Reformers, but also many Anabaptist, Pietist, and Arminian influences. At times it produced notable scholarship, but it also went through some periods in which anti-intellectualism was dominant, particularly in the period following the infamous Scopes trial. Following the Second World War, however, Carl F. H. Henry, Harold John Ockenga, J. Howard Pew, Billy Graham, and others sought to lay foundations for a "new" evangelicalism more hospitable to serious scholarship and compassionate social action. The new evangelical intellectuals, however, repeated the mistake of earlier Protestants by failing to face squarely the question of intellectual *norms*. They rejected the apologetic of Van Til, who insisted on the rule of Scripture in all human thought, and sought in various ways and degrees to find common ground with unbelief. I believe this uncritical intellectualism paved the way for the rejection of biblical inerrancy by many evangelicals in the 1960s. For many of those evangelicals, a serious commitment to rationality demanded acceptance of the norms of critical biblical scholarship. Few even asked the question whether Scripture itself contained its own norms for scholarship,

24. I have criticized this notion in Gordon Clark and Van Til in my *CVT*, 141–49.

different from and opposed to those of the negative critics. So the sometimes sharp difference between evangelical and liberal scholarship has since the 1960s become a blur.

One breath of fresh air during this period, however, came from Francis Schaeffer and his followers, such as Os Guinness, Udo Middelmann, Ranald Macaulay, Jerram Barrs, and David Wells. They affirmed biblical inerrancy and insisted, like Schaeffer's teacher Van Til, that there was a sharp antithesis between those who believed in the biblical God and those who thought the universe was merely matter, motion, time, and chance. The latter position, they argued, destroyed all meaning and intelligibility. These writers argued their position learnedly and graciously, earning a wide readership and a position of respect, though not dominance, within evangelicalism.

These writers present a theology with real backbone, standing up courageously against secular thought and the secularizing movements within evangelicalism. But some difficulties remain. I cannot find in this literature any clear affirmation that Scripture contains its own distinctive epistemological norms, different from those of secular thought. Schaeffer, indeed, gave the impression that the secular philosophers of Greece affirmed an adequate concept of truth—"true truth" or "objective truth"—which was lost only in the wake of Georg Hegel's dialecticism. And the Schaeffer apologetic focused to some extent upon "objective truth" as an abstraction, rather than that distinctive kind of truth, that divine Word, that is identical with Jesus himself. To that extent, the Schaeffer movement also has not been fully consistent with the Reformation *sola Scriptura*.

7. EVANGELICAL CRITIQUE OF CULTURE

David Wells has expressed his debt to Francis Schaeffer, and the title of his *No Place for Truth* reminds us of Schaeffer's emphasis on "true truth." He reminds us of Schaeffer also in his conviction that the "modern" era is very different from previous times and therefore presents unique temptations to the church. Evangelicals, he thinks, have fallen prey to those temptations, to such an extent that God's truth no longer rules in the churches.[25]

In Wells' analysis, modernity has fostered a new way of thinking, which he characterizes in various ways, including:

25. Compare Schaeffer's alarms about the "Great Evangelical Disaster," in his book of that title (Westchester, IL: Crossway, 1984). To him, the disaster was particularly the evangelical compromise of biblical inerrancy. The focus of Wells' attention is somewhat different.

1. Subjectivism: basing one's life upon human experience rather than upon objective truth.[26]
2. Psychological therapy as the way to deal with human needs.[27]
3. A preoccupation with "professionalism,"[28] especially business management and marketing techniques as the model for achieving any kind of common enterprise.[29]
4. Consumerism: the notion that we must always give people what they want or what they can be induced to buy.[30]
5. Pragmatism: the view that results are the ultimate justification for any idea or action.[31]

The effects of this mentality on the church, according to Wells, have been entirely detrimental. ("This book is insistently antimodern," he says.[32]) Because of the influence of modernity, theology no longer rules in the church.[33] Therefore, God himself becomes unimportant, "weightless," in Wells' memorable term.[34] Although the church believes in God's existence, his existence makes no difference to the church's practical decision-making. God becomes "user-friendly," not the holy, transcendent, awesome God of Scripture.

Therefore, says Wells, theology no longer governs the church in any meaningful way.[35] Sermons don't seek to set forth God's Word, but baptized equivalents of the latest cultural preoccupations ("felt needs"): psychic well-being, success in marriage, and so on.[36] Theories of church growth and the practice of "megachurches" substitute management and marketing theory for biblical principle, and view congregations the same way businesses regard consumers of their products. So churches cater to the wants of people rather than to their true spiritual needs. Seminaries aspire to become professional schools, training ministers in these worldly values and skills.[37]

26. David F. Wells, *No Place for Truth* (Grand Rapids: Eerdmans, 1993), 118, 142, 172, 174, 264, 268, 278, 280, and many other places; *God in the Wasteland* (Grand Rapids: Eerdmans, 1994), 101–11.
27. *Wasteland*, 61, 77–84, 115, 153, 176, 202.
28. *No Place*, 218–57.
29. Ibid., 60–87.
30. Ibid., 63–87, 100.
31. Ibid., 67.
32. Ibid., 11.
33. Ibid., 218–57.
34. *Wasteland*, 88–117.
35. *No Place*, 95–136; *Wasteland*, 186–213.
36. *No Place*, 250–57; *Wasteland*, 149–51.
37. *No Place*, 113–15.

Wells' books are wonderfully erudite and eloquently written. And there is much truth, certainly, in his indictment of evangelicals as individuals and as churches. Some, however, have criticized his position as one-sided. Marva Dawn says:

> Wells' passion for truth needs to be balanced with an equally immense passion for love. He does indeed caution us appropriately to avoid an overly simplistic acceptance of technology that does not recognize the values of the attendant milieu. Moreover, he rightly bemoans the loss of biblical fidelity, which reduces the gospel's subversive power. However, his remarks do not seem to contain enough concern for how that truth can be communicated to the modern generation, which has no context for receiving it. The Church needs careful creativity to find the best means for promulgating the truth and educative processes by which we can train the uninitiated in habits for cherishing it. Unfortunately, many books that emphasize the pole of love within the dialectic discuss reaching the world outside the Church only in terms of marketing strategy.

Dawn's comments raise the important question of how we can achieve such a balance in our critique of culture and of the church.[38]

There is a remarkable irony about Wells' two books. On the one hand, his main theme is that theology should play a much larger role in the church's thinking, practice, evangelism, and worship. On the other hand, there is very little theology in either *No Place for Truth* or *God in the Wasteland*. There are a few theological observations, mostly about the transcendence of God, the importance of history, revelation, and eschatology.[39] But Wells' primary tools in these books are the disciplines of history and sociology. Through them, he discerns a process of change in American life over the last two hundred years, and he is able to trace changes in the church over the same period. Thus, he is able to define the "modern" mentality and show how the church has capitulated to it.

What is the alternative? Here Wells does not go much beyond the negative point that we must reject the modern mentality. Although he does not quite say this, the structure of his argument strongly suggests that we ought to go back to the traditions of the church as they existed before the modern mentality took over. *No Place* begins with a very long discussion of the history of Wenham, Massachusetts: how it changed over two hundred

38. Marva Dawn, *Reaching Out without Dumbing Down* (Grand Rapids: Eerdmans, 1995), 60–61.

39. *No Place*, 270–82; *Wasteland*, 118–85.

years. He titles the chapter, nostalgically, "A Delicious Paradise Lost."[40] Doubtless he would not advocate that we merely turn back the clock. But the only guidance he gives us is that the old was better. Thus, he gives aid and comfort to the most immovable traditionalists, and no help at all to the "reformers."

Or perhaps what he really wants us to do is to develop a strategy for present-day ministry by a "way of negation": everything the modern marketers do, we will do the opposite. So the Wellsian church becomes a kind of mirror image of the marketer-consumer church: an exact reversal. But what is the opposite of consumerism? Giving no thought at all to the nature of the community to which one seeks to minister? Surely that is not what Wells would have us do. So mere negation is not much help. And as we know, mirror images retain many of the characteristics of the realities they reflect. That should at least give us pause.

As Dawn says, there is imbalance in Wells' books. But the more fundamental problem is that of his *method*. A plea for the primacy of theology must itself, surely, be theologically grounded, not grounded merely in history or sociology. And surely our methods of evangelism and principles of worship must be based on Scripture, indeed *sola Scriptura*. Now, of course, scriptural principles must be applied to situations, and to understand the situation it is legitimate to consider data from history, sociology, and other sciences. But Scripture alone provides the ultimate norms for evaluating these data. So far as I can see, Wells never actually tries to formulate biblical principles of evangelism, church planting, or worship, nor does he call our attention to other writings in which this work has been done. Rather, he somewhat oddly tries to derive these principles from his historical-sociological analysis itself, together with some broad concepts of divine transcendence and the like. Thus the reader is pushed toward either a blind traditionalism or a mirror-image reconstruction.

Simply opposing the modern model at every point is an entirely inadequate approach. I say that for *theological* reasons. I certainly wish to be counted among those whose thoughts and actions are based on principle, not pragmatism. But I confess to finding myself, on the basis of biblical principle itself, very often siding with those who are considered pragmatists rather than with those who are regarded as the most principled among us.[41] The fact is that when we seriously turn to Scripture for guidance, that guidance usually turns out to be more complex, more nuanced, than

40. *No Place*, 17–52.

41. We may recall that Jesus himself was considered something of a pragmatist, compared to the Pharisees, who proclaimed their allegiance to divine principle, but who in fact placed their tradition above God's Word. See, e.g., Matt 15:1–9.

anything we would come up with ourselves. Scriptural principle, typically, also leaves more room for freedom than man-made principles do, and as we saw earlier, it gives more encouragement to our creativity. Certainly, scriptural principle is more complex than any mere negation of existing cultural trends.

For one thing, Scripture itself does not merely negate the cultural trends of its time. It is true to say that in the Bible there is an antithesis between the wisdom of God and the wisdom of the world (1 Cor. 1–3), and between the church and the world (John 17:9–25; James 1:27; 4:4; 1 John 2:15–19). But Scripture never derives from this antithesis the conclusion that all our beliefs and actions must be opposite to those of the world. Unbelievers do know truth, although they suppress it (Rom. 1); so they can sometimes even teach God's truth with some accuracy (Matt. 23:1–4). And the church's missionaries must adopt at least some elements of the cultures they seek to reach with the gospel.[42] Says the apostle Paul:

> Though I am free and belong to no man, I make myself a slave to everyone, to win as many as possible. To the Jews I became like a Jew, to win the Jews. To those under the law I became like one under the law (though I myself am not under the law), so as to win those under the law. To those not having the law I became like one not having the law (though I am not free from God's law but am under Christ's law), so as to win those not having the law. To the weak I became weak, to win the weak. I have become all things to all men so that by all possible means I might save some. (1 Cor. 9:19–22 NIV)

There are, in other words, some areas in which Christians may and should be like those to whom they preach, so that their witness may be more effective. Obvious instances are speaking the language of one's community and observing to some extent the local customs in food and clothing. The same principle, according to the above passage, applies to some kinds of moral scruples. For example, Paul may have observed the Mosaic dietary laws when in the company of Jews, but not when in the company of Gentiles.

This flexibility is not religious compromise. Paul did not disobey God when he behaved sometimes as a Jew, sometimes as a Gentile. It was God's own Word, indeed, that gave him the freedom to behave either way. This is not relativism. There were many areas in which Paul did not have such freedom, many forms of worldly behavior that he plainly condemned (as Gal. 5:19–21). But there were also significant areas of freedom. And Paul's

---

42. For a full discussion of *antithesis*, see my *CVT*, chap. 15.

judgments as to where he was free and where bound were based not on any autonomous analysis of culture, but on the Word of God.

So let us think about our own time. Does Scripture condemn all "marketing" techniques in setting forth the gospel? Well, that depends on what is meant by marketing techniques. Certainly, there are similarities between selling and preaching. (To say that is, of course, to say very little: everything is similar to everything else in one respect or other!) Both activities convey information. Both seek to elicit a commitment. Both require a speaker to attract the attention of his audience. If marketing techniques are simply rules for clear communication, vivid ways of attracting attention and motivating commitment, then they should certainly be taught to preachers.

Does this analysis neglect divine sovereignty? I think not. Salvation is entirely by divine grace, and God needs no human help to draw sinners to Jesus. But God has freely chosen to use human means to accomplish this task, in most cases (Matt. 28:18–20; Rom. 10:14–15; 1 Cor. 1:21). As in other aspects of salvation, there is in evangelism both divine sovereignty and human responsibility. We must preach and teach.

But to preach and teach requires effort. We must speak clearly and persuasively, in order to reproduce the clarity and persuasiveness of the gospel itself. So we must learn rules for gospel communication just as a seller must learn techniques for communicating the virtues of his product. Many of those techniques are valid for all forms of communication. So it is not impossible to imagine that we might learn something of value from secular marketing theorists.

Now, of course, there are also many respects in which evangelism is different from marketing. The church's "product" is very different, eternally urgent, the ultimate in divine blessing. Our approach to communication should reflect the solemnity and holiness of our God. It should reflect our own willingness to humble ourselves in order to exalt the Lord. In these respects, we leave the secular marketing world far behind.[43]

Sometimes, then, we would do well to learn from the marketers, sometimes not. When marketers tell us that it is unwise to fill an auditorium beyond 80 percent of its capacity, we do well to listen, though we must never put such advice on a par with God's Word. Scripture never says that we must fill our buildings to the point of standing room before going to two Sunday morning services or two assemblies or a larger facility. So there is nothing wrong in taking the marketers' advice in the absence of more important considerations. But if marketers tell us that we must avoid the

---

43. Although this sort of self-abasing servant attitude deserves to be a model for Christians even in the marketing field!

subject of sin in order to keep the seekers comfortable, we must at that point disagree in the sharpest terms, for biblical principle is then at stake.

Is it wrong for preachers to address "felt needs" as an opening to preach the gospel? Well, many felt needs today are genuine spiritual needs, according to Scripture. People want to know how to make marriages work; the Bible answers that need (Eph. 5:22–33). People want to know how to avoid anxiety; Scripture addresses that concern (Phil. 4:6–7). Why should preachers not address these topics and answer them through the riches of the gospel of Jesus Christ? Of course, many other felt needs (the "need" for health, wealth, self-esteem, etc.) are either ambiguous or condemned by Scripture. Nevertheless, even these—with their scriptural evaluations—should be the subjects of preaching.

So biblical worship and evangelism should not be viewed as simple negations of every element of an unbelieving culture. Rather, there should be a discerning use of the elements of culture, governed by the values of God's Word.

Consider also the content of the church's preaching. Should the church's preaching focus on the objective rather than the subjective, on God and history rather than our response, on objective truth rather than human experience, as Wells argues? Here I tend to be more sympathetic with Wells than I have been in the preceding paragraphs, because I do believe that in general, preaching today needs to place a greater emphasis on the objective.

But again Wells misses nuances. In theory of knowledge, it is wrong to force a choice between object (what one knows) and subject (the knower). All knowledge involves both: you don't have knowledge unless you have both a subject and an object.[44] Therefore, Scripture records the objective truth of God and redemption; but it also records the experiences by which the biblical writers came to know these objective facts. And indeed there is in Scripture much teaching about believing subjectivity. The psalms are full of "I" and "we," full of personal testimonies about how God has entered human experience. We learn much in Scripture about our emotional life: about joy, fear, anxiety, peace, anger, erotic passion, and so on.

And there is a subjective side to salvation itself. The objective side is that Christ, the Son of God, lived a perfect human life, died for the sins of his people, rose from the dead, and ascended into heaven. The subjective side is that when he died for sin, we died to sin (Rom. 6:1–14) and rose with Christ to newness of life. God not only atones, but regenerates. We are new creatures (2 Cor. 5:17), partakers of Christ's abundant life (John 10:10).

44. And also, thirdly, a norm or standard. See my *DKG*.

Preaching, in Scripture, does not merely present the objective truths of the history of redemption. It also responds to those truths in a personal way, giving testimony of what God has done in the life of the preacher and what he can do in the lives of the hearers. The psalms are full of such testimony, as are the letters and sermons of Paul. And biblical preaching calls for its hearers to respond to it, both inwardly and outwardly. Biblical repentance is a change of heart that brings change in behavior, and it is a crucial goal of preaching (Acts 2:38–39).

Wells therefore loses credibility when he bases so much of his case on historical and sociological analysis, without giving substantial attention to the biblical values that must judge the culture. For one thing, our time is probably not much better or worse than past ages, contrary to Wells' Schaefferian rhetoric about the uniqueness of modernity. But in any case, we are to address culture today in the same way Paul addressed the culture of the first century: by the Word of God, communicated by all scripturally legitimate means available in the culture.

8. CONFESSIONALISM

The recent Cambridge Declaration of the Alliance of Confessing Evangelicals[45] seeks to recommend to the evangelical churches a renewed confessionalism. It is organized around the great *solas* of the Protestant Reformation: Scripture, Christ, grace, faith, and glory to God. Many emphases of this document are welcome and greatly needed. Naturally, I am pleased that the first article reaffirms *sola Scriptura* and follows the sentence: "These truths we affirm not because of their role in our traditions, but because we believe that they are central to the Bible."

The document is recognizably Wellsian. In the *sola Scriptura* section, we read, "Therapeutic technique, marketing strategies, and the beat of the entertainment world often have far more to say about what the church wants, how it functions and what it offers, than does the Word of God." The discussion goes on to say that in these and other areas to which Wells has given attention, the church should turn to Scripture, rather than the culture, for its message. True enough. But as in Wells' books, I believe that more needs to be said. The attempt of churches to learn from therapists, marketers, and consumers is not, in my mind, motivated by unbelief pure and simple. If lack of faith is one factor, there is also the motive of seeking to reach out to the world, to apply scriptural principles in a way that

---

45. I am working from a photocopied version without publication data.

is relevant to the present world and communicable to the unchurched. The strengths and weaknesses of this document are similar, then, to the strengths and weaknesses of Wells' own writings.

Positively, the document recommends a return to the attitudes and convictions of an earlier time:

> The faithfulness of the evangelical church in the past contrasts sharply with its unfaithfulness in the present. Earlier in this century, evangelical churches sustained a remarkable missionary endeavor, and built many religious institutions to serve the cause of biblical truth and Christ's kingdom. That was a time when Christian behavior and expectations were markedly different from those in the culture. Today they often are not. The evangelical world today is losing its biblical fidelity, moral compass and missionary zeal.[46]

The last sentence is surely true, but the rest of the paragraph seems rather naive in its assessment of evangelical Christianity in the early twentieth century. The missionary movement of those days was a wonderful thing in many ways, but as it was aided and abetted by the imperialism of the Western nations, it was not entirely countercultural, nor was it unambiguously righteous. The document, like Wells' books, calls us back to a nostalgia for a past age. That, in my view, is a frail reed. It also calls us back to a greater fidelity to Scripture. That is a strong element in the document. But it needs to be spelled out in detail: what does Scripture say about missions, church growth, marketing, as opposed to the notions prevalent in our culture today? We need a document that gives us positive guidance, rather than merely negating present trends.

I certainly favor a renewed confessionalism if it means a better appreciation for the teaching of the Reformation *solas*, indeed for the distinctive teachings of the Reformed faith. The argument of this paper, however, should help us to guard against certain abuses of the confessionalist position, such as (1) emphasizing confessions and traditions as if they were equal to Scripture in authority, (2) equating *sola Scriptura* with acceptance of confessional traditions,[47] (3) automatic suspicion of any ideas that come from sources outside the tradition, (4) focusing on historical polemics rather than the dangers of the present day, (5) emphasizing differences with other confessional traditions to the virtual exclusion of recognizing

---

46. Cambridge Declaration, 5.
47. Actually, as I have argued, it would be more accurate to derive from this principle a critical stance toward traditions.

commonalities,[48] and (6) failing to encourage self-criticism within our particular denominational, theological, and confessional communities.

A reaffirmation of confessionalism for our time ought to repudiate the commonly understood equation between confessionalism and traditionalism. It should rather reiterate a doctrine of *sola Scriptura* like that of Westminster at its best: one that will encourage careful thinking about the movements of our time rather than overstated condemnations and that will discourage romantic notions about past ages. A doctrine of *sola Scriptura* must actually, practically, point us to Scripture itself, rather than generalizations about historical trends, for our standards.

9. CONCLUSIONS

In a number of ways we can improve on Wells' analysis by a more consistent application of *sola Scriptura*: We can see more fully the ways in which modern culture has strayed from God's path but also understand how to use certain elements of that culture with God's blessing. *Sola Scriptura*, which is often perceived as a narrowing, limiting doctrine, actually opens our vision to behold a greater complexity in modern culture than we would otherwise recognize. And it is a *liberating* doctrine in the sense that it gives us greater freedom than any mere traditionalism or *via negationis* could provide. At the same time, it sets forth true restrictions on the use of culture with greater clarity and gives us direction to avoid the traps of the modernists and the evangelical accommodationists.

Westminster's emphasis on *sola Scriptura*, therefore, provides us with a powerful tool for the critical analysis of culture, one rarely found elsewhere in evangelical scholarship. It guards us against both secularism and traditionalism. We would be wise to stress this principle continually, neither compromising it nor forgetting to apply it to every matter of controversy.

Scripture, therefore, must be primary in relation to history, sociology, or any other science. It is Scripture that supplies the norms of these sciences and that governs their proper starting points, methods, and conclusions.[49]

48. For more observations on this subject, see my *ER*, now out of print. It is still available at http://www.frame-poythress.org/frame_books.htm.

49. This paper will serve as my reply to Richard Muller's "The Study of Theology Revisited: A Response to John Frame," *WTJ* 56 (Fall 1994): 409–17. I have not engaged Muller's arguments specifically, but then, he did not engage mine either. But his response leaves me still with the impression that his theological method, in order to avoid some aspects of hermeneutical circularity, gives priority to neutral or autonomous historical study over the methodological principles of Scripture itself.

> *Note (2010)*: In the original publication of this paper in the *WTJ*, Richard Muller and David Wells published replies. Below is my response to them.

REPLY TO RICHARD MULLER AND DAVID WELLS

I do thank Muller and Wells for participating in this discussion. I will examine their replies in alphabetical order.

Muller's position is quite straightforward: "Whereas *sola Scriptura* must be the doctrinal watchword in all matters of faith and life, it does not stand as a principle that can be applied to historiography."[50] On this point, he and I simply hold opposite views. I do think there is much truth in his analysis of the use of history to support heresy. He says that people who use history in this way are not in fact autonomous or neutral, but are themselves operating on theological assumptions. I agree, although these writers typically do make *claims* to neutrality. But that fact raises the question whether there is such a thing as historiography that is theologically neutral.[51]

Muller thinks such neutrality is not only possible, but normative: "Historiography ought not to be grounded in theological assumptions" (p. 311). He does accept that "historiography does have assumptions and presuppositions," but he tends to think that "they are minimal and belong to the realm of common sense rather than to the realm either of theological or philosophical system" (ibid.). He encourages a historical method that elicits "the meaning of texts with as little *tendenz* as possible" (ibid.).

But I keep asking, what does Muller do with the central biblical and Reformed claim that God's Word is to rule all areas of human life? If "all things" are to be done to the glory of God, does that include historiography, or does it not? And if not, why not? Muller himself says that "*sola Scriptura* must be the doctrinal watchword in all matters of faith and life" (ibid.). How can he then turn around in the very next clause and say that it does not apply to historiography? Surely historiography is part of life, something we do either to the glory of God or in the service of an idol.

50. Quoted in John M. Frame, "Reply to Richard Muller and David Wells," *WTJ* 59, 2 (Fall 1997): 311. The article spans pages 311–18.
51. For present purposes, I will use *autonomy* and *neutrality* as synonyms, and I will define this pair of terms as "acting without being subject to ultimate norms." Ultimate norms are norms that make an unconditional demand upon one's beliefs or actions, norms that cannot be negated by any higher principle. For Christians, the teachings of Scripture have such normative character, but of course there are competing claims to normativity. In my view, there is no neutrality or autonomy so defined; there are only claims to it. Those claims are false because in fact everybody always serves either God or an idol.

Perhaps he is putting a special emphasis on the word *doctrinal*, as if Scripture were a doctrinal watchword, but not, perhaps, a methodological watchword. But if doctrine bears on all of life, then surely it bears on methodology as part of life. We do today sometimes speak of "doctrine" as a discipline focused on the subject matter of church confessions, but Scripture itself does not limit the scope of its authority to any particular area of life. If we are to speak of doctrine in a biblical way, there is surely a sense in which it applies to everything.

This is not, of course, to say that Scripture gives us detailed instructions for repairing cars or drilling teeth. As in the passage I quoted from Van Til, "We do not mean that [Scripture] speaks of football games, or atoms, etc., directly, but we do mean that it speaks of everything . . . It is only if you reject the Bible as the Word of God that you can separate its so-called religious and moral instruction from what it says, e.g., about the physical universe."[52]

Surely there is something primal, something utterly basic, about our confession that God is Lord of *all* areas of human life. Certainly, Muller has heard that principle over and over again from the pulpit. Can he not see that there is at least a prima facie discrepancy between that confession and the distinctions he is trying to make? Knowing from his writings the depth of Muller's Christian commitment, I find it very hard to believe that he really wants to advocate autonomy over against God's lordship expressed in Scripture. Perhaps he can find some way to reconcile his position with that fundamental principle, but in his writing so far he does not even seem to have grasped the problem.

Now, I know it sounds a little crazy, especially in the present theological climate, to say that Scripture is the sufficient and ultimate rule for historiography. To say such a thing may seem to put us in the same boat with those who, say, advocate "biblical" recipes for bread, or who find in the Bible mysterious codes predicting events of modern history. But I thought that in my essay I had made the necessary qualifications. Scripture doesn't tell us what texts of Calvin's writings are most authentic, or in what year Luther was born. Yes, there is plenty of room for "reason." But Scripture is the *ultimate* norm, the norm over which none other takes precedence. And as the ultimate norm, it is sufficient; we need no more ultimate norms.

---

52. Van Til, *The Defense of the Faith*, 8. This point is very important in the current theological climate. Some evangelicals have taken the position that biblical inerrancy pertains only to its teaching about salvation, not to its teaching about anything else. Scripture itself, in my view, does not limit its authority in any such way, and the distinction itself breaks down upon analysis. But if biblical authority and inerrancy have unlimited scope, surely Scripture's sufficiency also applies to all areas of life.

Muller describes his position loosely as Thomistic. But even Thomas Aquinas, for all his zeal to distinguish the realms of faith and natural reason, admitted that Scripture had, at least, a veto power over the assertions of reason. Aristotle had argued that the world was eternal. Thomas felt the force of that argument, but he rejected it, primarily because its conclusion was contrary to Christian faith. Surely we must say at least that much about the relation of Scripture to historical method. David Hume's view of how to evaluate historical evidence is subject to many kinds of objections; but surely a Christian cannot ignore the fact that his view is unscriptural. If Hume were right, we could never accept testimony for any supernatural event. Muller himself, in effect, employs a biblical veto against the historiography of D. F. Strauss, Ritschl, Adolf von Harnack, and the modern advocates of "discontinuity," for he considers them theologically biased, and he rejects their particular bias, presumably because of its unscripturality.[53] (I assume he agrees at least that theological biases must be dealt with theologically.) But those theological biases are an integral part of the Ritschlian historical method. Therefore, Muller ought to agree with me that Scripture is relevant, at least in this respect, to the evaluation of historical methodology.

Does Scripture say anything positive about historiography, or does it merely claim veto power? Well, it couldn't very easily have veto power without having some positive content to impose over against unscriptural alternatives. In the case of Aquinas mentioned above, the positive content was the biblical teaching that the world had a beginning. In the case of historiography, we should be able to agree that Scripture presents a narrative of historical events that the historian has no right to question. It also presents, in Van Til's terms, "a philosophy of history as well as history."[54] It asserts that history is not a series of irrational, chance happenings, but a meaningful, teleological sequence governed by divine providence. It tells us that the human race is not getting better and better through the progress of civilization, refuting some of the more optimistic overviews of history.

And I believe that Scripture also provides us with a general epistemology, again in broad outline rather than detail. I have described this epistemology at great length in my *DKG*. It is, of course, an epistemology centered on God's word (in nature and Scripture) and on the illuminating work

53. This point is, of course, not the heart of his critique of such NT scholarship. His main point is to argue that their *tendenz* has led them into defective arguments and conclusions. But if their *tendenz* were correct, then we would have to regard their arguments much more positively. Muller's critique, certainly, assumes that Ritschl's *tendenz* is wrong. If that assumption is correct, it is a biblical assumption, and it is essential to Muller's case.

54. Van Til, *The Defense of the Faith*, 8.

of the Spirit. In Scripture, God tells us what knowledge is: thinking his thoughts after him. And Scripture distinguishes wisdom from foolishness, truth from falsity, right from wrong. It also aids our judgments of what is possible and probable, leading us to adopt standards very different from those of Hume, Strauss, Ritschl, Bultmann, and the Jesus Seminar. Historical claims must be judged, ultimately, by these principles. When we write history, we must ask in every case whether our assertion is wisdom, or whether it is foolishness in God's sight. Thus, whatever we believe, we believe by the permission of Scripture.

I have noted Muller's exception at this point. He replies with the example that he doesn't understand his computer software program by biblical principles and norms. I reply: (1) it is by biblical principles that you know that this is a rational world suitable for computing. If the biblical worldview weren't true, there would be no point to computing at all. (2) If Scripture told you to abandon your beliefs about the software, you would abandon them, for you are a Christian. And you would also abandon them if Scripture yielded epistemological principles that forced you to abandon those beliefs. But so far as you can tell, Scripture imposes no such obstacles to your beliefs. In that sense, you hold your beliefs about the software program by the *permission* of Scripture.

Note that I said *permission*, not *commandment*, though I do believe there are many beliefs that Scripture commands us to hold. Much has been written in recent philosophical literature about the "ethics of knowledge": what we are obligated to, permitted to, forbidden to believe. The implied correlation of ethics with epistemology shows even more clearly the importance of maintaining a Christian (that is, a biblical) view of knowledge, and to assess all our beliefs by Christian criteria.

Scripture does not tell us everything we need to know about historiography, but it does tell us quite a lot, and what it does tell us is normative and important.[55] And my point is that as the corpus of *ultimate* norms for historiography, Scripture is also sufficient. We don't need, and God has not given us, any more ultimate norms. That point, so developed, does not seem at all crazy to me. In fact, it seems like a necessary application of that primal Christian insight that God is Lord of all areas of life.

Autonomous historiography, then, understood as historiography that disavows the relevance of *sola Scriptura* for its work, is excluded. Understood as activity that disavows *any* religiously significant presupposition, it is impossible.[56] For in all areas of life, we either glorify God or deny him. We

---

55. History is one of the chief concerns of Scripture, unlike recipes for bread and the like.

56. Hence the usefulness of Muller's demonstration that Ritschl and others operated on theological presuppositions. My problem with Ritschl, of course, was not that he was

serve him or an idol. There is no middle ground. Understood as a *claim* to religious neutrality in historiography, it must be dismissed as arrogance.

Why, as Christians, should we ever want to do anything autonomously? Muller defends a certain kind of autonomy in the area of historiography by saying that "the alternative is a theologically controlled method that predetermines the result of an investigation and that, therefore, never offers the wandering systematic theologian a fixed documentary point from which to critique his own expertise" (p. 314).

On my view, clearly *some* results are predetermined. I cannot, while remaining a Christian, seriously entertain the historical hypothesis that Jesus' body is still in the ground. Cornelius Van Til used to offer his students tickets on an airline to go to Palestine to look for the body of Jesus. He got no takers. But I don't see that my view requires *all* results to be predetermined. Nothing in Scripture tells me how many years Calvin spent in Strasbourg; nor does it supply premises from which I could deduce that conclusion by good and necessary consequence.[57] The question is a genuinely open one, requiring rational examination of extrascriptural data, according to the norms of a Christian epistemology. And questions remain open in systematic theology, too, until we gain assurance of what Scripture actually says.[58]

On the subject of worship, I welcome Muller's agreement that marketing is not always bad. I do not, however, believe that marketing is *adiaphora* in the sense that Scripture says nothing normative about it.[59] I rather cringe when Muller cites the maxim that Scripture is a "nose of wax" that "can be bent in all directions unless there is a confessional context within which the work of interpretation takes place" (p. 315). If he is referring to the arbitrary way in which some people read Scripture, fine; but if he is saying that Scripture itself is so amorphous as to justify such arbitrariness, I take sharp exception. I will assume that he means the former rather than the latter. I do, like Muller, advocate confessional contexts of interpretation. But in that confessional context, Scripture is not a rubbery object of communal

---

actually able to do autonomous historical research, but that he exempted himself from the principles of Scripture, only to enslave himself to a nonscriptural assumption.

57. It does, I think, supply epistemological, especially ethics-of-knowledge, principles that will lead me into the truth if the data is there and I have the ability to find it.

58. There are, of course, different levels of assurance here, and other complicating factors that I can't discuss in the limits of this reply. See *DKG*.

59. I do have some problems with the notion of *adiaphora* as such, because it can be used to circumvent the universal scope of Scripture's concern, which I have defended earlier. But certainly there are some human choices that are between two goods rather than between right and wrong, and I don't object to the term *adiaphora* being used to describe these.

molding. It is the mighty, sovereign, clear Word of the living God, given to rule the interpretative activity of God's people. And when individuals, working outside the confessional context, err in their interpretations, it is still the perfect Word of God about which they are mistaken.

As to whether Scripture is a help in resolving questions about worship, music, and church planting: I sure hope it is, or else we are really at sea. On these questions, I suggest that readers look at my *CWM*. I see this book as a serious theological work, even though it deals with a popular subject. I try there to provide an example of how *sola Scriptura* can provide us with guidance in such areas.[60]

Perhaps all this sounds to Muller like "muddle-headed Dooyeweerdianism" (p. 315). I assure him that the Dooyeweerdians gave up on me many years ago as an incurable scholastic. I, too, have been a critic of Dooyeweerd and his followers. But God has used them, and especially their patron saint Abraham Kuyper, to remind me of God's claims on all of life. We all need to hear that message over and over again.

Now Wells. He says that my "shots" at him were "wildly amiss" (p. 316), a criticism that I am willing to consider seriously. But I don't see in his reply evidence that would justify such a strong retort. His description of his work in comparison with Augustine's *City of God* was illuminating, but it was not at all inconsistent with my own conception of what he was trying to accomplish.

He disavows my description of him as a "follower" of Francis Schaeffer. In the context of the paper we are discussing, it should be obvious to the reader (and I hope it will be obvious to Wells upon reconsideration) that I meant the Schaeffer reference more as a compliment than as a criticism. I characterize Wells' work (with that of others in this general tradition) as "a breath of fresh air" and "a theology with real backbone." I described his work as "wonderfully erudite and eloquently written," and I said that "there is much truth, certainly, in his indictment of evangelicals as individuals and as churches." I would add that Wells mirrors Schaeffer in his important work of analyzing the culture to help us understand how to respond to it as Christians. In his *City of God* labors, I mean only to encourage him, and I'm disappointed that he failed to detect that encouragement in my writing.

Of course, one way in which we can encourage one another is by constructive criticism, "iron sharpening iron," and certainly there is a lot

---

60. On a few specific matters: I do agree with Muller that *a cappella* psalms can be great aesthetically, but in my experience they have usually been otherwise. As for great composers in the Reformation tradition, I love Heinrich Schütz and the others Muller cites, but it is interesting that there are no Reformed composers on this list. I still believe that the Reformed churches have yet to come to terms with their intellectualism.

of that in my essay. But we need to be clear, first of all, as to what those criticisms are. I certainly never made what Wells calls "the remarkable assertion that for me sociology and history are authoritative, rather than Scripture" (p. 316). Rather, I commended the Schaeffer-Guinness-Wells (sorry, but that was the context of the commendation) stand for biblical authority and inerrancy. What I said specifically was that sociology and history, rather than theology, were Wells' "primary tools" in the books under consideration. I also said that in this literature I could not find "any clear affirmation that Scripture contains its own distinctive epistemological norms, different from those of secular thought." Now, Wells evidently failed to understand what I meant by this criticism. It does not mean that Wells is not committed to biblical authority. Rather, and I hope my remarks to Muller will have clarified this, it means that Wells does not in these books (except in very general terms) present distinctively biblical standards for evaluating the cultural movements he discusses.

It is with some pleasant surprise that I find him endorsing a principle of mine that Muller specifically negated, namely, that all our knowledge is by the permission of Scripture. That is the kind of confession I wish had been prominently displayed in his books. And to be consistent with that confession, it seems to me that Wells should seek to apply biblical principles to the cultural data with more detail and precision than he has so far.

Which leads me to the point about traditionalism. I don't believe that I said anywhere in my essay that Wells opposes everything modern, as he claims I did.[61] I thought I was clear in saying that the object of Wells' critique is "a new way of thinking" *fostered by* "modernity."[62]

He also thinks I misunderstood his evaluation of the past: "Nowhere have I said, or even hinted, that the old is better; taken as a whole, it is simply *different*" (p. 317). Well, now: when he describes eighteenth-century Wenham as "A Delicious Paradise Lost" in the title of the first chapter of *No Place for Truth*, are we not even permitted to take that as a *hint*? And I think it should be plain to most all readers that Wells thinks the present-day evangelical church is in much worse shape than the church of two hundred years ago. Wells, of course, is the best one to describe his intentions; but his readers and reviewers must be allowed to make judgments about what he has actually communicated.

Then he says that I have been unfair to criticize in his books the balance between truth and love. He replies that with classical theology, he sees "love as an expression of holiness" (ibid.). I applaud this point theologi-

---

61. I have more to say on these topics in *CWM*.
62. See the first paragraph of the section of my paper called "Evangelical Critique of Culture."

cally and logically. But I've seen too many churches divided by theological battles in which one or more parties use theological "truth" or principles of "holiness" as clubs with which to beat others over the head. When one remarks that the offending party is not showing love, we get the reply that real love is implicit in a concern for truth. And so, presumably, it's okay to use truth as a weapon, without any sensitivity or concern for people. Truth itself is love, and so we don't need to worry about love as long as we're sure of the truth. But if that is the case, doesn't Paul's statement about "speaking the truth in love" (Eph. 4:15) become redundant?

I'm certainly not accusing Wells of holding such an attitude. But to make the logical point that holiness and truth imply love is not to solve the practical problem of the balance between truth and love in the church, or in theological writings. And I still agree with Dawn that Wells, like many of us, needs to make some progress in achieving such balance. Our present exchange has only confirmed that evaluation in my mind.

As to my complaint that he has "not actually formulated the biblical principles that should guide evangelism, church planting, and worship," Wells cites some writings of his that deal with these topics. I apologize for neglecting these. But the *City of God* series should have, I think, summarized these principles at some length, so that readers could see how they relate to his present argument.

He does tell us that "I operate from the assumption that we already have the answers to these things and we can find them within the stream of classical Reformational thinking to which we are heirs. Modernity poses no question to which the answer, in principle, has not already been conceived" (p. 317). Would I be wrong to take this as another *hint* that for Wells "the old is better"? In any case, I would be interested to get his response to my arguments for contemporaneity in worship.[63] I believe these arguments are principled, not pragmatic in any pejorative sense. And they are even based, in one sense, on the Reformation *tradition*, particularly its insistence on worship in the vernacular.

Wells also says that my essay bypasses the important questions about the relation of history to systematic theology. I certainly agree that there is far more to be said on the subject. My reply to Muller above (along with my earlier review article about his *The Study of Theology*)[64] should give some indication of how I would answer at least some of those questions. More important, it should show why I think my concept of "something close to biblicism" sets forth the most important principles, for Christians, in deal-

---

63. In *CWM*.
64. "Muller on Theology," *WTJ* 56 (1994): 133–51 (Appendix C in this volume).

ing with those issues. Clearly, as Wells says, more needs to be said about the place of redemptive history in the understanding and use of the biblical canon, but I could not presume to develop anything like a complete hermeneutic in my essay.[65] Evidently Wells and I disagree, with regard both to his books and to my essay, as to what subjects most urgently need to be addressed for an adequate treatment of the issues. The question of when an author must discuss A in order to give an adequate account of B is itself an interesting issue, but I must for the present leave that to be resolved by the reader's intuition.

As to Wells' last three paragraphs, dealing with the task of theology, he may be surprised to learn that I agree wholeheartedly. Reading between the lines, however, I gather he is saying that my "Biblicism" essay was too insular, a "retreat" into a "safe haven" or "protected enclave" (p. 318) with people such as John Murray who do theology apart from history. I would like to assure him here that if my essay represented a retreat, it was a strategic retreat, a retreat to draw provisions for the spiritual warfare of our time. Strange as it may seem to him, I still think that the approach of Murray and Van Til gives us very powerful weapons in our struggle with "modernity." These weapons are those of God himself, the whole armor of God. As much as we exchange verbal fisticuffs on the pages of theological journals, let us never forget that in that larger struggle we are on the same side.

---

65. For some thoughts on these issues, see *DKG*.

TRADITIONALISM

Note: This essay on *sola Scriptura* and traditions supplements chapters 32, 37, and 38 of the present volume. It also deals somewhat with the liberal theological tradition discussed in chapters 3–7.

One of the largest problems today in evangelical and Reformed theology is the tendency toward traditionalism. I hope in this paper to take some steps toward analyzing this danger and commending its antidote, the Reformation doctrine of *sola Scriptura*.[1]

TRADITIONALISM AND *SOLA SCRIPTURA*

Traditionalism is hard to define. It is right and proper to revere tradition, since God has raised up many teachers for his church over the years who, through their writings, continue to speak to us. A teacher in the church does not lose his authority after he dies. So God does intend for us to learn from teachers of the past, or, in other words, from tradition. On the other hand, the Protestant doctrine of *sola Scriptura* teaches us to emulate the

1. I have previously addressed these issues in my books *ER* and *CWM*, and in "In Defense of Something Close to Biblicism," published in *WTJ* 59 (1997): 269–318, with responses by Richard Muller and David Wells. The latter essay is included in this volume as Appendix O. I also participated in an e-mail debate on this and other subjects with Darryl Hart in early 1998, available at http://www.frame-poythress.org. Note also my article "A Theology of Opportunity: Sola Scriptura and the Great Commission," available at http://www.frame-poythress.org/frame_articles/1999ATheology.htm.

Reformers in testing every human tradition, even the teachings of the church's most respected teachers, by the Word of God.

Traditionalism exists where *sola Scriptura* is violated, either by adding to or by subtracting from God's Word (Deut. 4:2). To subtract from the Word is to contradict or neglect its teaching. To add to it is to give to human teaching the kind of authority that belongs to God's Word alone (Isa. 29:13–14; Matt. 15:8–9). Too great a reverence for tradition can lead to both errors.

In this article, I will focus on one way in which evangelical and Reformed theologians are tempted to add to the Word of God: by seeking to resolve substantive theological issues by reference to historical traditions, without searching the Scriptures.

This error in theological method has, of course, been characteristic of Roman Catholic theology since long before the Reformation, and it was one of the Reformers' chief complaints against the Roman magisterium. It has also been characteristic of the liberal theology of the last several centuries. For liberal theology is, almost by definition, the attempt to present the Christian message on some basis other than that of the infallible authority of Scripture.[2] Liberals use Scripture in their theological work, to be sure. But they reserve the right to disagree with it. So in the final analysis they are on their own, basing their thought on human wisdom, human tradition.

How do liberals reach theological conclusions without appealing to the ultimate authority of Scripture? It isn't easy. But essentially, the liberal appeals to Christian tradition. With some exceptions, liberals do not like to present their work as mere speculation. They want to be recognized as Christian teachers, as members of the historic theological community. So they seek to position themselves within the church's theological tradition. I will mention three ways in which they do this, using my own nomenclature:

1. *Identification*: choosing a historical or contemporary movement and endorsing it, allowing it to set standards of truth.
2. *Antithesis*: choosing a historical movement and opposing it, making it into a paradigm case of error. (Thus, the mainstream of liberal theology has typically demonized especially modern "fundamentalism" and the post-Reformation Protestant theologians.)

2. By *liberal* I refer to the whole tradition from Enlightenment rationalism to the present that currently dominates mainstream theological discussion and ministerial training in the large denominations. It includes not only the "older liberalism" of Albrecht Ritschl and Adolf von Harnack, but also neoorthodoxy, existential theology, secular theology, liberation theology, postliberalism, and other movements.

3. *Triangulation*: identifying two or more historical movements thought to be of some value, identifying weaknesses in these movements, and defining a new position that supposedly overcomes these weaknesses.[3]

When I studied at Yale in the mid-1960s, the courses labeled *systematic theology* were actually courses in the history of liberal theology since Friedrich Schleiermacher. (Theology before Schleiermacher was called *history of doctrine*.) Whatever movement the professor espoused (process theology, narrative theology, Kierkegaardian individualism, etc.) provided the "identification." Fundamentalism or Protestant orthodoxy provided the "antithesis." Triangulation was the method urged upon the students for developing their own theological perspectives. Karl Barth had too much transcendence, Rudolf Bultmann too much immanence; so the students were encouraged to go "beyond" both, to a position that did justice to the insights of Barth and Bultmann, without going to such indefensible extremes. Doing their own triangulating, some professors pointed us to the "futuristic" theologies of Jürgen Moltmann, Gustavo Gutiérrez, and Wolfhart Pannenberg, in which the future provides transcendence and the concrete movement of history provides immanence. But more importantly, students were urged to go their own way, triangulating on whatever movements inspired them, to develop their own distinctive brands of theology.

EVANGELICAL TRADITIONALISM

Evangelical scholars often study in liberal institutions, and so it is not surprising that the methods of identification, antithesis, and triangulation have also entered evangelical theology, sometimes alongside a genuine concern for *sola Scriptura*. There is, of course, nothing wrong with the three methods themselves as long as Scripture supplies the norms for evaluation. But using them without biblical norms (as in the examples of my Yale experience) amounts to theological autonomy and the loss of *sola Scriptura*.

Most theologians in the evangelical tradition do confess *sola Scriptura*. But alongside that confession has arisen an increasing emphasis on tradition.

Thirty years ago, the best-known evangelical scholars were apologists, biblical scholars, and systematic theologians (Gordon Clark, Carl F. H. Henry, E. J. Carnell, Cornelius Van Til, F. F. Bruce, J. I. Packer[4]). Today,

---

3. These three methods form a Hegelian triad of sorts.
4. Bruce and Packer were, of course, historians, too. But during the 1960s, they were better known for biblical scholarship and systematic theology, respectively.

evangelical academic leaders are largely in the field of historical theology, or they are systematic theologians who greatly emphasize church history: Donald Bloesch, Robert Godfrey, Stanley Grenz, Hendrik Hart, Michael Horton, George Marsden, Alister McGrath, Richard Muller, Mark Noll, Thomas Oden, David Wells, et al.[5]

In addition, we should note (1) the movement toward a renewed confessionalism led by the Alliance of Confessing Evangelicals, and (2) recent "conversions" of people of evangelical background to communions giving more stress to the historic traditions of the church: Anglicanism, Roman Catholicism, Eastern Orthodoxy.

What lies behind these trends? An adequate answer to that question would probably require historians of the caliber of the men listed above. But here are a few suggestions that make some sense to me.[6]

1. Evangelical Exposure to Liberal Theological Methods

The academic stars of evangelicalism are chosen, to a great extent, by the secularist-liberal academic establishment. Those whose scholarship is most admired among evangelicals are those who have earned degrees or obtained appointments at outstanding secular universities. The secular academic establishment does not, of course, reward theologians who derive their conclusions from the divine, infallible authority of Scripture. But gifted evangelicals can do well in the secular environment if they write their dissertations and phrase their conclusions in *historical* terms. One could not, for example, expect Oxford University to grant a PhD to a dissertation defending biblical inerrancy. But it is not hard to imagine such a degree being given for a thesis on the *history* of the doctrine of inerrancy, in which the writer's own evaluations are couched in the modes of identification,[7] antithesis, and triangulation.

If an evangelical doctoral candidate has a bias in favor of sixteenth-century theology instead of nineteenth or twentieth, the secular establishment will not normally consider that attitude any sort of challenge, as long as in other ways the candidate respects the methods and standards approved

---

5. Let me make clear my profound respect for these men and the quality of scholarship they have maintained. My criticisms of evangelical historicism, which may in part apply to some of these brothers, are not intended in the least to dishonor them or to belittle their achievements.

6. For those familiar with my "perspectives," the following three suggestions can be classified as situational, normative, and existential, respectively.

7. Of course, in such a context one must identify with a movement that has the approval of the liberal establishment.

by the establishment. Indeed, the candidate's advisers and readers may regard his bias as a quaint sort of antiquarianism, a charming affectation appropriate to the academic vocation.

So it has been natural for evangelicals to focus on historical studies and methods, even when seeking to give some normative support to evangelical distinctives.

That is not wrong, in my estimation. It does not necessarily entail compromise. One does what one can do in such a situation. It has been going on a long time. I recall that when the Reformed scholar John H. Gerstner taught at the liberal Pittsburgh Theological Seminary, he held the title Professor of Church History, though in my estimation most of his interests were better classified as systematic theology and apologetics. Holding his conservative beliefs, he was not invited to teach systematic theology, but he regularly taught courses in the "history of" various doctrines: biblical authority, justification, and so on. Gerstner had a tremendous influence. R. C. Sproul attributes his Ligonier Ministries to Gerstner's theological inspiration.

Though the emphasis on history can certainly be justified by the inherent value of historical studies and by the pragmatics of evangelicalism's marginal position in the academic world, there is a downside. Scholars can[8] get into the habit of using the methods of identification, antithesis, and triangulation, without taking adequate care to find biblical standards of evaluation.[9]

a. *Identification*: They may sometimes attach themselves to some movement in the past or present that they come to virtually regard as a standard of truth.[10] In Reformed circles, this tendency leads to a fervent traditionalism, in which not only the confessions, but also the extraconfessional practices of the Reformed tradition, in areas such as worship, evangelism, and pastoral care, are placed beyond question.

8. I am not saying, of course, that study in liberal institutions leads *necessarily* to these distortions. Some students have resisted these influences successfully, J. Gresham Machen being a conspicuous example. But fallen human nature being what it is, it is not surprising that some have succumbed to these temptations.

9. I have used the example of David Wells in my "In Defense of Something Close to Biblicism," cited in note 1 above. See also my comments on Richard Muller, "Muller on Theology," *WTJ* 56 (Spring 1994): 133–51, Appendix C of this book. See also comments on Hart, Marva Dawn, and others in my *CWM*.

10. Hart, in the debate cited earlier, describes Reformed tradition as a kind of *presupposition*, in the Van Tillian sense of that term. Elsewhere in the debate, he does claim belief in *sola Scriptura*, but not very credibly in view of his enormous reverence for tradition. He expresses terror of ever departing from Reformed tradition in any respect, comparing that to the terror Luther experienced at the prospect of breaking fellowship with the Roman church.

In an atmosphere of such traditionalism, it is not possible to consider further reform, beyond that accomplished in the Reformation period itself. There is no continuing reformation of the church's standards and practices by comparing them with Scripture. Thus, there is no way in which new practices, addressing needs of the present time, can be considered or evaluated theologically. This is ironic because one of the most basic convictions of the Reformed tradition itself is *sola Scriptura*, which mandates continuing reformation, *semper reformanda*. At this point, Reformed traditionalism is profoundly antitraditional.

In other circles influenced by evangelicalism, there is an identification with evangelical feminism. Paul K. Jewett's *The Ordination of Women*[11] is so strongly governed by feminist assumptions that even the authority of the apostle Paul comes under question.

b. *Antithesis*: Such scholars tend also to focus on other movements that serve as paradigms of error. In Reformed circles, these movements usually include Roman Catholicism, Arminianism, the charismatic movement, dispensationalism, and such contemporary movements as liberalism, Marxism, feminism, and "pop culture." I am not an advocate of any of these movements, and I see them as deeply flawed. But I think it is wrong to make them *paradigms* of error, so that nothing true or good can ever be found in any of them. Our world is fallen, but it is also the object of God's common and special grace. Therefore, both good and bad are to be found in all people and social institutions.[12]

But one sometimes gets the impression in reading evangelical theology that it is wrong to find any good in such movements, or even to formulate our own positions in ways that "blunt our testimony" against these movements. It is almost as though a theology cannot be genuinely Reformed unless it is "set over against" these other movements in the sharpest way.

At its worst, this method becomes a *via negativa*: we attempt to define the truth by looking at a movement we don't like and defining our own

11. Grand Rapids: Eerdmans, 1980. His later systematic theological work, *God, Creation, and Revelation: A Neo-Evangelical Theology* (Grand Rapids: Eerdmans, 1991), also affirms the feminist movement and adopts sexual egalitarianism as one of its main structural motives. See pages 13–14, 322–25, and the sermons included in the book of the Rev. Dr. Marguerite Schuster.

12. I do hold a Van Tillian view of antithesis between the church and the world, between truth and error. But Van Til himself recognized the importance of common grace, and he spoke of a "mixture of truth and error" in the thought of unbelievers. He also recognized that antithesis in the proper biblical sense requires definition on biblical standards, not on the basis of our autonomous evaluations of historical movements. See my *CVT*, especially chapter 15.

position to be the opposite of that. Thus, ironically, the false movement becomes, by logical inversion, a standard of Christian truth. Antithesis becomes a perverse form of natural theology. But surely this is wrong. We should define the Christian message positively, from the clear revelation of God's Word. I consider the *via negativa* to be fatal to the doctrine of *sola Scriptura*.

c. *Triangulation*: Or evangelical scholars trained in the methods of liberal theology may seek to develop new and fresh forms of evangelicalism by the method of triangulation. I see some evidence of this in Stanley Grenz and Roger Olson, *Twentieth-Century Theology*,[13] in which everything turns on the concepts of transcendence and immanence and the challenge to evangelicals is to seek a "balance" that Immanuel Kant, Karl Barth, Paul Tillich, and others have failed to achieve. My response: Don't seek to balance the profoundly false notions of transcendence and immanence found in liberal theology, but go back to the Bible.

I also believe that the "open theism" of Clark Pinnock, Richard Rice, David Basinger, and others is essentially a triangulation between traditional Arminianism and process theology. Arminianism doesn't adequately safeguard its own concept of free will because of its affirmation of divine foreknowledge. Process theology overcomes this problem by denying foreknowledge, but its god is so immanent that it is not clearly distinct from the world. Ergo, open theism: God is transcendent, but does not have complete knowledge of the future. It would have been better, in my view, for Pinnock and the others to look harder at Scripture.[14] A more careful look at the Bible would have led them to question the heart of their system: the libertarian view of human free will.

2. Evangelical Weariness over the Inerrancy Debate

The "battle for the Bible" has virtually defined American evangelicalism from the time of B. B. Warfield until very recently. In the early days of that period, the battle was against the liberals, who defined themselves in effect as being opposed to biblical inerrancy. In the mid-1960s, however, it became evident that some within the evangelical tradition also found

13. Downers Grove, IL: InterVarsity Press, 1992.
14. I realize that their writings do include exegetical arguments, but I find these quite implausible. Ironically, it seems to me that their exegesis falls into the error that they regularly attribute to Calvinists: their exegetical conclusions are governed by their dogmatics. For my response to open theism, see *DG* and *NOG*.

it difficult to affirm biblical inerrancy, and the battle raged within the evangelical movement as well as with those outside. The International Council on Biblical Inerrancy held conferences and published a great many writings on the subject, before it disbanded. It remains to be seen where this discussion has led the evangelical movement.

Since inerrancy was often mentioned as the doctrine that defined evangelicalism over against its Protestant liberal rivals, the questioning of inerrancy within evangelicalism led to a profound identity crisis. The "limited" or "partial" inerrantists were not liberals; they were supernaturalists who held to the traditional "fundamentals" (virgin birth, miracles, blood atonement, physical resurrection, second coming) *except for* biblical inerrancy. But with such a deep rift on a central matter, how was the evangelical family to stay together?

There were different answers to this question among evangelicals. Some inerrantists simply read their opponents out of the movement. Others tried to recognize the remaining common ground, along with the differences. Questions of inerrancy sometimes, at least, resolved into questions of interpretation (e.g., the question whether Genesis 1 teaches a temporal sequence of divine creation in twenty-four-hour days), and increasing realization of that fact led some on either side to see the issue as something other than black-and-white. And there was a *rapprochement* from the far side as well: scholars from the liberal tradition were taking the Bible more seriously and coming to more conservative conclusions on historical and dogmatic questions. Thus, the gap between evangelicals and liberals narrowed, appearing in some cases to be a continuum rather than an antithesis.

With these developments came a weariness with the inerrancy debate. Today there is far less interest, even among those committed to a strong view of inerrancy, in proving the Bible right about every matter of history, geography, and science than there was twenty years ago. Further, some have sensed a need for a common-ground methodology that will enable inerrantists, limited-inerrancy evangelicals, and liberals to work together without constantly arguing the detailed accuracy of the biblical texts.

That methodology is essentially the methodology of historical scholarship. When Wolfhart Pannenberg, coming from the liberal tradition, declared the necessity of verifying all theological statements by (religiously neutral) historical scholarship, many evangelicals applauded.[15] They perceived this dictum as vindicating their evidential apologetic. And in effect,

---

15. For reasons *not* to applaud religious neutrality in apologetics, history, and theology, see my *AGG* and *CVT*. See also the above-mentioned articles, "Muller on Theology" and "In Defense of Something Close to Biblicism." By *religiously neutral* I mean scholarship in which the ultimate standards of truth are found somewhere other than Scripture.

many evangelicals of different convictions about inerrancy, and many liberals of different stripes, are now working together to develop theology on this model.

But a theology based on religiously neutral historical scholarship must find its standards of truth elsewhere than Scripture. And so the methods of this kind of theology tend to be the methods of identity, antithesis, and triangulation discussed earlier in this paper, rather than any direct and detailed appeal to biblical texts.

3. Evangelical Shame over Past Parochialism

Evangelicals have in this century often been called to reexamine themselves. Carl Henry's *The Uneasy Conscience of American Fundamentalism*[16] chastised evangelicals for their poor scholarship and their withdrawal from issues of social justice. The "new" evangelicalism of the postwar period tried to reconstruct fundamentalism along the lines suggested by Henry and others. In the debate over inerrancy from around 1967–1990, again the very nature of evangelicalism was up for discussion.

Meanwhile, other evangelicals found their tradition wanting in its lack of any sense of the great traditions of the church. Evangelicalism, it seemed, was not well connected to the roots of Christendom: the church fathers, Augustine, the fathers of the Eastern church, the great liturgical traditions of Catholicism and Protestantism. This was connected with the feeling that evangelicalism was liturgically inadequate: too simplistic, without a sense of transcendence or depth, aesthetically inane, culturally parochial. Some evangelicals studied carefully the traditions of the broader church, and some of them defected to church bodies that are not generally considered evangelical: Anglicanism, Roman Catholicism, Eastern Orthodoxy.

Others have remained within evangelical churches, but have urged upon their denominations a greater respect for broader Christian traditions. I applaud this development as a symptom of a reawakening of biblical ecumenism.[17] But insofar as this movement represents a weakening of the *sola Scriptura* principle, I fear that its ultimate thrust will be antiecumenical, for it will forfeit the only firm basis for a reunion of the church.

These developments have come, of course, through historical study, and they have both presupposed and confirmed a higher evaluation of the importance of tradition than has been common in evangelicalism. Indeed, conversations with former evangelicals who have crossed the wall into

16. Grand Rapids: Eerdmans, 1947.
17. See my *ER*.

these other movements often turn on the subject of *sola Scriptura*. Converts from evangelicalism often report that their turning point came with a radical questioning of *sola Scriptura*, leading to an identification of tradition (of course, *including* Scripture) as the fundamental source of revelation.

THE RESULTS OF TRADITIONALISM

As one committed heart and soul to the principle *sola Scriptura*, I find the trend toward traditionalism most unfortunate. It has, in my view, weakened the evangelical witness in our time.

1. It has bound the consciences of Christians in areas where Scripture gives freedom. Traditionalists have often insisted, for example, that popular music is entirely and always unfit for use in Christian worship. But where does Scripture say this? What biblical principle implies it? How does this scruple stand up against Paul's willingness to "become all things to all men so that by all possible means I might save some" (1 Cor. 9:22)?[18] The argument against the use of "contemporary worship music" is based largely on a historical argument about the genesis of the genre and its incompatibility with certain traditions.[19]
2. It has thus led to unnecessary divisions and partisanship among churches and denominations. That displeases our Lord (John 17; 1 Cor. 1–3).
3. Traditionalism has weakened the rational basis of Christian theology insofar as it has replaced exegetical arguments with historical-traditional ones. In Christianity, only Scripture is ultimately authoritative. Arguments based only, or largely, on traditions (either evangelical or nonevangelical) will not be persuasive to Christian hearts.
4. Many traditionalist arguments should be classified as genetic fallacies. For example, we sometimes hear the argument that something is good (e.g., Reformed liturgy) because it comes out of Reformed tradition.[20] That assumes that everything historically connected

18. All quotations of Scripture in this appendix are from the NIV.

19. There are also biblical arguments, but rather shallow ones, based on the assumption that contemporary worship music does not, reflect, for example, the transcendence of God. In my view, emphasis on divine transcendence (holiness, majesty, and power) is one of the strengths of this music. See my *CWM*.

20. This sort of thing is even worse, of course, when an idea is adopted because it "sounds" Reformed and another is rejected because it "sounds" Arminian. I have often encountered this kind of sloppy thinking among theological students.

with the Reformed tradition is good. So either the Reformed tradition itself is ultimately normative or the argument is a fallacy. Or, negatively, we sometimes hear that a song comes from the tradition of pop culture and is therefore unsuitable to Christian worship. This is an antithetical argument, as the former was an argument from identification. It is valid only on the assumption that there is nothing at all that is good in pop culture, an assumption impossible to prove and unlikely on a biblical view of common grace. It is hard for me to avoid the impression that traditionalism accounts for much of the poor quality of thought and argumentation that one finds in evangelical writings today.[21]

5. The traditionalist-historicist argument that the church must be completely separate from modern culture is hard to square with the Great Commission of Matthew 28:18–20. The biblical stance of Christians is not to hide from the world, but to go forth and win the world for Christ. We are not to be "of" the world, but we are to be "in" it. And to carry out the evangelistic mandate, we are to become like the world, like the prevailing culture, in some ways: Paul says, "I have become all things to all men so that by all possible means I might save some" (1 Cor. 9:22).[22]

   This raises the issue of communication, for as Christ's ambassadors, we must proclaim the gospel in the languages of the world. The movement toward contemporary worship music is essentially an attempt to speak the musical language that many people are speaking today. The traditionalist would forbid this and require us to use antiquarian music. But has he adequately considered Paul's emphasis on intelligible communication in worship (1 Cor. 14)?

6. There are distressing signs that some are seeking to *define* the evangelical and Reformed movements in traditionalist ways. I have called attention to this danger in the "Cambridge Declaration" of the Alliance of Confessing Evangelicals.[23] I have also heard

21. I speak, to be sure, as one who has been burned by reviewers who have attacked my writings without any meaningful argument, merely because I disagreed with traditions with which the reviewers identified. See, for example, the exchange between Mark Karlberg and me concerning my CVT in *Mid-America Journal of Theology* 9, 2 (Fall 1993): 279–308.

22. The argument that we must avoid any contamination of contemporary culture in our means of proclaiming the gospel seems to me also to be at odds with the exhortation of Abraham Kuyper to bring all of culture under the dominion of Christ (cf. Paul in 2 Cor. 10:5). Some aspects of culture—its immorality and selfishness—should be avoided. Scripture tells us what to avoid. But for the most part Scripture calls us to conquer, not to hide.

23. In my "Biblicism" paper, cited in note 1 above.

recently of a conference sponsored by that organization in which one speaker made a scathing attack on contemporary forms of worship and worship music. These issues, to be sure, are complex, and I certainly do not insist that all evangelicals agree with me. I have explored this issue in a book-length discussion,[24] and I freely admit that there is far more to be said. I am happy to see these matters freely and vigorously discussed. I wish, however, that ACE would see the value of presenting more than one view of these matters when, after all, they are not actually resolved by the confessions themselves.

This is a time of definition for evangelicals, especially those who, like me, genuinely wish to be known as *confessional*. And I fear that the message people are hearing in the ACE writings and conferences is that those who are motivated by the Great Commission to speak in God's praise the languages of our time are not fit to bear the name of evangelical. That suggestion, I think, is unhistorical, divisive, and untrue.

THE ANTIDOTE: *SOLA SCRIPTURA*

In this situation, the Reformation (traditional!) principle of *sola Scriptura*, the sufficiency of Scripture, needs to be heard anew. Scripture itself proclaims it:

> Do not add to what I command you and do not subtract from it, but keep the commands of the LORD your God that I give you. (Deut. 4:2; cf. 12:32; Josh. 1:7; Prov. 30:6; Rev. 22:18–19)

> These people come near to me with their mouth and honor me with their lips, but their hearts are far from me. Their worship of me is made up only of rules taught by men. (Isa. 29:13, which Jesus quotes against Pharisaic traditionalists in Matt. 15:8–9)

> All Scripture is God-breathed and is useful for teaching, rebuking, correcting and training in righteousness, so that the man of God may be thoroughly equipped for every good work. (2 Tim. 3:16–17)

Scripture does not, of course, tell us everything we need to know about everything. We must look outside Scripture if we want specific directions on how to fix a sink or repair a car. But Scripture tells us everything that God wants us to know "concerning all things necessary for His own glory,

24. CWM.

man's salvation, faith and life" (WCF 1.6). Scripture doesn't tell us how to repair a car, but it tells us how to glorify God in repairing a car, namely, by doing whatever we do "in the name of the Lord Jesus, giving thanks to God the Father through him" (Col. 3:17), and by working at it with all our hearts, "as working for the Lord, not for men" (v. 23).

Even in worship there are some things that cannot be derived from Scripture, "some circumstances concerning the worship of God, and government of the Church, common to human actions and societies, which are to be ordered by the light of nature, and Christian prudence, according to the general rules of the Word, which are always to be observed" (WCF 1.6). So there is room for tradition. But Scripture and Scripture alone has the final word. Nothing outside Scripture may be imposed as law on God's people. No mere historical argument, no critique of culture, no human tradition, not even a church confession can be ultimate law in God's church.

Some would argue that the church preceded Scripture. In one sense this is true. From Adam to Moses, there is no clear record of any written revelation. But when God gives his written Word to Israel, that Word stands as his written covenant with them, the written constitution of the people of God. That covenant document is to be the highest authority for God's people, the Word of the living God himself. Thus, the people are not to add or subtract; they are not to turn to the right or to the left. Open any page in Deuteronomy at random, and you are likely to find admonitions to obey all the commands, statutes, testimonies, words, judgments, and so forth in God's law, the written law.

The new covenant in Jesus is also subject to God's written Word (2 Tim. 3:16–17). No human wisdom must be allowed to take precedence over Scripture, either to allow what Scripture forbids or to forbid what Scripture allows.

So when questions arise concerning worship, we must ask first of all what Scripture commands. What are the things that Scripture requires? What are the areas in which Scripture gives us freedom to make decisions within the bounds of its general principles?

Where we have freedom to make our own choices (as, I believe, concerning music style), we still have to evaluate the possibilities. Are there contemporary styles of music that are incompatible with biblical norms for worship? I think there are. But if someone wants to argue that a particular style is incompatible with Scripture, he will need to show that he has carefully understood what the biblical principles are, and not just rely on genetic-fallacy historical arguments or arguments assuming that tradition should never be changed. And he will need to do justice to *all* the relevant biblical principles: not just the transcendence and holiness of God, but also the Great Commission and the importance of edifying worshipers.

Sola Scriptura, therefore, forbids us to absolutize tradition or to put the conclusions of historical scholarship on the same level as Scripture. Thus, it is a charter of freedom for the Christian, though, to be sure, Scripture restricts our freedom in a number of ways. Jesus' yoke is easy, and as we take that yoke upon us, we lose the tyrannical yokes of those who would impose their traditions as law. May God enable us to understand and celebrate his gentle bonds and his wonderful liberty.

THE SPIRIT AND THE SCRIPTURES[1]

Note: In this article, I explore the testimony of the Spirit to the Scriptures, both in Scripture itself and in modern theology (especially Karl Barth and G. C. Berkouwer). So it supplements the discussion of the Spirit in this book (chap. 42) and also the discussions of modern theology (chaps. 3–7).

The Holy Spirit is involved with the Bible in a wide variety of ways.[2] As the third person of the Trinity, he participated in formulating the eternal plan of creation and redemption, of which Scripture is a part (Eph. 1:3, "spiritual" referring to the Holy Spirit). Further, he was involved in the creation of the heavens and the earth, without which Scripture, God's Word to his creatures, would have had no role (Gen. 1:2; Pss. 33:6 ["breath" suggests "spirit" in Hebrew]; 104:30). Then he was the author of revelation, the one who revealed God's truth to the prophets (Isa. 61:1–4; Acts 2). Next, he was the one in charge of inspiration, the one who supervised the placing of God's Word in writing (1 Cor. 2:9–10; 2 Tim. 3:16 ["spirit"

---

1. This article was originally published in D. A. Carson and John D. Woodbridge, eds., *Hermeneutics, Authority, and Canon* (Grand Rapids: Zondervan, 1986), 213–35, a collection later published by Baker Book House, and still later by Wipf and Stock Publishers. I have used this article by permission of D. A. Carson. For stylistic purposes, this appendix has been copyedited for inclusion in this volume.

2. On the general subject of the Spirit's witness to Scripture, I should mention some valuable works (not elsewhere directly cited in the notes) that I have found helpful. One is Bernard Ramm, *The Witness of the Spirit* (Grand Rapids: Eerdmans, 1957); then, two by Arthur Pink: *The Holy Spirit* (Grand Rapids: Baker, 1970) and *The Doctrine of Revelation* (Grand Rapids: Baker, 1975). Although Pink is probably to be classed as a popular rather than a scholarly writer, his works are often remarkably thorough and insightful.

being implicit in the Greek word for "inspired"]; 2 Peter 1:21). Finally, by the internal testimony of the Spirit, he enables the "hearers" of the Word of God to savingly appropriate it (Rom. 8:14–17; 1 Cor. 2:10–16; 1 Thess. 1:5; 2:13; 1 John 2:27; 5:9). In all these ways, the Spirit validates God's Word—planning it, creating the media for its communication, authoring it, recording it, driving it home to human hearts.

The present study will be primarily concerned with the Spirit's work in revelation, inspiration, and internal testimony.

I. THE SPIRIT'S WORK IN REVELATION AND INSPIRATION

In the areas of revelation and inspiration, a vast amount of literature has been published.[3] It is not necessary, therefore, to elaborate or justify these doctrines in detail. This study, rather, will assume the main outlines of the current common orthodox position and will address some questions that focus specifically on the *Spirit's* activity. Scripture, it will be assumed, is the Word of God, recorded inerrantly by the Spirit in the original manuscripts of the biblical books. Thus, the Spirit is the author of Scripture. Scripture, however, also has a number of *human* authors; and the questions before us focus on the relationship of the divine author to the human authors.

In many ways, Scripture does not *appear* to be written by one divine author. It contains a wide diversity of literary styles, reflecting the divergent personalities, gifts, educations, and environments of its human authors. The authors borrow from one another and seek historical information in ways common to human writers of the biblical period. Sometimes, between one author and another, there appear to be contradictions, even misunderstandings, when, for example, writers of the New Testament appeal to those of the Old. Many evangelicals have sought to explain or reconcile these apparent contradictions; I will not add to that literature. My questions, however, are these: How does the Holy Spirit figure in all of this? What role does he play? How is the Bible different from what it would be if only

---

3. Some of the most useful works today are these: Wayne A. Grudem, "Scripture's Self-Attestation and the Problem of Formulating a Doctrine of Scripture," in *Scripture and Truth*, ed. D. A. Carson and John D. Woodbridge (Grand Rapids: Zondervan, 1983), 19–59; Meredith G. Kline, *The Structure of Biblical Authority* (Grand Rapids: Eerdmans, 1972); John Murray, "The Attestation of Scripture," in *The Infallible Word*, ed. Ned Bernard Stonehouse and Paul Woolley (Philadelphia: Presbyterian and Reformed, 1946); Cornelius Van Til, *A Christian Theory of Knowledge* (Philadelphia: Presbyterian and Reformed, 1969); Benjamin Breckinridge Warfield, *The Inspiration and Authority of the Bible* (Philadelphia: Presbyterian and Reformed, 1948); Edward J. Young, *Thy Word Is Truth* (Grand Rapids: Eerdmans, 1957).

human writers were involved? Should we not expect, in a book inspired by God, a greater uniformity, something more tidy, more easily distinguishable from merely human literature?

When questions of this sort arise, it is always well to ask, "What would be the alternative?" We can imagine a more "uniform" book—something like the Qur'an is thought by Muslims to be. Would that be an improvement on the Bible? Scripture is written so that we might believe in Christ and be complete in him (John 20:31; 2 Tim. 3:17). Would a more uniform text help us in those ways?

Put in this way, the issue appears less simple. Perhaps it really requires more insight into God's mind than he has chosen to give us. Do we know more than he does as to what it takes to save and sanctify? Perhaps it is best just to leave these matters in his hands. Yet from what he has revealed about his purposes in revelation, some further clarifications can be suggested.

A. COMMUNICATION

God's purpose in giving us the Bible is communication. Clearly, the art of communication is to speak the language of one's hearers. When God communicates, therefore, he speaks as humanly as anyone could possibly speak—the language that humans are used to, in ways that humans are used to hearing. In the incarnation, God became truly human, enduring all the sufferings and temptations of human life. Jesus did not live on earth with a halo or perpetually surrounded by hosts of visible angels. Many would not have known by looking at him that he was the true God made flesh. God did this so that Jesus might be sympathetic as High Priest, a true representative of humanity before God (Heb. 2:10–18; 4:14–16). Similarly, God's written Word is a truly human word, one that captures all the nuances of human life and human communication.

Some types of "uniformity" actually *hinder* communication. Utter constancy of style can be monotonous. Recounting every detail of a historical event with "pedantic precision" can detract from the point of the story. (If someone asks my age, and I give it down to the hour, minute, and second, surely I have, in most situations, placed a roadblock in the process of communication.) If God had spoken to the Hebrews using the precise language of twentieth-century science, he would have been thoroughly incomprehensible. If every apparent contradiction were explained in context, what would happen to the religious and emotional impact of the words?

Considerations such as these help to reassure us that God's ways, after all, are best. The humanity of Scripture ought not to be an embarrassment to us, a weakness in an otherwise powerful document. Rather, the humanity of Scripture is its *strength*. It is an index of the *success* of God in speaking our language, in communicating his Word clearly to us.

B. Variety

The truth of God is *many-faceted*. It includes teaching about eternity past, time, and eternity future. It tells of the various parts of God's creation— heaven, earth, stars, and seas. It speaks to men, women, and children of all ages. It speaks of salvation as a comprehensive change in our hearts, affecting every aspect of life.

Describing all these matters requires sometimes artistry, sometimes conceptual sharpness, sometimes analytical clarity. It requires the poetic gifts of David, the wisdom of Solomon, the passion of Amos for social justice, the brilliant arguments of Paul, the intuitive clarity of John, the historical scholarship of Luke. A "more uniform" text would be poorer than the Bible we have, for it would not display as clearly the incredible richness of our salvation in Jesus Christ.

C. Mystery

How, then, did the Spirit work as he inspired Scripture? The answer is: mysteriously. That is what we expect from him (John 3:8). He works, paradoxically, most divinely when he is speaking most humanly, for then he shows the perfection of his communication. Most writers on the subject of inspiration admit that Scripture tells us very little about the way in which God inspires. Sometimes what he does seems to be "dictation," however much we may wish to deny a "dictation theory" (see Isa. 6:9ff.; Rev. 2–3). Other times he works through methods of human reasoning (including an author's historical research—Luke 1:1–4). Sometimes he may give to a writer extraordinary knowledge of some historical information that is otherwise unknowable, but that is not usual. In every case the Spirit creates, by the human writer, a text that is God's Word, in the best form for communication.

II. THE SPIRIT'S INTERNAL TESTIMONY

More time will be spent on this aspect of the Spirit's work, since it is not as widely understood and expounded as are the doctrines of revelation and inspiration. Also, several problems that have emerged in recent theology deserve thorough analysis.

The Protestant Reformation contended for the gospel of justification by faith alone. But this doctrine contradicted the church tradition, or so it was said. So the Reformers argued intensively, not only about justification, but also about biblical authority and its relation to tradition. A crucial weapon in the discussion was the Reformers' doctrine of the "internal testimony of the Holy Spirit." Rome was willing to grant the authority of Scripture; but, she insisted, we cannot even know that Scripture is authoritative except by the testimony of the church. Thus, church tradition became, at that point at least, a more basic authority than Scripture. No, said Martin Luther and John Calvin. Our final assurance of biblical authority is not human tradition, but the witness of God's own Spirit within us.

Calvin developed this doctrine in more detail than did Luther, turning it into the centerpiece of his Christian epistemology.[4] In his *Institutes*,[5] he sharply denies that "the eternal and inviolable truth of God depend[s] upon the decision of men." On the contrary, the church itself is founded on the "writings of the prophets and the preaching of the apostles."[6] Although "sufficiently firm proofs are at hand to establish the credibility of scripture,"[7] "we ought to seek our conviction in a higher place than human reasons, judgments, or conjectures, that is, in the secret testimony of the Spirit."[8] Calvin denies that this doctrine leads to what we would today call subjectivism. He opposes those "fanatics" who forsake Scripture for alleged new revelations of the Spirit.[9] Word and Spirit go together, so that the Spirit is recognized in his agreement with Scripture.[10]

Later in the *Institutes*, Calvin again discusses the Spirit's testimony, this time in its relation to individual faith and assurance. Using many Scripture passages, Calvin indicates that faith is the work of the Spirit.[11] Without the Spirit, we are incapable of faith.[12] Only the Spirit can lead us to Christ.[13]

Since the Reformation, this doctrine has continued to play an important role in Protestant theology—but with a wide range of interpretations,

---

4. "The keystone of his doctrine of the knowledge of God." Benjamin Breckinridge Warfield, "Calvin's Doctrine of the Knowledge of God," in *Calvin and Calvinism* (New York: Oxford University Press, 1931), 113.

5. John Calvin, *The Institutes of the Christian Religion*, trans. Ford Lewis Battles, 2 vols. (Philadelphia: Westminster, 1960), 1.75.

6. Ibid.

7. Ibid., 81.

8. Ibid., 78.

9. Ibid., 93.

10. Ibid., 94–95.

11. Ibid., 541–42.

12. Ibid., 582–83.

13. Ibid., 581–82.

applications, and emphases, provoking numerous partisan debates. In our day, many have argued that the "orthodox" tradition that followed the Reformation (Turretin, Voetius, et al.) either ignored or seriously misunderstood this teaching, leading to similar deficiencies in the "Old Princeton" theology (Hodge, Warfield), which so strongly influenced modern evangelicalism.

The present study will deal with three areas in which the orthodox approach has been questioned: (A) the sovereignty, (B) the objects, and (C) the rationality of the Spirit's testimony. But first we must set the stage for this discussion.

As far as sovereignty is concerned, Karl Barth, especially, has charged that the orthodox thinkers inadequately appreciated the lordship of the Spirit in his testimony. They thought of Scripture as a finished, permanent deposit of divine truth, while, in Barth's view, they ought to have seen it as a human document that from time to time *becomes* God's Word to us as the Spirit sovereignly moves. On the orthodox view, Barth thinks, we may become complacent, believing that we "have" God's Word under our control.[14]

Moreover, in considering the objects of the Spirit's testimony, G. C. Berkouwer[15] and others have argued that the orthodox tradition held too "formal" a view—a view of the Spirit's witnessing to Scripture as a collection of inerrant truths on a wide variety of subjects. Berkouwer prefers to say that the Spirit witnesses to Christ, to the gospel of salvation, to our adoption as sons and daughters of God. The Spirit witnesses to Scripture also—but only as Scripture witnesses to these realities. Thus, the Spirit's concern is not to establish a "formal" principle of authority but to establish the "material" content of the gospel. He guarantees the truth of the gospel but not necessarily the accuracy of Scripture on such matters as history, geography, and science.

In regard to rationality, both Berkouwer[16] and others—such as Jack B. Rogers and Donald K. McKim[17]—think the orthodox tradition misconstrued the place of reason in relation to Scripture, constructing a system of rational arguments to buttress biblical authority rather than relying entirely on the testimony of the Spirit.

In what follows, these questions will be considered in more detail—without entering into the historical questions whether the modern critics have

14. Karl Barth, *Church Dogmatics*, 4 vols. (Edinburgh: T&T Clark, 1936–56), 1:1, 207ff., 523ff.

15. G. C. Berkouwer, *Holy Scripture* (Grand Rapids: Eerdmans, 1975), 39–66.

16. Ibid.

17. Jack B. Rogers and Donald K. McKim, *The Authority and Interpretation of the Bible: An Historical Approach* (San Francisco: Harper & Row, 1979).

rightly interpreted the orthodox tradition.[18] We will analyze the modern views, seeking to determine their meaning and their theological validity and to address the theological questions they raise. Although these views are complicated, I believe that this discussion will make the orthodox views look more compelling than their modern would-be replacements. In general, I will maintain that the modern formulations, while commendably reminding us of some biblical emphases, are too confused to stand serious theological scrutiny. These confusions can be overcome by formulations that, while recognizably orthodox, are stated to meet the contemporary questions.

A. The Sovereignty of the Witness

One of the most exciting things about the Spirit's testimony is that it is an intimate, even "direct," relation between ourselves and God. Listening to Scripture is not merely a transaction between ourselves and a book, even a very extraordinary book; rather, in Scripture we meet God *himself*. For Protestants (at least those outside "charismatic" circles), no experience offers a more profound closeness with God. It is this sense of the divine presence that pervades the Barthian analysis of the Spirit's witness. The same emphasis can be found in Calvin: "Thus, the highest proof of scripture derives in general from the fact that God in person speaks in it. . . . God alone is a fit witness of himself in his Word."[19]

Some modern writers, indeed, are even more bold in speaking of the closeness of our relation with God in the Spirit's testimony. Helmut Thielicke speaks of our having "a share in (God's) self-knowledge (1 Cor. 2:10f.; 13:12b)."[20] There is some danger of pantheism in this formulation,

18. Such historical work, defending the orthodox tradition, has been done well, for example, by John D. Woodbridge in his *Biblical Authority: A Critique of the Rogers/McKim Proposal* (Grand Rapids: Zondervan, 1982) and in "The Princetonians and Biblical Authority: An Assessment of the Ernest Sandeen Proposal," written with Randall H. Balmer, in *Scripture and Truth*, ed. D. A. Carson and John D. Woodbridge (Grand Rapids: Zondervan, 1983), 251–79. See also W. Robert Godfrey, "Biblical Authority in the Sixteenth and Seventeenth Centuries: A Question of Transition," in *Scripture and Truth*, 225–43; John H. Gerstner, "The View of the Bible Held by the Church: Calvin and the Westminster Divines," in *Inerrancy*, ed. Norman L. Geisler (Grand Rapids: Zondervan, 1979), 385–412; John H. Gerstner, "Warfield's Case for Biblical Inerrancy," in *God's Inerrant Word*, ed. John W. Montgomery (Minneapolis: Bethany House, 1974), 115–42. Richard B. Gaffin argues in "Old Amsterdam and Inerrancy," *WTJ* 45, 1 (Fall 1983): 219–72, that Kuyper and Bavinck—often appealed to by Rogers, McKim, and Berkouwer as representing a tradition opposed to "Old Princeton"—were firm believers in inerrancy.

19. Calvin, *Institutes*, 1.78–79.

20. Helmut Thielicke, *The Evangelical Faith*, 3 vols. (Grand Rapids: Eerdmans, 1974), 1:105. Cf. p. 323.

which Thielicke seeks to counter in various ways. Yet the Scripture passages present the Spirit's witness as something uniquely wonderful, which we cannot adequately describe without taking some theological risks.

But if the internal testimony brings us face-to-face with God, at the same time it brings us face-to-face with his sovereignty and freedom. The doctrine must be formulated so as to do justice to God's lordship in his revelation.

1. The Position of Modern Theology

Both "orthodox" and "modern" thinkers find value in these sorts of considerations. But the modern thinkers also find in them some weapons against orthodoxy. For one thing, consider the traditional orthodox distinction between inspiration and the internal testimony of the Spirit. Orthodox thinkers have traditionally insisted that "inspiration" and "internal testimony" are quite distinct, though both are works of the Spirit.[21]

In modern theologians like Barth, however, this distinction loses its sharpness. For them, first, inspiration in the orthodox sense does not exist; God does not place his words on paper. For God to inspire words in this way would compromise his freedom and sovereignty; God himself could not abrogate such words once he had spoken them. Thus, what the biblical writers experienced was not inspiration in the orthodox sense, but a kind of illumination similar to what we experience today in the Spirit's witness. Furthermore, the distinction between inspiration and illumination becomes difficult to draw for theologians who are impressed with the immediacy of the divine presence in the Spirit's witness. What can "inspiration" be, if it is not the internal testimony? What more can we ask than an intimate participation in God's own self-knowledge?

But there is further implication. If inspiration in the traditional sense is rejected, then there is also a change in the basis of biblical authority. In orthodox Protestant theology, the inspiration of Scripture renders it authoritative, though the witness of the Spirit is essential if we are to perceive and accept that authority. In much modern theology, however, particularly in the Barthian tradition, not only is the witness of the Spirit essential to our acceptance of biblical authority, it is the one factor that *makes* Scripture authoritative. Without his witness (and therefore without our faithful response), Scripture has no more authority than the best books of human wisdom.[22] On this view, Scripture lacks authority until

21. See, e.g., Carl F. H. Henry, *God, Revelation and Authority*, 6 vols. (Waco, TX: Word, 1976–79), 2:13ff.

22. See, e.g., Robert Clyde Johnson, *Authority in Protestant Theology* (Philadelphia: Westminster Press, 1959), 54: "Just as scripture could become an instrument of redemp-

we believe it. But why should we believe a book that, before we believe it, has no authority over us?

Thus, in much modern theology the internal testimony *replaces* the traditional concept of inspiration. It was the internal testimony, not inspiration, in this view, that motivated the original writing of Scripture, and it is the internal testimony (presently occurring, as we read and hear), not inspiration, that grounds our faith in Scripture. The Bible is not inspired, if by *inspiration* we mean a unique divine action in the past that guarantees the truth of the text at all times and for all readers. If the word *inspiration* is to be of use, it must be used as a synonym for the internal testimony, so that we today are "inspired" as were the biblical writers, though our inspiration may in some respects depend on theirs.[23]

This construction coheres well with three familiar concepts of neoorthodoxy. First, Scripture "becomes" the Word of God when the Spirit uses it to reach our hearts. Second, our response to the Word of God is a part of the revelation, so that there is no revelation without our (positive) response.[24] Third, the truth or error of the biblical text itself is irrelevant to faith, for the Spirit can reach the heart even by means of erroneous content.

These notions are thought to be essential to the freedom or sovereignty of God in the Spirit's witness. God is free to use, or not to use, any text as his Word, whether it be true or false. In the orthodox view, the Barthian argues, God is forced to honor a word spoken in the past; he is not free to contradict the canonical texts. Thus, we who "have" the canonical texts have God under our control.

But surely there is something odd about saying that an inerrant canonical text places God under our control. For one thing, Scripture never draws any such inference. In Scripture, God makes covenant promises, by which he *binds himself*. In Christ, all these promises are Yes and Amen (2 Cor. 1:20). God cannot lie or deny himself (2 Tim. 2:13; Titus 1:2; Heb. 6:18). Therefore, his Word abides forever (Isa. 40:8). These divine words constitute a body of truth, a "tradition" (2 Thess. 2:15; 3:6), a faith that was "once for all entrusted to the saints" and for which we are to contend earnestly (Jude 3).[25] God commands his people to obey all his written words, statutes, and ordinances and to pass them on to their children (Deut.

---

tion only by the action of the Spirit, so it could become theologically authoritative only under a personal relationship to the sovereign God through the personal presence of the Holy Spirit."

23. See Karl Barth, *The Holy Ghost and the Christian Life* (London: Muller, 1938), 23.

24. E.g., John Baillie, *The Idea of Revelation in Recent Thought* (New York: Columbia University Press, 1956), 64ff., 83ff.

25. All quotations of Scripture in this appendix are from the NIV.

6:4–9; 8:3; Pss. 1; 19:7–14; 119; Matt. 5:17–20; 1 Cor. 14:37; 2 Thess. 2:15; 2 Tim. 3:15–17; 2 Peter 1:19–21; 3:15–16).

Moreover, the biblical writers do not reason that these divine promises compromise God's sovereignty. On the contrary, God sovereignty is expressed through the irresistible power of his Word. "So is my word that goes out from my mouth: It will not return to me empty, but will accomplish what I desire and achieve the purpose for which I sent it" (Isa. 55:11). God's Word is an instrument of his sovereign rule. It is precisely the case that his sovereignty would be compromised if he did *not* speak such words.

Evidently we must use greater care in formulating our concept of divine sovereignty than has sometimes been shown among theologians. When we reason without such carefulness (relying on intuition, as it were), ambiguities emerge. To one theologian, God's sovereignty would be compromised if he were to utter an inspired, inerrant sentence. To another (and I believe this is the uniform position of Scripture), God's sovereignty *requires* the existence of such sentences.

The moral seems to be that "sovereignty" is a more complex concept than we often imagine. Use of it requires some careful thinking rather than jumping to conclusions that seem intuitive. What seems intuitive for one theologian will be counterintuitive for another. Intuition misleads us, because generally intuition does not make fine distinctions. Intuitively, we tend to formulate divine sovereignty by excluding anything that looks like it might be a "limitation" on God. When we reflect on the matter, however, we can easily see that sovereignty cannot be taken to mean an absence of all such supposed limitations. Only the most extreme nominalists would conceive of sovereignty in that way. Some "fine distinctions" are needed to tell us what *kinds* of "limitations" are inappropriate to divine sovereignty—that is, what sorts of "limitations" would *really* be limitations. Most theology books, even by Calvinists, recognize that God is "bound," at least by his own character—by, for example, his goodness, rationality, and transcendent greatness; God *cannot* be evil, stupid, or weak. God is also bound by his covenant promises, as we have seen from Scripture.

There is, therefore, no carte blanche sovereignty, sovereignty without any "limitation" at all. Thus, a theologian must take pains to justify the types of qualifications he allows. The orthodox thinker must justify his assertion that God limits himself to working within the framework of his covenant promises. (We have given an outline above of such a justification.) Barth, too, must justify the sort of limitation that he alleges, that God *cannot* guarantee the continuing truthfulness of written sentences. Barth, however, rarely if ever argues his distinctive view at this point; he seems to think that his particular view of God's sovereignty/limitation is intuitively obvious.

When such an argument is brought forward, we will again consider the Barthian position. Until that time, we ought to remain content with the position of the Reformers, which (as we have seen in summary) is the position of Scripture itself.

2. The Orthodox Position

a. Contrary to neoorthodoxy, there *is* such a thing as an inspired text. God calls his people not to listen to subjective inner promptings, but to listen to his "commands, decrees and laws" (Deut. 6:1).[26] God holds his people responsible to obey his written Word.

b. The Spirit and the Word go together. This is the major emphasis of both Calvin and Luther over against the Roman church on the one side and the "enthusiasts" on the other. The Spirit witnesses to the Word—not against it or in addition to it, as the neoorthodox construction suggests. Scripture always represents the witness of the Spirit in this fashion: the Spirit calls us to hear what God says (see John 14:26; 15:26; 16:13; 1 Thess. 1:5; 2:13). As Helmut Thielicke points out, the Spirit is poured out in fullness only after the crucifixion and resurrection (John 16:7), for he bears witness to the finished work of Christ (John 16:14). Thus, he "protects the givenness of the event." But, to complete Thielicke's point, the Spirit can witness to those objective events for us today only by witnessing to the apostolic *word* concerning those events, the word we have in Scripture.[27]

c. The Word is self-authenticating. It is the ultimate authority for the believer, and therefore it is the ultimate ground even for its own authority. We cannot test Scripture by anything more authoritative than Scripture. God's written Word, in fact, is the means of testing spirits (1 Cor. 14:37; 1 John 4:1–3). No one, therefore, may dare to place any teaching of the Spirit over against the Word of God.[28]

26. This emphasis on obeying God's written words pervades Deuteronomy and many other parts of Scripture. See also the texts listed earlier in this article. A valuable study of the centrality of written revelation within God's covenant kingdom is Kline, *The Structure of Biblical Authority*.

27. Thielicke, *The Evangelical Faith*, 1:129ff.

28. For Calvin, one main function of the doctrine is precisely to exalt the authority of Scripture, over against church tradition on the one hand and alleged modern prophets on the other. The idea that the internal testimony somehow removes the need for a fully authoritative Scripture is directly contrary to the intention of Calvin and the other Reformers. See Calvin, *Institutes*, 1.74ff.

d. What, then, is the ground of biblical authority? Is it to be found in inspiration or in the Spirit's testimony? There is some ambiguity here in the term *authority*. The term can be used in an objective or subjective sense. Objectively, a civil law, for example, has authority over me whether I even know about it or not. Subjectively, however, that law will not rule me (in the sense of influencing my conduct toward obedience) unless I know about it and receive it favorably. Similarly, Scripture has objective authority over us by virtue of its inspiration. We are responsible to obey it whether or not the Spirit has witnessed to us. If we disobey, we are subject to divine judgment unless God forgives us through Christ. The subjective authority of Scripture, however, comes through the Spirit's witness; we cannot obey from the heart until or unless the Spirit testifies *in* our heart.[29]

e. Thus, the sovereignty and freedom of God in the Spirit's testimony are seen not in God's ability to contradict or modify or add to his

---

29. Three addenda to this distinction: (1) There is some confusion among Calvin scholars—and possibly in Calvin himself—as to his views on this matter. Geoffrey Bromiley writes that Calvin "perhaps does not sufficiently differentiate" the self-authentication of Scripture from the Spirit's testimony (*Historical Theology: An Introduction* [Grand Rapids: Eerdmans, 1978], 225). Reinhold Seeberg indicates vagueness in Calvin: "Thus Calvin establishes the authority of the scriptures partly upon their divine dictation, and partly upon the testimony of the Holy Spirit working through them" (Reinhold Seeberg, *Textbook of the History of Doctrines*, 2 vols. [Grand Rapids: Baker, 1954], 2:395). The "partly . . . partly" formulation is understandable as an interpretation of Calvin, but it suggests at the same time Calvin's own vagueness as to the relation between the two factors. Wilhelm Niesel finds Calvin contradictory or "dialectical" here (see *The Theology of Calvin* [Philadelphia: Westminster, 1956], 30ff.). A good analysis of this issue, particularly as it relates to Calvin's statements, can be found in John Murray, *Calvin on Scripture and Divine Sovereignty* (Grand Rapids: Baker, 1960), republished in Murray, *Collected Writings of John Murray*, 4 vols. (Edinburgh: Banner of Truth, 1982); in this latter collection, see 4:183–90. See also Edward A. Dowey, *The Knowledge of God in Calvin's Theology* (New York: Columbia University Press, 1952), 106ff., esp. p. 111. (2) A good recent example of confusion created by a "partly . . . partly" scheme is the argument in David H. Kelsey's *The Uses of Scripture in Recent Theology* (Philadelphia: Fortress Press, 1975) that the "discrimen" for evaluating theological proposals is "the conjunction of certain uses of Scripture and the presence of God" (p. 160). The result is vagueness and subjectivism. See my review article on this book in *WTJ* 39, 2 (Spring 1977): 328–53 (Appendix H in this volume). (3) The distinction we have made between objective and subjective authority is, of course, the proper response to the neoorthodox idea that there is no revelation apart from our response. In the objective sense, they are wrong; in the subjective sense, they are right. Of course, their view actually is that there is no biblical authority in the objective sense. Yet some writers are remarkably inconsistent here. In Baillie, *The Idea of Revelation*, 134–48, the closing epilogue ("The Challenge of Revelation") exhorts the reader along this line: Don't criticize God for failing to reveal himself; criticize yourself for failing to hear. But what sense can we make of this exhortation if there is no objective revelation that exists apart from our response?

Word, but in his ability to drive it home to otherwise unwilling hearts and, indeed, to do everything he says he will do.

B. The Objects of the Witness

The chief burden of G. C. Berkouwer's important work *Holy Scripture* is his critique of what he calls "abstract" and "formal" views of Scripture. "Whenever the words 'abstract' and 'formal' appear frequently in the discussion," he says, "what is meant is that scripture is received as writing, as a book of divine quality, while its content and message as such are thereby not taken into account from the outset."[30] In discussing the Spirit's witness, then, Berkouwer wants to insist that the Spirit does not witness to scriptural authority in an abstract" or "formal" way; rather, the Spirit testifies to the "content and message" of Scripture, and his testimony to the authority of Scripture occurs only in that context.

Berkouwer further insists that this witness to the biblical "content and message" does not occur "apart from its connection with the condition of the religious subject."[31] It "first of all has a bearing on a person's sonship."[32] That is to say, the Spirit's witness to the Scripture is not a different witness from his witness to our adoption (described in Rom. 8:14–17).[33] Thus, the Spirit validates the context of Scripture in its application to a faithful son or daughter of God.

Negatively, Berkouwer says (interpreting Bavinck) that the Spirit's testimony

> does not supply direct certainty regarding the authenticity, canonicity, or even the inspiration of Holy Scripture; nor regarding the historical, chronological, and geographical data "as such"; nor regarding the facts of salvation as *nuda facta*, nor, finally, regarding the closedness of the canon, as if it were possible to solve the problems regarding canonicity with an appeal to the witness of the Spirit.[34]

Berkouwer is a subtle thinker, and often it is not easy to describe precisely what he has in mind. There are always qualifiers that take the sharp edges off his more controversial statements. Note above, for example, that he does not deny that the Spirit witnesses to the biblical text, only that he so

30. Berkouwer, *Holy Scripture*, 42–43.
31. Ibid., 43, quoting Bavinck.
32. Ibid., 43.
33. Ibid., 51–52.
34. Ibid., 44.

witnesses "in abstraction" from Scripture's "message."[35] Later on, in fact, he does clarify this point: "Reformed theology was not confronted with the dilemma of a dualism between authoritative scripture and the message it brings, because Reformed theology hears the message of salvation precisely in the witness of scripture."[36]

Nor does he quite deny that the Spirit witnesses concerning biblical authenticity, canonicity, inspiration, historical, chronological, and geographical data. If he did, then, of course, we would have to raise questions; for Scripture contains a great deal of material about such matters, and it is unclear why the Spirit would leave such data out of his purview. Rather, what Berkouwer denies is that the Spirit testifies to these "directly" or "as such" or "as *nuda facta.*" What, we want to know, is the "cash value" of all this? What is Berkouwer, concretely, trying to rule in and to rule out?

Sometimes it seems as though what Berkouwer wants is a certain order of topics: "On the basis of the New Testament, the confession of the Spirit is first of all related to salvation in Christ; and *then* the Word of God is discussed."[37]

But it is hard to believe that Berkouwer's concern is as trivial (and formal!) as a mere order of discussion. Is he concerned, rather, about an *emphasis*? Sometimes we get that impression. But *emphasis* in theology is itself a rather subtle matter. Berkouwer does not mean, evidently, that the author of a paper on the Spirit's witness, for example, must spend, say, 80 percent of the text discussing salvation and only 20 percent discussing biblical authority. And surely an intelligent theologian such as Berkouwer would not want to limit theological reflection to those topics "emphasized" in the NT, as if it were somehow impious to write about the veiling of women in 1 Corinthians 11. In what sense, then, are we required to "emphasize" matters of salvation when discussing the Spirit's witness?

---

35. This subtlety, however, makes it difficult to evaluate Berkouwer's criticisms of others. Has anyone ever taught that the Spirit does witness to the text "in abstraction from its message"? Has anyone, for example, argued that the Spirit witnesses to the isolated proposition that Scripture is God's Word, without at the same time witnessing to the message taught by that Word? Some theologians have, perhaps, failed to emphasize these connections as strongly as Berkouwer would like, but no one, to my knowledge, has ever denied them. When Berkouwer charges (p. 164) Edmund P. Clowney with "formalism" because Clowney wants us to hear what Christ says about the Bible (and not only vice versa), we wonder what is going on! Is Berkouwer really urging a much more radical view than he generally presents, namely, a denial that we should have any concern with the authority of the text? No one can rightly accuse Edmund Clowney of neglecting the Christological focus of Scripture—not unless he means by *focus* something radically different from what the rest of us mean.

36. Ibid., 53.

37. Ibid., 52–53.

Perhaps Berkouwer's point, after all, is not well described as a "matter of emphasis." But in that case, what is he saying? What does it mean to deny that the Spirit witnesses to historical data "as such"?

Berkouwer's chapter on the Spirit's witness leaves these matters rather unclear, but other parts of the book illumine his concern somewhat. In the chapter on "reliability," for instance, Berkouwer mentions differences in the Synoptic accounts, and concludes that the biblical concepts of witness, truth, and reliability are

> not in opposition to a freedom in composing and expressing the mystery of Christ; their purpose is rather to point in their testimony to that great light. . . . The aim of the portrayal was not to mislead and to deceive; it was not even a "pious fraud," for it was wholly focussed on the great mystery. This explains why the church through the ages was scarcely troubled by the difference pointed out long before, and by the inexact, non-notarial portrayal. A problem was created only as a result of attempts at harmonization and the criticism that followed. . . . But through a recognition of the true nature of the Gospels, the way is opened to hear and understand the one testimony.[38]

Here Berkouwer argues that since the purpose of Scripture is to proclaim the "great mystery," we should not expect a "notarial" precision in the biblical narratives. Scripture can adequately witness to its content and message without such exactness. Therefore, in making judgments about the "reliability" of Scripture, we must take into account its content, message, and purpose. Relating this discussion to the Spirit's work, then, we may say that, for Berkouwer, the Spirit does not testify to a "notarially precise" Scripture; he validates the *truth* of Scripture, but only that kind of truth appropriate to the message.

All of this is true enough as far as it goes, but it is scarcely new. Orthodox Protestants have long denied that biblical inerrancy entails "pedantic precision."[39] How, then, does Berkouwer differ from those orthodox thinkers whom he seems to be criticizing? Chiefly, I think, in the vagueness of his formulation and also in his special agenda: Berkouwer throughout the book seems to be urging on theological conservatives a greater openness toward current forms of biblical criticism,[40] often charging them with

38. Ibid., 252.
39. The phrase comes from Murray, *Collected Writings*, 4:175, but the point has been made by a great many authors. I still think one of the best treatments is Edward J. Young, *Thy Word Is Truth* (Grand Rapids: Eerdmans, 1957).
40. Berkouwer, *Holy Scripture*, 131ff., 227–28, passim.

"fear"[41] or with avoiding questions[42] when they are not as open as he would like. But he rarely indicates that there are any limits at all to this openness. (He does, to be sure, indicate that Rudolf Bultmann's demythologization is unacceptable.)[43] The reader is left with a vague feeling, then, that he ought not to fuss too much over biblical criticism, that he should be open to almost any critical proposal. That vague feeling seems to be the "bottom line" of Berkouwer's analysis.

I suppose, then, that in evaluating Berkouwer's view we should ask whether he has succeeded in justifying this vague openness to biblical criticism. And of course, the answer is no. Certainly, Scripture's purpose is to proclaim Christ, and it is worth pointing out as Berkouwer does (and most all the orthodox do) that this purpose does not necessitate "pedantic precision." But there is nothing about this purpose to warrant a vague openness concerning the theories of modern biblical scholarship.

On the contrary, there is much in Scripture to warn us *against* such openness. Scripture teaches us that we live in a fallen world, in which the fashionable currents of human learning are opposed to God and to his gospel (Rom. 1; 1 Cor. 1–2). It warns us over and over again about the danger of false teaching from within the church (Matt. 7:15–20; Gal. 1; 2 Thess. 2; 1 Tim. 1:3ff.; 4:1ff.; 2 Tim. 3:1ff.; 2 Peter 2). Thus, if we are really to read Scripture in terms of its central message, we will be *suspicious* of modern biblical scholarship, particularly when it comes from those who have renounced the Bible's own supernatural worldview. This does not mean that there is no truth in the writings of modern scholars; the question before us is one of our attitude or disposition toward them. Berkouwer has not succeeded in justifying his recommendation of sunny optimism.

41. This is one of the leitmotifs of the book: ibid., 22, 135, 145, 184, 248–49, 272. It is disturbing that a man with Berkouwer's reputation as a responsible scholar would spend such a large part of a book impugning (gratuitously, I think, for the most part) the motives of others. Is it really the case that those who differ with Berkouwer on these issues hold their positions out of fear? Is it not equally plausible (and perhaps equally irresponsible!) to suggest that Berkouwer's own formulations arise out of his fear of being rejected by the academic establishment? And of course, we must also raise the question whether certain types of fear are justified.

42. This, too: ibid., 11, 16, 25–26, 30, 135, 145, 150–51, 178, 183, 185, 189, 193, 207, 248–49, 365. Again, I think this talk is gratuitous. Maybe some conservative thinkers have sought to avoid difficult questions, but I hardly think that charge can be brought against such people as Warfield, Wilson, Van Til, and Machen. With at least equal plausibility, we could ask why Berkouwer is so vague in his formulations; is it perhaps to avoid the difficult process of speaking clearly to issues that are troubling the church? Is he avoiding something?

43. Ibid., 253ff.

Otherwise, much of Berkouwer's concern is legitimate. He is right in saying that we should not fear to investigate the difficult questions.[44] Berkouwer is also right to insist that the Spirit does not merely witness to the authority of a book. He witnesses to the gospel message, to what the book says. Believing Scripture is believing that message.[45] At the same time, believing the message entails believing the book,[46] for the message is the book's content. And although the book is centrally focused in certain great events—Jesus' life, death, and resurrection—it speaks out about everything in creation, including history, geography, and science. It speaks of a God who made the heavens, earth, and sea and who acted in earthly history and geography to save us from our sins. It urges us to do *all* things to his glory, whether we are preachers or carpenters or historians or scientists (1 Cor. 10:31). As long as we read Scripture responsibly (yes, "in relation to its message"), we need not fear (as I believe Berkouwer does)[47] studying its implications for these and all areas of human life. Berkouwer's view is not only wrong but greatly harmful, insofar as he discourages such study, which study is in essence the attempt to "take captive every thought to make it obedient to Christ" (2 Cor. 10:5).

Does the Spirit tell us what books belong in the canon? Does he help us decide between rival interpretations? Does he help us with scholarly questions about literary genre, variant readings, and the like? Not in the

44. Robert Dick Wilson, one of the great orthodox scholars of "Old Princeton," took as his motto the sentence "I have not shirked the difficult questions." Whatever else we may say about the Old Princeton theologians, we certainly have no right to accuse them of fearfulness.

45. This can be an important point. Does a cultist who claims to believe in biblical inerrancy but denies the gospel of Christ qualify as a Bible-believer? Not in the eyes of God.

46. This is clearly the position of Calvin: "Faith is certain that God is true in all things whether he command or forbid, whether he promise or threaten; and it also obediently receives his commandments, observes his prohibitions, heeds his threats. Nevertheless, faith properly begins with the promise, rests in it, and ends in it" (*Institutes*, 1.575). In the second sentence, Calvin expresses Berkouwer's concern for the material content of the gospel; but in the first sentence he expresses a "formal" concern (though *formal* hardly seems the appropriate word to describe the profound attitude of obedience expressed here): to urge obedience to what God says, whatever he says. Cf. Anthony N. S. Lane, "John Calvin: The Witness of the Holy Spirit," in *Faith and Ferment* (papers read at the 1982 Westminster Conference), ed. Robert S. Bilheimer (Minneapolis: Augsburg, 1983). George Hendry, *The Holy Spirit in Christian Theology* (Philadelphia: Westminster Press, 1956), criticizes Calvin because (Hendry thinks in contrast with Luther) he made Scripture itself not only an instrument but also an object of the Spirit's witness.

47. As we have seen, Berkouwer frequently charges his conservative brethren with fearfulness—but there is more than one kind of fear. It is well to remind ourselves of the biblical admonitions to fear God rather than human beings. And as we have also seen, there are plenty of admonitions in Scripture to "beware" of false teaching. (Whether the word *fear* is appropriate to describe this watchfulness is unimportant; the issue itself, however, is important.)

sense of whispering in our ears the solutions to these problems! On that question, the Reformers, the orthodox, and Berkouwer are agreed: Scripture never represents the Spirit's work as the giving of new information *about* the Bible. No one, for example, ought to claim that the Spirit has given him a list of canonical books; the actual list comes through historical and theological investigation of the contents of these books. Yet the Spirit has certainly played an important role in the history of the canon. By illumining and persuading the church concerning the true canonical books, he has helped the church to distinguish between false and true. He has motivated the church to seek out reasons for what he was teaching them in their hearts.[48]

Thus, the Spirit gets involved in everything we think and do as Christians. There is no area from which he, or his Scriptures, may be excluded. In that Berkouwer calls us to read those Scriptures responsibly, he should be applauded. But insofar as he discourages (as he does, at least by the ambiguity of his proposals) the comprehensive application of Scripture to all of life in opposition to unbelieving thought, he is not a reliable guide.[49]

C. The Rationality of the Witness

Now let us consider the question concerning the relation of the Spirit's testimony to evidences and rational arguments. Here it will be necessary to discuss some more general aspects of Christian epistemology.[50]

Knowing always involves a knower, a knowable content, and some "laws of thought" or criteria for determining what is true about the knowable content. To put it more succinctly, knowing involves subject, object, and norm. These three factors are distinguishable in theory but very difficult to separate when we look at the actual experience of knowing. Where does the "subject" end and the "object" begin? Philosophical battles (between idealists such as Berkeley and Hegel and realists such as Moore and Russell) have been fought over this issue. Sometimes it seems that all our knowledge

48. Some of the Reformed confessions suggest that the witness of the Spirit is the basis for our confession of the canon. See the important distinctions made by Auguste Lecerf in an interesting (and somewhat subtle) analysis of this question, *An Introduction to Reformed Dogmatics* (London: Lutterworth, 1949), 318–63. See also Berkouwer, *Holy Scripture*, 67ff.; Herman Ridderbos, *The Authority of the New Testament Scriptures*, ed. J. M. Kik, trans. H. de Jongst (Philadelphia: Presbyterian and Reformed, 1963).

49. On the question of the relation of "central message" to "peripheral matters" in Scripture, see also John M. Frame, "Rationality and Scripture," in *Rationality in the Calvinian Tradition*, ed. Hendrik Hart, Johan Van Der Hoeven, and Nicholas Wolterstorff (Lanham, MD: University Press of America, 1983), 295ff.

50. I have discussed these matters at greater length in ibid., 293–317, and in *DKG*.

is really self-knowledge: after all, everything in my mind is *my* experience, is it not? But then, where is the "object" that stands over against the self? Other times it seems that I have no self-knowledge at all. David Hume diligently searched his experience and couldn't find anything called *the self*. So the debate continues: either the self is swallowed up in the object or vice versa.

Similar problems arise in connection with the "norm." To the existentialist, the norm is indistinguishable from the self. (I am my own, and my only, law.) To the pure empiricist such as John Stuart Mill, laws are generalizations from sense experiences, merely shorthand ways of speaking about objects. Thus does the norm get lost in the subject or the object. But the reverse problem also occurs. In Plato—and perhaps in Immanuel Kant and others—subject and object both get lost in the norm. Knowledge for them is faithfulness to a preexisting ideal (for Plato) or categorical structure in the mind (for Kant); anything short of such norms is inadequate and, in an important sense, unreal.

Christianity, too, recognizes this triad. God reveals himself in the world (object), in his image (subject), and in his Word (law). As sinners, we hear but repress God's revelation in all three forms (Rom. 1). In saving us, however, God overcomes this resistance. He performs wondrous, mighty deeds in the world to save us (object) and sets forth their meaning and application to us in his Word (norm).[51] Also, he transforms our own hearts and minds so that we will be able to believe his deeds as they are proclaimed in his Word. This transformation is the work of the Holy Spirit. His witness to the Word illumines and persuades us so that we have a saving knowledge of God's revelation.

In Christianity, the three factors—subject, object, and norm—are closely related but distinguishable. Knowledge of any one brings with it knowledge of the others. We cannot know the world without taking God's law into account; when God reveals himself in the world, he also reveals his *ordinances* (Rom. 1:32). We cannot know ourselves except in the light of God's Word. But likewise, we cannot know the Word unless it comes to us through the world and through ourselves. We read the Bible as an object in the world among others, and we come to understand it through our own mental—and spiritual—gifts. Hence, it is not surprising that many have reduced some of our three elements to others. Besides, non-Christian thinkers have a special problem here. For the Christian, there is a God who has created the world and self and has spoken his norm-word. Thus,

51. Here, of course, I am not thinking of the norm as *law* in distinction from *gospel*. Here the word is both norm and good news at the same time.

the Christian has confidence that object, subject, and norm will cohere; all three lead to the same place. But those who reject the theistic premise have no such basis for confidence. Therefore, they are tempted to choose one of the three, the one in which they have most confidence, as the *only* element of knowledge.

The Christian, though, knows that however inseparable these elements are in our knowledge, they are not identical. I am not the world, nor vice versa. God gave humans dominion over the world (Gen. 1:28). Nor is God's word identical with the world or with myself. God's word is Creator (Gen. 1; Ps. 33:6; John 1); the world and self are creatures.

Now, the testimony of the Spirit to the written Word has a specific function in this triadic structure. The Spirit himself, as we saw earlier, is active in all aspects of revelation—creation, incarnation (Luke 1:35), prophecy, inspiration.[52] But the internal testimony, as distinct from these other aspects of revelation, is focused on the *subject* of knowledge. The internal testimony is not new revealed words (norms; see section I, above), nor is it a new saving act in history (object). Rather, in the internal testimony, the Spirit operates in our hearts and minds, in ourselves as subjects, to illumine and persuade us of the divine words and deeds.[53] This fact has important practical consequences for us when we seek God's guidance. When we lack knowledge of God's will, our need is not necessarily a need for new factual information (object), and it is never a need for new revelation in addition to Scripture (norms). Rather, most often (I think) it is a need for inward change, a need to reconcile ourselves to what God has already revealed. Guidance need not be either mystical (revelation apart from the Word) or intellectualistic (arising from a merely academic study of Scripture). Our pride and doctrinal misunderstandings often lead us to think that if we have problems, either we can solve them through our own resources (intellectualism) or they are God's fault (because of inadequate revelation). But Scripture continually directs our attention to our own sinfulness as the source of such problems—to our need of the Spirit.[54]

Now, since our theological question deals with the relation between the Spirit's witness and "rational argument," we must give some atten-

52. Note here in the term *theopneustos* the implicit reference to the Spirit (*pneuma*).

53. For the distinction (with biblical justification) between *illumination* and *persuasion* in the Spirit's witness, see John Murray, "The Attestation of Scripture," in Stonehouse and Woolley, *The Infallible Word*, 1–52.

54. This is not to deny that sometimes our problems are intellectual, at least in part. But I do not believe that our problems are ever the result of a lack of revelation (see Luke 16:27–31; Rom. 1:18–21; 2 Tim. 3:16–17; 2 Peter 1:3).

tion to human rationality.[55] Reason may be defined as a person's capacity for forming judgments, conclusions, inferences. So understood, reasoning is something we do all the time, not merely in academic or theoretical work. When a football quarterback sees a telltale motion in his opponents' backfield and moves to avoid the defensive players, he is reasoning; he has drawn an inference as to what the opposing players will do, and he has acted upon that inference. Logic is the science of inference, but people regularly draw inferences without having studied that science. Inference may fruitfully be seen as an *ethical* matter—and, therefore, as much a matter of conscience as of logical skill. A valid inference is an inference that we *ought* to acknowledge; and that "ought" is a *moral* "ought."[56]

So understood, reasoning takes place every time we make some use of God's revelation (in nature or Scripture). When a Christian is tempted to cheat on his taxes and resists that temptation, reasoning has taken place. He has drawn the conclusion—from Scripture, preaching, or conscience—that stealing is wrong, and he has drawn the further inference that cheating is stealing and therefore also wrong. Thus, every act of obedience to the Lord involves reasoning, whether or not some explicit argument is formulated.

Therefore, when we acknowledge Scripture as God's Word (also an act of obedience!), that acknowledgment is also a rational inference. We have looked at the data of Scripture and have come to this particular conclusion. Even if we "leap" to this conclusion by "blind faith," we have somehow come to the conclusion that our blind faith *ought* to leap to this conclusion rather than some other—meaning, of course, that our "blind faith" has not really been blind at all. Even a blind-faith conclusion is a conclusion, an inference.

Such reasoning can, of course, be bad reasoning. Sometimes people offer inadequate reasons for believing in Scripture. But we cannot conclude that *all* such reasoning is bad. To say that would be to say that there are no good reasons for believing the Bible. But that would mean that faith in Scripture is unwarranted; and that in turn would mean (recalling our ethical interpretation of logical inference) that we have no obligation to believe in Scripture. Scripture, then, would not have any authority at all.

Every warranted confession of Scripture, therefore, is a rational confession, a sound inference from experience. But then, what role remains for

---

55. I have treated this subject, too, at greater length in "Rationality and Scripture," 304ff.

56. What else could it be? Nothing else but morality compels us to acknowledge valid inferences. We are not physically forced to draw them, and we are not always motivated to draw them by self-interest. Why, then, should we accept such inferences, if not because we simply ought to?

the testimony of the Spirit? Just what we said before. The Spirit's work is in the subject. Scripture tells us that sin blinds us to the truth (Rom. 1; 1 Cor. 1–2). This means that sin keeps us from acknowledging those things that we *ought* to acknowledge; it keeps us from acknowledging warranted conclusions, rational conclusions. The work of the Spirit is to remove those effects of sin, to overcome that resistance. The Spirit does not whisper to us special reasons that are not otherwise available; rather, he opens our eyes to acknowledge those that *are* available (and that, at one level of consciousness, we know already, Rom. 1:21). Nor does the Spirit give us power to transcend reason altogether. That would mean either that no reasoning is involved at all (contrary to what we have established) or that the reasoning accompanying our conviction is invalid (but then our conclusion would be unwarranted, illegitimate).

According to our threefold scheme, therefore, in rational argument, norms (logical and others) are applied to an object (the data of experience). This process warrants a rational conclusion. But the sinner will resist this conclusion unless the Spirit opens his eyes. To come to rational conclusions, we need objects and norms, but we must also be the kind of people who can and will come to the right conclusions. The Spirit supplies that crucial third factor. He changes us so that we acknowledge what is rationally warranted.

Now, just as secular philosophers have tended to confuse norm, object, and subject, so Christian thinkers have often confused the Spirit's witness with the other elements of the Christian's knowledge. This sort of confusion often occurs, in my opinion, when theologians consider the relation between the Spirit's work and human rationality. Calvin himself is not immune from criticism on this score. It is possible that Calvin's teaching can be reconciled to the sort of model I have presented,[57] but some of his expressions are problematic. Note:

> We ought to seek our conviction in a higher place than human reasons, judgments, or conjectures, that is, in the secret testimony of the Spirit. . . . The testimony of the Spirit is more excellent than all reason. . . . Therefore, illumined by his

57. As argued, in effect, by Benjamin Breckinridge Warfield, *Inspiration and Authority*, and more recently in R. C. Sproul, John H. Gerstner, and Arthur Lindsley, *Classical Apologetics* (Grand Rapids: Zondervan, 1984), 162ff., 296ff. I won't go into this in detail, but I should say that their critique of my position is largely a misunderstanding, in my opinion. Actually, my view (and Van Til's) of the Spirit's testimony is very close to theirs, far closer than they realize. See my review of this book in *WTJ* 47 (Fall 1985): 279–99. This position, however, has been sharply attacked by Rogers and McKim (*Authority and Interpretation*), Berkouwer (*Holy Scripture*), and others.

power, we believe neither by our own nor by anyone else's judgment that scripture is from God; but above human judgment we affirm with utter certainty . . . that it has flowed to us from the very mouth of God by the ministry of men. We seek no proofs, no marks of genuineness upon which our judgment may lean.[58]

Here Calvin talks as though the Spirit's testimony and rational arguments were competing factors, as it were, contributing to our assurance of Scripture. It sounds as though arguments are an inadequate means of assurance, the Spirit's testimony an adequate means. Now, it is surely true that many arguments are unsound and do not truly warrant faith in Scripture and that, therefore, the testimony of the Spirit goes beyond those arguments. It is also true that even *sound* arguments without the Spirit's testimony will not lead anyone to saving knowledge of Christ and Scripture. Doubtless points of this sort were in Calvin's mind.

But Calvin's expressions might also be taken to mean that the case for the truth of Scripture is inadequate, and that we may come to belief in it only by irrational means. Such a view would certainly be illegitimate (and I think contrary to Calvin's own intent). Or these statements might be understood as meaning that the Spirit *supplements* the evidence, giving us a legitimate warrant in place of inadequate ones. But what could this mean but that (1) Scripture lacks objective authority apart from the Spirit's witness (a notion that we have refuted in section I), and (2) the Spirit gives us a new revelation to provide the adequate warrant, a notion that Calvin always rejects?

Such data have led to problems in the interpretation and theological use of Calvin's doctrine. We do not have the space for a historical excursus, but I do believe that the Dutch Calvinist theologians Kuyper and Bavinck, along with the philosopher Herman Dooyeweerd (not to mention Barth and Berkouwer, whom we discussed earlier), have pressed Calvin's teaching in a somewhat irrationalist direction. Similarly, the contemporary philosopher Alvin Plantinga has spoken of a "reformed epistemology" in which belief in God is accepted as "properly basic" (that is, not based on any reasoning or evidence). Jay M. Van Hook argues that although Plantinga can successfully defend the rationality of theistic belief on this basis (all systems of thought have to begin somewhere; therefore, Christianity has a right to begin with God), he cannot show the *irrationality* of someone who *denies* Christianity (holding that

58. Calvin, *Institutes*, 1.78–80.

something other than the biblical God, the Great Pumpkin for instance, is "properly basic").[59]

I think there is much value in Plantinga's concept of "proper basicality." God is the Christian's presupposition, the norm of all his thinking about everything else. More needs to be said, however, about how one distinguishes rational from irrational "presupposings" and about how the Christian presupposition has a rational basis in God's self-revelation.[60] And there is some danger now that Reformed people will avoid wrestling with such questions, thinking that the doctrine of the Spirit's testimony answers them sufficiently.

That doctrine, however, is not suited to that particular purpose. Scripture does not present it for the purpose of overcoming inadequacies in the rational basis of Christianity. The point we need to remember is that there is no competition between the rationality of the Scriptures and the witness of the Spirit. We do not need to make the case for Scripture somehow irrational or inadequate in order to do justice to the Spirit's testimony. If knowledge of God is to be possible, both rationality and the Spirit are needed—rationality so that faith will be warranted, indeed obligatory, and the Spirit so that our sinful unbelief, our refusal to accept our obligation, will be overcome.

The discussion above will seem rationalistic to some. For the record, let me indicate my belief that human reason has a great many limitations,[61] especially in matters of faith. I freely grant that the "knowledge of God" in Scripture is far more than a theoretical contemplation, that it involves obedience, love, and trust. Further, coming to know God is far from a merely intellectual or academic experience. It involves all our faculties (as well as those of the Spirit!); it is more like coming to know a friend than coming to know, say, wave mechanics. For that matter, even learning wave mechanics is not a "purely intellectual" process, whatever that may mean. Intellectual operations are always dependent on our experience, our emotional makeup, our religious and ideological commitments, and so on.[62]

It should be said, too, that the testimony of the Spirit works in the Spirit's typically mysterious way (John 3:8). As we have said, he does not whisper

59. Jay M. Van Hook, "Knowledge, Belief and Reformed Epistemology," *Reformed Journal* 31, 7 (July 1981): 12–17.

60. See my *DKG*.

61. See again my "Rationality and Scripture," 305ff.

62. See, e.g., Thomas S. Kuhn, *The Structure of Scientific Revolutions* (Chicago: University of Chicago Press, 1970). A considerable body of literature has developed over the past thirty years emphasizing that science is not a purely "objective" or "neutral" discipline, as many people still think it to be. This point has been made by N. R. Hanson and M. Polanyi, as well as by Christian thinkers such as Dooyeweerd and Van Til.

in our ears; but neither does he work predictably through the normal channels of education so that those with advanced degrees automatically have the greatest spiritual perception. He gives us, rather, a sort of "intuition" for things divine, as many writers have put it. We recognize Scripture as the Word in the same way we recognize white to be white or sweet to be sweet. Suddenly, that Word, which we had as unbelievers despised, becomes fresh and exciting and precious to us. Arguments and reasons that, perhaps, we have heard many times and rejected display their cogency suddenly before our eyes. We recognize the *loveliness* of the gospel and respond with joy.[63]

Nor do I wish to say that we must be able to supply proofs and arguments in order to justify faith. As I have said, much of our reasoning is very informal, like that of the football quarterback. Generally it is not formulated into syllogisms, and usually it would be difficult, I think, even for a professional logician to identify the premises and the logical steps. God has simply given us a *sense* of what is reasonable, and usually that is sufficient. (Note how all reasoning, not just that which deals with matters of faith, may involve something like the Spirit's testimony.)[64] On the other hand, if someone has the God-given skill to develop some kind of formal proof, I know of nothing in the doctrine of the Spirit's testimony that would prevent him from doing so.[65]

63. See Jonathan Edwards, *A Treatise on the Religious Affections*, in *The Works of Jonathan Edwards*, ed. Edward Hickman (Edinburgh: Banner of Truth, 1974), 281ff. Edwards' argument here is fascinating and perceptive in many ways. He says that in the internal testimony the Spirit reveals no new propositions to us and thus must reveal something of a different character from propositional truth. He settles on the "loveliness" of God and his Word; for unbelievers can know of God's existence, but they fail to acknowledge his loveliness, his desirability. Edwards' argument is useful in showing one of the important and neglected dimensions of the Spirit's work. At the same time, I would like to make some additional distinctions. In my view, unbelievers, even Satan, are capable of recognizing that God is lovely (objectively), while they prefer ugliness to loveliness (thus showing the irrationality of their unbelief). What the Spirit does is to give us a new heart, a heart that leads us to accept God's Word obediently. But that new heart of obedience is also a crucial epistemological capacity. It cures us of the irrationality of unbelief and frees us to acknowledge with word and life the reality of what is.

64. Valentine Hepp argued that the Holy Spirit also bears witness to general revelation—that is, that his witness is involved in all human knowledge—in *Het Testimonium Spiritus Sancti* (Kampen: Kok, 1914).

65. Of course, such a project would be under considerable disadvantage, for several reasons: (1) I believe that any valid proof of Christianity would be circular in a sense and thus not impressive to many people. See Cornelius Van Til, *The Defense of the Faith* (Philadelphia: Presbyterian and Reformed, 1963), and my "The Problem of Theological Paradox," in *Foundations of Christian Scholarship*, ed. Gary North (Vallecito, CA: Ross House, 1976). (2) It is very difficult to capture in a formal proof the logical force of all the elements that really persuade people of the truth of Christianity, such as the love demonstrated by a Christian neighbor, the joy on the face of a church soloist, or a sudden awareness of one's

III. SUMMARY AND CONCLUSION

In this study, I have sought to clarify some matters pertaining to the Spirit's work in revelation, inspiration, and internal witness. I have argued that although revelation and inspiration do not produce a "uniform" text, that fact need not be an embarrassment to us, unless it be an embarrassment of riches; for the Spirit gives us *more* than a "uniform" text, a text that conveys the truth with a fullness and clarity as appropriate to its depth and riches as is possible in human language.

Then I argued that debates over the sovereignty, objects, and rationality of the Spirit's internal witness ought themselves to be more carefully related to the riches of that inspired text. The weakness of theological discussions in these areas has been that they have seized on certain biblical concepts (such as "the sovereignty of God in revelation"), largely ignoring the qualifications, interpretations, and uses given to these concepts in the actual context of Scripture. Paradoxically, these modern theologians (most of whom would be quite opposed to the notion of "uniform" inspiration) have taken Scripture to be much more uniform than it really is! The biblical concept of sovereignty, for instance, is, as we have seen, much more nuanced than are the concepts of sovereignty in most modern theologies of revelation. The modern views owe more to philosophical discussions than to biblical data.

These methodological problems in modern theology are found in many areas beyond those discussed here. That fact will provide much for future study. For the time being, I advance this moral: if theologians would try to be more biblical in their doctrine of Scripture, they would be forming some habits that would be useful across the board, avoiding pitfalls in other areas of theology. It is important, then, even in the relatively "abstract" area of theological methodology, to hear the Spirit speaking in the Word. "He who has an ear, let him hear what the Spirit says to the churches" (Rev. 2:7).

---

sinfulness. (3) Finally, even if such a proof were sound and persuasive to normal (believing) minds, unbelievers would still resist it, and believers would not really need it.

Bibliography

American Heritage College Dictionary. 3rd ed. Boston and New York: Houghton Mifflin Co., 2000.

Aquinas, Thomas. *Summa Theologiae*. 1265–74.

Athenagoras. *A Plea for the Christians*. Available at http://www.monachos.net/content/patristics/patristictexts/313-athenagoras-plea-link.

Austin, J. L. *How to Do Things with Words*. Cambridge, MA: Harvard University Press, 1962.

Ayer, A. J. *Language, Truth and Logic*. New York: Dover, 1946.

———, ed. *Logical Positivism*. Glencoe, IL: Free Press, 1959.

Bahnsen, Greg. "The Inerrancy of the Autographa." In *Inerrancy*, edited by Norman Geisler, 156–59. Grand Rapids: Zondervan, 1979.

Baillie, John. *The Idea of Revelation in Recent Thought*. New York: Columbia University Press, 1956.

Barker, William S., and W. Robert Godfrey, eds. *Theonomy: A Reformed Critique*. Grand Rapids: Zondervan, 1990.

Barr, James. *Old and New in Interpretation*. London: SCM Press, 1966.

Barth, Karl. *Church Dogmatics*. Vol. 1.1, *The Doctrine of the Word of God*, edited by G. W. Bromiley and T. F. Torrance, translated by G. T. Thomson. New York: Scribner, 1936.

———. *Church Dogmatics*. Vol. 2.1, *The Doctrine of God*, edited by G. W. Bromiley and T. F. Torrance, translated by T. H. L. Parker, W. B. Johnston, H. Knight, and J. L. M. Haire. New York: Scribner, 1957.

———. *Church Dogmatics*. 4 vols. Edinburgh: T&T Clark, 1936–56.

———. *The Holy Ghost and the Christian Life*. London: Muller, 1938.

———. *The Theology of the Reformed Confessions*. Louisville: Westminster John Knox Press, 2002.

Bavinck, Herman. *Reformed Dogmatics*. Vol. 1. Grand Rapids: Baker, 2003.

Beale, G. K., and D. A. Carson. *Commentary on the New Testament Use of the Old Testament*. Grand Rapids: Baker Academic, 2007.

Beegle, Dewey M. *The Inspiration of Scripture*. Philadelphia: Westminster Press, 1963.

Berkouwer, G. C. *Holy Scripture*. Grand Rapids: Eerdmans, 1975.

Bilheimer, Robert S., ed. *Faith and Ferment*. Minneapolis: Augsburg, 1983.

Bloesch, Donald. *Holy Scripture: Revelation, Inspiration and Interpretation*. Downers Grove, IL: InterVarsity Press, 1994.

The Book of Church Order. Office of the Stated Clerk of the General Assembly of the Presbyterian Church in America, 2008.

Bouma, Hessel, et al. *Christian Faith, Health and Medical Practice*. Grand Rapids: Eerdmans, 1989.

Bromiley, Geoffrey. *Historical Theology: An Introduction*. Grand Rapids: Eerdmans, 1978.

Brunner, Emil. *The Divine Imperative*, translated by Olive Wyon. Philadelphia: Westminster Press, 1947.

———. *Dogmatics*. Vol. 1, *The Christian Doctrine of God*, translated by Olive Wyon. Philadelphia: Westminster Press, 1950.

———. *Truth as Encounter*. Philadelphia: Westminster Press, 1964.

Buber, Martin. *I and Thou*. 2nd ed. New York: Scribner, 1958.

Calvin, John. *Calvin's Commentaries*. Available at http://www.ccel.org/ccel/calvin/commentaries.i.html.

———. *The Institutes of the Christian Religion*, translated by Ford Lewis Battles. 2 vols. Philadelphia: Westminster, 1960.

Carson, D. A., ed. *Worship: Adoration and Action*. Grand Rapids: Baker, 1993.

Carson, D. A., and John D. Woodbridge, eds. *Hermeneutics, Authority, and Canon*. Grand Rapids: Baker, 1995.

———. *Scripture and Truth*. Grand Rapids: Zondervan, 1983.

Clark, Gordon H. *Religion, Reason and Revelation*. Philadelphia: Presbyterian and Reformed, 1961.

Coleman, Richard. "Reconsidering 'Limited Inerrancy.'" *JETS* 17 (1974): 207–14.

Committee on Biblical Authority of the Christian Reformed Church. *The Nature and Extent of Biblical Authority*. Grand Rapids: Board of Publications of the Christian Reformed Church, 1972.

Conn, Harvie M., ed. *Inerrancy and Hermeneutic*. Grand Rapids: Baker, 1988.

Conn, Harvie M., and Samuel F. Rowen, eds. *Missions and Theological Education in World Perspective*. Farmington, MI: Associates of Urbanus, 1984.

Dawn, Marva. *Reaching Out without Dumbing Down*. Grand Rapids: Eerdmans, 1995.

De Graaff, Arnold H., and Calvin Seerveld. *Understanding the Scriptures*. Toronto: Association for the Advancement of Christian Scholarship, 1968.

Dodd, C. H. *The Apostolic Preaching and Its Developments*. London: Hodder and Stoughton, 1936.

———. *In the Twilight of Western Thought*. Nutley, NJ: Craig Press, 1968.

Dooyeweerd, Herman. *A New Critique of Theoretical Thought*. Lewiston, NY: Edward Mellen Press, 1997.

Dowey, Edward A. *The Knowledge of God in Calvin's Theology*. New York: Columbia University Press, 1952.

Downing, F. Gerald. *Has Christianity a Revelation?* London: SCM Press, 1964.

Edwards, Jonathan. *A Treatise on the Religious Affections*. In *The Works of Jonathan Edwards*, edited by Edward Hickman. Edinburgh: Banner of Truth, 1974.

Eire, Carlos M. N. *War against the Idols*. Cambridge: Cambridge University Press, 1988.

Enns, Peter. *Inspiration and Incarnation: Evangelicals and the Problem of the Old Testament*. Grand Rapids: Baker, 2005.

Fletcher, Joseph. *Situation Ethics*. Philadelphia: Westminster Press, 1966.

Flew, Antony, and Alasdair C. MacIntyre, eds. *New Essays in Philosophical Theology*. London: SCM Press, 1955.

Frame, John M. "Above the Battle?" 2003. Available at http://www.frame-poythress.org/frame_articles/2003Above.htm.

———. *The Amsterdam Philosophy*. In *The Collected Works of John M. Frame*. CD and DVD collection. Phillipsburg, NJ: P&R Publishing; Whitefish, MT: Bits & Bytes, Inc., 2008. Available at http://www.frame-poythress.org/frame_books/1972Amsterdam.htm.

———. "Antithesis and the Doctrine of Scripture." 2006. Available at http://www.frame-poythress.org/frame_articles/2006Antithesis.htm.

———. *Apologetics to the Glory of God*. Phillipsburg, NJ: P&R Publishing, 1995.

———. "Certainty." 2005. Available at http://www.frame-poythress.org/frame_articles/2005Certainty.htm.

———. *Contemporary Worship Music: A Biblical Defense*. Phillipsburg, NJ: P&R Publishing, 1997.

———. *Cornelius Van Til: An Analysis of His Thought*. Phillipsburg, NJ: P&R Publishing, 1995.

———. "Covenant and the Unity of Scripture." 1999. Available at http://www.frame-poythress.org/frame_articles/1999Covenant.htm.

———. *Doctrine of the Christian Life.* Phillipsburg, NJ: P&R Publishing, 2008.

———. *Doctrine of God.* Phillipsburg, NJ: P&R Publishing, 2002.

———. *Doctrine of the Knowledge of God.* Phillipsburg, NJ: P&R Publishing, 1987.

———. *Evangelical Reunion.* Grand Rapids: Baker, 1991. Available at http://www.frame-poythress.org/frame_books.htm.

———. "God and Biblical Language." In *God's Inerrant Word*, edited by John W. Montgomery, 159–77. Minneapolis: Bethany Fellowship, 1974. Available at http://www.frame-poythress.org/frame_articles/1974BiblicalLanguage.html.

———. "In Defense of Something Close to Biblicism." *WTJ* 59 (1997): 269–318. Available at http://www.frame-poythress.org/frame_articles/Biblicism.htm.

———. "Machen's Warrior Children." In *Alister E. McGrath and Evangelical Theology*, edited by Sung Wook Chung. Grand Rapids: Baker, 2003. Available at http://www.frame-poythress.org/frame_articles/2003Machen.htm.

———. "Muller on Theology." *WTJ* 56 (Spring 1994): 133–51. Available at http://www.frame-poythress.org/frame_articles/1994Muller.htm.

———. "No Scripture, No Christ." *Synapse* II 1, 1 (January 1972). Reprinted in *Guardian* (January 1979): 10–11. Available at http://www.frame-poythress.org/frame_articles/1972No.html.

———. "The Problem of Theological Paradox." In *Foundations of Christian Scholarship*, edited by Gary North, 295–330. Vallecito, CA: Ross House, 1976.

———. "Proposal for a New Seminary." *JPP* 2, 1 (Winter 1978): 10–17. Available at http://www.frame-poythress.org/frame_articles/1978Proposal.htm. Republished with some revision as "Case Study: Proposals for a New North American Model." In *Missions and Theological Education in World Perspective*, edited by Harvie M. Conn and Samuel F. Rowen, 371. Farmington, MI: Associates of Urbanus, 1984.

———. "Rationality and Scripture." In *Rationality in the Calvinian Tradition*, edited by Hendrik Hart, Johan Van Der Hoeven, and Nicholas Wolterstorff. Lanham, MD: University Press of America, 1983. Available at http://www.frame-poythress.org/frame_articles/1983Rationality.html.

———. "Remembering Donald B. Fullerton." Available at http://www.frame-poythress.org/frame_articles/Remembering_fullerton.htm.

———. "Reply to Mark W. Karlberg." *Mid-America Journal of Theology* 9, 2 (Fall 1993): 279–308.

———. "Reply to Richard Muller and David Wells." *WTJ* 59, 2 (Fall 1997): 311–18.

———. Review of *A Biblical Case for Natural Law*, by David VanDrunen. Available at http://www.frame-poythress.org/frame_articles/2010 VanDrunen.htm.

———. Review of *Biblical Errancy: An Analysis of Its Philosophical Roots*, edited by Norman Geisler. *WTJ* 45, 2 (Fall 1983): 433–41. Available at http://www.frame-poythress.org/frame_articles/1983Geisler.htm.

———. Review of *Christ and the Bible*, by John Wenham. *Banner of Truth* (July–August 1973): 39–41. Available at http://www.frame-poythress .org/frame_articles/1973Wenham.html.

———. Review of *Christian Faith, Health and Medical Practice*, by Hessel Bouma, et al. *Christian Renewal* (June 18, 1990): 16–17. Available at http://www.frame-poythress.org/frame_articles/1990ReviewBouma .htm.

———. Review of *Classical Apologetics*, by R. C. Sproul, John H. Gerstner, and Arthur Lindsley. *WTJ* 47 (Fall 1985): 279–99.

———. Review of *Inspiration and Incarnation*, by Peter Enns. 2008. Available at http://www.frame-poythress.org/frame_articles/2008 Enns.htm.

———. Review of *The Last Word*, by N. T. Wright. *Penpoint* 17, 4 (August 2006). Available at http://www.frame-poythress.org/frame_ articles/2006Wright.html.

———. Review of *The Study of Theology*, by Richard Muller. *WTJ* 56, 1 (Spring 1994): 438–42. Available at http://www.frame-poythress.org /frame_articles/1994Muller.htm.

———. Review of *Systematic Theology*, by Gordon Kaufman. *WTJ* 32, 1 (November 1969): 119–24. Available at http://www.frame-poythress .org/frame_articles/1969Kaufman.htm.

———. Review of *The Uses of Scripture in Recent Theology*, by David H. Kelsey. *WTJ* 39, 2 (Spring 1977): 328–53. Available at http://www .frame-poythress.org/frame_articles/1977Kelsey.htm.

———. Review of *Van Til, Defender of the Faith*, by William White Jr. *WTJ* 42, 1 (Fall 1979): 198–203. Available at http://www.frame-poythress .org/frame_articles/1979White.htm.

———. *Salvation Belongs to the Lord*. Phillipsburg, NJ: P&R Publishing, 2006.

———. "Scripture Speaks for Itself." In *God's Inerrant Word*, edited by John W. Montgomery, 178–200. Grand Rapids: Bethany Fellowship, 1974. Available at http://www.frame-poythress.org/frame _articles/1974Scripture.html.

———. "The Spirit and the Scriptures." In *Hermeneutics, Authority and Canon*, edited by D. A. Carson and John D. Woodbridge, 217–35. Grand Rapids: Zondervan, 1986. Available at http://www.frame -poythress.org/frame_articles/1986Spirit.htm.

———. "A Theology of Opportunity: Sola Scriptura and the Great Commission." Available at http://www.frame-poythress.org/frame _articles/1999ATheology.htm.

———. "Traditionalism." 1999. Available at http://www.frame-poythress .org/frame_articles/1999Traditionalism.htm.

———. "Traditionalism and Sola Scriptura." *Chalcedon Report* (October 2001): 15–19, and (November 2001): 434–35.

———. *Van Til: The Theologian*. Phillipsburg, NJ: Pilgrim, 1976. Available at http://www.frame-poythress.org/frame_articles/1976VanTil.htm.

———. "The Word of God in the Cosmonomic Philosophy." *Guardian* (October 1972): 123–25, and (November 1972): 140–42.

———. *Worship in Spirit and Truth*. Phillipsburg, NJ: P&R Publishing, 1996.

Gaffin, Richard B. "Old Amsterdam and Inerrancy." *WTJ* 45, 1 (Fall 1983): 219–72.

Gaussen, Louis. *The Inspiration of the Holy Scriptures*, translated by D. D. Scott. Chicago: Moody Press, 1949.

Geehan, E. R., ed. *Jerusalem and Athens*. Nutley, NJ: Presbyterian and Reformed, 1971.

Geisler, Norman L., ed. *Biblical Errancy: An Analysis of Its Philosophical Roots*. Grand Rapids: Zondervan, 1981.

———, ed. *Inerrancy*. Grand Rapids: Zondervan, 1979.

Geisler, Norman L., and Thomas A. Howe. *When Critics Ask*. Wheaton, IL: Victor Books, 1992.

Gerstner, John H. "The View of the Bible Held by the Church: Calvin and the Westminster Divines." In *Inerrancy*, edited by Norman L. Geisler, 385–412. Grand Rapids: Zondervan, 1979.

———. "Warfield's Case for Biblical Inerrancy." In *God's Inerrant Word*, edited by John W. Montgomery, 115–42. Minneapolis: Bethany House, 1974.

Godfrey, W. Robert. "Biblical Authority in the Sixteenth and Seventeenth Centuries: A Question of Transition." In *Scripture and Truth*, edited by D. A. Carson and John D. Woodbridge, 225–43. Grand Rapids: Zondervan, 1983.

Grant, F. C. *Introduction to New Testament Thought*. Nashville: Abingdon Press, 1950.

Grenz, Stanley, and Roger Olson. *Twentieth-Century Theology*. Downers Grove, IL: InterVarsity Press, 1992.

Grudem, Wayne. "Scripture's Self-Attestation and the Problem of Formulating a Doctrine of Scripture." In *Scripture and Truth*, edited by D. A. Carson and John D. Woodbridge, 19–59. Grand Rapids: Zondervan, 1983.

————. "Shall We Move beyond the New Testament to a Better Ethic?" *JETS* 47 (2004): 299–346.

————. *Systematic Theology*. Grand Rapids: Zondervan, 1994.

Gutiérrez, Gustavo. *A Theology of Liberation: History, Politics, and Salvation*. Maryknoll, NY: Orbis Books, 1973.

Hall, David, ed. *The Practice of Confessional Subscription*. Lanham, MD: University Press of America, 1995.

Hart, Hendrik, Johan Van Der Hoeven, and Nicholas Wolterstorff, eds. *Rationality in the Calvinian Tradition*. Lanham, MD: University Press of America, 1983.

Hendry, George. *The Holy Spirit in Christian Theology*. Philadelphia: Westminster Press, 1956.

Henry, Carl F. H. *God, Revelation and Authority*. 6 vols. Waco, TX: Word, 1976–79.

————. *The Uneasy Conscience of American Fundamentalism*. Grand Rapids: Eerdmans, 1947.

————, ed. *Revelation and the Bible*. Grand Rapids: Baker, 1958.

Hepp, Valentine. *Het Testimonium Spiritus Sancti*. Kampen: Kok, 1914.

Hickman, Edward. *The Works of Jonathan Edwards*. Edinburgh: Banner of Truth, 1974.

Hodge, Charles. *Systematic Theology*. Grand Rapids: Eerdmans, 1952.

Holmes, Arthur Frank. *All Truth Is God's Truth*. Grand Rapids: Eerdmans, 1977.

Jewett, Paul King. *God, Creation, and Revelation: A Neo-Evangelical Theology*. Grand Rapids: Eerdmans, 1991.

————. *The Ordination of Women*. Grand Rapids: Eerdmans, 1980.

Johnson, Robert Clyde. *Authority in Protestant Theology*. Philadelphia: Westminster Press, 1959.

Jones, Peter R. *Spirit Wars: Pagan Revival in Christian America*. Escondido, CA: Main Entry Editions, 1997.

Kant, Immanuel. *Religion within the Limits of Reason Alone*. 1934; repr., NY: Harper and Bros., 1960.

Kaufman, Gordon D. *Systematic Theology: A Historicist Perspective.* New York: Scribner, 1968.

Kelsey, David H. "Appeals to Scripture in Theology." *Journal of Religion* 48, 1 (January 1968): 1–21.

————. *The Fabric of Paul Tillich's Theology.* New York and London: Yale University Press, 1967.

————. *The Uses of Scripture in Recent Theology.* Philadelphia: Fortress Press, 1975.

Kierkegaard, Søren. *Fear and Trembling: The Sickness unto Death.* 1941; repr., Garden City, NY: Doubleday, 1954.

Kline, Meredith G. *Images of the Spirit.* Grand Rapids: Baker, 1980.

————. *The Structure of Biblical Authority.* Grand Rapids: Eerdmans, 1972.

Klooster, P. "Toward a Reformed Hermeneutic." *RESTB* 2, 1 (May 1974): 5.

Kuhn, Thomas S. *The Structure of Scientific Revolutions.* Chicago: University of Chicago Press, 1970.

Kuyper, Abraham. *Principles of Sacred Theology,* translated by J. H. De Vries. Grand Rapids: Eerdmans, 1965.

Lane, Anthony N. S. "John Calvin: The Witness of the Holy Spirit." In *Faith and Ferment,* edited by Robert S. Bilheimer. Minneapolis: Augsburg, 1983.

Lecerf, Auguste. *An Introduction to Reformed Dogmatics.* London: Lutterworth, 1949.

Lessing, Gotthold Ephraim. "On the Proof of the Spirit and of Power." In *Lessing: Philosophical and Theological Writings,* edited and translated by H. B. Nisbet. Cambridge: Cambridge University Press, 2005.

Lewis, C. S. "Modern Theology and Biblical Criticism." In *Christian Reflections,* edited by Walter Hooper. Grand Rapids: Eerdmans, 1967.

Machen, J. Gresham. *Christianity and Liberalism.* Grand Rapids: Eerdmans, 1923.

McGowan, A. T. B. *The Divine Authenticity of Scripture: Retrieving an Evangelical Heritage.* Downers Grove, IL: InterVarsity Press, 2008.

————. *The Divine Spiration of Scripture: Challenging Evangelical Perspectives.* Nottingham, UK: Apollos, 2007.

————, ed. *Always Reforming.* Downers Grove, IL: InterVarsity Press, 2006.

McPherson, Thomas. "Religion as the Inexpressible." In *New Essays in Philosophical Theology,* edited by Antony Flew and Alasdair C. MacIntyre, 131–43. London: SCM Press, 1955.

Meek, Esther. *Longing to Know.* Grand Rapids: Brazos Press, 2003.

Moltmann, Jürgen. *Theology of Hope.* New York: Harper and Row, 1967.

Montgomery, John W., ed. *God's Inerrant Word.* Minneapolis: Bethany Fellowship, 1974.

Muller, Richard A. *The Study of Theology: From Biblical Interpretation to Contemporary Formulation*. Foundations of Contemporary Interpretation 7. Grand Rapids: Zondervan, 1991.

———. "The Study of Theology Revisited: A Response to John Frame." *WTJ* 56 (Fall 1994): 409–17.

Murray, John. "The Attestation of Scripture." In *The Infallible Word*, edited by Ned Bernard Stonehouse and Paul Woolley. Philadelphia: Presbyterian and Reformed, 1946.

———. *Calvin on Scripture and Divine Sovereignty*. Grand Rapids: Baker, 1960.

———. *Collected Writings of John Murray*. 4 vols. Edinburgh: Banner of Truth, 1982.

———. *Principles of Conduct*. Grand Rapids: Eerdmans, 1957.

New Spirit Filled Life Bible, edited by Jack W. Hayford. Nashville: Thomas Nelson, 2002.

Niesel, Wilhelm. *The Theology of Calvin*. Philadelphia: Westminster, 1956.

North, Gary, ed. *Foundations of Christian Scholarship*. Vallecito, CA: Ross House, 1976.

Olthuis, James H. *Ambiguity Is the Key*. Toronto: Association for the Advancement of Christian Scholarship, 1969.

Olthuis, James H., and Bernard Zylstra. "Confessing Christ in Education." *IRB* 42 (Summer 1970): 41ff.

Orr, James. *Revelation and Inspiration*. New York: Scribner's, 1910; repr., Grand Rapids: Baker, 1969.

Pache, René. *The Inspiration and Authority of Scripture*, translated by Helen I. Needham. Chicago: Moody Press, 1969.

Packer, J. I. *Beyond the Battle for the Bible*. Westchester, IL: Cornerstone Books, 1980.

———. *Fundamentalism and the Word of God*. Grand Rapids: Eerdmans, 1958.

Pannenberg, Wolfhart. *Jesus, God and Man*. Philadelphia: Westminster Press, 1968.

Pink, Arthur W. *The Doctrine of Revelation*. Grand Rapids: Baker, 1975.

———. *The Holy Spirit*. Grand Rapids: Baker, 1970.

Pinnock, Clark H. *Biblical Revelation*. Chicago: Moody Press, 1971.

Poythress, Vern. "A Biblical View of Mathematics." In *Foundations of Christian Scholarship*, edited by Gary North, 159–88. Vallecito, CA: Ross House, 1976. Available at http://www.frame-poythress.org /poythress_articles/1976Biblical.htm.

————. *God-Centered Biblical Interpretation*. Phillipsburg, NJ: P&R Publishing, 1999.

————. "Modern Spiritual Gifts as *Analogous* to Apostolic Gifts: Affirming Extraordinary Works of the Spirit within Cessationist Theology." *JETS* 39, 1 (1996): 71–101. Available at http://www.frame-poythress.org/poythress_articles/1996Modern.htm.

————. *Philosophy, Science and the Sovereignty of God*. Nutley, NJ: Presbyterian and Reformed, 1976.

————. "The Presence of God Qualifying Our Notions of Grammatical-Historical Interpretation: Genesis 3:15 as a Test Case." *JETS* 50, 1 (2007): 87–103. Available at http://www.frame-poythress.org/poythress_articles/2007Presence.htm.

————. "Problems for Limited Inerrancy." *JETS* 18, 2 (Spring 1975): 93–102. Available at http://www.frame-poythress.org/poythress_articles/1975Problems.htm.

————. *Redeeming Science*. Wheaton, IL: Crossway, 2006. Available at http://www.frame-poythress.org/Poythress_books/NAllPoythress RedeemingScience20061017.pdf.

Pratt, Richard. "Historical Contingencies and Biblical Predictions." Available at http://reformedperspectives.org/newfiles/ric_pratt/TH.Pratt .Historical_Contingencies.html.

Ramm, Bernard. *The Witness of the Spirit*. Grand Rapids: Eerdmans, 1957.

Ridderbos, Herman. *The Authority of the New Testament Scriptures*, edited by J. M. Kik, translated by H. de Jongste. Philadelphia: Presbyterian and Reformed, 1963.

Rogers, Jack. "Van Til and Warfield on Scripture in the Westminster Confession." In *Jerusalem and Athens*, edited by E. R. Geehan, 162ff. Nutley, NJ: Presbyterian and Reformed, 1971.

Rogers, Jack B., and Donald K. McKim. *The Authority and Interpretation of the Bible: An Historical Approach*. San Francisco: Harper and Row, 1979.

Runia, Klaas. "The Reformed Liturgy in the Dutch Tradition." In *Worship: Adoration and Action*, edited by D. A. Carson. Grand Rapids: Baker, 1993.

Runner, H. Evan. *The Relation of the Bible to Learning*. Pella, IA: Pella Publishing, 1960.

Ryle, Gilbert. *Dilemmas*. Cambridge: Cambridge University Press, 1954.

Sailhamer, John. *Introduction to Old Testament Theology: A Canonical Approach*. Grand Rapids: Zondervan, 1995.

Schaeffer, Francis A. *The Great Evangelical Disaster*. Westchester, IL: Crossway, 1984.

Schleiermacher, Friedrich. *The Christian Faith*. Edinburgh: T&T Clark, 1928.

Schrotenboer, Paul G. "The Bible, Word of Power." *IRB* 32–33 (January–April 1968): 1–4.

———. "The Bible as the Word of God." Unpublished discussion paper, n.d.

———. "Orthodoxy and the Bible." *CalCon* (February 21, 28, 1972): 1.

———. "Theology, Its Nature and Task." Unpublished discussion paper, n.d.

Seeberg, Reinhold. *Textbook of the History of Doctrines*. Grand Rapids: Baker, 1954.

Shepherd, Norman. "Bible, Church and Proclamation." Response to Prof. Johan A. Heyns. *IRB* 54 (Summer 1973): 60ff.

———. "The Nature of Biblical Authority." Unpublished lecture.

Skilton, John H., ed. *Scripture and Confession*. Nutley, NJ: Presbyterian and Reformed, 1973.

Spier, J. M. *An Introduction to Christian Philosophy*. Philadelphia: Presbyterian and Reformed, 1954.

Spinoza, Baruch. *Ethics*. 1674.

———. *Tractatus Theologico-Politicus*. 1670.

Sproul, R. C., John H. Gerstner, and Arthur Lindsley. *Classical Apologetics*. Grand Rapids: Zondervan, 1984.

Spykman, Gordon J. "A Confessional Hermeneutic." *RESTB* 1, 3 (December 1973): 9.

Stonehouse, Ned Bernard, and Paul Woolley, eds. *The Infallible Word*. Grand Rapids: Eerdmans, 1946.

Thielicke, Helmut. *The Evangelical Faith*. 3 vols. Grand Rapids: Eerdmans, 1974.

Toulmin, Stephen Edelston. *The Uses of Argument*. Cambridge: Cambridge University Press, 1958.

Van Baalen, Jan Karel. *The Chaos of Cults*. Grand Rapids: Eerdmans, 1938.

Vander Stelt, John C. *Philosophy and Scripture*. Marlton, NJ: Mack Publishing, 1978.

VanDrunen, David. *A Biblical Case for Natural Law*. Grand Rapids: Acton Institute, 2006.

Van Hook, Jay M. "Knowledge, Belief and Reformed Epistemology." *Reformed Journal* 31, 7 (July 1981): 12–17.

Van Til, Cornelius. *Christianity and Barthianism*. Philadelphia: Presbyterian and Reformed, 1962.

———. *A Christian Theory of Knowledge*. Philadelphia: Presbyterian and Reformed, 1969.

———. *The Defense of the Faith*. Philadelphia: Presbyterian and Reformed, 1963.

———. "The Doctrine of Scripture." Unpublished syllabus. Ripon, CA: Den Dulk Foundation, 1967.

———. *An Introduction to Systematic Theology*. Nutley, NJ: Presbyterian and Reformed, 1974.

———. "'It Says:' 'Scripture Says:' 'God Says.'" In Benjamin Breckinridge Warfield, *The Inspiration and Authority of the Bible*. Grand Rapids: Baker, 1948.

———. "Nature and Scripture." In *The Infallible Word*, edited by Ned Bernard Stonehouse and Paul Woolley, 255–93. Grand Rapids: Eerdmans, 1946.

———. "The Oracles of God." In Benjamin Breckinridge Warfield, *The Inspiration and Authority of the Bible*, 351–407. Grand Rapids: Baker, 1948.

———. *The Protestant Doctrine of Scripture*. Philadelphia: Presbyterian and Reformed, 1967.

———. "The Terms 'Scripture' and 'Scriptures' as Employed in the New Testament." In Benjamin Breckinridge Warfield, *The Inspiration and Authority of the Bible*, 229–41. Grand Rapids: Baker, 1948.

———. *The Triumph of Grace*. Philadelphia: Westminster Theological Seminary, 1958.

Von Meyenfeldt, Frederik Hendrik. *The Meaning of Ethos*. Hamilton, ON: Guardian Press, 1964.

Warfield, Benjamin Breckinridge. "Calvin's Doctrine of the Knowledge of God." In *Calvin and Calvinism*, 27–130. New York: Oxford University Press, 1931.

———. "The Idea of Systematic Theology." In *Studies in Theology*. Grand Rapids: Baker, 1981.

———. *The Inspiration and Authority of the Bible*. Philadelphia: Presbyterian and Reformed, 1948; repr., Grand Rapids: Baker, 1970.

Webb, William. *Slaves, Women and Homosexuals*. Downers Grove, IL: InterVarsity Press, 2001.

Wells, David F. *God in the Wasteland*. Grand Rapids: Eerdmans, 1994.

———. *No Place for Truth*. Grand Rapids: Eerdmans, 1993.

Wenham, John William. *Christ and the Bible*. Downers Grove, IL: InterVarsity Press, 1973.

White, William, Jr. *Van Til, Defender of the Faith*. Nashville: Thomas Nelson, 1979.

Wiseman, P. J. *Ancient Records and the Structure of Genesis*. Nashville: Thomas Nelson, 1985.

Wittgenstein, Ludwig. *Lectures and Conversations on Aesthetics, Psychology and Religious Belief: Compiled from Notes Taken by Yorick Smythies, Rush Rhees and James Taylor*, edited by Cyril Barrett. Oxford: Blackwell, 1966.

Wolterstorff, Nicholas. *Reason within the Bounds of Religion*. Grand Rapids: Eerdmans, 1976.

Woodbridge, John D. *Biblical Authority: A Critique of the Rogers/McKim Proposal*. Grand Rapids: Zondervan, 1982.

Woodbridge, John D., and Randall H. Balmer. "The Princetonians and Biblical Authority: An Assessment of the Ernest Sandeen Proposal." In *Scripture and Truth*, edited by D A. Carson and John D. Woodbridge, 251–79. Grand Rapids: Zondervan, 1983.

Wright, George Ernest. *God Who Acts*. London: SCM Press, 1952.

Wright, George Ernest, and Reginald Horace Fuller. *The Book of the Acts of God*. Garden City, NY: Doubleday, 1957.

Wright, N. T. *The Last Word: Beyond the Bible Wars to a New Understanding of the Authority of Scripture*. San Francisco: HarperCollins, 2005.

———. *The Resurrection of the Son of God*. Minneapolis: Fortress Press, 2003.

Young, Edward J. *Thy Word Is Truth*. Grand Rapids: Eerdmans, 1957.

Zylstra, Bernard. "Thy Word Our Life." *IRB* 49–50 (Spring/Summer 1972): 57–68.

Index of Names

Aaron, 88–89
Abraham, 3–4, 58–60,
    178–79, 297, 446
Adam, 3, 4, 5, 55, 56–58
Adams, Jay, 388, 577, 579
Aeschylus, 123
Anaximander, 17
Anaximenes, 17
Anselm, 374, 378
Aquila, 259
Aquinas. *See* Thomas Aquinas
Aristotle, 8, 17, 549, 594
Arius, 374
Athanasius, 136, 214–15,
    336n1, 575
Athenagoras, 141
Augustine, 241n2, 374, 575,
    597, 609
Austin, J. L., 478

Bacon, Francis, 556, 558,
    560
Bahnsen, Greg, 241, 543,
    578
Baillie, John, 153, 154,
    626n29
Barr, James, 28–29, 154–55,
    342, 467, 473, 570
Barrs, Jerram, 582
Barth, Karl, 15, 24, 55, 346,
    437–39, 467, 469, 471,
    473, 492, 494, 518,
    546n37, 549, 561, 603,
    607, 637

on divine transcendence,
    459–60
on event-revelation, 154
on history, 29, 30–32, 570
on identity between
    Christ and Word,
    41–43
on idolatry, 438–39
on inspiration, 460–62
on judgment, 158
on religious language,
    430–31
on revelation, 39n7,
    103–4, 125, 262, 342,
    427–28
on subjectivity of revela-
    tion, 36, 37, 41–42
Van Til on, 338
on Westminster Confes-
    sion, 551–52
on witness of Spirit,
    314n14, 620, 621–27
Barton, John, 535
Bartsch, Hans-Werner, 471,
    475
Basinger, David, 607
Bauckham, Richard, 19
Baur, F. C., 19, 193
Bavinck, Herman, 142,
    539n28, 549–51, 627,
    637
Baxter, Richard, 241n2
Beale, G. K., 190n10, 499,
    512n15
Beck, W. David, 557, 560

Beegle, Dewey, 560
Bengel, J. A., 570
Berkeley, George, 23n1, 632
Berkhof, Louis, 579
Berkouwer, G. C., 314n14,
    351n13, 383, 466n2,
    490, 492, 494, 497,
    549, 555, 556, 56–62,
    576, 620, 627–32,
    636n57, 637
Bloesch, Donald, 532, 536,
    604
Blomberg, Craig, 19
Bloom, Allan, 372
Borg, Marcus, 19
Bromiley, Geoffrey, 626n29
Bruce, F. F., 19, 603
Brunner, Emil, 24, 35–36,
    55, 101, 153, 154, 156,
    158, 338, 459–60, 467,
    518
Buber, Martin, 24, 36, 153,
    429n16
Bultmann, Rudolf, 19, 24,
    55, 160, 181, 341, 467,
    471, 472, 473, 481,
    494, 546n37, 556, 595,
    603, 630

Cain, 58
Calvin, John, 241n2, 349n8,
    535, 575, 631n46
    on accommodation, 175
    on biblical authority,
    165–66

655

Index of Subjects

Index of Scripture